Web Marketing
ALL-IN-ONE
FOR
DUMMIES®

by John Arnold, Ian Lurie, Elizabeth Marsten, Marty Dickinson, and Michael Becker

Wiley Publishing, Inc.

Web Marketing All-in-One For Dummies®

Published by
Wiley Publishing, Inc.
111 River Street
Hoboken, NJ 07030-5774

www.wiley.com

Copyright © 2009 by Wiley Publishing, Inc., Indianapolis, Indiana

Published by Wiley Publishing, Inc., Indianapolis, Indiana

Published simultaneously in Canada

For general information on our other products and services, please contact our Customer Care Department within the U.S. at 877-762-2974, outside the U.S. at 317-572-3993, or fax 317-572-4002.

For technical support, please visit www.wiley.com/techsupport.

Wiley also publishes its books in a variety of electronic formats. Some content that appears in print may not be available in electronic books.

Library of Congress Control Number: 2009922964

ISBN: 978-0-470-41398-2

Manufactured in the United States of America

10 9 8 7 6 5 4 3 2 1

WILEY

About the Authors

John Arnold's uncommonly effective Web marketing strategies are featured in popular Web marketing books, syndicated columns, blog articles, and seminars. John is the author of *E-Mail Marketing For Dummies;* and he is an engaging conference speaker, media contributor, and Web marketing consultant.

John's marketing expertise gained national attention when he helped to pioneer a small business marketing seminar series on behalf of the permission-based e-mail marketing company Constant Contact. Through the program, John taught e-mail marketing strategies to thousands of small business owners. During John's tenure, Constant Contact was named #166 on the Inc. 500 list of the fastest-growing private companies and later completed a successful Initial Public Offering (IPO).

John has since become a trusted source for practical, low-cost Web-marketing strategies. He continues to advise small business owners in person and online through his Web site at www.johnarnold.com.

Ian Lurie started his Internet marketing company, Portent Interactive, in 1995. He is a long-time Internet marketing geek, with a blog, a book, and occasional speaking gigs on the subject. If you care about this kind of stuff, Ian's been interviewed and/or written for *The Seattle Times,* the *Puget Sound Business Journal, Direct Magazine,* DMNews, and *Visibility Magazine.*

Ian's diverse background includes degrees in history and law; experience as an information designer, graphic designer, marketing copywriter, and programmer; two years working in a bicycle shop; and a brief stint as a political hack. As a child he used a TRS-80 Model One to print fliers advertising his lawn mowing business. The rest is history.

Ian has spoken at SMX Stockholm, SMX West, SEMpdx SearchFest, and the WSA, and he contributed to the most excellent book you have in your hands right now. Ian's blog, Conversation Marketing, is on Advertising Age's list of the top 150 marketing blogs. You can visit it at www.conversation marketing.com. You can visit his company at www.portent.com.

Elizabeth Marsten is the PPC Manager at Portent Interactive, a full-service Internet marketing agency based in Seattle, WA. She oversees all the pay per click (PPC) operations and staff and is also learning the ropes in affiliate marketing and managing many of the affiliate efforts at Portent Interactive as well. She is a regular contributor of PPC best practices on the Portent Interactive blog, along with the worst practices on the PPC spoof blog: www.ppcvillain.com.

Her PPC marketing experience started with an interview for office manager, which she didn't get but was instead offered the position of PPC specialist (which she initially thought was *pay per clip marketing* until she Googled it. Google asked her whether she meant *pay per click marketing*, which she did. From there on, she has lived PPC every day, all day, and still pretty much does. Her detail-oriented skills and obsessive need for order and structure have served her and her clients well in their campaigns, which have ranged broadly from office furniture and wedding invitations to glue guns and salt.

Marty Dickinson launched his first Web site — MusicMates.com — in 1996 as a hobby. Today, Music Mates is one of the largest musician referrals in the country. Marty soon began helping other business owners with their Internet strategies through services, writing, and workshop-style training.

Someone once asked him, "We'd like to hire you, but how do we know you will be around in six months?" So, Marty formalized his Internet marketing–services company by calling it HereNextYear, Inc. (`www.HereNextYear.com`). Since then, he has produced and managed nearly 100 of his own Web sites and has assisted with more than 200 client projects.

One of Marty's greatest enjoyments is to share his strategies through public speaking and writing. In particular, nontechnical business owners appreciate his ability to present complex subjects in an easy-to-understand language.

Michael Becker is a leader in the mobile marketing industry, taking on the roles of industry practitioner, industry volunteer, and entrepreneur academic. Michael is co-founder and EVP of Business Development at iLoop Mobile, Inc., a leading mobile marketing platform solutions provider and winner of the Mobile Marketing Association (MMA) Innovation of the Year Award (2007).

Michael sits on the MMA North American board of directors and global board of directors, founded and co-chairs the award-winning MMA Academic Outreach Committee, and founded and co-edits the award-winning MMA International Journal of Mobile Marketing, the world's leading academic journal focused on the use of the mobile channel for marketing. Also, Michael is a contributing author of *Mobile Internet For Dummies*, supports the Direct Marketing Association Mobile Council, has written numerous articles on mobile marketing, and is winner of the MMA Outstanding Individual Achievement Award (2007).

In addition to his practitioner and industry roles, Michael is a contributing author to *Mobile Internet For Dummies,* has authored more than 40 articles on mobile marketing, oversees an industry blog, and is pursuing his doctorate on the topic of mobile enhanced customer-managed interactions. In recognition of his contributions to the industry, Michael was award the MMA Individual Achievement Award (2007).

When he comes up for air, Michael enjoys quiet times at home in Sunnyvale, CA, with this wife and two kids — with his Smartphone on silent.

Dedication

John Arnold: To the One who causes all things to work together for good and reminds me that marketing is not the most important thing in life

Ian Lurie: To my family, who make me want to be a better person, every day

Elizabeth Marsten: Glennis and Jeff, also known as Mom and Dad

Marty Dickinson: For my family, who has always inspired me to live a life of service to others, and my many business mentors who have shown me how

Michael Becker: To all those looking to establish and develop flourishing intimate, interactive, relationships through a new, exciting, and rapidly maturing medium: the mobile channel

Authors' Acknowledgments

John Arnold: I would first like to thank my wife and kids for being my cheering section. Everyone should be so fortunate to have a tireless team of supporters under their own roof.

Next, I would like to thank Matt Wagner for running the ideal literary agency. This book wouldn't have been possible without his experience and guidance, and nor would any others.

Special thanks to the super team of professionals at Wiley Publishing. Thanks to Steve Hayes for his confidence in this team of authors from beginning to end. I would also like to thank Rebecca Huehls for the outstanding job in managing our editing process. Your ability to give constructive feedback to so many know-it-alls is second only to the graceful way you kept us on task and in line with what our readers need to understand.

Finally, thanks to the outstanding team of authors who contributed to the content in this book. Thanks for loving your customers more than your technical prowess, and thanks for your technical prowess. Thanks especially to Ian, who contributed nearly half of this book's page count.

Ian Lurie: I'd be nuts if I didn't first thank my wife and kids, too. My wife Dawn put the kids to bed many more times than normal while I sat, typing frantically to meet deadlines. My son Harrison and daughter Morgan put up with me constantly multitasking, recording, or scribbling notes while I helped them with their homework.

Thanks to John Arnold, too, for being a very tolerant and helpful editor and advisor while I peppered him with first-timer questions. Everyone at Wiley I've never met face-to-face but who gave me such great advice during this process: Thanks for giving me such a fantastic opportunity.

Finally, thanks to everyone at my company and to my clients. Your boss/consultant was very distracted during the writing of this book, and you all kept things running regardless. You've all taught me a lot in the past ten years. I couldn't have written a word without those lessons.

Elizabeth Marsten: Thanks to Ian Lurie for hiring me and bringing me on board in the first place and to John Arnold for answering all my inane questions and keeping us organized and on schedule. Thanks to Rebecca Huehls for being so encouraging and helpful during the editing process. And of course to my parents, who paid for the college education that laid the groundwork for my acquiring some sort of writing skills.

Thanks big time to the team at Portent Interactive, who all contributed in some way or another.

Marty Dickinson: My first thank you goes to John Arnold for extending the invitation to me for being a part of this important and timely work. Secondly, I'd like to thank Wiley Publishing for their process as a whole. The format in which we were to submit book content has made me a better communicator in anything I write or present on stage.

My clients and customers deserve some gratitude, too, for it is you who continue to give me the incentive to try new business-building strategies and share with you the ones that work.

And, finally, special appreciation goes to my loving wife Sue, my princess Jessica, and son Douglas for keeping my feet to the fire to meet writing deadlines. I love you all.

Michael Becker: I'd like to acknowledge the everlasting and loving support of my wife and kids, who have put up with countless late nights and travel over the years as I've pursued my dreams. They're incredibly dear to me, and I would be nowhere without them.

I'd also like to extend my appreciation to a number of my industry colleagues, including my co-workers at iLoop Mobile: especially Matt Harris, who has demonstrated incredible leadership; Mike Ricci for his tireless creativity and edits; Chris Wayman for his pursuit of excellence; and the rest of the iLoop Mobile team. I couldn't find a better group of people to work with. I would be remiss in not recognizing my associates at the Mobile Marketing Association, including Laura Marriott for her support over the years. I also want to extend my thanks to Michael O'Farrell, Executive Director of the dotMobi Mobile Advisory Group, who invited me to contribute to the group as well as his recently published title *Mobile Internet For Dummies*. I'd also like to recognize the team at the Direct Marketing Association, including Paul McDonnough, Lori An Pope, Ken Ebeling Julie Hogan, and Ramnath Lakshmi-Raton, who have all given me the opportunity contribute to the DMA's efforts in helping the industry embrace the mobile channel for marketing.

Finally, I'd like to extend my thanks to John Arnold, who invited me to contribute this effort and guided me through the entire process. His contributions to the work have been invaluable.

Publisher's Acknowledgments

We're proud of this book; please send us your comments through our online registration form located at `http://dummies.custhelp.com`. For other comments, please contact our Customer Care Department within the U.S. at 877-762-2974, outside the U.S. at 317-572-3993, or fax 317-572-4002.

Some of the people who helped bring this book to market include the following:

Acquisitions, Editorial, and Media Development

Project Editor: Rebecca Huehls

Development Editors: Kathy Simpson, Beth Taylor

Executive Editor: Steven Hayes

Senior Copy Editor: Teresa Artman

Copy Editors: Brian Walls, Becky Whitney

Technical Editors: Paul Chaney, Brian Bille, Richard Ting

Editorial Manager: Leah P. Cameron

Media Development Project Manager: Laura Moss-Hollister

Media Development Assistant Project Manager: Jenny Swisher

Media Development Assistant Producers: Angela Denny, Josh Frank, Shawn Patrick, Kit Malone

Editorial Assistant: Amanda Foxworth

Sr. Editorial Assistant: Cherie Case

Cartoons: Rich Tennant (www.the5thwave.com)

Production

Senior Project Coordinator: Lynsey Stanford

Layout and Graphics: Carl Byers, Ana Carrillo, Reuben W. Davis, Melissa K. Jester, Christin Swinford, Christine Williams

Proofreaders: Laura L. Bowman, Caitie Kelly

Indexer: Potomac Indexing, LLC

Publishing and Editorial for Technology Dummies

Richard Swadley, Vice President and Executive Group Publisher

Andy Cummings, Vice President and Publisher

Mary Bednarek, Executive Acquisitions Director

Mary C. Corder, Editorial Director

Publishing for Consumer Dummies

Diane Graves Steele, Vice President and Publisher

Composition Services

Gerry Fahey, Vice President of Production Services

Debbie Stailey, Director of Composition Services

Contents at a Glance

Introduction 1

Book 1: Web Presence 7
Chapter 1: Internet Business Basics 9
Chapter 2: Making Money Online 23
Chapter 3: Designing to Sell 49
Chapter 4: Creating and Connecting Multiple Web Sites 73
Chapter 5: Creating Exceptional Copy That Sells 97
Chapter 6: Encouraging Communication 121
Chapter 7: Getting Help with Your Web Presence 137

Book 11: Search Engine Optimization 151
Chapter 1: Getting Ready for SEO 153
Chapter 2: Choosing the Right Keywords 169
Chapter 3: Eliminating Search Engine Roadblocks 183
Chapter 4: Making Search Engines Love Your Site 199
Chapter 5: Understanding Blended Search 211
Chapter 6: Writing Great Copy for Search Engines (And Readers!) 221
Chapter 7: Building Link Love 235
Chapter 8: Analyzing Your Results 251
Chapter 9: Hiring an SEO Professional 257

Book 111: Web Analytics 261
Chapter 1: Setting Your Conversion Goals 263
Chapter 2: Tracking Traffic Volumes 279
Chapter 3: Measuring Your Best Referrers 291
Chapter 4: Measuring Visit Quality 303
Chapter 5: Using Conversion Goals 313
Chapter 6: Using Goal Funnels 329

Book 1V: Online Advertising and Pay Per Click 337
Chapter 1: Grasping PPC Methods 339
Chapter 2: Combining PPC and Search Engines 345
Chapter 3: Making Keyword Lists That Sell 379
Chapter 4: Writing Ads That Earn Clicks and Pay You Back 391
Chapter 5: Budgeting and Bidding on Keywords 403

Chapter 6: Legally Speaking: PPC and the Law 417
Chapter 7: Using Tools, Tips, and Tricks of the Trade 425

Book V: E-Mail Marketing 443

Chapter 1: Adding E-Mail to a Web Marketing Strategy 445
Chapter 2: Becoming a Trusted Sender 453
Chapter 3: Building a Quality E-Mail List 469
Chapter 4: Constructing an Effective Marketing E-Mail 483
Chapter 5: Making Your E-Mail Content Valuable 517
Chapter 6: Tracking Your E-Mail Campaign Results 531
Chapter 7: Maximizing E-Mail Deliverability 545

Book VI: Blogging and Podcasting 561

Chapter 1: Picking Your Blog Topic 563
Chapter 2: Getting Yer Blog On 571
Chapter 3: Writing Like a Blogger 585
Chapter 4: Tracking Other Blogs 593
Chapter 5: Getting Involved on Other Blogs 605
Chapter 6: Promoting Your Posts 615
Chapter 7: Introducing Podcasting 623

Book VII: Social Media Marketing 635

Chapter 1: Understanding Social Media 637
Chapter 2: Creating Your Social Media Desktop 651
Chapter 3: Creating Your Social Media Plan 665
Chapter 4: Navigating Top Social Media Sites 683
Chapter 5: Building Your Network 713
Chapter 6: Creating a Winning Social Media Campaign 721

Book VIII: Mobile Marketing 731

Chapter 1: Getting Started with Mobile Marketing 733
Chapter 2: Planning a Mobile Marketing Campaign 759
Chapter 3: Running Mobile Communication Campaigns 775
Chapter 4: Launching a Mobile Advertising Campaign 797
Chapter 5: Delivering Valuable Mobile Content 815
Chapter 6: Getting Paid for Your Mobile Marketing Efforts 831
Chapter 7: Tracking a Mobile Marketing Campaign 841

Index 857

Table of Contents

Introduction *1*

    About This Book 2
    What's in This Book 2
        Book I: Web Presence 2
        Book II: Search Engine Optimization 3
        Book III: Web Analytics 3
        Book IV: Online Advertising and Pay Per Click 3
        Book V: E-Mail Marketing 4
        Book VI: Blogging and Podcasting 4
        Book VII: Social Media Marketing 4
        Book VIII: Mobile Marketing 5
    Icons Used in This Book 5

Book 1: Web Presence *7*

    Chapter 1: Internet Business Basics 9
        Understanding the Internet Marketing Process 11
        Step 1: Get in control 11
        Step 2: Establish your products and services for sale 12
        Step 3: Communicate your solution 13
        Step 4: Build traffic to your Web site 13
        Step 5: Become the recognized expert in your field 14
        Step 6: Create a virtual sales force 14
        Step 7: Power-partner with others for exponential sales growth 14
        Moving ahead with the process 15
        Planning Your Web Site Strategy 15
        Defining your target customers and competition 15
        Developing your Web site goals and budget 17
        Knowing your limits 21

    Chapter 2: Making Money Online .... .23
        Discovering the Ways to Make Money on the Internet 23
        Promoting affiliate products 24
        Monetizing traffic 27
        Selling your own products and services 29
        Assembling an Internet-Based Buying Process That Converts 30
        Defining the components of an online transaction 30
        Shopping cart setup secrets 33
        Answering important questions 35

Doubling or Tripling Your New Customer Revenue.................................36
  Upselling 37
  Cross-selling 38
  Back-end selling 38
Generating Traffic...39
Creating Your Own Affiliate Program...40
  Setting up affiliate tracking...41
  Attracting affiliates 41
  Training affiliates 42
Joint Venturing for Exponential Sales Growth.......................................43
  Getting your facts straight...43
  Finding a joint venture host 44
  Presenting your plan 45

Chapter 3: Designing to Sell.....................................49

Branding Your Look 49
  Creating taglines and slogans..50
  Developing a branded logo..51
  Creating a consistent look with CSS..53
Styling Text on the Web...54
Using the Right Colors for Your Web Site 55
  Considering what colors convey 55
  Using Web-safe colors..56
  Combining colors for your Web site 57
Adding High-Impact Photos 57
Laying Out Content on Your Web Pages 59
  Evaluating layouts with a heat map application...........................60
  Using the upper-right quadrant (URQ) 62
  Inspiring action with the horizontal navigation bar.....................64
  Choosing scrolling over clicking..66
  Attracting attention with arrows, buttons, and more..................67
  Promoting specials in the right column...68
Completing the Web Site Pre-Flight Checklist 69
Designing for Optimum Usability 70
  Incorporating usability standards 71
  Testing live for usability 71

Chapter 4: Creating and Connecting Multiple Web Sites..........73

Choosing a Traditional Web Site 74
  Starting a traditional site from a design template.........................75
  Checking out template providers 75
Creating a Blog...77
  Introducing blogging tools..78
  Setting up a WordPress blog 79
Getting Specific with Mini-Sites 82
Reaching for Traffic with Content Sites 84
Asking for Questions with an Ask Site 85
Managing a Membership Web Site 86

Defining a true membership Web site 86
Evaluating membership site types 87
Calculating your revenue potential 89
Managing Content with a Content Management System 91
Justifying Joomla! 91
Definitely Drupal 92
Considering an alternative CMS 93
Creating and Maintaining Web Site Content 93

Chapter 5: Creating Exceptional Copy That Sells. 97

Understanding the Elements of Effective Web Site Copy 97
Writing headlines with a hook 98
Proving that you're a real human being... 100
Proving your solution does what you say it will do 102
Providing clear and easy calls to action 106
Driving Sales with Landing Pages 106
Creating educational content pages.. 107
Building your opt-in e-mail list with squeeze pages 110
Providing all the facts through sales pages.................................. 111
Writing Copy That Sells, Using The C.O.N.V.E.R.T. M.E. Formula 113
Captivate visitors with a headline that hooks 114
Offer reinforcement of your headline.. 115
Now address your visitors personally 115
Validate some facts.. 115
Expose your solution... 117
Recapture visitors' attention... 117
Test for action 117
Motivate by adding value and urgency... 118
Energize visitors to buy 119

Chapter 6: Encouraging Communication 121

Perfecting Your Form... 121
Choosing the right contact form.. 121
Exploring opt-in form types... 123
Adding a Tell-a-Friend Function to Your Pages 125
Considering Online Chat... 126
Creating Audio for Your Web Site 129
Adding Professional, Homemade Video to Your Web Site.................. 131
Getting started with video 132
Editing video... 133

Chapter 7: Getting Help with Your Web Presence. 137

Recognizing the Skills You Need Help With 137
Choosing an Internet Service Provider... 139
Finding good ISP candidates 141
Interviewing and selecting the right ISPs...................................... 144
Attracting the best ISP 146
Deciding whether to outsource 148

Setting ISP expectations and measuring results 148
Nurturing a good ISP partnership 150

Book II: Search Engine Optimization 151

Chapter 1: Getting Ready for SEO 153

Understanding Why Search Engines Exist 153
Knowing What Makes a Web Site Relevant 155
Avoiding Penalties 157
Setting Up Your Toolbox 159
Downloading and installing Firefox 159
Installing add-ons 159
Setting up and using Webmaster tools 165
Installing Xenu Link Sleuth 167
Creating Your SEO Worksheet 168

Chapter 2: Choosing the Right Keywords 169

Thinking Like Your Visitors 169
Understanding the Long Tail 170
Finding the Right Tools 171
Using keyword services 171
Working with the Google AdWords keyword research tool 171
Using Google Trends 174
Watching the news 175
Using your brain 175
Picking Great Keywords 176
Judging keyword relevance 176
Comparing competition and search volume 176
Checking demographics with adCenter Labs 177
Checking your industry with Google Insights 178
Testing with pay per click 179
Building Your Keyword List 179
Sizing Up the Competition 180
Finding your keyword competitors 180
Discovering your competitors' weaknesses 180
Ignoring your competition 181

Chapter 3: Eliminating Search Engine Roadblocks 183

Ensuring Search Engine Visibility 183
Checking your robots.txt file 184
Checking for meta robots tags 184
Eliminating registration forms 185
Eliminating login forms 186
Providing a Way to Browse 187
Using Ajax and DHTML 188
Avoiding All-Flash Pages 189

Avoiding Client-Side Redirects..190
Checking Your Site Using the Web Developer Toolbar 191
Avoiding Duplicate Content 191
    Finding duplicate content using Google 192
    Linking to your homepage the right way 193
    Using consistent URLs...194
Dealing with Broken Links 195
    Finding broken links 195
    Using a 301 redirect 195
Removing Code Bloat...195
    Coding using standards 196
    Removing inline JavaScript and CSS................................196

Chapter 4: Making Search Engines Love Your Site **199**

Structuring Your Site for Search Engines and People......................199
    Creating content clusters 200
    Deep linking for special cases 204
Keeping the Structure Clean and Clear.......................................204
    Keeping content in one place...204
    Writing great link text..205
    Using keyword-rich URLs...206
    Stepping away from the site map 207
Building a Semantic Outline 207
Optimizing for Trust..208

Chapter 5: Understanding Blended Search **211**

Optimizing Products 212
Optimizing News..213
Optimizing Images 214
Optimizing Video 215
Optimizing for Local Search...217
    Optimizing your local search listings................................217
    Getting reviews and bookmarks 218
    Optimizing your site for local search................................218

Chapter 6: Writing Great Copy for Search Engines (And Readers!) **221**

Writing Online Copy..221
    Avoiding stop and filter words..222
    Keeping it simple 224
    Using active voice 224
    Getting to the point 225
    Writing scannable copy 226
    Finding the right keyword density..................................227
Writing a Great Title Tag 227
    Getting past your brand...227
    Avoiding keyword stuffing..228
    Telling your story 229
    Making it readable 229

Writing a Great Description Tag...230
Connecting Headlines to Copy..231
Avoiding a Verbal Meltdown..232
Setting a Writing Routine..232
Hiring Writing Help...233

Chapter 7: Building Link Love 235

Understanding Link Votes..235
        Links that don't count...236
        Understanding nofollow...236
Writing Link-Worthy Content...237
Encouraging Links..238
        Using absolute URLs...239
        Saying thanks...239
Getting Easy Links..239
        Submitting to directories..240
        Submitting to design galleries......................................240
        Commenting on blogs...240
Leveraging Your Partners for Links..241
Asking for Links...241
        Building a contact list...242
        Being polite..242
Building a Widget...242
Creating Quality Links..244
        Including keywords...244
        Varying link text...244
        Getting relevant links...245
Staying Out of Trouble...245
        Link buying and selling...245
        Link exchanges...246
        Link networks...246
Creating Great Link Bait...246
        Brainstorming link bait...247
        Using images in link bait..248
        Using video in link bait...249
        Managing expectations...250
Researching Your Competitors' Links......................................250

Chapter 8: Analyzing Your Results 251

Using Your Tracking Worksheet...251
        Setting up the links page..254
        Entering your keyword list..254
Watching for Plagiarism...254
Knowing What to Do If Your Numbers Fall.............................255

Chapter 9: Hiring an SEO Professional. .257

Finding an SEO Professional..257
Checking Qualifications..258

Knowing What to Ask an SEO Professional 259
Knowing What to Expect 259

Book III: Web Analytics 261

Chapter 1: Setting Your Conversion Goals. 263

Knowing What's Possible (Or Not) 264
    Collecting data and what it can tell you 265
    Understanding the limits of reporting 265
    Minding visitors' privacy 266
Knowing How Reporting Tools Work 267
    Log file reporting 267
    Web bugs and JavaScript 268
Choosing Your Reporting Tool 269
    Deciding what you need 269
    Surveying your options 270
Making Sure Your Server Is Set Up 272
Setting Up Google Analytics 272
    Create your account 272
    Installing the tracking code 274
    Tracking site search 276
    Excluding your office 277

Chapter 2: Tracking Traffic Volumes 279

Seeing Why Hits Are a Lousy Metric 279
Understanding the Five Basic Traffic Metrics 280
    Tracking sessions (visits) 281
    Tracking unique visitors 283
    Tracking pageviews 285
    Tracking time on site 287
Tracking Referrers 289

Chapter 3: Measuring Your Best Referrers 291

Understanding Referrers 291
Checking Out the Referring Site Data in a Traffic Report 293
Analyzing the Referring Sites Data 295
Tracking Referring Keywords 299

Chapter 4: Measuring Visit Quality 303

Setting Quality Targets 303
    Setting benchmarks for pageviews per visit and time on site 304
    Calculating your loyalty benchmark 305
Applying Those Targets 307
    Checking your top content against your targets 307
    Drawing conclusions based on multiple targets 308

Learning More with Bounce Rate 309
    Analyzing your homepage 311
    Spotting bottlenecks and missed opportunities 312

Chapter 5: Using Conversion Goals 313

Determining Key Performance Indicators 313
Defining Conversion Goals 315
    Maintaining consistent goals 315
    Checking out conversion goal pages 316
    Figuring out your conversion goals 317
    Finding hidden goals 318
Attaching Monetary Value to Goals 319
    Valuing e-commerce conversions 319
    Valuing leads 320
    Valuing soft goals 320
    Valuing the immeasurable 321
Setting Up Goal Tracking 321
    Setting up e-commerce tracking 322
    Tracking goals manually 324
Interpreting Conversion Data 324
    The costly keywords 324
    The hidden gold mine 325
    The great landing page 326

Chapter 6: Using Goal Funnels 329

Finding a Funnel 330
Setting Up Goal Funnel Tracking 331
Interpreting Goal Funnel Data 333

Book IV: Online Advertising and Pay Per Click 337

Chapter 1: Grasping PPC Methods 339

Seeing How Pay Per Click Works 339
Knowing How Search Engines Determine Relevancy 340
Figuring Out Whether You Need PPC 341
    Benefits of using PPC 342
    Possible drawbacks of PPC 343

Chapter 2: Combining PPC and Search Engines 345

Selecting a PPC Search Engine 345
    Researching search engines 345
    Comparing the top three search engines 346
Using Google AdWords 347
    Creating an account 347
    Setting up your first campaign 349
    Setting daily budgets and bids 350

Setting up billing in AdWords.................................352
Expanding Google AdWords.................................355
Using Yahoo! Search Marketing.................................358
Creating an account and a campaign.................................358
Naming your ad group.................................362
Setting up billing.................................362
Configuring your account.................................364
Expanding Yahoo! Search Marketing.................................365
Using MSN adCenter.................................370
Creating an account.................................370
Expanding MSN adCenter.................................375

Chapter 3: Making Keyword Lists That Sell **379**
Choosing Keywords.................................379
Organizing Keywords in Ad Groups.................................380
Working with Match Types.................................381
Knowing the match types.................................381
Choosing the match type to use.................................382
Segmenting Keyword Lists by Destination URLs.................................383
Applying keyword destinations in Google.................................383
Applying keyword destinations in Yahoo!.................................384
Applying keyword destinations in MSN.................................385
Using Advanced Keyword Targeting in Yahoo! and MSN.................................386
Advanced keyword targeting in Yahoo!.................................386
Advanced keyword targeting in MSN.................................387
Expanding Keyword Lists.................................387
Adding keywords in Google.................................388
Adding keywords in Yahoo!.................................388
Adding keywords in MSN.................................389
Contracting Keyword Lists.................................389
Analyzing underperforming keywords.................................389
Deciding when a keyword should be deleted.................................390

Chapter 4: Writing Ads That Earn Clicks and Pay You Back **391**
Working with PPC Ads.................................391
Creating the headline.................................391
Crafting the body.................................392
Planning the display URL.................................393
Choosing the best destination URL.................................393
Writing PPC Ad Copy.................................394
Follow the benefits/features model.................................394
Craft the call to action.................................394
Focus on goals, grammar, and guidelines.................................395
Avoid common mistakes.................................396
Testing for Successful Ads.................................396
Conducting A/B tests.................................396
Using dynamic keyword insertion.................................399

Determining When to Change an Ad 400
    Using goals to make changes 400
    Using click-through rate to make changes 400
    Using conversion tracking to make changes 401

Chapter 5: Budgeting and Bidding on Keywords 403

Determining Your PPC Budget 403
    Researching your assets 404
    Deciding the duration and reach of your budget 404
    Considering ad schedules 404
    Setting and sticking to your budget 405
Entering Your Budget in the Big Three Search Engines 405
    Setting a budget in Google AdWords 405
    Setting a budget in Yahoo! Search Marketing 406
    Setting a budget in MSN adCenter 407
Budgeting by Campaign 407
    Estimating traffic 407
    Setting an example campaign budget 408
Bidding on Keywords 409
    Knowing how CPC is determined 409
    Deciding what to bid 410
Bidding by Day and Time 411
    Scheduling options in Google AdWords 411
    Scheduling options in MSN adCenter 414
Tailoring Your Spending 415
    Spending by industry 415
    Spending by niche 415

Chapter 6: Legally Speaking: PPC and the Law 417

Understanding Editorial Guidelines 417
    Ad editorial guidelines 417
    Keyword list guidelines 419
    Display and destination URL guidelines 419
    Trademark and copyright guidelines 420
Dealing with Click Fraud 422
    Recognizing click fraud 422
    Detecting click fraud 422
    Reporting click fraud 423

Chapter 7: Using Tools, Tips, and Tricks of the Trade 425

Using Offline Editors 425
    Google AdWords Editor 426
    The MSN adCenter editor 427
Using Keyword Traffic Tools 428
    Estimating traffic in Google 428
    Estimating traffic in Yahoo! 429
    Estimating traffic in MSN 430
Employing Geotargeting 431

Understanding Demographic Bidding..................................432
    Demographic bidding in MSN..................................432
    Demographic bidding in Google 433
Managing a Content Network Campaign 434
    Google's content network..................................435
    Yahoo!'s partner network..................................437
    MSN's content network......................................438
Choosing an Analytics Package 439
    Analytics in Google 440
    Analytics in Yahoo!...440
    Analytics in MSN 441

Book V: E-Mail Marketing 443

Chapter 1: Adding E-Mail to a Web Marketing Strategy 445

Understanding the Benefits of E-Mail Marketing...................445
    Asking for immediate action.................................445
    Gathering feedback...446
    Generating awareness 447
    Staying top-of-mind..447
Combining E-Mail with Other Media 447
Taking Advantage of E-Mail Service Providers 449
    Checking out leading providers 449
    Exploring provider benefits.................................450

Chapter 2: Becoming a Trusted Sender 453

Complying with Spam Laws 454
    Determining which e-mails have to comply 454
    Collecting e-mail addresses legally.........................455
    Including required content in your e-mails 455
Asking for Permission 457
    Deciding on a permission level 457
    Inheriting a list: Getting permission after the fact.......460
Minimizing Spam Complaints..462
    Allowing your audience to unsubscribe from receiving e-mails...463
    Keeping your e-mails from looking like spam 465

Chapter 3: Building a Quality E-Mail List. 469

Preparing Your E-Mail Database....................................469
Collecting Contact Information.......................................471
    Deciding what information to collect.......................471
    Getting to know your list members better 473
    Posting signup links online.................................475
    Collecting information in person 477
    Collecting information through print.......................478
Offering Incentives to Increase Signups 478

Giving subscribers immediate incentives....................................479
Giving subscribers future incentives 480
Building a List with List Brokers.....................................480
Sticking to quality 481
Renting to own 482

Chapter 4: Constructing an Effective Marketing E-Mail.........483

Creating From and Subject Lines That Get Noticed...............................483
Filling out the From line 485
Writing a Subject line 488
Branding Your E-Mails to Enhance Your Image................................491
Matching your e-mails to your brand............................491
Maintaining brand consistency with multiple e-mail formats......493
The ABCs of E-Mail Layout 495
Including Images in Your E-Mails 498
Choosing a file format for your images 498
Don't embed: Referencing your images 499
Including Text in Your E-Mails.....................................501
Including Links in Your E-Mails 505
Using text links 505
Making your images into links............................509
Adding navigation links.......................................510
Including a table of contents in your e-mails 511
Linking to files in your e-mails 513

Chapter 5: Making Your E-Mail Content Valuable...............517

Sending Valuable Offers..518
Creating content to promote something 518
Cashing in on coupons.......................................519
Including incentives...521
Using giveaways 521
Making gains with loss leaders 521
Extending urgent offers......................................522
Writing an Effective Call to Action 523
Giving Your E-Mail Content Inherent Value 525
Creating content to inform your audience 525
Adding tips and advice......................................527
Providing instructions and directions 528
Putting in entertaining content 528
Including facts and research 529
Finding Help with Content Creation..............................529

Chapter 6: Tracking Your E-Mail Campaign Results..............531

Understanding Basic E-Mail Tracking Data.............................531
Calculating your bounce rate.................................532
Calculating your non-bounce total 533
Calculating your open rate 533
Calculating your click-through rate..............................535

Tracking Non-Click Responses 536
   Tracking in-store purchases..536
   Tracking phone calls 538
   Tracking event attendance 538
   Tracking e-mail replies 538
Evaluating E-Mail Click-Through Data.....................................539
   Using click-through data to target your e-mail offers 539
   Using click-through data for intelligent follow up 542
   Using click-through data for testing your
   offers and calls to action...543

Chapter 7: Maximizing E-Mail Deliverability **545**

Managing Bounced and Blocked E-Mail....................................545
   Taking action on bounced e-mail.....................................547
   Reducing blocked e-mails 549
Reducing Filtered E-Mail..552
   Establish your sender reputation.....................................552
   Understand automatic content filtering...........................554
   Understand user-controlled content filtering 554
Understanding E-Mail Authentication.......................................558

Book VI: Blogging and Podcasting 561

Chapter 1: Picking Your Blog Topic **563**

Choosing a Blog Topic 563
Thinking about Your Blog Goals..566
Sizing Up Your Space 568
   Using Technorati..568
   Using Google Trends 569
   Using search engines..570

Chapter 2: Getting Yer Blog On **571**

Choosing Your Blog Platform..571
   Blogger and WordPress.org: Easy and free 571
   WordPress installed: A sports car....................................574
   Movable Type: A racing car...575
   Other blog options..576
Getting Your Blog Set Up 577
   Blog account setup 577
   Picking your blog look..578
   Configuring comments 580
   Setting up pinging 580
   Creating your RSS feed...582
Writing Your First Post 584

Chapter 3: Writing Like a Blogger **585**

Following the Three Blog S's 585
    Writing for simplicity 586
    Writing for scannability 588
    Writing sharp 590
Clearing Bloggage 590
    Setting your editorial calendar 591
    Keeping an idea list 591
    Writing ahead 592
    Finding guest bloggers 592

Chapter 4: Tracking Other Blogs **593**

Understanding Feeds and Feed Readers 594
Setting Up Google Reader 595
Using Folders and Tags to Organize Your Feeds 597
    Using folders to organize feeds 598
    Using tags to organize feeds 600
Reviewing Feeds Fast with Hot Keys 602
Creating a Shared Items Page 603
Avoiding Information Insanity 604

Chapter 5: Getting Involved on Other Blogs **605**

Connecting with Other Bloggers 605
Leaving Great Comments 606
    Tracking replies to your comments 607
    Avoiding foot-in-mouth syndrome 609
Linking to Other Blog Posts 609
Giving Credit Where Credit Is Due 610
Writing a Guest Post 610
Joining Blog Carnivals 611
The Art of Asking Nicely 613

Chapter 6: Promoting Your Posts **615**

Publishing Your Post 615
Letting the World Know: Using Pinging 616
Submitting Your Post to StumbleUpon 616
Submitting Your Post on Digg (Once in a While) 618
    The madness of Digg 619
    Knowing when you're Digg-worthy 619
    Other social voting sites 619
Submitting Your Post to Bookmarking Sites 620
Sending a Polite E-Mail 620
Participating in Online Communities 621

Chapter 7: Introducing Podcasting **623**

Podcasting 101 623
Setting Up Your Podcasting Studio 624

Getting the right recording software.............................625
Getting a good microphone..626
Setting Up Your Studio...627
Testing Your Setup...628
Supporting Podcasting on Your Blog................................629
Preparing Your Podcast Script...630
Recording Your First Podcast...630
Encoding and Uploading Your Podcast............................633
Promoting Your Podcast...634

Book VII: Social Media Marketing 635

Chapter 1: Understanding Social Media 637
Marketing, Social Media Style...637
Exploring Social Media..638
Posting and commenting on blogs 640
Connecting via social networks 642
Bookmarking sites 644
Microblogging...646
Media sharing sites...648
Popularity sites 648
Aggregators 649

Chapter 2: Creating Your Social Media Desktop 651
Setting Up Your Social Media Desktop with RSS 651
Setting Up Your Social Media Desktop in iGoogle..........653
Setting up an iGoogle homepage 653
Adding a Web site or blog feed to iGoogle 654
Adding a blog search result to iGoogle....................656
Adding feeds to iGoogle manually 658
Creating Your Social Media Desktop on Netvibes...........658
Setting up a Netvibes homepage...............................658
Adding content to a Netvibes homepage..................659
Creating Your Social Media Desktop on My Yahoo!........661
Setting up a My Yahoo! homepage 662
Adding content to you're My Yahoo! homepage 662
Deciding What to Track 663

Chapter 3: Creating Your Social Media Plan 665
Researching Your Audience..665
Starting with online communities.............................666
Researching with adCenter Labs 667
Getting more data with Quantcast............................672
Getting fancy with paid data services.......................673
Crafting Your Social Media Message................................674
Setting Your Social Media Style.......................................675

Preparing Your Social Media Profile 676
Choosing Your Target Social Media Sites................................. 677
Reviewing Your Site for Social Skills 678
    Creating great bait 679
    Employing RSS subscriptions... 680
    Make sharing easy 681
Setting Your Social Media Marketing Routine 681
Planning for the Long Social Media Marketing Haul 682

Chapter 4: Navigating Top Social Media Sites 683

Making Friends on Facebook 684
    Using the Facebook networking tools................................. 684
    Branding and publicity: Facebook Pages
      and Facebook Events 688
    Creating your own audience with Facebook applications........... 691
Socializing on MySpace... 692
    Getting started on MySpace 693
    Understanding what's different about MySpace................. 694
    The sneeze principle, revisited 695
Networking for Business on LinkedIn 696
Bookmarking Your Way to the Top.. 697
    Building your bookmarking reputation................................ 698
    Making bookmark connections 699
    Tagging bookmarks properly 699
Playing the Social News Game 700
    Getting "Dugg".. 700
    Behaving yourself 701
Growing Your Business with Media Sharing.............................. 701
    Using Flickr as a networking tool....................................... 702
    Spreading the word on YouTube.. 703
    Reaching more folks with TubeMogul.................................. 704
Talking in Discussion Forums 704
Using Microblogs as a Launchpad... 707
    Understanding microblogging.. 708
    Building a microblog following 708
    Avoiding microblogging overload 709
Building a Good Reputation in Yahoo! Answers........................ 710
Unleashing the Power of Niche Sites 712

Chapter 5: Building Your Network 713

Finding Friends 713
Keeping Friends 715
Expanding Your Network with Questions and Answers.......... 715
    Finding questions.. 716
    Make great answers.. 717
Obeying the (Unspoken) Rules 717
Knowing When to Stop.. 718

Chapter 6: Creating a Winning Social Media Campaign **721**

The Importance of Creating a Winning Social Media Campaign 721
Marketing by Providing Tools.. 722
Social Media Marketing with Content 725
    The hallmarks of a successful content campaign.......................... 725
    Providing entertainment with a content campaign...................... 727
Leveraging Networks to Create a Winning Social Media Campaign...... 728
Addressing Harm to Your Reputation 728
Applying These Lessons Everywhere... 729

Book VIII: Mobile Marketing **731**

Chapter 1: Getting Started with Mobile Marketing **733**

Understanding and Weaving Mobile into Marketing............................... 734
    Reviewing marketing and its elements.. 734
    Defining mobile marketing and its elements 735
Adding Mobile to Your Marketing Strategy.. 736
    Planning for the complexities of the mobile channel................... 736
    Partnering with mobile service providers 738
    Aligning all the players in the mobile marketing ecosystem 740
Understanding the Many Paths within the Mobile Channel 741
    Understanding SMS capabilities 742
    Enhancing your messages with MMS 744
    E-mailing your messages... 745
    Humanizing your messages with IVR 745
    Working the mobile Internet 746
    Building installed applications.. 747
    Making connections through Bluetooth 747
Examining Key Mobile Channel Enablers 748
    It's a snap: Using the camera.. 748
    Finding the way with location 748
    Ticketing and identification with NFC and RFID 750
Deciding How and When to Use a Particular Mobile Path 750
    Six considerations for mobile marketers....................................... 750
    Ratings for mobile technologies 752
Complying with Regulations and Guidelines 753
    Adhering to industry standards and best practices 754
    Steering clear of mobile spam.. 754
    Checking mobile SMS and content program certification 755
    Avoiding contact with the National Do Not Call Registry............. 756
    Safeguarding the privacy of children 756
    Protecting personal information.. 757
    Staying compliant in special cases 757

Chapter 2: Planning a Mobile Marketing Campaign **759**

Setting Up a Plan..759
Starting with a goal..759
Planning your coverage 760
Deciding who handles what...761
Choosing an approach 761
Understanding the Costs of Mobile Marketing.................................762
Calculating up-front costs and estimated timelines.....................762
Accounting for variable costs 763
Estimating your timeline 765
Working with Common Short Codes...765
Knowing what CSCs do...765
Acquiring a CSC 766
Deciding what type of CSC to use 767
Managing Opt-Ins..769
Placing an opt-in call to action in media.................................770
Executing opt-ins 772
Handling Opt-Outs...774

Chapter 3: Running Mobile Communication Campaigns **775**

Planning Your Communication Flow..775
Creating a user-flow diagram..776
Customizing a user-flow diagram..777
Considering optional user flows 779
Providing Text Promotions 781
Using quizzes to gather information and entertain.................782
Gathering input with open-ended survey questions...................784
Calling People to Action: Polling 786
Choosing a poll type...787
Setting poll options...788
Offering Incentives: Gifts, Freebies, Samples, and Coupons...................789
Managing prize promos, contests, and giveaways 789
Offering mobile coupons..790
Applying User-Generated Content...793
Mobile blogging...793
Social networking...794
Text-to-screen and experiential campaigns 794
Tell-a-friend (word-of-mouth) programs.................................795

Chapter 4: Launching a Mobile Advertising Campaign. **797**

Reviewing the Mobile Ad Players 798
Playing the role of mobile buyer...798
Playing the role of mobile publisher 799
Understanding the role of mobile advertising enablers...............799
Placing Ads on Mobile Internet Sites 800
Placing ads on your own site..800
Placing ads on a branded site 802

Advertising during page loads and downloads..............................802
Advertising on a network of mobile Internet sites 803
Placing outside ads on your mobile Internet site.........................803
Placing Ads in Mobile Messages...804
Combining advertising and SMS 805
Displaying ads with MMS 806
Going Local with Location-Based and On-Package Advertising...........806
Proximity advertising..806
Packaging and point-of-sale advertising and promotion 807
Speaking to Your Audience through Voice-Call Ads........................809
Adding Viral and Cause Elements to Mobile Advertising Campaigns....810
Managing viral marketing elements...810
Leaning on vanity marketing 812
Stimulating social interactions...812
Supporting a cause 813

Chapter 5: Delivering Valuable Mobile Content. 815

Sourcing Your Mobile Content 815
Sending Content via Messaging 816
Sending text alerts to a group 816
Sending personalized text alerts...819
E-mailing informative messages...820
Providing Mobile Enhancements and Applications 820
Providing branded wallpapers and screen savers 821
Delivering ringtones and other system sounds 823
Making Marketing Fun with Mobile Games and Applications.............824
Considering the challenges 825
Creating a mobile application or game 825
Serving Up Mobile Web Sites 826
Employing the mobile Internet..826
Creating a mobile Web site...827
Testing your mobile site 829
Broadcasting Audio and Video Content 829
Creating audio and video content 829
Delivering audio and video content 829
Offering Branded Utility Services 830

Chapter 6: Getting Paid for Your Mobile Marketing Efforts 831

Methods of Monetizing the Mobile Channel 831
Offering Your Content through a Carrier's Portal............................832
Developing a direct relationship..832
Entering into a channel relationship 833
Contracting with an intermediate company................................833
Making Money through Premium Text Messaging............................834
Putting PSMS to work: An example campaign............................835
Setting up a premium messaging program.................................836
Determining how much you'll get paid and when 837

Selling Your Content and Services via the Mobile Internet 838
 Using mobile Internet link billing...839
 Collecting credit card payments...839
 Getting paid through PayPal 840

Chapter 7: Tracking a Mobile Marketing Campaign 841

Building Your Marketing Database...841
 Creating the database 842
 Accessing your mobile marketing data...842
Creating Consumer Profiles 842
 Outlining demographic data..843
 Organizing psychographic data..844
 Planning for preference data...844
 Benefiting from behavioral data 845
 Looking out for location data..845
 Aligning with syndicated data...845
Populating a Marketing Database...846
 Collecting data through SMS 846
 Connecting through the Web 848
 Integrating CRM and mobile campaigns 848
Using Your Database to Deliver Targeted Programs 849
 Protecting list members...849
 Tracking opt-ins and opt-outs 849
Managing Feedback...850
 Responding to feedback..850
 Reporting on feedback 851
Tracking and Measuring Interactions: Clicks,
 Calls, Votes, and More...851
 Tracking methods...852
 Data storage and analysis...852
Tracking and Measuring Purchases 854
 Tracking transactions 854
 Reconciling reports 854

Index *857*

Introduction

*I*f your business, organization, or association needs to reach people who use computers for shopping, browsing the Internet, or interacting with others, you need Web marketing. And if you need Web marketing, you need this book.

Here are some reasons why.

Successful Web marketing requires you to place and maintain your messages on multiple Internet mediums because your prospects and customers use those same Internet mediums to help them look for products and services. You don't have to be a technical expert to reap the rewards of Web marketing, but you do need to understand how people behave when they fire up their Internet browser, e-mail program, or mobile phone; that way, your marketing messages are always top-of-mind when customers are ready to make a purchase.

Because people search for products and services online, you need a Web presence that can be found easily via search engines. People are more likely to do business with companies that stand out among the competition, so you need online advertising and pay per click (PPC) to attract interest.

The millions of folks who interact socially online act as an influence to others who share their interests and preferences. Thus, your marketing messages need to find their way to social media networks, blogs, podcasts, and viral communities. You need to be able to communicate with your prospects and customers when you have timely information, which means using effective e-mail marketing, really simple syndication (RSS), and text messaging.

To keep track of which marketing strategies get you closer to your goals, you need analytics and tracking. The rapid adoption of mobile devices with Web capabilities means that your marketing messages need to be available to folks with a mobile phone so they can find your offers anytime — and almost anywhere.

The breadth of topics covered in this book, combined with easy-to-follow tips, make this book perfect for your business, organization, or association. Keep this book on a nearby bookshelf or on your desk so you can reference it often. That way, you can allow the combined experience of these five seasoned authors — all experts in their own niche of Web marketing — to guide your plans and decisions to more successful outcomes.

About This Book

We know you're busy. After all, you're trying to market a business (or are just getting started), right? With that in mind, we wrote this book for time- and value-conscious people who are in charge of marketing a small-to-medium–sized business, organization, or association. If that sounds like you, we hope you've been using or exploring Web-marketing tactics. And if you haven't, you're in the right place.

No matter what your level of experience, you'll find this task-oriented reference book as your guide to describe the entire Web-marketing process step by step. This book is also a great resource for you if you're searching for a career in Web marketing or a Web marketing–related field.

What's in This Book

This book is really eight minibooks, each covering a topic related to Web marketing. Each minibook covers a topic in its entirety, so each is a concise — yet comprehensive — path to learn about the Web marketing topics you need to know about.

The content in each minibook and each chapter stands alone, so you don't have to read all the minibooks — or even all the chapters — in order. You can use this book like an entire series of books on the subject of Web marketing. Scan through the table of contents to find a single topic to refresh your memory or to get a few ideas before beginning a task, or you can read an entire chapter or a series of chapters to gain understanding and gather ideas for executing one or more parts of an entire Web-marketing campaign. When a topic is mentioned that isn't covered in depth in that chapter, you'll find a cross-reference to another minibook and chapter where you can find the details.

The following sections offer a quick overview of what each minibook contains.

Book 1: Web Presence

The "Build it, and they will come!" days of the Internet are long gone. With literally billions of Web pages online, according to Google, competition for customers online is fierce. Most successful business owners have turned to using multiple outlets to promote their products and services through the Internet. And many have outsourced teams of helpers to implement integrated, Internet marketing campaigns. How can you compete?

This minibook introduces you to the Internet marketing process of today: a step-by-step sequence to follow for using the Internet to its fullest potential for your business. Whether your business has reached a growth plateau or is just starting, simply locate where you are in the process and plug in!

Best of all, you don't need to be a Web designer or a programmer to put this section to immediate use for your business. Focus on understanding "the process" so you can find the right helpers to help establish — and explode — your online presence. This minibook shows you how.

Book II: Search Engine Optimization

Building a Web site is pointless if no one can find it, and three-quarters of everything that happens on the Internet starts with a hit on a search engine. *Big takeaway:* Ignore search engines, and you might as well turn away three of every four customers who ask for help.

The good news? A high ranking in organic, unpaid search results can drive thousands or even tens of thousands of customers to your site. The bad news? You can't bribe or buy your way to the top. You have to get there by building a site that's attractive to search engines and customers alike.

And that's the art of search engine optimization (SEO). Don't get rattled by the term: SEO isn't a black art. We demystify it so you can see how it's nothing but a series of steps and little things you do to move up in the rankings. This minibook walks you through the steps, getting you started on your way up the search result rankings.

Book III: Web Analytics

Web marketing is unique: You can track the performance of every ad, page, and product; measure the return generated by your marketing efforts; and quickly adjust your site and advertising to get the best result.

To do all that, though, you need Web analytics. This minibook starts with the general principles of traffic reporting and analytics — and the difference between the two. Then it demonstrates setting up traffic reporting and analyzing the data you collect.

Book IV: Online Advertising and Pay Per Click

Pay per click advertising can be a very complex — yet simple — medium to conquer. The concept itself is simple. You post an ad, someone clicks it, and you pay a fee for every time someone clicks. Where it gets complex is in the management of those ads, keywords, and budgeting. This minibook helps walk you through the most necessary concepts that you need to know to have a successful pay per click account.

Pay per click is a great way to get a spot for your Web site on the front page of search results and to get in front of people who are specifically looking for what you have to offer. If you're working on organic search engine rankings but just aren't there yet, pay per click is just one of the resources you should consider using for getting your message to an interested audience.

Book V: E-Mail Marketing

Every successful marketing strategy entails cutting through the clutter, and few places are more cluttered than the average consumer's e-mail Inbox.

E-mail marketing represents an opportunity to experience both the thrill of increased customer loyalty and steady repeat business as well as the agony of bounced e-mail, unsubscribe requests, and spam complaints. Whether you find thrill or agony in your e-mail marketing strategy depends on your ability to effectively deliver valuable and purposeful e-mails to prospects and customers who need your information.

This minibook combines time-tested marketing strategies with consumer preferences and best practices to help you develop and deliver professional-looking e-mails that your prospects and customers look forward to receiving. Additionally, this minibook shows you how to turn your prospects into loyal customers who make more frequent purchases.

Book VI: Blogging and Podcasting

Everyone's talking about blogging, to the point where it's hard to know what's truth and what's myth. When you look past the hype, though, you can see that blogging is a powerful business tool.

Using a blog helps you reach new customers, connect with influencers, tell the story behind your product or service, and build your site's SEO potential.

This minibook explains what blogs are and why they matter, how to set up a blog, principles for writing blog posts, and how to reach out to other bloggers to build traffic.

Book VII: Social Media Marketing

Social media is a buzzphrase that's used to describe a wide array of conversational tools in use on the Internet. These tools help Web users connect, converse, and make better use of the resources they find online.

Social media is also a business opportunity. You can reach out to customers, find new audiences, and talk to existing ones in more ways than ever.

This minibook explains social media; separates truth from fiction; and then demonstrates specific business strategies for major social media outlets, such as StumbleUpon, Facebook, and Twitter.

Book VIII: Mobile Marketing

The mobile phone is no longer simply a phone: It's evolved into a newspaper, map, camera, radio, shop, stereo, TV — and yes, it's still a phone, too.

An estimated 3 billion people are mobile subscribers around the world, and ResearchandMarkets.com expects the number to grow to 4 billion in 2008. The United States alone has 263 million subscribers according to the Cellular Telephone Industries Association (www.ctia.org). With traditional media channels fragmenting, the mobile channel is emerging as a powerful medium for business-to-business (B2B), business-to-consumer (B2C), and consumer-to-consumer (C2C) direct customer engagement. For the uninitiated, getting a firm grasp on how to leverage the mobile channel successfully for profitable interactive engagement and the mobile enhancement of marketing practices can be a significant challenge. This minibook will help you overcome this challenge.

In this minibook, you'll find the information you need to integrate mobile marketing successfully into your marketing plans. We define mobile marketing and show you how it fits within the broader practice of marketing. We review the mobile marketing ecosystem; best practices; myriad paths that make up the mobile channel; and a plethora of applications you can use to communicate, deliver, and exchange value with your audience. After you read this minibook, you'll have a strong grasp of the practice of mobile marketing and will be ready to engage your audience.

Icons Used in This Book

The Tip icon marks tips (duh!) and shortcuts that you can use to make Web marketing easier.

Remember icons mark the information that's especially important to know. To siphon off the most important information in each chapter, just skim through the paragraphs marked with these icons.

The Technical Stuff icon marks information of a highly technical nature that you can normally skip.

The Warning icon tells you to watch out! It marks important information that may save you headaches.

Information highlighted with this icon points out how a technique or tool works in the real world. We might recount something from our experiences or share something we've seen or heard. Nothing speaks louder than history, so don't skip these nuggets of Web marketing in action.

Book I
Web Presence

The 5th Wave   By Rich Tennant

"Guess who found a Kiss merchandise site on the Web while you were gone?"

Contents at a Glance

Chapter 1: Internet Business Basics............................9

Understanding the Internet Marketing Process 11
Planning Your Web Site Strategy...................................... 15

Chapter 2: Making Money Online 23

Discovering the Ways to Make Money on the Internet.................... 23
Assembling an Internet-Based Buying Process that Converts............. 30
Doubling or Tripling Your New Customer Revenue....................... 37
Generating Traffic... 40
Creating Your Own Affiliate Program 41
Joint Venturing for Exponential Sales Growth......................... 44

Chapter 3: Designing to Sell...............................49

Branding Your Look... 49
Styling Text on the Web.. 54
Using the Right Colors for Your Web Site 55
Adding High-Impact Photos 57
Laying Out Content on Your Web Pages 59
Completing the Web Site Pre-Flight Checklist 70
Designing for Optimum Usability 71

Chapter 4: Creating and Connecting Multiple Web Sites..........73

Choosing a Traditional Web Site 74
Creating a Blog.. 77
Getting Specific with Mini-Sites 82
Reaching for Traffic with Content Sites 84
Asking for Questions with an Ask Site 85

Chapter 5: Creating Exceptional Copy That Sells.................97

Understanding the Elements of Effective Web Site Copy 97
Driving Sales with Landing Pages 106
Writing Copy That Sells, Using The C.O.N.V.E.R.T. M.E. Formula 113

Chapter 6: Encouraging Communication 121

Perfecting Your Form.. 121
Adding a Tell-a-Friend Function to Your Pages 125
Considering Online Chat... 126
Creating Audio for Your Web Site 129
Adding Professional, Homemade Video to Your Web Site................ 131

Chapter 7: Getting Help with Your Web Presence................137

Recognizing the Skills You Need Help With 137
Choosing an Internet Service Provider............................... 139

Chapter 1: Internet Business Basics

In This Chapter

✔ Understanding the Internet marketing process

✔ Creating a Web site plan

✔ Knowing who your customers are

✔ Setting goals for your Web site

✔ Calculating your Web site promotion budget

✔ Deciding what to do yourself and when to hire an expert

*I*n 1995 — often called the "Olden Days" of the public Internet — the average computer connected online via a telephone line, reaching download speeds of merely 56 Kbps. We would wait patiently (often for several minutes) while images loaded, pages displayed, and long paragraphs of text rendered font sizes and color combinations to challenge our optical nerve endings.

And we didn't have many choices. For example, very few comparison shopping opportunities were available online. For many, the idea of having a Web-based shopping cart to accept product orders from a Web site was as far into the future of possibilities as owning a flying car.

Because of the manual effort and knowledge base required to create a Web site back then, business owners with forward-thinking minds but limited budgets would negotiate paying a few hundred dollars for a single basic Web page — or even a mini-page — just to have some type of presence on the Web. Web sites with multiple pages were restricted to the technical companies who could employ programming staff and designers. In short, having a presence on the Web of any kind was a luxury and more of a status symbol than anything.

Today, of course, the game has changed — considerably.

Your Web site is any and all of the following:

✦ **Most cost-effective sales vehicle:** It can accept orders 24 hours a day, 7 days a week without the need for employees to process the order by phone or in person.

✦ **Ultimate lead generator:** Even the smallest businesses can be in competition with the largest companies for attracting new customers worldwide.

✦ **E-mail list builder:** Inspiring visitors to give you their e-mail address for something they will get in return (such as a newsletter, a free report, coupons) allows you the opportunity to make routine contact with prospects so you can earn their trust over time.

✦ **Worldwide marketing outlet:** Even the smallest businesses can be in competition with the largest companies for attracting new customers anywhere in the world.

✦ **Market research spy:** Use online tools to "legally" know what your competition is doing to promote products and services on the Internet to help you make your own decisions of how and where to promote.

✦ **Fast market tester:** Make changes to prices and sales copy as often as you'd like and the changes happen immediately, usually with no cost associated (unlike print marketing).

✦ **Collections agent:** Credit cards are automatically charged at the point of purchase before the product is shipped or services are delivered.

✦ **Communications vehicle:** Company developments can be announced to a mass audience within a few hours or even minutes.

✦ **Support department:** The Internet offers one person the ability to provide immediate assistance to multiple customers at the same time by displaying FAQs and offering personalized attention with online chat and e-mail support.

✦ **Product delivery truck:** The Internet allows new product forms to be developed that require no shipping, such as e-books and MP3 audio downloads.

This chapter is meant for business owners, Web site designers, programmers, and other providers of Internet services alike. First, I introduce you to today's Internet marketing process. By understanding the process, you know the right time and sequence of steps to apply any strategy you glean from this minibook, such as having various Web site components in place before launching a Google AdWords campaign, or knowing your conversion rates before attempting to recruit affiliates to promote your product. I then help you assemble a realistic plan that will enable you to use the Internet to its fullest potential for the growth of your business.

Understanding the Internet Marketing Process

I want to be clear from the start. Your Web site is an important component to your success with the Internet, that's true. However, it's far from being the *only* piece of the pie. In and of itself, the creation of your Web site is really only about 5 percent (or maybe even less) of what you need to gain any real presence on the Internet. Sure, having your Web site appear on search engines is important, too. But, for most companies, search engine presence is only another 5–10 percent of the overall opportunity that awaits you.

Today's entrepreneur finds success by following a step-by-step process to grow and run his company via the Internet. The following sections outline this process for you.

Step 1: Get in control

The success or failure of your Internet marketing strategy determines whether food appears on your table next month and whether your bills get paid. You must be in control of any process that affects your lifestyle. Basic components you should be in control of include

✦ **Original Web site design files, including images, photos, and logos:** In the event that your designer suddenly becomes unavailable through other employment, discontinued interest in your project, or even death, having access to originals will allow you to transition easily to another service provider.

✦ **Web site hosting logins:** Every Web site needs a Web site hosting location where all the files are stored and accessed on the Internet. You should always choose your own hosting company and pay for that service directly to the hosting company. Any login user names and passwords supplied by that hosting company should be in your name and in your control. You might very well provide access to your Web site to helpers such as designers, programmers, and Internet marketers, but the only way you'll have the ability to change passwords in the event you want to change helpers is if you are in charge of your hosting account.

✦ **Backups of all content, pages, and HTML code:** In the event that you need to change Web site hosting companies or you decide to fire your copywriter or administrative staff who might supply or maintain your Web site content, always have a current backup of your Web site's pages. That way, if your hosting company pulls the plugs on their servers and goes out of business, you could still be up and running with another hosting provider within a matter of hours — *if you have good backups of your content.* Otherwise, if you don't have access to those pages, you would need to create all those documents from scratch. Not good.

✦ **Domain name logins and registrations in your name:** Your domain name is the heart of your Web site. It is the most critical component of all. As the business owner, you *must* own your domain name, have it registered in your name, and have exclusive rights to maintain it. Never let your designer, administrative assistant, or even your mother register your domain name for you. A domain name such as *YourBusinessName.* com is tied to the Web server where your Web site resides. If you decide to change hosting companies, the only way to change where the domain name directs is by logging into your *domain name registrar* (the company where you registered your domain name) and changing the appropriate settings. This is something only you should have control over.

✦ **Additional logins or passwords:** Beyond the basic Web site level, a variety of user names and passwords will be issued to you. These could include a Google AdWords account, article directory submission logins, visitation statistics reporting access, YouTube video accounts, social networking logins (as presented in Book VII), and third-party e-mail management systems (such as Constant Contact, discussed in Book V), to name a few. When you're implementing your own Internet marketing campaigns, be sure to have all account registrations in your name, using your e-mail address. That way, you always retain administrative rights to those promotional outlets.

However, if you choose to outsource the more time-intensive Internet marketing functions (such as Google AdWords, as an example), be open to the idea of a professional organization having the exclusive right to that account. After all, there is a great deal of magic that skilled Google AdWords managers will be reluctant to hand over to you should you choose to cut your ties with their services. In cases like these, you really are still in control: that is to say (cough), you are in control of whether you will pay that service provider for additional services next month. Make sure that your service provider supplies you with routine progress reports so that you can make that assessment accurately.

Step 2: Establish your products and services for sale

If you have a business, money needs to eventually transact, or you won't be in business for long. Part of the Internet marketing process is identifying what products your market wants, how or whether your competition offers anything similar, and what online methods you will use to transact that sale online and deliver the goods. Book I, Chapters 3, 4, and 5 offer an introduction to strategies that help you accomplish this step.

TECHNICAL STUFF

Getting your site files via FTP

If you use a Web designer outside your company, you can easily transfer copies of all your current HTML files, images, and photos by transferring your files with File Transfer Protocol (FTP) software. Here are the steps, but you should have your hosting company or designer walk you through the backup process if this is your first time:

1. **Download the free (LE) version of Core FTP at `www.coreftp.com/download. html` (for Windows computers) or Cyberduck at `http://cyberduck. ch`, which is also free.**

2. **After the program downloads, click Open to begin the setup wizard.**

The screen defaults to the Site Manager.

3. **In the Site Manager, enter a title related to your site.**

4. **Fill in the Host, Username, and Password as supplied by your hosting company.**

5. **Click Connect.**

You see all your Web site files on the right, and your computer files on the left.

6. **Click the main directory on the right side; when you see an arrow pointing left, click it.**

Your Web site files begin transferring to your computer.

Step 3: Communicate your solution

Your future customers will visit your Web site with a problem to solve. And, they're hoping you have the solution! Before launching any traffic-building campaign, assure that your Web site delivers the highest potential conversion rate.

REMEMBER

A *conversion* is the point at which a Web site visitor takes the next desired step with your business: for example, buying a product, subscribing to your newsletter, or picking up the phone to get more information. The percentage of visitors that convert — the *conversion rate* — is one of the most critical numbers to keep track of on a weekly, or even daily, basis.

I discuss the importance of conversion rates in "Create traffic and conversion what-if scenarios" later in this chapter. Book III offers more nitty-gritty details about setting and meeting conversion rate goals.

Step 4: Build traffic to your Web site

After your Web site is converting on a small scale, the next step is to increase visitation. This is where press releases, search engine optimization, articles, and podcasting (to name a few campaigns) come into play. There are more than 100 methods for driving traffic to a Web site. Your job is to research each type of traffic generator and decide which outlets are good fits for your budget and desired speed to market. Each minibook in this book provides detailed steps toward implementing the most impactful traffic builders used today on the Internet. Master those first — such as search engine optimization (Book II), pay per click advertising (Book III), and social networking (Book VII) — and you will naturally graduate to other traffic-building opportunities over time.

Step 5: Become the recognized expert in your field

People buy online from other people whom they know, like, and trust. The Web is a tremendous tool for achieving all three, and in a short amount of time and on a shoestring budget. You become the expert by sharing what you know about your industry. The blog is one of the greatest inventions in recent years for developing a following and becoming a perceived leader in your field. A blog is, by definition, a Web site like any other. It contains graphics, content, and formatting just like all traditional Web sites. However, a blog has additional firepower that, if used correctly, can automate almost the entire publicity distribution process for you, giving you the opportunity for near immediate visibility (see Book VI).

Another essential, and often overlooked or misused, component to becoming a recognized authority in your field involves using e-mail (see Book V).

Step 6: Create a virtual sales force

After you have traffic and proven conversion rates, you can recruit people to promote your products and services to others. These virtual ambassadors (most of whom you will never meet in person) are *affiliates*.

You don't have to pay affiliates until they sell something, but having even just four or five eager affiliates could easily double or triple your revenue inside one month's time. Without an affiliate program, you would be missing out on one of the greatest opportunities on the Web: letting others sell your products and services for you. The next chapter of this minibook covers affiliate marketing in more detail.

Step 7: Power-partner with others for exponential sales growth

Also known as a *joint venture, power-partnering* is similar to having an affiliate program but on a much larger level, both financially and personally. The process involves finding one very special person who's of high stature in an industry and then convincing that person to recommend your product or service to his very large sphere of influence. The results could mean literally thousands of sales for you within as short as one week's time.

Moving ahead with the process

The great thing about this Internet marketing process is that it works for every business type, large or small. The unfortunate stories you've heard from other business owners about their painful online experiences is probably because they didn't work the process. That process includes asking for help from people who have demonstrated Internet marketing skill and paying for such services in your annual marketing budget.

Going forward — seeing as how you now know the process — you can probably figure out where your business fits in. Maybe you have plenty of traffic, but your Web site isn't converting as many visitors to customers as you want. In that case, go to Step 3 in the process. Or, you're getting traffic and sales, but you're experiencing an unordinary amount of returns. Go to Step 2 and build a better product or service. Conversely, after you make it through the sequence and you're now becoming a recognized expert in your field, you want to set your sights on creating an affiliate program because a virtual sales force and ultimately a joint venture opportunity will be right around the corner.

With the Internet marketing process in hand, you can take a fresh and honest approach to creating your plan.

Planning Your Web Site Strategy

Just like how the Internet marketing process is a sequence, developing your online strategy is much the same. For example, you must know your customers and how much they're willing to spend before you can create goals for how much you can sell. You need to know your own capabilities and interests as well as how much you want to be involved with the mechanics of the project before you can determine your budget.

Defining your target customers and competition

Many business owners create a product first and then try to figure out who they can sell to. This method isn't optimal, though, because it doesn't offer a predictable outcome. Always be aware of who needs your product or service and your competition. These are your two keys to success, and you can do much of your research to gain this knowledge on the Internet.

If you already have a Web site up and running, identifying the most popular groups visiting your Web site is easy. Just look at the visitation statistics for the pages of your Web site to see the popular topics your audience is interested in.

However, if you're just in the development phase of your Web site, find an industry-specific forum (a Web-based discussion board) to find out what questions people are asking about your industry. The most popular topics and discussions in those forums will help you identify most popular needs — and, therefore, the most probable categories of people who will be visiting your Web site.

1. **Document three categories of needs.**

   At least three main groups of people will always visit your Web site in search of a solution. For example, if I were a doctor, I could know from history that new patients come to me because they

   • Have an insurance change and are forced to find a new doctor

   • Aren't getting their needs met with a former doctor and are looking for someone new

   • Are unhappy with the doctor staff or surroundings

2. **Identify competition.**

   Using Google.com, search for specific keyword phrases to see what competition might be present in your area of focus. For example, if you were a doctor with a specialty in dealing with stroke victims, you would want to search Google for *"stroke doctor"*, followed by your city or even your state.

3. **Spy on your competition by pointing your browser to Quantcast (www. quantcast.com) (see Figure 1-1) and entering the URLs of competing sites in the search box.**

   Continuing with the doctor scenario, you could look for the following pointed results:

   • Average number of visits per month

   • Average age

   • Percentage of male versus female visitors

4. **Estimate revenue potential.**

   Verify whether there could be enough business to make that product worthwhile.

5. **Calculate potential market share.**

   List the number of competitors and potential customers by region.

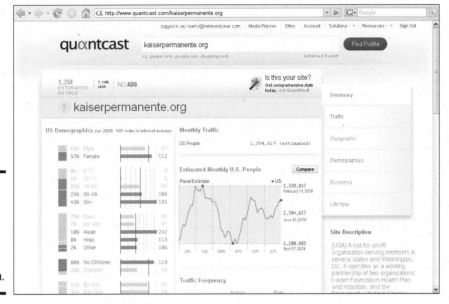

Figure 1-1:
Quantcast
reports
demo-
graphics
of your
competition.

Developing your Web site goals and budget

After you're confident that you have a product or service that's in demand, you can begin to develop the goals for your Web site. Here's a list of what you need to calculate those goals:

✦ How much profit do I need per month for my business to grow?

✦ How many new customers do I need each month to achieve that revenue level?

✦ What is the average sale quantity I need to make to accomplish my goals?

Too often, a business owner will create her operating budget from the ground up. First, she accumulates costs involved with setting up an office. Then, advertising costs are calculated. Business cards and brochures are quoted. At the end of the day, a required monthly sales revenue requirement is generated to assure a certain amount of growth per month or year for a start-up company. This approach is reversed when it comes to using the Internet to build a business. The following sections outline a better process to following when establishing a budget for Web marketing.

Start with your financial goals

There are so many proven models for building businesses online that you have no reason to "pick numbers out of a hat" any longer. In fact, you can pick virtually any financial number you want to receive per month or per year and have a very close idea of what kind of budget will be required to get you there. Use this formula to determine your own online marketing budget:

1. **Determine your desired annual gross revenue.**

   In other words, decide how much money you want to make by the end of a 12-month period. For this example, use the number that seems to be in everyone's sights these days: $1 million in gross annual revenue.

2. **Calculate your average sales value (ASV).**

   An *average sales value* is the total dollars received for all purchases within a given time frame divided by the number of purchases made. It is neither cost related nor profit oriented. Average sale value is simply a number for you to use as a marker to help determine how many overall sales of all products combined you need in the future to reach a desired gross revenue.

   You might have only one product or service to sell right now — and that's okay. You can work on that later! Maybe you've been in business for years, with multiple product lines, a variety of pricing, and a number of purchases for each price point per month. In either case, you need an average sale value to work with to determine your Internet marketing budget. For the following example, keep it simple, and say you have an average sale value of $27 for an e-book you created.

3. **Project your required sales per day.**

   I created a basic Excel spreadsheet showing common average sale values and how many sales per year you would need to arrive at $1 million in gross revenue. Here's the formula I used, where DR is desired revenue, ASV is average sale value, and SPY is sales per year:

   ```
   DR / ASV = SPY
   ```

   According to Figure 1-2, and continuing with the $27 e-book example, you need 37,037 sales of your e-book over one year's time. Broken down further, that translates to an average of 3,086 orders per month, or 102 orders per day. Remember that is *on average*. So, the first few months could be considered ramp-up time during a new product launch phase, and you could still hit that number by the end of the 12 months if you play the numbers.

These are simple calculations to make, but sometimes you don't really see it until you truly *see it* on paper.

Figure 1-2:
Annual,
monthly,
daily sales
needed for
revenue
goal.

# of Sales Needed for $1,000,000 in Gross Revenue per Year			
Average Sale Value	# Sales/Year	# Sales/Month	# Sales/Day
$10	100,000	8333	274.0
$27	37,037	3086	101.5
$100	10,000	833	27.4
$200	5,000	417	13.7
$500	2,000	167	5.5
$1,000	1,000	83	2.7
$5,000	200	17	0.5

REMEMBER

The numbers you calculate here are starting points. In Book I, Chapter 2, you find out how the you can turn a simple $27 sale into a $100 sale or more by using upselling, cross-selling, and back-end selling techniques. Then, if every $27 sale turns into a $100 sale, you would need only 27 sales per day (versus 102) on average or 833 sales per month (versus 3,086) to arrive at your desired $1 million revenue goal.

With a better idea of how many sales you're after per year, month, and day, read on to discover how to calculate the Web site visitation you need to arrive at those numbers.

Create traffic and conversion what-if scenarios

Next, create a similar spreadsheet to show how improving your conversion rates can reduce the amount of traffic you need to make the same revenue as well as the amount of sales per month. (If you're unfamiliar with conversion rates, refer to the section "Understanding the Internet Marketing Process" earlier in this chapter.)

To determine your required visitation per month to meet your sales revenue goals, use the following formula, where S is the number of sales you need, C is the conversion rate (which is a percentage), and V is the amount of Web site visitors needed to produce those results:

$S\ /\ C\ =\ V$

Adding this formula to a spreadsheet (see Figure 1-3) using Excel or Google Docs is not only critical to your creation of a budget and overall Internet marketing plan, but it enables your ability to dream a bit as well. Although I used 1% as a starting point and .05% would be more realistic as an average, why not triple the number displayed in the sales column or double your conversion rate to see how that reduces the number of visitors you need to acquire? Go ahead; no one is watching. It's okay to dream!

# of Visitors per Month Needed to Achieve Monthly Sales Goal of 3086 at $27 Each		
Monthly Sales Desired	Conversion Rate	Monthly Visitation Required
3,086	0.10%	3086000
3,086	0.50%	617200
3,086	1.00%	308600
3,086	1.50%	205733
3,086	2.00%	154300
3,086	3.00%	102867
3,086	5.00%	61720
3,086	10.00%	30860

Figure 1-3: Web site visitor traffic needed per month.

Continuing with the $27 e-book example and the goal of making $1 million in revenue by the end of a year, the formula would look like this:

```
3,086 / 0.01 = 308,600
```

Or, in simple language:

> 3,086 (sales per month) divided by .01 (a 1% conversion rate) = 308,600 visitors needed per month to reach your goal

 Notice how much the needed monthly visitation drops with each small increase in conversion rate. Many marketers have proven that spending your effort testing ways to increase conversion rates — rather than focusing solely on increasing traffic — is far easier (and certainly less expensive).

Here are a few significant insights for analyzing information like this:

✦ **Predictability:** You can predict how much revenue your business will see next month — and over the coming months — based on the traffic you generate over just one week's time.

✦ **Reactivity:** When you recognize that visitation decreases suddenly or your conversion rates drop, you have the opportunity to investigate why — and make immediate changes. A shift of even one-quarter of a percentage rate increase or decrease could mean the difference of thousands of dollars.

✦ **Testability:** One of the greatest features of the Web is that practically anything online can be changed. Gone are the days when you have to pay a designer to build your Web site once and never get to change anything. Today's tools allow you to constantly test, tweak, and try new things to increase conversion rates and visitation. You don't have to wait until you see a severe drop in visitors or sales to do something about it. You can always be working toward increasing those results!

You can easily see the importance of continually monitoring visitation and conversion rates. Such good practices make up the basic fabric from which you make all online promotion decisions going forward.

Book III of this resource goes, in depth, into multiple Web analytics tracking setup and strategies.

More than half of prospective clients who seek Internet strategy help don't know their visitation or conversion rates. Get the answers before you call a service provider for help. Their first two questions will be to ask you those rates.

Calculate how much to spend per visitor

After you determine how many sales you need to meet your goals and how much traffic you need to generate your desired sales volume, the next logical step is to calculate how much money you can afford to spend to get the traffic. Again, I use a basic Excel spreadsheet (shown in Figure 1-4) to demonstrate.

Figure 1-4: Expense allowance per visitor.

# of Visitors per Month Needed to Achieve
Monthly Sales Goal of 3086 at $27 Each

Monthly Sales Units Desired	Total Monthly Sales at $27	Conversion Rate	Monthly Visitation Required	Cost Per Visitor Break Even	Cost Per Visitor at 20% Net
3,086	$ 83,322	0.10%	3086000	$ 0.03	$ 0.02
3,086	$ 83,322	0.50%	617200	$ 0.14	$ 0.11
3,086	$ 83,322	1.00%	308600	$ 0.27	$ 0.22
3,086	$ 83,322	1.50%	205733	$ 0.41	$ 0.32
3,086	$ 83,322	2.00%	154300	$ 0.54	$ 0.43
3,086	$ 83,322	3.00%	102867	$ 0.81	$ 0.65
3,086	$ 83,322	5.00%	61720	$ 1.35	$ 1.08
3,086	$ 83,322	10.00%	30860	$ 2.70	$ 2.16

This number is significant for your operating budget process because it allows you to create a specific marketing projection based on predicted results. For example, you could have 20 percent of your budget allocated to organic search engine optimization services, 10 percent toward your continued learning, 50 percent going to Google AdWords, and 20 percent allocated toward offline marketing efforts. Simply change the numbers in the formula to create your own instant what-if scenarios.

Knowing your limits

Many of us start a business because we want to be our own boss: to make all the decisions and be responsible for all functions. By the time the business is up and running, though, you've likely discovered just how many decisions need to be made and how many functions there are to do — and how much time they all consume. For example, using the Internet to bring leads and sales to your business can easily be a full-time job for at least one person. Even the most cutting-edge online strategies won't move forward until you turn the keys in the ignition.

Answer these questions to help you decide how much you want to be involved with the day-to-day operations of a Web site strategy:

+ What am I really, *really* good at?

+ Which skills make sense for me to improve, and for what tasks should I hire someone who already has the necessary skill set?

+ What do I enjoy doing that I could do all day long and not require payment?

+ What type of work do I absolutely despise?

Use Table 1-1 to rate your ability and willingness to perform the following functions (rank from 1–5, where 1 = low, and 5 = high). Then add each line for your total.

Table 1-1	Rating Yourself on Key Web Marketing Tasks		
Tasks Description	*Ability*	*Interest*	*Total*
Web site design	1 2 3 4 5	1 2 3 4 5	_____
Programming	1 2 3 4 5	1 2 3 4 5	_____
Web server administration	1 2 3 4 5	1 2 3 4 5	_____
Content writing	1 2 3 4 5	1 2 3 4 5	_____
Copywriting	1 2 3 4 5	1 2 3 4 5	_____
Publicity	1 2 3 4 5	1 2 3 4 5	_____
Accounting	1 2 3 4 5	1 2 3 4 5	_____
Sales	1 2 3 4 5	1 2 3 4 5	_____
Research	1 2 3 4 5	1 2 3 4 5	_____
TOTAL			_____

For any task where your total is less than 6, it would likely be in your best interest of time to pay someone to perform that role for you. Anything for which you score an 8 or higher, you might find total enjoyment from performing that task on your own. The middle ground offers opportunity for learning and growth.

Nearly everyone who's truly successful on the Internet has a team of people who bring special skills to the table. The Web changes so quickly that any one person keeping up with everything is impossible, especially after you have a successfully selling product or service on your hands.

Chapter 2: Making Money Online

In This Chapter

✔ **Identifying the components of accepting a sale online**

✔ **Turning one sale into two or more**

✔ **Building traffic for free and for a fee**

✔ **Building a virtual sales force**

*M*aking money on the Internet is like panning for gold: Your fortune can be made instantly, or you can spend a lifetime chasing the dream. Had a goldpanner in the late 1800s known what we know about the Internet today, he would've realized that directly panning for gold to feed his family wasn't his only income opportunity. For example, he could have also rented his spot on the creek, or sold drinking water to other panners, or taught beginners his secrets of goldpanning for a small fee. And after he had a proven claim, he could've recruited others to pan for him or pay others to sell usage of his claim.

When you think of making money from the Internet, what's the first thing that comes to mind? Selling your own product through your Web site is probably at the top of the list. Or, maybe you offer a service and want people to pay online so you can help them. Both of those, of course, are relevant ways to make a sale on the Internet — but there are several others.

In this chapter, I introduce you to a variety of ways to make money online, including the tools and tactics to help you mine online for traffic and revenue.

Discovering the Ways to Make Money on the Internet

Of the many ways to make money by using the Internet, they all fall into three main categories:

✦ Promoting affiliate products

✦ Monetizing traffic

✦ Selling your own product

In the following sections, I take a look at each more closely.

Promoting affiliate products

An *affiliate product* is an item that someone else produces, delivers, and supports. All you have to do is recommend that others visit that company's Web site. When someone makes a purchase through that Web site as a result of your recommendation, you get paid a sales commission. Affiliate programs don't usually require you to create a Web site to promote them. They are also commonly free to join.

A domain name at `www.bestdomainplace.com` is an example of an affiliate product that I promote to my own clients (see Figure 2-1). Whenever someone buys a domain name or any of the other Internet services offered, I get a small commission on the sale. The product is then delivered and supported by the main company. All I have to do is supply some customizations and the traffic.

This is how an affiliate program works:

1. Find an affiliate product.

Your first step is to find a product that you're interested in recommending. Your interest can stem from a topic that your customers have shown interest in that you don't offer, or maybe a trend you recognize in your industry. My domain affiliate program, for example, stemmed from my witnessing too many business owners with domain names registered by their Web designers — meaning that the business owner didn't truly own his own domain name! My affiliate program offered me the opportunity to help them transfer their existing domains to a system in which they had full administration rights to their own domain names.

Likely, your first affiliate products of interest will come from items you've already used and are impressed with, such as a good book, a software program, or maybe a CD set. And affiliate programs can be quite lucrative — offering more than $1,000 per sale — so you don't have to settle only for small-dollar-value products.

Here are two main ways to find affiliate programs to consider:

- *Search on a search engine.* To find an affiliate product on a search engine, search for an industry-specific topic or an exact product, followed by the words *"affiliate program"*. See the example in Figure 2-2.

- *Use an affiliate aggregator,* such as ClickBank (`www.clickbank.com`) or Commission Junction (`www.cj.com`), where all the money and affiliate payments are handled.

Figure 2-1:
Example of
an affiliate
product.

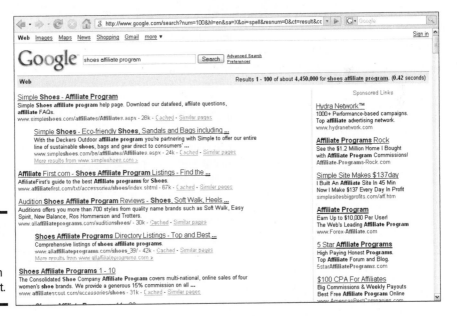

Figure 2-2:
Search for
an affiliate
program on
the Internet.

2. **Access your unique affiliate link.**

   Visit the company's Web site and add an affiliate account there. You will be directed to an administration area, where you can find a link to use in your promotions. When people click your affiliate link and make a purchase, you get credit for sales that originate with your recommendation.

   In the example in Figure 2-3, I accessed the affiliate admin area for promoting a conference. For every person who signs up through my affiliate link, I get $1,000 as a commission check!

3. **Promote your affiliate link.**

   After you have the link to promote, copy and paste it for use in your e-mails and on your Web site.

When I join an affiliate program, I always register a domain name to forward to my unique affiliate link. That way, I don't have to remember a long string of numbers and letters every time I want to promote my link to someone. Plus, promoting an affiliate product verbally is a lot easier if I can have people visit a domain name that's tied to the affiliate link. That way, I still get credit for the sale.

Visit the administration area frequently because that's where you find important statistics related to your affiliate product, such as the number of visitors to your affiliate link, the number of sales per month, conversion rates, and most importantly, the dollar figure you can expect to receive in your bank account for those referred sales.

Figure 2-3:
Example of a unique affiliate link URL.

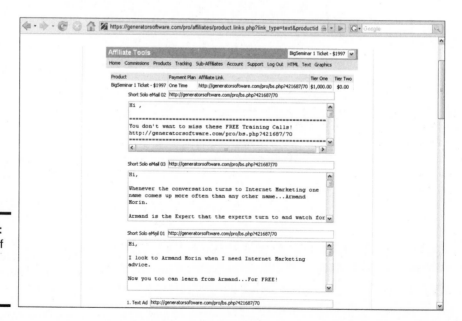

Monetizing traffic

If you can attract Web site visitors, you can turn that traffic into money —
monetize — without promoting affiliate products or attempting to sell your
own. Here are a few examples of monetizing traffic:

✦ **Google AdSense ads:** AdSense is the most popular method of advertising on the Internet today. Within a few minutes, Google supplies a
bit of code that you add to your site, and you begin making money
immediately when someone clicks the provided links. Google makes
it especially easy for you by instantaneously figuring out what ads to
display on your page that have the most potential of being clicked. Get
started by adding a Google AdSense account at `www.google.com/
adsense`.

AdSense ads don't typically produce large revenue from small Web sites
with low visitation. So, to make any real money with AdSense, be prepared
to build a site with lots of pages like the example at `www.leadership
articles.net`, where literally hundreds of pages have been optimized
for high search engine–results positioning. Notice the Google ads at
the top.

The whole intention with AdSense ads is to drive your traffic to other
people's Web sites. So, it's usually not a good idea to display AdSense
ads on pages where you're selling your own product!

✦ **Traditional banner advertising:** When you work directly with an advertising client to display her ads on your Web site, you're using traditional
banner advertising. The three ways to offer traditional banner ads on
your site to business owners include

• *Cost per click (CPC):* When you use this method, it's up to you to
track how many times visitors to your Web site click an ad's link.
Google Analytics is free statistics-tracking software that allows
you to track what are called *Banner Ad Exits,* appropriately named
because visitors will be exiting your Web site through the banner ad.
Here is a shortcut URL to Google's explanation of how to use Google
Analytics to track banner ad usage:

`http://tinyurl.com/5579ju`

Then you report that number of clicks to your advertising client and
charge them accordingly. You decide the amount you charge per
click. Personally, I like to have this type of advertising prepaid. So, I
might charge, say, 3 cents per click for an inventory of 10,000 clicks,
for a total of $300.

If your advertising client wants to produce her own ad (which is usually the case), you'd better hope that she creates an ad that attracts
clicks, or her ad will just be taking up space on your Web site.

Wondering about the difference between cost per click and pay per click? Technically, when the money comes from the bank account, there is no difference between PPC and CPC. Your perspective in the transaction may influence how you see things, however. Certainly the easier of the two to understand is "pay" per click, meaning as the business owner, you will "pay" every time someone clicks your ad. On the other hand, "cost" per click is accurate too because, to the one who actually "pays" for the clicks, a higher or lower "cost" per click can be experienced based on how you create your ad, the landing page, and so on.

✦ **Cost per 1,000 page views (CPM):** With this method, you're not reliant upon the quality of ads for you to get paid. An advertiser simply pays you in advance to showcase his ad on a page of your Web site for a certain number of times that the Web page is accessed by visitors. Typically, CPM rates range between $4 and $10 per 1,000 pageviews, but prices can easily be higher for niche audiences.

If you intend to sell traditional advertising on your Web site, be prepared to show advertisers detailed reports of pageview visitation and click-through rates. A *click-through* occurs when a visitor to your Web site clicks the ad you're promoting and is brought to another Web location. Your advertiser will expect to see proof that he got what he paid for, or he could ask for his money back. See Book III, Chapter 2 for information about how to track traffic volume.

The Interactive Advertising Bureau (IAB) Web site at `http://tinyurl.com/yps483` provides a nice display of the most common banner ad sizes. And, with IAB media company members being responsible for almost 90 percent of all online advertising in the United States, this resource is certainly the industry standard for banner ad best practices.

✦ **Pay per call (PPC) and pay per lead (PPL):** These fairly new methods of advertising have been gaining popularity over the past couple of years and are usually managed by third-party companies, such as Ingenio Pay Per Call (`http://paypercall.ingenio.com`), and might include using banner or text ads to get your visitors to take action with their promotions. The great appeal with a company such as Ingenio is that you don't pay a dime until you get a phone call from a lead.

✦ **Call per action (CPA):** With this method, the advertiser has to pay only when a sale is made. This is the ultimate form of paid advertising because the pressure is really on the promotional agency to close the deal so that its efforts get rewarded. Actually, CPA advertising is a lot like having your own affiliate program because the third party is paid only when you get a sale.

Selling your own products and services

At first glance, the idea of selling your own products and services online would seem to be the most profitable path because you get to keep all the money. This isn't always the case, especially in the short term. With affiliate programs, proven content is normally already provided for you, so ramp-up time is fast, and your investment is low. With monetizing traffic, the ads on your pages are commonly already tested and proven to work.

Selling your own products and services can prove to be the most challenging because you have so much work to do before you can begin selling. However, there is no substitute for creating your own product if you want creative control and long-term growth potential. Here are some guidelines to follow when offering your own products and services for sale online:

✦ **Information products are still king.** An information product — which can be as simple as a how-to book — is still the easiest and least expensive product to produce and deliver. Virtually anyone with a computer can use a word processing program to write a how-to book and then convert it to a PDF (Portable Document Format) file. You can use a free, online PDF converter at `www.pdfonline.com/convert_pdf.asp`, which will send an e-mail to you with your converted PDF document.

✦ **Audio is queen.** If typing isn't your forte or style, buy recording equipment and talk into a microphone to create 30- to 40-minute MP3 audio files to sell. For as little as $75, you can buy a digital recording device with a lapel microphone for hands-free recording. Or, make a complete CD set showcasing your knowledge. After you get started with audio, you will quickly realize the unlimited opportunity potential available by producing recorded products and promotional content.

Another great use of audio would be to interview an expert the next time you attend a conference. Host a short ten-minute Q&A, add the sound file to your blog, and send a notice to your opt-in list that you added the recording for their review.

✦ **Video is HOT, HOT, HOT.** Every Web site can enhance the buyer's experience by offering video, especially when there is a product for sale. Software can be demonstrated, shoes can be modeled, e-books can be featured, and services can be displayed. Video sells online, and video products sell, too. Professional video can now be produced in your own home for a one-time purchase of just a few hundred dollars in software and equipment.

✦ **Webinars are the ultimate education tool.** A *Webinar* is an online session in which you walk through a presentation or training session on your computer while an audience views your presentation online and hears your voice from their computer. The best part about Webinars is that they can be recorded and offered as a product for sale. Microsoft's www.gotomeeting.com — owned and operated by Citrix — has video and audio recording built in to its Webinar tools.

✦ **Create a whole product line.** For every information product you produce, you can create an entire product line by offering the nearly identical product in e-book form, MP3 audio recording, video, Webinars, and in-person seminar training.

The following sections in this chapter focus on the tools needed to accept and promote online sales of your own product. Of course, many of the techniques described here can be applied to promoting affiliate products and monetizing traffic, but examples shown are more directed toward selling products online.

Assembling an Internet-Based Buying Process That Converts

Sure, you must have a Web site that's graphically satisfying to visitors to entice them to become interested in — and find — your offer (as discussed in Book I, Chapter 3). Of course, you must have promotional copy that inspires a prospect to take action with your offer (as presented in Book I, Chapter 5). Perhaps the most important component of all is the actual buying process you provide. Without a smooth buying process, you could lose not just some sales but all your sales potential. The following sections walk you through the elements of online transactions and offer tips to ensure that customers who buy your products have a positive experience on your site.

In the sections that follow, I focus on marketing. If you're building a site yourself or need to work directly with a technical team, you likely need to understand at least some technical aspects of Web design, site organization, and security as you move from marketing concepts to actually implementing your buying process. For help, check out *Building Web Sites All-in-One For Dummies,* 2nd Edition by Doug Sahlin and Claudia Snell (Wiley).

Defining the components of an online transaction

Every online transaction has three main components: the transaction page, the merchant account, and the payment gateway. The following sections introduce each component and offer tips for getting started.

The transaction page

The *transaction page* is where buyers enter their contact information and credit card number. For the transaction page, you may use a formal shopping cart or a custom form:

✦ **Shopping cart:** The most popular way to sell products and services is through an Internet-based ordering system known as a *shopping cart.* You're probably familiar with the system through your own online shopping: Just as you use a cart to shop in a grocery store — picking certain items off the shelf, adding them to your shopping cart, and then proceeding through the check-out lane — a Web site visitor clicks an Add to Cart button for purchasing items online. The difference is that an online shopping cart system allows you to set up your entire store on the Internet, complete with products, services, categories, sale discounts, and, of course, a transaction page where visitors see credit card payment types accepted, fields to enter their billing information, shipping, and tax. See "Shopping cart setup secrets," a little later in this chapter, for my tips on working with shopping carts.

✦ **Custom form:** Not all transaction models can fit into the mold of a prepackaged shopping cart, but require a custom form instead. A custom form allows you to have any combination of product purchases on the same page. The downside is that custom forms take a lot more work to create and integrate with the payment gateway.

See `www.thunderridgeski.com` for a good example where a season pass purchaser might also buy a pass for his wife and two children, along with a locker. The form allows for the transaction to take place all on the same customized, secure page.

Whether you choose to use a third-party shopping cart versus a custom order system will largely be based on cost and turnaround time. When you use a commercial shopping cart, you can be live for selling your product within just a few hours, provided that you already have an Internet-capable merchant account and gateway.

The merchant account

You must have an arrangement with a company to accept credit card information for your online transactions, using an Internet-capable merchant account. This special kind of merchant account is designed to accept and track credit card transactions over the Internet. This Internet-capable merchant account could be PayPal, or you could get your own through a bank.

The merchant broker I recommend to all my clients for the lowest transaction fees possible is Lew Kelly with Expedient Financial Services, Inc. Lew has been selling merchant accounts for more than six years. I refer all my clients to him because nobody knows more about the merchant account business than he does. Lew's phone number is 303-256-7501. He welcomes the opportunity to give you a free consult by phone if you're out of state, or an in-person visit if you're within metro Denver and the front range of Colorado. Lew will educate you about how almost all merchant accounts charge you more than they should per transaction without you even knowing it. But, then he will make your life easy by completing all the paperwork with you and even getting the next step of the process set up for you: namely, the gateway.

Using only PayPal at the beginning for accepting payments online is a good idea while you get your feet wet with online transactions. As soon as possible, though, get your own merchant account. There is no precise measurement I'm aware of, but I would guess that as many as 25 percent of your Web site visitors simply won't buy from you if you accept payments only through PayPal. Some might be fearful of being the victim of PayPal's next hacking, while others will question whether you're really an established business. To be fair, if you don't offer a PayPal payment option, an estimated 10–20 percent of potential customers won't buy from you, either, because they pay for everything online via PayPal.

The payment gateway

A *payment gateway* is a tool that ties the transaction page with the merchant account. Authorize.Net is an example of a payment gateway and has been my choice for more than 12 years of accepting orders through the Internet. Authorize.Net (www.authorize.net) is also the only gateway I've found that allows the use of custom forms, such as the one used in this Web site, featuring the Thunder Ridge ski resort in New England (see Figure 2-4).

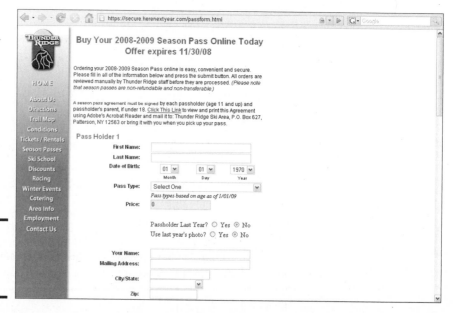

Figure 2-4:
Custom order form example.

Shopping cart setup secrets

From a revenue standpoint, it is absolutely critical to set up your shopping cart to sell — and well. In Table 2-1, I outline helpful actions to take as you set up your shopping cart and explain the benefit of each action.

Table 2-1	Shopping Cart Setup Secrets
Shopping Cart Setup Action	*Benefit*
Customize the look of the order page to match the appearance of the rest of your Web site.	Users aren't distracted by an abrupt change in look and feel.
Assure all images are uploaded to a secure directory.	An error message won't display when visitors click from your sales page to the order page.
Display the item description, quantity being ordered, and price on the order page.	Buyers are assured they're paying for only what they want.
Display that either credit cards or PayPal can be used as the payment source.	You show willingness to accommodate customers' preferences.
Remove all navigation buttons from the order page.	This prevents tempting the buyer to exit the purchasing process.
Create a custom Thank You page for each individual product sold.	This give you the possibility for cross-selling.
Create an auto-responder for each product, which is an e-mail or sequence of e-mails automatically sent to a customer upon purchase.	You can add a customer to a specific list to market later with back-end sales offers.

My shopping cart of choice for more than five years now has been 1ShoppingCart (http://1shoppingcart.com) because of its all-in-one feature set and because it's one of the few shopping cart systems that offer free technical support by telephone. My favorite features of 1ShoppingCart include

✦ **Ease of use:** Customers can easily add and maintain products to the shopping cart.

✦ **Premade graphics:** The system creates Add to Cart buttons for you: Just copy and paste the code to your Web site.

✦ **Customizability:** The capability to make your order pages look just like the rest of your Web site.

✦ **Payment options:** 1ShoppingCart enables you to offer payments through PayPal, your merchant account, both, or neither. That's right — you can use 1ShoppingCart to accept credit card information without actually processing the order online.

✦ **Coupons:** Using coupons enables you to run specific promotions and track their effect on sales.

✦ **Custom thank you pages:** This is one of the rarest features of low-end shopping carts and one of the most important for increasing sale value per customer. When folks make a purchase through your shopping cart, they already have their credit card on the table. This is the best time to get them to buy more. Only through the use of a custom Thank You page can you make that special offer while their credit card is still out of their pocket and you have their undivided attention.

✦ **Built-in affiliate program:** You don't need to find a third-party, affiliate-tracking system to manage your shopping cart. It's all integrated already. ("Promoting affiliate products," earlier in this chapter, introduces third-party affiliates.)

✦ **Digital download capable:** If you have an e-book or MP3 audio files, you can set them up in the system to be downloaded upon purchase instead of hosting the files on your own server.

✦ **Built-in auto-responders and mailing system:** An *auto-responder* is an automated system that sends a message (that you create) to someone that requests information from you. There is a direct correlation between folks receiving automated or routine e-mails from you and their willingness to purchase your products or services.

Any sales trainer will tell you that you need to be in communication with a prospect at least seven times before he is willing to buy from you. On the Web, this number is typically even higher. Why? Because everyone is a skeptic online. So, you must prove over time that you are worthy of doing business with. Setting up automated responses gives you the opportunity to gain trust from your prospects so they will buy from you. A great way to attract your audience to join your auto-responder list is to offer opt-in forms on your Web site to download free reports. When someone buys your product, he can automatically be moved to a customer list and removed from the prospect list.

✦ **Free technical support by phone:** This is the most important feature, as well as the hardest to find these days. If you choose to sell products online, it's only a matter of time before you will want some help. Never subscribe to a shopping cart system that doesn't offer support.

1ShoppingCart is a great solution for the small or beginning marketer. After your sales reach the next level of complexity, you'll want a system more integrated with your sales efforts. When that time comes (or if you're there now), I recommend looking into NetSuite (www.netsuite.com) and Infusionsoft (www.infusionsoft.com) as upgrades. For nonprofit organizations, check out a full Customer Relationship Management (CRM) system, such as Convio and Crown Peak (www.convio.com; www.crownpeak.com), which are the emerging leaders in the field.

Answering important questions

Before someone takes the final step and uses a credit card to make a purchase through your ordering system, a series of questions go through his mind within a matter of minutes. Many of these questions can and should be addressed in your sales letter or on your product sales page (as described in Book I, Chapter 5). But, these questions must also be addressed during the check-out process, or it could kill the sale.

People want to buy from you. After all, your offer is the solution to their problem. All you have to do is not stand in their way. Too often, Webmasters put too much effort into graphics instead of paying attention to writing copy that sells, or to the shopping cart itself, which provides a smooth order process. By human nature, your audience consciously or unconsciously looks for reasons to not buy from you. Your job is to minimize those obstacles by providing the information they need to make an informed decision to buy while at the same time providing an easy buying procedure.

Here are just some of the questions your Web site visitors will be asking themselves before placing an order:

✦ **How do I get what I ordered?** Clearly describe your delivery method. Will there be an immediate digital download link available, or will purchasers be required to drive somewhere for pickup?

✦ **How long will it take to get what I ordered?** Mention whether you have the items in stock or whether a fulfillment house needs to burn a series of CDs that will be sent to your customer in the next three weeks, for example.

✦ **Is this site secure?** Make a statement to your prospects that invites them to look for an image of a closed padlock in their browser while on your order page.

✦ **Is this company legitimate, or did it make an outlandish offer it can't really fulfill?** Use testimonials to prove you can do what you say you can do.

✦ **Did I make the right decision?** Assure buyers that their purchasing choice was a good one by offering a follow-up e-mail.

✦ **What will be done with my contact information after the order?** Assure your customers that their contact and billing information is held strictly confidential.

✦ **Whom do I contact if there's a problem with my order?** Provide a phone number or an e-mail address where people can get in touch with you if they have any questions.

✦ **Where do I go to get a refund?** Mention this in your guarantee. (See Book I, Chapter 4.)

✦ **Did I get everything I was supposed to?** Provide a checklist of all items that are to be received so that your customer can cross-check what arrived.

✦ **Should I expect more communication from the seller?** If your product offer includes more communication from you — such as, weekly coaching, a bonus e-course, or ongoing support, for example — be sure to state what to expect in the offer.

✦ **When will my credit card be charged?** It has become more common to have a statement right in the header of the shopping cart that requires people to agree to payment terms, like, "I understand and authorize that upon purchase, my credit card will be charged $975 payable to HereNextYear, Inc."

✦ **Am I ordering the right product?** Reassure the buyer that this product is right for him. A popular way to do this is in the postscript statements at the bottom of the page. For example

> *P.S. Remember, if your company has experienced more than a 2% turnover in the past six months, this team-building program is tailor made for you!*

✦ **Am I getting the best price possible for this purchase?** Another element of effective copywriting (as discussed in Book I, Chapter 4) is to tell your readers that you have scoured the Web and have found that no one has what you're selling, for the price you're offering.

✦ **Have I completed the sales process yet, or do I have something more to do?** If there are three steps to the buying process, mention that there will be three steps involved. When the final step is complete, display onscreen that the visitor has completed the process.

✦ **Is it really worth the price?** Reassure the buyer that your product is worth not only the price you're charging, but a whole lot more as well. Back up that statement with real reasons to increase the value of the purchase.

Doubling or Tripling Your New Customer Revenue

Doubling or tripling the initial sale amount for new customer purchases begins with having more products to offer. These can be your own products or affiliate items. Make a list of all the products you could possibly promote, and you're on your way to maximizing every new customer sale.

The next step is to think about your range of products and their cost. Every business should have products for sale with multiple price levels, known as *price points*. A consultant, for example, could feature products ranging from free to several thousand dollars, as shown in Table 2-2.

Table 2-2	A Consultant's Possible Price Points
Product Type	*Price Point*
Industry report	Free
E-book	$27
2-hour seminar	$50
3-CD set with training manual	$97
Silver-level coaching program	$149 per month
1-day boot camp workshop	$250
5-week live Webinar training course	$497
Gold-level coaching program	$300 per month
Platinum-level coaching program	$997 per month
One-on-one consulting onsite	$4,500 per day

With your product range and price points in place, you can upsell, cross-sell, and back-end sell your products to existing customers. Although it's no secret that the easiest people to sell to are your existing customers, a point often overlooked is that people always want more. They will pay for an initial problem to be fixed and then pay more for related issues to be addressed. Your task is to simply inform them that "more" is available and give them an incentive to take advantage of it. That's where upselling, cross-selling, and back-end selling come into play, as you discover in the following sections.

Upselling

Upselling is nothing more than convincing someone to buy a more expensive version of what he already decided to buy. You've likely been asked, "Would you like cheese on that? Fries with that?" Or, if you've ever ordered a gin and tonic, you were probably asked whether you preferred a name-brand gin versus the house stuff. Sure, the bartender was trying to be a good host, but he was also trying to make a better sale. Using the earlier example of selling an e-book, an upsell opportunity is when someone buying the e-book for $27 gets to the order page and is made a special offer to purchase a 3-CD Set with Training Manual, instead, for $97.

Cross-selling

Cross-selling is most easily defined as promoting accessories during the purchase process. Using the preceding example, say someone buys the e-book for $27. Then, the Thank You page features a special offer that the purchaser can add the 2-hour seminar CD set to her purchase. That's cross-selling.

Cross-selling can occur before or after the initial sale is made — and sometimes in both instances! You really have to know your audience, though, when trying to cross-sell. If you offer too many accessories before the point of purchase, the buyer may get distracted, confused, or just plain annoyed by feeling pushed to buy more. Overzealousness can kill a sale.

I prefer to get the initial sale and then offer additional options immediately after that first purchase is complete. The promotion is made on a custom Thank You page. If you've ever bought something on the Internet, you eventually get to a page that reads, `Thank you for your order and please print this page for your records.` This is the page you want to customize to maximize your potential for increasing your initial purchases from one dollar value to the next.

In Figure 2-5, you see one of my most popular Thank You pages, where the reader is given an incentive to buy two of my training manuals at one, low cost. By the time the customer gets to this Thank You page, he has already spent $27 with me. By inspiring him to take immediate action and spend another $70, the total transaction becomes $97. About half of my $27 initial purchases turn into $97 sales, using this method.

Back-end selling

When people become associated with your business, whether as a customer or even just as a newsletter subscriber, you have the opportunity to offer solutions to them. *Back-end selling* is promoting products on the "back end" of an action they took with you. There are so many giveaways of information and tangible items on the Internet today that could otherwise be sold for money because of this simple reason: There is often more value in the back-end sale.

Here are some simple examples of back-end selling:

✦ An e-mail newsletter promoting a new product release offered only to current customers

✦ A follow-up phone call or in-person meeting with a customer two weeks after the product has been received

✦ A personalized letter sent by postal mail addressed specifically to the person who purchased your product

If you have enough affiliate products in your arsenal, you can pick the perfect moment to suggest a recommendation for purchasing.

After your systems are in place for accepting sales online — complete with upsells, cross-sells, and back-end offers — you're ready to take the next step in the Internet marketing process: namely, driving visitors to your Web site. Read on for details.

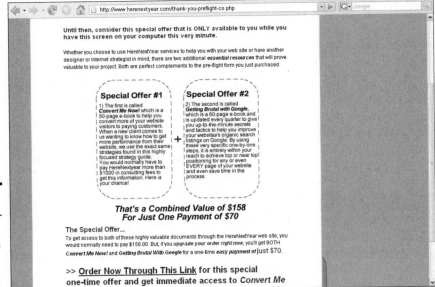

Figure 2-5:
Make cross-sell offers on a custom Thank You page.

Generating Traffic

Business owners often ask me, "How can I get my Web site on top of Google?" When I ask them why they want to accomplish that goal, they respond with, "Because it's free!" Um, not really. Generating traffic to your Web site of any kind is far from free. You either have to spend your own time to attract visitors, pay for visitors directly, or hire helpers to do the work required to get the visitors. You could always follow the detailed steps offered throughout this book on your own, but don't forget that your time has value. Let me repeat: *No traffic is totally free.*

Having said that, here are five core categories of traffic on the Web that virtually all businesses can benefit from:

+ **Free search:** Although effort and time have a cost, many search engines and directories don't require you to pay a fee to get listed. Google, MSN, Yahoo!, and dmoz are good examples. And, by getting the pages of your Web site visible on the preceding search engines alone, you will have the potential of being in front of more than 80 percent of all search engine and directory traffic. Optimizing your site content can help you appear higher in search engine results, as Book II explains.

+ **Paid search:** With the growth in development of measurement tools (such as Google Analytics, for example), paid search has become an accepted and essential form of promotion for any product or service.

Earlier in this chapter in the "Monetizing traffic" section, I discuss CPC, CPM, PPC (call, not click), PPL, and CPA. Each applies to how you can pay to receive targeted traffic as well.

✦ **Supplying content:** Just when you think every topic of content has been covered, new angles and opinions emerge. Supplying content to the Web through blogs, really simple syndication (RSS), press releases, articles, and forums, and the growing surge of content pushing to cellphones are traffic-generating processes that are available for you right now to pursue. Internet users will always search for content. You just have to find out what they're searching for and supply them with unique content. More on this topic can be found in Book I, Chapter 5.

✦ **Offline efforts:** Don't overlook your opportunities to use offline resources to promote your Web site. More than 900 radio talk shows throughout the United States alone need guest experts every day. Offer a giveaway to listeners every time you're on the radio. Networking events, associations, leads groups, and schools and churches are always looking for interesting speakers to deliver short, 30-minute messages to their audience. Deliver content-rich information and suggest a visit to your Web site for a free download or for more information about your company. And, always provide the opportunity for people to be added to your e-mail list.

Joe Sabah has appeared on more than 650 radio talk shows around the country, most by never even leaving his home. He produces a handy contact list and program at www.sabahradioshows.com for getting on radio talk shows.

✦ **Referrals:** Of course, no visitor is a higher-quality visitor than a referral. Referrals will spend more time on your Web site and are much more likely to buy from you because they have reached a certain level of trust in you because of the referral.

Whether referrals come from offline or online, always strive to increase visitors who are referred by someone else. One of the great ways to do just that is to start your own affiliate program, which I explain how to do in the next section.

Creating Your Own Affiliate Program

Not long after you gather some experience as an affiliate promoting other people's products do you start to imagine how you would benefit from having others promote your products and services. Plus, you will discover things they're doing right as well as what needs improvement when it comes to helping you sell their products. Use these experiences and incentives to create your own affiliate program so that others can sell your products and services for you. Even a moderately successful affiliate program can quickly propel your business to a new level that would've been impossible (or at least extremely difficult) to attain on your own.

Setting up affiliate tracking

All Web-based affiliate programs require three essential components, including

✦ **An affiliate center:** This is where affiliates can add an account for themselves; check their sales; and get links, ads, and scripts to promote.

✦ **A reliable, integrated connection to the product being sold:** Don't allow an affiliate to promote your products with links that don't work! Least-worse case, you'll be embarrassed. Worst case, your affiliate will likely never promote your products again.

✦ **A payment-tracking system:** To stay on an affiliate's good side, you need a mechanized way to determine when and how much you need to pay each affiliate.

Fortunately, 1ShoppingCart offers all these features rolled into one, which is why it's my choice for affiliate-program software and the one I recommend to many of my clients. See "Shopping cart setup secrets" earlier in this chapter for details on 1ShoppingCart.

Attracting affiliates

After your affiliate center is complete, announce to your clients that you're looking for people to recommend your products and services to others — and that you do pay referral fees. The easiest people to recruit for promoting your products to others are those who have used your products and services. Your customers often become your best salespeople.

For example, here is a short letter that I recently sent to one of my client lists announcing a new product being added to my affiliate program for them to market.

> *Hello [firstname] and welcome to Friday. You may remember hearing that we've been working on the most recent quarterly edition of our "Getting Brutal with Google" search engine optimization manual.*
>
> *I'm happy to say that it's now complete!*
>
> *So, not only am I including this quarter's edition, but I'd like to give you an invitation as well to get involved with our affiliate program. If you like how Getting Brutal has worked for you, why not recommend it to other business owners you know?*
>
> *When they buy through your affiliate link, you will get 50% of the purchase price! It's an easy sale. Simply visit HereNextYear.com and look for the "Affiliates" link at the bottom of the page and sign up. We'll help you every step of the way from there.*

Training affiliates

Having a small network of affiliates will bring in some additional sales, but the general rule is that you will need 20 affiliates for every 1 who produces any sales. That means to have 50 producers, you would need to have more than 1,000 registered affiliates. This ratio can be greatly reduced through continuous opportunities for training. Here are some ways you can train your affiliates:

✦ **Conduct a weekly conference call.** Keep this call short: say, no more than 40 minutes. And always have someone on the call who is being interviewed — maybe an industry expert or a sales trainer. Conference calls where one person talks the whole time are boring, and are usually long-winded and disorganized. Create an agenda for what will be covered on the call and follow it. Always start on time and end on time.

I've used Free Audio Conferencing (www.freeaudioconferencing.com) for all my conference calls for three years now and have had as many as 85 people on the call with no technical glitches.

✦ **Record the conference calls.** Most conferencing systems will provide a means for recording your calls at the press of a button. Send an e-mail to your affiliate list with a link to the recorded call immediately after the call is complete so that any affiliate can listen to it again and share it with others. And, if some folks missed the call, you can give a little promotion in the e-mail about what was covered and why they should listen.

✦ **Provide one-on-one assistance.** Until your affiliate group gets too large to manage by phone, provide some individual coaching to each new affiliate beginning right after a member signs up.

✦ **Provide the tools to use in their promotions.** Being an affiliate for more than 30 different products and services, I can tell you firsthand that *I am lazy* when it comes to promoting other people's products! I don't want to write my own sales copy and pay my designer to create banner ads for products that aren't mine. I want the company I'm promoting to provide all that for me. The more they provide me, the more I will promote them. See how that works? When you're on the other side of the fence, trying to build and launch your own affiliate program, you must be willing and even excited to put the effort into making sales copy, images, promotions, audio, and even potentially video for your affiliates to use in their efforts to promote your products. Know that your affiliates will be lazy, too, and will look to you to have all those resources produced for them. Consider all the resources your affiliates might need to help sell your offers, and they will be more dedicated to promoting you.

Register for your own affiliate program so that you can identify areas of the signup process that need improvement.

Joint Venturing for Exponential Sales Growth

In 2004, when I began teaching Internet strategy through workshops, my first audience had ten people. One of those attendees was a fellow marketer and speaker who happened to have 7,500 devoted opt-in readers of his newsletter. Together, we conducted 14 workshops over the course of a year for nearly 1,000 of his subscribers. He supplied the meeting room and the food; I produced the sales copy for the e-mails he was to distribute to his list and set up his shopping cart to accept the registrations; and off we went. The first two workshops sold out in 24 hours. The next two sold out one month in advance, in 72 hours. I was suddenly on the fast track to a speaking career!

I share that example to illustrate the true power and speed of joint venturing and to differentiate it from a simple affiliate program. I could've easily rented a hotel meeting room and promoted to my affiliates to sell the workshop for me. Joint ventures are different, though: They're more involved, yet often far more lucrative. There are rules, though, and a protocol. The following sections explain how to pursue a joint venture relationship to potentially double or triple your business in size, stature, and sales volume within a matter of a few months.

Getting your facts straight

Compared with affiliates, which are quick to promote products to their lists and to people they know, joint venture hosts are very selective. Notice that I use the word *host* instead of *partner*. That's because a joint venture host is more like the master of ceremonies at a seminar than like a true business partner. Joint venture hosts don't care about looking at your accounting books or having an influence on who you hire for employees. They just want to sell your product in mass quantities and get a big check in the mail from you! It's the host's job to give you a raving recommendation to his multitudes of followers, and your task is to provide the goods to the host's followers. Before you approach a potential host for a joint venture, you must have all your ducks in a row, including

✦ **Sales:** Documented proof of your success selling your own products and services.

✦ **Visitation and conversion rates:** Documentation of how many people visit your Web site per month, and also how many of those visitors convert to customers resulting from your Web site, sales copy, and shopping cart. If your host drives 50,000 visitors to your sales page tomorrow, what kind of sales could be expected? In Book III, you can read all about using Web analytics tools to capture these numbers.

✦ **Affiliate performance:** How many affiliates you have. And, how many sales your affiliates have produced for you so far as well as your affiliate's conversion rates.

Affiliates will typically get better conversion rates than even you (as the Web site owner) because the visitors are coming as a result of a personal referral. Conversion rates from a joint venture host can be even higher because the receiving audience knows that the host's high profile recommendation is at stake. If they're recommending it, it *must* be good!

✦ **Fulfillment:** How many orders you could fill in a week's time. For example, imagine if Mark Victor Hansen (of *Chicken Soup for the Soul* fame) were to send a recommendation out to his entire list (more than one million people!), and had 50,000 orders to fill in 24 hours. How many mailers could you stuff in a week's time? Know your delivery capabilities before you even start talking to a joint venture host.

Finding a joint venture host

One of the problems with joint venturing is that it's not new anymore. Internet-based joint ventures started as far back as 1995 when I was getting started online. Today, anyone with a substantial list and visible profile probably has 50 to 100 people per month or more clamoring after them to do a joint venture. Even if you can get in the door to talk to the golden goose of your industry, chances are good that you'll be met with a response like, "Who the heck are you, and why should I be listening to you?"

My suggestion is that you start with smaller joint ventures first. Follow this simple sequence to locate joint venture partners, and you will have plenty of opportunities to go after the big guys after you build a track record:

✦ **Attend networking events and seminars.** You need to meet people and let them know you're looking for joint venture hosts to help take your product to new levels. Create a 20-second *elevator pitch* that announces what your product is, the conversion rates you're getting from your Web site, and how much a potential joint venture host might make with a list of 10,000 or more subscribers that you both would be promoting, too. Numbers talk, and joint venture hosts listen to numbers.

✦ **Participate in online forums.** You probably won't find T. Harv Ecker or Anthony Robbins participating in online forums much, but you'd be surprised how many multimillionaires do spend an hour or more daily offering advice online (anonymously, of course). Add a signature line (as shown in Figure 2-6) in your forum bio stating that you're seeking joint venture hosts, and add a link to your Web site.

✦ **Ask your affiliates and clients for referrals.** Your affiliates and clients likely know someone who could be a possible joint venture host for you. Ask them what vendors they use who might be able to roll out your product or service as a value-added offer to their customers.

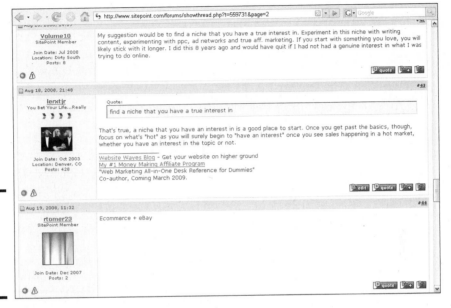

Figure 2-6:
Add a
signature
line in
a forum
posting.

Finding joint venture hosts really isn't difficult. You'll discover that just by using the three preceding resources alone. The trick is to convince the right hosts to do business with you and make things happen. You need to have a plan and present it well.

Presenting your plan

Depending on the size of the host's company, you might be expected to conduct a formal presentation to a group of staff with your plan. If you start small, however, many joint ventures can be assembled over a cup of coffee at your local coffee house or sometimes even via a phone call. Use your instincts to read how formal the meeting should be. But, be assured that the more professional, organized, and successful you appear, the more seriously your project will be considered. The following sections help you put together your materials and make your pitch to a potential host.

Gather your presentation materials

The first step is putting together a nice binder with materials your host will likely want to see. Buy a high-quality, portfolio-style, three-ring binder notebook that can lie flat on a desk. You need something in which you can easily insert pages. Don't forget to pick up a box of sheet protectors for the elements that go in your three-ring binder. In this notebook, I suggest you include the following.

✦ Printout of the sales volume you're experiencing

✦ One-page report of your affiliates and how much they make by selling your product

✦ Visitation statistics report showing how many people visit your Web site on a monthly basis and where those visitors are coming from

✦ Full copy of your sales letter or product sales page

✦ List of testimonials from happy customers

✦ Report of returns and refund requests

✦ Photos of you with high-profile experts in the industry (if you have them)

✦ Sample joint venture host agreement, which typically includes

- *The terms of the revenue sharing:* What percentage of the sale are you willing to offer your host, and how long after the promotion occurs are you willing to pay commissions for sales generated? For example, if you get a phone call from someone a year from now who saw a promotion run by your host offering a special price, will you accept the sale? Will you pay your host the due commission for that sale?

You have to promise a high-enough percentage to attract the attention of a good host in the first place: 50, 60, and sometimes even 100 percent of the revenue is given to the host for his support of your product.

- *The expectations for each involved:* I prefer to write sales copy for my hosts when they promote to their audience. After all, I know my products — and how to sell them — a lot better than they do. So, I will add a sentence in the agreement that the host will "use my promotions as written or slightly modified to meet their natural speaking tone," for example.

- *Any limitations:* Most likely, you will sell the same product outside your hosting agreement, using your own promotion efforts, affiliates, or other joint ventures. Your agreement needs to claim your right to ownership of your product and the right to continue to sell it in any way you choose. And it should state that your host will not be receiving commissions for sales generated from alternate promotions.

- *Commission payments and returns:* What date of the month will you be reconciling orders and making a payment to your host? And, how will you account for returns? I suggest making your payment at the end of each month following the date a sale is made, similar to what I suggest earlier in this chapter (in the section of this chapter). This gives you enough time to process any returns and deduct those orders from the amount of commission due your host. This procedure should be included in your agreement.

- *Disputes:* Decide how a formal dispute will be handled.

- *Intellectual property rights:* Remember that this is your product you're offering to your host's followers. Be sure to include in your agreement that you still own all rights to your products.

- *Confidentiality:* During the course of a joint venture project, you will likely be exposed to insider information as to how your host conducts business. For some of the joint venture deals I've worked with, I've been granted access to the host's online shopping cart to set up our product promotion to be available on his Web site! Now, that's trust. You will wind up revealing some secrets of your own as well. It will be comforting to your host that you hold his practices in high regard and will not share any of his personal or business information with others.

Explain your value

Joint venture hosts have a substantial public following. They got to where they are because they (more often than not) genuinely care about people. When you arrive at your meeting with your potential joint venture host, be ready to promote a joint venture opportunity with the host's audience in mind:

- ✦ How will his followers benefit from your product?

- ✦ What can they expect as a result from using what you produce?

- ✦ Why are you the best person to make this offer to his list?

A host is always pressed for time, so you need to present how easy your joint venture process will be. Be prepared to do all the work and even bend over backward for your host. You must present that your host will

- ✦ **Make a ton of money without spending a boatload of time.**

- ✦ **Be on the top of your priority list.**

- ✦ **Get special treatment.** You might even decide to make a completely separate Web site just for your host to promote your product.

- ✦ **Benefit from your sales ability.** You will surely need to prepare customized sales copy for e-mails to be sent to your host's list, for example.

- ✦ **Be involved in the process.**

- ✦ **Have a new team player at his side.** You might well be invited as a guest speaker for a teleconference or even brought up on stage for a few minutes at an event in front of hundreds of people!

My point is not to scare you away from joint venturing. Quite the opposite, actually. Realize the excitement that awaits by moving toward a joint venture opportunity. Think bigger than your normal day-to-day online sales strategies that trickle in from your search engine optimization (SEO) efforts and Google AdWords campaigns. Sure, those are all important. But, they are most important to generate numbers you will eventually use to present your offer to future joint venture hosts. A huge growth opportunity awaits for your company. Following the Internet marketing process from A to Z is what will get you there.

And one last point: Dress well. Joint venture hosts might wear jeans and a T-shirt to a meeting, but they appreciate it when you honor their stature by dressing professionally. I always wear a dark fancy suit and tie when meeting with potential joint venture hosts to set the tone for a professional meeting.

Chapter 3: Designing to Sell

In This Chapter

✓ Understanding the purpose of Web site design

✓ Preventing distraction from the sales process

✓ Using branding basics

✓ Keeping it legal

✓ Testing for usability

The design of a commercial Web site has only one basic purpose: to assist visitors through the sales process. Sure, graphic artists will tell you that design is a crucial element of establishing branding recognition and showing uniqueness. Technical support staff for a software company might suggest that design be used for current customers to quickly get to the support area of the site when they have a problem. A nonprofit organization might view design as a means of displaying documents of research and treatment options in a prominent place on every page of the Web site.

And all these design imperatives are true and realistic. But, in each of those cases (and others), accomplishing those goals through effective design eventually brings more revenue.

This chapter is devoted to using several design techniques to guide your Web site visitors through your online sales process without distracting them. You discover how to think about the affect of elements that appear on your site: branding, colors, fonts, and graphics. After making these key decisions, you're ready to consider how to pull these elements together in your site layout — and in particular, ways that make best use of important areas on a Web page. You also find tips along the way to help you design a site that's easy to use. The last section in this chapter explains easy ways to test your site's usability.

Branding Your Look

If you read any book on marketing or branding, you will see common examples of the ultimate goal of branding, such as Xerox "owns" the word *copiers*. McDonald's "owns" *hamburgers*, Levi Strauss "owns" the word "jeans." What word or phrase does your product or service own or aspire to own?

Branding is a simple concept to understand yet sometimes a painstaking process to implement. Big companies pay marketing firms thousands of dollars to have expert teams produce branding strategies, over weeks and months of brainstorming. So, if you've been struggling with your branding for a while, you're not alone.

If you're new to this term, you will find many definitions for the word *branding*. To me, branding is simply getting prospects and repeat customers to see and remember your product as the only solution to their specific problem or need. Other alternative items might be similar, but nothing on the market is exactly like what you offer. Of course branding is accomplished by all the things you hear about in formal definitions like creating a logo, establishing corporate identity, product packaging, advertising, bonding with customers, and establishing loyalty.

Every word you write and every image you place on your Web site can help you build visitors' perception of you as a leader of your field. People buy from leaders and innovators, not from followers.

The following sections explain branding strategies that will help your visitors form a positive perception of you when visiting your Web site.

Creating taglines and slogans

Taglines and *slogans* are short phrases that convey important ideas to customers. During the branding process, your tagline should be created even before your logo design begins because the meaning of your tagline will have an influence on that logo design. Create a branding tagline for your own Web site that will mirror your branding image but won't change over time. For example, Carpet Exchange (www.carpetexchange.com) has a great tagline — *Your floor store* — displayed online under its logo, as shown in Figure 3-1. It's short and meaningful, and even rhymes!

Use www.rhymezone.com and www.morewords.com to come up with words that rhyme if you would like your tagline to rhyme.

A branding slogan is a little different in that it changes depending on the type of promotion you're running. JELL-O is a good example. One of its slogans is *Every Diet Needs a Little Wiggle Room.* But, when winter comes around, it could change this tagline in promotions to *Every Vacation Needs a Little Wiggle Room.*

Figure 3-1:
Pair a
tagline with
your logo.

Developing a branded logo

Perhaps one of the most overlooked elements of doing business in general — let alone online — is the importance of having a meaningful logo. Many Internet marketing gurus will tell you not to waste your time or money producing a logo. But, if you are promoting a real company on the Web, a good logo is a vital ingredient: It helps you communicate a lot about your business to a Web site visitor in a fraction of a second. When people see your logo (or lack of one), they can immediately rate various elements of your business in their minds. This act of evaluation might even occur in their subconscious. Some of these include your

✦ Level of professionalism

✦ Ability to create or innovate

✦ Enthusiasm for your product

✦ Level of traditionalism

✦ Attention to detail

Visitors will associate words to your business based on the appearance of your logo, such as funny, silly, exciting, desperate, growing, content, or curious. So, be careful what you ask your designer to create for you.

When it comes to your Web site, it's more important than ever to at least have a logo to identify your business, if not a logo for each of your products too! The following list invites you to take a look at some good logos that are memorable but also define the business and even the personality of the business:

✦ www.TheAccidentalLawyer.com — The Accidental Lawyer logo features a somewhat common approach to a law firm logo in that it has the roman pillar theme in the background. What's not so common is the linking between that traditional image and The Accidental Lawyer name with the hat on top of the letter A. This tells me, maybe only on a subconscious level, that this is a law firm that links tradition with business sense, and just the right amount of personality and charisma.

✦ www.ContractorsAccess.com — I chose to feature this logo because I didn't know what the company did until I saw their logo. Now I understand that they offer the high-rise equipment you see window washers standing on, among other things. So, a logo alone can sometimes bring it all together to tell a visitor what your business does.

✦ www.monkeybizness.com — On the other end of the spectrum, there is Monkey Bizness, with the tagline "where kids monkey around." Everything about this logo is playful and not too serious, from the font type used to the coloring and the slight animation of the monkey jumping up and down.

The point of mentioning these three logos is that each paints a memorable picture in your mind. And, that's what branding is all about: creating something that remains in people's minds for days, weeks, or months to come.

Professional designers are your best resource for creating a logo that matches how you want your business to be perceived. Keep in mind that logos take time to conceptualize and create. So, be prepared that by the time you approve a logo, you might see several iterations, costing several hundreds of dollars. The best scenario from a time standpoint is when your Web site designer is also the creator of your logo. That way you don't have to worry about the logo designer getting the right formats to your Web designer and waiting for that communication to take place. But, many Web designers do not work with logos and require a logo to be submitted before beginning work on your Web site. In that case, here are two low-cost methods for getting a logo created.

One shortcut to logo production is to hold a contest between many designers. At 99designs (online), you can post your logo design request for as little as $39, plus whatever you're willing to pay to the winner. Usually, you need to offer enough — say, $100 or so — to give incentive for designers to jump on your projects. But, it's often just as professional a result (and faster) than using a traditional designer for logo creation. Here's how it works:

1. Visit `http:99designs.com`.

2. Start a free account.

3. Click Launch a Contest and describe the project.

4. Post your "brief" and set a price amount.

   $39 is required to post your contest.

5. Respond to designers as they post their logo concepts and ask for refinements.

   Within a few days, you'll have several logos to choose from produced by different graphics experts.

6. Choose the winner.

   The payment in the form of credits is sent to the designer, and the designer then sends the completed logo files to you by e-mail.

Another resource for logo creation (one that I've used a few times over the years) can be found at `www.1800MyLogo.com`. The package deals range from $289 to $399, and while these are great prices, the key is in their process. After completing an extensive questionnaire about your business, target, and your personal likes and dislikes related to logos and schemes, each design team member creates his or her own version of a logo for you. So, you get several comps (compositions) to choose from. Then you pick a few that you like and send notes back with changes to make and toss out the rest. After a week or so, you have the final logo you've always wanted. The process works very well.

Creating a consistent look with CSS

If you're working with a Web designer, you need to know whether your designer is formatting your fonts, as well as the rest of your site, with Cascading Style Sheets (CSS). This is important because a Web site can be designed on one computer yet appear totally different on the next. This is a browser and operating system issue as well as a display issue. The most dramatic differences can be seen if you look at a Web site on a PC versus a Mac, or on Internet Explorer versus Firefox, or on different monitors. Consistency, though, must be a key element when branding your site, and CSS is the common thread that allows that consistency to be maintained.

Among other things, using CSS helps ensure that

✦ Larger fonts don't appear too large.

✦ Smaller letters don't come across as unreadable.

✦ Text and other elements have a consistent look on every Web page.

✦ Rows and columns appear the same width and height.

✦ Spacing between images and text is the same.

✦ Border colors and thickness are identical.

CSS styles can get pretty involved, and the details of crafting them are beyond the scope of this book. If you're interested in learning more, see *CSS Web Design For Dummies* by Richard Mansfield. If you're designing your own site, *Web Sites Do-It-Yourself For Dummies* by Janine Warner can walk you through the nuts and bolts of creating your site, including styling Web page elements with CSS. And *Building Web Sites All-in-One For Dummies,* 2nd Edition (Doug Sahlin and Claudia Snell), can help you use CSS in Web design.

If you're not interested in designing your Web site, that's fine. Just share this information with your designer so that, together, you can plan for the appropriate CSS components to help every page of your site appear visually consistent, no matter what type of computer, monitor, or browser people use to view it.

Styling Text on the Web

Web site visitors rarely read text word for word on a Web site; instead, they scan information and wait for something to catch their interest. One important element of a Web site that captures people's interest and attention is font size and font type.

✦ **Font size:** Some designers like to push the limits by using huge fonts or really tiny text.

The Internet is a great place to test different methods, but don't get too carried away, or your sales can suffer quickly.

✦ **Font type:** I recommend using one of these fonts listed in order by popularity: Arial, Verdana, Trebuchet, Georgia. These are by far the most widely used and readable fonts on computer screens and browser types. Specifically, here's what I think are the strengths of each font:

• Arial is great for headlines and subheadings.

• Comic Sans gives a site an informal look and is a good font type to use if your business has a more casual audience.

• Georgia is a good all-around font for screens with easy-to-read text for primary content and italics.

• Trebuchet is another good all-around font but only in standard 10, 11, or 12 point — or larger sizes like 18, 20, and 24.

• Verdana is the most readable font overall among Web-based text fonts, but Trebuchet is becoming increasingly popular.

When using text on your Web site, don't capitalize everything in a sentence. In all capitals, it's like you're yelling at your visitors.

Using the Right Colors for Your Web Site

Web site visitors react to color more than you might realize. That reaction can mean the difference between a visitor buying a product online with confidence versus a person being blinded by ghastly color combinations and hitting their Back button in less than three seconds. Talk to your designer about potential uses of color. If you don't have a Web designer chosen yet, make color options a point of discussion before hiring that helper. We all make decisions daily based on the colors we see, so color should be an important component of your Web site's design.

The following sections invite you to consider how color sets the tone for your Web site as well as how technical aspects affect color on the Web.

Considering what colors convey

Here is a summary of how most people interpret and react to colors:

+ **Blue** (most popular) suggests honesty, trustworthiness, calming, and loyalty.

+ **Black** displays authority, sophistication, power, elegance, and technical prowess.

+ **White** symbolizes purity, peace, and youth: neutral and clean.

+ **Red** excites with passion, energy, and excitement.

+ **Pink** suggests innocence, softness, and sweetness.

+ **Green** invites feelings of nature, growth, and regeneration.

+ **Dark green,** however, implies wealth and conservatism.

+ **Yellow** is optimistic and cheery, yet can come across as too dominating if overused.

+ **Purple** is associated with wealth; sophistication; and mystical, spiritual tones.

+ **Brown** is genuine, although it often emotes sadness.

+ **Orange** conveys happiness, freedom, creativity, playfulness, and confidence.

+ **Gold,** as you would expect, suggests expensive taste as well as prestige.

+ **Silver** also emotes prestige but is cold and more scientific.

+ **Gray** has a more corporate, somber, and practical appeal.

Accounting for color-blindness in a design

Did you know that more than 1 in 12 visitors to your Web site might be color-blind? Did you also know that 90 percent of all color-blind people have the most problem seeing red and green? Here are some facts you might not have known about people with a color weakness. They can

✔ Distinguish between black and white.

✔ See all shades of yellow and blue.

✔ See dimmer shades of yellow, such as gold.

✔ Have trouble seeing greens and reds.

✔ Distinguish bright colors when contrasted with dark.

Keep these points in mind as you choose colors for your site. A site with lots of reds and greens might be hard to read for people who are color-blind. To make your site more accessible, try yellows and blues, or use colors with a highlight and dark contrast.

Putting some of these pieces together, take a look at the color mixtures chosen for www.MyGoldSecurity.com which features a trustworthy blue coloring in the header, with gold coins featured, of course. But, a silver coloring is used for the navigation bar, which makes sense with the scientific element of investing.

Now it's your turn. If you have an existing Web site, study the colors. Do the colors work together to convey a meaning that is consistent with your business? If you do not yet have a Web site or are working on a re-design, this is a great opportunity for you to make a list of two or three colors to include in your design, plus a few you want to stay away from.

Using Web-safe colors

At one of my advanced Internet strategy workshops, I showed a Web site onscreen for the small group to evaluate. My laptop was connected to a large widescreen monitor. One of the colored text sections had a blue background with red text in the middle. I definitely do not recommend that color combination, because it blinded me. But the text appeared *purple* on the widescreen monitor! This goes to show that even modern screens of today display colors differently, so you need to test your colors on multiple screen types to know what your visitors really see.

Years ago when CRT monitors were only capable of displaying 256 colors, there were 216 colors that were considered "safe" in that they displayed appropriately on monitors of the time. These Web-safe colors became the standard recommended for use on the Internet. Today, all LCD monitors can view the whole spectrum of 16 million colors. But, when it comes to text, I still use the same Web-safe colors, because people are used to seeing those colors. Blue underline links and red headlines are two examples of Web-safe colors that I use for every Web site because those are certain colors that people have come to expect.

Here is a great resource to see the most widely used Web-safe colors in the color spectrum, along with their Pantone Matching System (PMS) color associations:

`www.visibone.com/colorlab`

PMS is a way for printers, paint manufacturers, graphic designers, and others to communicate exact colors to each other. Because all colors can be matched by using a mixture of varying levels of red, green, and blue, their properties can be documented and shared using what are called *hue values*.

Combining colors for your Web site

If your Web site uses a blue header for the top of your Web pages with an orange left column, what third color could you use that would match the other two? If you had to think about the answer, chances are you'll appreciate the free Color Calculator tool, offered by Sessions Online by School of Design at

`www.sessions.edu/career_center/design_tools/color_calculator/
    index.asp`

The tool helps you choose three colors based on the color wheel.

Adding High-Impact Photos

What do people look like when they're using your product or service? What lifestyle do they lead now that they finally took your advice? Good design means using photos well to describe more than just your company image: for example, the outcome of using your product or service. Here are some real-world examples:

+ **Product shots**

  • If you have a dude ranch vacation destination, show a group on horseback, all smiling because they're having a wonderful time in the beautiful country surroundings. Figure 3-2 shows a Web site promoting the Bitterroot Ranch in Wyoming (`www.bitterrootranch.com`). The purpose of the dude ranch is evident; and if we were to take a trip to the same place, that's the look we would expect to receive.

- If you sell jewelry, have a photo of a woman looking at her new diamond ring as her husband-to-be peers over her shoulder. Showing interaction of a buyer with a product, rather than showing just a picture of the item itself, sells the product better.

✦ **Concept shots**

- If you sell perfume, show a couple getting close.

- If you're a personal success coach, show a photo of parents spending more time with their children.

Create a vision in your mind of the positive outcome people will enjoy by using your product or service. That's the image to create using photos throughout your Web site.

To get these photos, you can either create your own or purchase them:

✦ **Creating your own photos:** To create your own photos, you can hire a photographer in your area, or try shooting and editing your own photos. Your best bet is to take high-resolution photos, crop and correct them if needed, and then size them for the Web. Details about digital photography are beyond the scope of this book, but *Digital Photography For Dummies,* 6th Edition, by Julie Adair King and Serge Timacheff (Wiley) explains how to compose, edit, and size photos.

Whether you create your own photos or buy them, use photo editing software to make sure they're optimized to display quickly when someone visits your Web site. Images that take too long to download will cause you to lose customers. Adobe Photoshop Elements is a popular choice for the recreational user. Often there is software that comes with the purchase of a digital camera that will do just fine. Gimp software is a nice free substitute which you can download at www.Gimp.org.

When you get to the editing stage, you want to change the resolution setting to 72 ppi (pixels per inch) and save or export the file in .jpg format.

✦ **Buying photos:** An alternative to hiring a photographer is to purchase photos from an online gallery or a stock photo house. iStockphoto (http://istockphoto.com), BigStockPhoto (www.bigstockphoto.com), and Clipart.com (www.clipart.com) are a few resources to get you started.

Downloading photographs or images from a Web site to use on yours is a potential infringement of copyright and can be punishable in fines. If you must use existing photos and images, use a reputable company for your purchases and keep a printed copy showing proof of purchase for every image you use from their gallery.

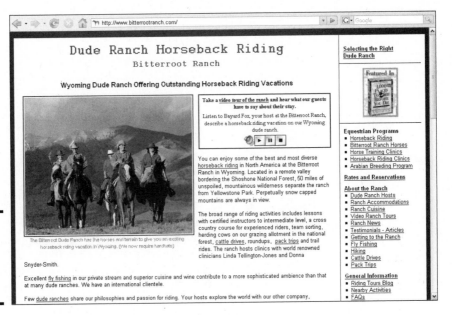

Figure 3-2:
Choose
photos that
sell the
outcome.

Laying Out Content on Your Web Pages

Good Web design is more than adding fancy colors and a visually exploding, movie trailer–like *splash page;* the layout needs to complement your branding while also inspiring visitors to take action. The "action" I'm referring to is your visitor either clicking one of the links provided in the layout or progressing through the content on the page. Google is a good example. It uses a minimalist design, but its layout is very strategically created to provide only the information you want in a quick and easy way. When people think of visiting Google, they know to expect simple results — fast.

One of the easiest ways to identify a layout design for your Web site is to search through templates available for sale. Template Monster (`www.templatemonster.com`) and Website Templates (`www.websitetemplates.com`) are two good places to start. You'll see hundreds of Web site designs that you can purchase for as little as $30, or you can simply get design ideas and have your designer create a look for you that uses ideas from the templates. Chapter 4 of this minibook has more details on working with templates.

In the sections that follow, you discover how to evaluate visitors' experiences on your current site layout (or the layout of your competitors). You also find tips for making the most of key areas on a page. Every page of any Web site should feature multiple opportunities for a visitor to take action of some kind. Those opportunities might include

+ Calling you for more information

+ Signing up to receive a free report

+ Subscribing to your newsletter

+ Making an online purchase

+ Visiting another page of your Web site

In addition to the images, text, colors, and words displayed on your site, the placement of these key components is the most significant decision you make on your entire Web site.

Evaluating layouts with a heat map application

Designing a Web site is very similar to designing a store. In fact, your Web site really is a store — a virtual store on the Internet. Grocery store chains have spent millions of dollars in market research watching and documenting how shoppers enter the store, turn right or left, and then graze their aisles. You need to know how a visitor enters your Web site and what their eyes look at. For example, if you decide to have a sale this month, you might want to add a special sale image, say, at the top of your right column. Wouldn't you want to know if the majority of your visitors are seeing that special notice?

Fortunately, you don't have to pay thousands or even hundreds of dollars to know what your visitors look at first, when they enter your Web site, and where their eyes go next. You can use the free heat map tool at Feng-GUI online (`www.feng-gui.com`) to upload an image of your Web page. Feng-GUI then displays how most people might be looking at that particular page when they see it for the first time. In Figure 3-3, notice how the D26Toastmasters homepage is most commonly viewed in the top-right corner initially, but then attention is moved to the middle of the page and finally half-way down the page.

The following steps explain how to create a similar map of your own site:

1. **Open your browser window and visit the homepage of your Web site (or any sub-page).**

If you don't have a Web site yet, you could use a heatmap analysis of a competitor's Web site to see what their visitors are interested in.

2. **Take a screen shot of your homepage (press the Print Screen button on your keyboard).**

3. **Open Microsoft Paint or your favorite graphics editor and paste your screen shot into a new document.**

Paint is available on most Windows machines; choose Start⇨All Programs⇨Accessories⇨Paint. When a new document opens, simply right-click your mouse and then choose Paste from the contextual menu that appears. Your homepage should now appear in Paint.

Figure 3-3:
Heat map
simulation.

4. **Save your screen shot in Paint as a JPG image (to keep the file size small) by choosing File⇨Save As. Give your image a name and then choose .jpg from the Save as Type drop-down list.**

5. **Point your browser to www.feng-gui.com and click the Browse button to find and upload the JPEG you just created.**

6. **Click the Heatmap button.**

   You see the most important areas of the page that of your visitors' eyes gravitate toward.

Ask yourself the following questions after running a heatmap simulation, whether you use your competitor's Web site or your own as the example:

✦ **Are these areas of the page where the attention of my visitors *should* go first?** For example, is your logo so dominating in the upper-left corner that your visitors see it first and immediately start scanning down the left navigation of your page, bypassing completely the fact that you have a special for the month appearing in your top-right corner?

✦ **What feature should I have in place where the majority of my visitors look first when they land on that page?** For example, if I was to create an educational content page (see Chapter 5 of this minibook), the first thing I would want visitors to see is a captivating headline centered at the top of the page. But, on a professional speaker's Web site, I would want a meeting planner to see topics I might have available for keynotes in the top-right corner.

✦ **Is there anything visual about this page that is a huge turnoff and a reason why so many people might leave the site prematurely?** See Table 3-1 for common possible reasons why people leave Web sites.

Table 3-1	Why Visitors Leave Web Sites		
Category	*Examples*	*How Long After Problem Noticed Do They Leave?*	*Reason for Leaving*
Visual	Graphics don't line up. Graphics aren't consistent with content. Too much graphics with not enough content. Too many animated images.	Less than 5 seconds	Visitor believes content or product will be of less quality and looks for something better.
Textual	Headline isn't related to search results. Text is too hard to read. Poor grammar and spelling.	Up to 10 seconds	Visitor becomes skeptical that solution is genuine.
Functional	Page loads too slowly. Links don't work. Searches don't display results. Too many animated images.	Up to 30 seconds	Visitor leaves for fear of pop-ups, viruses, and loss of time.

The visual component of your Web site is the first thing visitors see and is the most common reason why visitors leave in less than five seconds.

Using the upper-right quadrant (URQ)

The upper-right quadrant of a page on your Web site is one of the most critical areas of any individual Web page because it's the first place people see when they arrive. In Figure 3-4, practically anything you would want to do on this Web site is featured in the URQ, including requesting a quote, contacting staff, viewing samples, calling for a quote, or making a request online.

Another use of the URQ would be to eliminate a buying objection before the question even arises. In the site shown in Figure 3-5, the URQ is used for the sole purpose of showing visitors that the company has been in this online business for quite a while — since 1995!

Actions in the upper-right quadrant

Figure 3-4:
Upper-right
quadrant
(URQ)
actions.

Eliminate objections

Figure 3-5:
Use the URQ
to eliminate
objections.

There are no rules as to exactly what should be placed in the URQ, but this is an important area to test and modify often to see whether leads and sales increase or decrease. Yes, even a simple change to the upper-right quadrant of your Web site can impact your results. Here are some additional things to test in the URQ of your Web site:

✦ A special promotion that you've never offered

✦ Important company news, like a finalized merger

✦ A testimonial or celebrity endorsement

✦ A photo with a recognized authority figure in your industry

✦ An award image

Inspiring action with the horizontal navigation bar

Have you ever visited a Web site to look up movie start times, register for an event, or get directions to the location of a store? If so, then you know how annoying it can be when you can't find the information you need that should be featured in an obvious place.

Proper use of the top horizontal navigation bar (the links or buttons you see going across the top of a Web page) is critical for increasing leads and sales for your business. The top navigation area serves one purpose — to get a visitor to go to another page. Part of the trick is knowing what obvious utilities or content should be featured. The other is how to graphically produce the links to lead your visitors to those important sections. Determining what people expect can be discovered by:

✦ **Reviewing competing Web sites:** Visit some of the Web sites you are in competition with. Run a heat map test on them to see where their visitors are looking. See "Evaluating layouts with a heat map application" earlier in this chapter for details.

✦ **Participating in forums:** Search for a forum (otherwise known as a discussion board) focused on discussions with people in your industry. Pay attention to the forum categories and topics participants are talking about. These could become specific titles for your main navigation.

✦ **Knowing your target audience:** Find people in your own network who fit your target audience and ask them what they would expect to see when arriving at your Web site.

Many visitors know exactly what they're looking for, and you want to provide that information immediately. Your challenge is to decide what actions your Web site visitors will want to take and feature them prominently in the top navigation area.

TIP

Checking clicks with Crazy Egg

Crazy Egg (www.crazyegg.com) is an online utility that can show you what people are clicking on any page of your site. This service is $9 per month for tracking up to ten pages of your Web site, and it's interesting to see the images that people click that aren't even active links.

To add the code, follow these steps:

1. **Add a new account.**

2. **Click the Add New Page button.**

3. **Provide a name for the link you're going to create so that you can identify it later.**

4. **Visit your Web site and copy the full URL of the page you want to monitor.**

5. **Paste the URL from that page into the Crazy Egg field on the add new account page.**

6. **Choose either a length of time you would like to test this particular page or number of visits.**

7. **Add any descriptive text to describe the testing project and click the "Save" button.**

8. **On the dashboard screen that appears, click the What's My Code link.**

9. **To make the connection between Crazy Egg and your Web site, add the brief line of HTML code to the page of your Web site that you would like to track. Insert the code right before the </body> tag.**

If you have no experience with HTML or maintaining Web site content, then simply send an e-mail to your Webmaster to have the code added.

After you add the code, you can see where visitors click by logging in to your Crazy Egg account and clicking the View Results button. Recently, Crazy Egg helped me to discover that about 10 percent of visitors to one of my product sales pages were clicking on a screen shot I had on that page. They were probably hoping to see an enlarged version of the screen shot. Now I know to add that feature to my sales page because a good number of people are expecting to be able to click on that image.

Here are a few additional rules I follow when creating a horizontal navigation bar for a Web site:

✦ **Location:** Web sites usually have a banner at the top of the page featuring a logo on the left and then some other graphics in the middle and right. I prefer horizontal navigation to be directly under the banner. That way, a visitor can first focus on the upper-right quadrant of the page, and then scan across the graphics to give the visitor confidence that he's at a Web site worth investigating further. Then allow his eyes to naturally move down where the horizontal navigation bar catches his eye.

✦ **Type:** Navigation bars include either buttons or text links. Sometimes when you put your mouse over a navigation link, a menu of options unfolds. These are called menu trees, which contain either text links or buttons. Which is better, text links or buttons? That is more of a personal preference on your part. What is important is that your text or buttons are easy to view and identify. Do that much and you'll get the click. And, again, that's the only goal of your navigation bar — to get the click.

✦ **Number:** People like odd numbers. If we see anything on the Web that is in even numbers, we're wondering where the next item is. So, I recommend having three, five, or seven items on your horizontal navigation bar. In fact, limit the number to seven to avoid a cluttered navigation bar.

✦ **Order:** When you have a strong URQ that draws the eye of your visitor to the upper-right part of your page first, the next natural place the visitor will look is from right to left across your top navigation buttons. What feature would you like your visitors to see first on that nav bar? I usually choose a Home button on the left and a Contact button on the right because I want everyone to know how they can contact me and I don't want people hunting around for how to get to my homepage. What goes in the middle is directly related to whatever the primary offers are.

✦ **Words:** The top navigation bar should be designed to get people to actually *do* something. People like to *do* things online. They like to search, view, register, find, review, subscribe, add, get, contact, evaluate, demo, download, play, go to, and discover things for example. Use the words in your top nav bar to get people engaged with your Web site — to get them to do something. Consider using the following navigation bar:

Search Products | View Events Schedule | Subscribe Now

instead of this one:

Products | Events | Newsletter

Choosing scrolling over clicking

There is a belief that no one wants to scroll down a Web page — that people would rather click for more information. But, if you think about it, the only reason we click through links instead of scroll is to get to a page where the correct information is featured. When we get to the right page, we expect there is enough information to satisfy our curiosity and we're happy to scroll when we are on a Web page that provides us with the information we are looking for.

Valuable content (as described in Book I, Chapter 5) is what inspires people to want to scroll to read more and consider all the details they need to make an informed decision. Good design is what allows content to be added in a format that is consistent with other pages on the Web site. A good example of this is a report on your favorite local news Web site, such as the one shown in Figure 3-6.

If I were to despise scrolling so much, I would never know the details of the 11–0 win that the Colorado Rockies enjoyed in Cincinnati. But, because the content is of enough interest to me, I'm willing to scroll to read it.

See how you have to scroll to read the entire article? But the subject is captivating enough so that it's worth it to us, the readers, to do so.

**Book I
Chapter 3**

Designing to Sell

Figure 3-6:
Content
worth
scrolling for.

Attracting attention with arrows, buttons, and more

Specific elements on a Web page also encourage visitors to take action. Here are some next-action design elements to try:

✦ **Red arrows:** One of the most commonly used graphics online is to have a big, red arrow pointing to something important. Why are they so popular? Because red arrows instruct people what to do, and people want to be directed. Think of using arrows as a courtesy to your visitors by guiding them to where they should be interested in going.

✦ **Guarantee Sections:** Guarantees might be written in text, but it's the graphic piece that brings attention to it. After people are made aware that there is a guarantee, they're often more willing to take the next step.

✦ **Outlined text boxes:** A page full of content needs to be divided into sections, or it will just look long-winded without purpose. But an outlined text box draws attention.

✦ **Inline text links:** Throughout the content of a page, consider featuring links to other pages where more topic-specific content can be found. These *inline links* should always be underlined and blue in appearance. Designers will try to be creative and convince you to use other colors. Programmers will use CSS styles to remove the underline from all text links because they believe the page looks less cluttered without a bunch of links all over it. But, let's face the facts. Blue, underlined text links have been around since the word *hyperlink* was invented. When we see it, we know it's a link. Why blue? Well, let's look at some other colors as potential links:

- Red is probably not a good color for links because red means "stop" in our society. We have red stop signs, red stop lights, even red corvettes make us stop and look.

- Green is not a horrible choice for a link. After all, we look at green as meaning "go" whenever we're sitting at a stop light. The problem with green is that it doesn't stand out very well on a white background unless you use a larger font or bold the text. And, bolding every text link would really drive designers crazy!

- Yellow, orange, and even white links could be used when reverse text is concerned. Reverse text is when you have a very dark design forcing you to use very light colors for the text. In that case, try a lighter shade of blue for your links so they stand out.

Yes, the color blue will be your best fit for a text link color. Not just because of tradition or because it's what the pros do, but because blue works and we are conditioned to look for blue when we want more information on a topic. People look for blue, underlined links. And we don't want to let them down.

Promoting specials in the right column

The right column of a Web site is a perfect place to showcase special offers, weekend sales, new product launch dates, and advertising. Weblogs (blogs) reflect the power of the right-column promotion and often feature their authors' most beloved affiliate products there, as shown in Figure 3-7. Book IV takes a closer look at online advertising. If you're new to blogs, see Book VI.

Figure 3-7:
Promoting
specials
in the right
column.

Completing the Web site Pre-Flight Checklist

Just as you would want to crunch numbers and run what-if scenarios before launching a new company, you want to put your plan to paper for your Web site design as well. Collect information on these 25 top items when submitting your project scope to a Web site designer for a price quote:

✦ Company information, including name, address, phone, and e-mail

✦ How long you have been in business

✦ The primary goal of your business (what you sell)

✦ A description of your business in 25 words or less

✦ A list of three groups of people that might benefit from your product or service

✦ Your branding slogan

✦ The main domain name for your Web site (I use www.uownitdomains.com to search for available domain names and then register them.)

✦ A list of at least three Web sites you like and what you like about them

✦ A list of at least three Web sites you dislike and what you dislike about them

✦ A list of at least three competing Web sites

✦ A description of your potential customers' demographic profile, which you can find by searching www.quantcast.com for a high-traffic Web site related to your target industry

✦ Whether your potential customers are Internet savvy or technically challenged. (You learn this by attending seminars or networking events where your target audience is present and talking with them.)

✦ What you would expect if you were one of your potential customers

✦ The goals of your Web site (sell product online, generate leads, and so on)

✦ Whether visitors ever need to print pages from your site

✦ What the top navigation buttons will be

✦ What the left navigation buttons will be

✦ What special features will be displayed in the right navigation area

✦ What should be included in the footer of every page of the site

✦ Whether you will supply photos, or whether the designer should include photos in the quote

✦ Whether you will supply content, or whether the designer should include copywriting in the quote

✦ Whether you will supply a logo, or whether the designer should quote a price for logo creation

✦ Whether the Web site will require an online shopping cart

✦ Whether you already have an Internet-capable merchant account

✦ Whether there will be an online newsletter signup form on the Web site

If you need help with any of these points, check out related sections earlier in this chapter.

Designing for Optimum Usability

Assuring that your Web site is usable by your audience is partly the responsibility of the designer and partly the responsibility of the programmer. If something as simple as a link to another page isn't functional, for example, a visitor will quickly become frustrated and leave the site searching for a better solution. The following sections introduce you to usability standards, many of which might be familiar to you if you've read earlier sections of this chapter. You also discover how to test your site to ensure it meets usability standards.

Incorporating usability standards

Follow this ten-step checklist to evaluate the usability of your new Web site before its launch:

✦ Have all links on the site been tested to be functional?

✦ Is there a CSS file containing all font sizes, color, and table border details?

✦ Is alt text (alternative text) used for all images that have a possible description?

✦ Are links descriptive of what the user will see on the landing page?

✦ Does the site operate similarly on multiple browsers, versions, monitors, and operating systems?

✦ Can the navigation be easily followed and understood?

✦ Are text links underlined and blue?

✦ Does individualized metadata exist on each page of the Web site?

✦ Is there a link to the homepage on every sub-page?

✦ Are the URLs descriptive of what will be found on each page?

After you're sure that your Web site has passed the usability basics test, now it's time for the ultimate test — a live test for usability.

Testing live for usability

Usability testing is one of the most neglected aspects of creating and launching a Web site. Maybe you have had your friends or family take a look at the new design, but have never brought in a *focus group* (folks who've never seen your Web site). After all, who has time for that?

If your Web site is a hobby for you, usability testing might be put on the back burner. However, if you're in business and you plan for your Web site to be a major contributor to your annual revenue, usability testing is absolutely essential.

You should always test your own Web site for usability by viewing it with multiple browsers, multiple versions of those browsers if possible, multiple screen sizes, and multiple computer platforms (PC versus Mac). But the ultimate test to see how truly usable your Web site has become is to invite people to your location and have a focus group with a live review session. That way, you can be present in the room to see visitors' first reactions. Here are some things to consider when testing for usability with a live group.

+ **Test each person on the same computer.**

+ **Give each reviewer a checklist of things to try to find on your Web site.**

+ **Write their comments as each navigates the site.**

+ **Don't say a word.**

  Offer no assistance. That's what a usability study is!

+ **Share the results with the group at the end and allow for open discussion.**

+ **Be grateful for all feedback you receive.** Remember, if one person has a problem with your Web site's usability, there will be another thousand future visitors who will experience the same issue. So, don't be offended or angry; just fix the issue.

"Hot seats" are becoming more popular at seminars and workshops. In essence, a member of the audience volunteers to have her Web site brought up onscreen for all in the room to critique. If you ever have the opportunity to be in the hot seat, jump at the chance! Having several first-time visitors provide unbiased, immediate feedback about your Web site is worth the entire price of your registration.

The best news of all is that the work you do on the design, layout, branding, and usability of your Web site will serve as a tremendous training ground for when you begin to plan for promoting your core business through multiple Web sites.

Chapter 4: Creating and Connecting Multiple Web Sites

In This Chapter

✔ Defining the different kinds of Web sites

✔ Selecting which Web site types are right for your business and you

✔ Creating and maintaining your Web site content

✔ Launching and connecting multiple Web sites to broaden your reach and Web presence

*I*f 1995–2005 could be considered the infancy stage of the Internet, the years since could easily be called the competitive stage. These days, every industry online, right down to the most remote niche markets, is fiercely competitive. Successful business owners know that the only way to penetrate increased competition is to be visible in as many places and modalities as the Internet marketing budget allows. To accomplish the feat of gaining visibility, the practice today is to have multiple Web sites connected to each other as well as to a main Web site to promote a single business.

In this chapter, I introduce you to a variety of Web site types. Some may apply to you and your business more than others. My hope is that you discover ways to include in your marketing plans the idea of implementing multiple Web sites to supplement your main company Web site. When you expand your reach with multiple Web sites, your overall Internet traffic increases along with your leads and sales.

I begin with the most popular form of Web site, which I refer to as a "traditional" Web site. You get some shortcuts to get started on the design front. Then, I cover some other Web site types: blogs, mini-sites, squeeze pages, ask sites, content sites, and membership sites. If your competition hasn't already implemented these multiple types of Web sites to feed their main site, they will soon!

Creating and connecting sites helps you to become competitive, and updating those sites helps you to stay competitive. Content needs to be updated routinely to keep search engines interested in listing your Web site favorably in their search index and to keep your information current and engaging for readers. That's why I wrap up this chapter with an overview of popular software products for creating and maintaining your sites.

As you decide how to create your sites, I'd like to emphasize the importance of you being in control of any launched Web site, including graphics, user names and passwords, backup files, and content. This chapter isn't just about Web site types and connecting them; it's about keeping you in the driver's seat.

And as you build your network of Web sites, remember that good design and good content apply to each page of each site. More about specific design elements can be found in Chapter 3 of this minibook. After your design is approved, it's time to add content. This is the message you want to convey to your visitors, so take your time when crafting your message and use the components of Chapter 5 in this book to write effective copy in order to get your visitors to take action with you by either buying online, calling you on the phone, or requesting more information by e-mail.

Choosing a Traditional Web Site

A traditional Web site is created offline with a computer and then transferred to a Web server (your Web site hosting account) online to be displayed to the world through the Internet. Although you could technically use Microsoft Word to produce extremely basic HTML pages of a traditional Web site from your own computer by using the Save As HTML command, the majority of smart business owners hire Web designers to do this task.

Due to the reliance on a designer, the client is required to supply content, a logo, images, photos, audio, video, and anything else desired on the traditional Web site. Then the designer builds the pages one by one, page by page. To create the pages, the designer (and his or her team) uses relatively pricey Web authoring tools, such as Dreamweaver, Flash, and programming or markup languages, including PHP, ASP, HTML, CSS, and JS.

After the traditional Web site is launched, the client submits changes or additions to the Web designer for scheduled maintenance.

Because a traditional Web site is 100 percent customizable, it's the best way to go if you want your site to be unique among your competition and if you have any type of special feature that needs to be integrated into your Web site. The only limitation of a traditional Web site is your budget and how much you are willing to spend to get what you want.

Unlike the other Web site types I discuss in this chapter, a tradtional Web site is most often created with form first and function later. CasinoSoftware Solutions.com is an example of a traditional Web site: The goal for the site was a very specific and customized look featuring the company's software in the header and a casino look in the background. Having full flexibility in the areas of design and layout is the main reason for implementing a traditional Web site.

Starting a traditional site from a design template

If designing an entire site from scratch makes you a little weak in the knees, I'd strongly recommend that you begin with a template. A template is a design layout that someone else has already produced, and templates offer the easiest and most cost-effective way to begin building a traditional Web site. You can find such templates for free or for a nominal price.

With design elements already decided upon — such as how your headings and body text look, as well as basic page layout — you can easily add the content you want and have your new Web site up and running in a matter of hours. Templates can also be used as a starting point. Because the purchase of a template almost always results in your receipt of original graphics files, you can cut down on design fees by having your designer modify only small parts of the template to make the design your own. Plus, some template design companies offer customization for an affordable fee.

Figure 4-1 shows an example of a Web site template that costs just $45, and you get all original files to customize the graphics as you wish. For $450, you can have this layout all to yourself, and the option for anyone else to buy and use it for a Web site will be removed.

I chose this particular template because it satisfies most of the suggested design components as discussed in Chapter 3 of this minibook, including effective use of the upper-right quadrant (URQ), top navigation positioning for primary sections where visitors can take some kind of action, three-column format, the "safe zone" on the left side, text links in the footer, and a nice wide content area. This template is primed for selling.

One problem with using a template design is that other people might be using the same look and feel for their Web site. Some templates available online might have been used for 100 Web sites or more. So, if uniqueness is important to your business, going with a custom look and feel is probably the better choice.

Checking out template providers

Here is a short list of some online template providers for you to sample. Even if you're already working with a designer, browse template sites to find inspiration for your own site's look and feel. For even more results, just search for *"Web site templates"* in your favorite search engine.

✦ **For a fee:** You can expect to pay from $20 to $500 for a Web site template. Check out these vendors for some samples:

- www.WebsiteTemplates.com

- www.Top1000Templates.com

- http://webtemplatebiz.com

✦ **For free:** You can certainly find free Web site templates online, but they might not be as full-featured, attractive, or customizable as those you'd pay for. The following sites offer free templates:

- www.FreeWebsiteTemplates.com

- www.FreeWebTemplates.com

- www.TemplatesBox.com

Take care to make sure you have rights to use a free Web site template for a commercial Web site without infringing on a copyright. You find such restrictions or permissions within the Terms of Use area of the template site's download area.

✦ **Template customization providers:** From $10 to a few hundred dollars, you can have a designer customize your template or help with adding content to your site. The following sites offer template customization:

- www.TemplateTuning.com/prices.php

- www.TemplateMonster.com

Figure 4-1:
Start with a Web site template to speed your deployment.

Creating a Blog

A Weblog — or, *blog,* for short — is a Web site, nothing more. Well, maybe a little more. Okay, a lot more! A blog is designed for two things: speed of editing and automation of delivery. I'll explain.

Blogs are indeed just like traditional, custom Web pages in many ways. Just like you can add a new page to a traditional Web site, you add a *post* to a blog. The post might display on the homepage with other posts, but it always has its own individual page as well. Figure 4-2 displays how multiple partial posts are displayed on a homepage.

Figure 4-2:
A blog
homepage
can show
multiple
posts.

When a visitor clicks the headline for a post, the visitor is brought to an individual post page that displays the entire article, as shown in Figure 4-3. It's this individual page that you can use on multiple Web sites as a resource link, thereby connecting your multiple Web sites together.

This section introduces you to some of the basics of adding a blog to your network of sites. In Book VI, you find more details about choosing your blogging software, getting started with blogging, and turning your blog into a successful Web marketing tool.

Figure 4-3: An individual blog post page.

Introducing blogging tools

Behind most blogs is a blogging tool: WordPress, Blogger, TypePad, and Moveable Type are popular examples. Each requires an account, and some require you to download software. Others only require you to log in from the Web.

Using WordPress as an example, after logging in to your blog account, you can add a new post by clicking Write⇨Post, as shown in Figure 4-4. The Microsoft Word–looking icons within WordPress blogging software make creating your first blog post a breeze. There is no HTML editor to purchase and no code to learn — sweet!

WordPress — the most popular, self-hosted blog software, by far — can be downloaded at www.wordpress.org for free. Plus, it offers the easiest way, in my opinion, to add affiliate links to every post as well as include audio and video in posts.

At WordPress.com, you can have your blog hosted for free. However, you are not allowed direct access to the files and you do not have the opportunity to install any plug-ins. I've heard that the developers of WordPress might shut down your account if they discover you're making money with your blog while hosting on their server. So, if you plan your blog to be an income generator, ask your hosting company whether it supports WordPress. (Most hosting companies already have WordPress installed and can offer it to you at no additional charge.) I know for a fact that Best Hosting Place (www.besthostingplace.com) offers this feature.

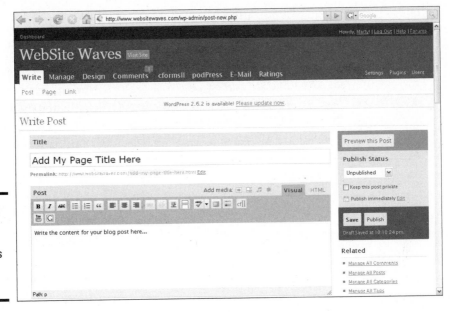

Figure 4-4:
Writing a
post with
WordPress
blog
software.

Another benefit of most blog software is how simple blogs are to install. You must know how to link a PHP script with a MySQL database, but even someone with beginner knowledge in this area can perform this task for you within 15 minutes or so. A full discussion of PHP and MySQL databases is beyond the scope of a Web marketing book, but you can read about these topics in depth in *PHP & MySQL For Dummies,* 3rd Edition, by Janet Valade (Wiley). You can find related articles and other related books at www.dummies.com.

Setting up a WordPress blog

The following steps offer an overview of the steps for installing a WordPress blog and then getting it up and running:

1. **Register a domain name related to your industry or create a new directory for a blog on your current site.**

   For example, one of my blogs uses the domain name www.website waves.com for its focus on what's happening in the world of Web sites.

   If you already have a Web site and are adding the blog to your Web site, create the directory www.*yourwebsitedomain*.com/blog instead of registering the domain name.

2. **Load the WordPress software.**

   Call your preferred Web site hosting company and have it install and configure WordPress for you. Or, download the WordPress blog software script from WordPress.org and connect it yourself to a MySQL database.

3. **Log in through admin and adjust the settings and preferences as you desire.**

   For example, under Settings, you can add a blog title, set your discussion preferences, set your privacy so that your blog is visible to search engines, and much more.

4. **Install plug-ins, which you can search for by clicking the link at the bottom of the Plug-ins page.**

   Here's a list of some important plug-ins I recommend installing to maximize your search engine optimization capability and automation of promotion:

   - *Askimet:* To reduce spam comments
   - *WP-Cache:* To reduce server load
   - *Related Posts:* To offer visitors links to other posts you've written on the same topic
   - *PodPress:* To allow you to easily add MP3 audio recordings and video to your blog posts
   - *All-in-One SEO:* To help make every post optimized for search engines
   - *Google XML Sitemap:* For immediate notification to Google that a new post has been made
   - *Stats at WordPress:* To keep a firm handle on visitation to your blog
   - *WP-Email Tell a Friend:* To add a link with a form that allows readers to tell others about your blog posts
   - *AdSense Manager:* To monetize your blog posts with Google AdSense ads

5. **Add a FeedBurner (www.feedburner.com) account, which helps automate the promotion of every post.**

6. **Promote your blog through a number of channels including**

   - *Blog directories,* such as BlinkList (http://blinklist.com)
   - *Other search engines,* such as MSN.com and Open Directory Project (ODP; www.dmoz.org)
   - *Social networking sites,* such as Squidoo (www.squidoo.com), LinkedIn (www.linkedin.com), and Twitter (http://twitter.com). Book VII covers social media marketing.

Book I
Chapter 4

Creating and
Connecting Multiple
Web Sites

7. **Add a page to your blog called** *About Us* **or** *About the Author.* **Then, provide a description of your business with a link to your main Web site, as shown in Figure 4-5.**

TIP

This last step is key to the topic of this chapter: connecting multiple sites. In Figure 4-5, notice the link to HereNextYear, Inc. in the text — this is an important example about how a main Web site is promoted from a blog. A simple link such as this one drives traffic to your main Web site where visitors can take further action with you, such as buy a product from your shopping cart, call you to consider your services, or just sign up for your newsletter.

You can find details for many of the these steps in Book VI. For example, Book VI, Chapter 2 introduces the different blog software (also called *platforms*) in more detail and explains how to use FeedBurner to add RSS capabilities to your blog. Book VI, Chapter 6 is dedicated to promoting your posts. However, because this book's focus is on Web marketing, you find just a taste of actually using a specific platform in this book. After you make your choice, check out www.dummies.com for platform-specific books and free articles that can help you with whatever option you choose.

Link to main site

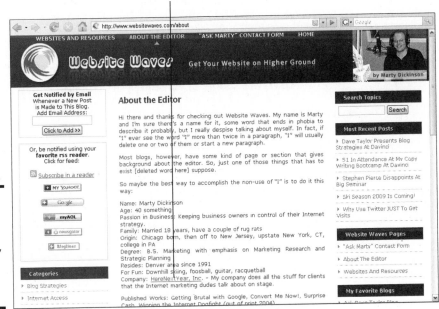

Figure 4-5:
A sample
About the
Editor page,
with a link
to the main
Web site.

Getting Specific with Mini-Sites

You used to be able to just make a Web site with a bunch of pages, and people would find their way through the pages. Remember the phrase *surfing the Web?* Today, fewer people just randomly surf through pages of content. Instead, they use the search engines to find the most relevant results possible. This change in the way people use the Internet has led marketers to create mini-sites (also called *micro-sites*) in order to stay competitive.

Mini-sites are usually an offshoot from or supplementary to a main Web site. Say, for example, you manufacture 20 different dolls for children, and all your dolls average online sales of just 5 per day each, except one doll that sells 20 per day. For that best-selling doll, you would want to register its specific product name as a domain name and create a mini-site that features up to ten pages about the doll. By adding this mini-site, you not only provide a specific mini-Web site just for that product and everything there is to feature about that product, but also bring those visitors to your main company Web site to make a purchase.

There are a few other types of mini-sites, including sales pages (otherwise known as one-page sales letters) and squeeze pages. (Squeeze pages are single-page mini-sites that have the sole intention of "squeezing" the visitor to perform only one task — to enter their name and e-mail address into a form to receive more information. I describe squeeze pages in more detail in Chapter 5 of this minibook.) For this discussion, though, the important key is to know how to direct traffic from the mini-site to the main site where visitors can be converted to leads or customers.

Here are three ways to connect mini-sites with each other and your main site:

✦ **Text linking:** You can add links to other mini-sites in case you have another mini-site that's more appropriate to that visitor. In Figure 4-6, you can see my squeeze page to encourage visitors to ask me any question about Web site design. But, if their burning question is really about SEO, they see the Ask Marty About SEO link at the bottom of the page. Clicking that link takes visitors to a separate mini-site where they are instructed to ask a specific question about SEO rather than Web site design.

✦ **Thank You–page linking:** When someone buys a product that you're promoting on a mini-site — or maybe a visitor opts in to a newsletter form — you can post a recommendation on the Thank You page to visit other mini-sites.

For example, after someone completes a form on one of my mini-sites, a Thank You page appears, as shown in Figure 4-7, which begins with "Hello and thanks for signing-up to ask Marty your question about blogging." Now, the visitor can, of course, continue through that link to ask their question, but the bigger intention is to get their question answered, and many more that they might not have thought about, by inspiring them to click the UltimateBlogChecklist.com link and sign up to get access to that document. The visitor is then converted to a subscriber and given the choice to enroll in a free e-course about blogging.

Figure 4-6:
Linking
from one
mini-site to
another.

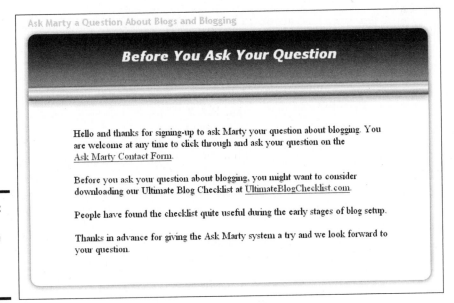

Figure 4-7:
Recom-
mendation
from a
Thank
You page.

✦ **Auto-responder linking:** When folks sign up to receive my free e-course, I suggest they visit `BlogSetupSecrets.com` where a product is for sale. This technique — one of my favorites — is highly effective. Planting a recommendation within an e-mail that's sent automatically is one of the great wonders of the Internet. See an example in Figure 4-8.

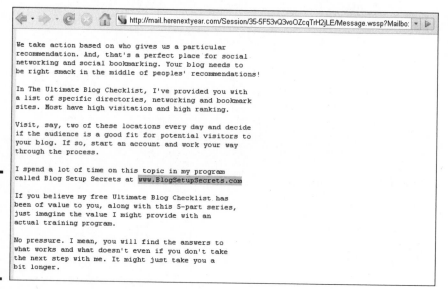

Figure 4-8:
Send a
suggestion
via an auto-
responder
message.

Reaching for Traffic with Content Sites

A *content site* is designed to feature dozens — if not hundreds, or even thousands — of pages surrounding a specific topic. These content pages are each optimized for organic search engine positioning, often using an automated process.

A content site is typically used to simply drive traffic to pages that feature Google AdSense ads, in hopes of monetizing the pages. (That's always my objective, as well, with content sites.) However, the greater purpose is to cast a wide net: Your content site can introduce you to a wide variety of people searching for multiple topics related to your industry. Down the road, a percentage of them will buy your product or at least contact you for more information.

For example, one of my Web sites (Music Mates; `www.musicmates.com`) contains an automated voting script so that folks can vote for their favorite local musician or band, anywhere in the country. More than 2,000 of these pages are indexed on Google. When you search specifically for those voting sections (such as *"best Denver rock band"* or *"best Miami country guitar player"*), the individual voting page results for that phrase are usually in the top three on Google (see Figure 4-9).

You can hire a programmer to create such a utility for your own content Web site. Or, you can subscribe to a system like Unique Article Wizard (`www.uniquearticlewizard.com`) to select content you want to post to your Web site automatically when it's made available.

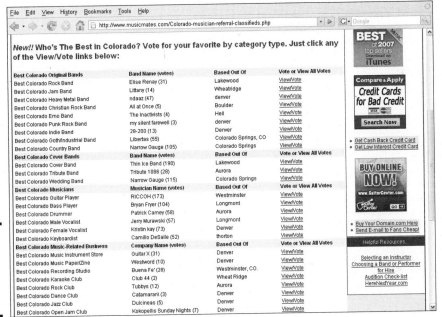

Figure 4-9: Music Mates.com voting script page.

Asking for Questions with an Ask Site

An Ask site is a mini-site and also a squeeze page that has one main purpose: to get visitors to ask you questions so that you can begin a relationship with them. Refer to Figure 4-6 for an example of an Ask Web site where I'm encouraging visitors to ask me a topic-specific question.

A by-product of Ask sites is that eventually you get asked the same questions over and over. From this pattern, you can gain an idea of what information people are hungry to learn about for any particular topic. Then, you can hold a Webinar or teleconference — or even produce a book or other product — to address their questions.

The following steps give you an overview of the process for creating an Ask site and connecting it to your network of Web sites:

1. **Register a domain name specific to the topic you are welcoming questions about.**

   `AskMartyAboutWebsiteDesign.com` is an example of an Ask page where visitors are encouraged to ask a question about Web site design.

2. **Set up a brief Web site that resembles the look of a squeeze page but with the intention of the visitor asking a question.**

3. **Incorporate a form to capture the visitor's name and address when they ask their question.**

4. **Create links to any additional Ask sites you might manage.**

   In fact, you could create literally hundreds of ask sites specific to topics covered in your industry. The first Ask Marty sites you see in this example were created by using MarketingMakeoverGenerator (`http://marketingmakeovergenerator.com`) in less than 90 minutes by using a clone feature. After I had one site set up, I could easily copy it and customize it to each topic.

5. **Add links from other Web sites to your Ask sites so that search engines will index them in their listings.**

Managing a Membership Web Site

The hottest topic among Internet marketers for the past couple of years has been membership Web sites because of the lure of a term near and dear to every entrepreneurial heart: *recurring revenue.*

We all dream of having thousands of dollars added to our bank accounts each month without requiring additional effort on our part. Member-based Web sites can produce such a financial effect although you should be aware that they are hardly an escape from continued effort.

Fortunately, membership sites have been around for many years, and we've gotten to know a lot about what makes them attract new members and retain current ones. The following sections explore these topics, as well as some initial steps to take.

Defining a true membership Web site

A membership Web site is one that allows and inspires Web site visitors to acquire a user name and password to view protected content through the Web. A member-based Web site doesn't always have to cost money to join.

Consider Yahoo! Groups. When you join a group, you become a member. You receive announcements whenever new content is added, and you're invited to share in resources provided to the group. The same principle applies to a true membership Web site, just on a larger scale.

Evaluating membership site types

The term *membership Web site* is often scary to people. And, in certain cases, it should be. Creating and maintaining a membership Web site can be the most complex or simplest process of your entire Internet-marketing strategy, depending on what you want to feature and how you want the content to be accessed. Here are some types of membership Web sites to help you choose which one might be right for you:

✦ **Adding a password-protected directory:** If you have a Web site of any kind right now, chances are you could have your Webmaster or hosting company simply add a directory that's password protected to your account. Then, you could add new content to that directory and offer access to your customers or Web site visitors. In this event, every member would have the same user name and password to access the password-protected area.

✦ **Using a third-party script to apply to your Web site:** For years, aMember software (www.amember.com) has been the gold standard for membership Web sites. Here are the steps to using aMember:

   a. *Create a Web site as you would normally.*

   b. *Earmark a section of your Web site where all member content will be made available to members, such as members.yourdomainname.com or yourdomainname.com/members.*

   c. *Install the aMember software script and connect it with a MySQL database.* aMember offers installation procedures as an additional service. Figure 4-10 displays a sample administration area for aMember software where you can see the two levels I assigned. On the left, you can see how I can add new users and manage admin options for the member program.

   d. *Configure aMember to allow various levels of membership.* For example, Level 1 might be a free membership, whereas Level 2 could be chargeable for $30 per month. Level 3 could be a much higher-end payment — into the hundreds of dollars per month, depending on the value of what you offer in the member area.

e. *Connect your shopping cart to the member area.* If your membership area will require an access fee, you need some mechanism for accepting both the initial payment and recurring monthly payments automatically. My personal choice for this component is 1ShoppingCartFree.com. Not that the cart is free, but it is for a 30-day trial. But, 1ShoppingcartFree.com has telephone support for its cart plus a custom add-on module for the sole purpose of working with aMember. An additional one-time fee is required for the add-on.

f. *The next piece you need is a gateway for the payments to be authorized and deposited into your bank account.* I prefer using Authorize.Net (`www.authorize.net`) for my gateway processing, which has a low monthly fee of only $10 plus a small per-transaction fee of $0.10.

g. *Finally, you need something to put into the membership area that will be of high enough value to attract members and keep them.*

The secret to attracting members for a membership Web site and keeping them is an *anchor*. For you, an anchor might be a monthly or weekly telecoaching program that's for members only. For me, an anchor is a set of tools that business owners use on a daily basis to implement and track their Internet marketing processes instead of trying to keep everything on Excel spreadsheets. I call it the Internet Marketing Organizer. Figure 4-11 shows an example from inside my membership area where clients can keep track of what steps they've taken with a variety of Internet-marketing tasks.

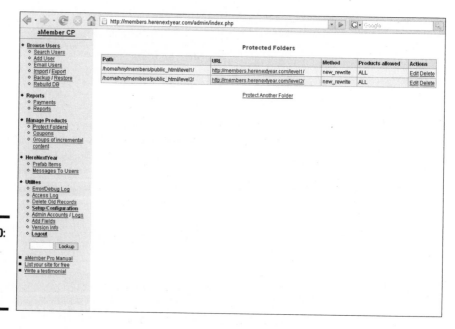

Figure 4-10:
The aMember admin screen.

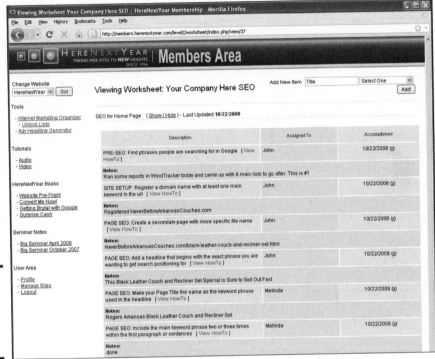

Figure 4-11: Attract members with an anchor.

REMEMBER

Think of an anchor as Web site hosting. After you find a Web-hosting company that works and doesn't go down all the time, you will keep your site hosted there until the end of time, right? That's an anchor. It doesn't matter what else is offered in the Web site membership area if you have an anchor that's valuable enough to your members. They'll keep using your system and paying you for years to come.

Calculating your revenue potential

Membership Web sites are cumulative. If you can keep your member retention high, your income will double or triple or grow by even more over time. Member sites that are promoted correctly have little problem getting 100 paying members within a month or two.

A few things need to be ironed out before you go live with your new member Web site, however. These include

✦ **Price:** How much will you charge for your member access? Most member Web sites have a free level and then from two to five paid levels. Whatever price you offer for a member level per month should equate to more than 20 times the value over the course of a year. So, if you decide to charge $27 per month for your Level 2 membership, that would be $324 per year. Your value needs to be at least $6,000 over the course of the year for people to feel they're truly getting a good deal.

✦ **Involvement:** How involved do you want to be when it comes to adding new content and new features to your membership area? The average, moderately successful Web site will have new content added at least once weekly. That way, you can send an e-mail blast to your members telling them to log in to the membership area to get access to the new content.

You must stay in frequent contact with your members lest they forget about your membership program. Releasing new content that they don't have to pay for is a great reason to contact them. And, they'll appreciate that you're keeping them up to date.

✦ **Cost:** The average membership Web site takes about one quarter of one person's time to manage per week. If that person is just you, be careful to calculate how much revenue you must earn to make it worth your while. It won't be long before you'll want to bring in some help after you get some members to serve.

Here's an example of how to calculate your revenue potential. Using the scenario I present in Figure 4-12, I factored a membership fee of $27 for a low-cost member site (and it's very unusual to offer only a $27 member level). I figured a high 30 percent churn rate of lost members and a very pessimistic projection for addition of new members. Still, with all those negatives, you could still be earning more than $34,000 per year.

If I change only the monthly fee from $27 to $79, check out Figure 4-13 to see how your income potential grows.

Most successful member programs have a lower level of pricing at anywhere between $5 and $30, a mid-range price of $50 to $100, and a third level of pricing anywhere between $300 and $1,500 per month. Now you should be getting a feel for why membership sites are so tempting to business owners today.

Figure 4-12: Spreadsheet for membership revenue potential at $27 per month.

	A	B	C	D	E	F
1		New Members	Lost Members	Total Current Members	Fee	Total Revenue
2	Month 1	10	3	7	$27.00	$189.00
3	Month 2	25	7.5	17.5	$27.00	$472.50
4	Month 3	35	10.5	24.5	$27.00	$661.50
5	Month 4	50	15	35	$27.00	$945.00
6	Month 5	70	21	49	$27.00	$1,323.00
7	Month 6	100	30	70	$27.00	$1,890.00
8	Month 7	125	37.5	87.5	$27.00	$2,362.50
9	Month 8	150	45	105	$27.00	$2,835.00
10	Month 9	200	60	140	$27.00	$3,780.00
11	Month 10	250	75	175	$27.00	$4,725.00
12	Month 11	350	105	245	$27.00	$6,615.00
13	Month 12	450	135	315	$27.00	$8,505.00
14	Yearly Income					$34,303.50
15						
16						
17						

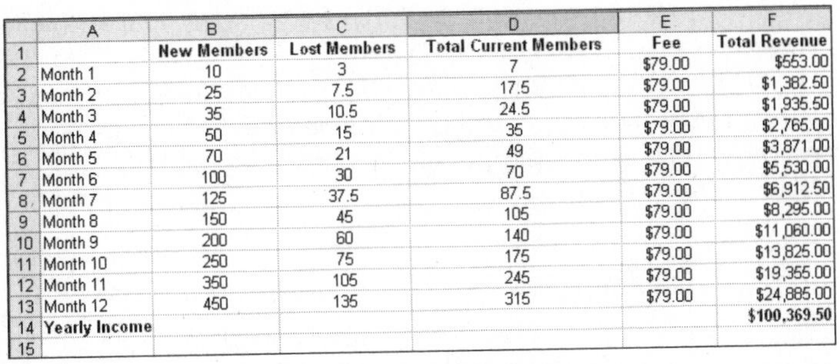

Figure 4-13:
Spreadsheet
for
membership
revenue
potential
at $79 per
month.

	A	B	C	D	E	F
1		New Members	Lost Members	Total Current Members	Fee	Total Revenue
2	Month 1	10	3	7	$79.00	$553.00
3	Month 2	25	7.5	17.5	$79.00	$1,382.50
4	Month 3	35	10.5	24.5	$79.00	$1,935.50
5	Month 4	50	15	35	$79.00	$2,765.00
6	Month 5	70	21	49	$79.00	$3,871.00
7	Month 6	100	30	70	$79.00	$5,530.00
8	Month 7	125	37.5	87.5	$79.00	$6,912.50
9	Month 8	150	45	105	$79.00	$8,295.00
10	Month 9	200	60	140	$79.00	$11,060.00
11	Month 10	250	75	175	$79.00	$13,825.00
12	Month 11	350	105	245	$79.00	$19,355.00
13	Month 12	450	135	315	$79.00	$24,885.00
14	Yearly Income					$100,369.50
15						

Managing Content with a Content Management System

Business owners have always wanted to manage their own Web site content instead of calling a designer every time even a minor change is needed. Unfortunately, too many shy away from the opportunity even if it's made available to them for fear of the process taking too long or just being too technical.

Developments of today have made managing Web site content easier and less technical than ever before. Earlier, I covered one form of content management system (CMS) when I talked about Contribute, but Contribute is a computer-based software program. In the following sections, I introduce you to the major players in Web-based CMS so that you can maintain content from any hotel room with an Internet connection, no matter what computer you are using.

Justifying Joomla!

Joomla! is CMS software that allows you to make changes to the pages of your Web site from your browser. After the design of the site is installed, you can add as many new pages as you want so your designer doesn't have to. Using Joomla! (`http://www.joomla.org`; free) has two huge benefits that make it very desirable to business owners:

✦ **Open source:** A programmer can customize how open source software works.

✦ **Extensions:** Joomla! has an enormous following where programmers have created modules — *extensions* (similar to plug-ins for WordPress) — with tremendous functionality, such as shopping carts and classified ads.

One drawback to Joomla! is its learning curve. And, you almost always need someone with PHP programming experience to install it. As easy as it might appear from this admin screen, Joomla! can be quite overwhelming to someone with no Web site–management experience.

For help, check out *Joomla! For Dummies* by Steve Holzner and Nancy Conner (Wiley).

For a larger organization, the benefits outweigh the learning curve. Joomla! is great when multiple people on a team are responsible for updating certain areas of Web sites.

Definitely Drupal

Drupal (http://drupal.org; free) is the main competitor to Joomla! in that it is also CMS software for updating, adding, and managing pages. But, Drupal has two additional benefits. Its front-end look is entirely customizable, and the HTML code it produces is much cleaner than that of Joomla! Better code has a positive impact on search engine positioning.

Drupal also has a large following of developers and users, but they are definitely weighted on the programmer side. Whereas Joomla has a visual approach to appeal to day-to-day administrative-level users, Drupal requires at least basic HTML knowledge to maintain.

Clearly Joomla! and Drupal serve one similar need: that is, enabling you to manage content. However, they differ in many important factors as well. Table 4-1 lists how my staff of designers, programmers, and administrative helpers have rated Joomla! versus Drupal. If you choose to use either, your choice can be made based on what's most important to you and your team from this list.

If you decide Drupal is the system for you, *Leveraging Drupal: Getting Your Site Done Right* by Victor Kane (Wiley) helps you use Drupal components to pull your site together.

Table 4-1	Comparing Joomla! and Drupal	
	Joomla!	*Drupal*
Popularity	👍	👎
Ease of learning	👍	👎
Number of design templates available	👍	👎
Ease of adding custom theme	👎	👍
Search engine–friendliness	👎	👍
Number of add-ons available	👍	👎
Quality of add-ons available	👎	👍
Favored by programmers	👎	👍
Favored by designers	👎	👍

	Joomla!	*Drupal*
The CMS more people move to	👎	👍
User management	👎	👍
Ease of making global changes	👎	👍
Best process for organizing articles	👎	👍
CSS (Cascading Style Sheet) efficiency	👍	👎
E-commerce/shopping cart solution	👍	👎

Considering an alternative CMS

Choosing the CMS system that's right for you is a very important challenge, to say the least. If you choose the wrong one, you might find yourself wanting to switch to the other after just a few months.

Implementing a Joomla! or Drupal CMS system isn't as easy as you might hear. Each business is different, as is each Web server. Configurations, setup, customizations, usage, and speed all need to be considered when evaluating which CMS is truly right for your purpose.

Having someone at your side who has proven skills in PHP and MySQL programming will be absolutely essential to the success of your CMS system. And, you will want modifications and additions along the way. Plan to spend at least between $4,000 and $6,000 or more for implementation of either.

Here is my suggestion: Consider using WordPress instead of Joomla! or Drupal. Hmm. Didn't I talk earlier about WordPress as blogging software? Well, yes, I did. However, WordPress is also a very robust and easy-to-use CMS. Carefully consider what WordPress has to offer. It could be your most logical choice for your entire Web site and CMS system as well.

Creating and Maintaining Web Site Content

Ask any designer and he'll tell you the hardest part of creating any Web site is getting the content from the client. As the owner of your business, it's up to you to provide the words, photos, images, audio, and video for the pages. The designer's job is only to assemble the content you provide and add it to your Web site.

The other issue when it comes to Web sites is how to maintain your online content. Most designers enjoy creating a Web site, but when you call them to update a block of text, they may take days to respond.

You can use software packages — HTML editors — to maintain the content for your Web site. Here are some recommendations:

✦ **Adobe Dreamweaver** is the most popular HTML editor available (see www.adobe.com/products/dreamweaver). The sting of its hefty price ($399) is softened a bit by its power and function. Dreamweaver is also the industry standard; most designers and programmers use Dreamweaver to create and manage Web sites. If you're brand-new to using HTML software, finding a one- to two-day Dreamweaver class in your area would be strongly recommended to shorten your learning curve.

An HTML editor (like Dreamweaver) is used only to produce *pages and content* for delivery on the Internet. You don't use an HTML editor to create graphics or edit photos. For that type of work, look into Adobe Photoshop (www.adobe.com/products/photoshop/photoshop) or freeware (such as GIMP; www.gimp.org).

Dreamweaver files are created and edited offline (on your computer) until you're ready to display them on the Web. Then you transfer those files to your Web site. For this task, I prefer using Core FTP (a free, file-transfer program), as shown in Figure 4-14. You can find more about this FTP (File Transfer Protocol) client at www.coreftp.com.

✦ **Adobe Contribute** ($199; www.adobe.com/products/contribute) is an editor that connects directly to the posted files on your Web site to make changes. The main benefit of Contribute is ease of use with its Microsoft Word–like interface. Designers like Contribute for its ability to protect pages or components within a page, thereby preventing their clients from permanently damaging major elements, such as page layout, navigation buttons, and main graphics.

The beauty of using Contribute is that a designer can create a Web site in Dreamweaver and then offer his client the ability to maintain pages of the site with Contribute.

✦ **XSitePro** ($297; www.xsitepro.com) can be thought of as a less-expensive alternative to Dreamweaver with the ease-of-use factor offered by Contribute. XSitePro includes 200 templates from which you can choose and then add content and publish your new Web site from scratch in less than ten minutes. Figure 4-15 shows a typical editing screen within XSitePro.

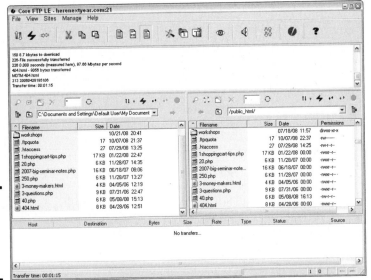

Figure 4-14:
Core FTP
offers easy
file transfer
to your site.

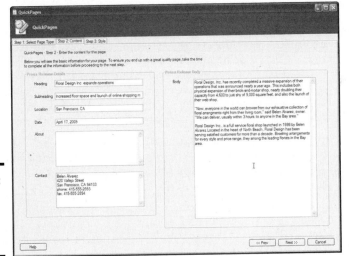

Figure 4-15:
Try the
XSitePro
Web page
editor.

Chapter 5: Creating Exceptional Copy That Sells

In This Chapter

✔ Writing clear, effective, and compelling copy for your Web site

✔ Using landing pages to drive sales

✔ Motivating customers to buy from you

*E*ven the prettiest Web site won't convert a single visitor to a customer unless you use well-written content to entice and inspire taking immediate action. Regrettably, lesser-quality content isn't typically the first thing on the chopping block when one tries to figure out why a Web site hasn't been earning its keep — but after you read this chapter, you'll understand why content should be one of the first things you examine closely for any improvement possible.

Fortunately, the Internet has been around for a while, so I've had lots of time to learn about what sells online from others' experiences as well as my own. You can follow proven strategies when it comes to writing content for your Web site. And, of course, there are several taboos to avoid. This chapter reveals the same system of creating content that I use when promoting my own products and services on the Internet.

Understanding the Elements of Effective Web Site Copy

Everyone is a skeptic on the Web. I'd be very surprised if you haven't heard about — or maybe even experienced firsthand — some type of online credit card fraud. Or, maybe you know someone who bought a birthday present online, only to receive the package three weeks after the birthday (if at all).

As a Web site owner and producer of content, your responsibility is to prove to your visitors that you're worthy of earning their business. The following sections offer tips to help you evaluate current copy or write fresh copy that reassures visitors and helps turn them into customers.

Writing headlines with a hook

You have five seconds or less before a visitor to your Web site decides to either read more on any particular page of your site or leave (see http://www.panalysis.com/bounce_rate_study.php). The first line of copy on your page needs to prove to your visitors that they arrived at the informational page they were looking for. A headline is the easiest way to accomplish this task.

A *conversion rate* is the percentage of Web site visitors that take some kind of action with you as opposed to leaving your Web site. This action can be a phone call, completing a contact form, walking into your retail store, or buying online through your shopping cart. Conversion rates can vary dramatically by making even a single change to the headline of a page. A headline has one purpose: to get people to read more. To accomplish that, your headlines must

+ Be intriguing and inviting

+ Prove to your visitors that they're at the right place

Sometimes, accomplishing both of the preceding objectives in just a few words can be like two repelling magnets. People spend weeks and even months testing new headlines to get them just right.

I find writing headlines to be the most challenging part of the copywriting process. So, I created a tool to help me, which I offer for free to all my clients. Here's how it works:

1. **Point your Web browser to**

   www.actionheadlinecreator.com

2. **To generate possible headlines, answer the four questions on the form and then click the Generate Headlines Now! button.**

   The headlines generated appear in alphabetical order, as shown in Figure 5-1. As an example, I used a fictitious product that you use to help get better gas mileage.

3. **Save the generated headlines for editing and future use by exporting to Excel.**

   I prefer exporting my headlines to Excel so that I can enter a few additional columns to the right of the spreadsheet including a Date Tested column and a Results column.

   Click the Download As CSV button, and then send the headlines to yourself or someone else by e-mail.

If you don't like any of the suggestions, you can always click the Clear! button, change the answers to the four questions, and re-run the report.

4. In Excel, massage the words to fit.

One of the headlines the tool produced is *A Breakthrough in How To Save Gas . . . In Only in First Tank Full!* This suggestion is a good example of when you need to massage a headline that doesn't initially seem to be a good fit into something that works. Let's take a look at some ways we could change this headline to fit a possible promotion on a sales page.

- The first part of the headline I might keep. "A Breakthrough in How to Save Gas" isn't bad. But, I'd also want to test "A Breakthrough in Saving Gas" because it has a more fluid sound to it.

- The second part needs more work. First of all "In Only in" is not even grammatically correct. So, that would have to go.

- "In Only First Tank Full" doesn't sound right to me either. So, how about "See Results in First Tank Full"

My final headline to test would be, "A Breakthrough in Saving Gas...See Results in the First Tank Full!"

5. To save your revised headlines for future use, choose File⇨Save, give your file a name, and then click OK.

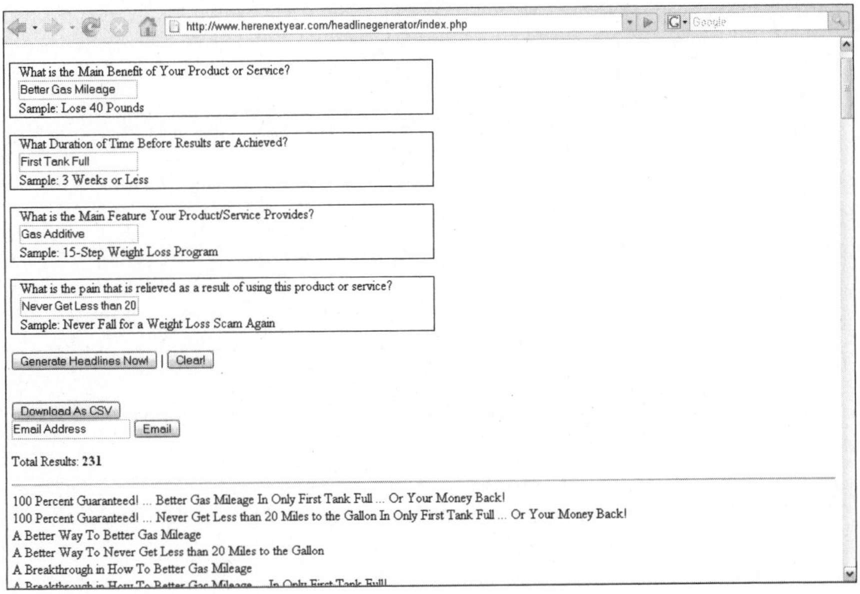

Figure 5-1:
Use this online tool to help you generate headlines.

(Screenshot of an online headline generator tool at http://www.herenextyear.com/headlinegenerator/index.php showing the following fields:)

What is the Main Benefit of Your Product or Service?
Better Gas Mileage
Sample: Lose 40 Pounds

What Duration of Time Before Results are Achieved?
First Tank Full
Sample: 3 Weeks or Less

What is the Main Feature Your Product/Service Provides?
Gas Additive
Sample: 15-Step Weight Loss Program

What is the pain that is relieved as a result of using this product or service?
Never Get Less than 20
Sample: Never Fall for a Weight Loss Scam Again

Generate Headlines Now! | Clear!

Download As CSV
Email Address Email

Total Results: 231

100 Percent Guaranteed! ... Better Gas Mileage In Only First Tank Full ... Or Your Money Back!
100 Percent Guaranteed! ... Never Get Less than 20 Miles to the Gallon In Only First Tank Full ... Or Your Money Back!
A Better Way To Better Gas Mileage
A Better Way To Never Get Less than 20 Miles to the Gallon
A Breakthrough in How To Better Gas Mileage
A Breakthrough in How To Better Gas Mileage ... In Only First Tank Full!

After you write your headline, remember to give it prominence and make it fit aesthetically on your Web page. Here's how I recommend you format and place your main heading:

✦ **Center the headline.**

✦ **Put the headline in a different color than the rest of your text to make it stand out.** Red is a good color for headlines because it stops people in their tracks to read what is so important. Blue is another good color for headlines because of its authority.

✦ **Make the font size of the headline two to four times larger than the rest of your text.**

✦ **Don't use punctuation to conclude a headline unless you're using a question mark (um, if you're asking a question in your headline).**

Proving that you're a real human being

We buy things from people we know, like, and trust. Your Web site is an opportunity to start that relationship and then build upon it. Here are some ways to increase the human factor of any specific Web page, or the Web site overall:

✦ **Write from your heart, not from the dictionary.** For example, a CPA firm can take a dry sentence like this:

> *We prepare individual, joint, unincorporated small business tax returns.*

And personalize it, as follows:

> *So many new clients would tell us their business and individual tax return horror stories with other CPA firms. We just knew we were really on to something special when they would thank us for making the process so easy.*

✦ **Add a good photo to your Web page.** Adding a genuine and original photograph of yourself or your team to any Web site header or landing page turns a dry faceless pile of words into a personal endorsement from you. Every time I have added a real photo to one of my own project sales pages, where there were only words on a page before, both my opt-in rates and my sales conversion rates have increased — but only when the right photo was chosen. (Some photos of people just look plain scary, and I'm not sure why folks choose to use them.) Have a professional, studio-produced photo taken and pass it around for all your friends and family. If your picture captures the true essence of who you are, they'll tell you so. And, that's the picture to use for your Web site. Figure 5-2 shows a great example of an effective photo, courtesy of Marcia Pessemier at LimelightPresentations.com.

✦ **Introduce yourself and your product with video or audio.** Video and audio are the highest forms of introduction available for placement on a Web site (see Figure 5-3). With today's tools, almost anyone can learn to create their own professional-looking videos from home for less than $1,000.

At www.animalbehaviorassociates.com, you can find an example of a homemade video for a business that would've cost between $2,000 and $5,000 to produce in a studio with professional editors.

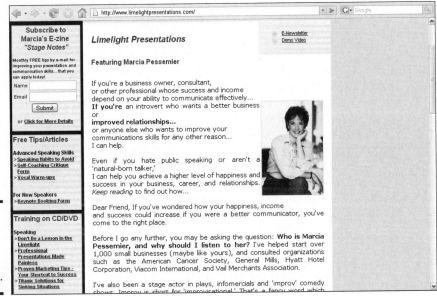

Figure 5-2:
Use a photo
of yourself
that tells
who you are.

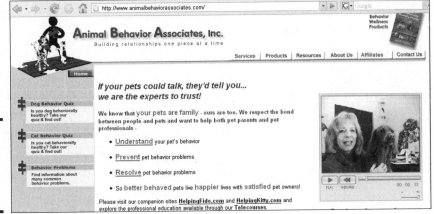

Figure 5-3:
Use video
to introduce
yourself on
a Web site.

One of the most popular questions about audio and video is whether to begin the playback immediately when visitors land on the page or to give them the option to click a Play button. The answer, as you might have guessed, is to test your own results. (You test by using Web analytics, the focus of Book III.) Try both ways by having your video start immediately for a couple of weeks and then have your video editor change the setting to force a playback button. If you have to pick one or the other and stick with it, I would suggest having the automated playback begin immediately when visitors land on the page, but then offer a Stop button as well so that they can turn off the player if desired.

✦ **Encourage contact by phone, e-mail, or live chat.** Welcoming communication builds visitor confidence and sets you apart from the rest of the many companies that use the Web to avoid communicating with their customers.

✦ **Describe how you were once in the same position as your visitors by telling your story.** Consider this fictional example of a divorce attorney attempting to sell her services:

> *22 years ago, my high school marriage grew apart, only to land in divorce court with an attorney who had never been married and just didn't understand. I lost everything — including my dignity — and I vowed I would learn to fight for others to never let an experience like that happen to them. Now, with 18 years experience in divorce law, I have a reputation for always. . . .*

If I wrote that correctly, you were probably hoping there was more to the story! And, that's exactly the point about copywriting for the Web. It's all about getting people engaged so they want to learn more about you.

✦ **Display your longevity and commitment to an industry.** One of my favorite, professional speaker coaches is Patricia Fripp. If you are a corporate executive looking for a speaking coach for an upcoming sales rally, for example, you probably wouldn't need to search any further after landing on Fripp.com (`www.fripp.com`; shown in Figure 5-4). Everything about the Web site exudes a dedication to the speaking industry — and only the speaking industry.

Proving your solution does what you say it will do

"Entrepreneurism is simply the act of solving problems at a profit."

— T. Harv Ecker

When it comes to writing promotional copy, there comes a point where you need to stop presenting more features and benefits and start proving that your offer solves the problem. Here are several methods for proving to your visitors that your product or service solves their problem:

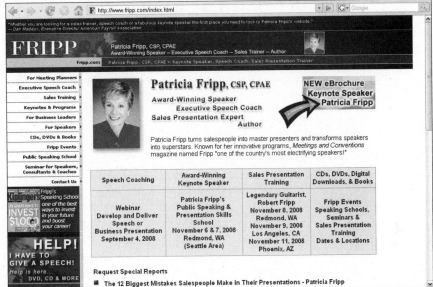

Figure 5-4:
Earn trust by
displaying
dedication
to an
industry.

✦ **Use testimonials in your Web site copy.** The best testimonial you can
have on a Web site is video of a customer telling the world how your
product or service helped his specific situation. A recorded audio file
is an adequate substitute. Printed testimonials are acceptable but are
believable only if you can print a first and last names of the testimony
provider, along with the city and state he or she lives.

You must be given authorization to use someone's full name and residence for a testimonial!

When asking for a video or audio testimonial, you can help your customers decide what to say by giving them a checklist. You can use the following list for virtually any video or audio testimonial occasion and even
try it yourself next time you attend a seminar where testimonials are
being taken onsite:

• Your name and Web site address

• Why you attended (or purchased a product)

• Your result

• Strong recommendation for others in similar position to attend next
time (or buy now)

• Repeat your name and your Web site address

✦ **Provide links to letters of recommendation.** A three- or four-line testimonial is adequate, but getting a formally written letter of recommendation printed on your customer's letterhead with a signature of the person at the bottom is exceptional. An example of a full letter of recommendation can be found at www.thinklikeaspy.com/lor/LFG.pdf. When you receive such a letter, you will need to have it scanned. Save the scanned copy as a PDF or JPG image, upload it to your Web site, and add a link from within a page on your Web site to the document.

✦ **Share that you've tried similar products.** You should always know your competition and the quality of product or service they are delivering. Buy as much as you can afford of your competitors' products so that you can speak wisely about how your offer fills gaps that the other products do not address. Most importantly, you must mention on your page that you're familiar with similar products but that certain elements of your product are what really sets you apart from the rest. Here's an example:

> *Now, I've personally spent more than $20,000 out of my own pocket buying products that claimed I would learn how to speak 2nd-year college level Spanish in 30 days. None of them worked because none of them offered V.R.I., my patent-pending, one-of-a-kind Voice Recognition Interpreter tool where the automated attendant automatically tells you how to correct a sentence before you've even completed one! I can tell you for certain that nowhere else can you find this product anywhere on the market today, and soon it will change the way people learn languages forever!*

✦ **Show that no competing product is as easy to use.** Today, people are doing the work of five people at their day jobs. The last thing they need or want is to learn something difficult or implement something that takes time to figure out. We want speed of implementation and speed of results. Convince your prospective customer that your solution is simple. And, if it's not simple, you need to work on its methodology so that it *is* simple.

Continuing with the Spanish training example, you could use verbiage like this to describe the ease of use:

> *Learning a foreign language is known as one of the most difficult things to do, especially as an adult. I discovered why this was true after trying every Spanish CD and book I could find. When I created this product, it was really for myself first. I needed a Spanish-learning process that was so easy that my mother at age 73 could figure it out! And, you know what? My mother and I have complete conversations today...in Spanish! She just loaded the CD into her computer and pressed the play button. That was it. No manuals. No complex reading or study. It was all right there on her computer.*

Don't invite your visitors to "check out the competition" — because they will! In the automotive sales business, salespeople will do anything they can to get you to buy their car while you're on the lot, because they know once you leave there is slim chance you will return to buy their car.

✦ **Describe the product's popularity.** We all like to be part of something that's popular, and we shy away from being the first to experience something new.

Include a paragraph in your Web site copy that suggests to readers that they're really missing out on something and that your product is used by either a large number or a wide variety of people. For example:

> *Last month alone, more than 350 people made the choice to learn Spanish in 30 days or less using my system.*

The objective of conveying your popularity is not to lie! Never lie to your audience. You don't need to fabricate numbers to be seen as popular even if your business is in the start-up phase. Simply identify something about your business that really is popular and talk about it. Here are some examples — just add your own number and change the topic to be more descriptive of your business:

> *Of the more than 100 people I talked to last month who had attempted to learn Spanish through some other means, only 2 reported that the system they tried worked.*

> *100 people who started learning Spanish using my product last month can't be wrong.*

> *Of the last 100 people who used my learning Spanish system, the success rate has been a whopping 94%!*

Creating video on your own

Here's what you need to produce a home video on a Windows machine:

✔ **A digital video camera**

✔ **A tripod**

✔ **A microphone**

I use the Audio-Technica Pro 41 (`www.audio-technica.com`; $217).

✔ **Sony Vegas Movie Studio 9 (`www.sony creativesoftware.com/movie studio`; $99)**

Tip: For all the pieces, video training, and support you need to get started with video for your Web site, check out InternetVideoGuy.com (`www.internetvideoguy.com`). I know the owner (Mike Stewart). He is the foremost authority on producing home-based video and has my full endorsement. More detailed steps about recording audio and video for your Web site can be found in Book I, Chapter 6.

Providing clear and easy calls to action

How many Web sites have you visited where you find yourself pulling out your credit card ready to buy, but the sales page never gives you a link to click or an Add to Cart button to press? Make it easy for your visitors to take the next step with you:

+ **Display a phone number in plain view on every page of your Web site.**

+ **Use different sizes of both links and buttons throughout your copy to take customers to order forms.**

+ **Test different text on buttons and links and then monitor which brings the best conversion rate possible.**

  There are two ways to test the effectiveness of links and buttons on a sales page. First, you can use Google Analytics as further described in Book III to track the exact path a Web site visitor takes through your Web site from the page they enter through the entire ordering system. The other way is by split testing (or A/B testing) during a Google AdWords campaign, as described in Book IV, Chapter 4.

+ **Keep your text links blue and underlined.** People are used to clicking links that are traditionally formatted as blue and underlined. Use a variety of graphic images to direct your visitors what to do next. See Chapter 3 of this minibook for more information on design.

+ **Try providing a form at the end of your copy instead of links to other pages.** The less you force people to click things to get to the next step, the more chance you have of them taking that next step.

+ **Reduce the number of distractions.** For other pages of your site, it's natural to offer navigation buttons, special offers on a variety of products, and other news items. When it comes to a sales page, though, reduce the distractions so that a visitor isn't tempted to deviate from the buying process.

According to test results by my good friend Eric Graham, "The Conversion Doctor," your conversions will increase by adding a red border around your Buy Now buttons. If you add an effect where the red border turns green when you mouse over the button, your conversion rates will increase even more!

Driving Sales with Landing Pages

Whether your visitors find you through search engines or banner ads, or by typing your Web site address into their Web browser, the first page of your site that people see is the *landing page.* If your landing page copy isn't exactly what your visitors are looking for, they will leave your site and search for someone else's landing page that offers more relevant results.

This section introduces you to three of the most popular types of landing pages used to cast a large net, capture a wide range of visitors, and/or receive targeted traffic — educational content pages, squeeze pages, and sales pages.

Create topic-specific pages throughout your Web site and drive traffic to those subsequent pages instead of trying to bring in all your traffic through the homepage. When a visitor lands on your homepage, too many choices are usually available. The visitor doesn't typically see what he was looking for within a few seconds and just clicks the Back button.

Creating educational content pages

Because most people search the Internet for answers to specific problems, create pages on your Web site to educate people on those issues. These *educational content pages* can develop into dozens, or even hundreds or thousands, in number, for any Web site. Figure 5-5 shows an example of an educational content page.

Book I
Chapter 5

Creating
Exceptional Copy
That Sells

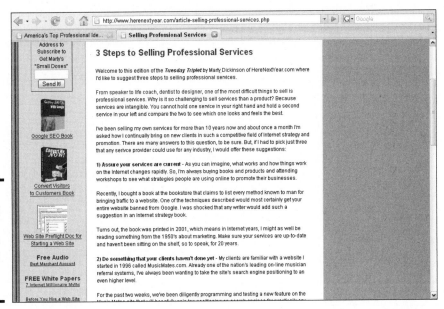

Figure 5-5: Educational content pages drive more traffic to your Web site.

Educational content pages are

✦ Fast and easy to create because they are so short.

✦ Enjoyable to read because they focus on one, specific topic.

✦ Attractive to search engines because they are heavily optimized for specific keywords related to the problems people are searching for.

✦ An opportunity to tell visitors there is more involved with the solution and that you have just the product or service to suggest.

✦ One of the least-expensive ways to cast a large net to attract a wide variety of visitors in a short amount of time.

The following steps outline key tasks for a successful educational content page. When you create your pages, make sure you follow all the steps:

1. **Research where the traffic is.**

   Before you write an educational content page, or plan to revise an existing one, find out what exact phrases people are searching for related to the topic you want to write about. Use the free keyword suggestion tool from Wordtracker (`http://freekeywords.wordtracker.com`). If you have a Google AdWords account, you can use Google's search tool, which not only gives you an estimated search count by month but a graphical report showing how many competitors are advertising for that keyword phrase. Your time is much better used by writing content pages for what people are searching for already rather than coming up with your own topics and hoping people somehow find them. See Book III for more details on keyword research.

   Be sure to include the search phrases you find, as follows:

   • *Create a headline that begins with the keywords people are searching for.*

   • *Use the exact keyword phrase people are searching for when you give your content page a Page Title and File Name for basic search engine optimization standards.*

   In Book II, you can find more detailed help with search engine optimization.

2. **Introduce the problem.**

   A paragraph that's three to ten sentences usually works well.

3. **Suggest what the reader can do right now on his own to work toward a solution.**

   Add three to five bullet points or numbered steps. Never use only one suggestion, or two or four suggestions (people respond better to odd numbers).

4. **Add a summary paragraph after you have completed the bullet point section of your content page.**

   Use no more than four or five sentences.

5. **Explain how you can help with the problem.**

   This goes beyond what the reader can do and involves either a product you offer or a service you provide.

6. **Introduce yourself.**

   Write a three- to five-sentence signature line that introduces you to the reader more formally.

7. **Link to your educational content page on other pages of your Web site.**

   You want visitors and search engine spiders to find the page. When you're creating these links, be sure to include a link to the content page on both your traditional site map and Google Sitemap areas. (See the nearby sidebar for details on site maps versus Google Sitemaps.)

Don't confuse educational content pages with article pages. An *article* is something you write to be displayed on someone else's Web site. Article pages are typically longer than 400–600 words and often reference other Web sites or sources. Content pages are very raw and to the point, and are designed to be showcased only on your Web site.

Search engines have been working on reducing the amount of duplicate content on the Internet. Resist the temptation to duplicate your content pages and change only a few words on each page in the hopes of getting more search engine visitors because you have more pages online.

The benefits of site maps

What I'm calling a "traditional" site map is a page of your Web site that was created only for the purpose of displaying links to all main sections of your Web site. You may have stumbled onto a site map page in the past; usually links to a site map appear on the bottom of the page. The idea with a site map used to be to allow a simple way for visitors to find anything on the Web site if they could not find the topic through the standard navigation buttons and links. But, the site map has another purpose, which is to be an easy way for search engines to find all your important pages and get them added to their search engine index. Site map pages almost never have fancy graphics for the links, but have text only links, thereby making it easy for the search engines to crawl through the site.

A Google Sitemap is a little different: It's Google's way of keeping in direct contact with your site so that it knows immediately of any changes to your Web site. When you add a new page or change an existing page, adding a Google Sitemap helps to alert Google so that indexing of those new or changed pages can update their list more quickly. More on traditional site maps and Google Sitemaps is provided in Book II, which covers search engine optimization.

Building your opt-in e-mail list with squeeze pages

Squeeze pages are short and simple pages that introduce additional content available to readers — but only if they're willing to register by providing an e-mail address. Figure 5-6 displays a squeeze page.

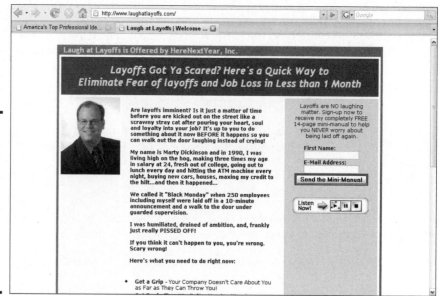

Figure 5-6: Squeeze pages convert more visitors to opt-in subscribers than the homepage does.

A squeeze page is a great way to accept targeted traffic for a very specific topic of interest and inspire visitors to register to be on your mailing list. Commonly, more than 20 percent of your first-time visitors to a squeeze page will complete and submit the opt-in form. Some points to keep in mind while creating a squeeze page include the following:

✦ **Great headlines are critical.** Going without a headline on a squeeze page or having one displayed that's not relevant to the topic is a traffic killer. See "Writing headlines with a hook" earlier in this chapter.

✦ **Show a good photo of yourself.** Conversion rates for a squeeze page always increase when you have a good photo of yourself (or whoever is writing to the visitor). See "Proving that you're a real human being" earlier in this chapter for tips on including a photo.

✦ **Write as if you're talking to someone one on one.** Squeeze pages are very personal. Take away all the corporate flair, and just talk to your visitors as if they're right in front of you.

✦ **List the benefits of why someone should opt in to your list.** What will they get exactly, and why is it worth giving up their e-mail address to receive?

✦ **Promise to give away something after they do sign up.** This could be a free report, e-course, or consult; sound files; or a coupon. Be creative. When you provide something of true value for free, an impressed subscriber will consider more strongly that your for-pay offer must have exceptional value as well.

✦ **Keep your subscription form to two fields — Name and E-mail Address:** Every additional field beyond those two will reduce your number of opt-ins substantially.

The term *opt-in* is a rather one-sided agreement. The Web site visitor agrees to give you an e-mail address so that he can get exactly what you were offering for free. It does not give you the permission to mercilessly barrage the subscriber with e-mails day and night until the end of time. In fact, think of every e-mail you send to your list to be like a fresh batch of chocolate cookies. If it doesn't taste great every time, the subscriber can unsubscribe anytime.

The best system I've ever seen for creating squeeze pages is the Web-based software MarketingMakeoverGenerator (www.marketingmakeover generator.com). With no design or programming skills, you can have your own squeeze page up and running in about 30 minutes.

Book V, Chapter 3 offers more tips for building your e-mail list.

Providing all the facts through sales pages

A *sales page* serves three purposes:

✦ To educate the visitor with the facts about a specific product, service, or event

✦ To give the reader enough facts to make an informed buying decision

✦ To provide the mechanism to actually take the next step in the buying process

Whereas educational content pages teach and squeeze pages build your list, sales pages are designed to convert readers into paying customers. Source Medical Equipment (www.sourcemedicalequipment.com) offers a good example of product sales pages that convert visitors to paying customers. Figure 5-7 displays one of its product pages.

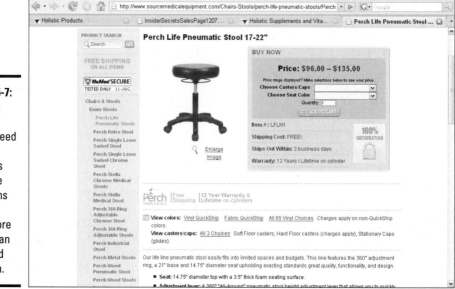

Figure 5-7:
Product sales pages need to offer answers to all the questions people ask before making an informed decision.

Sales pages come in a variety of shapes and sizes, and there is no general rule for how long or short a page should be for your particular product. The most important rule is to give just enough information to allow someone to make an educated decision. One word more is too much, and one word less is not enough.

I love to attend Internet strategy workshops and conferences. For a free, one-hour, brown-bag lunch seminar being held in my office building at noon, I might decide to attend after getting a simple one-paragraph announcement in an e-mail describing what the topic is that's being covered. To convince me to pay $2,500 and fly to another state and be away from my office and family for five days to attend a conference, I would want to know lots of specifics to make sure the trip would be worth my time and money. I use this example to suggest that you need to provide more information about your product as the price rises. Don't expect to sell a $100,000 diamond with three bullet points of text and a price. Conversely, you probably don't need a 20,000-word sales page to sell a $17 e-book.

Whether long or short, all good Internet sales pages have the following identical components:

✦ A main headline

✦ A description of the problem and why it's important to have the problem solved or alleviated

✦ Accurate and descriptive content to describe how, exactly, your product or service will solve the problem

✦ Proof that the item does what you claim or is what it appears to be

✦ A way to take immediate action whether by buying online or by picking up the phone to call

The trickiest thing about a sales page is the order in which to display those five elements. To make things easier to follow for myself, I created what I call the C.O.N.V.E.R.T. M.E. formula.

Writing Copy That Sells, Using The C.O.N.V.E.R.T. M.E. Formula

When someone buys something online, it's known as a *conversion* because the purchaser *converted* from a visitor to a paying customer. Only after you have proven yourself to your visitors can you focus on converting visitors to paying customers.

The following section outlines my step-by-step process that you can work through to create Web site copy that converts visitors to customers. The first letter of each step (and subsequent section) works as a mnemonic device to spell *c-o-n-v-e-r-t m-e* to help you remember the steps in the process. The following steps summarize the nine steps in the C.O.N.V.E.R.T. M.E. formula:

1. **Captivate visitors.**

   Write a headline with a hook.

2. **Offer just one testimonial.**

   Place one testimonial under the headline.

3. **Now address your visitors.**

   Use typical, letter-style formatting.

4. **Validate some facts.**

   Show industry percentages to reinforce the problem.

5. **Expose your solution.**

   Clearly define your problem solver and how it works.

6. **Recapture attention.**

   Don't let visitors leave just because you unveiled the secret.

7. **Test for Action.**

   Determine whether they're ready to buy right now.

8. **Motivate with value and urgency.**

   "But wait!" It's for real!

9. **Energize visitors to buy.**

   Give assurance that your offer really is a good deal.

To demonstrate the components of a successful online sales letter, I use the example of a working Web site, promoting a self-published book called *What's a Mom to Do?* which can be found at UnlimitedMom.com (`www.whatsamomtodobook.com`; see Figure 5-8).

Captivate visitors with a headline that hooks

Whoever wrote the suggestion that headlines should be short is probably broke. The secret to a good or bad headline is testing, not the number of words. You must test headlines for every page of your Web site where a product is sold or where someone is encouraged to take action of some kind, be it by phone, e-mail, chat, or completing a contact form. I even test headlines for educational content pages! Now, that's a lot of testing.

Testimonial

Headline

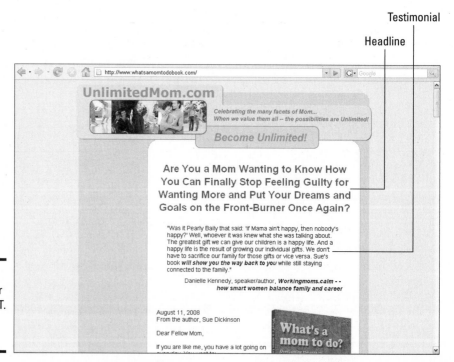

Figure 5-8:
Example for
C.O.N.V.E.R.T.
M.E.
formula.

Refer to Figure 5-8 for an example of the headline used on UnlimitedMom. com. See "Writing headlines with a hook" earlier in this chapter for tips on writing headlines. To test headlines, you need to watch your bounce rates. A bounce rate is the percentage of overall visitors who visit the page on your Web site and immediately leave. You can tell what your bounce rate is by looking at your visitation statistics logs within Google Analytics, which display the overall percentage of visitors who have left your site immediately, or under just a few seconds, on any particular page of your Web site. When you make a single change to your headline and then see your bounce rate percentage drop after a few days, you know you've made a better headline. Google Analytics is further described in Book III.

Offer reinforcement of your headline

Not too many things will generate interest and hope that a solution is possible better than a well-planned testimonial. Pick one of your best and add the testimonial right under the headline that you added to your site in the preceding section (refer to Figure 5-8). You can also use a sub-headline or an interesting statistic to reinforce your headline.

Even better than just choosing what you feel is your best testimonial would be an endorsement from a celebrity or a recognized authority in your field. You can begin the process of getting a celebrity endorsement by contacting their agent or management company and offering to send your product to them for free evaluation.

Now address your visitors personally

A personalized letter allows me to have a conversation with a reader as if we're on the phone with each other. For example, Figure 5-9 shows how you can quickly engage a reader by addressing them personally with a letter on your Web site. Notice how right after the Dear Fellow Mom salutation, there is a bullet point list of issues that moms face daily. This list builds rapport with the reader and gets her to the next stage, where you are to validate some facts.

Validate some facts

Before you go deeper into the components of the actual solution, attempt to make a bond with a wide variety of people who might be experiencing the issue you can resolve for them. This is accomplished by adding some facts and figures that address those groups. Use facts and figures that speak to the following issues when possible, as shown in Figure 5-10:

✦ More money

✦ More time

✦ Something fast

✦ Something easy

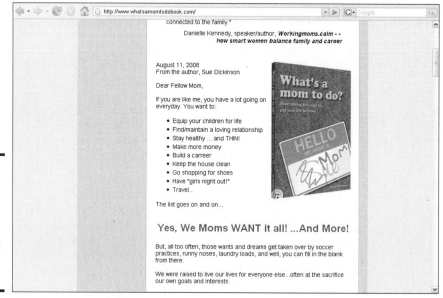

Figure 5-9: Addressing the reader personally begins a one-on-one conversation.

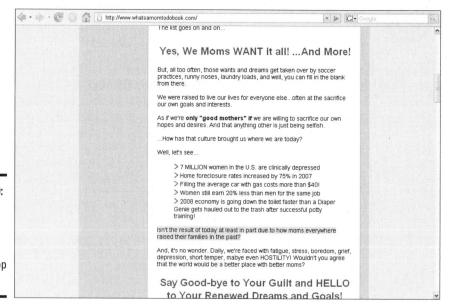

Figure 5-10: Providing facts and figures makes readers stop and think.

It's also important in this step to transition the conversation you're having with the prospect away from facts you've revealed to the idea that there is hope for a solution. A solution does exist. After you point out that a solution is possible and that one exists, it's time to expose your solution.

Expose your solution

Now it's time to rope in the visitors after they read the facts and figures by exposing exactly what your solution is. What kind of product or service are you offering? Use solution phrases to suggest an answer that is going to be unveiled shortly. Then, let your visitors know precisely what it is you're going to provide to them and what problems you will help them solve. For example, you can start your sentences with these:

✦ *Now, You Too Can . . .*

✦ *And, Just When You Thought There Was No Solution . . .*

✦ *This New Opportunity Will . . .*

These are just a few examples of how solution sentences begin. In my continuing example, I chose *Say Good-bye.*

Be prepared that you'll spend just as much time (if not more) creating and testing the wording of these solution statements as you will spend creating a captivating headline. The extra effort is worth it!

List your benefits clearly with bullet points and highlighting to make them easy to scan because most people won't read them word for word. Use action words that have energy and enthusiasm and that encourage people to keep reading.

Recapture visitors' attention

Solution sentences and benefits lists can get pretty long sometimes. The fact that some people scan through sales pages differently than others comes into play here. Maybe your reader skipped over the facts and figures area but started to read some of the benefits. Or, maybe the bullet points were skipped all together.

After you expose your solutions, it's time to recapture the attention of your visitors, as shown in Figure 5-11. This can be done several ways, but the strategy I chose for this working example was a little bit more rapport-building.

Notice how I use the phrase *It Worked for Me* to bring the reader back. But, it is in the next few sentences where I recapture the attention of the reader. Then I'm able to build additional interest in the solution by showing a table of contents for the book.

Test for action

At this point, you will have some readers that are convinced they should give your product or service a try. They just need one last nudge.

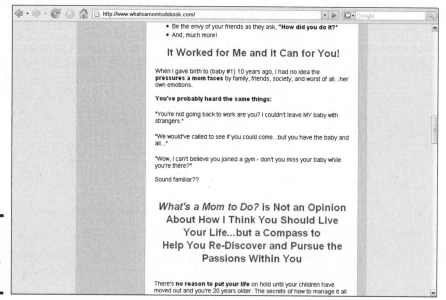

Figure 5-11:
Recapture
the reader's
attention.

One of the best ways to get people over the hump of making a decision to take action with you, whether by calling you on the phone, submitting a contact form, or making an online purchase, is to offer more testimonials. Hopefully, one of the testimonials will resonate with the reader as someone else having been in a similar situation where their problem was solved, and a purchase may result from that single testimonial. Then, use a sub-headline format to give a strong suggestion to buy right now.

+ If you want them to click a link to buy, suggest it like this:

  Click Here to Order Now

+ If you want the visitor to visit another page to learn more about dog food, tell them to click a link as follows:

  Learn more about dog food.

+ If you want them to call you right now, tell them specifically to

  Pick up the phone right now and call 800-555-1212 for your special . . .

Motivate by adding value and urgency

Although a few potential customers might be willing to buy at that point of testing for action, most will not. The majority of your buyers will require additional incentive or increased value of the purchase price. One way to set the stage for people to act on your value proposition and urgency is to put them at ease with a guarantee, as shown in Figure 5-12.

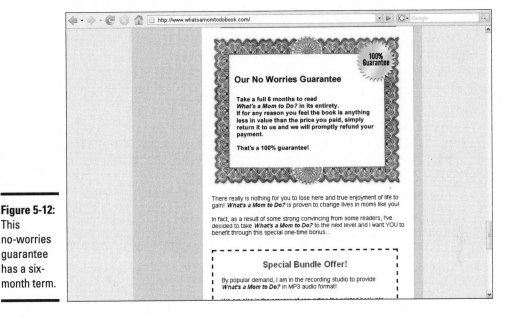

Figure 5-12:
This
no-worries
guarantee
has a six-
month term.

Now, we're all sick of hearing those ghastly television infomercials, "BUT WAIT! There's MORE!" But, that is the type of idea you want to convey to your readers, whether or not you use the exact wording. You want your prospective buyers to know that your offer is worth the full purchase price, but you also want to offer a special incentive to place their order right now.

The key to this step is adding time sensitivity to the offer. Here are some examples:

✦ *You MUST order by midnight tonight because this item will no longer be available.*

✦ *You MUST order now because this item will sell out by noon today for sure.*

✦ *I only have 14 of these left in stock. You must order now or risk never seeing an offer like this again!*

In my running example, I created a special bundle offer to pre-sell a new feature that would be produced a month later (refer to Figure 5-12).

Energize visitors to buy

At this point, you have tested for action and provided all the motivation possible by adding value to the sale. Figure 5-13 shows how I wrapped things up and did my best to encourage my visitors to buy.

✦ **Suggest a specific action again, such as** *Click Here to Buy Online Now or Call This Number Now.*

✦ **Sign your name or use your initials.**

For your own security, use a different signature than you would on a personal check.

✦ **Add three post script (P.S.) statements.**

People respond better when things are presented in three's. See Figure 5-13.

Some visitors will completely bypass everything you write in a sales letter only to look at the P.S. statements at the end. Use this format to capitalize on this fact:

✦ **P.S.:** Your statement No. 1

✦ **P.P.S.:** Your statement No. 2

Make this one a powerful reminder of the most important benefits.

✦ **P.P.P.S.:** Your statement No. 3

Then provide one final action statement here or the order link.

If you sell a product online, your merchant account provider will probably require that you have a Terms of Use page and also a privacy statement. I would like to suggest that you also post a Disclaimer page, especially if your product or service has the potential of improving one's financial or health status.

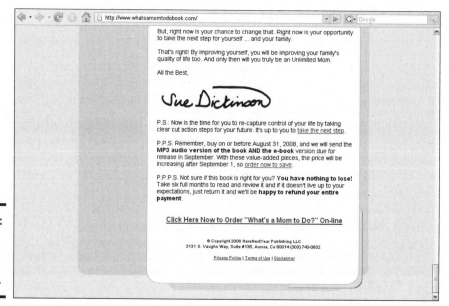

Figure 5-13:
Example of signature and P.S. statements.

Chapter 6: Encouraging Communication

In This Chapter

✔ Understanding the extras that make Web sites work

✔ Selecting and implementing forms

✔ Incorporating powerful communication techniques

A Web site should help build rapport with new prospects and introduce existing customers to new products and services. In this chapter, you explore a number of tools that can help you communicate with prospects and customers and them with you. You also improve your capability to learn about your customers and their questions — and what about your business is and isn't working for them. The bottom line is that adding communication tools to your site will help turn it into a safe and efficient leads- and sales-producing machine!

Perfecting Your Form

If you've ever added your name and e-mail address to a page on a Web site, you have experienced using a form. You probably also know how frustrating it can be to complete a form and submit it only to be met with an error page, realizing that your form submission didn't work! Web forms have been an integral part of Web site functionality since even before the first company Web site went live — for good reason, too. Forms allow visitors to do things, such as make contact with the Web site owner, opt in to a newsletter, or tell friends about a Web site they should become familiar with. In the following section, I cover all these functions in more detail.

Choosing the right contact form

Having a contact form on your Web site is quite possibly the most important utility your Web site will ever have. Positioned correctly, a contact form can save a sale from being lost or perhaps inspire someone to make contact with you for a vital question. Plus, if your e-mail goes down, a form can be set up to write the contents to a backup file. Figure 6-1 shows an example of a typical contact form.

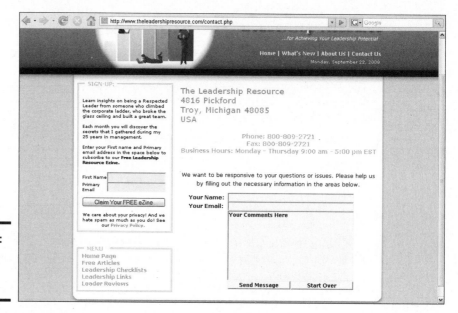

Figure 6-1:
A sample contact form.

Every good contact form has five key components:

✦ **Form field headings:** Be very descriptive with your form field headings. Rather than just using *E-mail* to identify that you want the visitor to add their e-mail address in a particular form field, be specific: for example, *Add Your Primary E-mail Address Here.*

✦ **Form fields:** The actual form fields can be made easily within most any HTML editing software, such as Dreamweaver, GoLive, or FrontPage. They should be either to the right of each form heading or directly below them.

Keep the number of fields very limited for a contact form. If you try to get your visitors' life history in a single form submission, they will almost surely leave. Most newsletter opt-in forms display only a first name and an e-mail address on a Web site so that the signup process is fast. Think of a contact form as similar to a newsletter opt-in form, but do provide a larger text box for comments or a question in addition to fields for name and e-mail address.

✦ **Submit button:** Using the word *Submit* on a submit button isn't very inviting or engaging to a potential lead. But, submit buttons are easy to change. So, test some different wording, such as

- *Please Respond Quickly*

- *Tell Me More!*

- *Yes! I Want to Know*

✦ **Backup file:** E-mail is getting increasingly unreliable. Never trust precious leads to only arriving in your Inbox by e-mail. Your form contents can be set up to write to a data file that you can access daily.

✦ **Form-processing program:** This piece of the puzzle makes the form do what you want it to do when a visitor clicks that all-important submit button.

A form-processing program can come in different shapes:

✦ **Custom form-processing program:** Most Web programmers (and many designers) can quickly create a simple custom form program for you in less than an hour.

Before contracting a programmer to create a custom program for you, find out from your Web site–hosting company whether your Web server is using Linux or Windows. This will be the first question a programmer will ask to help determine which programming language to use when creating your form processor (typically PHP or ASP).

✦ **Freeware:** These small programs are written by programmers looking for exposure by offering various programs for the Web, including form processing. Be aware that you will often need to customize the programs on your own to match your Web site. PHPJunkYard (`www.phpjunkyard.com`) is a good resource for such programs.

✦ **Third-party forms processors:** If you're not a programmer and don't have access to one, consider employing a company that allows you to produce and manage your own forms. Wufoo (`www.wufoo.com`) offers such a service with which you specify how your form looks and operates within its Web-based system (as shown in Figure 6-2). Simply copy the code that Wufoo provides and then paste it onto any page of your Web site where a form is desired. Wufoo can be used for a variety of forms, not only contact forms.

Exploring opt-in form types

When you opt in through a form on a site, you choose (of your own free will) to receive more information about something. An opt-in form is a bit different than a contact form: A contact form is meant to initiate one-on-one conversation, whereas an opt-in form promises content of value. Here are some examples of opt-in forms.

✦ **Newsletter subscription form:** Probably the most common of all the opt-in forms on the Web is the subscription to a free newsletter, such as the one shown in Figure 6-3.

Including an opt-in form in a prominent place on every page of your Web site is entirely acceptable and encouraged. After all, it's a safe bet that more than 80 percent of your visitors will *not* buy your product or call you on the phone for more details, no matter how good of a copywriter you are. But, they might just have enough interest to opt in to get to know you first.

✦ **Free e-course registration:** Use sequential auto-responder software, like what AWeber Communications (`www.aweber.com`) or 1ShoppingCart (`www.1shoppingcart.com`) offers. With this kind of software, a Web site owner can assemble a series of e-mails once, in a course format, to be delivered every day, every other day, once weekly, or virtually any combination, in the same order, for each person that signs up.

✦ **Squeeze pages:** When you land on a Web site where the only action you can take is to add your name and e-mail address, you are being "squeezed" into opting in to receive more information. *Squeeze pages* — commonly used to promote conferences and higher-ticket items — are where you must opt in to gain access to a large amount of detail. Online, visit `www.startawebsitedesignbusiness.com` to see how this site "squeezes" you into applying for a free, five-day recorded e-course. I introduce squeeze pages in Book I, Chapter 5.

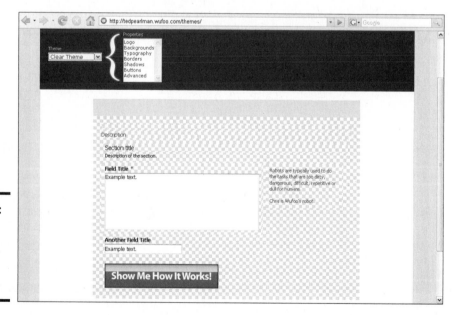

Figure 6-2:
A sample form processor created in Wufoo.

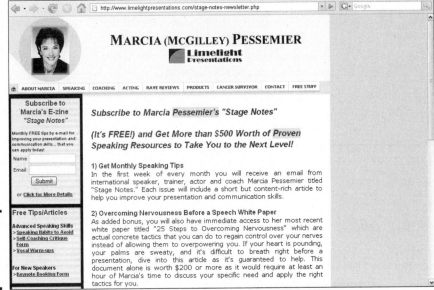

Figure 6-3:
An example
newsletter
opt-in form.

Adding a Tell-a-Friend Function to Your Pages

When you experience something worthwhile, you want to tell someone, right? If you believe the content of your Web site is of value to others, make it easy to tell their friends about it! Install a Tell-a-Friend feature on every page of your site, as shown in Figure 6-4, found at `www.ultimate dreamguide.com`.

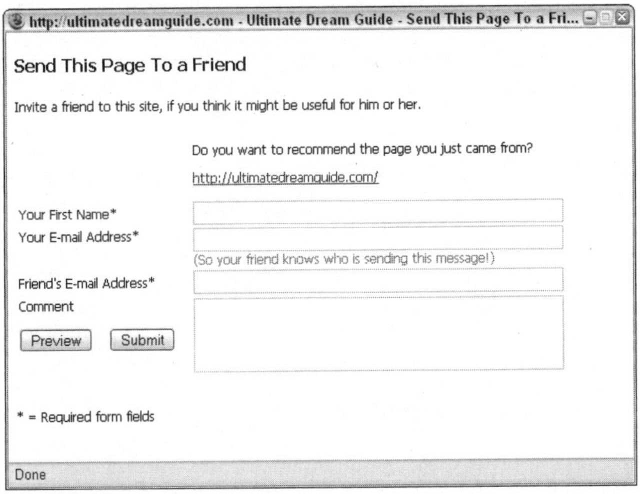

Figure 6-4:
This Tell-a-
Friend script
shows the
exact page
to visit.

Adding a Tell-a-Friend feature typically involves adding a script to a Web page. Free Tell-a-Friend scripts are easy to find. Try either of the following:

✦ Search your favorite search engine:

- *If your Web site is hosted on a Linux server:* Search for *"free tell-a-friend script php"*.

- *If your Web site is hosted on a Windows server:* Search for *"free tell-a-friend script asp"*.

✦ Use a commercial e-mail package (such as from Constant Contact; `www.constantcontact.com`) that offers built-in Tell-a-Friend functionality. See Book V for more about e-mail packages.

Considering Online Chat

When I evaluate a piece of software for which I might require support, the first thing I look for is whether the company offers online chat. I don't want to wait for e-mail, but I also don't want to talk to a support technician or salesperson on the phone unless I really have to! The answer is online chat, which is increasing in popularity every year. You can see the online chat option on my Web site in Figure 6-5.

If you're looking to add online chat to your site, here are the general steps to follow:

1. **Find an online chat provider.**

You can search the search engines for *"free online chat software"* or *"free support desk software"*, but I prefer to use Provide Support, which offers easy customizability and supports its product through online chat, of course. Visit `www.providesupport.com` to read about how you can pay as little as $15 per month (for a single user, or *operator*) to offer full online chat capability on every page of your Web site.

2. **Set up your account.**

Including the following items as you set up your account can make your online chat feature truly helpful as a lead generator and customer service tool:

- *Craft a description page* that details exactly what online chat is (seeing as how most people haven't used the feature yet and might mistake the phrase "online chat" as being something more of an "adult" chat room!).

- *Customize your graphic header* to look like the rest of your Web site.

- *Develop a custom exit survey* for instant feedback and gaining list subscribers.

- *Create a mechanism for chatters* to have the entire conversation e-mailed to them for reference.

3. **Add the code to your Web site.**

   For every page of your Web site, adding an online chat image is a simple copy-and-paste process. You can also easily copy the provided HTML code produced by the chat software and e-mail it to your designer or assistant to add to your pages for you.

4. **Monitor your computer.**

   When a Web site visitor lands on your Web site and chooses to chat with you using Provide Support's chat software, the sound of a phone ringing will emanate from your computer speakers. Click the Accept Call button, and you're ready to answer your visitor's question! You can see a chat in progress in Figure 6-6.

   Even though the button is labeled Accept Call, the Provide Support chat software allows you to communicate only through typing. So, it's really not a phone call, per se. However, because you're not actually on the phone, that means you can be chatting with five, ten, or potentially more prospects or customers all at the same time! How's *that* for efficiency?

Online chat option

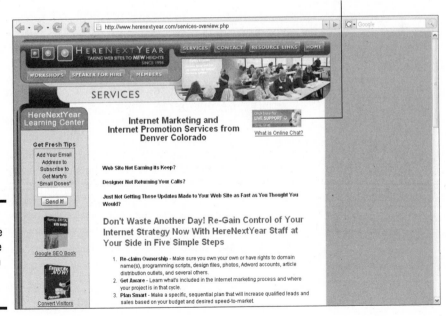

Figure 6-5:
An example of an online chat button on a Web site.

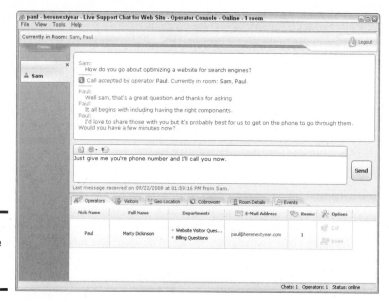

Figure 6-6:
Chat online
with a
visitor.

5. Gain valuable user behavior information about your visitors.

Sure, Google Analytics will track the path of a Web site visitor through your Web site, but only an online chat system can allow you to actually watch a visitor migrate through your pages in real-time.

One of the most important benefits of watching your visitors travel through your Web site in real-time is to discover possible reasons why they're leaving without taking further action with you. For example, if someone spends, say 20 seconds on the first page they see on your Web site, then a full minute on the second page after they click a link, then only a few seconds on the third page before exiting your Web site entirely, it's nothing to be alarmed about. But, if the next 30 visitors do the same exact thing, you'd better make a quick change to the third page because you're losing visitors!

Whenever I launch a sales page on my Web site for a new workshop, I add a special banner on my pages and watch the first 20 or so visitors who click on that banner. If they get to the workshop page and leave in under 5 seconds, I know I need to change the headline of that sales page. If visitors give me a good solid minute or more before deciding to buy or leave, I know my copy is engaging enough to keep their interest.

If you're bold, you can even call out to your visitors and ask whether they have any questions about the page they're reading at that particular time!

You must be very careful about calling out to a Web site visitor before he chooses to chat with you! People are so used to being anonymous in their Web travels that it easily freaks them out when a chat window interrupts their reading. Use this feature with extreme caution and social grace, or you will lose that visitor forever.

Creating Audio for Your Web Site

Today's Internet is too competitive to rely on written words alone to earn the trust of prospects and customers. You need to take the next step and differentiate yourself by being vocal with your visitors through the use of audio. You can and should learn to record audio, edit your recordings, and post audio files to your Web site. All you need is the right equipment, a process to follow, and a willingness to get involved.

1. Choose the right equipment.

The three things you need to record audio are

- *A good quality microphone:* I prefer what's called a *condenser mic,* which is similar to what you would see in a radio station. Surprisingly, you can find very good condenser microphones for less than $300. You also need what's called a "boom stand" so that you can mount the microphone in the stand and swing it out of the way when you're not talking. Boom stands are typically $20–$40.

- *Sound-editing software:* Sound Forge Audio Studio (from Sony; $54.95; `www.sonycreativesoftware.com/products/soundforge family.asp`) is one of the leaders in the audio field and has been my own editor of choice for nearly three years now.

- *A sound card mixer:* Use a mixer to bring your sound from your microphone to the software through your computer. The EDIROL UA-25 for $295 (`www.roland.com/products/en/UA-25`) is a worthy choice for most cases.

2. Seek step-by-step instruction.

The fastest and least costly way to learn how to produce audio is to watch video tutorials. Mike Stewart (`www.internetvideoguy.com`; known as the Internet Audio Guy) offers extensive online tutorials for recording and editing audio. In fact, he promotes a package you can purchase, which includes a microphone, software, and a sound card mixer.

3. Decide what's worth recording.

If you have a page of your Web site that asks people to follow a process, you run the risk of your visitors not understanding what to do next or thinking it will just take too much time. This is a perfect opportunity to give them some inspiration with a short audio message letting them know that the process is more simple and faster than they might imagine at first.

Book I, Chapter 1 explains common possible reasons why people leave Web sites.

4. Prepare your editing software for recording.

Figure 6-7 shows Sony Sound Forge in ready position. By clicking the red circle, recording begins.

5. Edit your recording.

Figure 6-8 shows a recorded file in edit mode. You can see where I was louder or softer, denoted by the height of marks. By highlighting any point with a mouse, I can select my um's and ah's to delete them, or replace a selection with new content.

6. Save the recording for publishing on the Internet.

MP3 format settings typically sound fine for Web playback, and the MP3 format is compatible with a wide variety of music players. (Just make sure your MP3 settings set the Hz for the recording around 44,100 Hz so the recording is clear but not too large for the Web.)

7. Publish your audio file to your Web site.

With an MP3 file in hand, I could simply upload the file to my Web site, add a link, and have people start listening. But, for this particular promotional message, I want it to appear on the homepage of my HereNextYear.com Web site. And, I want anyone to be able to play the audio without downloading my file or having to open any software. The solution is Xiosoft Audio (www.InstantAudioGenerator.com), where you can upload your raw MP3 files and produce the code to copy and paste the files to your Web site within minutes.

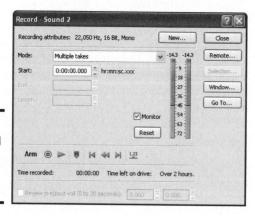

Figure 6-7:
Sony Sound Forge recording screen.

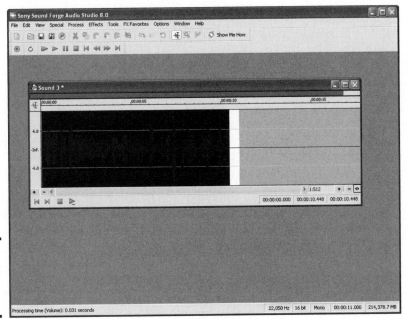

Figure 6-8:
Audio peaks
and dead
spots.

Adding Professional, Homemade Video to Your Web Site

The best way for two people to communicate has always been face-to-face. There is no better or faster way to make a first impression than to get a person in a room and have a one-on-one conversation while looking each other in the eye.

Adding video to your Web site is the closest substitute to an in-person meeting. Although the presenter does not get to look the Web site visitor "in the eye," Web video does give the opportunity for the prospect to evaluate the presenter. Video on the Web is the ultimate way to display to your viewing audience that you are a real person who can be believed and trusted. Video on a Web site can be used for demonstrating a product, interviewing an expert, introducing a special offer, leading an instructional course, or providing simple entertainment.

Considering the enormous popularity growth of YouTube, the progress that online video has made within just the past year on the Internet, and the advent of technical advancements and lower hardware prices, there's no excuse for overlooking video.

Getting started with video

The following tips can help you get started with video on the Web:

✦ **Develop your online audio skills first.** When you work with video, you have two major pieces to learn: video itself as well as audio. Trying to learn both at the same time could prove a bit discouraging. Audio is fast to learn and very easy to create. Moving to work with video will be much easier after some audio experience. The section "Creating Audio for Your Web Site" (earlier in this chapter) explains how to get started with audio.

✦ **Purchase the right equipment.** Like with audio, selecting the right equipment for video is vital to your inspiration as well as success, including

 • *A video camera:* Most video cameras will do the job for basic video.

 • *A high-quality microphone that connects to your computer and that you can walk around with:* Never use the built-in microphone that comes with the video camera. For every inch you move away from the microphone, sound quality decreases rapidly. I use the Audio-Technica Pro 70 ($178.00) (www.audio-technica.com), which is a wireless lavaliere microphone with a 15-foot cord attached. With a mic like this, I can use my hands to demonstrate things while recording audio and video at the same time and also maintaining high-quality sound.

 • *Video-editing software:* Vegas Movie Studio 9 (from Sony; www.sony creativesoftware.com/moviestudio) surprised me by how simple it was to use, and for only $99. See the next section for the basic steps in editing video.

If you plan to do a lot of recording indoors, such as in an office room, invest in some good lighting. For about $300, you can buy two standing photographer lights to make your video shine.

✦ **Get training.** Detailed instruction is a must if you want to save hours of wasted trials, and even weeks or months of trial and error on your own. Seek your training on video so that as your skills increase, you pick up new things each time you watch the training videos (if you have them available). Again, I suggest contacting Mike Stewart for a complete package, including hardware and software, through www.internetvideo guy.com where he also provides free support for what he teaches.

✦ **Start simple.** Video is not to be done on a large scale until you master the process with small recordings.

So many Web site owners are turning to YouTube to host their videos because it's free and also because of simplicity. Videos can usually be uploaded to YouTube directly from the camera. Then, it's just a matter of copying and pasting HTML code from YouTube to your Web site to have the full player display. The limitation is that YouTube only allows for videos 100MB or less in size, and most video cameras will produce a 100MB video in only 5 or 6 minutes of recording time. By using video-editing software, as described in the following section, you can change the size and format of your video to meet the requirements of YouTube or any other video hosting service.

Editing video

The following steps outline the basics of editing video, using the video-editing software of your choosing:

1. **Import the raw recording file to your computer (or external drive).**

2. **Open your video-editing software and then the video file.**

   Because raw files from a video camera are quite large, only a few minutes of recording can easily exceed 100MB in size. When getting into video, I recommend investing in an external hard drive. The one I use is the Iomega Desktop Hard Drive Silver Series 500GB external hard drive, which I purchased for around $130. This translates to more than 50 hours of raw recording storage capability at its highest resolution rate.

3. **Edit your video.**

   You may have already seen videos on the Web that begin with a music intro and a moving collage of images or designs to capture your attention. Then a person begins talking, and the screen changes to what looks like a software screen or an amazing view of mountains or the ocean. While the narrator is still talking, the video immediately changes to something even more engaging! Stop! Your beginning video does not need to be nearly that complex.

   When beginning video editing, there are only a few things you need to focus on, including that your video is

   - *Centered:* If the image being videotaped is you, make sure you are in the middle of the finished video! Use your video-editing software to crop, enlarge, or reduce the main image area so that the main feature takes up most of the space in the video window.

   - *Audible:* If your audio came in too soft or is overpowering, use the audio controls to adjust to a normal speaking voice level.

   - *Viewable:* One of the most challenging elements of capturing quality video is lighting, particularly with video taken indoors, because indoor lighting is usually so soft. You can make adjustments to lighten or darken your video from within video-editing software, but for more predictable results, experiment with lighting options *before* video recording begins.

- *Fluid:* When you're shooting your video and you forget what to say or get tongue-tied, just let the camera keep rolling, pause for a moment, and then say your line again. Removing a part of your video during editing is as simple as highlighting a section with your mouse and pressing Delete.

- *Natural:* It would seem "unnatural" to have only a black square visible to your audience before they press the Play button to view your video on your Web site. So, use your video-editing software to capture one of the screens from your video to be your first screen. Also use your editing software to remove any dead space at the beginning and end of your video. This way, when a person clicks Play, the video begins immediately and closes out immediately at the end.

4. Render your video as an AVI file.

Save your edited video as a video for Windows in AVI format. You could transfer this AVI file to a DVD if you wanted to. You can also use AVI files for higher-end streaming video for the Internet. But the more popular, faster, and least expensive approach to publishing video online today is to use FLV formatted video.

5. Convert your AVI video file to FLV, as shown in Figure 6-9.

FLV stands for FLash Video. Flash, now owned by Adobe, is the main software product used to create animations and interactivity on the Internet, let alone full-blown multimedia presentations offline. When you land on a Web site and the entire page is made up of a slew of moving parts, it was probably designed with Flash.

To allow an FLV file to play, it needs what is called an FLV player. Think of it like a television set. You have a signal coming in from your cable or satellite dish, but you need a "player," an actual TV set to put the signal into a viewable format. FLV players, of course, are produced with Flash software.

FLV has become the leading video format on the Internet and is in large part why video has emerged as a tangible tool online over the past few years. We used to have to produce video files in multiple formats if we wanted to feature video at all. At minimum, we would have to feature MPG format (for Windows computers) and QuickTime (for Macs). But, because you can view a Web site made with Flash software on both PC and Mac computers, you can also view video produced with a single video format: FLV.

Does that mean you need to run out and buy Adobe Flash software to convert your AVI file to FLV and then create a player? No. There are many programs available to help you with these two steps. Some of them are even free, and can be found by searching for *"free flv converter"* and *"free flv player creator"*.

My program of choice is FLV Producer, which can be found at `www. flvproducer.com` for a one-time purchase of $97.00.

6. Create the video player.

Embed the prepared video file into its own video player using the same FLV Producer software. Simply select style choices, and the HTML code will be produced for your video (see Figure 6-10).

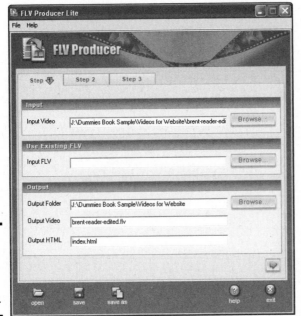

Figure 6-9:
Convert
your AVI
files to FLV
for the Web.

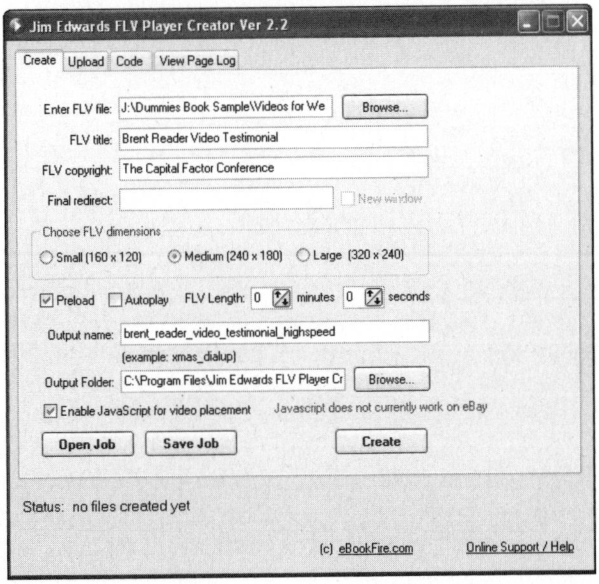

Figure 6-10:
Set the size
of the video
player.

7. **Upload all files produced from the FLV conversion to your Web site.**

   FLV Producer allows you to add your FTP user name and password (see Chapter 1 for more about using FTP to transfer files) within its software so that a simple press of a button will allow for uploading of all the needed files to your Web site.

Chapter 7: Getting Help with Your Web Presence

In This Chapter

✔ Identifying Internet tasks worth paying for

✔ Finding the right people to help

✔ Assuring you get what you pay for

✔ Staying in control of it all

In a perfect world, most business owners dream of walking in their office one day to find a full-time staff person sitting behind a desk, building and promoting their Web sites exclusively for 60 hours per week (for $10 per hour). In reality, your budget would need to be more like $60,000, $80,000, or possibly more than $100,000 per year to attract a person skilled in design, programming, database management, sales, marketing, publicity, customer service, search engine optimization (SEO), pay per click (PPC) campaign development, and all the dozens of secondary online promotion components. And, that person would be worth every penny!

Even then, you would spend your days worrying about the employee's personal Web site projects being worked on during business hours when you're on your conference calls or at business development meetings. And, it would only be a matter of time before some of those side projects would be making a higher revenue than you'd be willing to pay in salary. Why should someone of that caliber work for you when he can make more money on his own?

The short answer is that if a person is capable of bringing real increases in leads and sales for your company, you probably won't be able to pay him enough to keep him for the long term.

As a result, business owners near and far turn to out-tasking and outsourcing their Internet-related agenda. In this chapter, you are introduced to the many types of helpers available to you — broadly called *Internet service providers* — and how to hire them to help with your projects.

Recognizing the Skills You Need Help With

What are you really good at? How do you enjoy spending your days? Do you like sitting in front of your computer screen for hours? Or are you more of a people person? Is your time better spent on the phone talking with prospects or in an online forum giving free advice? Do you jump out of bed in the morning to race to your computer at 5 a.m. to check your Google AdWords click-through rates, or would you rather meet your colleagues on the golf course for a morning of networking?

To maximize the Internet for your business, there are ten main positions to fill: an Internet marketing team, if you will. For most business owners, accomplishing all ten roles solo — successfully, that is — is impossible.

✦ **Vice President Internet Marketing (VPIM):** Keeps everything together; creates, directs, and monitors the plan and results; adheres to the budget; holds helpers accountable to their performance and deadlines

✦ **Marketing expert:** Creates the brand, logos, taglines, and *stickiness* (the ability of a brand or product to remain in someone's mind over time); promotes consistency among all promotions and packaging

✦ **Web site design expert:** Works with the marketing expert to create the Web site's look and feel that combines brand consistency with proven sales strategy

✦ **Internet marketing expert:** Researches competition; works with the sales expert to optimize the Web site and content for maximum sales conversion; builds the opt-in list and prepares e-mail campaigns and newsletters; conducts organic SEO (see Book II); manages CPC ad campaigns; implements inbound link campaigns, article creation, and syndication; manages blog setup and training; monitors shopping cart setup and testing; oversees audio and video production; provides progress reports to VPIM

✦ **Sales expert:** Writes effective and compelling sales copy; creates auto-responder sequences; trains affiliates; finds and attracts joint venture hosts; conducts tele-seminars, Webinars, and workshops to build product awareness; identifies customer needs

✦ **Publicity expert:** Writes and distributes press releases; finds opportunities for the VPIM to participate in talk radio shows

✦ **Programming expert:** Works with the Internet marketing expert to alter or customize tools that help increase sales, such as shopping carts, lead forms, and online registration scripts

✦ **Content manager:** Changes Web site content routinely and quickly upon request

✦ **Coach or mentor:** Provides cutting-edge techniques; notices mistakes before you make them; helps the team improve its skills

✦ **Business owner:** Stays involved; relays customer approval to the rest of the team

To attempt to perform all these functions on your own is a recipe for destruction over time. So, consider which of these skills you have no interest in performing yourself and make plans now to find resources to help.

Choosing an Internet Service Provider

You can't possibly do all the work yourself that the Internet requires for maximizing leads and sales to their fullest potential. You need to build a team or hire a team that's already established. By having such a team at your side, you'll be amazed how many more hours of the day are available to you. And, if the right team members are chosen, your sales and leads will likely increase dramatically within only a few weeks of hiring.

To that end, I strongly recommend that you hire an Internet service provider (ISP). No, I'm not talking Comcast or AT&T. I'm talking about people who provide services to help increase your leads and sales on the Internet. Same words, but different.

Ten years ago, the term *Internet service provider* defined a company that would host your Web site or provide you with a connection to the Internet. Today, an ISP is anyone or any entity that offers any type of service that directly or indirectly helps you conduct business online: a broad definition to be sure.

You can probably find thousands of ISPs in your area: folks with full-time, non-Internet-related jobs by day who moonlight or even volunteer their time as self-proclaimed experts by night. On the other end of the spectrum, established companies with departments full of employees are ready to dedicate an entire team of experts and a combined 100 hours or more per week to your project. And as you might expect, several levels of ISPs fall between these two extremes. Which level of help is right for you? Table 7-1 can help you with that decision.

Table 7-1		ISP Types	
ISP Type	*Benefits*	*Challenges to Expect*	*Typical Budget*
Hobbyist	Lowest cost possible Easy to barter with Highest percentage of time allocated to your project because it's usually their only project	Lowest probability for fast results because every request requires experimentation and learning curve Loss of interest Loss of time-sensitive opportunities	Free to $15/hour

(continued)

Table 7-1		ISP Types	
ISP Type	*Benefits*	*Challenges to Expect*	*Typical Budget*
Semi-pro	Easy to negotiate price Only 1 to 3 projects going at a time, which means you still get priority attention Work with the same person although contracted helpers	Hard to contact during the day because he's still at the day job or has family obligations on weekends High rate of burnout Quality of performance reduces over time	$15–$50/hour
Full-time soloist	Same person works on your project over time Accessible on weekends if emergency arises Knows business very well because they make their living online Always on the cutting-edge of new strategies	These one-man shows do it all and get sidetracked by such administrative time-drainers as driving deposits to the bank and bookkeeping Longer lead-times for completed work Often claim to own the Web site even though you paid for it	$50–$200/hour
Small company team	You benefit from cumulative range of knowledge among team Team is paid based on results, so they're motivated to excel Extensive tracking systems are in place Low turnover	Often, the highest priced option You could become confused as to whom you should be talking to on the team Possible lag-time in accomplishing tasks if team members don't agree with each other	$100–$300/hour Monthly programs from $1K to $10K Possible revenue sharing
Large ISP	Best chance of the ISP being around in a year or two Best chance of offering 24/7 support Best chance of having entire team under one roof	High turnover Rarely talk to same person twice Best chance for a buyout or merger and therefore package offering changes and price changes Best chance for services to be "canned" instead of customized	Wide range of prices

Which ISP should you choose to help with your project? It largely depends on your budget, your commitment to running a business versus feeding a hobby, and your desired speed to market. For example, someone working a full-time job may want to start a business on the side and get a Web site to get things rolling and test the waters. In this case, a hobbyist or semi-pro ISP is a perfect fit. Conversely, most large companies only feel comfortable hiring high-end agencies. Small to mid-sized businesses enjoy long-term rewards and individual attention by dealing with the same people over time with the small company team.

Countless Web site designers have started by designing a free Web site for their church or for a friend and decided to leave their corporate job to make their millions as a Web designer. A month or two later, they're starving for work, lacking the necessary skills on many fronts, and crawl back to their former employers.

Others new to the world of self-employment accept any project that comes their way just to make a few bucks. They spend three times as long as they were compensated for just to figure out how to accomplish the task. After a few long nights, hours of trial and error, and an unhealthy dose of uncertainty, the ISPs of this caliber often just disappear without notice.

Finding good ISP candidates

The best ISP referrals typically come through other business owners in your network. By asking for referrals from people you know, you can hear about their experiences first-hand.

If you get no referrals to a good ISP from other business professionals in your network, don't worry. The old saying, "Good help is hard to find," rarely applies when looking for a good ISP on the Internet, thanks to middleman-like services such as E-lance, Rent-a-Coder, and Craigslist. The challenge becomes selecting the right person or team from a sea of talented designers, programmers, and marketers while weeding out those who lack experience.

The following sections offer tips for finding good referrals as well as introductions to popular middleman resources.

Personal referrals

Begin your search for good personal referrals by reviewing Web sites owned by friends or business acquaintances. Search the search engines for related keyword phrases to their industry and see whether their Web sites appear on the first page of Google. When you visit those Web sites and evaluate them, look for components of proofing and copywriting that sells. If both are present, chances are good that the Web site was produced by a knowledgeable and reliable team that produces results! Ask for a referral to the site owner's ISP.

Elance

Elance (www.elance.com) has for years been one of the more popular middlemen systems for posting design, programming, and Internet marketing projects. After a project is posted, it's often only a day or two before a dozen or more bid on your project. Today, Elance has categories for writing, administration, sales, finance, engineering, and legal, in addition to Internet development. Figure 7-1 displays an Elance posting.

Here's how it works:

1. After you begin your account, add a posting of your project by selecting categories and filters and adding a description of what kind of help you want.

2. ISPs respond to your posting and provide a bid for doing the work.

3. Once you correspond with a few of the ISPs and select the ISP of your choice, you transfer the payment for the project to an escrow account within Elance.

4. When you agree the project is complete, you receive the files and the ISP receives the funds.

 One of the great features of Elance is the ability to read reviews for an ISP's work over just the past six months or overall. You can also see how much revenue that ISP has earned through Elance projects, which will build your confidence that they can do the job right for you.

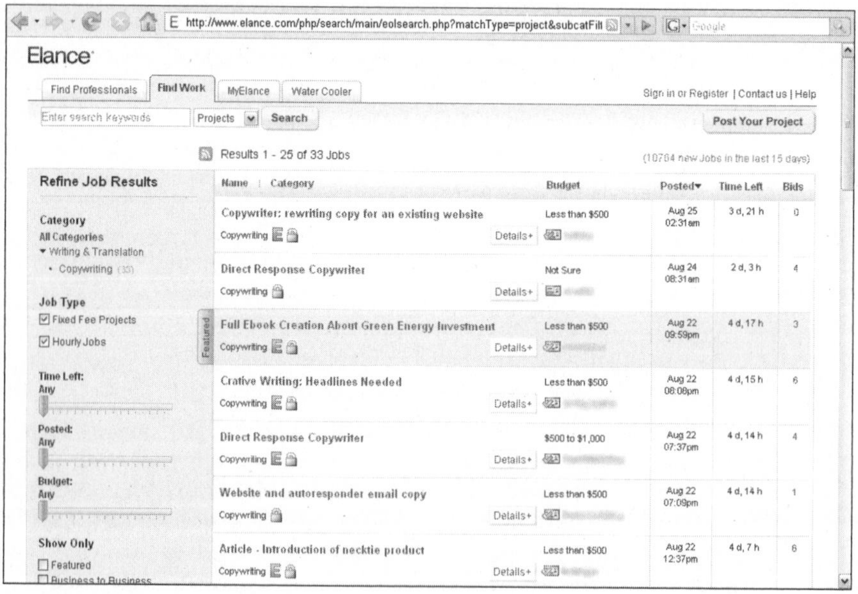

Figure 7-1: Sample Elance project posting.

RentACoder

RentACoder (www.rentacoder.com) is similar to Elance in that the business owner can make a project posting for free and the money is put into escrow until the project is complete. When payment is issued to the ISP, RentACoder keeps 15 percent or less depending on the project type. RentACoder also offers ratings so you can get a feel for how well a coder meets expectations.

RentACoder is focused on projects that involve the creation of software. Software, of course, is a broad category that could mean anything from simple HTML coding to Oracle database development. You'll find a few marketing-related categories too, like content writing and wiring sales pages and search engine optimization (SEO), but RentACoder has been long-known more for finding people to help with development projects.

Payment to the ISP is made by RentACoder and works similarly to Elance in that the project posting is free for the business owner and the ISP pays a percentage of the money received (15 percent) to RentACoder. Figure 7-2 features a sample project posting on RentACoder.

Craigslist

Craigslist (www.craigslist.org), shown in Figure 7-3, has become a favorite when looking for Internet service providers. Business owners prefer Craigslist because of speed. Within a matter of a few hours, an interesting posting can generate 20 or more replies and communications can begin. Although Craigslist is beginning to charge $25 per listing in a particular category in some cities, most feel the cost is justified because of the enormous feedback that results.

ISPs like Craigslist because it's completely free to review posts and reply to them. Because payment for projects occurs between the business owner and the ISP, Craigslist receives no additional compensation for the job. Another advantage to ISP's with Craigslist is that all the communication is behind the scenes, whereas Rent-a-Coder and Elance publicly post project quotes.

Best of all, the Craigslist Web site is sorted by city, so you are more likely to get responses from local helpers than with Elance or RentACoder. After contracting help from all over the world for years, my project teams are now almost completely localized. This enables me to meet each helper individually and build a more lasting and trusting relationship than I can with someone overseas, who I might communicate with only by e-mail.

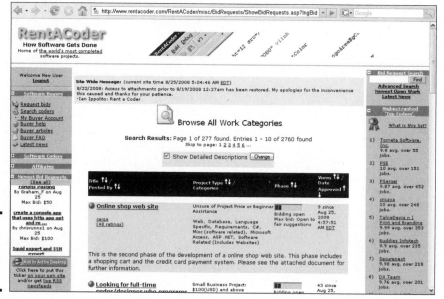

Figure 7-2:
Sample
RentACoder
posting.

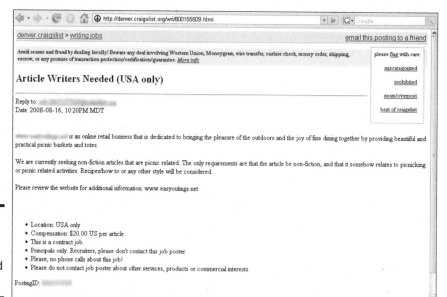

Figure 7-3:
Sample
Craigslist
help wanted
posting.

Interviewing and selecting the right ISPs

Finding a person or team of people to help you promote your business on the Internet is much more than the equivalent of contracting a carpenter to re-face your kitchen cabinets or a plumber to fix your sink. It's more similar to hiring an ER doctor to shock what could be your dying business back to life! You cannot afford to make wrong choices. After you review the ISP types to choose from (refer to Table 7-1) and gather a pool of potential candidates through referrals or middlemen (see the preceding section), follow these steps to choose the ISPs that are right for you:

1. **Contact the potential ISP by e-mail and phone with some questions ready, such as "How long have you been in business?"**

   However long it takes them to respond to your contact attempt is how long you can expect a response to take when you're a client. Be ready for the possibility that even your first contact attempt could turn into a free consultation to see whether your project is a good fit with the ISP's focus. Listen for the element of enthusiasm in your project. The last thing you want is a service provider that is not interested in what you plan to offer the world through your business.

2. **Find out how the ISP charges (by block of time, by project, or by both), not what they charge for.**

   This demonstrates to the ISP that you know the business — if only a little. Determine whether the ISP requires prepayment, partial down payment with the rest due upon completion, or simply net invoice amount due in 30 or 60 days (often called net-30 or net-60). All these options have benefits; you just need to be aware of what to expect.

3. **Ask what the ISP's typical turnaround time has been for similar projects they've worked with and if there would be additional charges for rush orders.**

4. **Find out whether the ISP offers additional services related to the project.**

   For example, a Web site design company might recommend a preferred hosting company.

5. **Find out how long the ISP has been doing this work.**

   An ISP with five or more years in the business has a pretty good chance of still being in business the next time you need something added to your Web site. Few feelings are worse than being in need of immediate help from your ISP and hearing "This phone has been disconnected . . ." on the other end when you call. I know because it's happened to me!

   Plus, an ISP that has been around for while probably has experience working with a number of clients in a variety of industries. So, you gain the benefit of having strategies applied for your project that produced results for another company in a related industry. Someone who has not had that industry experience will probably need to exercise some additional trial and error to get it right.

   On the other hand, having helped clients with hundreds of projects since 1996, I can say I do tend to stick with what works. So, if you're looking for someone to go totally against the grain for your project, you may want to seek out someone that doesn't have much experience. The most important thing is that you want the truth. If a service provider lies about the number of years in business, he's bound to lie about other elements of your project, too.

You can quickly find out their claim to length of service by asking for some Web site projects they worked on in the early years and ask how they believe things have changed since they began in the business.

6. **Try to determine how you can be assured the ISP will be around in six months or more.**

Listen closely when you ask this question because you can usually hear nervousness in someone's voice if he's on the brink of going bankrupt. Be wary of hiring a person or team desperate for a sale.

Attracting the best ISP

Most ISPs I know prefer to do business with people who have some experience working with helpers to complete Internet tasks and projects. If you sound like a first-timer, chances are you might be ignored. So don't ask general questions, claim to have the world's next greatest idea, or use exclamation marks and triple question marks when e-mailing ISPs. Have your project well defined before you call, offer to e-mail your wish list during the call, and communicate with upbeat language throughout the e-mail.

Here are a few more do's and don'ts for attracting an ISP to work on your project.

Do: Say, Say, Say

"My Web site visitors would benefit if . . ."

"What safe font types do you recommend that would be consistent with my market?"

"I like some of the components of this other Web site. Can you produce something similar?"

"Are you taking on any new SEO projects?"

"How do you monitor accomplishments and benchmarks on a project?"

"What are your payment options?"

"I'm taking my involvement with the Internet to a higher level."

Don't: Don't Ask, Don't Tell

"How much do you charge for a Web site?"

"I know exactly what I want."

"Can we use some font other than boring Arial or Verdana?"

"I'd like you to just go to this other Web site and make the same design for me."

"Can you get my site on top of Google?"

"Do you have a money-back guarantee?"

"Can I pay you when the project is complete?"

"I'm brand new to the Internet."

Finally, don't settle for your helpers owning any part of your Web site or withholding user names and passwords. Demand to have all original graphics and program files sent to you before final payment; and require that all accounts, user names, and passwords for hosting, databases, domain names, or third-party applications be in your name. Web site designers in particular have an issue with giving away their original artwork. Set them at ease that you will always go to them for changes to graphics but that you should have originals on-hand in the event that they become unavailable for a long period of time or in case the relationship terminates.

There are exceptions to the rule of ownership. For example, if you hire someone to manage your Google AdWords campaign, it is common practice for an ISP to not allow clients direct access to the AdWords account. For one, it would be easy for a novice to delete months of work and testing within seconds inside an AdWord campaign. Second, there are proprietary techniques one learns with experience, and an ISP would not want the client to cut and run without continuing to pay for those benefits received. You learn many of those techniques in Book IV.

One way to assure who owns what and specific tasks to be performed for the amount of money transacted is to have a written contract. Personally, I'm not one to spend time on lengthy contracts. In fact, I have clients who have been with me for ten years or more and we have yet to have the word "contract" come up in a conversation. Call me "old school," but if a prospect requires something in writing longer than a single page, it's probably not going to be a good working relationship anyway because a level of trust has not yet been established. I would prefer to work on a small project with a new client requiring no contract first to see how we work together, than to begin our working relationship with a huge project that requires hours of contractual paperwork before beginning the task. Be prepared, however, that some ISPs go overboard in the other direction requiring contracts signed at each phase of completion. In my opinion, these hours of lawyer fees and time delays waiting for approvals could be better spent making you money online! Be sure to ask what, if any, the contractual process is for any ISP you begin working with.

The "Do's" help to establish a rapport with the ISPs you interview about your project. When an ISP has a greater comfort level that you know what you're doing, you often get a better-quoted price. If not, at least your ISP will take more interest in your project when you express a certain level of professionalism and courtesy.

Deciding whether to outsource

If you decide to outsource your project to another country in a different time zone, be prepared for some challenges to occur in the areas of communication and time lag. Typically, your main contact will speak your native language, but only on a basic level. So, communicate on a basic level. Expect turnaround times for all requests to take at least 12 hours . . . even if an emergency arises.

And, prices are increasing. You used to be able to get a development project bid at $5,000 in the United States for a few hundred dollars overseas. Now, pricing isn't nearly as competitive.

Outsourcing does certainly have its opportunities, especially when you can guarantee ongoing work hours, month after month. For example, you can fairly easily find overseas ghost writers to produce blog posts and articles for you on a weekly or even daily basis for just a few hundred dollars a month.

If you can guarantee a set amount of work for a programmer, the same is true. A colleague of mine has a full team in India that he personally trained to construct code in his style. Today, he pays each member of the team $1,000 per month as a salary to do tens of thousands of dollars of work in value to him per programmer.

Setting ISP expectations and measuring results

Whether your ISP is helping with the production of a mere banner ad or rolling out your next millionth-visitor-in-a-week traffic campaign, you and your helper must be very clear on what the goal is for the project. How will your expectation be met? Do you require a certain number of new sales or more traffic? Maybe the completion of the project has nothing to do with traffic or sales, but is merely a convenience to you. Whatever the goal, write it down and have a mutual agreement on the outcome. Here are some specific steps you can take to assure your goals are met:

✦ **Request frequent communication:** When you're working on a time-sensitive deadline, an update per day by e-mail is not too much to ask and keeps you confident that your project is being worked on.

✦ **Become aware of potential roadblocks:** Ask whether anything might prevent the deadline from being met. If you have an absolute deadline for the project to be completed, you might require upfront that a fee reduction should be granted for every day after the deadline that the project is not launched. For example, if you hire an ISP to produce an online registration form for an upcoming conference, you might require that the form is live two weeks prior to the last day of the "early bird" special pricing offer. If the registration form is not complete until two or three days before the early bird date, you would lose significant registrations. If it is truly the ISP's fault for not getting the form live in time, a reduction in fee would certainly be warranted. But, if that ISP was waiting for content from you and could not go live without the approved information, the standard fee would be in play.

✦ **Use repetition:** Announce the goal on every phone call and decide together whether you're closer to or farther away from reaching that goal since your last conversation.

✦ **Give encouragement:** ISPs like to know when they're on the right track. Even though a project might not be complete, you can make complimentary comments on the job done so far. ISPs like to work for people they like. So, a little ego stroking pulls some weight when working with helpers.

✦ **Ask for activity reports:** With the help of an online project tracker (there are many to choose from), you can request progress reports at any time. If you pay your helpers in blocks of time or by the hour, keep a close watch on what has been accomplished for the time spent.

I've had good experience working with Basecamp when multiple people are on the same project team and need to coordinate who is in charge of completing which tasks by a certain date. Basecamp has a monthly fee starting at $24 and requires a bit of a learning curve.

My main project report system, however, is called DotProject. This free, open-source software is installed on the Web server and is totally customizable. As a result, my colleagues and I are able to produce simple reports for any of our clients within seconds that display the dates of tasks performed, description of the tasks, who performed them, and the total amount of time that each task required. When it comes to tracking billable time, it doesn't matter if your ISP uses complex customized software like ours or a simple e-mail once a week, as long as there is some mechanism in place to provide you with that information when you need it.

✦ **Request sales and cost reports:** If you have a company managing a promotional campaign, demand reports at least once per week. Even with the most complex Google AdWords campaigns, running a sales report takes less than ten minutes. It's your money: Know where it's being spent.

✦ **Offer to check off a completed project:** When your project is close to completion, offer to sign off on the project. ISPs love clients that want things finalized. Extend the courtesy of acknowledging when a project is complete.

One man's outsource is another man's basement

I heard a story of a business owner who hired an overseas development company just because, "That's what everyone is doing." He found out a few weeks later that the "company" was actually just a guy working out of his basement — in Chicago!

If you request a report and notice an abrupt change in communication by your ISP, be on alert that something might have gone wrong. Helpers tend to disappear into their caves when things don't go as planned or aren't completed within the time they thought the project would go live. Be sympathetic at first. Unforeseen factors can creep into any project at any time even for the most experienced firms. But, don't let it go too long. Be patient, yet persistent, when needed.

Not every client/ISP relationship is going to work like a charm. If things are not going how you planned, be the proactive business owner and confront your helper to either get your money back or get the project fixed. This is why I always hire a new helper for only small tasks at first. If someone can't get a $50 project completed for me in time and the way I ordered it, there's no chance he could make me happy with a large project.

Nurturing a good ISP partnership

When you find an ISP that you like and trust over a period of months, offer a little more incentive than a project fee or hourly rate to keep you and your project at the forefront of his mind. Devise a plan that offers a small compensation per month based on sales. This invitation is best made when the ISP is not expecting it. Offering such an incentive accomplishes several objectives:

- ✦ **Builds confidence:** The ISP is certain that you approve of his work.

- ✦ **Strengthens the team:** People like to be part of teams that accomplish things. Monetary incentives help your ISP understand that he really is a valued part of the team.

- ✦ **Sparks creativity:** Most ISPs start to get creative when they know they're going to get a piece of the pie. You will get occasional e-mails from them that read, "You didn't ask me to do this, but the idea just struck me and I had to try it out. What do you think about it?"

Book II

Search Engine Optimization

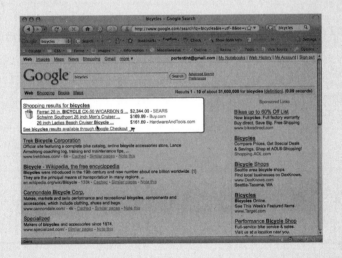

Contents at a Glance

Chapter 1: Getting Ready for SEO **153**
Understanding Why Search Engines Exist.................................... 153
Knowing What Makes a Web Site Relevant 155
Avoiding Penalties 158

Chapter 2: Choosing the Right Keywords. **169**
Thinking Like Your Visitors.. 169
Understanding the Long Tail.. 170
Finding the Right Tools.. 171

Chapter 3: Eliminating Search Engine Roadblocks **183**
Ensuring Search Engine Visibility.. 183
Providing a Way to Browse 187
Using Ajax and DHTML 188

Chapter 4: Making Search Engines Love Your Site **199**
Structuring Your Site for Search Engines and People.......................... 199
Keeping the Structure Clean and Clear....................................... 204
Building a Semantic Outline 207
Optimizing for Trust... 208

Chapter 5: Understanding Blended Search **211**
Optimizing Products 212
Optimizing News... 213
Optimizing Images 214

**Chapter 6: Writing Great Copy for Search Engines
(And Readers!)** **221**
Writing Online Copy.. 221
Writing a Great Title Tag.. 227
Writing a Great Description Tag... 230

Chapter 7: Building Link Love **235**
Understanding Link Votes 235
Writing Link-Worthy Content... 237
Encouraging Links 238

Chapter 8: Analyzing Your Results **251**
Using Your Tracking Worksheet.. 251
Watching for Plagiarism.. 254
Knowing What to Do If Your Numbers Fall 255

Chapter 9: Hiring an SEO Professional. **257**
Finding an SEO Professional.. 257
Checking Qualifications 258
Knowing What to Ask an SEO Professional................................. 259

Chapter 1: Getting Ready for SEO

In This Chapter

✔ Understanding why search engines exist

✔ Discovering what matters to a search engine

✔ Staying away from tricks and penalties

✔ Setting up your toolbox

✔ Making an SEO worksheet

Search engine optimization (SEO) is a long-term effort. It requires a lot of work and patience and a consistent strategy.

This chapter helps you prepare for a lengthy campaign by explaining why search engines exist. You find out what works and what doesn't in the SEO world. I also cover how to set up your SEO toolbox and help you put your SEO worksheet together.

Understanding Why Search Engines Exist

Search engines drive the Internet. If you're going to grow your business online, you're probably going to depend on such search engines as Google, Yahoo!, and Microsoft Live Search to deliver a huge chunk of your customers and clients. A high placement in the search engine ranking pages (*SERPs*, if you want to feel all geeky) can drive tremendous growth.

You can leave those rankings to chance and hope for the best. Or you can use *SEO*, the practice of providing the best possible target for search engines.

SEO is a huge field, with thousands of little details that come together to make a successful campaign. If you're looking to dig deeply into this topic, get *Search Engine Optimization for Dummies*, 2nd Edition, by Peter Kent (Wiley). If you want to improve your search rankings and steer clear of trouble, this book is for you.

When you're learning SEO, it's hard to separate tricks from solid strategies. To understand how search engines work, you need to know why they exist.

Search engine terms to remember

Crawl refers to what a search engine does when it reads and indexes a Web site.

Organic or natural search results are unpaid listings on a search result page.

Search engine ranking pages (SERP) are the result pages you see when you complete a search on a major search engine.

Spiders or robots (bots) are software that the search engine uses to crawl your site.

Black hat SEO uses tactics specifically designed to improve search rankings and fool the search engines into providing a higher ranking than a Web site should actually receive according to that search engine's algorithms.

White hat SEO uses tactics to make a Web site as acceptable as possible to both visitors and search engines, without attempting to manipulate the search engines.

Search engines deliver relevance. Relevance means visitors click on search results and are happy with what the search engine found for them. When that happens, visitors come back, traffic to the search engine rises, and the search engine company's stock goes up.

For example, if I go to Google and type in **pastrami**, I expect to click a result and find a site about pastrami. If I click a result and instead find a Web site about bread, I might not use Google again. Google wants to deliver the most useful Web sites relating to pastrami because it's good for their business. Same for every other search engine on the Internet.

Don't be fooled by hucksters who offer to help you move up in the rankings. They tell you they can trick the search engines into giving you a high ranking, even if you don't deserve it.

These tricks might include adding thousands of links on hundreds of Web sites; duplicating pages on your site; buying or stealing content from other sites and using it on yours; or connecting you to *linking networks* where hundreds of sites exchange links. Or, when asked how they will improve your rankings, the con artist might just say, "It's a secret."

Regardless, these people are trying to get you to believe they can get you a top ranking for *pastrami* even if you sell salami, or if you only sell a little pastrami.

Using tricks like these may get you some initial success, but they cost money, and you risk getting penalized by the search engines. Penalties cause you to disappear from the rankings or move down to four or five pages of the listings without warning. That can get expensive. I go over more about this in the "Avoiding Penalties" section later in the chapter.

Search engines don't like to be fooled. If you're selling salami and engage in some trickery to gain a high ranking for pastrami, the search engine's programming team will remove you from the rankings.

Knowing What Makes a Web Site Relevant

Search engines want to know which Web site is the most important for a particular concept. These concepts are represented by *key phrases. New York hotels, chocolate candy, bicycles,* and *wedding dresses* are all examples of key phrases.

Search engines are hierarchical thinkers. After reading billions of pages of content by using little software programs called *spiders,* search engines determine the relevance of each of those pages for a key phrase based on a complex series of rules.

**Book II
Chapter 1**

**Getting Ready
for SEO**

When you go to a search engine and type in a key phrase (*wedding dresses,* for example), the search engine picks the best matches by looking at the following in hierarchical order:

1. A site's authority on the subject of wedding dresses, as demonstrated by links from other sites about wedding dresses

Every link from other, relevant sites is a vote for the target site's authority.

2. Whether wedding dresses are the main focus of each site, as demonstrated by site structure

3. Which pages on those sites are most dedicated to wedding dresses

4. Whether those pages are more relevant than all the other pages in the search engine's index

All you have to do is get yourself to the top of each of those pyramids, and you're rich!

Well, maybe it's not *that* simple. Thousands or even millions of other sites are all vying for that same top spot. To really compete, you're going to need to know how Web pages are built and how search engines read them. If you know how search engines read sites, and you know how to build them, you can provide what search engines want: a structure that indicates what a page is really about.

Table 1-1 describes the factors that make a Web site relevant as well as the factors that have little or no impact on a site's rankings.

Table 1-1			What Matters in SEO
Factors	*Matters*	*Doesn't Matter*	*Why*
Title tags	X		Title tags are at the very top of the hierarchy for each page. They're the first thing search engines look at. If the key phrase shows up in the title tag, search engines flag the page as relevant to that phrase.
Keywords meta tag		X	The keywords meta tag was so horribly abused by SEOs that search engines largely ignore it.
Description meta tag	X		The description meta tag actually affects your rankings, but is usually shown as the page 'snippet' in the search engine results.
Headings (H1, H2, and so on)	X		Headings provide a content outline to the search engines when they crawl your pages. If the target key phrase shows up in a heading, that demonstrates relevance.
Paragraph copy	X		The more copy you have on your site the easier it is to rank well. Don't just stuff copy with keywords, though. More on this in Chapter 6 of this book.
Bolded key phrases		X	Bolding keywords in your paragraph text doesn't help.
Hidden text		X	Hiding text on your page and stuffing it with key phrases may seem like a neat trick. But search engines root this stuff out, and if you're caught, they'll penalize your site.
Site age	X		Older sites have higher rankings. You can safely assume that a two-year-old site will have more leverage than a two-week-old one.
Trust factors	X		Having a physical address on every page can definitely help make you look more trustworthy.
Image captions	X		Text captions near images help with image search results.
Bullets and lists			Bullets are more easily scanned, which makes for better linking opportunities. But they don't directly impact rankings.

Factors	Matters	Doesn't Matter	Why
Links	X		Links equal authority. Authority equals greater relevance. Don't just buy junk links, though. You need relevant links from relevant sites.
Link text	X		If the link to your site reads `Click Here`, that tells the search engines that your site is relevant to click here. If the link reads `Wedding Dresses`, it tells the search engine your site is relevant to wedding dresses. See how that works?
File names	X		Keyword-rich file names on images and individual pages insert keywords into the site hierarchy.
URL	X		Keyword-rich Web addresses can be a huge help, because every link to your site that uses the URL as the link text creates a keyword-rich link. This only works within reason, though.
Submitting a Web site		X	You can certainly submit your Web site to Google, Yahoo!, and Live, but it's better for these search engines to find you through links on other sites.
Number of clicks on my search listing		X	Click your listing as much as you want. The search engines still won't move you up.

Avoiding Penalties

Web site owners often make the mistake of looking for the Miraculous Path to Search Engine Greatness. One does not exist. SEO is a long process. You need to write, optimize, build links, and slowly work your way up.

If you *do* find a short-term fix that works, it won't last. The road to a No. 1 ranking is littered with the shells of Web sites that tried all sorts of trickery and shortcuts.

At some point, you, your boss, your spouse, or your business partner is going to ask, "Why does this other site rank higher than ours?" You might discover that the other site bought 4,000 links, or they have 1,000 near-duplicate pages. Then you'll ask yourself, "Why shouldn't I do that, too?"

Search engines aren't the keeper of ethics or laws. Strictly speaking, there's no ethical reason not to play games with them in an attempt to get a higher ranking. However, this is a lousy business plan. I can point to only one or two cases where someone got away with trickiness for more than a few months. Assuming that your business plan allows for growth over a period of years, it pays to practice *white hat* SEO tactics — rely on content and natural link growth, with a little help here and there — rather than tricks.

Read about white hat and black hat SEO in the sidebar, "Search engine terms to remember."

I make absolutely no moral judgment about *black hat* SEO. As Michael Gray, a great SEO pro, once said, "Google is not the government." Black hat SEO professionals try to find loopholes and clever ways to fool search engines into providing a higher ranking than a site might actually deserve within that search engine's ranking system. They're not breaking any laws, or doing anything unethical. They're just balancing risk versus benefit: Black hat SEO is very risky, but can provide a huge benefit. But it also nearly guarantees you'll get caught at some point.

Search engines demand relevance, not tricks, and assuming you want your rankings to have a life span beyond a couple months, you should give the search engines what they want. Although it takes longer, following the rules gives you a more resilient online business.

Anyone guaranteeing you a No.1 ranking, offering to submit you to 3,000 search engines, or contacting you out of the blue is probably going to rip you off. Also beware of tools that promise instant SEO ranking improvement with little or no effort. If it sounds too good to be true, it probably is.

An SEO tale of woe

In late 2004, a business owner named Jake received a call from a company promising him great search rankings. He worked with a white hat search engine optimization company and slowly began moving up in the rankings. Unfortunately, he became impatient.

He decided to find a new SEO company. This company's experts explained that they would modify his Web site to include dozens of hidden links that search engines would see, but visitors would not. In exchange, they'd add Jake's site to all of their other clients' Web sites. Best of all, the results were guaranteed: Top 10 rankings on Google and Yahoo! within two months.

Jake hired them, and within a few weeks, his site ranked in the Top 10 for nearly every key phrase. He was ecstatic.

Then, a week later, traffic to his site plunged. He checked the rankings: He'd vanished from the search engines. Why? Google and Yahoo! had both found the hidden links, detected that they were indeed hidden, and removed his site from their indexes.

It took six months for Jake to get back into the search engines. In the long run, his coffee business lost far more than it gained.

Setting Up Your Toolbox

Some fantastic tools are available to help you see how a search engine will evaluate your Web site. Use the tools mentioned in the following sections to set up your SEO toolbox.

Downloading and installing Firefox

Firefox is a Web browser by the Mozilla foundation. It's speedy, allows for tabbed browsing, and most importantly, has hundreds of add-on tools that can help you with SEO. To download and install Firefox, follow these steps:

1. **Go to www.mozilla.org/firefox.**

2. **Click the Free Download button.**

3. **After the download is complete, install Firefox.**

Firefox runs on Mac OS X, Microsoft Windows, and Linux.

Installing add-ons

Firefox's number one feature is that it allows developers to create their own add-ons. You can find a huge collection of add-ons at http://addons.mozilla.org. The ones you want for SEO include the following:

+ **SeoQuake,** which collects and displays a few dozen relevant search engine statistics, including pages in the Google index, pages in the Yahoo! index, keyword density on the page, site age, and page rank.

+ **Live HTTP Headers** shows what your Web site is telling a search engine about each page.

+ The **Google Toolbar** gets you a few details about your site as seen by Google.

+ The **Web Developer Toolbar** lets you change how Firefox displays a Web page. It's great for testing how your site looks without images or styles (how a search engine sees it).

+ **Yellowpipe Lynx Viewer Tool** enables you to see the Web page in a text-only Web browser — another good way to preview how a search engine will see your site.

These five tools are really just the beginning. Dozens of other Firefox add-ons are available, including Rank Checker and SEO for Firefox.

To install an add-on, follow these steps:

1. **Open Firefox.**

2. **Go to http://addons.mozilla.org.**

3. **Browse or search for the add-on you want.**

4. **Click Add to Firefox.**

5. **Restart Firefox when indicated in the add-on installation window.**

Adding and using SeoQuake

Install SeoQuake by using the steps in the previous section. After you install SeoQuake, a tiny icon appears in the lower-right corner of your browser window, as shown in Figure 1-1.

Click the icon to activate SeoQuake.

Do not leave SeoQuake on all the time! SeoQuake *scrapes* the search engines for information. If you leave it on, you're basically pestering Google, Yahoo!, and Live Search. They don't like that.

Visit your favorite Web page. You can see the handy SeoBar at the upper left of the page. Click the arrow to expand the toolbar, as shown in Figure 1-2.

Hover over any of the items to see what they are and then click on any item to get more detail. Clicking the Google Links item, for example, shows you a listing of all incoming links that Google sees for the page.

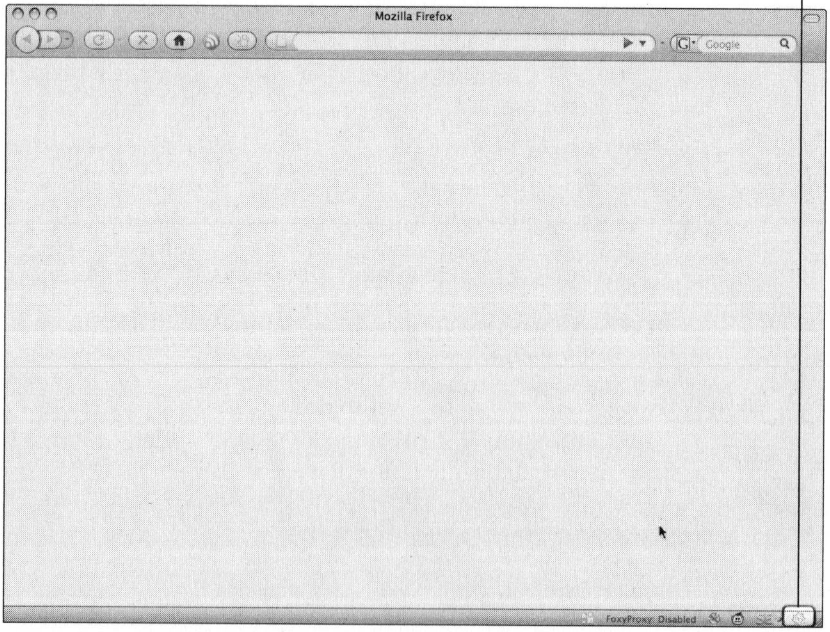

SEOQuake icon

Mozilla Firefox

Google

FoxyProxy Disabled

Figure 1-1:
The SeoQuake icon.

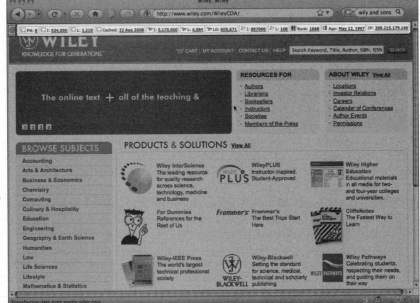

Figure 1-2:
The SeoBar
provides
SEO
information
goodness.

Check the following items for your site as well as for your competitors' sites:

- ✦ **Google links,** which shows the number of links to the site as seen by Google.

- ✦ **Yahoo! linkdomain** results provide the number of links to the Web site from other Web sites, as seen by Yahoo!.

- ✦ **Google and Yahoo! index** gives the number of pages indexed by each search engine.

- ✦ **MSN links and index.**

- ✦ **Site age.**

- ✦ **Density** is a critical feature. You can check a site to see which phrases are most popular/common on that page. This is a great insight into how optimized a page is for a specific phrase.

- ✦ **Links** that are set to `nofollow`. SeoQuake strikes through any links that have the `rel` attribute set to `nofollow`. You find out more about that in Book II, Chapter 7.

If you want to geek out, you can also get specific data about links from within the site to one page, the page's `robots.txt` file, and the IP address of that Web site.

No search engine ever tells you the full story regarding links and indexed pages. Because SeoQuake pulls its data in large part from the search engines, take the results with a grain of salt. However, it's a great way to compare Web sites and measure progress.

You can have SeoQuake show up in your toolbar, too. I don't — I have got enough stuff up there — but if you want to, choose View⇨Toolbars and then choose SeoQuake Toolbar.

Adding and using Live HTTP Headers

Install Live HTTP Headers by following the steps in the "Installing add-ons" section.

To use the tool, choose Tools⇨Live HTTP Headers. Browse to the Web page you want to check. A lot of gobbledygook streams by in the Live HTTP Headers window, as shown in Figure 1-3.

For now, you care about only one thing: the first HTTP note. If it reads `200 OK`, as shown in Figure 1-3, your Web server is telling all visiting browsers — including search engine spiders — that everything is fine and they should index this page normally.

Test your site's Page Not Found error page, too. Go to `www.yoursite address.com/asdfasdf` and replace `yoursiteaddress` but keep the `asdfasdf`. Chances are that page doesn't exist. The HTTP note should read `404`. If it reads `200`, tell your Webmaster he needs to fix that. I talk about this more in Book II, Chapter 3.

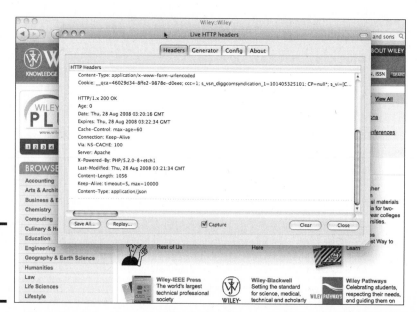

Figure 1-3: Using Live HTTP Headers.

Adding and using the Google Toolbar

Some SEOs love it, and others hate it, but the Google Toolbar provides one bit of data that no SEO professional can seem to live without: Google Toolbar PageRank.

1. **To install it, go to `toolbar.google.com`.**

2. **Click Download Google Toolbar.**

3. **Click Settings in the toolbar, and then click the More link (as shown in Figure 1-4).**

Make sure that the PageRank and Page Info are selected.

Google Toolbar PageRank is *not* an accurate measure of Google's real PageRank for your site. The actual PageRank scale goes from 0 to the millions (or billions) and keeps changing. Google Toolbar PageRank goes from 0 to 10 and updates only occasionally.

Adding and using the Web Developer Toolbar

This tool is the most complex of any I discuss in this chapter. If you're scared by terms such as *CSS* and *JavaScript,* skip ahead to the next section. The Web Developer Toolbar is handy but is not required.

Install the Web Developer Toolbar by following the steps in the "Installing add-ons" section.

Book II
Chapter 1

Getting Ready
for SEO

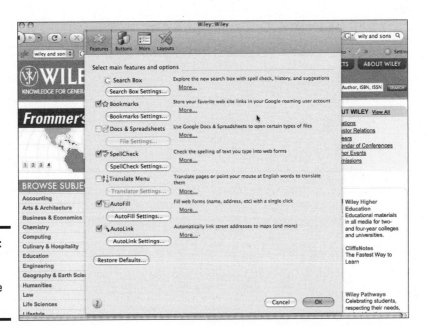

Figure 1-4:
The More panel for the Google Toolbar.

After it's installed, choose View➪Toolbars➪Web Developer Toolbar. Make sure that it's selected. The Web Developer Toolbar, as shown in Figure 1-5, appears in Firefox.

The main tools you want to use are Disable➪JavaScript and CSS➪Disable All Styles. By disabling JavaScript and styles, you get a more accurate picture of what the average search engine sees when it crawls your Web site.

Take some time, play around, and see how it all works. Just be sure that you look up from the monitor once in a while. The Web Developer Toolbar is highly addictive.

Adding and setting up Yellowpipe Lynx Viewer

Yellowpipe Lynx Viewer lets you see how your site looks in the text-only Web browser Lynx. You can get another look at how search engines see your site.

Install it by following the steps in the "Installing add-ons" section. After it's installed, right-click any page you're viewing and then choose Yellowpipe Lynx Viewer Tool. The pop-up window shows you the page in a text-only browser, as shown in Figure 1-6.

This add-on is a great test of any site for basic SEO friendliness. If the Lynx view is blank or starts with gibberish, the site might have problems. If links are nonexistent, that's a problem, too.

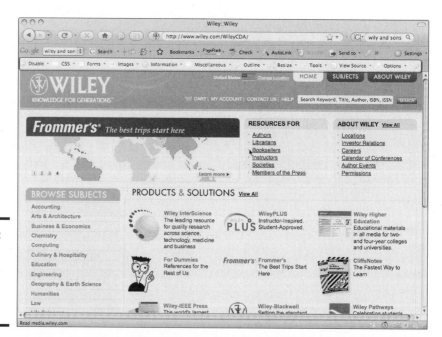

Figure 1-5:
Using
the Web
Developer
Toolbar in
Firefox.

Figure 1-6:
The Lynx
view of a
Web site.

Setting up and using Webmaster tools

The major search engines provide insight into your site's SEO, too. Yahoo!,
Live Search, and Google all have Webmaster tools that can

✦ Notify you if they find problems, such as duplicate content

✦ Show you who is linking to your site

✦ Report the most common queries used to find your site

✦ Tell you the last time the search engine crawled your site

✦ Allow you to modify (in a few cases) how your listings appear

The Webmaster tools sites for the various search engines are

✦ **Google:** www.google.com/webmasters/tools

✦ **Yahoo!:** siteexplorer.search.yahoo.com

✦ **Live Search:** webmaster.live.com

To use Webmaster tools, follow these steps:

1. **Set up an account with each search engine, as directed.**

2. **Verify site ownership by either uploading an authentication file or
adding a meta tag to your site, as directed by the search engine.**

If you have no idea what this step means, talk to your Webmaster to get
it set up.

Using Google Webmaster tools

The Google Webmaster toolset includes more than 20 gadgets. You want to explore them all, but you can't do without these three:

✦ **Diagnostics⇨Content Analysis** tells you, at a glance, whether any pages on your site duplicate title or description meta tags, or whether they're missing those tags.

✦ **Links⇨Pages with external links** tells you which pages on your site have links from other sites. And you can drill down to find out where those links come from.

✦ **Statistics⇨Top search queries** allows you to peek at the key phrases (and your rankings for those phrases) that drive traffic.

You can export these reports to TSV format if you're a real datahead, too.

Google Webmaster tools are a *must have.* Don't leave them out of your toolbox!

Using Yahoo! Site Explorer

Yahoo! Site Explorer is simpler than Google's toolset. But it provides a deeper look at incoming links.

Site Explorer shows you

✦ All the pages on your site that Yahoo! has indexed

✦ The last crawl date of each of those pages

✦ Incoming links

Because Yahoo! tends to include more links in its index than Google, it can be a far better competitive research tool.

Two reports you want to check often are

✦ **Inlinks:** Show Inlinks Except from this domain and to Entire Site. In Figure 1-7, the options in the pop-up menus near the top are set to Show Inlinks from All Pages and to Entire Site.

✦ **Pages:** You can see which pages are included in the Yahoo! index and which aren't.

You can export these reports to TSV format, too.

Using Live Webmaster tools

Microsoft's Live Search Webmaster tools are a treasure trove. Some of the service's reports overlap with Google Webmaster tools, but I recommend checking out the following:

+ **Crawl Issues** shows pages that Live's spider can't find in the File Not Found issue type.

+ **Keywords Report** allows you to type in a key phrase to see which pages Live considers strong for that keyword.

+ **Outbound Links** is unique. You can get a single report showing all the links you have pointing at other Web sites.

And, yes, you can export all these reports to TSV format.

Installing Xenu Link Sleuth

Xenu Link Sleuth is a great little program that crawls any Web site, giving you a list of broken and working links. It's also free, by the way. To install it, follow these steps:

1. Go to `http://home.snafu.de/tilman/xenulink.html`.

2. **Double-click the program, type in the Web address you want checked, and then click OK.**

   You can change the other settings to crawl a site faster or slower.

Use Xenu to find broken links. When Xenu detects broken links, it also shows you the page on which it found the link, so it's relatively easy to find problems.

**Book II
Chapter 1**

**Getting Ready
for SEO**

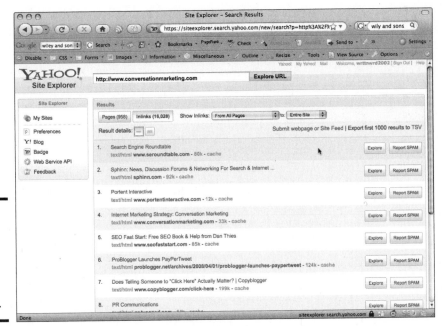

Figure 1-7:
The Inlinks report, set to show incoming links from other sites.

Xenu is available only for Microsoft Windows. Luckily, Peacock Media has a tool called Integrity that comes awfully close to Xenu's features. Best of all, it's free, too. You can download it from `http://peacockmedia.co.uk/integrity`.

Creating Your SEO Worksheet

SEO can take a long time. Plus, changes you make today might impact your rankings months from now, so it's important that you keep a record of relevant data and changes you make over time. That way, you can refer back to those changes and better understand what worked and what didn't.

If you're serious about SEO, you're going to need to track a number of different statistics over time, including:

✦ **Traffic from organic search:** Your Web analytics package (see Book III for in-depth Web analytics information) should show you clicks from unpaid search rankings.

✦ **Keyword diversity:** The number of key phrases driving traffic to your Web site. Again, your Web analytics package will give you this.

✦ **Incoming links, by search engine:** The number of links reported by Live, Yahoo!, and Google.

✦ **Indexed pages, by search engine.**

✦ **Sales/leads/other results from organic search:** If your site has a goal, and your analytics package allows it, record the results you get. Traffic is great. Sales are better.

✦ **Keyword rankings:** Notice how this is last? That's because *keyword rankings don't matter.*

Keyword rankings don't matter. Traffic and results do. Although ranking No. 1 for a phrase or two is one way to get those extra visitors, getting 500 Top 10 listings for less prominent phrases may get you far more visitors and sales, leads, or whatever else you need. Don't obsess about keyword rankings. Obsess about traffic, keyword diversity, and success.

Record these numbers by month. You can record them by week if you're really obsessive. Whatever you do, don't check them every day — you may lose your mind, and I don't want that on my conscience.

See Book II, Chapter 8 for information on search engine analytics and analyzing your results.

Chapter 2: Choosing the Right Keywords

In This Chapter

✔ Picking keywords your visitors (not you) want

✔ Discovering keyword tools

✔ Using the right selection criteria

✔ Researching your competitors

For now, keywords (or, more accurately, key phrases) are the focus of successful search engine optimization. Someday search engines may be able to index and rank sites based on *concepts* — by knowing that cars and autos are the same thing — but until then, you need to make some pretty specific choices.

Search engine optimization (SEO) is a long-term undertaking. You may wait months before you see any results. Choose the right keywords and you can see a nice lift in traffic after all that effort. Choose the wrong keywords and your months of effort won't help your business. In this chapter, I go over how to pick the right keywords to bring traffic to your business Web site.

Thinking Like Your Visitors

Before I talk about tools, you must understand that you are not optimizing for the keywords *you* like or think should be associated with your product or service. You are optimizing for the keywords *potential customers* associate with your product or service.

For example, say you sell salad through the Internet. You've found a miraculous way to keep vegetables crisp and prevent lettuce from wilting, and you ship salad to suburban dwellers everywhere.

You research keywords and find that no one searches for *salad.* They search for *"mixed greens"* instead. You have a choice to make. You can insist on optimizing for *salad,* because that is what you sell. Or, you can optimize for *mixed greens,* get visitors, and then educate them as to why *salad* is better.

Don't try to shove your own beliefs about your product or service down the throats of your customers by picking the keywords *you* think they should use to find you. That never works in marketing, and it really doesn't work in search engine optimization. Understand what your visitors will use to find you. You can educate them as to why you're different, and why they should care, after they arrive on your Web site.

If a customer searches for *bicycles* and clicks a link to your site, she'll expect to see information about bicycles. If you sell cars, don't optimize for *bicycles* and then try to tell folks why cars are better. That just frustrates them. Go with your strengths: Optimize for *cars*.

Understanding the Long Tail

You never optimize for a single word; you optimize for a keyword and the hundreds or thousands of permutations on that word. So, if you're targeting *broccoli,* you're probably also targeting *cream of broccoli soup, broccoli recipes,* and *broccoli coleslaw.* These *long-tail* phrases — longer niche phrases that don't get as many searches — are the real beauty of search engine optimization. By optimizing for one word or phrase, you get the benefit of improved rankings for many more.

Go back to the *salad* example I use in the preceding section. You decide to optimize for *mixed greens.* After six months of hard work, you're still stuck on the fourth rankings page for that phrase. But your traffic from organic searches has gone up 300 percent. For these reasons, you're not sure whether you should fire yourself or give yourself a raise.

Taking a look at your traffic report, though, you notice something interesting. Traffic from longer phrases that include the words *mixed greens* has gone up. Phrases such as the following are now major traffic generators:

> *mixed spring greens*
> *mixed greens online*
> *buy mixed greens*
> *mixed greens salads*
> *really great mixed greens*
> *where can I buy mixed greens*

All these phrases are driving traffic to your site. Together, the six phrases drive more traffic than *mixed greens* would have.

Behold, the long tail! By optimizing for one phrase, you really optimized for six longer ones. Even though you didn't move up in the rankings for the target phrase, you did move up for these others, and they brought you traffic.

Long-tail phrases work for two reasons:

✦ You can optimize for many of them at once by focusing on one shorter phrase.

✦ Searchers that visit your Web site from long-tail phrases are generally better targeted and better customers. If folks comes to your Web site from a long-tail search result and you have what they want, they're likely to buy.

So the next time you're sweating bullets, staring at your rankings report, and wondering why you haven't moved up, check your traffic report, too. The long tail might pay off big.

Finding the Right Tools

Luckily, you don't have to guess to find keywords. You can use some of the great tools available to help you with your initial brainstorming.

Using keyword services

Several companies have launched keyword services designed just for search engine optimization pros looking for the right targets. These services include

✦ **Wordze:** www.wordze.com

✦ **Keyword Discovery:** http://keyworddiscovery.com

✦ **Wordtracker:** www.wordtracker.com

All services cost a small monthly fee, but they are a good investment. They provide at-a-glance reports showing keyword demand, competition, and quality, as shown in Figure 2-1.

Be sure to know where these tools get their data! For example, none has access to Google organic search numbers (Google doesn't release that data). They're good at extrapolating, but you want to supplement your research with the tools I describe in the rest of this section.

Working with the Google AdWords keyword research tool

Google recently updated its keyword research tool to show search volumes. That makes the Google keyword tool the only source for Google keyword search data.

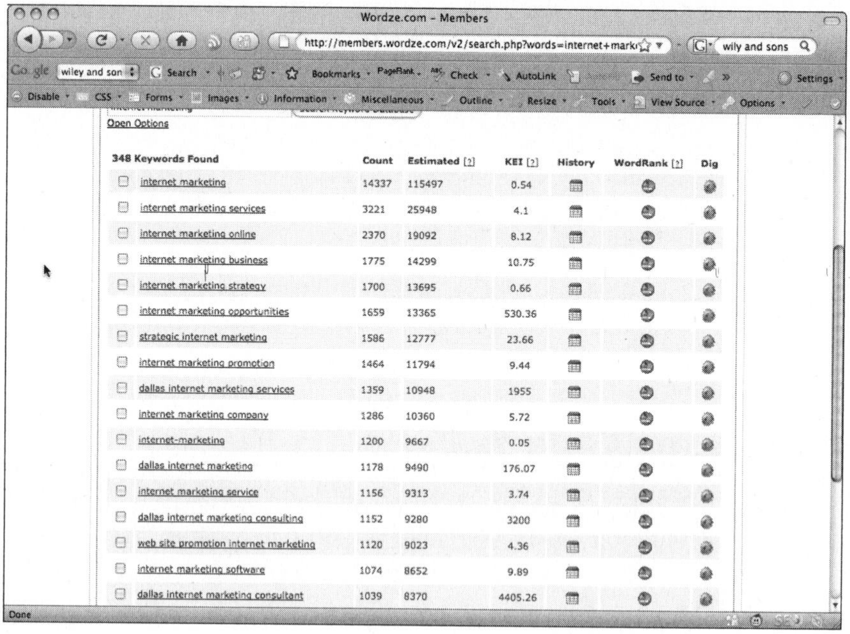

Figure 2-1:
Wordze
shows you
related
keywords,
searches
per month,
and
competition
(Keyword
Effective-
ness Index,
or KEI).

To show search volumes, follow these steps:

1. **Go to** `http://adwords.google.com/select/`
`KeywordToolExternal`.

2. **Type in a phrase in the text box, click the Get keyword ideas button,**
and you get a report like the one shown in Figure 2-2.

The report shows searches performed in the previous month, average
monthly search volume over the past 12 months, and advertiser
competition in Google AdWords.

3. **Click the Choose Columns to Display option list and then choose Show**
Search Volume Trends.

Doing this adds an additional column to the report. You see trended
search data listed by month.

4. **Go back to the list and select Show Highest Volume Occurred In to**
look for any seasonal trends for your keywords, too, as shown in
Figure 2-3.

Don't worry about the Match Type or cost-related options. They are used for
pay per click (PPC) marketing research. See Book IV to find out more.

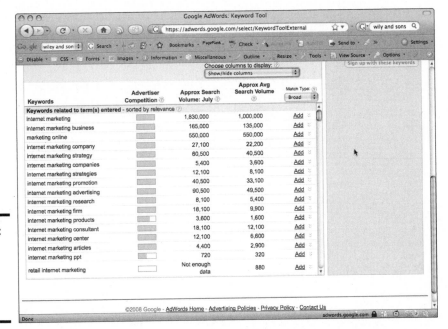

Figure 2-2:
Using the
Google
AdWords
keyword
tool.

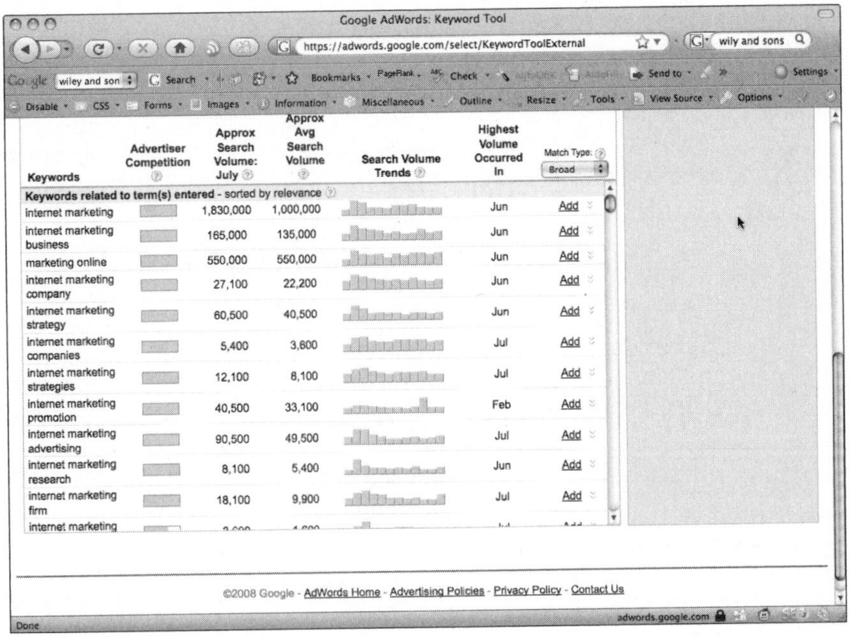

Figure 2-3:
Viewing the
seasonal
trends and
highest
volume.

You have a few other options:

✦ **You can filter results to remove some keywords.** To do this, click the Filter My Results option and enter keywords you don't want in your list.

✦ **You can also get keyword ideas based on a Web site's content.** Click Website Content and enter a Web address. Google's tool checks the page and pulls keywords based on the words and phrases on that page. The Website Content option is a great way to get ideas for keywords you hadn't thought of. You can also verify that your page is optimized for the right phrases and check competitors' pages.

I know what you're thinking: Why use any other keyword tools? Google has the lion's share of the traffic anyway.

Although Google does get most of the traffic, the Google keyword tool is designed for pay per click marketers. If you rely solely on it, you may miss some great niche phrases simply because they don't get a lot of bids in Google AdWords. Use the other keyword tools I describe earlier, too, to ensure that you get an accurate picture.

Using Google Trends

All major search engines favor content that focuses on hot key phrases. For example, say that a famous movie star loses 45 pounds on a diet solely composed of mixed greens. The story hits newsstands, and suddenly everyone is searching for *"mixed greens diet"*.

If you knew that, you could add a few articles to your site about the mixed greens diet. The search engines would see that and quickly move you up in the rankings. You'd get a nice burst of traffic.

If only there were a way to check on trending phrases. . . .

Oh, but wait, there is! Google Trends. Go to www.google.com/trends. Type in any phrase, and you can see whether search volumes are rising or falling. The report even shows specific news stories and whether they affected search volumes.

The top section is the *search volume index,* the rise or fall in searches for that phrase. The bottom section is the *news reference volume,* which tells you online media mentions of the phrase.

You can get more advanced reporting at www.google.com/insights/search, including seasonality, geography, and categories.

You can see a list of the top 100 hot phrases by clicking the More Hot Trends link, as shown in Figure 2-4.

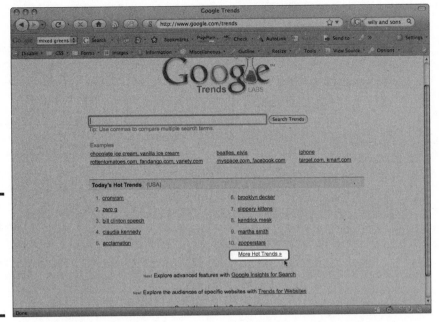

Figure 2-4:
Clicking the More Hot Trends link produces the top 100 phrases.

Watching the news

We are media driven. It pays to keep current on TV, radio, and print news. If a relevant story seems to be gaining a lot of ground, work it into your Web site.

Going back to the (now somewhat silly) mixed greens example earlier in this chapter: If you see on the news that Mark Starguy is the movie star who lost 45 pounds on the mixed greens diet, you might want to mention his name here and there. Chances are other folks watching the news will remember the star's name and *diet,* but not *mixed greens.* If you show up for *Mark Starguy diet,* you're set.

Using your brain

All the computers in the world can't match your brain for its ability to manipulate language. Don't rely on keyword tools alone. They will eventually lie to you (or at least tell a small fib): Keyword tools lack your insight into your customers. They can use only the data they have, and that means sometimes they'll miss important subtleties, such as the difference between *auto* (as in *automobile*) and *auto* (as in *automatic*).

Your brain is the last line of defense against keyword paralysis. If the tools are showing you keywords that simply make no sense, go with your gut and try a different approach.

I don't have any nice screen captures of you using your brain. You have to use your imagination.

Picking Great Keywords

After you decide what tools to use, it helps to know the criteria for choosing a great keyword. You need to judge relevance, competition, and value.

Judging keyword relevance

Question whether the keyword you found is really relevant to your business. For example, *mixed greens* could mean mixed greens for salad. It could also mean mixed green paint.

After you choose a keyword, test it by using all the tools I describe earlier in this chapter. Make sure that you don't see any equally correct but totally irrelevant meanings creeping into the search results.

No keyword is 100 percent relevant. If more than half of the long-tail phrases using that word are relevant to your business, though, you probably have a winner.

Comparing competition and search volume

If you're facing 200 million other Web sites that are all vying for the No. 1 spot, you might want to choose a different keyword.

Go to Google, Yahoo!, and Live Search and search for the phrase you've chosen. Look at three competitive factors:

- ✦ **The number of competing sites:** If you find more than 10 million competing pages in the search results, you might be facing an uphill battle.

- ✦ **Where you rank:** If you're already on the second page of the results, you might not care how many sites are competing with you.

- ✦ **Your ability to compete:** If you have a daily newsletter on your site about mixed greens, you might be super-competitive, even if a mob of other sites are trying to beat you. You're adding new, highly relevant content every day, and search engines love that. That steady content growth gives you an advantage.

Always balance competition against search volume. Some terms might be so relevant and offer so many potential visitors that any level of competition is worth it. For example, the phrase *wedding dresses* gets over one million searches per month. It's also one of the most competitive phrases on the entire Internet. But one million searches makes *wedding dresses* so potentially valuable that, if you have any chance of gaining a front-page ranking for it, you have to try. Other keywords might offer only a tiny trickle of traffic — and thus, very little competition.

Your best strategy is to mix your keyword list and optimize for both of the following:

+ **High-volume, high-competition keywords** that require a long effort on your part before you gain any rankings

+ **Low-volume, low-competition keywords** that can produce results sooner

This strategy lets you build traffic sooner while still aiming for the home run phrases later.

Checking demographics with adCenter Labs

Another great way to test keyword validity is to compare demographic data for that phrase. Microsoft's adCenter Labs offers a great tool to do that.

Go to `http://adlab.msn.com/demographics-prediction`. Type in the keyword you want to test. You get a report like the one shown in Figure 2-5.

Does the report show that the demographics for the keyword match your customer base? If so, you likely chose a great keyword. But, if the demographics don't match your customer base, you might want to rethink your keyword choice. However, you might have just found an unexpected audience, too!

**Book II
Chapter 2**

**Choosing the Right
Keywords**

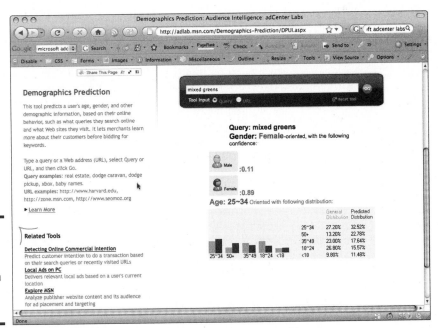

Figure 2-5:
Test keyword validity with adCenter Labs.

Checking your industry with Google Insights

You can also make sure that the keyword you chose fits your industry. (See my example of *mixed greens* and *mixed green paint* earlier in the chapter.) You can use Google Insights to double-check your assumptions about your keyword's relevancy by following these steps:

1. **Go to** `www.google.com/insights/search` **and type in your keyword in the text box.**

   Obviously, I'm using *mixed greens* in this example.

2. **Click the All Categories drop-down list, choose Food & Drink, and then click the Search button.**

   Pshew. Looks like *mixed greens* really *is* about leafy stuff.

3. **If you're still worried, click All Categories and then choose Home & Garden⇨Home Improvement.**

   If you get the result shown in Figure 2-6, you know that you're in good shape.

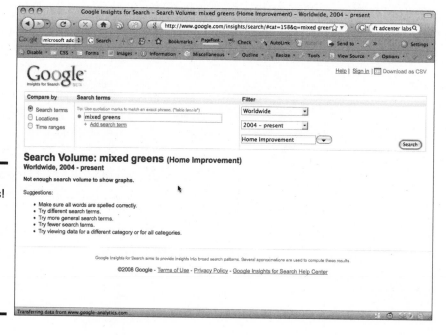

Figure 2-6: Good news! Mixed greens apparently have nothing to do with paint.

Testing with pay per click

Because a search engine optimization campaign can take months to really affect your business, you may want to test your keywords by using a faster method — pay per click (PPC) marketing.

Because you can start and end a PPC campaign in a matter of minutes, doing so is a great way to get a rough idea of keyword viability.

Variables including budget, ad wording, competition, and landing pages can skew your results. Make sure that you use your head when you review results. Read Book IV to find out how PPC works.

Book II
Chapter 2

Choosing the Right Keywords

Building Your Keyword List

As you select keywords, I recommend that you keep a record. I use a spreadsheet like the one shown in Figure 2-7.

games	875,296	1,120,000,000
free games	211,779	1,110,000,000
game	171,060	1,730,000,000
free online games	159,422	795,000,000
online games	128,390	1,080,000,000
chess	97,995	59,900,000
dress up games	79,615	46,600,000
video games	76,415	1,080,000,000
addicting games	69,728	1,710,000
play game	53,098	602,000,000
pc games	49,519	548,000,000
flash games	48,930	221,000,000
mahjong	47,968	21,400,000
free game downloads	40,693	261,000,000
play games	39,220	599,000,000
funny games	37,906	187,000,000
online game	32,993	997,000,000
computer games	32,044	475,000,000
board games	29,432	220,000,000
kids games	28,973	218,000,000
arcade games	27,791	80,000,000
free games online	26,613	726,000,000
fun games	25,955	553,000,000
bejeweled	24,598	7,380,000
free game	23,190	946,000,000
car games	22,840	536,000,000
video game	21,401	944,000,000
download games	20,863	938,000,000
card games	19,827	354,000,000
shooting games	19,624	54,800,000
family feud	19,622	2,790,000
diner dash	19,056	3,050,000
games online	17,749	1,110,000,000
free online game	17,617	845,000,000
bookworm	17,254	9,120,000
cake mania	17,211	4,870,000
racing games	16,859	123,000,000
math games	15,988	45,900,000
computer game	15,978	437,000,000

Figure 2-7: Keep a keyword spreadsheet to help you remember selections.

Keeping a spreadsheet helps me remember which keywords I selected, which ones I ignored, and why.

Your keyword list shouldn't be static. As you come up with new ideas, add them to the list. If you're a hardcore SEO geek like me, you might keep a small pad of paper with you at all times so you can scribble down new phrases when they occur to you. If you're a more sane person (or have better ways to use your time), just keep your spreadsheet up to date.

Sizing Up the Competition

Always keep your eyes on the competition. If they're smart, they're keeping their eyes on you, too. Watch how your competitors rank for particular keywords; watch what they're doing to try to beat you in the rankings; and always look for places where you have an advantage. SEO is a zero-sum game: There is only one No. 1 spot. So make sure that you're always tracking competitors.

Finding your keyword competitors

Hopefully, who your competitors are isn't a mystery. Go to Google, Yahoo!, and Live Search, and search for your target keywords. Consider the top ten sites to be your primary competitors.

Use some of the tools I talk about in Book II, Chapter 1 to learn about your competitors. Use the following:

✦ **SeoQuake** tells you how many links your competitors have, shows you their keyword density, and shows how many pages they have in the respective search engine indexes.

✦ **Yahoo! Site Explorer** can show you exactly what those links are, so you can go after them, too.

✦ **Yellowpipe Lynx Viewer** tells you whether they're pulling any funny business by showing different content to the search engines than they're showing to the public.

Discovering your competitors' weaknesses

Chances are that several of the top ten sites for a specific phrase aren't doing a very good job of optimizing their Web sites. They're in the top ten by luck, or because no one else has done much SEO, either.

You need to find those sites' weaknesses. If you can optimize your site better than they can, you have a good shot at replacing them in the rankings. Refer to Book II, Chapter 1 for details on the tools you can use.

Use SeoQuake to see whether you can increase the keyword density — the percentage of total page text occupied by your key phrase — for target phrases on your site. I never recommend going above 5 to 7 percent keyword density. But if your competitors have 200 words on a page and 10 instances of a phrase, you can certainly put 250 words on a page and have 15 instances of the same phrase.

Use the Web Developer Toolbar to see whether your competitors have built a good relevance hierarchy on their sites. (I discuss the importance of this topic in Book II, Chapter 1.) If they don't have the target key phrase or a related phrase in their title tags or headings, you can get a huge advantage by putting the phrase in those elements.

Use the Web Developer Toolbar to check for image ALT tags and other elements, too. ALT tags don't do much, but every little bit helps!

Figure out where your competitors have fallen down on the job. It's not magic. The vast majority of Web sites on the Internet do a horrible job of SEO. Research the basics, and chances are you can find lots of ways to outrank them.

Ignoring your competition

The vast majority of sites do a horrible job of SEO. If a keyword you selected looks just fantastic, but none of your competitors are using it, it might be their problem, not yours. What if all your competitors insist on optimizing for *salad,* even though no one searches for it?

You know your business and your customers. If your competition seems to be optimizing for key phrases that make no sense, *and* you can't find any evidence that customers are searching using those phrases, trust your judgment — ignore your competition.

The success of your business, not a top spot for a specific phrase, is what really matters.

Chapter 3: Eliminating Search Engine Roadblocks

In This Chapter

✔ **Ensuring search engine visibility**

✔ **Avoiding problems**

✔ **Finding and fixing broken links**

✔ **Minimizing code bloat**

*O*ne way or another, business owners often block search engines from reading their content. And by doing so, they're cutting off a huge segment of their audience. If a search engine can't find your content, it can't index it, which means that it can't determine relevance. When this happens, you don't get ranked.

In this chapter, I cover a range of ways to ensure visibility, find and fix problems, and avoid problems that create search engine roadblocks. I also demonstrate how when a search engine reads your Web site, it does so as the simplest, least-flexible Web browser in the world. In the rest of this chapter, I touch on only a few of the thousands of ways to create search engine roadblocks. If you use a little common sense, though, you can easily test your Web site for problems: Use the Web Developer Toolbar to check your entire site with CSS and JavaScript turned off; fix broken links; and write good, clean, fast-loading code.

Ensuring Search Engine Visibility

I've seen four Web sites in the last year disappear from the Google rankings because a developer put a tagline on every page of the site that read:

```
meta name="robots" content="noindex,nofollow"
```

Chances are that the developer put that tag there to prevent search engines from reading the site while she was building it. It's like covering a painting until it's unveiled. Leave that tag in place, though, and search engines ignore not only that page but also every single link on that page — which is like forgetting to remove the cover from the painting before the big show.

In the following sections, I explain how to make sure that you're not actively blocking search engines from crawling pages on your Web site.

Checking your robots.txt file

Go to www.*yoursiteaddress*.com/robots.txt. You might get a Page Not Found error. That's okay for our purposes. You might also see a file that looks like this:

```
User-agent: *
Disallow: /blog.htm
```

It might have other lines in it, too. This file is called the robots.txt file. It tells search engine crawlers, also known as *robots,* what to do when they visit your Web site.

If you want to become a robots.txt geek, visit www.robotstxt.org. You can find out everything you ever wanted to know about guiding robots around your site.

What you *don't* want to see in your robots.txt file is this:

```
Disallow: /
```

This line tells a visiting search engine crawler to ignore *every page* on your Web site. A developer may add this line when he is building the site to prevent search engines from crawling it while it's under construction. If it is left there by accident, your site is invisible to search engines.

If your robots.txt file has any Disallow commands in it, check with your Webmaster or developer to make sure there's a reason. Disallow can be used to hide pages that change a lot, hide duplicate content, or keep search engines out of stuff you just don't want them crawling. Just make sure that you're not accidentally hiding content they *should* see.

Checking for meta robots tags

Using the meta robots tag is another way to hide pages from search engines. Go to any page on your Web site and view the source code. You don't want to see

```
<meta name="robots" content="noindex,nofollow">
```

If the meta robots tag is there, and it contains either noindex or nofollow, or both, remove it. There are valid reasons to use this tag: You might want a search engine to ignore this page because it's a duplicate of another; you might feel the information on the page is inappropriate for search results; or the developer might have hidden the page during development. But you should know those reasons. If you don't, delete the tag.

Do not trust your developer to remove the meta `robots` tag. When they build your site, they're working hard, writing code so fast their fingers smoke. Forgetting to remove that one little line of code is easy when you're facing a tough deadline and still have 4,000 lines of code to write. Remind them!

Eliminating registration forms

Don't put registration forms in front of great content! Visitors often have to complete these forms before they can download some kind of premium content, such as a white paper, or before they can read some articles on a site. Companies put them in place because they want leads — they want contact information for interested potential customers.

If you have any registration forms hiding white papers, newsletters, or other information, remove the forms.

Your salespeople might howl. Your head of marketing might yell. Your CEO might stamp her feet. Remain calm and ask them for a one-month test — and here's why:

You spent two months writing a white paper. You put it up on your Web site, and you want to get something in return. So you add a little form that forces visitors to give you their e-mail address and name before they can read the paper.

That form hurts you in two ways:

✦ It greatly reduces the number of people who will read the content. You wrote that content to spread the word about your company, so you want people to read it.

✦ Search engines can't fill out forms, so they'll never see that great information. Which means, if you wrote a white paper on making a perfect carrot cake, folks searching for "*perfect carrot cake*" will never see your information. Never mind whether they call. They won't even know you're there.

Here are the arguments you may get in favor of keeping the forms, and the reply to each of them:

✦ **"We won't get any leads. People will just read the pages without contacting us."** Actually, by eliminating the form, you expand the number of people reading this information by a factor of ten or more. Because they're already looking for information, they're good prospects. Make sure the phone number and other contact information is in the paper, and they'll be in touch. I've tested this time and again in the last ten years. It never fails.

✦ **"Someone will steal our content."** Welcome to the Internet. That's going to happen regardless. Place a link to your site on every page of the article or paper. That way, any would-be plagiarists create a link back to your site.

✦ **"We need to see a return from this."** You will. Search engines generate the lion's share of traffic online. By removing the registration form, you gain far more leads and customers than you lose.

✦ **"I won't be able to reach people who read the article, because I won't have their contact information."** Actually, you can reach them by posting another great article. And another. You can build your reputation as an authority, reach more readers, and have far more marketing opportunities.

Dump the registration forms.

Eliminating login forms

You've probably already guessed that login forms are bad, too. If you haven't, well, they're bad.

Web site owners might include login forms for the following reasons:

✦ They feel that they need to add value for registered members.

✦ They want to force registration.

✦ They don't want company secrets getting out.

Remove the forms anyway. If you remove your registration forms, you'll remove the need to add value for registered members. Also, hiding a few white papers behind a login doesn't give perceived value to members.

If you really have top-quality training content, tools, or products for sale for which you're offering a preview, then keep the login. Otherwise, you don't need that form.

When it comes to company secrets, you need to think carefully. Is this information really a secret? Or is it just information you'd rather people didn't know? In both cases, a login form won't help you.

If you don't want people to find it, don't put it on the Internet. Someone will find the information, somehow, someday, and republish it to their heart's content.

Dump the login forms.

Providing a Way to Browse

Search engines move from page to page on your Web site by following links. They can't fill out forms, which means they can't use that search box you've got on your site (ironic, huh?). They also can't use a quick navigation box such as the one shown in Figure 3-1.

Figure 3-1: Search engines can't follow form-based navigation.

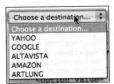

So, if you have any of the following, make sure that there is a way to click through and browse the entire database by using regular HTML links:

✦ A location database that shows a list of local stores or other addresses

✦ A searchable directory of products

✦ An address book for your company's staff

✦ Any other data stored in a database and searched using a form

I use the *mixed greens* example in Chapter 2 of this minibook. Your site sells salads. On your homepage, you have a form that lets folks pick what ingredients they'd like on their salad, and then see which pre-made salads they can order that fit their requirements.

If that form is the only way to find product information, and you don't have any regular links, you're blocking search engines from finding your products. *Remember:* Search engines can't use forms.

To fix the problem, add a link that says Browse All Products. Then let visitors drill down from there by ingredients, categories, or both.

Another example: You have a searchable database of stores offering your products. Visitors type in their address or postal code, and the site displays nearby stores. Great for visitors, but not good for search engines, because they can't use a search form (ironic, isn't it?).

Add a link that lets visitors click instead of search, by choosing their state and then their city.

Search engines can follow that link, find all those pages, and add more content to their index of your site. Make sure that all your content is browseable.

Using Ajax and DHTML

Ajax is a trendy new way to build Web applications. It allows a Web page to load new information without requiring a new page load. That delivers faster, smoother Web interaction and generally makes visitors happy. *DHTML* is a method used to create things like drop-down menus, simple animations, and special effects. You don't need to understand the technologies to understand the risk they pose in SEO.

Ajax loads content by using JavaScript. Search engines can't read JavaScript, so any content you load using Ajax is effectively hidden from the search engine. If you have content you really want a search engine to find, don't deliver it using Ajax.

Ajax is a nifty way to build great Web applications, including shopping carts and search tools. Just be sure you don't hide text content behind an Ajax application.

DHTML also loads content by using JavaScript. Same problem. You can make DHTML menus like the one shown in Figure 3-2 in such a way that a search engine can still find the links.

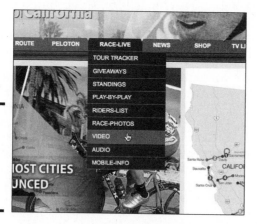

Figure 3-2:
Using DHTML to create a drop-down menu.

Ask your designer to make sure that they build the menus to *degrade gracefully*. A Web page that degrades gracefully provides basic navigation and all content in a sensible way, even if the browser visiting it doesn't support JavaScript or DHTML.

Don't trust your designers, either. They're totally focused on designing something great. You can verify whether your page's DHTML navigation degrades gracefully. Open the page in Firefox. Using the Web Developer Toolbar, disable CSS and JavaScript. If you can still see the links that are in the drop-down menus, then your page is perfect. If you can't, go ask the designer to redo them. Ask nicely. She is probably tired at this point.

Avoiding All-Flash Pages

Adobe Flash is a great way to create beautiful, interactive animations for your Web site. Unfortunately, search engines can't read Flash animations. Remember, search engines visit your Web site as a super-simple Web browser. Flash is a plug-in that you have to add to your Web browser — without it, you can't see any Flash content. Search engines don't have that plug-in built into their software, so they typically can't read any of the content.

Also, Flash compiles links, fonts, and structural information differently than a typical HTML page. So even if a search engine *does* manage to read the content, it may read it as gibberish.

Finally, Flash is often used to load multiple pages of text, videos, and other motion graphics onto a single HTML Web page. That creates the same problems as Ajax, by hiding all but the very first snippet of information from visiting search engines.

Google and Adobe recently announced that they're working together to make Flash more search friendly, but they aren't there yet. Although Google might crawl a Flash animation, it still can't organize and categorize the content in the animation and may ignore much of the text copy in the animation.

You can still use Flash animations. The Portent Interactive homepage, shown in Figure 3-3, is a good example.

You might be using Flash in a way that could hurt your SEO efforts. Pay attention to the following warning signs:

✦ Visitors click from page to page on your Web site from within Flash, without actually going to a new page.

✦ When you view the page using Yellowpipe Lynx Viewer, you see a blank page, or your page doesn't show large amounts of text.

✦ Your designer can't look you in the eye when you ask whether the Web site is SEO ready.

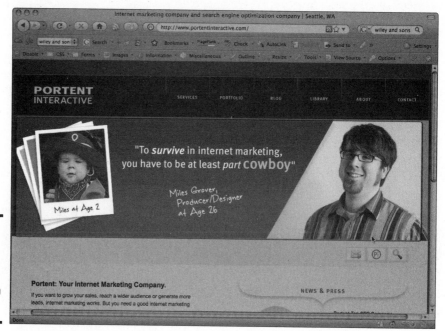

Figure 3-3:
Portent
Interactive
homepage
uses a Flash
animation.

Designers often use Flash because it's the only way they know to get just the right fonts on the Web. However, Cascading Style Sheets (CSS) are now advanced enough to let them get almost the same look and feel with a regular HTML page. See *CSS Web Design For Dummies* by Richard Mansfield (Wiley) for more information.

Avoiding Client-Side Redirects

When search engines first appeared, many Web developers looked for ways to show them super-relevant content. Sometimes, that super-relevant content was just lists of keywords on an otherwise blank page. Developers knew they didn't want visitors to see that gibberish, so they used something called a *client-side redirect* to forward human visitors to a more friendly, comprehensible page.

These redirects used either JavaScript, to reroute a visiting browser, or a meta `refresh` tag, to do the same thing. Because search engines don't support JavaScript, and didn't understand meta `refresh` tags at the time, they stopped dead, while visiting Web browsers redirected human visitors, who didn't even notice the redirect.

Search engines would see the super-relevant gibberish and give the Web site a high ranking. A nice trick, but one that search engines really didn't appreciate.

Search engines want to rank your site based on the same content that human beings see. The redirection tactic, known as *cloaking,* became anathema.

Because of that history, search engines don't like to see any kind of *client-side redirect.* It's still one of the cardinal sins of search engine optimization. Make sure your Web team members know that they shouldn't use either method to reroute people around your Web site.

 If you must redirect visitors from one page to another (say, because you have deleted the old page and now have a new one, or you've moved to a new Web address), use a server-side or 301 redirect. Your Web developer will know how to set this up. If he doesn't, find one who does.

Checking Your Site Using the Web Developer Toolbar

You can find all of the problems I've described so far by using the Web Developer Toolbar. If you don't know what this is, turn to Chapter 1 in this minibook.

In Firefox, go to your Web site. Using the Web Developer Toolbar, disable JavaScript, meta redirects, and CSS. Click around your site. If you can get to every page without clicking on Flash, you're in good shape. Write down the pages you couldn't reach.

Hopefully, you can fix the problem. But if you can't fix it, you can provide an alternate way for search engines to get to those pages, such as a link in the footer of your Web site.

Avoiding Duplicate Content

Nothing hurts a search engine's quest for relevant content as much as finding the exact same words on two different pages. There are three reasons duplication is bad:

+ **Duplication used to be another tactic to fool the search engines.** Webmasters would take one Web site and replicate it across many different domains, linking them all together. That would fool early search engines into seeing many relevant sites interlinked, and therefore cause the engines to artificially inflate rankings. You don't want to risk being associated with this tactic — penalties are rare but severe.

+ **Duplicate content creates confusion.** If a search engine finds the same content on two pages of one site, or two pages on two different sites, it has to basically guess which page should be ranked. Having duplicate words also makes it hard for a search engine to decide *which* page should be ranked.

✦ **Other Webmasters who link to your content might link to either version.** All links to your site are votes. If half of all Webmasters link to one page on your site and the other half link to the duplicate, you've split your vote and lose authority.

Most of the time, duplication is an accident. It's created by inconsistent linking, bad pagination scripts, or other sloppy Web site building practices.

In the following sections, I go over how you can detect duplicate content so that you can avoid it.

Finding duplicate content using Google

You can find duplicate content on and off your Web site by using search engines. To do so, follow these steps:

1. **Go to Google and type** `site:www.`*yoursiteaddress*`.com.`

(Type your actual Web site address.) Doing this shows all pages from your site that are currently in the Google index.

2. **Click through all the result pages.**

If you get to a message that reads `In order to show you the most relevant results, we have omitted some entries very similar. . .`, you have pages that Google considers duplicates.

3. **Click Repeat the Search with the Omitted Results Included.**

The additional pages are your duplicates.

You can also find duplicate content with a more basic search. Copy one sentence from somewhere on your Web site. Make sure it's not a sentence that others are likely to use. On Google, search for that sentence, in quotations marks. An example is shown in Figure 3-4.

Google returns all pages in its index that include those words, in that order. This lets you find other sites that have copied your writing as well as pages on your own Web site that are duplicates of each other.

No matter how hard you try, you can never create a site that is 100 percent duplication free — it's impossible. The important thing is to make sure that you don't duplicate entire pages or sets of pages from one page to the next or, even worse, one Web site to another.

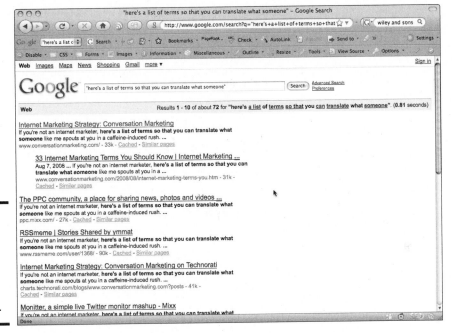

Book II
Chapter 3

Eliminating Search
Engine Roadblocks

Figure 3-4:
A Google
search,
using
quotes
to find
duplicates.

Linking to your homepage the right way

To a search engine, all three of the following URLs are unique pages on the
Internet:

```
www.mydomainname.com
mydomainname.com
www.mydomainname.com/index.html
```

Although they're all pointing at the same page, search engines see each URL
as unique. This is the most common form of duplication on the Web.

If you have your homepage in a file called `index.html` and you link to it
three different ways, search engines will find it at those three locations, with
the exact same content. The search engine then has to figure out which page
is the *real* page and ignore the rest.

In the worst case, other folks randomly link to each of the three addresses.
You do the same on your own Web site. Search engines find all three links,
splitting the relevance votes those links can deliver. Instead of getting three
votes to one page, you get one vote each on three different pages that all
compete with each other for authority in the search engines.

You can use a simple fix. Always link to your homepage exactly like this:

`http://www.`*yoursiteaddress*`.com/`

Exactly like that, except replace *yoursiteaddress* with your actual Web site address.

Then, set up a 301 redirect from *yoursiteaddress*`.com` to `www.`*yoursiteaddress*`.com`. (See the "Using a 301 redirect" section for instructions on how to do this.)

That will reduce link confusion and prevent homepage duplication.

Using consistent URLs

Database-driven sites can often use very complicated page addresses (URLs), such as:

`http://www.mysite.com?pageid=1&content=234&category=thecategory`

That's because database-driven sites use variables like `pageid` and `content` to determine what to display on each page of the site.

These page addresses don't present a search engine roadblock — search engines can handle dynamic addresses. However, if you link to this page like this:

`http://www.mysite.com?pageid=1&content=234&category=thecategory`

and also like this:

`http://www.mysite.com?pageid=1&content=234`

and both links work, guess what? You have duplicate content. This isn't the same as the homepage linking issue discussed in the previous section. Dynamic, database-driven sites can create thousands upon thousands of duplicate pages, because they're generating these links the moment a browser visits the site. They automatically create the page addresses on request. So potentially *any* link format that works could end up being read by a search engine.

Incorrect homepage linking may create two or three duplicate pages. Incorrect database-driven site links can create copies of every single page on your site.

Make sure you link to each page the same way.

Dealing with Broken Links

Broken links stop search engines in their tracks. If a search engine reaches a broken link, it can't find the page you intended (obviously) — but it might also give up on your Web site or reduce the relevance of your site. So you need to find those busted links and fix 'em.

Finding broken links

You can find broken links by using Xenu (on the PC) or Integrity (on the Mac). See Book II, Chapter 1 for instructions.

After you run the tools, put your results in a list.

Then, using your list as a guide, find all the broken links that you can fix and correct errors so that each link is once again functional.

Using a 301 redirect

Sometimes, though, a link is broken because it points to a page that is no longer there. In that case, you can use a *301 redirect.*

301 — the code the server sends to visiting browsers and search engine crawlers — means "This page isn't here any more — go to this other page, instead." When a search engine sees that, it follows the redirect, applies all the link relevance of the old page to the new page, and replaces the old page with the new one.

It's *very* important that you use a 301 — *not* a 302 — redirect. A 302 redirect says, "This page isn't here, but it'll be back soon." If a search engine sees that, it doesn't pass any link relevance and doesn't replace the old page with the new one.

You can set up a 301 redirect on either of the most popular Web servers out there — Internet Information Server (IIS; Microsoft) or Apache. If you don't know how to do this, talk to your Webmaster for instructions. Trust me, though: If you aren't familiar with these Web servers, ask your Webmaster to set these up.

Removing Code Bloat

Search engines like to see a high ratio of content to code: As few lines of code as possible per line of content. There are a few simple ways to remove code bloat and maximize the ratio of code to content.

Coding using standards

If you code using standards XHTML and CSS 2.0, you can automatically minimize code bloat. These standards keep the code that controls how things look in a single, separate CSS file, and put all the content in the XHTML page. This setup maximizes that ratio of content to code.

One critical benefit of coding with standards is that you can stop using HTML tables for layout purposes. Tables are meant to display data, not graphics.

If you want to become more familiar with XHTML, take a look at *HTML, XHTML & CSS For Dummies,* 6th Edition, by Ed Tittel and Jeff Noble (Wiley).

Removing inline JavaScript and CSS

Another code bloat culprit is JavaScript that's inserted right into the page, as shown in Figure 3-5.

That JavaScript code doesn't have to be there. Instead, you can move it into a separate `.js` file and include it by using JavaScript, such as

```
<script language="javascript" type="text/javascript" src="thescript.js">
```

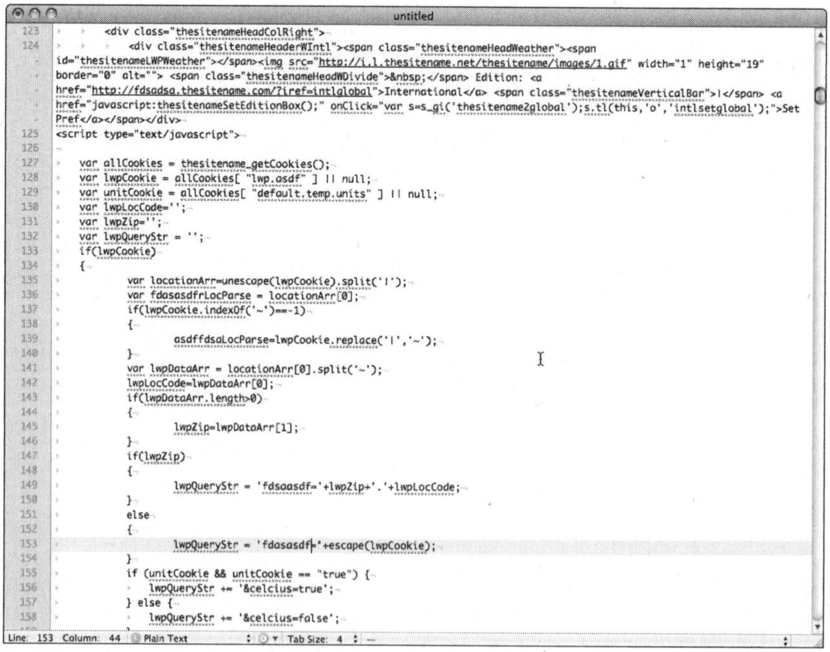

Figure 3-5:
Inline
JavaScript
in the
source of a
page.

You just removed 20 lines of bloat from your page.

You can do the same thing with blocks of CSS information, as shown in Figure 3-6.

Move that CSS code to a separate .css file by using this code:

```
<LINK REL="StyleSheet" HREF="style.css" TYPE="text/css">
```

Congratulations! You just removed another ten lines of code bloat.

Removing inline JavaScript and CSS has an additional benefit. When you put JavaScript and CSS information into separate files, visiting Web browsers will *cache* the information on the users' hard drives. They download the scripts and CSS once and then load it from their own hard drives from then on. That speeds site performance and means you use less bandwidth. Also, by putting these files in one place, you can more easily make site-wide changes and additions.

**Book II
Chapter 3**

**Eliminating Search
Engine Roadblocks**

Figure 3-6:
Remove
inline CSS.
Naughty
developer!

```
33  <link rel="search" type="application/opensearchdescription+xml" href="/tools/search/thesitenamecomvideo.xml"
    title="thesitename.com Video" />
34
35  <script type="text/javascript" language="javascript">
36  pagetypeTS='homepage';
37
38  var overrideVideoAd = '/thesitename_adspaces/2.0/homepage/asdffdsaasdf.ad';
39  </script>
40  <style type="text/css">
41  <!--
42  .thesitenameElexRFoot p
43  {position:relative;}
44  .thesitenameElexRFoot p span
45  {position:absolute;right:0;}
46  .thesitenameElexPrimary
47  {position:relative;}
48  .thesitenameElexPrimary span a
49  {position:absolute;right:0;top:5px;font-size:10px;}
50  * html .thesitenameElexPrimary span a
51  {right:20px;}
52  * html .thesitenameiReportBox .thesitenameiReportMoreMain a
53  {width:302px;}
54  -->
55  </style>
56
57  <script language="JavaScript" type="text/javascript">var thesitenameCurrTime = new Date(1219897360118); var
    thesitenameCurrHour = 0; var thesitenameCurrMin = 22; var thesitenameCurrDay='Thu';</script>
58  <script type="text/javascript">
59      var thesitenameDocDomain = '';
60      if(location.hostname.indexOf('thesitename.com')>0) {thesitenameDocDomain='thesitename.com';}
61      if(location.hostname.indexOf('thesitename.com')>0)
    {if(document.layers){thesitenameDocDomain='thesitename.com:'+location.port;}else{thesitenameDocDomain='thesitename.com';}}
62      if(thesitenameDocDomain) {document.domain = thesitenameDocDomain;}
63      // DO NOT PUT ANYTHING BENEATH THIS!
64  </script>
65
66
67  <script type="text/javascript" src="http://i.cdn.thesitename.com/thesitename/.element/js/2.0/ad_head0.js"></script>
68
69  <script type="text/javascript"
    src="http://i.cdn.thesitename.com/thesitename/thesitename_adspaces/thesitename_adspaces.js"></script>
```

```
Line:  38  Column:  71   Plain Text          Tab Size:  4
```

Chapter 4: Making Search Engines Love Your Site

In This Chapter

✔ **Creating and maintaining a great site structure**

✔ **Building great on-page structure**

✔ **Optimizing for trust**

Search engines want relevance. In this chapter, I discuss how you can make your Web site more attractive to search engines by creating content clusters and using deep links. I also go over how to maintain your Web site after you optimize it.

After you understand how to structure your Web site, you can use a semantic outline to create an appealing structure for each page. I also cover how to optimize your Web site for trustworthiness.

Structuring Your Site for Search Engines and People

Think of your Web site as a pyramid. At the top, you have the homepage. One click away from the homepage, you have the second layer of content. Two clicks away, you have the third layer. Each additional click moves you another layer down in the hierarchy until you can't click any further away from the homepage. That's the bottom layer. Search engines award more relevance more readily to content that is closer to the top of the site pyramid.

You can bring content to the top of the pyramid by

✦ Creating content clusters so that you create individual, high-relevance *hub pages* within the site structure. You can then link to these high-relevance pages from your homepage and move the entire cluster up the hierarchy.

✦ Deep linking to extremely important pages directly from the homepage, which moves this content up the hierarchy.

Creating content clusters

You can use *content clusters,* groupings of related content, to help build relevance. When you link two or more related pages to each other and to a central *hub* or index page from which a visitor can find all of those related pages, you create a cluster of relevant content.

These links lend authority, just as links from other sites lend authority. If you can link ten pages to and from a single hub page, that creates more relevance than if you had a single relevant page all alone. So, there's strength in numbers — the more related pages you can link in clusters, the greater authority you can generate for your site.

Always link like with like. Keeping your content clumped together has two benefits:

✦ **Customers are happier.** Visitors to your site want to find all related content grouped together, like in a library. Content clusters and the hub pages that drive them make it far, far easier for visitors to see those groupings and find what they need.

✦ **Hub pages and clusters make search engines consider your site more relevant.** You concentrate authority from many relevant pages in a single hub page. And, you can link to that hub page from your homepage, which moves the entire cluster of content up in the site hierarchy.

Figure 4-1 shows a structure of a pretty good bicycle shop Web site with average navigation. Visitors can browse the usual sections — Products, About Us, and so on.

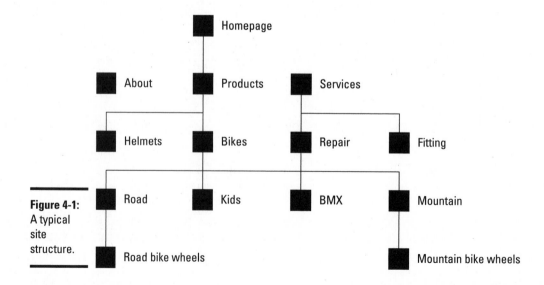

Figure 4-1:
A typical
site
structure.

The problem is that people don't look for "*products*"; they search for "*bicycle repair*" or "*custom built wheels*" or "*kids bikes*". The bike shop Web site shown in Figure 4-2 might offer exactly what's needed, but the information is scattered around the site structure.

For example, if I come to this site looking for a set of mountain bike wheels, in the current site structure, I have to click at least two times just to begin my search. Plus, search engines come to the site and find the only bicycle wheels–related content four clicks from the homepage. That's four levels down the pyramid. To a search engine, that means wheels aren't very important on this Web site. So, the site's going to have a harder time gaining a decent ranking for wheels-related key phrases. Figure 4-2 illustrates the problem.

To fix the problem, you need to create a wheels-related content cluster around a single hub page that lists the links to all of those wheels-related pages. Then all those wheels-related pages need to link back to the hub page, as well. You don't have to reorganize your existing site, or make any massive changes. Instead, follow these steps:

1. **Find all the related pages on your Web site.**

   In the bicycle wheels example, the owner will find all wheels-related content.

2. **Create a single hub page that references all of these other pages.**

   In this case, the owner creates a single page about wheels.

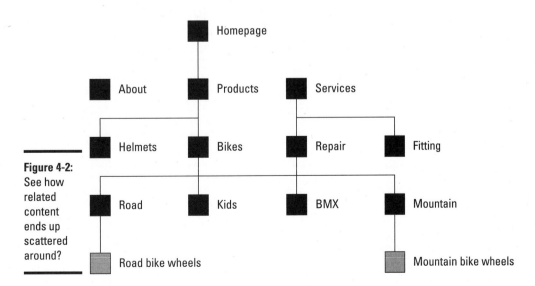

Figure 4-2:
See how related content ends up scattered around?

3. **Link to that hub page from each of those other pages.**

   To see how the bicycle shop owner would do it, see Figure 4-3.

4. **Link to the hub page from the homepage of your Web site, or from another Web page that is no more than two clicks from the homepage.**

   In this case, the owner creates a link from the homepage to the wheels page.

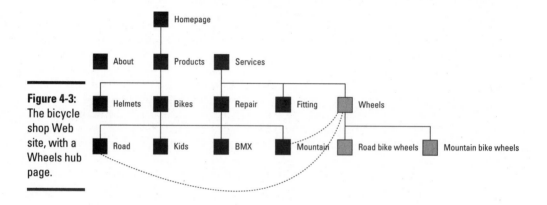

Figure 4-3:
The bicycle shop Web site, with a Wheels hub page.

What did the bike shop owner just accomplish? Three things:

✦ He made it far easier for customers to find information about the wheels he sells. Visitors can now click the Wheels link on the homepage and immediately find what they need, rather than wandering three or more clicks from the homepage to try to find it.

✦ Search engines now see lots of wheels-related content one click from the homepage. The wheels-related content has been moved up in the site hierarchy.

✦ Search engines now see a single Wheels hub page with at least two other relevant pages linking to it. Remember, the links from the other two pages are votes. The new hub page is therefore more relevant to *wheels* and related phrases than the other two pages were when they were separated in the site hierarchy.

A hub page can't just be a list of links. It must have real utility for people as well as search engines.

Here's another example: Groomstand.com competes in a very difficult search engine optimization area — groomsmen gifts. When I first started working on the site, it had hundreds of pages of content about groomsmen gifts, but these pages were spread throughout the site hierarchy. I created a single groomsmen gifts shopping page, with product images and descriptions (shown in Figure 4-4). Then I linked to that page from the homepage of the site, and from every groomsmen gift–related page. That gave visitors a single page to browse when shopping for these types of gifts. It also gave search engines a single page that had tremendous authority for the phrase *"grooms-men gifts"* because hundreds of relevant pages on the site linked back to it. Finally, it placed that authoritative page one click from the homepage, thereby moving the entire content cluster within just one click of the homepage.

You don't need to modify your Web site. You simply link to the same pages in a different way. The original structure can remain in place.

This kind of cluster consolidates related content, which funnels link relevance to a single page — the hub page. It lets you take the *votes* those pages have and point them at that single page, making it a super-relevant centerpiece for your Web site.

I rarely recommend creating a cluster of fewer than five Web pages. Unless you're working on a very noncompetitive key phrase, you can end up too diluted to move up in the rankings because you aren't sending enough votes from other pages on your site to that page.

Creating content clusters around hub pages builds a site structure that's better for search engines and people. It'll help you get higher rankings *and* improve your site's appeal to visitors.

Book II
Chapter 4

Making Search Engines Love Your Site

Figure 4-4:
The Groomstand Groomsmen Gifts hub page.

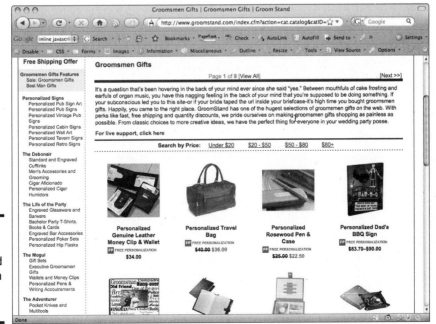

Deep linking for special cases

A *deep link* is a hyperlink that goes directly to a page more than one click from the top of the site pyramid (the homepage). If another Web site links directly to a single product in your store, bypassing the homepage and any category pages, that's a deep link. You can also create deep links within your own site, by linking from your home or top-level pages to individual pages deep within your site's structure.

You'll most often do this to get a little extra boost for a page that's already on its way up in the rankings. Occasionally, a single page on your Web site suddenly shows up on Page 2 of the search engine result pages. Search engines consider it relevant for your target phrase.

If that page is a hub page, pat yourself on the back! If it's not, try this: Add a link to the page that's suddenly on Page 2 from the homepage of your Web site. By doing that, you move that page to the second level of your site's hierarchy, no matter how many clicks from the homepage it originally was.

Search engines attach more importance to content that's closer to the top of your Web site. If you link to this page from the homepage of your site, you move it to the top of the site hierarchy. You get more structural relevance.

Deep linking will rarely take you from no ranking to Page 1, but it can give you a boost, and it can place compelling content where visitors will find it.

Keeping the Structure Clean and Clear

After you do the work to create and improve a search engine optimized site structure, you'll want to maintain it.

That means never moving content around, reinforcing that structure with great link text, using keyword-rich URLs (if possible), and avoiding some common site map issues. This section provides tips for accomplishing all four goals.

Keeping content in one place

Many large sites (particularly publications) create an archive section. After a few months, old content is moved to this section. So a page that used to be

    www.mynewspapersite.com/june/2007/sports

becomes

    www.mynewspapersite.com/archive/sports

Search engines lose track of the content. And when they find it again, it's likely buried in the site hierarchy, five to ten links from the homepage.

The fix is simple: *Don't move your content. Ever.*

Make sure your Web site is set up to accommodate a lot of content without an archive. Pages that stay where they were originally placed get you far more SEO leverage. If you archive content, you're effectively playing now-you-see-it, now-you-don't with the search engines.

I'm not saying you can't use archives. I'm just saying don't move your content to create them. Here's an example: If your business is a newspaper, your site might have thousands of pages of content per year. Your sports section probably has hundreds of pages, too. You can't keep all of that content linked from the sports section homepage. The page will get larger and larger, making it impossible for visitors to find anything.

So, you create an archive hub page, and one sub-hub page for each month of each year. On August 1 (as an example), you remove all links to July content from the sports section page and place them on the July archive sub-page. You didn't actually move the July pages. If they were at `www.newspaper site.com/2008/07/` before, they're still there now. Search engines and visitors can still find those pages at the same address, and you made room for new content and maintained links to the old.

Writing great link text

The text contained in a link provides a hint to both search engines and visitors. A link tells them what they're going to see when they follow the link.

Search engines look at link text to gain insight into the target page's content. If you have a page that talks about bike wheels and a link that reads Click Here, for example, search engines have no idea. Although Click Here is accurate, using something like Click Here for More About Custom Wheels — or even just Custom Wheels — is far better.

Take a link's text and write it on a blank sheet of paper. Read it. Does it identify the page at which it points?

If your Web site has any of the classic links shown in the left column in Table 4-1, consider your options. Use the examples as a guide to come up with something more relevant.

Table 4-1	Link Text Ideas
Original Link	*Better Link Examples*
Products	Business Gifts Computer Software Bicycles
About Us	Best Bicycle Shop Our Software Geeks 5 Years of Dentistry
Services	Internet Marketing Services Dental Services Bicycle Repair

Your Web site designer might say that your site design doesn't have room for long links. However, I think that tweaking the design to allow for a few extra characters is better than having your online store sit, unused, because no one can find it. If you can't change the design, create enhanced links elsewhere on the homepage.

Use great link text and you reinforce your site structure, and the meaning of the content within that structure, to both search engines and people. So, you boost your chances of a high ranking.

Using keyword-rich URLs

Even if you can't get a keyword-rich domain name, you still have control over page addresses. For example, I really want `Seattle-bicycles.com`, but it's not available. So, I go with a less-perfect domain name, `brityup.com`. Hmmm.

I can still add relevance to my page URLs, by naming pages and folders with key phrases: `Brityup.com/bicycle-repairs/` or `Brityup.com/kids-bicycles.html`.

You need to use some common sense when doing this. If you create a stretched page or folder name, such as `bicycle-repairs-in-seattle`, you're trying too hard, and search engines are likely to ignore it. The page and folder names need to make logical sense, be brief, and not read like you're trying to shoehorn in every key phrase you're targeting.

As I write this chapter, it appears that Google is reducing the importance of key phrases in Web page addresses (URLs). I don't recommend turning your site on its head just to make your URLs more keyword-rich. But, if you're adding new pages or creating a new site, consider how you can work keywords into your page addresses.

Stepping away from the site map

You probably have a page on your Web site that lists every section and page — the site map. Search engines tend to ignore pages with more than ten links in the body of the page itself. That prevents Web site owners from creating related links pages with thousands of sites and then using those pages to build links for the sole purpose of improving rankings. Search engines want you to build your site for visitors, not around them. Long link pages are a sure sign you're doing the latter, not the former, so search engines typically ignore pages that have lots of links and no other content.

Step away from the traditional site map! If you must have one, put fewer links and include some descriptive text, too, so you get more of a directory than a site map page. Create a nested structure of pages that let visitors browse through an outline of your site, instead of a single page with dozens or hundreds of links. There's nothing wrong with a site map — it just won't help much with your SEO efforts.

Building a Semantic Outline

After you get a handle on the basics of structuring your Web site for search engines and people, you can create a structure for each individual page. Every page has a *semantic* outline — an outline that explains the meaning and structure of content on the page.

Search engines look for a semantic outline that conforms to XHTML and HTML conventions, starting with the title tag at the top.

The following is a good example:

> Title tag
>
> H1 (level 1 heading)
>
> H2, H3, and so on (lower-level headings)
>
> Paragraph text
>
> Links, captions, and other stuff

Don't underestimate the importance of the other stuff. But any SEO effort must optimize your title tags, heading tags, and paragraph text on every page. If you don't have your target key phrase in the title tag, level 1 heading, and somewhere in your body text, your other efforts won't get you anywhere.

Begin your title tag with your key phrase, like this:

```
<title>Bicycle Repair and Sales - Ian's Bike Shop</title>
```

If you must put your brand name in the title tag, put it last. Ideally, though, leave it out entirely.

Also, make your title tag unique and relevant to each page. Repeating the same title tag throughout your Web site hurts your efforts to build keyword diversity and may get you penalized by the search engines.

Your heading elements should be enclosed in proper heading tags:

```
<h1>Bicycle Repair Services</h1>
```

You can get the same appearance by simply bolding the text and increasing the font size, like this:

```
<span style="font-weight:bold;font-size:18pt;">Bicycle Repair Services</span>
```

But that doesn't help as much. The heading is no longer defined as a heading within the page's semantic outline, so search engines won't accord it the same importance.

Use only one h1 element on a page. If you have additional headings, they should be level 2 and level 3 headings, nested appropriately. Think of your page as a traditional outline. Each outline has one item that states what the entire outline is about — your title and h1 elements. Under that top-level item, you have your first major topic. That's an h2 element. Under that, you might have more subtopics, which would be h3, h4, and deeper elements. Then under each of those, you might have descriptive text. Those are your paragraph elements.

Make sure the ideas put forth in the title tag and heading tags support the paragraph copy, too. For example, loading up the title tags with keywords such as *repair* won't help if the page you're titling talks about buying new bikes. The semantic outline should fit together, just like the outlines you created in elementary school.

A great semantic outline makes sense to people and search engines alike. If you feel like you're twisting your writing to create the outline, reconsider what you're doing.

Optimizing for Trust

Not many people know this, but search engines are now including trust in their ranking algorithms. This new concept, called TrustRank, is how search engines separate legitimate Web pages from spam. The search engines analyze pages and links for factors that make the pages seem more or less trustworthy, such as

+ Is the site a known distributor of illicit software or viruses?

+ Is the site supported by a legitimate business enterprise?

+ How long has the site been in operation?

Luckily, optimizing for trust is fairly simple. Do the following:

+ **Use an old domain name.** After you establish a Web address, keep it. If you must move, use 301 redirects to pass as much of the trust along as possible. (Read about 301 redirects in Chapter 3 of this minibook.)

+ **Get your site evaluated by one of the security services, such as ScanAlert.** Then put their *sticker* on your site. Search engines actually do look for this. SEO geeks have spent hours going over patent applications, notes from search engineers, and all sorts of obscure tests. After a lot of debate, it's now consensus that security stickers help, if they're legitimate.

+ **Put your physical address and phone number on every page of your site.**

+ **Take all reasonable security precautions.** If your site is ever attacked and exploited to distribute a virus or steal data, search engines may flag it and move you down in the rankings, or show a dire warning, such as the one shown in Figure 4-5.

+ **Don't link to sites you know to be borderline scams or that may have a low TrustRank.** You can check sites' TrustRank at `www.trustrank.org`. Also, have a look at the SEOmoz nifty Trifecta Tool at `www.seomoz.org/trifecta`. You can also join the U.S. National Better Business Bureau and apply for accreditation. After you receive it, you can place the official BBB Accredited Business seal on your site, too.

Book II
Chapter 4

Making Search
Engines Love
Your Site

The site you are trying to visit has been identified as a forgery, intended to trick you into disclosing financial, personal or other sensitive information.

Suggestions:

- Return to the previous page and pick another result.
- Try another search to find what you're looking for.

Or you can continue to http://adwords.google.com.selectlogin.cn at your own risk.

If you are the owner of this web site, you can request a review of your site using Google's Webmasters Tools.

Advisory provided by Google

Figure 4-5: Danger! This page may be bad for you.

TrustRank is even harder to measure and quantify than PageRank. It's newer, the search engines have kept their measurement methods far more secret, and the definition of trust is far harder to define, anyway — but it's also easier to maintain. Behave yourself, don't cheat (by buying or otherwise spamming links), and don't link to other folks who might be cheating.

Chapter 5: Understanding Blended Search

In This Chapter

✔ **Knowing what gets blended**

✔ **Optimizing products**

✔ **Optimizing news**

✔ **Optimizing images**

✔ **Optimizing video**

✔ **Optimizing for local search**

*I*n May of 2007, Google released a new version of its search results dubbed *universal search*. Other search engines followed suit. The SEO industry calls it *blended search*.

Blended search mixes relevant news, image, video, and other content right into the traditional Web search results on a search result page.

If a search engine decides that some other type of content (a photograph, for example) is more relevant than the top ten Web search results, then the search engine replaces one of those Web search results with the image.

Blended search presents more opportunities for you to grab real estate on the first page of search engine results. Every image, video, and press release you do, as well as your physical location, give you a shot at a Top 10 ranking.

In this chapter, I give you the factors search engines appear to use to rank blended content, and explain why they really aren't that different from the normal Web content ranking factors.

As with many SEO topics, I could write an entire book on blended search optimization. This chapter is intended to give you the basics. If you want to get more elaborate, I strongly suggest talking to a professional search marketer.

Optimizing Products

Product pages on your Web site end up in the regular search rankings. But you have a second way to get them into the search engines — the product feed. A *product feed* is basically a spreadsheet of all of the products in your store. You give that spreadsheet to the search engines, and they use it to create an index of your products. Products submitted through a feed show up in the blended search results, as shown in Figure 5-1.

Figure 5-1:
Blended results for product listings.

Google, Yahoo!, and Live Search all provide ways for you to submit a list of products and prices. You can do so for free at `www.google.com/base` and `www.productupload.live.com`; `www.searchmarketing.yahoo.com/shopsb` charges you by the click.

Make the items in your product feed *more relevant* than the regular Web search items that a major search engine would show on its first page. That's the only way your product will show up.

Here are five ways to optimize your product feed:

✦ **Submit a complete feed.** Although it might be tempting to submit a product name and price and be done with it, you should carefully fill in all the details. That way, if someone searches for *"700c bicycle tire"*, he'll find you because you completed the Size field.

✦ **Submit individual products manually.** You can actually submit products one at a time, using a Web form instead of a spreadsheet. I know, this sounds horrible. But if you manually edit your feed, you can optimize product descriptions and other fields for best impact.

✦ **Include images.** A listing with an image draws far more clicks than a listing without.

✦ **Update your feed.** If you're selling products, update your feed to match your inventory cycle. You don't want out-of-date pricing, products you no longer sell, or incorrect information on the Internet.

✦ **Use custom fields.** For GoogleBase, add custom fields that make sense. For example, if you're selling shoes, you might add a custom field called Stars and list the stars currently wearing those shoes. If folks search for *"shoes that Suzy Starlet wore"* and your site shows up, they'll buy.

Optimizing News

Google, Yahoo!, and Live also blend news headlines into their search results now. Figure 5-2 shows news results blended right into a search result.

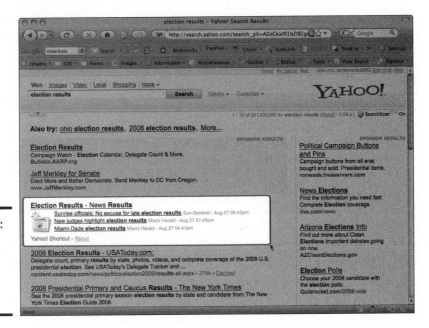

Figure 5-2: Blended news search results on Yahoo!

If you send out a press release, try the following tips to get into the blended search results:

✦ **Optimize your press release.** Do all the stuff in this book! Making your press release relevant by including your target phrase in the headline, paragraphs, and other elements will definitely help.

✦ **Avoid using sales language, such as *best deal* or *fastest service*.** Press releases should be informative, not salesy. Don't write a marketing piece.

✦ **Use a newswire.** Unless you're going to go through the pain of getting your Web site's press area accepted into the news sections of all three major search engines, you want to submit your press release by using one of the Web-savvy newswires, such as PRWeb.

Optimizing Images

Getting an image included in a search result can generate a lot of traffic. I've seen clients increase traffic by as much as 200 percent in a single day because an image from their Web site landed on the front page of Google, Yahoo!, or Live Search.

Images typically show up at the top of the search result, as shown in Figure 5-3.

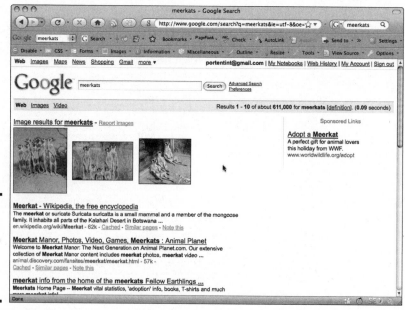

Figure 5-3: Images blended into a normal search result.

The image rankings aren't as competitive as the traditional Web rankings for most key phrases, so they might offer you an opportunity to grab a good position for phrases that are otherwise out of reach.

However, search engines can't actually *see* images. So they use a number of cues to determine image relevance. Use the following tips to optimize images:

+ **Use original images.** If you lift an image from another Web site, a newspaper, or something else, you have little chance of getting ranked. You may, however, get sued.

+ **Use high-quality images.** You want images that are sharp and easy to interpret.

+ **Optimize the content around the image.** If you have a picture of a carrot on a page, make sure the page is well optimized for *carrot,* too. Put a text caption under the image that has the word *carrot* in it, too.

+ **Use the correct formats.** Photographs should be in JPG, not GIF, format. GIF allows only 256 colors. JPG allows millions and is a more logical choice for a photograph.

+ **Make images accessible.** Put photographs in a separate images folder from the graphics that comprise your Web site layout. Make sure that the folder isn't disallowed in your `robots.txt` file.

+ **Consider hosting your image on a third-party service, such as Flickr.** If your image gets a lot of views and/or comments, you get an additional rankings boost. You'll sacrifice direct traffic and links to your site, though, so you need to weigh the benefit of a huge audience on a site such as Flickr against link building.

+ **Give the image a keyword-rich name.** If you name an image `dpc12312432.jpg`, it's hard for a search engine to determine relevance. If, on the other hand, you name the image `carrot.jpg`, a search engine can immediately determine what it's crawling.

Optimizing Video

Video and images in blended search are similar in the following ways:

+ File names must contain relevant terms. If the file name explains the meaning of the video — `bicycle-wheels-sale.mov`, for example — you'll get a good ranking.

+ Overall page relevance helps determine video relevance.

+ Originality, quality, and format can all make a difference.

A video search result can be just as compelling. See Figure 5-4 for an example.

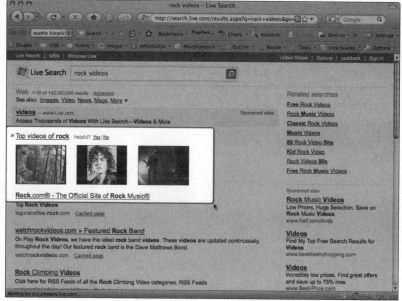

Figure 5-4:
Video
blended
search
result on
Live Search.

In addition to these factors, to optimize video you need to

✦ **Make sure you place the video on your Web site and let your current customers or readers know it's there.** Number of views and *velocity* (how many views you get in how short a time) can boost you in the rankings, particularly if your video is hosted on a service, such as YouTube.

✦ **Consider putting all your videos in an RSS feed.** If you aren't sure what an RSS feed is, have a look at *Syndicating Sites with RSS Feeds For Dummies* by Ellen Finkelstein (Wiley). The RSS feed can give a search engine *hooks* to find all of your videos.

✦ **Be organized.** And even more so with video than with images because videos typically show on pages with little or no text. Thus, organization might be the only clue a search engine has as to the meaning of the video. Put all your videos in a single directory. Create a set of pages, one video per page, that lets search engines find all the content.

✦ **Weigh the benefit of putting a video on a site such as YouTube, and potentially getting a lot of views in a short time, against getting the links and direct traffic from having that video on your Web site.**

✦ **Give your videos a relevant file name and surround them with relevant content.**

TIP

If you upload a video using a service such as YouTube, be sure to have lots of friends in your network first. Read Book VII for more information. More friends equals more views in less time, and this can mean a front-page ranking.

Optimizing for Local Search

If you're a local business, a top local search listing can drive customers faster than any other online marketing technique. A top ranking such as the one shown in Figure 5-5 puts you at the very top of the search results.

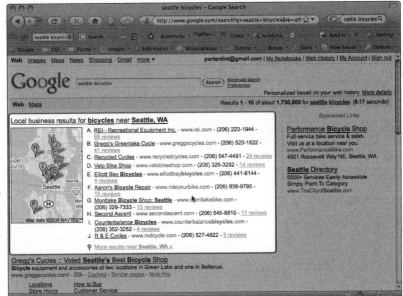

Figure 5-5:
A top local listing might mean a top search listing.

Local search optimization isn't difficult. But it *does* require a very sustained effort, around three different factors:

✦ Listings, on the local search engines and the directory sites they reference

✦ Reviews and bookmarks on those same sites

✦ Local data on your Web site

Optimizing your local search listings

The first step in local search optimization is making sure that your business is in each major search engine's local search directory. To do so, follow these steps:

1. Search for your business on Google Local, Yahoo!, and Live Search.

2. Make sure you fill out all fields requested by the search engine, including the description and hours.

3. Submit your Web site to Yelp.com (`www.yelp.com`), Superpages.com (`www.superpages.com`), Yellowpages.com (`www.yellowpages.com`), and CitySearch.com (`www.citysearch.com`).

   The major search engines crawl these sites to determine relevance and location. Note that there are other sites, too. These basics will get you started.

4. Make sure that your business is assigned to the correct category in the local listings.

Getting reviews and bookmarks

Now that you have the listings, it's time to get some attention. This requires the most sustained effort on your part, because you have to get past customers to review your business. Search engines look at the quantity of reviews and bookmarks as one indicator of relevance.

✦ Send a polite note to all of your customers or provide them with a coupon or other incentive, inviting them to review your business at Google, Yahoo! or Live Local. The more reviews you get (even if they're not all good), the more easily you'll move up in the local rankings.

✦ Provide an easy way for folks to bookmark your location on the mapping service of their choice. More bookmarks or saved locations on Google, Yahoo!, or Live Local mean a higher ranking, too. You can link to your local listing and let your visitors take it from there. See Figure 5-6 for an example.

Optimizing your site for local search

With all of these steps, it's easy to forget that you can optimize your own site, too. Use the following tips to optimize your Web site for local search:

✦ **Make sure your physical address is on every page of your Web site.**

✦ **Put your metro area location in a few title tags on your Web site.**

✦ **Have a very good contact page, with directions.**

✦ **Consider geotagging your Web site.** There's no direct evidence this impacts rankings yet, but it probably will soon. You'll need to read up on the geotagging of meta tags, which at the time of this writing still isn't a finalized standard.

✦ **Get links from other local sites.** Join your local Chamber of Commerce, for example, and get a link from its Web site.

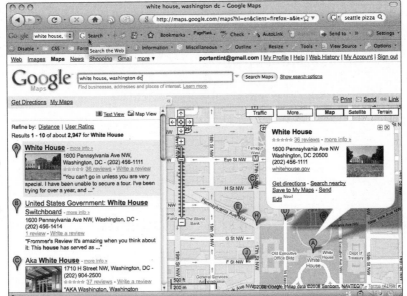

Figure 5-6:
A link to this Google page lets visitors easily bookmark your location.

Chapter 6: Writing Great Copy for Search Engines (And Readers!)

In This Chapter

✔ Writing online copy that attracts customers, boosts sales, and helps grow your business

✔ Writing title tags and headings (that people will click)

✔ Setting a writing routine

✔ Finding writing help

Like it or not, search engines care about words, so you're going to have to put your hands on a keyboard and write some stuff about your company or hire someone else to do it.

Keep the following in mind:

✦ Writing great copy takes time and practice, not necessarily natural talent.

✦ Hiring someone else to write is an option, but it's going to cost you. If you pay $5 for a page of copy, it will read like you paid $5 for it — lousy.

✦ Setting a routine makes writing easier.

In this chapter, I give you some tips for writing great copy that both search engines and your visitors will like.

Writing Online Copy

You haven't even started writing yet, but I bet the two thoughts going through your mind are

> "I don't have anything to write about!"

and

> "How many times should I repeat a key phrase on a page?"

Brainstorming tips

Can't think of anything to write? Try these five tips:

- Think about what your customers most often ask and write detailed answers to each of those questions. One well-written page can reduce calls and questions and make your customers happier. Plus, if that's the question they're asking, chances are they're typing it into the search engines, too.

- Write down the most ridiculous claim your competitors make. Then answer it, professionally and succinctly, but allow just a little of your passion to creep in. Those "Rank #1 on Google for $99!" e-mails provide me with endless fodder.

- Go to your favorite search engine. Search for the latest news about your industry or product. If something in there gets you riled up, seems really clever, or otherwise grabs your interest, write down your thoughts.

- Look at every product or service you offer. If you can break them up into smaller sub-products or services, do it, and write about each of those. For example, bicycle repair can be broken up into tune ups, wheel truing, frame repair, and painting. Accounting can be divided into tax, bookkeeping, and cash flow.

- Don't worry about writing for the Web the right way. Get your thoughts written down first. Then you can tweak the copy for best impact. If you try to put together the perfect sentence before you write down that great idea, you might forget the idea before you hit the first key. Plus, the first way you write something is often the best.

After it's all written down, it's time to start editing. Start by removing so-called "stop" or "filter" words. (See the "Avoiding stop and filter words" section.)

You spend every day immersed in your business, so it might feel routine to you, but for your customers it's a whole new world. You have a wealth of knowledge and information they've never seen or have forgotten. If you can clearly communicate that to them, you'll attract loyal customers. Even better, you'll demonstrate relevance and move up in the search rankings, too.

As for the second question: The maddening answer, borrowed a bit from Mozart, is "Precisely as many times as necessary. No more, no less." Search engines won't tell you "make sure you use 2 percent keyword density!" Remember that they want relevance — not keyword density.

Avoiding stop and filter words

Stop words are words that search engines typically ignore in your search, including those shown in the following list.

a	in	where
about	is	who
an	it	will
are	la	with
as	of	www
at	on	
be	or	
by	that	
com	the	
de	this	
en	to	
for	und	
from	was	
how	what	
I	when	

Although stop words don't directly hurt your attempts to get a high ranking, they don't help either.

> "Our bicycles are really great, and anyone who comes here will wonder why they didn't before."

Becomes:

> "Our bicycles really great anyone comes here wonder why they didn't before."

So, loading up on stop words can have unexpected results. Try to minimize stop words. It's good technique, too. Stop words tend to slow a reader's progress as they try to learn what it is you're telling them. Fewer stop words means clearer writing.

Filter words are those that may actually cause a search engine to ignore other content on the page. No one's proven that search engines actually penalize sites for using specific terms, but you can safely assume that words commonly associated with some industries, such as adult entertainment, may hurt your rankings.

You're giggling right now, I know. What are the odds you'd end up writing naughty language on your Web site?

It's easier than you think. Take this sentence for example:

"John was an adult who had a date with destiny."

Adult and date, in close proximity, might just trigger some search filters.

And try this example:

"The Bushtit is a small bird."

Quit snickering — it's a real animal. I had a client once who couldn't seem to move up the search rankings. His Web site was likely getting dinged for having this word on the page. The problem went away as search engines matured and got better at determining the true meaning of words, but it's a great example of accidental filter words.

There are also stop *characters* that can confuse a search engine while it tries to crawl your Web site. Any special character — such as an ampersand (&) or a copyright or bullet symbol should be replaced with an *entity*. An entity is a computer-friendly definition of a special character. The entity for &, for example, is *&*. Check with your developer and make sure he takes care of that. He'll know what an entity is — and if he doesn't, you should find another developer.

Keeping it simple

Online more than anywhere else, simple writing is best. People still have a tough time reading text on a screen. Most Internet users tend to scan for answers and keywords before they read.

So always look at how you can shorten what you've written. Here are a few tips and examples:

+ **Pare down the number of words whenever possible.** "Then things went from bad to worse" can just as easily be "Things got a lot worse."

+ **Avoid slang and colloquialisms.** "They couldn't see the forest for the trees" might also be "They were stuck on the details."

+ **More syllables won't make you sound smarter — folks will just skip the sentence altogether.** "Our expertise is unrivaled in our industry" could read "We're the best."

Using active voice

Many of us were taught to write in the passive voice, like this.

It's better to say, "Many of us learned to use passive voice."

See the difference? I turned "were taught" into "learned." Instead of some mysterious third party out there who taught us, I got straight to the point. Active voice is always clearer, easier to read, and often far easier to optimize for a search engine.

Here are a few examples:

✦ **Okay:** "Bicycles are repaired by our mechanics" is fine, but it's slow, wordy, and doesn't include *bicycle repair,* which is the real target phrase.

✦ **Better:** Instead, try, "Our mechanics perform top-notch bicycle repair." It's not actually a shorter sentence, but it reads better *and* it includes your target phrase.

✦ **Okay:** "Mixed green salads are good for you!" That reads pretty well, but it misses a few opportunities to deliver more marketing punch, and if your target phrase was *mixed greens health benefits,* you missed that opportunity, too.

✦ **Better:** You can use active voice and write, "You already know mixed greens' health benefits."

✦ **Okay:** "We are Frank's favorite CPA firm."

✦ **Better:** "Frank says, 'I love this CPA firm!'" No big difference, SEO-wise, but it's a shorter sentence and makes Frank the speaker — the words are coming directly from him because active voice is used.

Getting to the point

Standard college and primary school writing style tells you to write as shown in the chart in Figure 6-1.

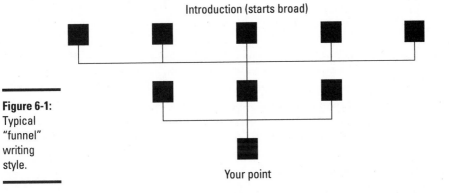

Introduction (starts broad)

Figure 6-1:
Typical
"funnel"
writing
style.

Your point

However, search engines lend more weight to text at the top of the page, not at the bottom. If your point is all the way at the bottom of the page, two things happen:

✦ **Search engines accord it less relevance.** If your point includes your target phrase, you want to move it up.

✦ **Readers are likely to give up before they get all the way down the page.** Your point is often your value proposition. You want to say that first.

So learn to make your point and state your value proposition at the very top of the page, not at the bottom. Compare these two brief product descriptions:

Our bicycle tires are made by hand. They also feature a Kevlar belt. They use our patented long-wear formula. And they are rigorously tested by our laboratory. So they'll remain flat-proof for years.

They're flat-proof? Why didn't you tell me that in the first place! Try this instead:

Our flat-proof bicycle tires feature a Kevlar belt. They're hand-made and rigorously tested by our manufacturing team. With our patented long-wear formula, they'll remain flat-proof for years!

Much better. Not only did this version tell me that these are flat-proof bicycle tires, it also worked the value proposition right into the first sentence, so search engines will give this page high relevance for the phrase "*flat-proof bicycle tires*".

Writing scannable copy

I can take the previous example one better, though, by making it more scannable. Remember, online readers tend to scan, not read. So, breaking your most important points into separate bullets and short, punchy paragraphs can help your readers. Using this format also provides a structure search engines can more easily filter for the most important points.

You can revise the last example from the preceding section this way:

Our flat-proof bicycle tires

- *Feature a Kevlar belt*

- *Are hand-made*

- *Are rigorously tested*

- *Will remain flat-proof for years, thanks to our long-wear formula*

You can see how much easier it is for a reader to pull out the important features of this product.

Finding the right keyword density

I can bet that you're now grinding your teeth in frustration, still wondering just how many times you should use a keyword.

I can't give you a solid answer, but here are some tips that should help:

1. **Write your copy *first*, without considering your key phrase at all.**

2. **Look at your competitors' pages.**

   How many words do they have on a page? How many times do they repeat their target phrases?

3. **Review what you wrote.**

   Try to include ten percent more copy than did your competitor.

4. **Use the same keyword density that they did, with a maximum density of three to four percent.**

   Any more than that sounds ridiculous. Look for places where you used synonyms you can easily replace with your target phrase.

Writing a Great Title Tag

Writing a title tag involves more than putting your keywords first. Search engines display the keyword tag at the top of each item in the search engine result pages (SERPs). Figure 6-2 shows an example:

A well-written title tag might increase the odds that a searching customer will click your listing. If you balance the need for SEO with the need for an impactful title tag, you generally get more clicks *and* a higher ranking.

Getting past your brand

First, *don't put your brand first.* I've said this before, and it bears repeating. Your brand will be front-and-center when customers land on your Web site. In the meantime, focus on getting a high ranking and a click.

Here's an example:

```
<title>Harrison's Bikes: Seattle Bicycle Repair</title>
```

The brand went first. That placement reduces the relevance of the tag for *Seattle bicycle repair* because search engines more heavily weight the first words. Plus, readers won't see the benefit in clicking unless they read the whole title tag. Why make them work for it? Instead:

```
<title>Seattle Bicycle Repair: Harrison's Bikes</title>
```

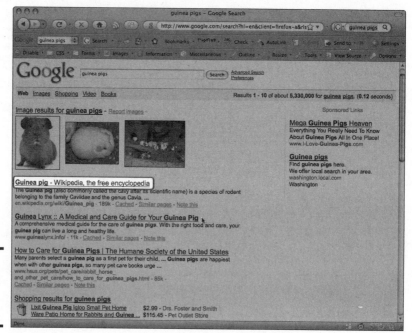

Figure 6-2:
The title tag in a SERPs listing.

The key phrase is first. Even better:

```
<title>Seattle Bicycle Repair and Sales</title>
```

It leaves out the brand in favor of another keyword.

You can make a title tag as long as you want, but keep in mind that search engines ignore anything longer than 65 characters. The phrase at the end won't affect relevance as much as the one at the beginning.

Avoiding keyword stuffing

Try not to put a given keyword into a `title` tag more than once. Twice if absolutely necessary. Search engines have long hated `title` tags like this:

```
<title>Bicycles and Bicycle Repair with Bicycle Sales at
    Harrison's Bicycles</title>
```

Plus, doing so is a terrible way to introduce customers to your company — the writing is poor and is hard to read.

Telling your story

Your `title` tag may well be the very first thing your customers see. It should say something important about you. If there's something that sets you or your business apart — an award, a unique service, or something else — try to work it into the tag:

```
<title>Bicycle Repair and Sales - Rated Seattle's Number 1
    Bike Shop: Harrison's Bicycles</title>
```

Note that this `title` tag doesn't repeat any keywords. To a search engine, *bicycle* and *bicycles* are different words.

This `title` tag maximizes the chances that a customer will click. Rated No.1? Sign me up!

Making it readable

After all this work, it pays to re-read the `title` tag and make sure it makes sense.

Like link text, a `title` tag should make sense all on its own. It needs to be totally self contained. So,

```
<title>Bicycle Repair and Sales</title>
```

is okay, but it's missing important information, such as location. The tag

```
<title>Seattle Bicycle Repair and Sales</title>
```

is far better. Now I know it's in Seattle. Plus, search engines award greater relevance in local searches because I added *Seattle* to the title tag.

If you have a database-driven site and are editing your title tag using a maintenance or administrator control panel, you probably won't have to enter the `<title>` and `</title>` tags. The content management system will do that for you.

Make sure your `title` tag can stand on its own. It'll probably have to at some point. If folks create a link to your site, they might use the `title` tag as the link text. If your `title` tag clearly defines the page it titles, then the link will clearly describe the page to which it points.

If you have a database-driven site, such as an online store or a site powered by a content management system, make sure you can edit your `title` tags! Every database-driven site can and should do this. If it doesn't, have a developer change it. It's worth the effort. Without editable `title` tags, your site doesn't have a prayer in the rankings.

Writing a Great Description Tag

So far, I've largely ignored the meta description tag. That's because it doesn't directly affect ranking.

But a well-written description tag *can* cause more searchers to click through to your Web site. Search engines often use the description tag as the *snippet* in a search listing, as shown in Figure 6-3.

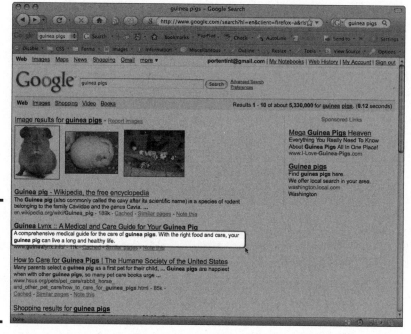

Figure 6-3: A search snippet using a meta description tag.

So, you can edit the description tag and optimize it for your customers.

If you don't have a description tag, search engines will grab other text from your Web page. There's no easy way to predict what search engines will grab, either, and it can lead to meaningless search listing snippets. Use a description tag whenever possible.

Here's an example, which also shows the code for a description tag:

```
<meta name="description" content="Harrison's Bike Shop
    is located in Seattle's Alki neighborhood. Our award-
    winning bicycle repair mechanics can fix any problem!
    In business since 1902. Open 7 days a week. Call us at
    222.333.4444."/>
```

Why did I bother inserting `bicycle repair` in front of `mechanics`? It seems wordy, but search engines boldface the words you search for in the snippet, as shown in Figure 6-4. That will increase the chances of a click.

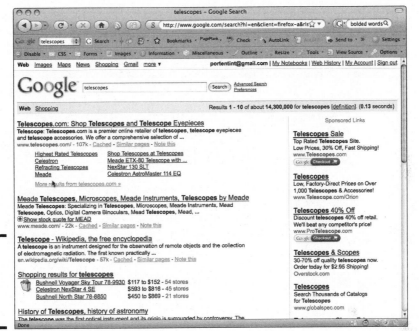

Figure 6-4: Bold keywords in a search result.

**Book II
Chapter 6**

**Writing Great Copy
for Search Engines**

Notice how I put a call to action — `Call us` — and the phone number at the end of the description. Sometimes, customers call you without even visiting your Web site. That's even better.

If your call to action is `Order online` or `Call for more information`, put that in your description tag, too. If your competitors' Web sites *don't* say "order online" and you do, you just gained an advantage.

If you have a database-driven site, such as an online store or a site powered by a content management system, make sure you can edit your description tags, too! Modify them as you learn what attracts more clicks.

Connecting Headlines to Copy

The heading is the first text your customers see. Like your `title` tag, it needs to stand on its own and contain your key phrase.

Unlike your `title` tag, though, it should directly support the paragraph beneath it. The `title` tag can be relevant to the entire page without referring to the first paragraph on that page. But even a level 1 heading needs to have some connection with the first paragraph of copy.

If your writing gets to the point (see the "Getting to the point" section), this shouldn't be a problem. Your point should be clear in the paragraph immediately following the headline.

Here's an example: Assume the first paragraph on the page discusses the award-winning service of Harrison's Bikes. The heading could be

```
<h1>Award-Winning Seattle Bicycle Repair</h1>
```

That ties into the paragraph copy, connects to the `title` tag, and includes the target key phrase *"Seattle bicycle repair"*.

Writing a great heading is an art all its own. The best authorities on the subject are David Ogilvy and Brian Clark of Copyblogger. You can get *Ogilvy on Advertising* by David Ogilvy at any bookstore. You can read Brian's great tutorials on writing great headlines at `www.copyblogger.com`.

Avoiding a Verbal Meltdown

Title tags, headings, descriptions, keyword density . . . it's easy to forget about the writing.

Avoid a verbal meltdown like this:

> "Bicycle repair at our Seattle bicycle shop is award-winning. Our bicycle repair experts will repair your bicycle 7 days a week. . . ."

Ultimately, you're writing for your customers. Yes, keywords matter. Yes, you want that top ranking. However, that's meaningless if your customers click the Back button after ten seconds on your Web page.

Setting a Writing Routine

One other way to avoid a verbal meltdown is to set a routine. I write about my company three times a week for 30 minutes. I don't worry too much about *what* I'm writing. I just spend 30 minutes writing down what comes to mind.

Two-thirds of the time, I can edit that copy and then put it right up on my site. The other one-third of the time, I end up with a nice list of ideas I can use later.

Follow these steps to set your writing routine:

1. **Find at least 30 minutes a week and put it into your calendar.**

   This time is absolutely sacred. Don't surrender it to meetings, television, or anything else.

2. **Get an egg timer or some other way to keep time.**

3. **Go someplace quiet, if you can, or put on headphones to block out distractions.**

4. **Set the timer.**

5. **Write for 30 minutes straight.**

   Do not stop to ponder sentences or decide whether you should use *toward* or *towards*. Just write, write, write. The idea is to get a complete brain dump.

6. **At the end of the 30 minutes, stop.**

7. **Later that day or the next, review what you wrote.**

It might be ready to post to your Web site or blog. If it is, pass it to a friend for a quick read. He might catch typos you missed. (Typos matter — search for *philsophy* online, and you'll see all the sites that misspelled *philosophy*. Those sites can't gain a high ranking for the correct spelling.)

If it's not ready to post, keep it anyway. Fiddle with it. See whether you can build on one or two paragraphs to create a complete page.

Brainstorming before you write each week is helpful. See the "Brainstorming tips" sidebar earlier in this chapter.

Hiring Writing Help

Business owners rank the fear of writing slightly below the fear of public speaking. And they fear both more than death.

If you just can't bear the thought of having to write your own Web site copy, do the brainstorming I describe at the beginning of this chapter. Then go to a site such as Elance (`www.elance.com`) and hire a writer to create your content. Book I, Chapter 7 covers Elance and other ways to find help in more detail.

Just realize you'll have to have someone — preferably an SEO pro — optimize that copy and create the title and description meta tags.

Or, hire an SEO copywriter. Doing so might cost more, but you get a more polished product.

Chapter 7: Building Link Love

In This Chapter

✓ Discovering why links matter

✓ Encouraging links

✓ Getting the easy links

✓ Staying out of trouble

✓ Creating link bait

*L*ink building — getting other sites to link to yours — is critical to your search engine optimization efforts. However, many people ignore the rest of SEO and focus entirely on acquiring links. Link building is not the only component, and ignoring all the other stuff I discuss in this minibook, such as great copy, great code, and a well-structured site, in favor of link building is a mistake.

In this chapter, I explain why links matter, how search engines weigh them, the factors for quality links, and several tactics for building links to your site.

This chapter is very technical and detailed, so keep some perspective. I'm not suggesting that you spend the next two years writing link bait. I suggest that you do everything up to and including the suggestions in the "Leveraging Your Partners for Links" section. For everything after that section, read and learn. If you have time and a big budget, go for it. If you don't, take it as advice in case you're ever bedridden for a month with nothing to do but putter with your Web site.

Understanding Link Votes

To a search engine, every page on the Internet has a certain number of votes it can hand out to other pages through links. The exact number of votes each page has differs, depending on the site's overall SEO strength.

This voting concept first hit the search world in 1998, when Google launched the beta version of its now-dominant search engine. They called the voting system PageRank.

To make things even more complicated, every vote can be worth more or less to your SEO efforts depending on the relevance of the linking Web site, the text in the link, and dozens of other factors that search engines won't divulge (but users can try to guess).

Link *velocity* — the rate at which your site acquires new links — matters, too. If you get 2,000 links overnight and then nothing, that likely won't help as much as getting 10 new links per day for 200 days.

So, every link you get is a vote. Each vote is weighed by search engines according to relevance and other factors.

A lot of links is better. And links, like everything else, start with content.

Links that don't count

A link helps you only if it links directly to your Web site. If a link first goes to some type of ad tracking server and then to your site, the search engines won't consider it a vote.

To check whether a link is direct, follow these steps:

1. **Navigate to the linking page and roll your cursor over the link.**

2. **Look in your browser status bar and see where the link points.**

    If it shows your page address, as in Figure 7-1, it's a vote. If it shows a redirection address or simply Done, as in Figure 7-2, it's not a vote.

Figure 7-1:
This link is a vote.

Figure 7-2:
This link is not a vote.

Some Webmasters get tricky and use JavaScript to make it *look* like a link is a vote. Don't worry about it — they're in the minority, and the effort to find those fake votes probably isn't worth it.

Understanding nofollow

Another form of links that don't count are `nofollow` links. The major search engines now recognize a special command that Webmasters can add to any link on their Web site:

```
<a href=http://www.harrisonsbikes.com rel="nofollow">
```

That `rel=nofollow` command tells a visiting search engine to ignore that link. SEO geeks refer to that link as *nofollowed*.

Clearly, nofollowed links aren't worth much. You can easily detect them by using SeoQuake, though. In SeoQuake, nofollowed links have a line through them, as shown in Figure 7-3.

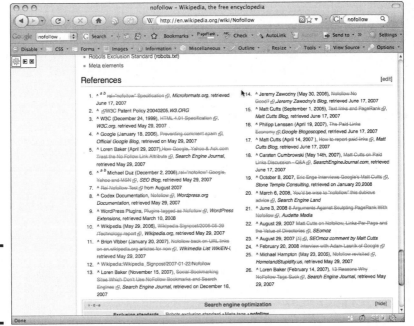

**Book II
Chapter 7**

Building Link Love

Figure 7-3:
Nofollowed
links in
SeoQuake.

All search engines do not treat nofollowed links the same. Some might actually follow the link but accord it no value. Others might ignore it altogether. Search engines' rules and policies for `nofollow` seem to change with the phase of the moon, so I won't try to say which engine does what here. Using a `nofollow` command might not prevent a search engine from crawling content. It's not a security tool.

Writing Link-Worthy Content

The best way to acquire links is to attract them naturally, with interesting, useful information. The importance of writing great content appears in almost every blog post on the subject of link building. Try these tips:

✦ **Be original.** Copying or rewriting someone else's content might get you noticed in court, but it's not going to help you build links.

✦ **Write quality stuff.** This goes without saying, I hope, but publish polished content. Have others help you edit before you go live.

✦ **Avoid the sales pitch.** No one will link to your services page if it just includes a sales pitch. You need to write something that has general value.

✦ **Write for easy scanning.** See Chapter 6 of this minibook for information on copywriting.

✦ **Include images.** Even if they're just silly, images make folks more likely to link to your site.

✦ **Have a punchy headline.** "Treatise on link building" won't get attention the way "10 Ways to Link Building Nirvana" will. Again, see Chapter 6 in this minibook.

You just never know what will turn out to be link worthy. I've spent days sweating over one article, only to have it ignored, while another page (see Figure 7-4) I wrote in 30 minutes with my kids thumping around the house in the background attracted dozens overnight.

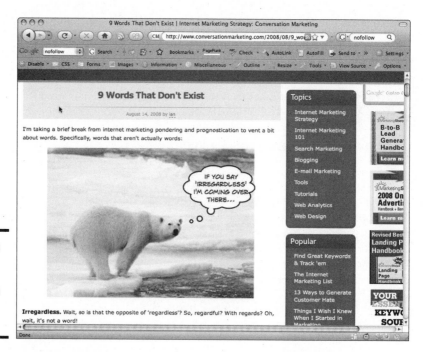

Figure 7-4: This page attracted 200 links in a day. Go figure.

Encouraging Links

You can encourage links by making it easy for folks to link to your site, too.

✦ **Make your page URLs easy.** I'd much rather link to

www.harrisonsbikes.com

than to

www.harrisonsbikes.com/index.aspx?category=1&products=2&special=
no&catid=234&productid=12312

✦ **Consider providing an easy way to bookmark each page on your site.** See Book VII for more information.

✦ **Provide an easy way for customers to forward links to friends.** You never know when a tool such as the one shown in Figure 7-5 will prompt a visitor to forward your page to their friend, the top 100 blogger.

Figure 7-5:
Encourage
forwards.

Using absolute URLs

When you link to one page of your site from another, use an *absolute* URL:

www.harrisonsbikes.com/products.html

instead of a *relative* URL:

/products.html

Although the latter is easier from a development standpoint, the former means that, if someone steals your page copy (it happens), they'll inadvertently link back to you, too.

These links won't be worth much, but they can help, and you may as well get the benefit.

Saying thanks

A simple thank you can go a long way. If folks link to you, send them a note to say you appreciate it. Remember, they just voted for you. They might vote again, too.

Getting Easy Links

Some links are no-brainers. Although they're not the highest-value votes on the Internet, your competitors have them. Go get them because they're easy and because they level the playing field.

Submitting to directories

Thousands of directories are out there. Search engines track a sizable chunk of them and count links to you from those sites as votes.

Many of these directories are free. Start with the following:

✦ **DMOZ.org:** It'll take a long time to get into this directory, but submit your site and be persistent. A link from DMOZ is worth it.

✦ **Chiff.com:** A free directory with a good reputation and a long history online.

✦ **Any and all local business directories in your area:** The Chamber of Commerce, the Better Business Bureau, and neighborhood associations are all a good start.

✦ **Industry associations:** If you belong to any industry associations, be sure you're in their directories, too.

Some pay directories that are worth the investment include the following:

✦ Best of the Web at BOTW.org

✦ The Yahoo! Directory at `dir.yahoo.com`

✦ JoeAnt.com

Submitting to design galleries

If you have a site that's 100-percent XHTML compliant, you can submit it to one of the many galleries that feature standards-compliant sites.

You can also submit to galleries that feature particularly striking designs. Clearly, though, your Web site must be particularly striking.

Be honest in both cases! If you spam every directory site hoping they won't check for standards-compliance or design quality, you'll be disappointed.

Commenting on blogs

When you leave a comment on a blog, the blog author usually asks for your Web address, as shown Figure 7-6. Enter your Web address, and the blog typically adds a link back to your Web site from the post.

Before you go to every blog on the Web and start entering comments (such as, "Interesting!") just to get a link, understand that the search engines long ago closed this loophole: Most blogs nofollow links from comments (see "Understanding nofollow" earlier in this chapter). Some, however, have stopped doing this because blog software has gotten better at filtering out short, useless messages entered strictly to create links.

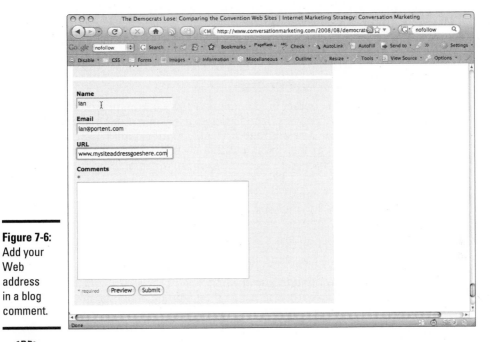

Figure 7-6:
Add your
Web
address
in a blog
comment.

Comment when it makes sense and when you really have a comment. You might get the additional benefit of a link.

Leveraging Your Partners for Links

If you own a large company and you have distribution partners or local retailers, ask them to link to you. You might want to provide an incentive, such as a discount on merchandise or additional training. Regardless, links from partners are often an untapped resource.

If your company sells or distributes products from another, larger company, ask the company to include a link to you in their distributor directory (assuming that they have one).

Asking for Links

Confession time again — I never actually ask for links. From personal experience, I know that any Webmaster with a Web site of even minimal importance receives at least ten e-mails a day begging for links. I know where I put those e-mails — in the trash bin.

However, other link builders report success using this technique. The math *does* make sense: If you ask 1,000 sites for links, and only one percent listen, you still gain ten links. If you have the time, it can work.

Building a contact list

First, you need a contact list so that you can work on building a relationship with these folks that goes beyond begging for links. Send them an occasional helpful note about a new article they might find useful. Wish them a happy holiday. Remember their birthday. If you ask people who know you for a link, they're more likely to help out. Follow these recommendations to help you get started:

✦ **Start with folks you know.** If you have a relationship with other Web site owners, start by contacting them. You have a far better chance.

✦ **Find sites related to your industry and see whether they allow you to contact the Webmaster.** If they do, add them to your list, too.

✦ **Find blogs related to your industry.** Add them to a separate list, because you want to market to them via social media, not by sending e-mail. See Book VII for more information.

Don't spam. If the site doesn't have a Webmaster contact address on it, don't contact them. You're already interrupting people who likely don't know you.

Being polite

Send an e-mail to each Webmaster. Send it once. If you don't hear back, cross them off your list. You tried. Maybe you ended up in their spam folder, or maybe they just ignored you. In either case, sending to them again and again will, at best, annoy them.

Make your e-mail very brief — no more than three sentences. Get right to the point, with a message like this:

> *I'm the owner of Harrisonsbikes.com. Since we sell the bikes you review, I'd greatly appreciate a link. Thank you!*

That's it. You've taken but a few seconds of the Webmaster's time. Trust me; she will appreciate it.

Building a Widget

You can also build links by giving people a tool to put on their own Web sites. Widgets are fairly commonplace now and can serve a wide variety of purposes. Widgets can

✦ **Provide the latest headlines from another Web site**

✦ **Show weather information for your area**

✦ **Show information about the site on which the widget is placed**

✦ **Play video**

YouTube and other services use widget-style code if you embed their video in your site.

If you include a link back to your own Web site as part of the widget, as shown in Figure 7-7, then every person who uses your widget gives you a link.

Follow these rules for widget link-building:

✦ **Don't overdo it.** Google, in particular, is sensitive to *widgetbait* link-building tactics. If this is your sole link-building strategy, you're headed for trouble.

✦ **Make it original.** Avoid using weather prediction widgets, fortune telling widgets, and random photo widgets that are available. Make yours very relevant to your business. Harrison's Bikes, for example, might have a widget showing results from local bike races.

✦ **Make it simple.** Provide a single chunk of code that Webmasters can cut and paste into their own Web sites. It must be a one-step process. If it isn't, they won't use it.

**Book II
Chapter 7**

Building Link Love

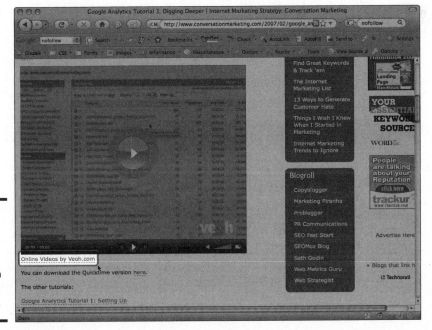

Figure 7-7:
A widget
that
includes a
link back to
the source
site. Links!

✦ **Make it fast.** If your widget grabs information from your Web site before loading, make sure it's fast. Nothing drives Webmasters crazier than a slow-loading widget that slows the load time of their own Web site.

✦ **Include a link.** Make sure that the widget includes a link back to your Web site and make sure it's a direct link.

There are companies that do nothing but develop widgets. Get in touch with them if you have an idea you'd love to see come to life. Elance.com is a good place to start.

Creating Quality Links

If you have control over links made back to your Web site, you can do a few things to maximize the quality of the votes they provide. I cover these tips in the following sections.

Including keywords

A link with relevant keywords in it provides a much better boost to your SEO efforts around that key phrase. For example:

```
<a href="http://www.harrisonsbikes.com">Seattle Bicycle Repair</a>
```

is far better than:

```
<a href="http://www.harrisonsbikes.com">Harrison's Bikes</a>
```

When search engines see a link with `Seattle Bicycle Repair` as the link text, they will assume that the Web site to which it points is about Seattle bicycle repair and count that link vote towards relevance for that phrase.

Don't turn down a branded link — they're still helpful. Even an image link with no text at all can help. But a keyword-rich link is pure gold.

If all the `a href` stuff made your head swim, don't worry. It's just HTML. Pay attention to the bolded text — that's what matters for this section.

Varying link text

The flip side of keyword-rich links: You don't want dozens of identically worded links. Ideally, you want some variation in link text.

The main time to worry about this is if you're reaching out to a partner network or using a widget to get a lot of links using one strategy. If you do that, try to use at least five different versions of link text. Variety gets you more votes.

Getting relevant links

A link from a relevant site is far more useful than a link from a site that has nothing to do with your business.

If you happen to get links from irrelevant sites, don't worry about it, but do focus your efforts on relevant sites.

Staying Out of Trouble

You can get into trouble when link building because for years, link building has been abused as an SEO strategy. So search engines have put automatic filters and whole teams of engineers and editors in place to check for

+ **Sudden, unexplained link growth**

+ **Links from *bad neighborhoods***

    That's SEO shorthand for a group of sites known to be sleazy. If you go out and acquire 100 links from sites selling suspicious pharmaceuticals or get-rich-quick schemes, you might end up associated with them in the search engines. That will hurt your ability to get a high ranking.

+ **Signs that you're selling links**

+ **Any other sign that you're getting links purely to improve your ranking**

Yes, they know we're out there doing just that. They just want us to go too far in the process. And no, they won't tell us what too far is. Fun, huh?

There are a few classic ways to get yourself into trouble, though. Steer clear of the topics in the next few sections.

Link buying and selling

There was a time when anyone with a budget could go out and buy dozens of links from quality Web sites, thereby helping their rankings. Ah, the good old days.

Alas, it wasn't to be. In 2007, Google cracked down hard on Web sites that were selling links. As a result, those sites either dropped entirely out of the Google index or fell so low in the rankings that they might as well have.

If you sell links, you risk severe penalties from search engines. They *really* don't like that. Yes, there are all sorts of ridiculous double-standards. It doesn't matter. Shaking your fist because you got dumped from the rankings but another site didn't won't help you after you're penalized.

Don't sell links.

And, if you buy links, you risk:

✦ **Acquiring a lot of links suddenly and tripping the search engines' spam alarms**

That can result in a temporary but automatic drop in the rankings — that's no fun at all.

✦ **Getting caught up in the mess if a link broker is discovered and his Web sites are banned**

✦ **Spending a lot of money on links that end up worthless**

Don't buy links.

Link exchanges

Exchanging links with another Web site probably won't hurt you, but it won't help, either. Search engines figured out this trick years ago and ignore any reciprocal links.

Link trading *can* hurt if you end up in a bad neighborhood. If you're linking to those sites, and they link back to you, they may take you down with them if they get penalized.

Link networks

Never, *ever,* join a link network. Most of these networks ask you to provide link text and a URL. Then they seed your URL out among many other sites, in exchange for you posting a few links from their network.

It sounds good, but it makes inclusion in a bad neighborhood even more likely than a link trade. Plus, you give up all control over who links to you and how. And, these networks are known as the worst offenders when it comes to SEO cheating.

Don't use link networks. Ever.

Creating Great Link Bait

Link bait is currently the most misunderstood, worst-employed link-building strategy. Few people are good at using it.

By definition, link bait is any piece of content written or created in such a way that it's going to attract a lot of links. Before I go too far, though, you need to understand the following:

✦ **Almost all great link bait is in the form of a list.**

"Top 10 ways to . . ." is a formula that just seems to work.

✦ **Great link bait typically includes images.**

✦ **Great link bait is easy to scan.**

Brainstorming link bait

This kind of link building starts with a really compelling idea. You can use a few strategies. Here are my favorites.

Cracking up the readers

If you take a look at Digg.com — Digg often shows some of the most successful link bait pieces — note that at least half the front-page pieces at any one time are funny, or at least ironic.

Humor can work very well. Just be sure you don't cross the boundary between funny and tasteless, unless you really mean to.

The Guinea Pig Olympics, shown in Figure 7-8, collected links faster than guinea pigs make baby guinea pigs.

Book II
Chapter 7

Building Link Love

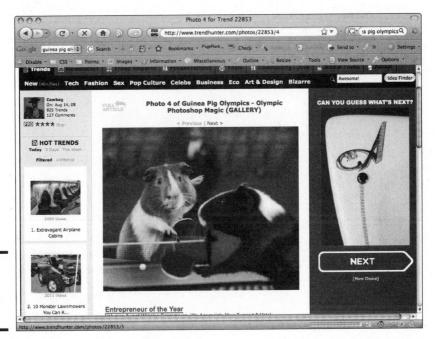

Figure 7-8:
The
Guinea Pig
Olympics.

Making the reader angry

Making readers angry is risky. If you can make a controversial statement that generates discussion on other Web sites, you can attract a lot of links from blogs, discussion forums, and online groups. That's great link building. Go too far, though, and you could end up alienating your audience.

I recommend using controversial link bait only after you have a few other successes, and you have a dedicated audience. They're more likely to forgive, and more likely to defend you — which, of course, generates more discussion and more links. I won't show any examples. They might just make you mad.

Puzzling your readers

If you're a top-notch writer, you can write something to get your readers buzzing about what you meant. For this to work, though, you need a large audience (for the buzz) who is pretty patient with you. Most folks go online for answers, not questions.

Examples include famous bloggers saying they're quitting blogging (they never do), pundits apparently reversing their opinion (they're actually not), and really bizarre April Fools' Day announcements (see the "Cracking up the readers" section).

Offering great content

Obviously, if you can offer great information, you can attract links in short order. Examples of informative link bait include the following:

The 30-second T-shirt fold

Step-by-step instructions on using Photoshop to do any number of things

Instructions for fixing a common problem in a popular car

The best way to enjoy a popular theme park

Ten bizarre facts about an animal, invention, country, or famous person

Some of these might seem silly. But if you think about it, they'd be a lot of fun to write.

And that might be the single most important item to keep in mind: Great link bait should be fun to write. If you don't enjoy writing it, most folks won't enjoy reading it — and you won't make much progress.

Using images in link bait

Images are the core of just about any successful link bait piece. Sometimes the images are directly involved, as in the Guinea Pig Olympics in Figure 7-8.

Sometimes they're just supporting material, as shown in Figure 7-9. Note how these images have all been modified in somewhat silly ways. Both of these examples are humorous link bait posts — in this type of article, it makes sense to use images as props for the joke.

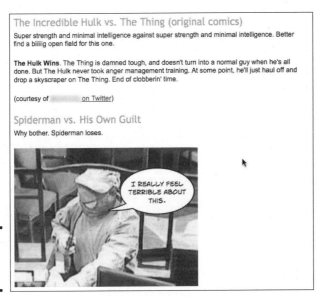

The Incredible Hulk vs. The Thing (original comics)

Super strength and minimal intelligence against super strength and minimal intelligence. Better find a biiiiig open field for this one.

The Hulk Wins. The Thing is damned tough, and doesn't turn into a normal guy when he's all done. But The Hulk never took anger management training. At some point, he'll just haul off and drop a skyscraper on The Thing. End of clobberin' time.

(courtesy of _____ on Twitter)

Spiderman vs. His Own Guilt

Why bother. Spiderman loses.

I REALLY FEEL TERRIBLE ABOUT THIS.

Figure 7-9: Comic book matchups.

 Host these images on your Web site, not by using a service such as Flickr. It's possible an image will become stand-alone link bait. If it does, you want the links pointing at your Web address, not at Flickr.

Using video in link bait

Video might *seem* like the perfect link bait, and using video can be very effective. However, it typically requires a lot of work, or a lucky break — say, you're the first person to capture a particular event on video, or you happen to film something hilariously funny happening in everyday life.

The more likely route is that you carefully prepare and produce a fantastic video. That's not easy: In my experience, a high-quality, 30-second YouTube video can take ten hours to create.

Videos you might want to prepare include the following:

✦ A how-to piece around one of your products or services

✦ An interview with a leader in your industry

✦ Ten ridiculous things you can do with your products

There are other possibilities. An ad agency in San Francisco did a video of its entire team lip-syncing a popular song. I'm not sure how their clients felt knowing that their highly paid team spent the day singing, but it did attract links.

Like images, you want to host the video on your Web site, not on YouTube. Otherwise, you end up helping YouTube build links, which won't really do much for your Web site.

Managing expectations

Link bait is not magic! It takes a lot of work and a long time. Manage your expectations for success by knowing that

✦ **If you create ten top-notch link bait pieces, you can expect one to succeed.** If you're expecting 100 percent success, you're being very unrealistic.

✦ **Link bait, by definition, needs to be attention-getting.** Writing something about how wonderful your product or company is will not work.

✦ **Link bait is a long-term investment.** Sometimes it can be months, even a year or two, before a piece of link bait really starts attracting links.

Researching Your Competitors' Links

One easy way to find good links is to see who links to your competitors. I use the following strategies to research competitors' links:

✦ **Use LinkDiagnosis.com.** If you visit this Web site in Firefox and install the LinkDiagnosis Firefox add-on, the Web site will generate detailed reports regarding your competitors' links.

✦ **Use Yahoo! Site Explorer to generate a list of all links to your competitors' sites.**

✦ **Do a blog search on Yahoo!, Google, or Live Search for your competitors' brand names.** The results might show blogs that reviewed their products. Those blogs might be willing to review yours, too — in which case, you might get a link.

✦ **Do a Google News search to find out which newswires your competitors use.**

After you build a list, check each link. Politely contact the bloggers, buy space in the same Web site directories, and figure out how you can attract links from the other Web sites. Something made those sites decide to link to your competitor. Read what the competitor wrote on the page that attracted the link and look at what the linking site said about it. That should give you a clue as to what will attract similar links in the future.

Chapter 8: Analyzing Your Results

In This Chapter

✔ Using your tracking worksheet

✔ Knowing what you should track

✔ Detecting plagiarism

In Chapter 1 of this minibook, I discuss how to set up an SEO worksheet. In this chapter, I go over how to put it to good use so that you can keep track of how your campaign is performing over time.

SEO is a long-term process. Changes you make now may take months to actually impact your traffic, so you need your worksheet to provide a long-term look at what worked and what didn't.

Using Your Tracking Worksheet

You should now have a worksheet that looks something like Figure 8-1. If you haven't set up your worksheet yet, get going!

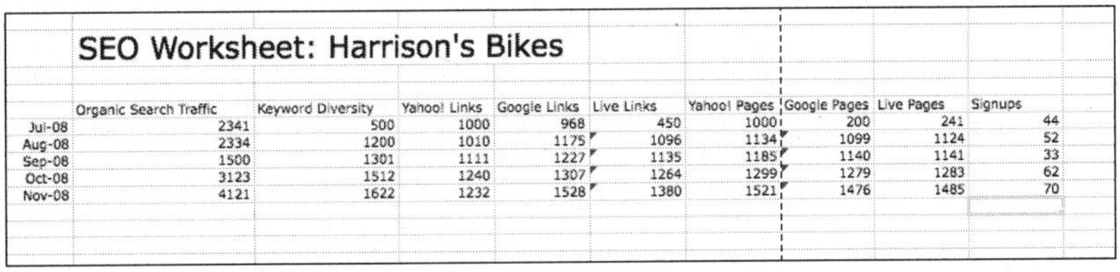

Figure 8-1: Basic SEO tracking worksheet.

SEO Worksheet: Harrison's Bikes

	Organic Search Traffic	Keyword Diversity	Yahoo! Links	Google Links	Live Links	Yahoo! Pages	Google Pages	Live Pages	Signups
Jul-08	2341	500	1000	968	450	1000	200	241	44
Aug-08	2334	1200	1010	1175	1096	1134	1099	1124	52
Sep-08	1500	1301	1111	1227	1135	1185	1140	1141	33
Oct-08	3123	1512	1240	1307	1264	1299	1279	1283	62
Nov-08	4121	1622	1232	1528	1380	1521	1476	1485	70

The tracking worksheet helps you do the following:

✦ **Boost morale.** Search engine optimization is a long-term game. Progress may happen in months . . . or years. You can look back six months and see you really have gotten a lot more traffic and conversions.

✦ **Match up changes in search with changes in sales.** If your offline or phone-driven sales jump 90 percent and your search traffic jumped 90 percent the same month, but nothing else changed, chances are your SEO efforts helped create that burst.

✦ **Obtain a big-picture look at what helped search engine optimization.** If you added ten new pages in March and your keyword diversity jumped 50 percent in April and May, that's valuable intelligence you can use to guide your next steps.

If you're getting fewer than 10,000 visits per month, you can update the worksheet monthly. If you get more than that, you might want to consider weekly updates, but you must consider how much time you have to devote to updating your worksheet. If you're reading this book, you probably have other responsibilities, such as paying bills and running your business. Prioritize accordingly.

The following list explains each of the basic statistics on your worksheet, and where to find this data in Google Analytics or on the search engines themselves. See Book III for more about Web analytics in general.

✦ **Traffic from organic search:** Choose Google Analytics⇨Traffic Sources⇨ Search Engines, and then click the Non-Paid link next to Show. See Figure 8-2.

✦ **Keyword diversity:** Choose Google Analytics⇨Traffic Sources⇨ Keywords. Then click the Non-Paid link next to Show. See Figure 8-3 for the number you need.

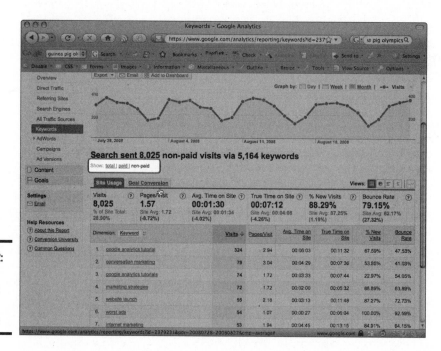

Figure 8-2:
The non-paid filter in Google Analytics.

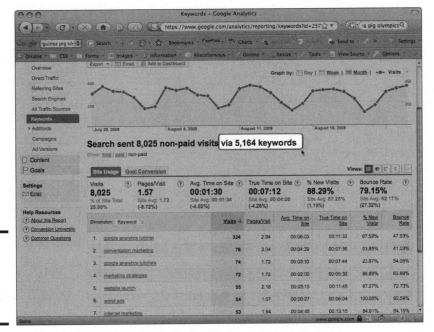

Figure 8-3:
The keyword diversity metric.

✦ **Incoming links, by search engine**

- *Yahoo!:* Yahoo! Site Explorer
- *Google:* Choose Google Webmaster Tools⇨Links⇨Pages with External Links.
- *Live Search:* Choose Live Webmaster Tools⇨Backlinks.

✦ **Indexed pages, by search engine**

- *Yahoo!:* Yahoo! Site Explorer
- *Google:* Choose Google Webmaster Tools⇨Index Stats.
- *Live Search:* Choose Summary⇨Indexed Pages.

✦ **Conversions from organic search:** Choose Google Analytics⇨Traffic Sources⇨Search Engines. Then click the Non-Paid link next to Show and select the Goals tab. Goals must be set up to use this metric. See Book III for instructions.

For an example of the non-paid filter in Google Analytics, see Figure 8-2; and to view an example of the keyword diversity report, see Figure 8-3.

Setting up the links page

You want to track which links you have and which ones you want, too. Add a tab to your worksheet. On that page, have columns for the following:

✦ The competitor and other links you want to get

   See Chapter 7 of this minibook for more about researching competitors' links.

✦ The date you requested the link

✦ The date you got it

Having these columns helps you keep track of your link campaign and ensures that you don't pester Webmasters with multiple e-mails.

Entering your keyword list

See Chapter 2 of this minibook for more information on keyword research.

Add a tab to your worksheet. On that page, have columns for the following:

✦ The keywords you're targeting

✦ Your current ranking on Google, Yahoo!, and Live Search

✦ Changes from the previous report

This information is the *least* important data you'll collect — traffic and conversions matter far more. See Book II, Chapter 2 to understand why. Don't go nuts updating the keyword list every day. Checking once per month is more than enough.

Watching for Plagiarism

Strictly speaking, watching for plagiarism isn't part of analyzing your campaign results. But plagiarism can hurt your brand and your SEO campaign. Because search engines don't like duplication, an unauthorized copy of writing on your Web site can really hurt you. So you should check for folks who are copying your Web site at least as often as you check these statistics.

Keep another tab in your spreadsheet to record copycats and when you contacted them.

You can find copies by using search engines or you can use a handy tool — Copyscape.

To use the search engine method, follow these steps:

Chapter 9: Hiring an SEO Professional

In This Chapter

- ✓ Figuring out how to find candidates
- ✓ Checking qualifications
- ✓ Asking the right questions
- ✓ Knowing what to expect

After reading this minibook, you might decide that you need to hire an SEO consultant instead of trying to improve your search rankings yourself. And hiring a consultant might be a wise decision. Search engine optimization is a time-consuming and demanding Internet marketing task.

Finding an SEO Professional

A good SEO professional is someone you work with for months or years. She can advise you and help you make long-term improvements to your Web site. And she is also aware of your business objectives beyond higher rankings or more traffic. Try the following places to start your search:

- ✦ **Talk to other business owners.** Find out whether they've worked with anyone; and if so, how they liked them. Referrals are still your best information source.

- ✦ **Check industry associations and analyst Web sites,** such as SEMPO at www.sempo.org or SEOmoz at www.seomoz.org. Both have market-places where you can request bids, and both provide lists of members or recommended vendors.

- ✦ **If you're looking for someone local,** search for "*(your city/town name) search engine optimization*". Really, if an SEO consultant can't get a Top 10 ranking for that search, you might want to reconsider.

Avoid looking in the following places:

- ✦ **In your Inbox:** Never, ever talk to an SEO professional who e-mails you out of the blue.

- ✦ **Any Web site or professional who guarantees you a ranking:** No honest SEO professional does this.

✦ **Any Web site or professional who asks you to put links to their other clients on your Web site:** That's a link exchange network, as described in Chapter 7 of this minibook.

✦ **Any Web site or professional who mentions optimizing your meta tags:** You've probably read enough now to understand why optimizing meta tags is only five percent of the battle.

Checking Qualifications

After you have your list of firms, you can narrow your search by checking a few qualifications. It's very important to perform an initial check because it helps you focus your search on the consultants who best fit your needs. Take these steps:

1. **Search Google Blog Search for the company name.**

   Make sure there aren't dozens of angry posts about horrible things the company's done. There are bound to be a few — everyone gets a few folks angry at them some time. But if you see a long history of complaints, think twice.

2. **Visit a firm's Web site in Firefox, with the Google Toolbar installed.**

   What is its PageRank? Don't worry if it's low. But if it's 0, the company might have been penalized by Google. If it has been, do you want those folks working for you?

3. **Type the first key phrase in their title tag into the three major search engines (Google, Yahoo!, and Live Search).**

   How does the company rank?

4. **Read its blog (and it had better have one).**

   What's the company's philosophy? Does it "play it very safe" and "white hat"? Or push the limits of what the search engines will tolerate? Make sure you find a firm you're comfortable with.

5. **Call the firm.**

   Talk to representatives on the phone or in person and make sure these are people you like. They're going to be working with you a lot.

You want a firm that has demonstrated competency, that has folks you can work with, and that will stick around if you decide to work with them for a few years.

Ask for references if you want. Realize, however, that only a moron would give you *bad* references. I know that it's comforting to hear how wonderful the agency you're about to hire really is. Just realize you're probably not going to get a clear picture this way.

One qualification you don't need to worry about is experience in a similar industry. It's just not that critical to SEO success. Whatever your industry, the challenges of gaining a good ranking remain largely the same.

Knowing What to Ask an SEO Professional

Before you start working with an SEO consultant, you must either meet him or talk to him on the phone. Find out the answers to the following questions:

✦ **What is the consultant's SEO process?** What can you expect to see happen in the first month? The process should make sense to you. If he can't explain it, don't hire him.

✦ **What is the first thing he would do on your site?** The SEO professional should look at your Web site before speaking with you. Or, he should ask whether he can look later. Either way, don't demand a lot of information — this is what you pay them for, and they shouldn't have to give information away for free. Instead, look for a sensible recommendation that demonstrates they gave your site some thought.

✦ **How are results reported?** If he mentions ranking reports, don't hire him. Traffic matters more than rankings. Any good SEO will know that.

✦ **How long has he been an SEO professional?** There's no specific right answer here, but a response like, "Six months," should give you pause.

✦ **If you're unhappy with the service, can you end your contract before the scheduled end date?** Many unethical agencies bind you to a contract and charge your credit card month after month.

✦ **How often will he speak with you?** Your SEO professional needs to periodically review results and strategy with you.

✦ **Does any service cost extra?** Many SEO firms charge extra for copywriting and other work. That's fine — just make sure you know before you start.

Don't worry about specific answers to these questions, except where noted. The main thing you're trying to get is an impression of the person or company you'll be working with. SEO is marketing, and it requires a lot of communication between you and your consultant.

Knowing What to Expect

More SEO campaigns have fallen to incorrect expectations than any other form of marketing. Here's what you should know before you start:

✦ **SEO takes a long time.** I typically require a minimum one-year contract with any SEO client. Two years is better. If you try to sign an SEO professional to a shorter contract, you'll likely either rush her (so she won't do solid long-term planning), or you'll chase off the best practitioners.

✦ **Don't expect fast results.** See the preceding bullet.

✦ **Do expect regular reports.** These should include all the data I talk about in Chapter 8 of this minibook.

✦ **Expect that your SEO professional wants a certain amount of work from you.** He is going to give you lots of recommendations and requests for changes to your site. He'll ask for content, and he'll want information about your competitors. That's a good thing.

Costs vary widely from one SEO to the next. Some charge as little as $99.95 per month. Others charge $10,000 or more per month. The difference? The level of service. For $99.95 per month, expect very little. The SEO firm answers the phone when you call, probably won't do any work outside of a few automated directory submissions, and might not get you results. At the top end of the pay scale, an SEO professional writes SEO-optimized articles for your Web site, regularly analyzes your site for potential problems, researches keywords, and generally does whatever it takes to move you up in the rankings.

Most SEOs charge based on a monthly fee. They might also offer one-time reviews where they check your Web site, write a report recommending changes, and then ride off into the sunset. If you have your own development team, this second option is a good one. If you don't, though, the monthly engagement works better.

Good SEO professionals often negotiate their fees depending on how challenging they think your campaign will be, how much work they're expected to do, and how long you plan to work with them. If you have a site that's already well optimized but needs a little help and you're hiring them for a year, expect your monthly fees to be lower. If you have a site that's an SEO disaster, and you're in a very competitive industry, *and* you want everything done in three months, you're going to pay more per month.

When it comes to cost, the real question is what makes sense to you and your budget. Don't hire a *bargain* you don't trust. Your money will be wasted.

Book III
Web Analytics

The 5th Wave   By Rich Tennant

"Sales on the Web site are down. I figure the
server's chi is blocked, so we're fudgin' around
the feng shui in the computer room, and if that
doesn't work, Ronnie's got a chant that should do it."

Contents at a Glance

Chapter 1: Getting Started **263**

Knowing What's Possible (Or Not) 264
Knowing How Reporting Tools Work 267
Choosing Your Reporting Tool 269
Making Sure Your Server Is Set Up 273
Setting Up Google Analytics 273

Chapter 2: Tracking Traffic Volumes **279**

Seeing Why Hits Are a Lousy Metric 279
Understanding the Five Basic Traffic Metrics 280
Tracking Referrers 289

Chapter 3: Measuring Your Best Referrers **291**

Understanding Referrers 291
Checking Out the Referring Site Data in a Traffic Report 293
Analyzing the Referring Sites Data 295
Tracking Referring Keywords 299

Chapter 4: Measuring Visit Quality **303**

Setting Quality Targets 303
Applying Those Targets 307
Learning More with Bounce Rate 310

Chapter 5: Using Conversion Goals **313**

Determining Key Performance Indicators 313
Defining Conversion Goals 315
Attaching Monetary Value to Goals 319
Setting Up Goal Tracking 321
Interpreting Conversion Data 325

Chapter 6: Using Goal Funnels **329**

Finding a Funnel 330
Setting Up Goal Funnel Tracking 331
Interpreting Goal Funnel Data 333

Chapter 1: Setting Your Conversion Goals

In This Chapter

✔ Seeing the differences between reports and analytics

✔ Setting expectations

✔ Discovering how analytics software works

✔ Setting up Google Analytics

You build your site, launch it, and wait. And wait. And wait some more. Is it working? Are you getting visitors? Are they doing what you want them to do? How will you know?

Enter the traffic report. A *traffic report* is a list of numbers and information about how folks are using your site, as shown in Figure 1-1. It is also the foundation for Web analytics.

Figure 1-1:
A traffic report.

Web analytics comprises using a traffic report to draw conclusions and adjust your marketing strategy. So, if a traffic report is the pencil and paper, Web analytics is the process of putting pencil to paper and creating a blueprint for your next steps.

The distinction between traffic reports and Web analytics is critical: Many traffic-reporting packages — including my favorite (Google Analytics) — refer to themselves as *Web analytics packages.* They are not, however. There is only one Web analytics tool: your brain. Don't forget it.

In this chapter, you find an introduction to Web analytics and traffic reports. Discover what's possible with analytics but also what's beyond its reach. I explain the basics of how traffic-reporting tools work and offer guidance on choosing one from the options available as this book goes to press. The chapter wraps up with a step-by-step explanation of getting set up with Google Analytics.

This entire minibook takes a very high-level look at analytics. It gives you the bare essentials to monitor and improve your site. It does **not** teach statistics. If you want to read about statistical analysis, rolling averages, and the like, you'll want to take a look at *Statistics For Dummies* or *Statistics Workbook For Dummies,* both by Deborah Rumsey (Wiley).

If you want to get a more in-depth look at Web analytics, check out *Web Analytics For Dummies,* by Pedro Sostre and Jennifer LeClaire (Wiley).

Knowing What's Possible (Or Not)

Traffic reports are useful tools, but a reality check is helpful as you begin venturing into the world of Web analytics. Specifically, you need to understand what you can and can't do when determining your key performance indicators (KPIs) — sales, leads, or other statistics that directly affect your business — and that's the first step in any Web analytics plan.

This section offers an overview of what data traffic reports can collect and what you can glean from that data. You discover the limits of that data and what effect your data collection has on your visitors' privacy. (***Hint:*** Not much, unless they agree to it.) Read on for details.

Ultimately, the purpose of analytics is to establish a narrative so that you can tell which changes have a positive or negative effect on your site and on your business over time. That helps you figure out what works and what doesn't, which leads to improved results.

Collecting data and what it can tell you

Traffic reports, at a minimum, show you

+ How many times people visit your Web site

+ Which pages are most popular

+ What sites send you visitors

+ How much time visitors spend on your site

Those are the basics. Additionally, most traffic-reporting tools now provide more powerful features, including

+ E-commerce sales tracking

+ Conversion goal tracking (more on this later)

+ Search-keywords reports that show which keywords folks use to find you

+ Campaign performance measurements so that you know which e-mail marketing pieces, banners, and other ads generate traffic

With most traffic-reporting tools, you can

+ **Find out your best sources of traffic and business** — such as search engines, a specific Web site, the e-mail you just sent, or something else that you didn't expect — so you know where to focus your advertising dollars and effort.

+ **See which pages on your site get the most or least attention** so you learn what your site visitors like — and give them more of it.

+ **Figure out which parts of your *shopping cart*** (that one log-in form, for example, or an intimidating billing information page) **drive away visitors** so you can tweak it to improve check-out rates.

+ **Discover which pay per click (PPC) advertising campaign generates the best return on investment (ROI)** so you can spend more on the keywords and ads that deliver the best results.

Understanding the limits of reporting

Traffic reporting isn't black magic. You can't peek at your visitors through their monitors and learn every detail of their lives. Nor should you.

However, most traffic-reporting tools cannot

✦ **Tell you someone's identity:** Virtually all (99 percent) traffic reporting is anonymous. Although most reporting tools know that person A visited your site at 12 noon on Thursday, looked at four pages, signed up for the e-mail newsletter, and then left, they don't know who person A actually *is.* Personally, I think that's a good thing. Paranoia about traffic reporting is bad enough without that kind of intrusion.

✦ **Accurately determine where someone lives:** They can sometimes do this, but not consistently.

✦ **Deliver 100 percent accuracy:** And this is okay. See "Choosing Your Reporting Tool," later in this chapter.

Minding visitors' privacy

There's a lot of hysteria about traffic reporting, analytics, and privacy. Folks are horrified that Web sites might be tracking where they came from, which pages they clicked on, and how long they stayed on a particular site.

Humbug.

The data that Web servers collect is anonymous and aggregated. That is, if I visit an online store, the store owner knows *someone* came and looked around. The owner doesn't know it was me, though, unless I already created an account on the site, logged in, and gave him permission to watch me.

Compare this with the many security cameras, credit card reports, and phone records kept by every retail company on the planet, and you can see that Web statistics tracking is just not much of an intrusion.

As a Web site owner, though, you must act responsibly:

✦ Have a clear privacy policy on your site explaining what, if anything, you do with data you collect.

✦ Never collect and store personal information unless you're capable of protecting it — and then, only if necessary.

✦ If you're using a traffic-reporting service, stick with a reputable provider, such as Google Analytics, Yahoo! Web Analytics, or Omniture. Research both and make sure that if there's ever been a security breach, the provider handled it.

✦ Never, ever, ever provide your analytics data to a third party unless you were granted permission by your audience.

Knowing How Reporting Tools Work

When you know a little bit about how reporting tools work, it's easier to understand what a specific reporting tool can or can't do for you. Reporting tools have two ways of collecting data:

✦ Processing log files

✦ Receiving data from JavaScript-based Web bug reporters

Some tools use one method or the other. Many tools, such as Urchin (from Google; `www.google.com/urchin/index.html0`), use both log files and a JavaScript bug.

Geekery ahead! But it's helpful to understand the basics of reporting technology, so I recommend you wade through this section. Although I use words like *JavaScript,* you don't need to actually understand log files or JavaScript code. You just need to know what's going on behind the scenes in your traffic reports.

Log file reporting

When someone visits your Web site, your Web server records basic information in a file called a *log.* Exactly what your server records might vary, but it usually includes

✦ When the visitor arrived

✦ What pages the visitor looked at

✦ Where the visitor came from

✦ Possibly, a unique identifier so that the server knows when that visit ended

Log file–reporting tools crunch through the thousands (or millions!) of lines of the server log file and create understandable reports based on the data. Tools range from simple, free packages (such as Webalizer; `www.webalizer.com`) to sophisticated packages (such as Urchin, which actually includes an option to use both JavaScript and log data).

This approach has some drawbacks:

✦ If you don't control your server, you might not control what the server logs. That can lead to poor reporting.

✦ Log files can get big — fast! — occupying a lot of space on a server.

✦ Web servers can have a lot of trouble distinguishing between different *sessions:* a single visit to a site by a single person. This can lead to inaccurate data.

Still, log files are simple; and if your Web server is properly configured, the data is available when you need it. You don't need to modify your site, either.

Web bugs and JavaScript

Other tools require that you actually place either a Web bug or special JavaScript in each page of your site. See Figure 1-2 for an example. The JavaScript "fires" when someone visits your Web page. It then sends back data to the analytics service about the visitor, the page the visitor is viewing, and where the visitor came from.

This approach allows for greater precision: Reporting tools can use sophisticated JavaScript to more accurately measure when a session starts and ends. They can also interpret all sorts of additional campaign data, thereby giving you greater ability to track campaign performance.

However, Web bugs require that you add code to every page of your site. And, because they use JavaScript, they can slow page performance or fail completely if the visitor's browser doesn't process JavaScript.

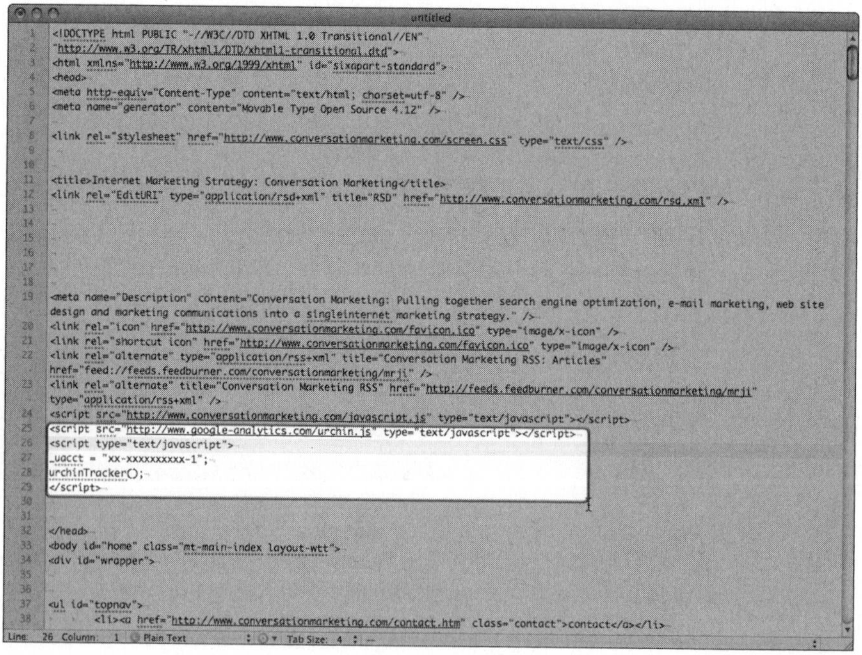

Figure 1-2:
A Web bug in the source code of a Web page.

Choosing Your Reporting Tool

You want to choose the right reporting tool from the start. Although switching to another tool is indeed possible, it's not easy because all reporting tools deliver slightly different data. So, I recommend sticking with one.

In this section, I show you a few options, explain the pluses and minuses of different solutions, and help you prepare for your installation.

Deciding what you need

No Web traffic–reporting tool is totally accurate. Different Web browsers might generate different results for JavaScript Web bugs, and log files might fall victim to server errors or privacy-blocking software. Thus, all traffic-reporting tools will overcount some items but undercount others.

The best you can hope for is consistent inaccuracy: By using the same tool, in the same manner, over time, you can ensure that your margin of error stays consistent, and that you have consistent metrics for proportional comparison, even if they're not precise.

Here's the main lesson of consistent inaccuracy: Choose your traffic-reporting tool carefully so that you don't have to change tools again later on. Data reported by different tools can vary by as much as 30 to 40 percent. It's no fun trying to explain to your boss why pageviews suddenly fell by 30 percent. Stick with one reporting tool. If you *do* have to switch, run both tools side by side for a while so that you can figure out the differences and allow for them when you finally turn off the old software.

The following tips can help you choose a reporting tool that you can hopefully stick with:

✦ **A balanced approach is best.** Use a JavaScript-based tool for sophisticated tracking; keep those log files around just in case. If you can use a tool that uses both, even better.

✦ **Consider what kind of data you'll be collecting.** See the earlier section, "Collecting data and what it can tell you," for a list of possible data you'll want.

✦ **Convenience matters.** Make sure your reporting tool will do things like e-mail you reports automatically so you don't have to constantly log in to review data. That takes time. The e-mailed report also acts as a reminder and ensures that you will regularly check your data.

✦ **Clarity matters, too.** When you look at the reports, do they make your head spin? If the answer's yes, either this isn't the right tool for you or you need some training before you dive into the data.

✦ **Flexibility is key.** Finally, look at the tool's custom reporting capabilities. Can you export data to Excel? Generate your own reports? If you can't, then this tool will probably outlive its usefulness for you pretty quickly.

Surveying your options

As of this writing, at least a dozen very good Web traffic–reporting tools are available. Some are free; some aren't. Table 1-1 outlines examples of what you can find on the market as this book goes to press.

Table 1-1	Web Traffic–Reporting Tools		
Tool	**Description**	**Cost**	**Web Address**
Omniture SiteCatalyst	The premium Web analytics tool, Omniture's system allows you to track conversions, segment your audience, and watch click behavior.	At least $500 per month. It's not an impulse buy.	www.omniture.com
Google Analytics	This tool offers a wide feature set, including conversion tracking and segmentation. It also integrates with Google AdWords (of course), is easy to set up, and includes more advanced features (such as click behavior).	Free	www.google.com/analytics

Tool	Description	Cost	Web Address
Yahoo! Web Analytics (formerly IndexTools)	Yahoo! Web Analytics promises to integrate with Yahoo! Stores. It's not available as of this writing, so you'll need to research it, but it looks like a very powerful toolset.	Free, but only to Yahoo! Store owners. Not yet released.	`http://web. analytics. yahoo.com`
ClickTracks	Lyris's Web traffic–reporting toolset is unique in that you get reports using a piece of desktop software. It boasts one of the simplest conversion and ROI-tracking toolsets available.	$995 one-time for the limited Desktop edition; $180/month minimum for the more powerful Pro edition	`www.click tracks.com`
Webalizer	This log-based reporting solution is popular on many Web hosts.	Free	`www.webalizer. com`
Sawmill	Sawmill is an old analytics favorite. It's a powerful, configurable, log file–processing tool.	Lite: $189 Pro: $399 Enterprise: $1,849	`www.sawmill.net`

You can, of course, build your own tool. But with as many options as there are, you'd need a really good reason. Start with one of these solutions or another out-of-the-box solution. You can add your own analytics tools later if you really need to. Chances are that you won't.

In this minibook, I use Google Analytics for most of the examples. It offers a great feature set and is free. Plus, most of the procedures for using Google Analytics will work just as well in other packages.

Making Sure Your Server Is Set Up

If you're using a log file–based solution, you need to make sure your server will log the data you need. That includes

- ✦ **Session time**
- ✦ **Referring cookie data**
- ✦ **IP address data**
- ✦ **HTTP status code**

    You don't need to know what this is. If you record it, your reporting tool will do the rest.

I won't go into the details of how this works. Contact your Webmaster to make sure that your server is configured to track all visit data, and you'll be all set. If you don't, though, and your server isn't tracking everything, there's no way to go back and get it later.

If you're using a JavaScript Web bug–based system, you don't need to worry about this.

Setting Up Google Analytics

After you choose your reporting tool, you have a setup process to follow. In the following sections, I explain how to set up Google Analytics, which takes four steps. First, you set up your account. Google Analytics offers JavaScript-based reporting, so you then need to add that script to each page in your site. Tracking search terms your visitors type also takes a little up-front work. And of course, you don't want people in your office skewing your results, so you find out how to exclude them from your traffic reports.

Google Analytics also offers goal and e-commerce tracking. *Goal tracking* reports completed lead forms, purchases (but not dollar amounts), or views of any page on your site that, if viewed by a visitor, indicates you achieved one of your KPIs. *E-commerce tracking* is goal tracking plus specifics regarding items sold and dollars collected. For details on these, see Chapter 5 of this minibook.

Create your account

To create your account, follow these steps:

1. **Go to www.google.com/analytics.**

2. **Click Sign Up Now.**

    If you don't already have a Google account, you need to create one (see the setup screen in Figure 1-3).

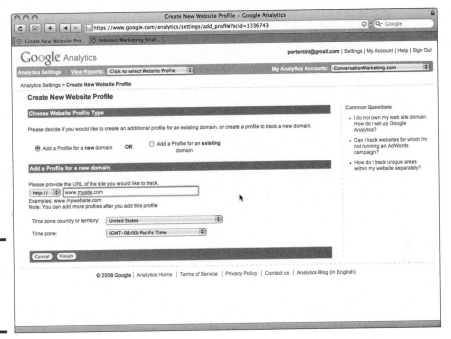

Figure 1-3:
The Google Analytics setup screen.

Book III
Chapter 1

Setting Your
Conversion Goals

3. **Enter the Web address you want to track and then click Finish.**

On the next page, Google Analytics provides you with the tracking code you need to add to your Web site to enable tracking (see Figure 1-4).

4. **Copy the code and paste it into a text editor so that you have it for later.**

If you're given the option, use the New Tracking Code — not the Legacy Tracking Code. The new code version gives you access to many cool features. If you're not given the option, don't worry: You're getting the latest code.

The code is slightly different for each site in your profile. Don't reuse the same code between multiple sites.

5. **Click Finish again.**

Your account is added, and you have the tracking code.

If you look at your Website Profiles page, you'll see that the Web site you entered was added. You'll also see, though, that it reads, `Tracking not installed`. That's the next step.

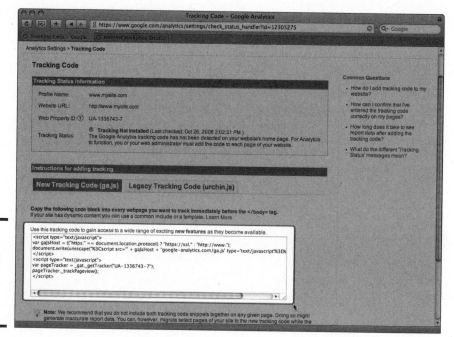

Figure 1-4:
Grabbing the Google Analytics tracking code.

Installing the tracking code

Remember that tracking code you copied in the last step? You need to install it on your Web site so that it can start sending data to Google Analytics.

This procedure varies depending on whether you have a blog site, a traditional site, or a CMS-driven site. (*CMS* stands for content management system.)

1. **Access your site with whatever editing tool you're using.**

   If you have a blog, you'll want to look at the Templates or Design tool. If you have a traditional site, you'll probably use a File Transfer Protocol (FTP) tool. If you're using a CMS, you'll want to edit your site template.

2. **Copy the Google Analytics tracking code to your Clipboard by first selecting all the code and then choosing Edit⇨Copy in the text editor where you pasted it.**

3. **In your editing tool, paste the tracking code right before the closing </body> tag on each page of your site.**

   - *If you're using a blogging tool or a CMS,* you might have to paste the code only once.

   - *If you're using a traditional Web site,* you might need to paste the code into each page. It's worth the effort, trust me.

4. **Save the edited code to your Web site.**

Finding the tracking code again

If you didn't copy the tracking code when you set up your account, here's how you can find it again:

1. **Log into Google Analytics.**

2. **Click Edit next to the Web site profile for which you need the code.**

3. **Click Check Site Status.**

   The code you need is at the bottom of the page, under the heading Instructions for Adding Tracking.

5. **If necessary, republish the site to update your code.**

   See Figure 1-5 for an example of properly installed Google Analytics code. This is how it should look.

6. **Wait a half hour or so. Log back into Google Analytics and look for the profile you added.**

   It should now read, `Receiving data`. It will likely be 24 hours before you see any actual data, but your code is properly installed.

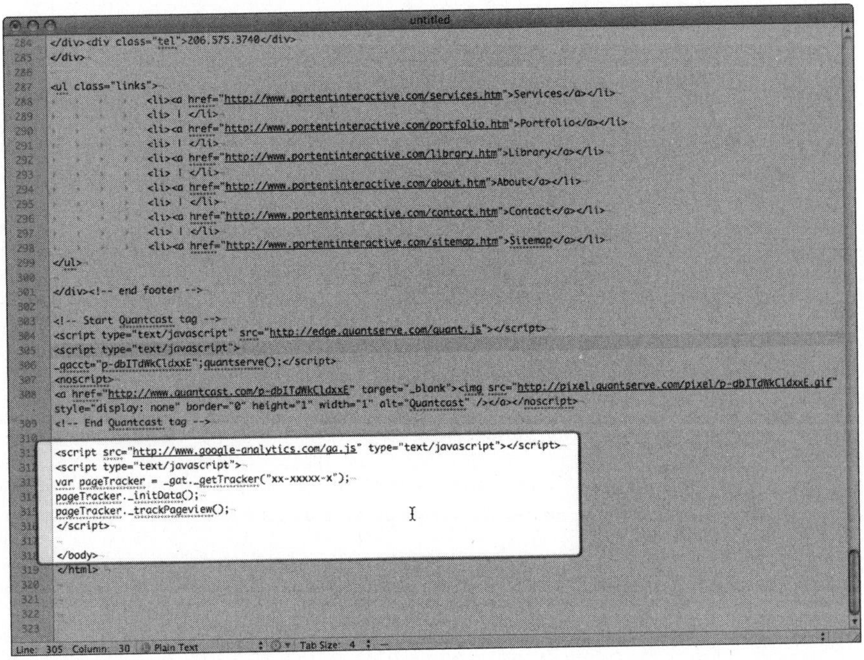

Figure 1-5:
Properly installed Google Analytics code.

Tracking site search

If you have a search box on your Web site, it makes sense to track what folks type into it. You can learn a lot about your audience. I talk more about analyzing site searches in Chapter 4 of this minibook.

To set up a site search, follow these steps:

1. **Log into Google Analytics.**

2. **Click Edit next to the Web site for which you want to track site search.**

3. **Click Edit at the top of the page, next to Main Website Profile Information.**

4. **Select the Do Track Site Search radio button (see Figure 1-6).**

5. **Leave this page open in your browser. Open a separate browser window for the next few steps.**

6. **In the new browser window, go to your Web site.**

7. **Search for *"buggy bumpers"*, using your site's search tool.**

8. **Look at the address of the search result page.**

    You should find the words `buggy bumpers` in the address, as well as a query attribute (such as `q=` or `search=`). See Figure 1-7 for an example.

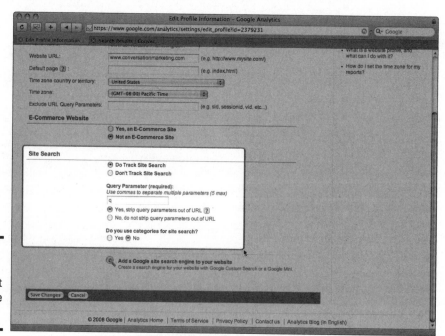

Figure 1-6:
Search tracking, set up in Google Analytics.

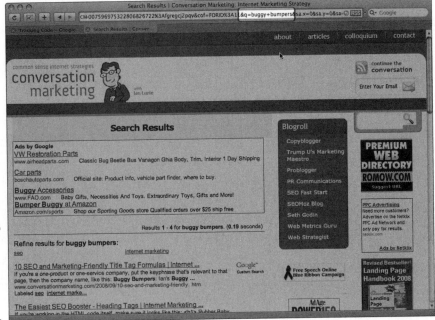

Figure 1-7:
The search
query
attribute on
my blog.

9. **Enter the query attribute into the Query Parameter field in Google Analytics.**

10. **Click Save Changes.**

    You're done. Within a few hours, you'll start seeing the phrases people search for on your site.

Excluding your office

Your analytics package won't distinguish between customers and folks at your company unless you tell it to. Because you want the most accurate numbers, set up a filter to exclude everyone who works at your organization.

That kind of filter depends on the IP addresses used by your office. If you don't know what that means, it's best not to fiddle with it. Instead, contact your Webmaster or your Internet service provider for help finding the IP address.

Then you set up the filter, as follows:

1. **Log into Google Analytics.**

2. **Click Edit next to the Web site profile that needs the filter.**

3. **Under Filters Applied to Profile, click Add Filter.**

4. **Select Add New Filter for Profile.**

5. **Give the filter a name you'll remember, such as *Exclude IPs*.**

6. **Under Filter Type, choose Exclude All Traffic from an IP Address.**

7. **Type in your IP address.**

   See Figure 1-8 for a completed filter.

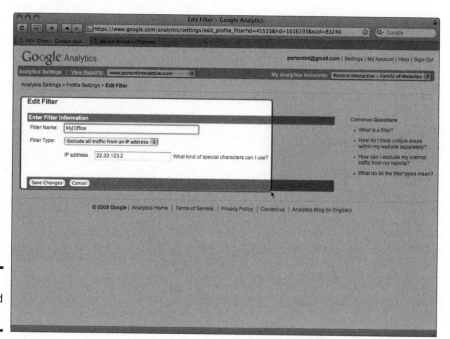

Figure 1-8:
A completed
IP filter.

You might need to exclude multiple addresses. You can create a separate filter for each one, or you can use regular expressions (also called *regex*). regex is beyond the scope of this book and involves very high level development expertise. Of the 25 people who work for me, only 2 have really mastered regex, and I'm not one of them.

Chapter 2: Tracking Traffic Volumes

In This Chapter

✔ Avoiding hits

✔ The five basic metrics

✔ How to interpret basic data

All the fancier metrics for tracking traffic and user behavior that you can read about later in this book are built on the five basic ones I cover in this chapter. You need to understand these five metrics — and how to interpret them — if you're going to do more advanced analysis and learn to use that data to improve your site.

I use Google Analytics for most of the examples in this book. The reports and such are much the same from one reporting package to another, though. Follow along with these examples, and you'll be able to apply what you glean here to any reporting toolset.

Seeing Why Hits Are a Lousy Metric

First off, though, you need to avoid one metric when tracking traffic and user behavior: hits.

You probably hear a lot of folks talk about hits. "I got a million hits last month!!!" is a claim I hear a lot.

That's great, but hits are almost meaningless when it comes to measuring audience or marketing performance. Simply defined, a *hit* is any one *file* downloaded from your Web site, any one time. Every image, script, and stylesheet linked to a page counts as one file — and, thus, one hit. Seeing as how one page can contain 1 file or 1,000 files, hits don't tell you much from a marketing viewpoint.

Look at Figure 2-1, which shows a single Web page. That page, though, holds dozens of images. Do the math, and you can see that a single view of that page generates about 80 hits. Take it a step further: If ten people visit the page, that's 800 hits. Wow!

Figure 2-1:
One page, 80 hits. Ten visitors, 800 hits.

On the other hand, a simpler page — such as the Google homepage — contains only a few files. Do the math again to see why these base numbers are important: A view of one of your simpler pages might be just as important to your business as a view of a more complex page — *but the simpler page generates fewer hits.*

Having laid out the preceding argument why hits aren't necessarily the end-all–be-all metric that people assume, I have to stress that hits are indeed a valuable measure. They're great for measuring server load and also a good way to figure out how to speed page load times. But because they're a lousy marketing metric, avoid relying on them.

Understanding the Five Basic Traffic Metrics

Traffic, in terms of Web visitors, actually comprises five different ingredients:

✦ **Sessions (also called *visits*):** A *session* is any one person visiting your Web site any one time. If I visit your site ten times in a week, my visits count as ten sessions, whether I stayed on the site for 5 minutes or 50.

✦ **Unique visitors (called *uniques* if you want to sound terribly professional):** A *unique visitor* is any one person visiting your Web site any number of times during a defined period. If I visit your site ten times in a week, I still count as only one unique visitor.

✦ **Pageviews:** A *pageview* is any one visitor viewing one page of your site, one time. A page must have a unique address, or *URL*. If I visit your homepage but then click a link and visit say, `contactus.html`, those are two pageviews.

✦ **Time on site:** This is the total amount of time one visitor spends on your site in the course of a single session. Average time on site is an invaluable measure of visit quality and visitor interest.

✦ **Referrers:** If I click a link at Google.com and land on your site, then Google is the *referrer*.

Any traffic-reporting toolset — even the most basic — must provide these five metrics. If yours doesn't, replace it. These five metrics typically show up right on the first page — the *dashboard* — of your traffic reporting package, as shown in Figure 2-2.

Tracking sessions (visits)

Because a session is defined as any one visit to your site, sessions are a good general measure of site use and load (more on this in a moment). Think of sessions as foot traffic in a traditional retail store: The same people might go in and out of the store, but that doesn't matter. If the store's full, it's full.

In your traffic-reporting tool, you'll find sessions either under a section called Sessions (surprise!) or Visits, as shown in Figure 2-3.

Figure 2-2:
The five metrics in Google Analytics.

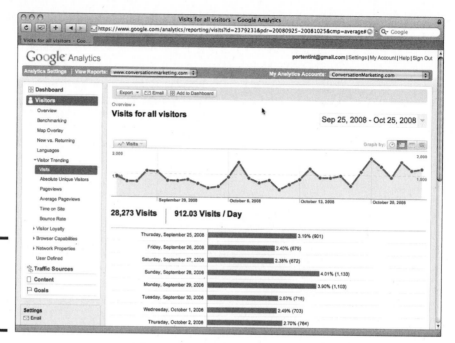

Figure 2-3:
The Visits
report in
Google
Analytics.

Don't use sessions to measure the following:

✦ **Audience size:** If someone visits, leaves, and then returns to your site many times, one person can generate multiple sessions in any time period. So, sessions can be far higher than unique visits (a more accurate measure of audience).

✦ **Ad performance:** Advertising — whether pay per click ads, e-mail, banners, or other creative elements — is created to bring you new customers. Because sessions don't differentiate between new and repeat visitors, they're not a good measure of ad performance. Counting unique visitors (see the next section) is far better.

Do use sessions to see

✦ **How busy your site is in the broadest possible terms:** More sessions mean more traffic, which may also mean a higher load on your Web server. Sessions are a good way to judge how much strain your site is under.

✦ **Conversion rate based on foot traffic to your site:** If you want to know how many visits it takes to get a sale or lead, you need to know how many sessions you get in a given time period.

✦ **General interest in your site:** Even though one person can generate many sessions, sessions are still a great way to see how much interest you're generating. At a high level, whether five or ten people generated those 100 sessions isn't critical. The average level of interest remains the same.

✦ **Peak times of day, month, or year:** Many businesses are cyclical by day or season. Peaks or lows in sessions might fit a pattern that tells you your customers are more active at a specific time of day or year. In Figure 2-4, the session graph of one day shows a common cycle.

Figure 2-4:
A typical daily traffic curve.

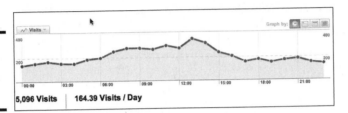

Among analytics experts, sessions can sometimes get a bad reputation. Folks will skip them and move on to unique visitors, which appear to provide better data. However, sessions do provide valuable information.

Tracking unique visitors

Unique Visitors reports are a good measure of audience size, ad performance, and the effect of blog mentions or other *noise* — news reports about you or a competitor, for example — on your site.

Don't use unique visitors to measure the following:

✦ **Per-visitor interest:** Unique visitor data will tell you how many people come to your site. On its own, though, it tells you nothing about how much they liked the site. Combine this data with pageviews and time on site to make that kind of analysis. (You can read about pageviews and time on site earlier in this chapter.)

✦ **Overall site activity:** If 100 unique visitors come to your site in a week, that might seem like a small group. However, if they each come to the site 100 times, that's 10,000 sessions. Use sessions to track site activity, not unique visitors.

Do use unique visitors to measure

✦ **Audience size:** Unique visitors are a great absolute measure of your audience in a given time period. After all, 10,000 sessions are great. If this represents only 100 unique visitors, though, your audience isn't that big.

✦ **Overall ad performance:** If you just purchased an ad — say, on a blog — and your unique visitor count increases, that could mean the ad's working for you. You want to dig deeper with pageviews and referrers, but unique visitor count is a good initial clue.

✦ **Changes over time:** Watch unique visitors over time. If your audience (unique visitor count) suddenly doubles in size after that local news coverage, you know that story had an impact.

✦ **Comparison with sessions:** A single visitor generating ten sessions in a week is still only one unique visitor. By comparing unique visits with sessions, you can see how many folks return to your site more than once. In many businesses, a high ratio of sessions to unique visits is good: It indicates visitor loyalty.

See how these metrics build on each other? Sessions alone are useful, as are unique visitors, but sessions compared with unique visitors is even better.

Any traffic-reporting package can deliver a unique visitors report much like the one in Figure 2-5. However, log file analysis tools (such as older versions of Urchin or WebTrends) require additional setup to report unique visitors. Otherwise, they'll report sessions only. Check your traffic reports to make sure you're measuring unique visitors. They're a must-have metric.

Figure 2-5:
A Unique
Visitors
report.

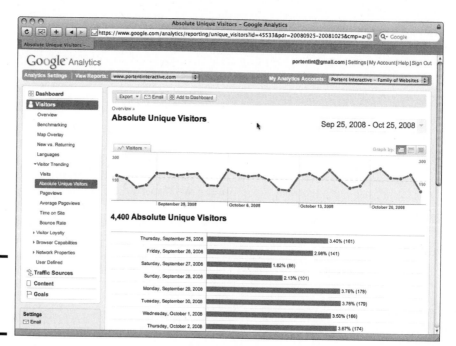

Tracking pageviews

If unique visitors are the people, then pageviews are their footprints. Pageviews are the measure of interest in specific areas of your site. Most traffic-reporting tools will give you a few different ways to look at pageviews, as shown in Figure 2-6:

✦ **Overall pageview count for your entire site:** Look for a Pageviews report to see the aggregate view.

✦ **A page-by-page look at which pages get the most attention:** Look for a report called Top Content or Top Pages to see a comparison of popular pages.

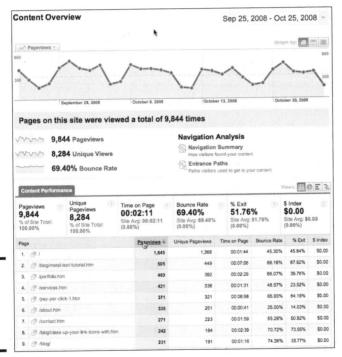

Figure 2-6: Aggregate and page-by-page reports.

**Book III
Chapter 2**

**Tracking Traffic
Volumes**

Don't use pageviews to measure audience size. One visitor may view 100 pages, while another may only look at 1. Having one customer who walks through your store and looks at every product isn't as good as having ten who look at a few products each. The same holds true on the Web. Pageviews are an awful measure of audience size.

Do use pageviews to measure

✦ **Visitor interest:** Combined with visitor data, pageviews are a great reflection of visitor interest. Pageviews per visit, as shown in Figure 2-7, are one indicator of just how interested your audience is in what you're showing them. If someone stays on your Web site and looks at ten pages, chances are that visitor is more interested than someone who stays on your Web site and looks at only one page.

✦ **Content performance:** Pages that get more pageviews are better performers. They also tell you what your audience wants to hear. A page that gets 4,000 views in a month is probably drawing more interest than a page that gets 1,000.

✦ **Ad performance:** Most traffic-reporting tools show pageviews per visit generated by specific referrers. (See the section "Tracking Referrers," later in this chapter.) Ads that generate more pageviews per visit are usually better performers.

Again, see how the different metrics can be combined? Pageviews are a great measure of raw site usage. Pageviews per visit (per session) give you an added dimension: visitor interest.

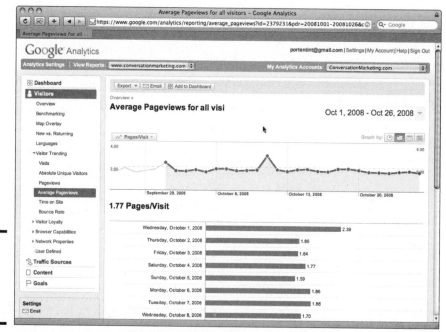

Figure 2-7:
Pageviews
per visit
in Google
Analytics.

Tracking time on site

Time on site is a useful metric when combined with pageviews, visits, sessions, and average time. Together, they give a more complete view of site performance and user interest. Consider the examples in the following sections.

Balancing pageviews with time on site

Time on site is the perfect balance for pageviews. Pageviews can be inaccurate, and here's a real-world example. If I come to your site, look at ten pages for five seconds each, hate what I see, and then leave, you might *think* you just got a quality visitor. I did, after all, look at ten whole pages. That's a lot of pageviews for a single visitor.

But — and here's the rub — I was on the site for only 50 seconds. Yikes.

If you track time on site, you can compare time on site with pageviews to make sure that you're getting an accurate measure of visitor interest. Most Web-traffic tools now show time on site and time on page right alongside pageviews and sessions.

In that example, the #2 page is a stronger performer than it might seem. Although it's only #2 in pageviews, it's showing more than seven minutes average time on page. Visitors really take their time to read that content.

Weighing sessions and unique visitors with time on site

You can use time on site to balance session or unique visitor counts, too. If your unique visitor count spikes suddenly because of a surge of traffic from a site like StumbleUpon (see Book VII on social media marketing), that's great. However, also checking average time on site helps you assess how valuable that traffic surge really was.

✦ **If average time on site plunged,** you might have gotten a lot of new visitors, but they were far less interested and probably won't give you much long-term benefit. Figure 2-8 shows one instance where that happened to me last April: I was excited at first, and then realized that I'd not done much to help my blog grow. The average time on site is less than one minute.

Sigh.

✦ **If, on the other hand, your average time on site stayed consistent even when your number of visitors jumped,** then those additional visitors spent at least as much time on your site as the rest. That's good: You added more quality members to your audience. Figure 2-9 shows one burst of traffic from StumbleUpon that did just that for me, in August: Much better!

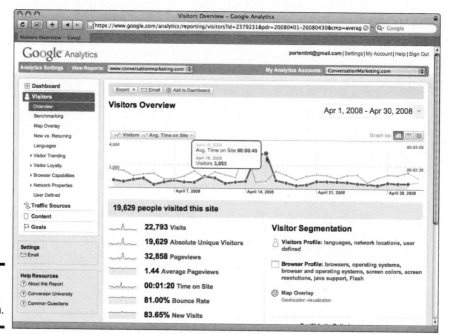

Figure 2-8:
More visits,
no attention.

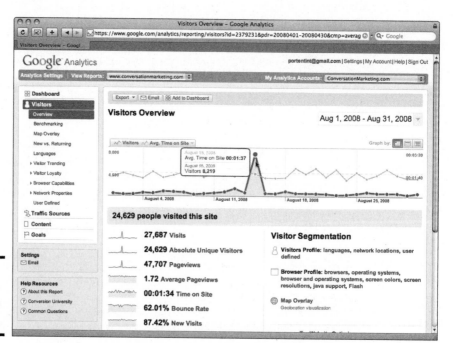

Figure 2-9:
More
visits, same
attention.

Tracking Referrers

Referrers complete the basic traffic-reporting toolset. A *referrer* is a Web page that points to your Web site. When someone clicks a link, that Web page becomes a referrer. Referrers come in many flavors:

✦ A traditional Web page that might have a link to your site

✦ A link in an e-mail that someone reads in a Web-based e-mail reader, like Hotmail or Gmail

✦ A search result on a search engine

So, a referrer tells you where visitors came from when they reached your site.

Think about it: If you ran a vegetable stand and every single person who walked up had a sign on their forehead that read, "I saw your ad in the news-paper" or "John at the corner store told me about you," you'd immediately know which advertising worked and which marketing didn't.

Referrers are like that kind of sign. Combine them with the other metrics in this chapter, and you can see which referrers generate quality traffic, as shown in Figure 2-10.

Figure 2-10:
Time on site and pageviews/ visit, by referrer.

Combine them with sales and conversion data (more on this later in this minibook), and you can actually measure return on investment (ROI) from many of your online marketing efforts.

That makes referrers a must have in your analytics toolset. If your reporting tool doesn't show referrers, get a new tool.

The following chapter is dedicated solely to referrers. They're that important!

Chapter 3: Measuring Your Best Referrers

In This Chapter

✔ Defining a referrer

✔ Analyzing referrers

✔ Special cases: Using tags

*I*f I had to be marooned on a deserted island with only one metric, it'd be referrers. A bit melodramatic, I know, but no Internet marketing campaign can survive — let alone succeed — without 'em.

I give you the basics on referrers in Book III, Chapter 2. But the business intelligence you can gain from this seemingly simple stat goes far, far deeper. It pays to have a really solid understanding of this metric, which is why measuring referrers is the sole subject of this chapter.

If you're using a log file–based tracking solution, make sure your server is set up. Otherwise, you could miss a lot of valuable referrer data. (Flip to Book III, Chapter 1 for details on tracking solutions that use log files versus JavaScript.)

You can apply referrer data to improve your online business in so many ways. This chapter barely scrapes the surface of referrer tracking. Here, you find out where referrer information comes from, basics about stats you find in your referrer data, and examples for analyzing referring site data. In the next few chapters, you discover how to start combining other metrics — such as conversion rates and visit quality — to help you get even more value from this data.

Understanding Referrers

Geekinese alert! I have to get a little technical in this section so you'll understand exactly how referrers are tracked, and what the tracking data means. Don't let it scare you off. You're a smart person. You bought this book, after all.

Here's how referrer tracking works in the background as you (or your visitors) use the Internet:

1. You use a search engine, visit a Web site, or receive an e-mail message.
2. You click a link on the page.
3. That link directs you to another Web site.
4. When you land on that other Web site, the Web server that powers that site asks your Web browser where you came from.
5. Unless you turned off this feature, your Web browser delivers that information — the *referrer* — to the Web server.
6. The Web server logs the data.
7. If you're using a JavaScript Web bug–based traffic-reporting tool (see Chapter 1 of this minibook), your reporting tool logs it, too.

That referrer data typically includes

+ **The referring site address, such as** www.yahoo.com
+ **The complete referring URL**

   For example, if I came from a search for *"buggy bumpers"* on Yahoo!, the URL might be `search.yahoo.com?p=buggy+bumpers`. If I came from the `contactus.htm` page on a company site, the URL might be `www.thesite.com/contactus.htm`.

With that data, any good traffic-reporting tool can determine

+ Where a visitor came from
+ If the visitor came from a search engine, what keywords that person used to find your site
+ The specific page on the referring site from which the visitor came
+ Sometimes, whether the visitor clicked a specific ad or link on that page

You can see why referrer data is so valuable. With it, you can figure out which Web sites, keywords, and ads generate sales, leads, or other quality visits to your site.

Without referrer data, you're driving with your eyes closed. But enough negativity. Time to talk about driving with your eyes open.

Augh! My privacy!

A lot of folks get the heebie-jeebies when I tell them that every Web server knows the site that referred you. Trust me: It's not that bad. You **can** turn off your browser's ability to deliver this data if you want. But 99 percent of the time, Web servers just know that some nameless person came from site A or B. They don't know who that person is. The only time they'll specifically know that you are who you are is if you create an account on that site and give them permission to track that data. Hopefully, you trust them at that point.

Checking Out the Referring Site Data in a Traffic Report

Most reporting tools don't show referrer data front and center on the main dashboard. You need to drill down to find it. Using Google Analytics as an example, this section walks you through the steps of finding your referring sites and introduces the common metrics you see along with those sites.

Although the following steps focus on Google Analytics, you can use these basic steps to work with most reporting tools. To find your referrals, follow these steps:

1. **Go to www.google.com/analytics to get to Google Analytics.**

   Book III, Chapter 1 explains how to get started with Google Analytics.

2. **Click Referring Sites in the sidebar on the left.**

   If you're using a different traffic-reporting tool, Referring Sites might be called Traffic Sources, Referrals, or Links. Be sure to click around if you don't see the referrer reports right away.

   If you can't find it at all, your traffic-reporting tool might not be properly configured. If that's the case, it's time to have a chat with your Webmaster.

3. **Check out the overview page to see which Web sites send you traffic.**

   The graph shows the flow of traffic from referring sites. The list below the graph shows all of the sites that sent you traffic.

   In Figure 3-1, the graph at the top and the Site Usage tab shows a list of referring sites for the specified time period. (Note that I'm using my blog as the guinea pig here. The data is for sample purposes only.)

Figure 3-1:
Referring sites in Google Analytics.

On the Site Usage tab, you see six different categories of information. Here's what each category means:

✦ The **Source** is where the visitors came from: the site.

✦ **Visits** tells you how many clicks you got from that referring site. Note that these are visits, and not *unique visitors*. Some reporting tools use one, some use the other. See Book III, Chapter 2 for the difference.

✦ **Pages/Visit** shows the average number of pages visitors looked at on the site after coming from this referrer.

✦ **Avg. Time on Site** shows the average time that visitors spent on the site after coming from this referrer.

✦ **% New Visits** tells how many visitors came to the site from this referrer who hadn't previously visited the site in this time period. Ah-HAH! A new statistic. This data can help you see whether the referrer is sending you new visitors, or just referring the same visitors to you again. Both might be valuable: A new visitor is a potential new customer.

✦ **Bounce Rate** shows how many people came from this referrer, looked at one page on the site, and then left without looking at any others. A high bounce rate isn't necessarily bad, but it bears investigation.

Some referrer reports include an item called *Direct* or *Not Set:*

✦ **Direct:** Someone came to your site by typing your Web address directly into their Web browser. Because this visitor didn't click a link to get to your site, there is no referrer.

✦ **Not Set:** This might mean the same thing; or, it might mean that for whatever reason, the reporting tool couldn't interpret the referrer.

Analytics isn't an exact science.

In the next section, you drill a little deeper into the referring sites data and check out examples of what you can glean by investigating your referring sites.

Analyzing the Referring Sites Data

You can turn a Referring Sites report into real business intelligence by asking yourself three questions, as outlined in the following steps. I use my report (refer to Figure 3-1) as an example of what you can discover, high-level, by asking these questions:

1. Which sites send me the most traffic?

- StumbleUpon is far and away my biggest referrer.

- Google is second, which is a little unusual. On most sites, you'd expect Google to be first.

- Then comes images.google.com, which is really a surprise, so I'll check on that later. Hopefully, it's not that picture of me at last year's holiday party.

2. Which sites send me the most attention?

- If I balance time on site and pages/visit, though, StumbleUpon isn't the best site. It generates a healthy two pages per visit (not bad for a blog), but less than 1:30 time on site.

- Google generates almost as many pageviews per visit and far more time on site.

- About.com also sends me quality visitors who pay attention. So does 45n5.com.

3. What insights can I gain?

The answers to this question are a bit more open ended than the preceding ones, but here are a couple of examples to give you an idea of what you might do with your referral data:

- Because StumbleUpon sends me a lot of traffic, but those visitors don't stick around very long, I need to see whether I can improve the *stickiness* (the length of time they stay on my site) of my site for StumbleUpon users. This might prove difficult, but that site is a huge traffic generator, so I need to try to take better care of that audience.

- I can't let go of the Google Image Search referrals. They only show a time on site of about 21 seconds. That's very low compared with my site average (1:35), so I'm concerned that my site might be broken for folks coming from Google Image Search, or that I'm delivering something that they really, really don't like. I need to find out what image is sending traffic my way. I don't want to offend people, and I don't want to show them a busted site, either. On the other hand, if it's a graph or chart I created, these referrals could tell me how to get more visitors.

The following steps outline an example of how you might dig a little deeper into your referral data by using Google Analytics, using that Google Image Search referral as an example:

1. **From the Referring Sites overview page, click images.google.com in the Sources column on the Site Usage tab.**

What appears on the screen is shown in Figure 3-2.

Okaaaay, that's not much help. I want to know what keywords generated those referrals.

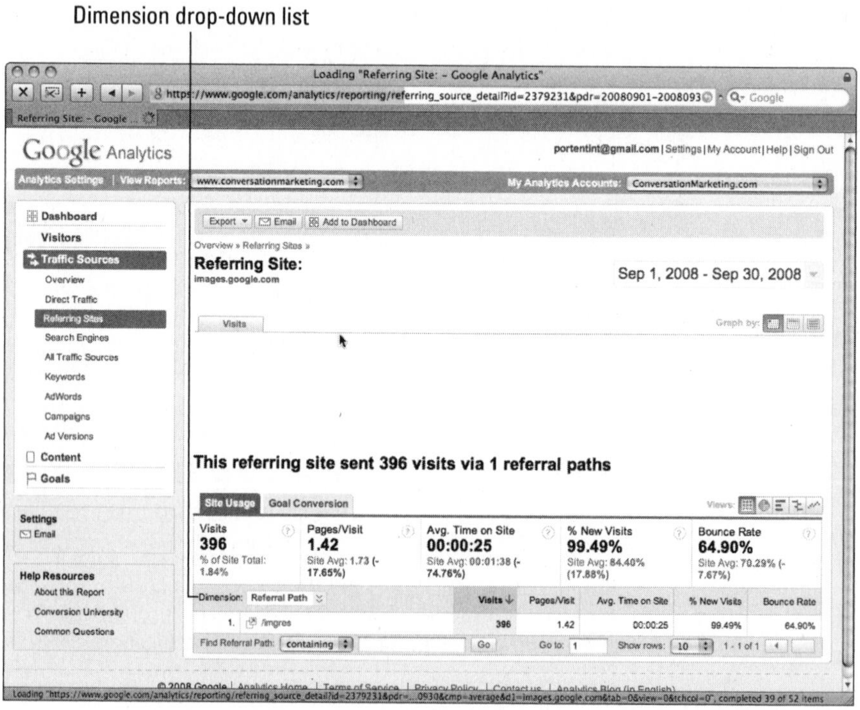

Figure 3-2: This information is not very helpful.

2. **To see the keywords, choose Keyword from the Dimension drop-down list.**

   The result is another dead end (although keywords aren't always a dead end, as the next section explains).

   Sigh. You'll get used to dead ends like these if you do Web analytics long enough. Luckily, there are other options.

3. **Choose Landing Page from the Dimension drop-down list.**

   The Landing Page option shows which pages on the site generated these referrals, as shown in Figure 3-3.

Figure 3-3:
See which landing pages generate referrals.

This referring site sent 396 visits via 67 landing pages					
Site Usage Goal Conversion					
Visits **396** % of Site Total: 1.84%	Pages/Visit **1.42** Site Avg: 1.73 (-17.65%)	Avg. Time on Site **00:00:25** Site Avg: 00:01:38 (-74.76%)	% New Visits **99.49%** Site Avg: 84.40% (17.88%)	Bounce Rate **64.90%** Site Avg: 70.29% (-7.67%)	
Dimension: Landing Page	Visits ↓	Pages/Visit	Avg. Time on Site	% New Visits	Bounce Rate
1. /2008/03/im-the-snidely-whiplash-of-seo.htm	69	1.33	00:00:35	100.00%	73.91%
2. /2008/01/11_internet_marketing_trends_t.htm	60	1.42	00:00:17	100.00%	61.67%
3. /2007/05/microsoft_acquires_aquantive_f.htm	35	1.43	00:00:40	100.00%	60.00%
4. /2007/08/every_time_you_say_web_20_a_ki.htm	28	1.64	00:00:19	100.00%	60.71%
5. /2008/05/internet-marketing-advances-i-like.htm	21	1.57	00:00:14	95.24%	57.14%
6. /2007/10/stump_ian_ask_your_internet_ma.htm	13	1.38	00:00:16	100.00%	61.54%
7. /2008/04/38_things_i_wish_i_knew_when_i.htm	11	1.64	00:00:11	100.00%	45.45%
8. /2008/02/handier_than_hobbits_why_you_r.htm	9	1.33	00:00:03	100.00%	66.67%
9. /2008/04/whats_marketing_peek_into_a_ma.htm	9	1.33	00:00:01	100.00%	66.67%
10. /2008/05/13-ways-generate-customer-hate.htm	9	1.67	00:00:13	100.00%	55.56%
Find Landing Page: containing	Go	Go to: 1	Show rows: 10	1 - 10 of 67	

Interesting. The results show that my number one landing page was a post I wrote that mentions and contains an image of Snidely Whiplash (a cartoon character from the Rocky and Bullwinkle series). See Figure 3-4 for the post.

4. **I go to Google Image Search and do a quick search on *"Snidely Whiplash"*.**

   What do you know? The image from my blog post is right up at the top of the page in Figure 3-5. I just got some pure gold information: At least some of my Google Image referrals are relatively worthless. They're folks looking for Snidely Whiplash, but I write an internet marketing blog, so I shouldn't expect much from that traffic. Nor do I get much: only 21 seconds per visit. But I don't need to worry about that low visit time, either. Nothing's wrong. Some visitors are just ending up in the wrong place because Google's sending them there. My site's working fine.

Book III Chapter 3

Measuring Your Best Referrers

Figure 3-4:
My Snidely
Whiplash
post.

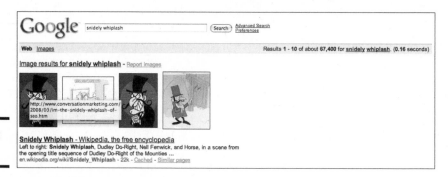

Figure 3-5:
I'm No. 1.

There are no hard and fast rules for what's "good" or "bad" traffic. That's why I haven't written anything like, "More than one minute is a good time on site stat." You have to see what's average for your site and go from there.

See how powerful referrer data is? In just a few minutes, I diagnosed a possible problem, found the source, and eliminated it. But wait, there's more!

Tracking Referring Keywords

If you're getting traffic from search engines (and you'd better be), folks are finding you by searching on keywords. Knowing which keywords they're using to find you gives you a hint as to the questions they might need answered when they first land on your site.

This section holds true for both paid and unpaid keywords. I don't buy any pay per click ads for my blog, so the examples you see here involve unpaid keyword traffic only.

The following steps walk you through an analysis of referring keywords, using Google Analytics and my blog results for the month of September as an example:

1. **Go to www.google.com/analytics and log in. Then click your profile to see the report.**

2. **Click Traffic Sources in the sidebar on the left and then click the Keywords option that appears.**

   The referring keyword report that appears will usually look a lot like the referring site report. See Figure 3-6 for keyword traffic to my site in September of 2008.

Figure 3-6:
The referring keyword report.

3. **Review your keyword report for results that are consistent — and check for anything new or unusual.**

   Looking at this report, I know right away that *Google Analytics Tutorial* is my top traffic generator. And I know why: I did a series a long time ago, and it still generates traffic. A quick look at search results on Google shows I'm No. 1 and No. 2 for the phrase.

   The next few keywords aren't surprising, except for *marketing strategies*. That's a tough keyword, and I've never had any respectable ranking for it on any search engine.

4. **To find out the referring sites for a keyword, click it in the results list. On the page that appears, choose Source from the Dimension drop-down list.**

   I clicked the keyword *marketing strategies* and changed to the Source to see whether I could learn more. Figure 3-7 shows that I get the most traffic from this keyword from Google. Hmm.

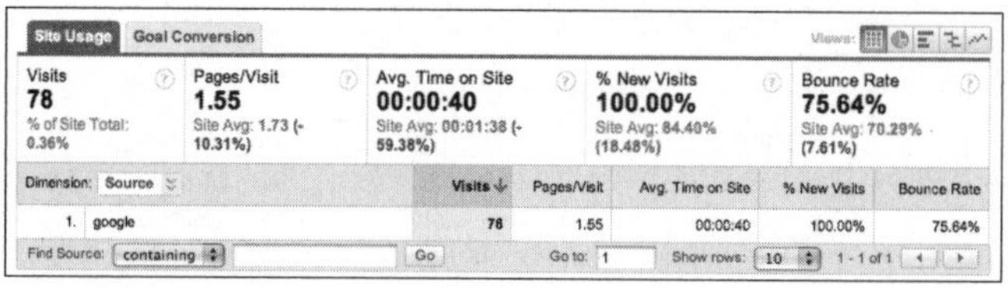

Figure 3-7: Sources for *marketing strategies.*

5. **Based on my result, I go to Google and find out I'm suddenly near the top of page 2 for the phrase. That explains it.**

   Seeing as how the pageviews/visit and time on site aren't bad, and I'm getting traffic even though I'm not yet in the top ten rankings, I should probably look at writing more on the subject so that I can move onto page 1.

   One other keyword leaps out at me: *Landing page.* I'm getting 1.28 pageviews per visit but barely eight seconds onsite. That's awful, and I want to find out why.

   You can see the page in Figure 3-8. But what you don't see — and visitors don't see either — is that the real meaty information is far, far down the page because of the huge image. ***Insight:*** I should either reduce that image's size, or move it farther down the page to improve page performance. Or at least learn that lesson for next time.

Getting fancy

I know how exciting referring site data can be. If you find that the basics outlined in this minibook just aren't enough, you might be interested in more advanced topics, such as

✔ **Custom tagging and campaign management:** Use these tools to track every banner, keyword ad, blog post, and anything else that sends traffic to your site on a very individual, targeted basis. Check out *Web Analytics For Dummies,* by Pedro Sostre and Jennifer LeClaire (WIley), or read the

documentation for your traffic-reporting toolset for more information.

✔ **Referrer-based page customization:** You can actually grab this referrer data on the fly to customize pages so they provide the best user experience. Amazon. com uses this data as part of their product recommendations on their homepage. If that makes your brain hurt, you're not alone. But it is a powerful feature on many sites.

Figure 3-8:
The guilty
page.

Chapter 4: Measuring Visit Quality

In This Chapter

✔ **What makes a good visit**

✔ **Tracking repeat visitors**

✔ **Using pageviews and time on site**

Measuring visit quality involves tracking what's typical for your site and using what you know to set benchmarks. You might notice that I mention nothing about absolute measures of quality visits.

Measuring visit quality is not a science. What you find in this chapter is simply a process for setting some benchmarks that you can try to improve upon. Your mission, should you choose to accept it, is to

✦ Build traffic, but not at the expense of these benchmarks.

✦ Increase time on site and pageviews per visit.

✦ Keep these benchmarks in mind as you look at other statistics.

Note that this chapter assumes you're familiar with the basic measures discussed in Chapters 2 and 3 of this minibook. If you're looking for information on tracking some form of conversion like a sale or a lead, you won't find that here; flip to Chapter 5 in this minibook, instead.

Setting Quality Targets

Take a look at Figure 4-1. How can you tell which referrers are generating good or bad visits? Argh: It's nothing a bunch of numbers — but, it's not as hard to decipher as it might look.

To make these numbers mean something, you have to set parameters for *good* and *bad*. If you're looking for hard-and-fast ways to do this, I'll warn you now that you're in the wrong place. Because every Web site is different, every business has a different profile of a "quality" visit.

You need to set target numbers for the kinds of visitors you want. Even if you have a goal on the site — such as a sale, lead, or white paper download — you still need these separate measures of visit quality. The key is to figure out what your benchmarks are so you can focus on improvement rather than producing a perfect set of numbers.

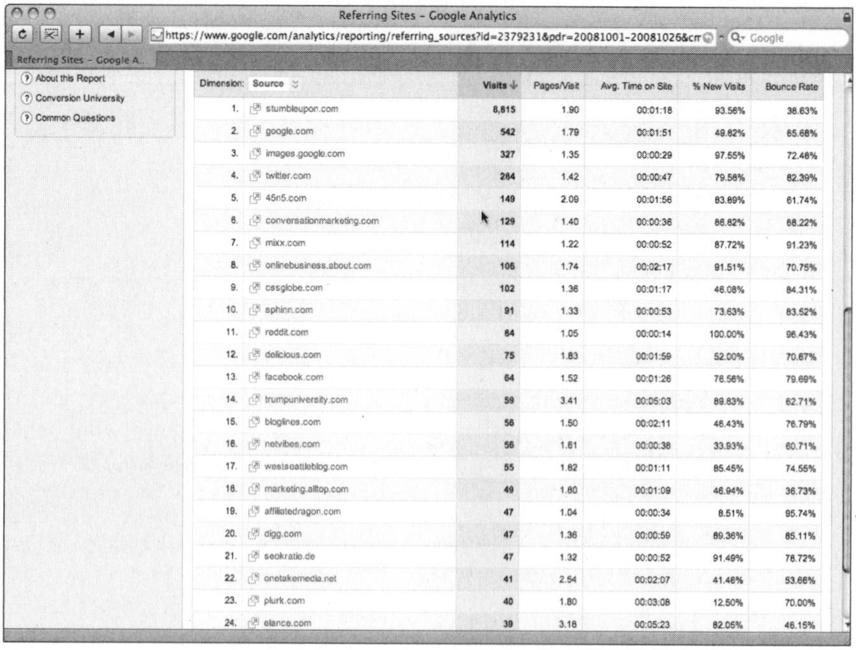

Figure 4-1:
A whole lot
of numbers.

So why not just focus on sales or whatever your ultimate goal is? Well, because even if visitors don't make a purchase, they might still show enough interest to return later, or tell a friend, or do something else you want them to do. You can't just rule out visitors who don't buy anything. Rather, think of their potential: They might still have a lot to offer your business.

The following sections walk you through setting these benchmarks for your business.

Setting benchmarks for pageviews per visit and time on site

To set benchmarks for these numbers, you need to have been running your traffic-reporting tool for at least two to three months. That gives you enough data to set your benchmark, which you do by following these steps (which use Google Analytics as an example):

1. **In Google Analytics, from the main dashboard, click Visitors in the sidebar on the left.**

2. **Click the Visitor Trending option and then click Average Pageviews.**

   This opens the pageviews per visit report, as shown in Figure 4-2. For details on accessing this report in a different tool, you need to check your documentation, but know that this is the report that you want.

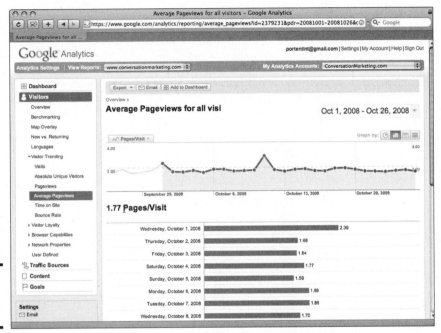

Figure 4-2:
The Pages/
Visit report.

3. **Look at the average for the past two to three months.**

   In Google Analytics, I do this by setting the date range to the last two to three months. The Pages/Visit number just below the chart now shows you the average.

   That average is your target. You want to improve upon that. Visits that exceed this average are good. Visits that don't aren't necessarily bad, but they're not as desirable. See "Applying Those Targets," later in this chapter, for the details.

4. **Navigate to your Time on Site report and, again, find the average for the last two to three months, which will be your target.**

   In Google Analytics, you can do this by clicking Time on Site in the sidebar on the left. It's located under the Average Pageviews option.

Calculating your loyalty benchmark

This section explains how to find out how many returning visitors you have and how to use this as a benchmark for increasing the percentage of returning visitors, which reflects visitor loyalty. The following steps help you set the target, again using Google Analytics as the example reporting tool.

1. **Open the report that calculates your percentage of repeat visitors.**

   In Google Analytics, the best place to start is the New vs. Returning report, shown in Figure 4-3. To access this report, click Visitors in the sidebar on the left. Then click the New vs. Returning option. Note that I use a one-month timeframe in this case. For this benchmark, the timeframe isn't that important. Just be sure you use a sufficiently long time period to account for weekly rises and falls in traffic, as well as any seasonal changes.

   In other reporting tools, you can look for the Returning Visitors or Visitor Loyalty report. The data will be the same: a comparison of one-time and returning visitors.

2. **Take a look at the percentage of returning versus new visitors.**

   In Google Analytics, you find this info on the Site Usage tab (toward the bottom of the screen). In Figure 4-3, my returning visitor percentage is 14.56%, so that's my loyalty target, which I'll want to increase. At the same time, I want to continue adding new visitors. My current number of visits is 20,293, so that's the target I want to improve upon.

Figure 4-3:
The New vs.
Returning
report.

Applying Those Targets

After you have your targets defined, it's time to apply them. In analytics, *applying your targets* means that you're using your benchmarks and seeing whether you improve upon them. If you improve upon them, your site is improving. If you don't improve, you need to continue tweaking your site to improve.

You can apply your targets across every statistic, turning those reports into true analytics. In the following sections, you take a look at a couple of examples.

Checking your top content against your targets

Look at the Top Content report in Figure 4-4.

You can use the time on page data to decide which page is your best as far as visitor attention. If time on page for one page is above the average for the rest of the site, you know that page is beating the *benchmark* — target — that you set. That means that the page is doing its job. It also means you should review that page to figure out why folks like it and spend more time there. Then apply what you learned to the rest of your site.

Figure 4-4:
A Top
Content
report.

For example, in the Top Content report in Figure 4-4, one page has visitors spending 2:13 minutes on the page. That's the highest time on page for any of my top pages! I need to review that page and see what exactly is so interesting to visitors, and whether I can apply the same ideas to the rest of the site. If I can, I might be able to improve the entire site.

Don't get too myopic. If you focus on the time on page data and ignore the pages themselves, you might miss something important: If visitors spend twice as much time on one page, perhaps that page has twice as much information. Always look at this data in context.

Drawing conclusions based on multiple targets

In this section, you see an example of how you can bring the different statistics together. Take a look at the referrer report (All Traffic Sources) in Figure 4-5. Look at pages/visit, average time on site, and percentage of new visits. If a single referrer brings you above-average counts of new visitors, pages/visit, *and* time on site, you know the referrer's a winner.

However, if the numbers start to mix, drawing conclusions gets harder. What if you have a page that brings a lot of new visitors, but lousy page/visit and time on site numbers? Table 4-1 outlines the rules I usually use for referrers of all types.

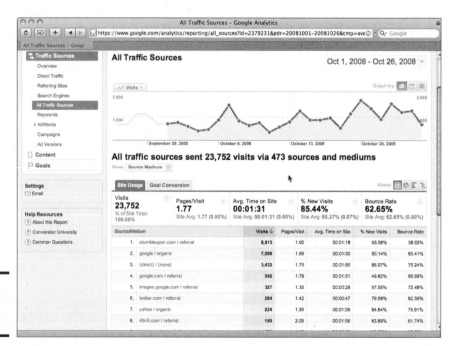

Figure 4-5:
A referrer report.

Table 4-1			**Drawing Conclusions from Multiple Targets**
Pages/ Visit	*Time on Site*	*New Visitors*	*Conclusion*
Above Average	Below Average	Below Average	Might be good or bad. You're getting some interest, but the first page folks land on isn't working for them, so they're moving on to other pages on your site pretty quickly. On the bright side, maybe that page is very easy to figure out, and visitors are responding. Test different page configurations to learn more.
Below Average	Below Average	Above Average	Not good. You're getting new visitors, but they don't like what they're seeing. Look at revamping that first page, and make sure you're reaching the right audience. It's possible this referrer is so perfect that visitors find what they need very quickly. Check conversion rates.
Below Average	Above Average	Above Average	Probably good. This referrer is sending folks who take their time and read everything on the page. Make sure you have a good, clear call to action, though. The low pageview count might indicate that visitors don't know what to do. Check the bounce rate (see the next section).
Above Average	Above Average	Above Average	Clearly a winner. Check conversion and bounce rates to make sure, but this referrer is sending you lots of new, high-quality traffic.

Book III Chapter 4

Measuring Visit Quality

Learning More with Bounce Rate

You can further measure visit quality with *bounce rate*. A bounce occurs if someone visits one page of your Web site and then leaves without clicking to any other pages.

Bounce Rate reports like the one in Figure 4-6 tell you the percentage of visitors who bounce.

Which bounce rate?

In Internet marketing, *bounce rate* can refer to two different things. As used in this chapter, *bounce rate* means the number of people who visit your site, view one page, and then leave without clicking to any other page. In Book V, though, *bounce rate* means the rate at which e-mails sent to a list never reach the recipient. Both are correct uses of the term. Any time you see bounce rate in a traffic report, though, it's referring to the bounce rate I talk about here.

Bounce rate is the ultimate arbiter of visit quality. It shows you

+ Pages that just drive people away
+ Pages that draw visitors further into your site
+ Most important, problems with landing pages

Figure 4-6: A Bounce Rate report.

Analyzing your homepage

Bounce rate is a great statistic to analyze for your homepage. Unless you have a one-page Web site, chances are you want as low of a bounce rate as possible. The report in Figure 4-7 shows how small changes in homepage content and layout can affect bounce rate. Between April and June of 2007, I put a lot of time into changing my site's design to lower the bounce rate: I added easier navigation, cleaned up the pages, and added a better search tool. So the bounce rate plunged. When traffic rose steeply in October, bounce rate increased again.

As I publish new stories on my homepage, I can see the effect those stories have on bounce rate. That, in turn, tells me what my audience likes or doesn't like. I can learn from that and deliver stuff they really like.

Sometimes, a high bounce rate is okay. If you have a blog, for instance, a lot of readers will drop in from an RSS feed or a link on another site, read something, and then leave. The more article-focused your site is, the less bounce rate might matter.

Book III Chapter 4

Measuring Visit Quality

Figure 4-7:
The bounce rate for my homepage.

Spotting bottlenecks and missed opportunities

One of the best things you can do with visit quality measurement is find bottlenecks or missed opportunities in your site: namely, places where a lot of visitors who might have otherwise become customers end up leaving or going off course.

Look at the content report in Figure 4-8, which shows a list of pages with time spent on each page and bounce rate.

See item 10? It has a 92% bounce rate. That's not always a bad sign. As I mention earlier, if many readers are finding their way to this page from other blogs, they might simply read and then move on.

However, any top-ten page on your site that's shedding over 80 percent of visitors is probably costing you some valuable opportunities. Yeah, you might have a bad bounce rate, but if you know about it, you can do something about it. You could add more links to other articles, for example, or look at whether something in the page is driving visitors away.

	Page	Pageviews ↓	Unique Pageviews	Time on Page	Bounce Rate	% Exit	$ Index
1.	/	45,899	33,274	00:01:30	52.91%	43.58%	> $0.00
2.	/2008/03/the_internet_marketing_list_58.htm	34,128	28,147	00:03:02	82.83%	79.30%	> $0.00
3.	/2008/05/13-ways-generate-customer-hate...	25,506	23,096	00:02:30	91.34%	87.91%	$0.00
4.	/2008/08/9_words_that_dont_exist.htm	16,721	9,967	00:01:52	48.75%	54.88%	$0.00
5.	/2007/02/google_analytics_video_tutoria_1...	13,173	10,832	00:02:17	52.41%	45.65%	> $0.00
6.	/2008/02/10_principles_of_internet_mark.htm	10,637	6,039	00:01:43	45.35%	52.24%	$0.00
7.	/2007/07/google_analytics_tutorials_all.htm	9,397	5,442	00:00:21	21.34%	18.39%	$0.00
8.	/2008/08/reviewed_google_checkout_paym...	8,439	7,986	00:00:44	86.80%	66.33%	$0.00
9.	/cmonline/intro.cfm	8,314	6,599	00:01:31	0.33%	49.41%	$0.02
10.	/2008/04/linkadage-selling-edu-blog-space...	8,267	5,785	00:04:18	92.01%	89.33%	$0.00
11.	/2007/02/google_analytics_tutorial_3_di.htm	6,260	4,863	00:02:15	34.94%	29.06%	$0.00
12.	/2007/02/google_analytics_video_tutoria.htm	6,190	5,000	00:02:46	51.78%	31.42%	$0.00
13.	/2008/04/38_things_i_wish_i_knew_when_i...	6,107	4,986	00:03:03	73.38%	65.29%	$0.00
14.	/2008/01/11_internet_marketing_trends_t.htm	6,034	4,768	00:02:12	73.91%	68.23%	$0.00
15.	/internet_marketing/	5,687	3,888	00:01:11	51.67%	22.05%	$0.00
16.	/2007/11/65_easy_ways_to_improve_onlin...	5,542	3,411	00:01:54	52.62%	56.10%	$0.00
17.	/2007/03/google_analytics_tutorial_4_wo.htm	5,057	4,297	00:02:55	62.35%	45.64%	> $0.00
18.	/internet-marketing-book/	4,605	4,238	00:01:42	62.59%	51.65%	$0.09
19.	/2007/09/streaming_video_creating_a_pro...	4,668	4,309	00:02:49	81.49%	79.99%	$0.00
20.	/2008/09/10-seo-and-marketing-friendly.htm	4,473	2,966	00:01:42	66.20%	60.09%	$0.00
21.	http://www.stumbleupon.com/refer.php?url...	4,105	2,587	00:02:31	80.00%	53.89%	$0.00
22.	/2008/05/stumbleupon-traffic-is-worth-s.htm	3,641	2,512	00:01:58	59.36%	61.21%	$0.00
23.	/web_analytics/	3,674	2,575	00:01:14	49.22%	27.05%	$0.00
24.	/2007/12/social_media_press_release_the...	3,514	2,260	00:01:55	61.40%	61.72%	$0.00

Figure 4-8:
A content report.

Chapter 5: Using Conversion Goals

In This Chapter

✔ Setting conversion goals

✔ Analyzing goal conversions

✔ Technical issues with goal tracking

✔ Interpreting conversion data

A major step in moving from reporting to analytics is knowing what you want to measure in terms of your business goals. This goes beyond visits or traffic, and usually moves to leads or sales or something similar.

In the biz, we call those *conversions*. A conversion occurs any time a visitor changes from a visitor to a customer (a sale) or a potential customer (a lead). Conversions can also occur when a visitor somehow takes a significant step toward offering value to your business. I talk more about that later in this chapter. Regardless, a visitor converts into something more valuable than a passerby. Get it?

Although tracking pageviews, time on site, and traffic quality is helpful, you need to know how your site's helping you achieve those goals. This is where Web analytics really shines. Virtually all major Web analytics packages — including free ones, such as Yahoo! Analytics and Google Analytics — support sophisticated goal tracking.

In this chapter, I talk about selecting, tracking, and analyzing conversions; and I use Google Analytics in my examples. I suggest following along using that tool, if you can. If not, just focus on the concepts I present here because after you understand those, you can apply them to any traffic reporting package.

Determining Key Performance Indicators

Goals are based on specific metrics that drive your business and Web site. These metrics — what make or break success — are *key performance indicators,* or KPIs. KPIs track the health of your online marketing efforts, for the good (success KPIs) or for the not-so-good (warning KPIs).

A KPI is *not* the same as a conversion goal! A KPI is a general measure of success for your business. It can be applied to your business's online efforts, offline work, brick-and-mortar store, Web site, or anything else. A conversion goal, on the other hand, is a specific event: an online sale or an in-store sale. You measure KPIs in terms of conversion goals. Don't confuse the two.

Before you go any further, write down your KPIs.

The ideal KPI will

✦ **Give you at-a-glance insight:** This gives you information as to how your Web site is performing.

✦ **Stand on its own as a measure of success or failure:** You shouldn't need to look at other data to get a basic idea of site performance.

✦ **Make business sense:** Interpreting a typical KPI won't require an expert Web analyst.

✦ **Be long-lived:** KPIs can change, but not often. You want to be able to compare KPI data day by day, month by month, and year by year. (See "Maintaining consistent goals" later in this chapter for more on the importance of consistency.)

Success KPIs are those that, if they increase, indicate you're doing well. They might include

✦ Number of sales

✦ Number of leads

✦ Conversion rate for leads or sales

✦ Number of E-mail a Friend submissions

✦ Number of e-mail newsletter signups

✦ Number of white paper (or other) downloads

Warning KPIs are those that, if they increase, mean something could be wrong. They might include

✦ Cost per sale

✦ Cost per lead

✦ Form abandonment rate

✦ Complaint frequency

✦ Bounce rate

No two businesses are exactly alike, so chances are you'll have some unique KPIs. The most common KPIs are

+ Cost per sale

+ Cost per lead

+ Revenue

+ Return on investment

For a very detailed look at all things Web analytic, check out *Web Analytics For Dummies* by Pedro Sostre and Jennifer LeClaire (Wiley).

Go write down at least two (preferably more) KPIs for your Web site. After you have your KPIs, you're ready to move on to the next step — setting your conversion goals.

Defining Conversion Goals

Goals? KPIs? What's the difference? It might seem like they're the same, but they're not. KPIs measure performance. Goals measure *success* and only success. All goals are KPIs. Not all KPIs are goals. Dizzy yet?

KPIs are signs of a response to your message and site. Goals are what happens when the visitor does what you want him to. Goals are always narrowly defined success KPIs, such as

+ A sale

+ A lead

+ An e-mail newsletter signup

+ A download of a specific article

+ A view of a specific page

Maintaining consistent goals

You *must* select goals you'll have around for the duration of any campaign. Consistency is critical.

For example, say you're doing a new product launch campaign. As part of that campaign, you're offering to send visitors a free product in exchange for an e-mail signup. You need to track those e-mail signups throughout the launch campaign! If you switch from tracking e-mail signups to, say, tracking product purchases halfway through, you'll have no way to compare performance of different advertising strategies.

Many goals will exist for the entire life of your business: Sales and leads are great examples. In those cases, it's important that you track those goals the same way over time.

For example: You're tracking the sales conversion goal based on views of the final check-out page. Then you decide to track the final order confirmation page, instead. That will throw off your numbers and make it impossible to track performance over time.

Checking out conversion goal pages

Here's one hallmark of a great conversion goal: a specific, unique *goal page* that indicates conversion. The following examples illustrate what I mean:

✦ **If I buy something from your online store,** the last page I see is the one that reads "Thank you for your business!" and has my order information on it. You know, for certain, that anyone reaching that page bought something and therefore did something you wanted them to do.

✦ **If I subscribe to an e-mail newsletter,** I usually land on a Thank You for Your Subscription page. That page is the goal page for e-mail signup. See Figure 5-1 for an example.

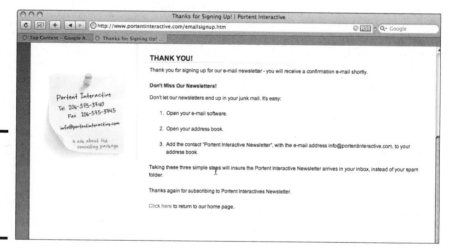

Figure 5-1:
The goal page for an e-mail newsletter signup.

✦ **If I then complete the Contact Us form** on your Web site, the resultant Thank You page for that form is a goal page, too.

A goal page almost always marks the *end* of the goal process. In other words, it marks a *conversion*. The visitor has become a customer, lead, or subscriber. The visitor has converted from being a generic audience member to a participant in your business.

So you need to change your goals?

Always maintain consistent goals. If you do have to change, do the following:

1. **Measure the old and new goals side by side for a full business cycle (a week, a month, or longer).**

2. **Compute the average difference.**

3. **Apply that formula to future calculations.**

   Be very careful when you use this kind of percentage conversion because there's no way you're going to get even 75 percent accuracy. But, it's better than nothing.

Figuring out your conversion goals

Now, it's time to define the goals and goal pages for your site. Earlier in this chapter, I ask you to write down some KPIs. Review them. Do any of them map easily to a specific goal on your site? For example, a KPI of *revenue* would map to the Thank You for Your Order page in your shopping cart.

✦ **If your KPIs are some of your goals,** find the goal page for a completed conversion for each goal. Then visit that goal page and copy and paste that page's address (as shown in Figure 5-2) next to the KPI (as shown in Figure 5-3).

✦ **If none of your KPIs are goals,** look at your site again. If you still can't find anything, read the next section to learn a bit about finding those hidden goals.

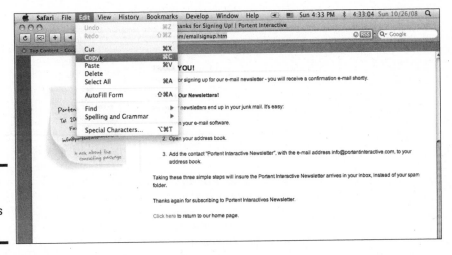

Figure 5-2:
Copy the goal page's address.

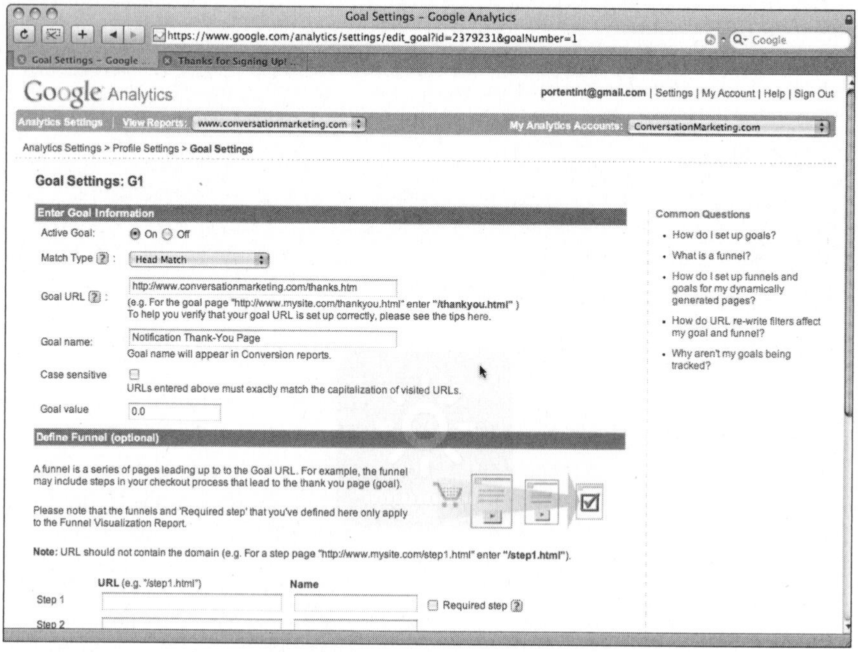

Figure 5-3:
The goal
and the
goal page
address.

Finding hidden goals

Your site might not have any clear, well-defined goals if it

+ Doesn't have e-commerce

+ Lacks an e-mail newsletter (shame on you!)

+ Doesn't collect leads

Regardless, all sorts of measurable goals reside in your site. They might be hiding, but they're there. You just have to coax them out.

Hidden goals might include

+ **A download:** If you have a white paper, brochure, or other information on your site in PDF, folks might download it. If they download it, chances are they're more interested than the average passersby. With a little work, you can track those downloads as a goal.

+ **A pageview:** If folks view one particular page on your site, does that tell you they're going to call? Think about those folks who view the Contact Us page. You can easily track that as a goal.

+ **A video:** If a visitor watches your entire video about your corporate philosophy, that's definitely a win. Someone with a bit of technical expertise can help you track completed views as goals, too.

+ **A Forward to a Friend link:** Does your site have a Forward This Page to a Friend tool? That's definitely a goal. Track how many folks forward pages to friends; those people are interested enough to recommend you.

+ **A ZIP code search:** If you have lots of stores and a visitor tries to find one, that's a conversion.

There are even fancier hidden goals: You can track all visitors who look at more than seven pages on your site as a conversion, for example. Tracking these types of goals generally requires a fair amount of expertise, though, so I'm not going into them here.

Hidden goals are rarely worth as much as a sale, but they're still conversions because visitors who complete them have taken a step toward working with you. Track those visitors, and you get a peek at how your site is performing in terms of your business.

Attaching Monetary Value to Goals

Goals don't mean much if you can't attach some real value to them. All goals have some worth to your organization. It's important to track that worth because you need to see whether you profited in landing that conversion.

For example, say I sell a widget in my online store for $100. Yay! Unfortunately, when I look at my ad spending, I see that I spent an average of $120 per sale. Hmm. That conversion actually cost me.

Attaching and tracking value keeps you focused on growth, and keeps you from spending two dollars to earn one.

Valuing e-commerce conversions

Easy, right? An e-commerce conversion is worth the sale amount, minus any costs:

```
ECOM Value = Sale Amount - (shipping + handling + other)
```

You'll want to figure out the average value of an e-commerce conversion, too, if possible.

But you need to figure out another critical metric: namely, the *lifetime* value of that conversion. How much will that new customer earn for you over time? You must know this! It could be perfectly reasonable to spend $120 to get a $100 sale if the lifetime value of that customer is $500.

Here's how you can figure it out, where *Customer Lifetime* is the average length of time a customer buys from you with no additional outside influence:

```
Lifetime Value = (Total Sales/Year ÷ Number of Customers) ÷ Customer Lifetime
```

By knowing the lifetime value, you put your sales in context and make sure you don't shut down an ad buy that's actually paying off for you in the long run.

Valuing leads

Attaching a value to a lead is a bit more difficult. Someone fills out a Lead Request form, which is one of those really common Please Send Me More Information forms you find on many Web sites. That doesn't directly translate into value for your company.

So, you need to figure out the value of a lead, using averages:

```
Lead Value = [Lead to Customer Conversion Rate] X [Avg. Customer Value]
```

Here's an example. Say I run a business where my Web site generates 100 leads per year; of those leads, 10 percent become customers. The average customer pays $10,000 per year for a consulting contract. So

```
10% X $10,000 = $1,000
```

My average lead value is $1,000.

You *do* need to be able to compute the value of a customer and the conversion rate of leads to customers. That's important to your business regardless of Internet marketing, though. If you don't already know customer value, divide total sales over at least one year by the number of customers in that year. It's not perfect, but it'll do.

Valuing soft goals

Soft goals, like a white paper download, are even harder to track. The connection between that conversion and an ultimate conversion to customer is distant. So take any numbers you compute here with a grain of salt.

To figure out the value of a soft goal, you must know the following:

✦ **Total goals:** The number of downloads, or pageviews, or whatever else.

✦ **Estimated conversion rate:** This is the hard part. You might not get enough information to track conversion rates directly, so you have to estimate based on four different statistics:

   • Total *unique visitors* (each visitor returning to your site any number of times) to your site

   • Percentage of those visitors who complete the goal (% Goal)

   • Percentage of unique visitors who become customers (% Conversions)

✦ **Average value of those customers** (Avg. Value)

Then calculate conversion rate, as follows:

```
Soft Goal Value = % Goal X % Conversions X Avg. Value
```

Here's an example of a soft goal–value calculation: Say I have a white paper on my site. I know the following:

✦ My site receives 10,000 total unique visitors per year.

✦ Ten percent of those visitors (1,000 people) download the white paper (% Goal).

✦ I keep track of their names, so I know that 10 percent of the white paper readers become customers (% Conversions).

✦ And I know that in one year, I get $250,000 in sales from 25 customers, or an average value of $10,000/customer (Avg. Value).

So, the value of one white paper download to my business is:

```
10% X 10% X $10,000 = $100
```

And, one white paper download is worth $100 to my business.

Valuing the immeasurable

Some goals can't be easily valued. A voter doesn't carry a monetary value (hopefully). Neither does a potential parishioner in a church.

There's no great way to attach a consistent value to these goals. But you *can* assign point values to them.

I usually assign an arbitrary value: one point per new person who visits a political Web site, for example. Then, compute the cost of each point over the longest possible time period, and use that cost as your measure. Work to improve on that cost, and you have a cost instead of a value, but it's still a baseline metric.

Setting Up Goal Tracking

Setting up goal tracking is straightforward — if you know the goal page.

I've seen broken or badly configured shopping carts where the last checkout page isn't so easy to track. Be sure to test and verify that your goal page really is unique within your site, and that multiple goals don't share a single page.

In a program like Google Analytics, you identify the goal page to the program, and it does the rest. Here's how:

1. **Log into Google Analytics.**

2. **Click Edit next to the Web site for which you want to track the goal.**

3. **Under Conversion Goals and Funnel, click Edit next to any goal that's not configured.**

4. **Open a new browser window and go to your Web site.**

5. **Complete the form, checkout, or other process you want to track.**

6. **Copy the address of the final page in the process.**

   It'll usually be a Thank You–style page. See "Checking out conversion goal pages" earlier in this chapter for an introduction to goal pages.

7. **Paste that address into the Goal URL field.**

8. **Name the goal, leave the other settings alone (you can learn more about those in Google Analytics Help, later), and then click Finish.**

   After your goal is configured (refer to Figure 5-3), Google Analytics reports all goal completions.

You can then compare paid search keywords, organic search keywords, advertising, e-mail campaigns, and most other aspects of site traffic in the context of goal conversion.

Setting up e-commerce tracking

If your site includes a store, you'll probably want to know how much money you're earning from each traffic driver — a search engine result, a review on another Web site, a link from a blog — or ad on the site.

To set up this tracking in Google Analytics and in most other reporting tools, you need to alter the final page of your checkout process to send the sales data to the tool. The code will typically resemble Figure 5-4.

If that looks like gibberish, don't try to set up e-commerce tracking on your own. Instead, talk to your developer or Webmaster about getting set up.

Even if you have to pay someone to get e-commerce tracking working, though, it's worth it. Figure 5-5 shows you just how much detail you can get with e-commerce data built into your analytics report. In Figure 5-5, I can actually see the value of a pageview on a single page, based on how many customers made a purchase after seeing that page. That kind of insight can help you steer customers to the pages that will best answer their questions and likely get them to buy.

```
script type="text/javascript">
    var pageTracker = _gat._getTracker("UA-XXXXX-1");
    pageTracker._trackPageview();
    pageTracker._addTrans(
        "1234",                    // Order ID
        "Mountain View",           // Affiliation
        "11.99",                   // Total
        "1.29",                    // Tax
        "5",                       // Shipping
        "San Jose",                // City
        "California",              // State
        "USA"                      // Country
    );

    pageTracker._addItem(
        "5678",                    // Item Number
        "DD44",                    // SKU
        "T-Shirt",                 // Product Name
        "Green Medium",            // Category
        "11.99",                   // Price
        "1"                        // Quantity
    );
    pageTracker._trackTrans();
</script>
```

Figure 5-4:
Sample
e-commerce
tracking
code.

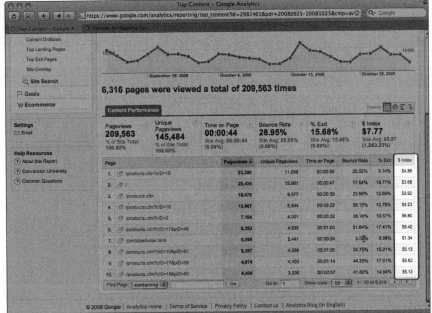

Figure 5-5:
Dig deep
with
e-commerce
tracking.

Book III
Chapter 5

Using Conversion
Goals

Tracking goals manually

If for some reason you can't set up goal tracking in your traffic-reporting tool, all is not lost.

Remember that your goals have goal pages. You can still track those pages by pageview. In Figure 5-6, I can see goal conversions by looking at the top pages report.

1. **In Google Analytics, go to the Top Content report.**

2. **Look for the page that is your Thank You page at the end of the check-out process or that appears after the reader completes the information request, or whatever else represents a completed conversion goal.**

   In Figure 5-6, for example, I can see that I had one conversion because I had one unique pageview on my e-mail signup confirmation page.

You can check what's driving traffic to that goal page, too, by clicking the /emailsignup.htm link in the Page column of the report. See Book III, Chapter 3 for a refresher on tracking referrers.

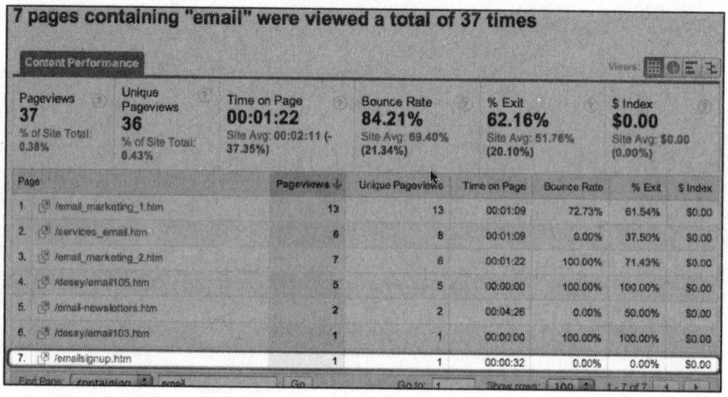

Figure 5-6:
Top pages
showing
conversions.

Interpreting Conversion Data

After tracking is set up, the reporting tool shows you conversion data for your goals in a separate report. That data requires some interpretation. The following sections offer a few examples of typical problems and opportunities you might find.

The costly keywords

In the report in Figure 5-7, you see a list of keywords generating traffic to the site. Note that I had to blur out the actual keywords in this example to protect the innocent. Your report will show actual keywords instead of blurs.

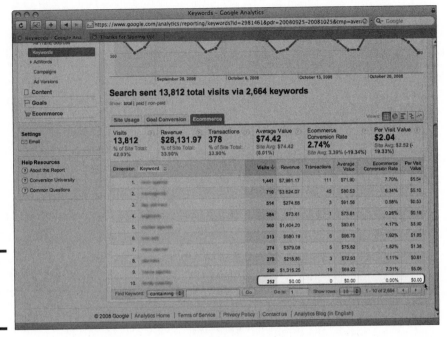

Figure 5-7:
The keywords report.

Some of these keywords are clearly not pulling their weight, such as the keyword that's not generating any revenue in Figure 5-7. If you're spending money on a keyword, consider whether those are dollars well spent. In my example, I might want to let go of the keyword that isn't generating any revenue for me.

Almost any paid search campaign, no matter how well managed, can benefit from an occasional review of actual conversion performance. See Book IV for more about paid search.

The hidden gold mine

Sometimes, one page or product on your site generates a far higher conversion rate than the others. A report like the content report with dollar index in Figure 5-8 can reveal them.

In that report, it's clear that one page is generating incredibly high value because it has a very high $ index. It might be a fluke; but then again, it might not. But it certainly pays to check.

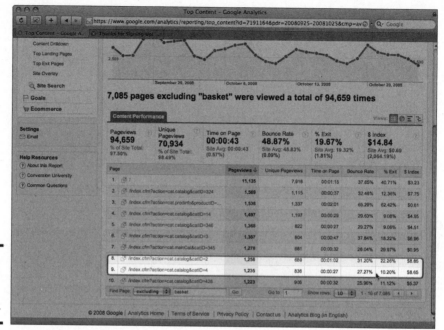

Figure 5-8:
Content
report with
dollar index.

The great landing page

Along the same lines as the Hidden Gold Mine, conversion data can show you the one page on your site that drives the best or worst conversion rate when it acts as a landing page.

A *landing page* is any page from your site at which visitors from other sites arrive. They *land* there.

Because search engines and other Web sites link to whatever page on your site they choose, every page of your site could be a lander. So you need to spot which pages are becoming landing pages, and adjust them to best answer visitors' questions.

Look at the report in Figure 5-9. It shows a few pages that have become major landing points for visitors coming from other sites.

You can use that data to find the landing pages that get the most traffic, and then make sure they're also driving proportional conversions. If they are, great! You've confirmed that things are working. If they aren't, you can tweak them to do a better job.

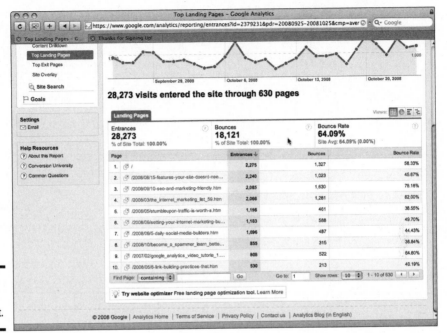

Figure 5-9:
Landing
page report.

Chapter 6: Using Goal Funnels

In This Chapter
✔ **Finding funnels**

✔ **Setting up funnel tracking**

✔ **Analyzing funnel data**

Some goals have multiple steps from beginning to end: A shopping cart check-out process, a multiple-page form, and a survey are all good examples. Such multiple-step processes are *funnels*.

Funnels consist of many small conversions in succession. If visitors complete only the first few pages, they don't complete the ultimate goal. Remember that the goal is a conversion that ties directly to a KPI, like a completed sale, or someone requesting more information from your sales force. See Chapter 5 in this minibook for a refresher. Conversions are what drive your KPIs: They're what help you succeed.

For example, in a shopping cart, each page of the checkout process is a small goal. The visitor must first enter a billing address and click Next Step. That's one goal. Then the shopper must select Shipping and click Next Step again. That's another goal, and so on, until the shopper clicks Place Order, which is the goal you care about. When someone clicks Place Order, he pays you money. That money goes to revenue, which is a KPI.

If a visitor completes the first goal — entering billing information — and then abandons the order, you need to know about it. Something might have happened. For example, a usability issue might have become obvious, a link might be broken, or a 25-field form might have intimidated the user into leaving.

Find out where these bailout points are, and you can greatly improve goal-conversion rate.

But more goal funnels exist than just checkout. Figuring out how to find them is a good first step.

Finding a Funnel

Any time you have multiple steps in a conversion process, you have a funnel. Some funnels occupy multiple pages but only a single endpoint and goal, such as the checkout process shown in Figure 6-1. A three-page, lead-generation form, such as the one shown in Figure 6-2, works the same way. These point-to-point processes are linear. The visitor starts at one end of the funnel and concludes on the final goal-conversion page. They're the easiest funnels to track.

Figure 6-1:
A typical
checkout
process.

Figure 6-2:
A multiple-
page lead-
generation
form.

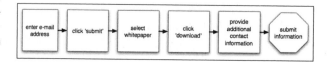

Finding the right funnel and tracking it can get more complicated if you have a funnel with one starting point and multiple endpoints. For example, the process shown in Figure 6-3 has three valid goals to track: an e-mail signup form, a download, and a purchase.

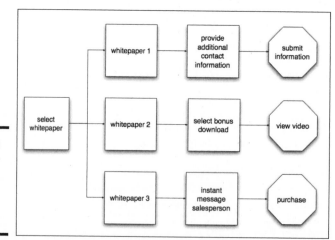

Figure 6-3:
A multiple-
step,
multiple-
goal
process.

AJAX: Friend or foe?

AJAX — Asynchronous JavaScript and XML — is a nifty technology that allows developers to change what's displayed on a Web page without actually reloading the page. It's a great way to create beautiful Web sites and interfaces (such as Flickr). However, it's an analytics nightmare. Until recently, analytics was built around tracking pageviews. AJAX, however, reduces pageviews. So, a multiple-step process that's handled by AJAX, instead of taking you from one page to the next, can be tricky to track.

The single entry point and multiple exit points comprise a funnel, but any end-point is a conversion. Deeper conversions are better, but they all generate value to the business. Don't rule out this type of funnel. It still matters! By tracking depth and results, you can find ways to improve conversion rates at all levels.

Other goal funnels on your site might include the following:

✦ **Forward to a Friend:** This one has two steps. Click to start the process, and then enter a friend's e-mail address and forward the page.

✦ **A dealer search:** The visitor first enters a ZIP code and then clicks a result and clicks Contact This Dealer. This funnel is another one that's worth tracking.

✦ **AJAX-driven process:** This funnel folds numerous pages into a single page. It's still a funnel, however. Tracking it requires a little JavaScript expertise, but if you made the investment in the process, it's worth the extra work.

Regardless of your final goal, look at any conversion process on your site that requires more than one button or link to complete, and you have a funnel.

Setting Up Goal Funnel Tracking

Some reporting packages, such as Omniture Site Catalyst (`www.omniture.com/en/products/web_analytics/sitecatalyst`), allow you to track a basic goal funnel by using the Pathfinder Report or the Fallout Report Builder. For other packages, such as Google Analytics, you need to know the unique address of each page in the checkout process and then add those addresses to a goal funnel report.

I use Google Analytics and a shopping cart in the following example. This procedure works in just about every reporting tool that includes funnel tracking. Follow these steps.

1. **Step through the checkout process and record the URL of each page in the process.**

   In Figure 6-4, I cut and pasted each page's URL into a spreadsheet as a temporary notepad.

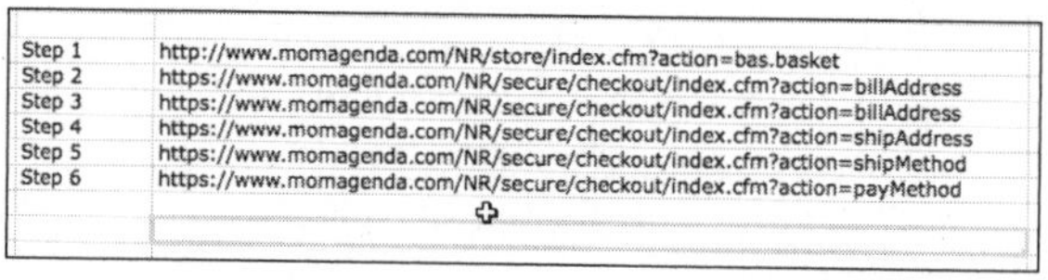

Figure 6-4:
The
checkout
process,
page by
page.

Step 1	http://www.momagenda.com/NR/store/index.cfm?action=bas.basket
Step 2	https://www.momagenda.com/NR/secure/checkout/index.cfm?action=billAddress
Step 3	https://www.momagenda.com/NR/secure/checkout/index.cfm?action=billAddress
Step 4	https://www.momagenda.com/NR/secure/checkout/index.cfm?action=shipAddress
Step 5	https://www.momagenda.com/NR/secure/checkout/index.cfm?action=shipMethod
Step 6	https://www.momagenda.com/NR/secure/checkout/index.cfm?action=payMethod

Figure 6-4: The checkout process, page by page.

2. **In Google Analytics, open the Profile Settings page.**

3. **In the Conversion Goals and Funnel section, click Add a New Goal or click the goal to which you want to add the funnel.**

   Book III, Chapter 5 explains how to set up goals in Google Analytics.

4. **On the Goal Settings page that appears, set up your goal.**

5. **In your new or existing goal, add the funnel for tracking by entering the unique address of each page in the checkout process under the URL.**

6. **Give each page a name you'll understand.**

   Figure 6-5 shows you an example.

7. **Save your new funnel.**

   Within a few hours, you have goal funnel data.

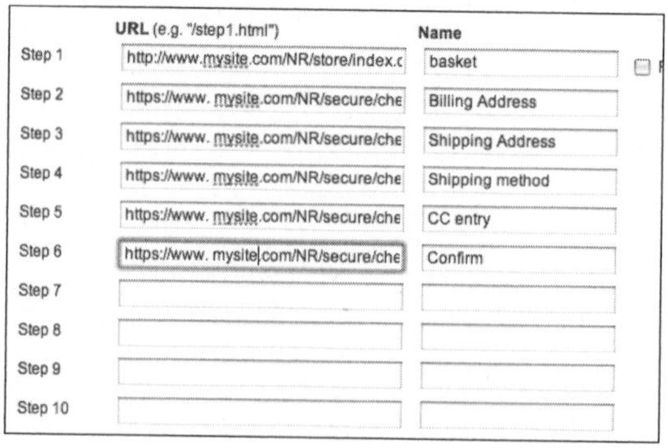

	URL (e.g. "/step1.html")	Name	
Step 1	http://www.mysite.com/NR/store/index.c	basket	
Step 2	https://www. mysite.com/NR/secure/che	Billing Address	
Step 3	https://www. mysite.com/NR/secure/che	Shipping Address	
Step 4	https://www. mysite.com/NR/secure/che	Shipping method	
Step 5	https://www. mysite.com/NR/secure/che	CC entry	
Step 6	https://www. mysite.com/NR/secure/che	Confirm	
Step 7			
Step 8			
Step 9			
Step 10			

Figure 6-5: Setting up a goal funnel for check out.

Some carts use the same page throughout so that even as customers move from billing to shipping to payment information to place an order, the page keeps the same URL. Don't despair: You can work around this situation in several ways. For example, go to Google Analytics (`www.google.com/analytics`) and type **goal funnel** in the Search box at the top of the page to see its solution. Or, talk to your developer.

Interpreting Goal Funnel Data

After you have the data, you need to use it. The typical reporting tool shows you a report resembling the one shown in Figure 6-6.

This report shows you, step by step, how many folks move through the process. I always check funnel reports for these items:

✦ **The biggest abandonment point:** In Figure 6-7, you can see that only 53 percent of visitors proceed from their shopping baskets to the page where they enter their billing addresses. That's a loss of customers in the checkout process. If you can reduce that abandonment at that point, you can greatly improve the overall conversion rate.

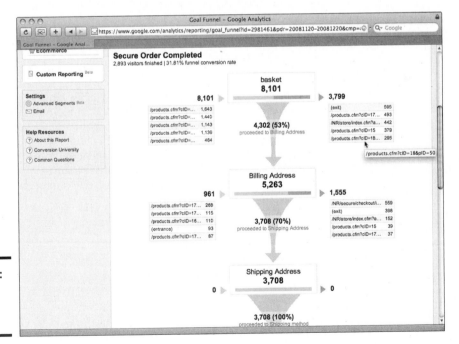

Figure 6-6:
A goal funnel report.

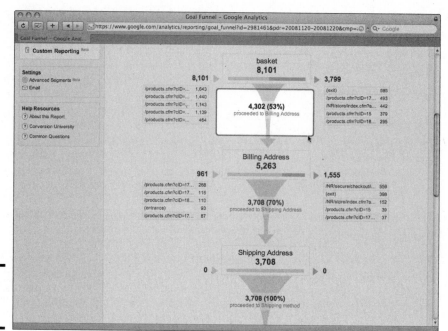

Figure 6-7:
The bailout
point.

♦ **Unexpected entry points:** Figure 6-8 shows where site visitors are entering the checkout process at the Billing Address page. I didn't expect that. My checkout process starts at the Cart page, and that's what I assumed was my entry point. But if you think about it, that must mean that people are adding products to their carts, looking around a bit more, and then moving to the Checkout page. It might make sense, therefore, to add a Proceed Directly to Checkout step.

Put the two together, and you can make one immediate improvement to this cart: Let customers go directly to the Checkout page without first approving their shopping baskets. That would probably reduce instances of bailout.

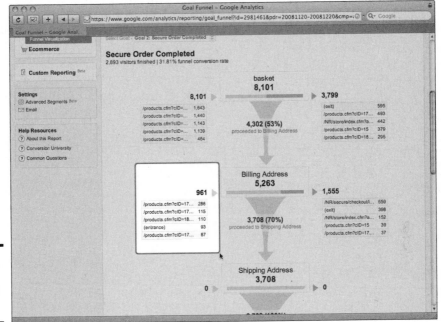

Figure 6-8:
An
unexpected
entry point.

Book IV

Online Advertising and Pay Per Click

The 5th Wave   By Rich Tennant

"We have no problem funding your Web site, Frank. Of all the chicken farmers operating Web sites, yours has the most impressive cluck-through rates."

Contents at a Glance

Chapter 1: Grasping PPC Methods 339

Seeing How Pay Per Click Works 339
Knowing How Search Engines Determine Relevancy........................ 340
Figuring Out Whether You Need PPC 341

Chapter 2: Combining PPC and Search Engines 345

Selecting a PPC Search Engine.. 345
Using Google AdWords 347
Using Yahoo! Search Marketing.. 358
Using MSN adCenter.. 372

Chapter 3: Making Keyword Lists That Sell 379

Choosing Keywords 379
Organizing Keywords in Ad Groups.. 380
Working with Match Types 381
Segmenting Keyword Lists by Destination URLs.............................. 384
Using Advanced Keyword Targeting in Yahoo! and MSN................. 386
Expanding Keyword Lists 388
Contracting Keyword Lists 390

Chapter 4: Writing Ads That Earn Clicks and Pay You Back 391

Working with PPC Ads 391
Writing PPC Ad Copy 394
Testing for Successful Ads 396
Determining When to Change an Ad 400

Chapter 5: Budgeting and Bidding on Keywords 403

Determining Your PPC Budget... 403
Entering Your Budget in the Big Three Search Engines 405
Budgeting by Campaign.. 407
Bidding on Keywords 409
Bidding by Day and Time 411
Tailoring Your Spending... 415

Chapter 6: Legally Speaking: PPC and the Law 417

Understanding Editorial Guidelines 417
Dealing with Click Fraud 422

Chapter 7: Using Tools, Tips, and Tricks of the Trade 425

Using Offline Editors 425
Using Keyword Traffic Tools.. 428
Employing Geotargeting 431
Understanding Demographic Bidding.. 432
Managing a Content Network Campaign 434
Choosing an Analytics Package 439

Chapter 1: Grasping PPC Methods

In This Chapter

✓ Getting to know pay per click

✓ Understanding search engines and relevancy

✓ Deciding whether PPC is right for you

*P*ay per click (PPC) — also known as *cost per click (CPC)* — is a type of paid advertising, such as paid search, sponsored listings, sponsored links, and partner ads. In a PPC model, the advertiser pays the site that hosts the ad space only if a user clicks its ads and goes through to the *destination URL* or *landing page* — the location on the Internet where the person who clicked the ad ends up.

In this chapter, you discover how pay per click works and find tips to help you decide whether you need to add PPC to your Web marketing strategy.

Seeing How Pay Per Click Works

PPC ads are often used in search engines like Google, Yahoo!, and MSN, generally along the top and right sides of the pages that contain search results. These ads don't appear unless someone performs a search in that engine, and the ads that *do* appear are those that the engine deems most relevant to the user's search results (see "Knowing How Search Engines Determine Relevancy," later in this chapter). This way, someone who searches for a baseball glove (see Figure 1-1) isn't shown ads for shoes.

To get the advertiser's ads to show up alongside relevant searches on a search engine, the search engine walks the advertiser through the following steps during PPC account creation. Each search engine's process is a little different, but here are the most basic steps you should be prepared to complete:

1. **Create a PPC account with the search engine.**

   See Book IV, Chapter 2 for details on creating an account with each of the major search engines.

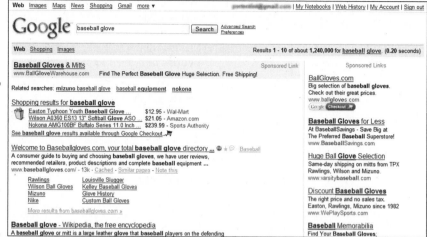

2. **Create campaigns and ad groups around the products or services to be advertised.**

   A *campaign* is where you set many of your options, such as budget and geography. *Ad groups* are tightly targeted groups that make up the campaign and that house your ads and keyword lists. For more information on both topics, see Book IV, Chapter 2.

3. **Determine a list of keywords.**

   Keywords are words and phrases that describe, or are features of, the products or services to be advertised.

4. **From the list of keywords, create ads that use those keywords to better explain to potential customers what benefits, features (such as styles and colors), or sizes are available.**

So when a user searches for, say, women's red high-heel pumps, she sees ads that are specifically tailored to people who are searching for that product. The search engine determines how well the advertiser's campaigns and keywords match the search; if they match well, the search engine displays the advertiser's ad on the result page. I describe this matching process in the following section.

Knowing How Search Engines Determine Relevancy

How do search engines determine what ads to show when? And to what degree can they really calculate which advertiser is more relevant than another? Each engine has an algorithm developed in house that sorts out which ad to show, when to show it, where on the result page to show it, and how much to charge the advertiser.

Depending on the search engine, many known factors determine relevancy, along with several unknown factors. Most search engines use the following known factors to determine relevancy:

- ✦ **Keyword list:** Do the keywords in the keyword list match what the person typed?

- ✦ **Ad copy:** Does the ad mention what the person is looking for?

- ✦ **Landing page:** Does the ad go to a page that has what the person is looking for?

- ✦ **Bid:** How much are you willing to pay to get that visitor?

  The amount of your bid in conjunction with these other factors determines where on the page your ad will display and how much you'll actually pay. (For more information on bidding, see Book IV, Chapter 5.)

For a complete list of known factors for a specific search engine, consult the engine's help center.

Search engines keep some relevancy criteria unknown to the public to keep the playing field level for all advertisers and to preserve a good user experience. This system cuts down on false advertising and misleading, spam-type ads; it also rewards advertisers who are adhering to the rules and editorial guidelines of the search engine.

Figuring Out Whether You Need PPC

PPC advertising has evolved as a way for companies, people, and sites to purchase a spot on the first page of search results. Often, the first result page has room for only about ten results, and few people click to see what's on page 2, 3, or beyond. So if your site has low *natural search rankings* (where your Web site appears in the search results), PPC is a way to buy a spot in front of the most people.

Suppose that your law firm practices landlord–tenant law, but your Web site is pretty outdated, and you haven't gotten a chance to do any search engine optimization updates (see Book II for more on SEO). When a user searches for, say, *"landlord tenant lawyer"* or *"landlord law firm"*, your firm's Web site is on page 10 of the search results.

That page is buried pretty far back, so the chances of getting noticed by people who are specifically searching for your type of law firm are low. Often, instead of going through the search results page by page, searchers change their search terms and try again. In this case, your firm stays buried. So how do you find new clients?

Certainly, you want to work on your SEO, but that project takes time — not only to research what to do, but also to implement and wait for the results. In the meantime, you can buy yourself a spot on that first page of results and be seen by people who are looking for the service you provide. For this example, your law firm can even create geotargeted campaigns (see Book IV, Chapter 7 for help on geotargeting) that show your ads only to people in the geographic region that your law firm serves. Whether that region is a metropolitan area or an entire state, PPC gets your firm's name directly in front of people who are already interested in what you do.

Benefits of using PPC

Trying out PPC advertising has many benefits:

+ It's a form of advertising that anyone can do.
+ It gives advertisers a lot of control of their budgets and audiences.
+ It has a great amount of accountability in terms of where the sale occurred, how much it cost, and which keyword and ad triggered the sale.

If PPC advertising is done correctly, the results can be measured very accurately to give the advertiser an idea of what the next steps should be.

Getting measurable results

PPC not only allows you to purchase a spot in front of potential clients, but it also allows you to test things quickly. If you're redesigning an outdated site but aren't sure which version of the Contact Us page you want to use, for example, you could set your campaign to send half of your visitors to one page and the other half to another page. Then you can measure the response in easily interpretable results, such as these:

+ What keywords did people use to find your site?
+ How many people filled out the form on a landing page?
+ How many people called the firm directly?
+ How many people left the site after visiting the landing page?

With PPC, you can drive visitors to your pages quickly and often, rather than wait for visitors to appear naturally.

Spending your money wisely

PPC enables you to set daily budgets for an account, campaign, and edit bids on a per-keyword basis. If you're trying to determine which keywords to target for SEO purposes, you can use PPC to measure the success and popularity of those keywords for yourself and, at the same time, limit the amount spent on that experiment. You can also set your budget to spend by time of day or geographic region and even turn your ads off when necessary, either automatically or manually. PPC gives you a lot of flexibility for managing both the amount spent and the frequency of your ads.

Finding niches

Particularly if your company is in a highly competitive market, you can use PPC to find a niche that isn't as competitive as others or that you can specialize in. Searchers give you a lot of information when they come to your site: what keywords brought them there, what pages they visited, how quickly they left, and what they bought or downloaded. To return to the law-firm example, if you find that you're receiving conversions from the keyword phrase *"lawyers for landlords"*, you can build a specific ad group and ad around that keyword to target searches better — and at a better cost to you. (See Book IV, Chapter 5 for more on budgeting and spending.)

Possible drawbacks of PPC

So far in this chapter, you've had a brief introduction to PPC and discovered some of the benefits of creating and running a PPC campaign. But beware — PPC isn't for everyone or every company. Fortunately, you'll know quickly whether your PPC campaign is working out. If not, consider whether you should seek a professional consultation or call the experiment quits.

Here are some situations that could limit the success of your PPC campaigns:

+ **Not enough budget to spend for your industry:** If you're trying to generate leads for a machine that retails for $80,000 and are spending only $500 a month for PPC, you're not spending enough. If your product is expensive, and the average cost per lead for the industry is expensive, don't expect to bid $1 and get 500 leads.

+ **Poorly designed Web site:** You can bring all the visitors to your site that you want, but if your site is hard to navigate, the shopping cart is difficult to understand, or you don't provide information about things like shipping time and charges, people are going to be far less likely to buy. You may have what they want, but if they can't find it or the cart fails, they can't buy.

+ **Slow page loads:** If it takes longer than a couple of seconds for the pages on your site to load, chances are that the visitor is going to leave and search for another site. Slow load time creates a poor user experience — and now it's also a factor for Google AdWords in determining relevancy (see "Knowing How Search Engines Determine Relevancy," earlier in this chapter). The slower your site is, the lower it is in the list of search results.

+ **Not enough volume:** Sometimes, the problem simply is that not enough people are searching for the keywords you're bidding on. If your niche is too targeted, you won't be able to bring new traffic to your site. In this case, you should expand your keyword list before calling it quits. (For tips on working with keywords, see Book IV, Chapter 3.)

Book IV Chapter 1

Grasping PPC Methods

✦ **No analytics:** If you're not using an analytics program of some kind to track the results, how can you honestly tell what's working and what isn't? Guessing is never the way to go, especially because PPC is such a measurable form of advertising. See Book II, Chapter 8 for information on choosing an analytics package that suits your needs.

✦ **Setting it and forgetting it:** PPC campaigns need to be managed actively. Simply setting things up and logging in only once a month is a recipe for disaster. Particularly at the beginning, you need to log in daily — if not more than once per day — to tweak your keyword lists, budgets, and bids. When you have a better understanding of what's working and what isn't, you can cut back on the amount of management. Still, you should never just leave the campaign running unchecked.

This list might help you determine whether PPC is right for you or your company. The size and complexity of the campaigns you're considering might be too large, for example, and you should outsource the management or initial setup. You might be able to find a firm that will set the program up for you and even include lessons or continuing support as needed. Also, several companies have created PPC management software to help automate the process. These programs tend to be best for large accounts across several engines with budgets to match. If this situation fits your case, you'll need to do a lot more research, starting with a basic search for *"pay per click management software"*. The search engines themselves don't recommend one software program over another; in most cases, in-house teams manage accounts for their biggest clients and search marketing agencies.

At the very least, start small and build up. As you work with a search engine's program and get a better feel for it and for PPC management, you'll be much more efficient, and then you'll be able to create keyword lists and campaigns easily and bid with the best of them.

Chapter 2: Combining PPC and Search Engines

In This Chapter

✔ **Choosing which search engines to use**

✔ **Setting up a Google AdWords account**

✔ **Setting up a Yahoo! Search Marketing account**

✔ **Setting up a MSN adCenter account**

*N*ot all search engines have a pay per click (PPC) platform to display ads with their search results. Some search engines have partnerships with large search engines such as Google, Yahoo!, and MSN — all of which have their own PPC services — to show their ads on those engines, thereby generating revenue for the partners to split.

Before you start investigating smaller search engines, be sure that you've evaluated Google, Yahoo!, and MSN to see whether those search engines alone will meet your advertising needs. This chapter shows you how to set up an account in each of those search engines, expand that account, and adjust its settings to suit your preferences.

Selecting a PPC Search Engine

Before you bring out the credit card and keyword list, you want to make sure that you've done your homework when it comes to selecting a search engine's PPC platform. Although the search engines may seem to be pretty similar, they differ on some big points. Also, depending on the industry or field that you're advertising for, one engine could be much more beneficial than another in terms of return on investment (ROI), audience reach for volume and targeting, costs, and time spent managing your campaigns. In this section, I give you some research pointers.

Researching search engines

Before you set up a new account on a search engine for PPC advertising, be sure to research the engine to see whether it meets your needs and those of your industry. Some PPC platforms are geared to business-to-consumer sales, for example; others target business-to-business sales. Some engines have considerably more traffic than others and are on the rise; others are falling off.

The best way to check out a search engine is to use it yourself. Perform some searches for items in your keyword list (see Book IV, Chapter 3) to see how much competition there is, how fast the engine is, and what the result page looks like overall. If the engine's user interface is clunky and the ads are hard to find on the result page, those results are indicative of the performance of the ads. If you can't find what you're looking for, how would you expect anyone else to find it? If the ads aren't in prominent places on the result page (such as across the top or down the right side), users aren't going to look at them; they'll go straight for the prominent results or change their search to another engine.

Comparing the top three search engines

The top three PPC-platform search engines, in order of search volume, are Google, Yahoo!, and MSN. They're tops in terms of volume of traffic (searches performed), quality of results, quality of the ads that appear with the results *(relevancy)*, and the average cost per click (CPC) compared with ROI. Here's how the top three compare:

+ **Google:** This engine is by far the most sophisticated PPC search-engine platform overall, and it delivers the best bang for your buck. It has the most traffic and the best management tools, and garners you results faster than any other search engine. Through Google, you should be able to find out what works and what doesn't work within a short period.

   The audience that uses Google is greatly varied; therefore, a large, diverse audience will be searching for your product or service.

+ **Yahoo!:** This engine is the second-most-popular search engine in the United States and has the largest presence worldwide. If your target audience is primarily overseas, you should definitely consider a Yahoo! account.

   Yahoo! also attracts a slightly younger audience than Google does, and offers more social tools, pop-culture news, and special-interest sections on its homepage — Yahoo! Answers, Games, Personals, Classifieds, and Shopping, for example.

   Yahoo! users tend to be less affluent than Google users, so keep both that fact and your product/service costs in mind.

+ **MSN:** This engine has less search volume than Google and Yahoo! do. Although millions of searches per day are nothing to sneeze at, depending on your industry, this volume can seem paltry by comparison.

In the following sections, I show you how to establish a PPC account with each of these three services.

Managing multiple PPC accounts

If you plan to have an account that encompasses more than one Web site, you'll want to look into setting up a main account so that you have to log in to each engine only once to access all the Web sites. Google provides a My Client Center account for this purpose; Yahoo! offers a Master Account; MSN's comparable account doesn't have a special name.

For Yahoo! or MSN, you need a customer service representative to help you set up the account. For Google, sign up for the Google Advertising Professionals Program at `https://adwords.google.com/select/professionalwelcome`.

Using Google AdWords

If you've decided to give Google AdWords a try, this section walks you through the process, from setting up your account to getting it activated and getting your ads running.

Creating an account

Follow these steps to sign up for AdWords:

1. **Go to the sign-in page for Google AdWords at `http://adwords. google.com/select/Login`, and click the Start Now button.**

The Choose Edition page opens, giving you a choice between the Starter Edition and the Standard Edition (see Figure 2-1).

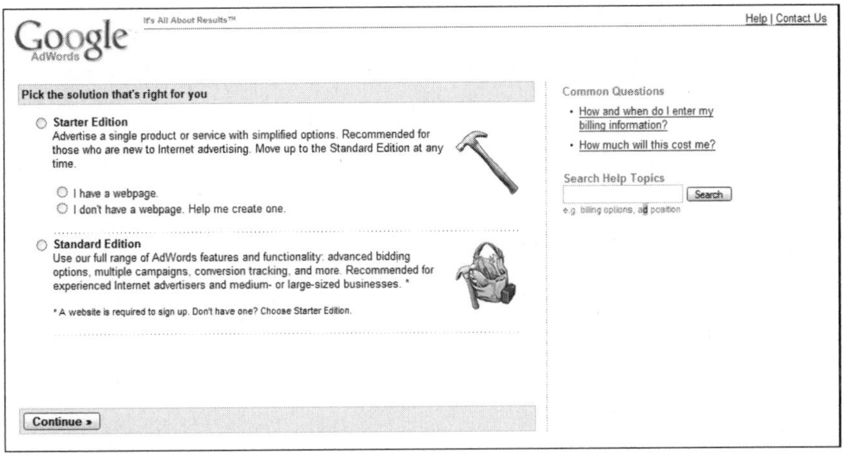

Figure 2-1:
Select the Standard Edition.

The Starter Edition is for those who aren't comfortable dealing with the full AdWords interface to begin with. It offers only text-ad options, can sell only in one region (meaning that you must pick a targeted location, ranging from a single city to the entire United States), and is the better choice if you have only one product or service and a single Web page. You can upgrade from Starter to Standard at any time, however.

For this exercise (and to complete the procedures in the following sections), choose the Standard Edition, which gives you access to the full range of AdWords tools, allows for multiple campaigns, and provides advanced bidding features.

2. **Select the Standard Edition radio button.**

The Create Google Account page opens.

3. **In the Which Best Describes You? section, select the appropriate radio button.**

If you already have a Google account, select the top radio button (I Have an Email Address and Password I Already Use with Google Services Like AdSense, Gmail, Orkut, or iGoogle).

If you don't have a Google account, select the bottom radio button (I Do Not Use These Other Services), and follow the prompts. Figure 2-2 shows a sample account-creation form.

Figure 2-2:
To get started, select the top radio button or create a new Google account.

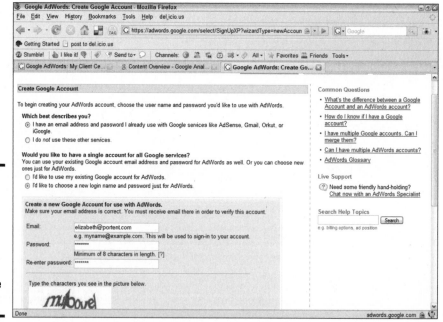

4. **Use your Google-account user name and password to sign in to AdWords.**

5. **Select the currency you'll be paying in (USD is the default), and click Continue.**

   Google sends an e-mail message to your Google-account e-mail address.

6. **When you receive the e-mail, click the link in it to go to the AdWords verification page.**

Setting up your first campaign

After you create and confirm your AdWords account, you're ready to set up your first campaign. Follow these steps:

1. **Sign into AdWords.**

2. **Click the Create Your First Campaign button.**

3. **Select the language in which you want your ads to display.**

4. **Select where you want the ads in this campaign to display.**

   The entire United States and Canada is selected by default. If you want to change that setting, click the blue Change Targeting link in the Target Customers by Location section. A Google map window pops up, allowing you to edit your preference (see Figure 2-3). For more on geotargeting, see Book IV, Chapter 7.

   The Create an Ad page opens.

5. **Fill in the Headline, Description (Line 1 and Line 2), Display URL, and Destination URL text boxes.**

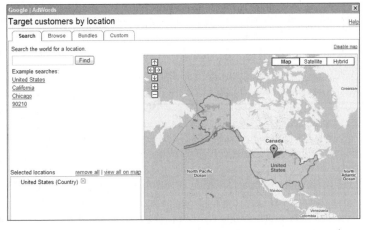

Figure 2-3: When you click the Change Targeting link, a pop-up map shows your current targeting.

Figure 2-4 shows an example of what your page might look like at this point.

For details on writing your ads and for definitions of the different parts of the ads, see Book IV, Chapter 4.

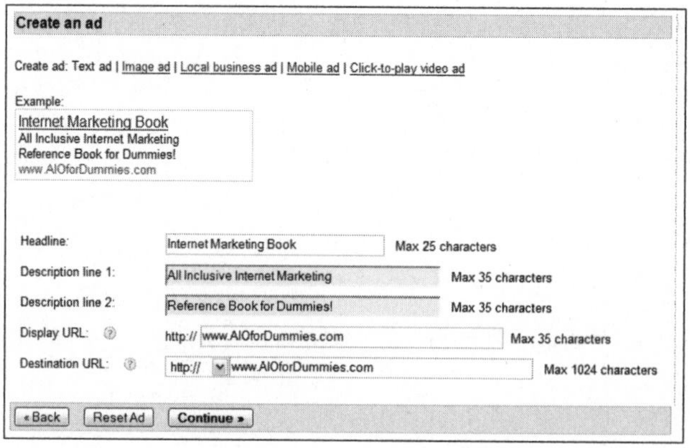

Figure 2-4:
Enter your
ad text,
display
URL, and
destination
URL in this
page.

6. Click the Continue button.

The Choose Keywords page opens.

7. In the text box, type the keywords that you want to add to your campaign, or use the Search option to find related keywords.

For details on creating a keyword list, see Book IV, Chapter 3.

You can click the Back link at any time to edit information. Also, Google allows you to change many settings even after you set up and launch a campaign — add or remove keywords, use the keyword-generation tools, and edit match types, for example. For more information on these features, see Book IV, Chapter 3.

Setting daily budgets and bids

After you enter your basic keyword list (refer to the preceding section), the Standard Edition's Set Pricing page asks you for your daily budget and bids. Figure 2-5 shows an example page already filled out.

To configure the settings in this page, follow these steps:

1. In the text box in the first section, enter your daily budget.

Later, if you prefer, you can change this setting to monthly; you can also change the daily or monthly amount as often as you want. For more information on setting budgets and bidding, see Book IV, Chapter 5.

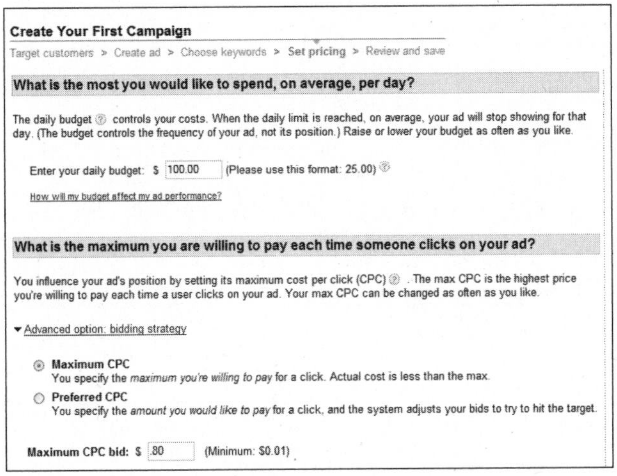

Figure 2-5:
The Set
Pricing page
is where
you set
your daily
budget and
preferred
bidding
strategy.

> **Create Your First Campaign**
>
> Target customers > Create ad > Choose keywords > **Set pricing** > Review and save
>
> **What is the most you would like to spend, on average, per day?**
>
> The daily budget ⓘ controls your costs. When the daily limit is reached, on average, your ad will stop showing for that day. (The budget controls the frequency of your ad, not its position.) Raise or lower your budget as often as you like.
>
> Enter your daily budget: $ |100.00| (Please use this format: 25.00) ⓘ
>
> *How will my budget affect my ad performance?*
>
> **What is the maximum you are willing to pay each time someone clicks on your ad?**
>
> You influence your ad's position by setting its maximum cost per click (CPC) ⓘ . The max CPC is the highest price you're willing to pay each time a user clicks on your ad. Your max CPC can be changed as often as you like.
>
> ▼ *Advanced option: bidding strategy*
>
> ◉ **Maximum CPC**
>   You specify the *maximum you're willing to pay* for a click. Actual cost is less than the max.
> ○ **Preferred CPC**
>   You specify the *amount you would like to pay* for a click, and the system adjusts your bids to try to hit the target.
>
> **Maximum CPC bid:** $ |.80| (Minimum: $0.01)

2. In the second section, select the appropriate radio button to set your CPC:

- *Maximum CPC:* Choose this option to specify the maximum amount that you're willing to spend per click.

- *Preferred CPC:* In preferred bidding, you tell Google what you want your average CPC to be for the entire campaign, and Google does its best to hit that target. Choosing this option means that Google decides when, how often, and for which keywords to show your ads to meet that average price.

The best practice is to start with the Maximum CPC bidding option. Maximum CPC is the easiest type of bidding to edit and keep an eye on, because what you see is what you get. If you choose the Preferred CPC bidding option instead, although you set a preferred price, the actual CPCs can vary a lot from that figure and can be confusing if you're just starting with PPC. (For more information on preferred bidding and other options, see Book IV, Chapter 5.)

3. In the text box below the radio buttons, enter the amount of your bid.

If your bid is too low, Google displays the message `bid is below first page bid estimate of X`. This message means that to get your ad to display in conjunction with that keyword on the first page, you must bid more.

4. Explore the CPC and traffic-estimator options (see Figure 2-6):

- *Want to Purchase the Most Clicks Possible?:* Click this first link to see, based on your keywords and ad, how Google thinks you should set your daily budget and maximum CPC in order for your ads to appear as often as possible.

**Book IV
Chapter 2**

**Combining PPC and
Search Engines**

This option is for traffic-driving, ad-impression purposes only; it doesn't take into account conversions or other goals of that nature. Google is just estimating how much it would cost to get the most visitors possible to your site.

- *View Traffic Estimator:* If you click this second link after entering your daily budget and maximum CPC, Google shows you how many impressions you can expect for that amount, ad position, clicks, and how much you might spend in a day. This tool is great to use to adjust your budget. If you make any changes, simply click the Get New Estimates button to see what effect your changes have on Google's estimates.

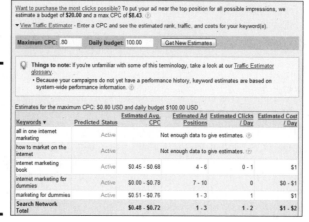

Figure 2-6: Example Google results for the keywords *"all in one internet marketing".*

5. **Click Continue.**

   The Review and Save page opens.

6. **Review your settings for language, geographic area targeted, ad, keyword list, and bids.**

7. **If you want Google to send you automated optimization tips, newsletters, and other information, check the appropriate check boxes.**

Setting up billing in AdWords

After you set up your account, the Billing Options page appears. This page gives you two options: set up billing now or set up billing later. If you choose to set up billing now, Google takes you to the Billing Preferences page, where you choose your options. If you choose to set up billing later, Google takes you to the Campaign Summary page of the campaign you just created. A message box across the top of the screen reminds you that for your ads to run, you have to enter your billing information.

To set up billing later, click the My Account tab anywhere in your account to see the billing options. Click the Billing Preferences link to enter your billing information. If you want to change your billing information at any time after setup, simply click the My Account tab and the Billing Preferences link. The Billing Preferences page is where you can change your billing address, form of payment, and credit card information.

When you're ready to enter your billing information, you see the page shown in Figure 2-7 only once: when you set your location and time zone. The time zone you enter here is the one Google will go by.

The selections you make on this page are permanent and cannot be changed later.

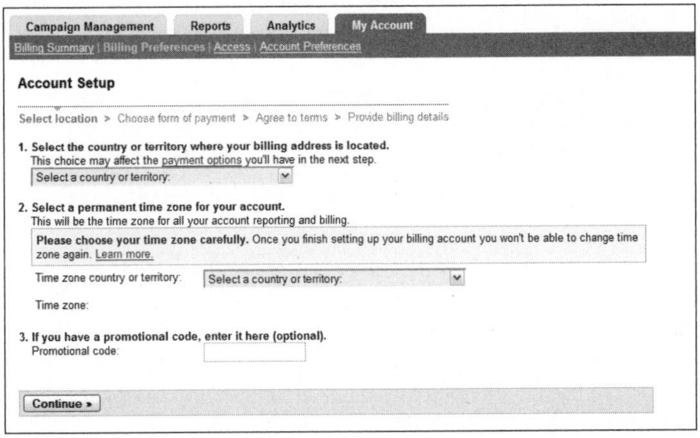

Figure 2-7: Choose the country for your billing address and time zone.

> **Campaign Management** | **Reports** | **Analytics** | **My Account**
>
> Billing Summary | Billing Preferences | Access | Account Preferences
>
> **Account Setup**
>
> Select location > Choose form of payment > Agree to terms > Provide billing details
>
> **1. Select the country or territory where your billing address is located.**
> This choice may affect the payment options you'll have in the next step.
> Select a country or territory:
>
> **2. Select a permanent time zone for your account.**
> This will be the time zone for all your account reporting and billing.
>
> **Please choose your time zone carefully.** Once you finish setting up your billing account you won't be able to change time zone again. Learn more.
>
> Time zone country or territory: Select a country or territory:
>
> Time zone:
>
> **3. If you have a promotional code, enter it here (optional).**
> Promotional code:
>
> Continue »

Next, after choosing your time zone, you see the Choose Form of Payment page (see Figure 2-8), which contains a lot of options. Your first choice is whether to set up postpay or prepay billing.

Postpay billing means that you pay Google after your account has accumulated clicks and cost. You have the option of paying by credit card or direct debit from a bank account:

✦ **Direct Debit:** If you choose the Direct Debit option, your AdWords account is tied to a bank account that Google can debit from after clicks have accrued. (You must be an AdWords business customer to choose this option; see the AdWords Help Center for more information.) The speed and amount that you spent determine how often Google withdraws funds.

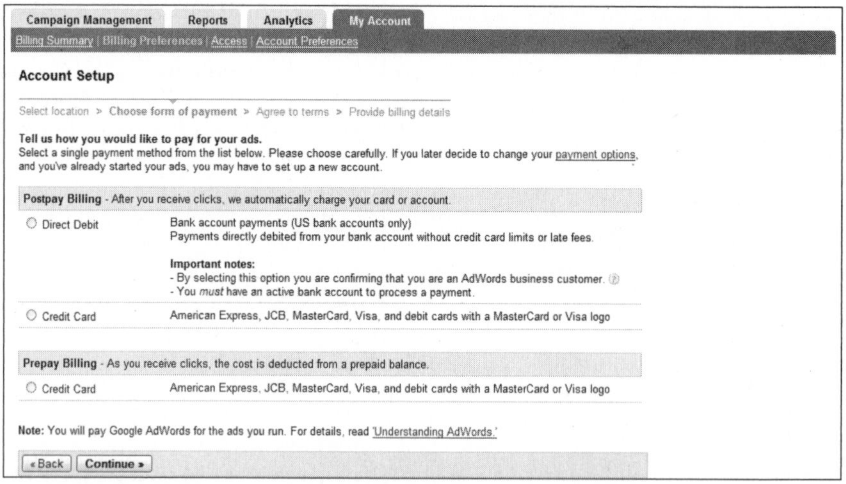

Figure 2-8:
Set your
payment
option.

✦ **Credit Card:** If you choose this option, Google charges your credit card for clicks in the same manner that it withdraws money from a bank account.

Prepay billing means that you deposit a set amount of money from which Google will debit clicks and costs. Your only option is to use a credit card. You set an amount for Google to charge you, and Google credits your AdWords account for that amount. Every so often, as the clicks add up, Google debits that amount from your account, and you have to refill the account as the balance lowers. You can elect to have the account refill automatically or do it yourself manually each time.

Google's billing cycle is 30 days. Your card is charged after 30 days or as you reach each of the following thresholds, whichever comes first:

✦ First billing threshold: $50

✦ Second billing threshold: $200

✦ Third billing threshold: $350

✦ Fourth (and final) billing threshold: $500

After you hit all these thresholds, $500 becomes your regular billing rate. If you are a large enterprise, however, you can request to go on invoicing and have your threshold increased.

After you select your billing option, Google presents its Terms of Service page. Review and agree to the terms of service; then click Continue. If you don't agree to the terms of service, you can't be an AdWords advertiser.

Next, Google displays the Billing Preferences page, where you input your billing information and credit card number. When you click the all-important Save and Activate button, Google charges your card a one-time, nonrefundable $5 activation fee.

Your account is live, and your first campaign is showing ads!

Expanding Google AdWords

When your account is active, you can add campaigns, ad groups, and keywords through the AdWords dashboard. In the following sections, I discuss all these expansion options.

When you expand a PPC account, always think beyond just keywords — think of the account as a whole or, at the very least, by campaigns. See Book IV, Chapters 3 and 4 for help with keyword lists and ad copy, respectively; see Book IV, Chapter 5 for help with budgeting and bidding.

Adding a new campaign

The Campaign Management tab contains a New Online Campaign link. If you click it, AdWords gives you two choices:

✦ **A keyword-targeted campaign:** In this type of campaign, you create a keyword list and ads, and bid accordingly. (I describe this type of campaign in the preceding sections.)

✦ **A placement-targeted campaign:** This type of campaign uses Web sites instead of keywords and shows your ads on Google's content network, which I cover in Book IV, Chapter 7.

For this exercise, add another keyword-targeted campaign to go with the one you created when you started your account. Follow these steps:

1. **Click the New Online Campaign link in the AdWords dashboard, and in the next page, choose Start with Keywords.**

The Start a New Campaign with Keywords page opens.

2. **In the Create This Campaign's First Ad Group section, type the campaign name and ad group in the text boxes (see Figure 2-9).**

3. **In the Target Customers by Language section, change the language, if necessary, by making a new choice from the drop-down menu.**

4. **If you want to change your targeting location (the United States and Canada are selected by default), click the Change Targeting link in the Target Customers by Location section, make your edits, and then click Done.**

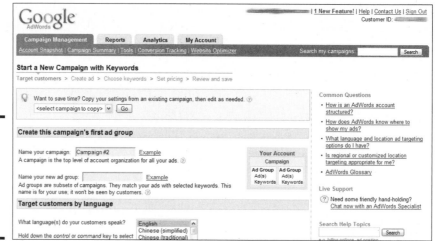

Figure 2-9:
Enter the
name of
your new
campaign
and ad
group.

5. **When you finish making your settings, click Continue.**

   You go to the Create Ad page.

6. **Fill in the Headline, Description (Line 1 and Line 2), Display URL, and Destination URL text boxes, and click Continue.**

   The Choose Keywords page opens.

7. **In the text box, type the keywords that you want to add to your campaign, or use the Search option to find related keywords; then click Continue.**

   The Set Pricing page opens.

8. **Set your daily budget and maximum bids.**

   For bidding and budget guidance, see Book IV, Chapter 5.

9. **Click Continue.**

   You go to the final review screen for your ads, keyword list, and targeting options. At any time during this process, you can click the Back button and edit as needed without losing any of your work.

10. **If the campaign suits your needs, click Save Campaign.**

    The Campaign Summary page of your account opens.

You can create another ad group for this campaign by clicking Create Another Ad Group in the Campaign Summary page (see the following section), but the best practice at this point is simply to save the campaign and review your work.

Adding an ad group to an existing campaign

After you create a campaign, you can go back at any time and add as many ad groups as you need. To add an ad group, follow these steps:

1. **Click the desired campaign.**

2. **Click the New Ad Group link.**

3. **Choose Start with Keywords from the drop-down menu.**

   The Name Ad Group page opens.

4. **Type the name of your ad group.**

   The Create Ad page opens.

5. **Fill in the Headline, Description (Line 1 and Line 2), Display URL, and Destination URL text boxes, and click Continue.**

   The Choose Keywords page opens.

6. **In the text box, type the keywords that you want to add to your campaign, or use the Search option to find related keywords; then click Continue.**

   The Set Pricing page opens.

7. **Enter your maximum CPC bid, and click Continue.**

   For help on setting bids, see Book IV, Chapter 5.

   The review-and-save page opens, allowing you to review your ad, keyword list, and bids.

8. **If you need to make edits in any of these sections, click the Back button to step back through pages or click the Edit link for the desired section.**

9. **When everything on the review page looks good to you, click Save Ad Group.**

Adding an ad to an existing ad group

To add an ad to an existing ad group, follow these steps:

1. **Click the ad group to which you want to add an ad.**

2. **Make sure that the dashboard is open to the Ad Variations tab and is displaying your ads.**

3. **Click Create an Ad Variation.**

   A template appears, providing blank fields where you can create your new ad.

4. **Enter your ad copy.**

   For information on ad testing and ad copy, see Book IV, Chapter 4.

5. **Click Save Ad.**

Additional AdWords settings

Google AdWords makes many tools available for free to users. In this book, I try to touch on most of them, but Google is continually adding and improving tools. To find out the latest tools and changes, visit the Help Center by clicking its link in the top-right corner of any AdWords page.

Using Yahoo! Search Marketing

Yahoo! Search Marketing doesn't require you to have anything more than an e-mail address to associate with the account, a valid credit card, and a few minutes for setup.

Yahoo! has an excellent online video that walks you through the signup process step by step; in the Start Advertising page (see Step 1 of the following section), click the Watch the Sign-Up Tutorial link.

Creating an account and a campaign

To create an account, follow these steps:

1. **Enter this URL in your browser to open the Start Advertising page (see Figure 2-10):**

```
https://signup13.marketingsolutions.Yahoo!.com/
    signupui/signup/loadSignup.do
```

Figure 2-10:
Start page for creating a Yahoo! Search Marketing account.

Start Advertising with Yahoo! Search Marketing in 5 Simple Steps

1. **Target Customers by Geographic Location**
Display your ad to customers throughout the entire market, or select specific regions or cities.

2. **Choose Keywords Related to Your Business**
Enter words or phrases related to the products and services your business provides.

3. **Tell Us How Much You'd Like to Spend**
Specify your daily spending limit and maximum bid.

4. **Create Your Ad**
Write the ad that will be displayed to prospective customers.

5. **Activate or Save Your Ad**
Review your ad and activate it by entering your billing information, or save it until you are ready to activate.

Need Assistance?

Need Assistance? We can recommend keywords or write ads for you. Learn more about Assisted Setup.

For a step-by-step guide to setting up your account Watch the Sign-Up Tutorial

Glossary of Terms

Select a Market

Market ? :
United States and Canada

Select a Time Zone

Your selection impacts your reports and campaign management. For instance, a campaign that is scheduled for a particular day starts at midnight, based on the time zone that you select. Please Note: Choose your time zone carefully. It cannot be edited in the future.

Time Zone:
(GMT-08:00) Pacific Time (US & Canada); Tijuana

2. **From the Market drop-down menu in the Select a Market section, choose the market in which you want your ads to be shown.**

   United States and Canada is the default setting, and you can't separate Canada from the United States. Also, the option covers English-speaking Canada only.

   You can't select multiple countries unless they're already grouped together.

3. **In the Select a Time Zone section, choose your time zone from the drop-down menu.**

4. **Click the Get Started button at the bottom of the page.**

5. **In the Target Customers by Geographic Location page, choose your target geographic area — the states or regions you want your ads to appear in — from the Target By drop-down menu.**

   The default setting is Entire Market. If you accept this setting, your ads will be shown to the entire market you selected in Step 1.

   If you want to narrow your target area, click the Specific Regions radio button in the Choose Your Geo-Targeting Preference section (see Figure 2-11); then choose the target area from the Target By drop-down menu. (If you choose Zip Code, also choose the radius in miles; the default is 5.)

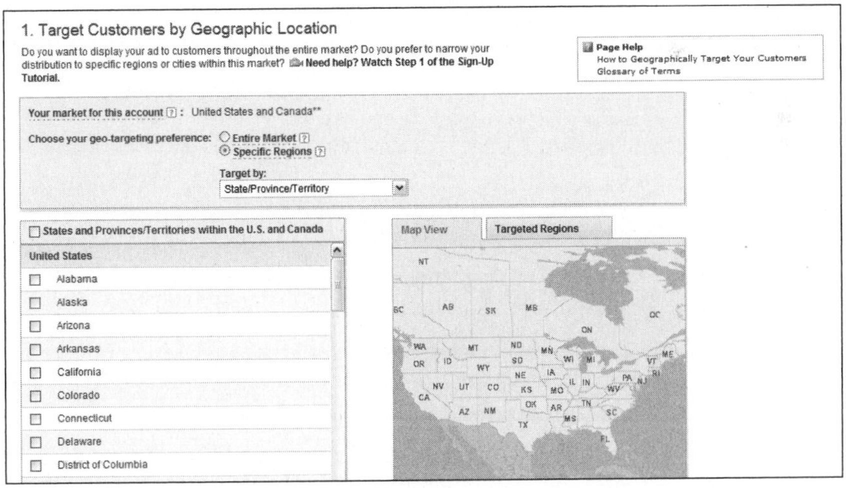

Figure 2-11:
Set your geographic targeting preference.

6. **When you finish, click the Next: Keywords button.**

   The Choose Keywords page appears. (For assistance on creating a keyword list, see Book IV, Chapter 3.)

7. **Type or paste your keywords in the Enter Keywords text box.**

**Book IV
Chapter 2**

**Combining PPC and
Search Engines**

8. **Look through the keywords provided by Yahoo! in the Consider Adding These Keywords list (see Figure 2-12), and click the Add button for each one you want to add.**

You can add a maximum 50 keywords during the setup process.

You can click the Get More Keywords button, but each time you do, Yahoo! widens its search, and you're more likely to have less relevant keywords appear.

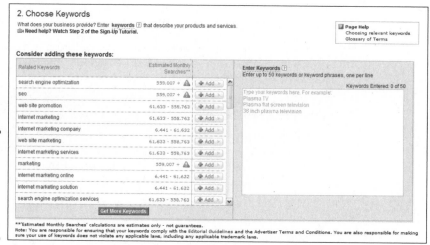

Figure 2-12: Enter keywords or choose Yahoo!'s suggestions.

Note the estimated monthly searches next to those keywords to make sure that the volumes meet your needs.

9. **When you finish adding keywords, click the Pricing button at the bottom of the page to open the Pricing & Budget page.**

This page is for setting your budget or the account's daily spending limit.

10. **In the Account Daily Spending Limit text box, enter your desired spending limit for the entire account per day, and click the Estimate button.**

Yahoo! displays a monthly estimate, a suggested maximum bid, and monthly impression and click estimates (see Figure 2-13). For budgeting and bidding help, see Book IV, Chapter 5.

If the estimated impressions, clicks, and costs don't seem to meet your needs, enter a different amount in the Account Daily Spending Limit text box and click Estimate again for an updated estimate.

11. **Click the Create Ad button at the bottom of the page.**

The Create Your Ad page opens.

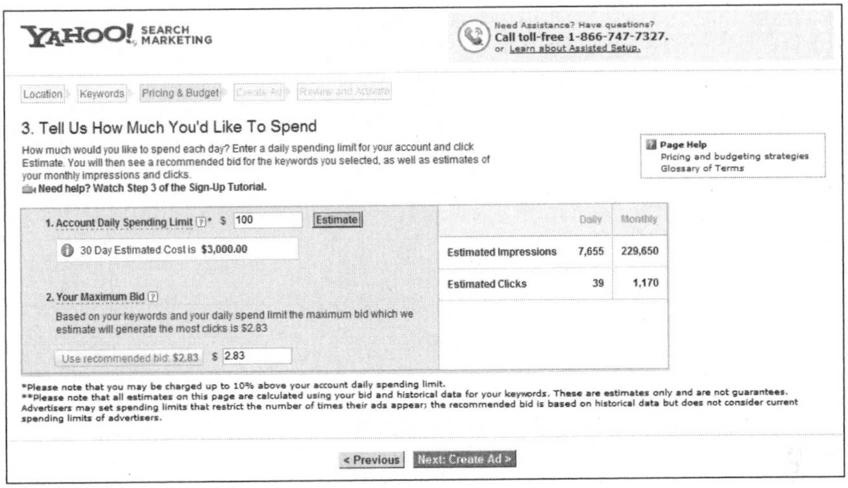

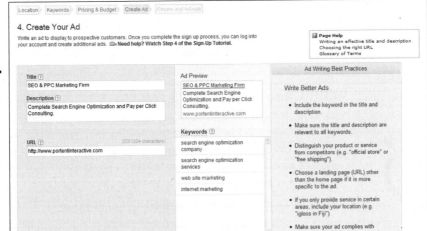

Figure 2-13:
Enter a daily spending limit for your account and a maximum bid for your ad group.

12. **Enter your ad copy:**

    - *Title:* 40 characters maximum, compared with 25 for Google and MSN

    - *Description:* 70 characters maximum

    - *URL:* The destination URL, or landing page, where users should go after they click your ad

    Figure 2-14 shows an example.

    You can't set the *display URL* (the URL that appears below the ad copy or description). Yahoo! uses the first part of the destination URL instead. If your destination URL is www.Yahoo!Ads.com/products, for example, Yahoo! uses www.Yahoo!Ads.com as the display URL.

Figure 2-14:
An example ad for a search engine optimization (SEO) and PPC marketing firm.

**Book IV
Chapter 2**

**Combining PPC and
Search Engines**

After you activate your account, you can change this setting. Open the ad group, click the ad to open it, make your edits, and click Save.

13. **Click Next.**

You go to the Review and Activate page — the final step in the signup process.

14. **Review your keywords, ads, and budget.**

15. **Enter a user name, password, and e-mail address for the account.**

16. **Click the Activate Now button.**

Your account is created.

Naming your ad group

During the setup process, you're not given the option to name your first ad group. If you want to change it from the default name (highly recommended), follow these steps:

1. **From within your new account, open the newly created ad group by clicking it.**

2. **Click the Ad Group Settings button to view the settings page for that ad group.**

3. **Click Edit in the Ad Group General Information box.**

4. **Change the ad group's name.**

The account isn't live yet; first, you have the fun of entering your billing information, adjusting settings and ads, or creating additional ad groups or campaigns. I cover these processes in the following sections.

Setting up billing

To set up your billing information, follow these steps:

1. **Log in to your new account, and click the Administration tab.**

2. **Click the account to which you need to add billing information.**

The main account information page opens, displaying a summary and billing and budgeting options.

3. **Click the Edit link next to Payment Method, below the Billing and Payment Information box.**

4. **To add a credit card, click the Add Payment Type link and choose PayPal or Credit Card.**

5. **Enter your payment information.**

6. **Click Save Changes.**

Now your payment information is on file, but your card hasn't been charged yet. Yahoo! runs on a prepay basis, which means that you select a dollar amount to add to your account, and Yahoo! debits from that amount as clicks occur on your ads. You can set your account to autorefill at a certain point by a certain amount; whenever your balance becomes low, Yahoo! automatically charges your card that amount and refills your balance. If you don't select autorefill, Yahoo! e-mails you each time your balance is low, and you need to add funds manually. I cover each option in the following sections.

Adding funds manually

If you want to add funds manually, follow these steps:

1. **Click the Administration tab.**

2. **Select the account to which you want to add funds.**

3. **Click the Add Funds link next to the account balance.**

4. **Select the card to be charged and the amount to be charged.**

5. **Click Submit.**

When you add funds manually, if you have more than one credit card on file, the drop-down menu for choosing a credit card to charge shows all the cards but no names — just the last four digits, the expiration date, and the type of card. Be sure to choose the correct card to charge.

Setting up autorefill

If you want the account to refill by a set amount automatically, follow these steps:

1. **Click the Administration tab.**

2. **Select the appropriate card and amount.**

Yahoo! will charge your card this amount whenever your balance becomes low — typically, when the account has less than a day's worth of budget left to spend. So if your daily budget is $40, and the account balance is $30, Yahoo! automatically charges your card with the refill amount.

To change this amount later, follow these steps:

1. **Click the Edit link next to Payment Method, below the Billing and Payment Information box.**

2. **Set the Activate Payment Type for This Account control to the credit card you want to use.**

**Book IV
Chapter 2**

Combining PPC and Search Engines

3. **In the Specify a Charge Amount section, click the check box titled I Would Like to Specify a New Charge Amount.**

4. **In the New Deposit Amount text box, enter the new autorefill amount.**

5. **Click Save Changes.**

Configuring your account

When you set up your account initially, Yahoo! asked you to set an account daily spending limit (refer to "Creating an account and a campaign," earlier in this chapter). This limit applies to the entire account. If you want to change this amount, click the Administration tab, select the account, and edit the amount in the Account Daily Spending Limit text box.

Account Tactic Settings

While you're in the Administration tab, you might notice a section called Account Tactic Settings (see Figure 2-15). This section allows you to enable or disable Yahoo!'s partner network, change the match type, and add negative keywords (or, as Yahoo! calls them, *excluded words*) for the entire account. *Negative keywords* are keywords that you don't want your ads to appear in conjunction with, such as *free* or *cheap*, for example. The settings you make in this section affect the entire account.

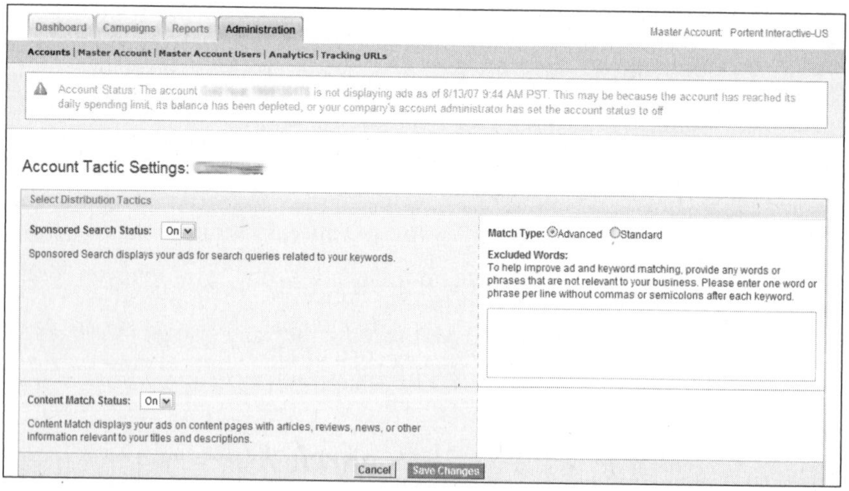

Figure 2-15: Sample Administration tab page.

By default, the search and content networks are enabled in every campaign. The *search network* consists of the sites where your ads appear when someone performs a search in Yahoo! The *content network* consists of sites that partner with Yahoo! to show ads by advertisers that have Yahoo! Search Marketing accounts. In exchange, the partner Web-site owners receive part of the CPC fee that Yahoo! collects from the advertisers. (For more information on the content network, see Book IV, Chapter 7.) If you want to disable the content network for your account, simply choose Off from the Content Match Status drop-down menu.

Keyword match types

You have two choices of keyword match types in Yahoo!: advanced and standard.

By default, all keywords are set to advanced match, which is the equivalent of broad match in other search engines. Advanced match means that ads are displayed for keywords that are broadly similar to the keywords in your list. This option also gives you the most potential for *impressions* (how many times your ad appears).

The other option, standard match, is the equivalent of exact match in other search engines. The user has to type that keyword exactly and search for it for your ad to show.

Yahoo! Search Marketing provides no middle ground between those two options. If your ad groups or campaigns have very popular keywords that are one or two words long, you'll want to change the setting to standard match; otherwise, you can leave advanced match enabled. You can also change this setting on a per-keyword basis.

To change the match type, follow these steps:

1. **Click the ad group you want to make changes in.**

2. **Click the keyword for which you want to change the match type.**

   A keyword details page opens. All settings on this page apply only to that specific keyword.

3. **Choose Standard from the Match Type drop-down menu.**

From this page, you can also change the bid for that specific keyword, as well as see average position and cost and traffic estimates, and set a destination URL for that keyword or alternative text. For more information on this subject, see Book IV, Chapter 3.

Expanding Yahoo! Search Marketing

When the initial setup is complete, be sure to check out all the tabs and links in the homepage Dashboard:

✦ **Performance tab:** This tab gives you a look at your account as a whole.

✦ **Campaigns tab:** This tab shows all the campaigns in the account.

✦ **Account Summary tab:** This tab contains shortcuts to pages where you can edit your account and daily budgets.

✦ **Administration tab:** This tab is where you edit settings and billing information.

✦ **Alerts section:** This section tells you when an ad has been rejected, funds are low, your credit card was charged, and so on.

✦ **Reports tab:** This tab allows you to create reports on the progress of your campaigns.

✦ **Preferences link:** This link, at the top of the dashboard page, allows you to edit your user profile and notification options.

Adding a campaign

To add a campaign, follow these steps:

1. **Click the account to which you want to add the campaign.**

2. **Click the purple Create Campaign button next to the account name (see Figure 2-16).**

Figure 2-16:
Click the
Create
Campaign
button.

Portent Interactive-US

Account: Portent Interactive-Affiliates

+ Create Campaign

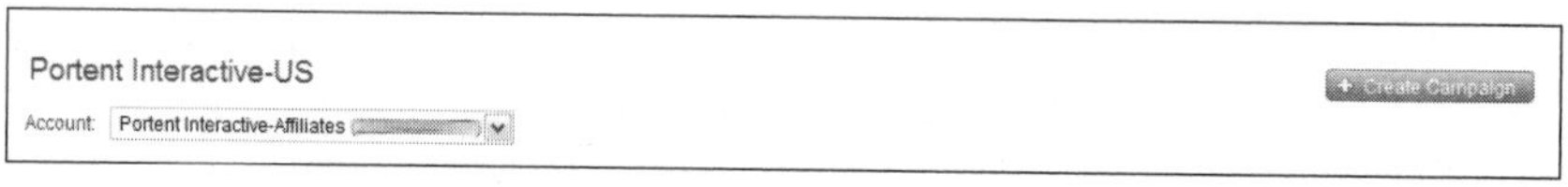

3. **Click the Get Started button in the overview screen.**

4. **Enter the name of the ad group in the Name text box.**

5. **Choose at least one Distribution Tactic option: Sponsored Search and/ or Content Match.**

6. **Select a match type: Advanced or Standard.**

    For more information on both options, refer to "Keyword match types," earlier in this chapter.

    At this point, your screen should resemble Figure 2-17.

7. **Click the Next: Choose Keywords button at the bottom of the page to open the Choose Keywords page.**

8. **In the appropriate text boxes, enter the keywords to be associated with that ad group, along with any excluded words you want to add to the account (see Figure 2-18).**

9. **Click the Next: Bid button at the bottom of the page.**

    The Ad Group Bid page opens.

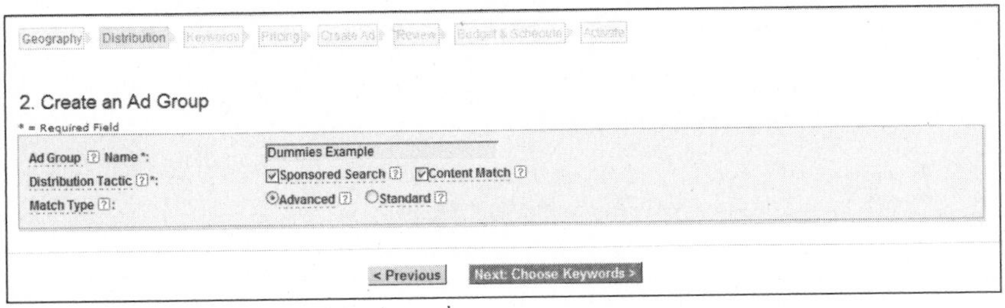

Figure 2-17:
Name your
new ad
group, and
make sure
that the
Distribution
Tactic and
Match Type
settings are
correct.

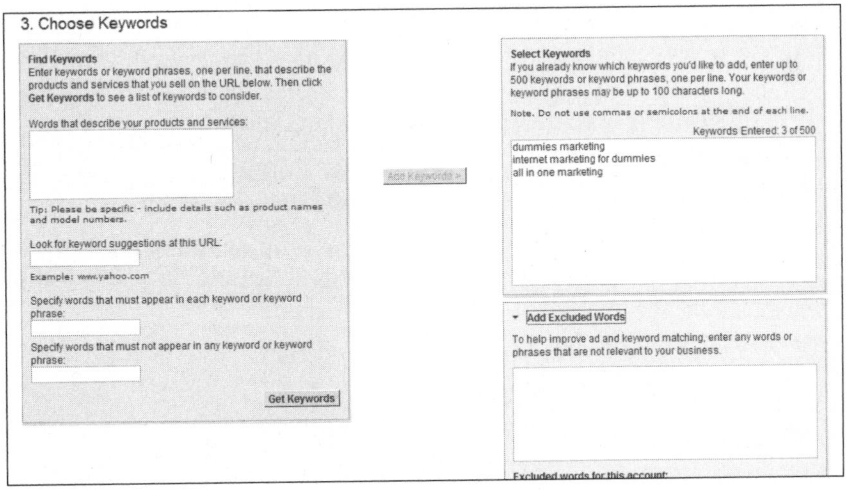

Figure 2-18:
Enter
keywords
and
negative
keywords,
or use the
keyword-
generation
tool.

10. **Enter your maximum CPC for the ad group, and click the Update Estimates button (see Figure 2-19).**

    The right side of the page displays Yahoo!'s estimates of impressions, ad positions, and clicks that your ad group will receive in both the search and content networks. Verify that the bids for both sections are what you are willing to pay per click. For bidding tips, see Book IV, Chapter 5.

11. **When you finish setting bids, click the Next: Write Ad button.**

    The Create Your Ad page opens.

12. **Type your ad copy in the appropriate text boxes.**

13. **Add a destination URL and a display URL.**

14. **Name your ad.**

15. **Click Save.**

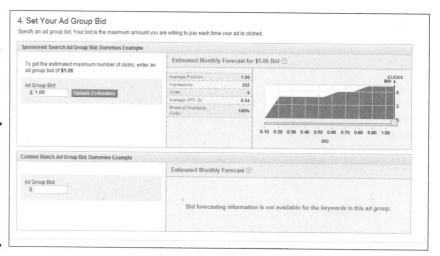

Figure 2-19:
Set and
adjust bids
for the
search and
content
networks.

16. **Click the Review button to move to the next step.**

17. **Review your new ad group. If you don't want to add more groups, click the Budget and Schedule Campaign button.**

18. **If you want to set a campaign daily spending limit (the most that campaign can spend in a day), select the Yes radio button and enter an amount.**

    By default, No is selected for all new campaigns.

19. **Set any date options:**

    • *If you want your campaign to start on a date other than the date when you created it,* click the little calendar icon to choose a start date.

    • *If you want your campaign to end on a specific date,* select the radio button next to the calendar icon, and choose an end date.

    No End Date is selected by default. If you're not sure what to do, accept the default setting. You can always go back later and set an end date or pause a campaign.

20. **Click Activate.**

    The Review and Activate Campaign page opens, displaying the entire campaign, ad group, and settings.

21. **If you're satisfied, click the Activate Campaign button.**

    You're done!

Adding an ad group to an existing campaign

To add an ad group to an existing campaign, follow these steps:

1. **Click the campaign to which you want to add the group.**

2. **Click the Create Ad Group button.**

   The Create an Ad Group page opens.

3. **Name your ad group, and click the Next: Keywords button.**

4. **Enter your keyword list in the appropriate text boxes, along with any excluded words you want to add to the account.**

   For help on using Yahoo!'s keyword-generation tool, see the following section.

5. **Click the Next: Bid button.**

   The Set Your Ad Group Bid page opens.

6. **Enter your maximum CPC for the ad group, and click the Update Estimates button.**

   The right side of the page displays Yahoo!'s estimates of impressions, ad positions, and clicks that your ad group will receive in both the search and content networks. Verify that the bids for both sections are what you are willing to pay per click.

7. **Click the Next: Write Ad button.**

   The Create Your Ad page opens.

8. **Type your ad copy in the appropriate text boxes.**

9. **Add a destination URL and a display URL.**

10. **Name your ad.**

11. **Click Save.**

12. **Click Done.**

    That's it! Your new ad group has been created.

Additional Yahoo! tools

Here are a few additional tools in Yahoo! Search Marketing:

✔ **Campaign Tune Up:** Yahoo! analyzes the selected campaign and makes suggestions based on the budgets you enter and the metrics you select. You can accept or reject the suggested changes. If you accept, Yahoo! uploads the changes automatically.

✔ **Campaign Optimization:** Yahoo! automatically manages the bidding for your keywords and the ads to be shown within your budget.

✔ **Optimize Ad Display:** By default, this feature is turned on, which means that Yahoo! determines which ad is most successful and shows it most often. If you want to conduct an A/B test (see Book IV, Chapter 4 for details), you need to change this setting to Off so that Yahoo! will rotate your ads evenly.

Using MSN adCenter

Microsoft's search engine is called Live Search, and the PPC ads served alongside those search results are provided through MSN adCenter.

Microsoft Live Search's search page is a lot like the one in Yahoo!, featuring news, popular culture, and weather features so that users will search on it out of convenience. MSN's audience is as diverse as Google's but tends to be more business oriented. If your focus is business-to-business leads or sales, definitely try MSN adCenter before Yahoo! Search Marketing.

Microsoft has been making strides to improve its PPC service's interface, tools, search quality, and volume. Programs such as Live Cashback, adCenter Desktop (an offline PPC ads editor), product search, and Gatineau (an analytics program) have all launched within the past year. For more information on offline editors and analytics programs, see Book IV, Chapter 7.

Creating an account

To create an MSN adCenter account, follow these steps:

1. **Enter this URL in your browser:**

    https://adcenter.microsoft.com/customer/SignupTargeting.aspx

2. **In the Target Your Customers page, choose language and geographic targeting options.**

All Available Countries/Regions is the best option to get started with. You would select the other options only if you plan to have multiple accounts for the same product or service. After adCenter is set up, you can edit the geographic target settings per campaign.

3. **Click the Continue button.**

The Create Your Ad page opens (see Figure 2-20).

4. **Enter the appropriate information in the Ad Title, Ad Text, Display URL, and Destination URL text boxes.**

For help with ad copy, see Book IV, Chapter 4.

5. **Click the Continue button.**

The Enter Keywords page opens.

6. **Type or paste in your keyword list.**

For information on creating your keyword list, see Book IV, Chapter 3. If you don't already have a keyword list, you can use the keyword-generation tools provided by MSN; Book IV, Chapter 3 also covers those tools.

7. **Click the Continue button at the bottom of the page.**

The Set Your Budget page opens.

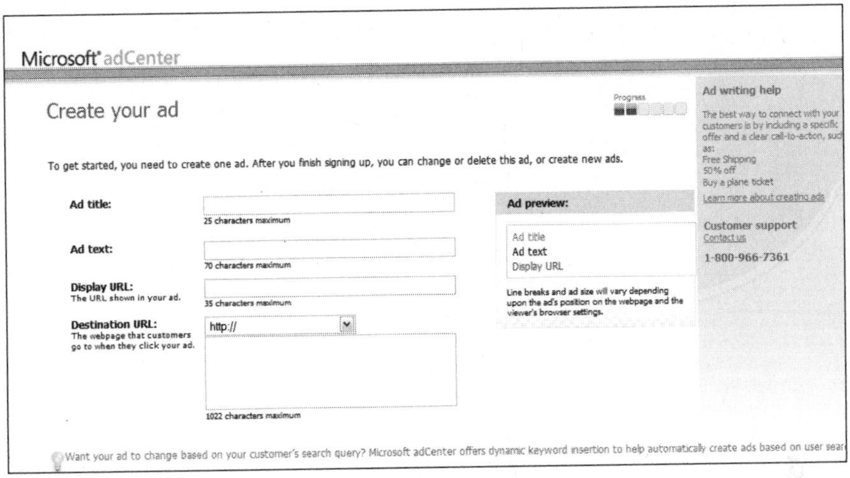

Figure 2-20:
A blank
MSN
adCenter
ad creation
page.

8. **Enter your monthly budget information, along with your maximum CPC (the most you're willing to pay per click).**

   You can edit the monthly budget and set daily budgets later, if you don't want to go by a monthly budget alone.

9. **Click the Continue button.**

   The Confirm Your Ad Campaign Details page opens. Figure 2-21 shows an example.

10. **Review the campaign details, making edits if necessary by clicking the appropriate Edit link.**

    If you make edits in any section, you have to click the Continue button from that section forward to return to the campaign-details page.

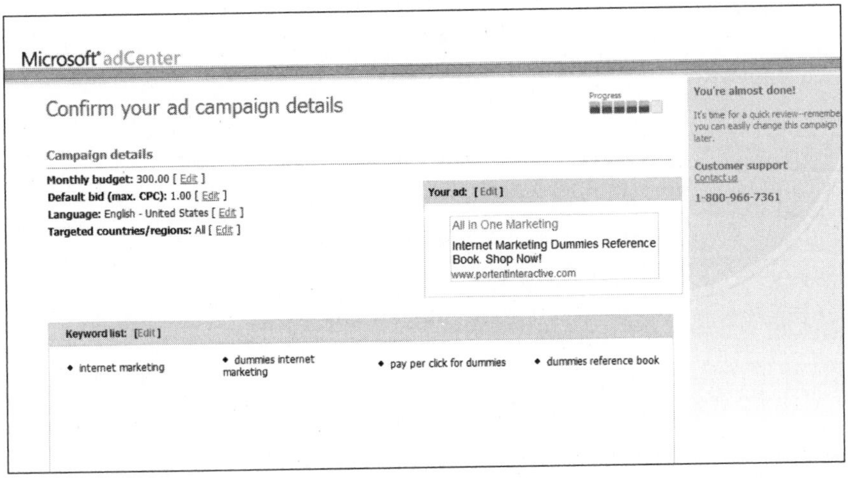

Figure 2-21:
Review this
page before
starting your
account.

**Book IV
Chapter 2**

Combining PPC and Search Engines

11. **Enter your account creation information, and click Continue.**

    The Activate Your Ad Campaign page opens.

12. **Enter your company and billing information.**

    Unlike Google and Yahoo!, MSN doesn't allow you to enter this information later; you have to provide it now to complete the account setup.

    Below all the billing information on the same page, you see a slew of options for e-mail, phone, and mail updates, as well as the terms and conditions of the account.

13. **Set your preferred method of contact.**

14. **Review the terms and conditions.**

15. **If everything is okay, select the check box to agree to the terms and conditions of service — and to the nonrefundable $5 setup and activation fee.**

16. **Click Submit.**

    That's it!

Choosing account settings

You need to tweak your account settings immediately following account activation, as your ads and keywords are live. To do so, follow these steps:

1. **Sign in to your account.**

   You should see everything from your initial setup in the dashboard.

2. **Select the campaign you just created and then click the Edit Campaign Settings link.**

   The Change Campaign Settings page opens (see Figure 2-22).

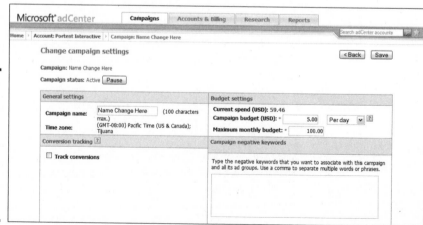

Figure 2-22: Edit the campaign name, budget, and negative keywords on this page.

3. Change the settings as desired.

You can pause the campaign, change the name of the campaign, and edit the budget settings. Upon setup, MSN had you set a monthly budget; if you want to set a daily budget, you do that on this page as well. You can also add negative keywords for the campaign. For more on negative keywords, see "Account Tactic Settings," earlier in this chapter, as well as Chapter 3.

4. Click Save.

5. Click the ad group you created during initial setup.

The Manage Selected Ad Group page opens.

6. Click the Edit Ad Group Settings link.

7. Change the settings as desired.

You can edit the name of the ad group; add negative keywords at ad-group level; and enable or disable the content network, which is all the MSN partners. You want to retain the search network, which is Live Search. For more help with the content network, see Book IV, Chapter 7.

8. Farther down the page, change the geographic targeting setting, if you want, by making a new choice from the drop-down menu.

9. Set your ad scheduling options, selecting an option in the Available box and clicking the Add button to move days of the weeks or blocks of time to the Selected box.

The default settings show your ads on all days at all times. If you know that you have peak hours or days of the week, however, choosing different settings (as shown in Figure 2-23) is a great idea. For best practices on ad scheduling, check Book IV, Chapter 5.

10. Click Save.

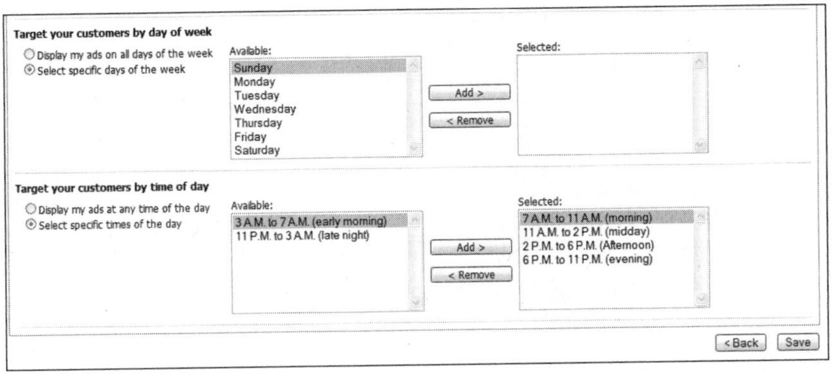

Figure 2-23: Target customers here to have ads appear only during selected days and times.

Book IV
Chapter 2

Combining PPC and Search Engines

Adjusting keyword lists and setting incremental bidding

When you entered your initial keyword list, the match type by default was broad, and the maximum CPC was applied to all keywords in that ad group. Now, however, you can set separate bids for specific keywords or change the overall maximum CPC.

You can enable incremental bidding and target users by gender or age by increasing your bid when MSN detects a user in your desired demographic (age, gender, or time of day).

To adjust your keyword list or use the incremental bidding tool, follow these steps:

1. **If you want to edit the match types, click the ad group for which you want to edit the keywords and then click the Edit Keywords link below the Keywords tab.**

   Your entire keyword list appears (see Figure 2-24). If you need more information on the different match types, see Book IV, Chapter 3.

Figure 2-24: A keyword list.

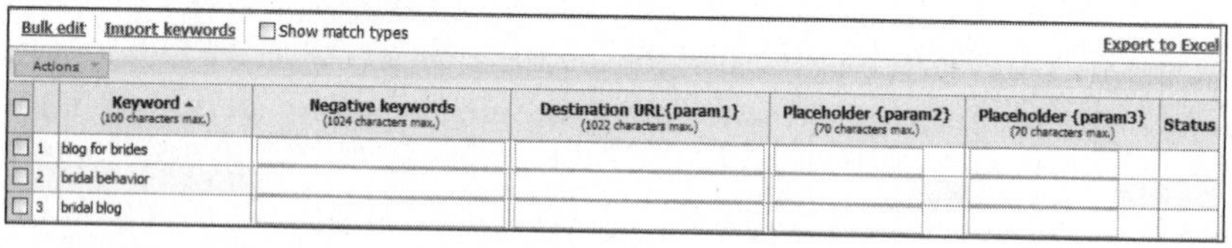

2. **Click the Show Match Types check box.**

3. **Change the match type per keyword to Phrase or Exact, add negative keywords, add keyword destination URLs, and add placeholder text.**

4. **Click Continue.**

5. **To create different bids for individual keywords, click the Advanced Bidding link, and check the Bid for Individual Keywords check box.**

6. **To bid separately for ads displayed on content pages, check that check box as well.**

   This option allows you to set a separate bid for ads on the content network. By default, MSN selects your maximum CPC for all networks. You want to be able to bid separately. Book IV, Chapter 7 goes over content network bidding practices in more detail.

7. **Click Continue when you finish.**

   You go to the Pricing page, which has options for changing your keyword bids and editing your budget.

   For this example, scroll down to the Set Incremental Bids for Targeting section (see Figure 2-25).

Incremental targeting increases the amount of your bid when MSN detects a user in the chosen demographic. If you set 10 percent for Female in the Gender section, for example, MSN increases your maximum CPC when females see your ad, so you gain better position more often.

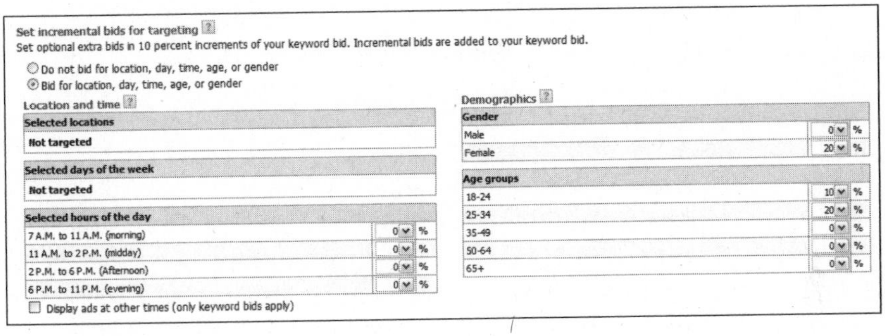

Figure 2-25:
To set incremental bids for this keyword list, make your choices from the drop-down menus.

Set incremental bids for targeting ?
Set optional extra bids in 10 percent increments of your keyword bid. Incremental bids are added to your keyword bid.

○ Do not bid for location, day, time, age, or gender
◉ Bid for location, day, time, age, or gender

Location and time ?		
Selected locations		
Not targeted		
Selected days of the week		
Not targeted		
Selected hours of the day		
7 A.M. to 11 A.M. (morning)	0	%
11 A.M. to 2 P.M. (midday)	0	%
2 P.M. to 6 P.M. (Afternoon)	0	%
6 P.M. to 11 P.M. (evening)	0	%
☐ Display ads at other times (only keyword bids apply)

Demographics ?		
Gender		
Male	0	%
Female	20	%
Age groups		
18-24	10	%
25-34	20	%
35-49	0	%
50-64	0	%
65+	0	%

8. **If you want to use this option, select the radio button labeled Bid for Location, Day, Time, Age, or Gender, and start choosing your bids from the drop-down menus.**

   Incremental bids must be set in increments of ten percent.

9. **Set your selected hours of the day, location, and days of the week for incremental bidding.**

   MSN will increase your bids by ten percent during those times and at those locations.

10. **Set your incremental bidding amounts based on males and/or females in the Gender section and based on age in the Age Groups section.**

11. **Click Save.**

Incremental bids add up quickly. You pay the increased price only if the user clicks your ad, but if you enabled a 10-percent boost for females and a 20-percent boost for ages of 18–24, and a 20-year-old female searches, your ad receives a 30-percent incremental bid boost. Technically, this user is in the key demographic that you're targeting, but incremental bids can get expensive fast, so consider your maximum CPC when you choose your incremental bids.

Expanding MSN adCenter

After you create your initial campaign and ad group, you'll want to expand them at some point. In this section, I show you how to add campaigns and ad groups, as well as how to increase the number of keywords in your keyword lists.

Adding a campaign

To add a campaign to your MSN adCenter account, follow these steps:

1. **Open the account to which you want to add a campaign, or click the large green Create Campaign button on your dashboard.**

   The Create a Campaign and Ad Group page opens.

2. **Name your campaign and ad group.**

3. **Select your targeting options.**

4. **Click Continue.**

   If you have an existing ad group that's very similar to the one you want to create, you can copy it (go to Step 5); if not, continue to Step 6.

5. **If you want to copy the settings of an ad group you already have in your account, check the Copy an Existing Ad Group check box; select the ad group you want to copy; and check the check boxes on the right side of the page if you want to copy the ads, the keywords, or both (see Figure 2-26).**

   If you copy an ad, that ad will be shared between those two ad groups, so if you edit one ad, the same edits are made automatically in the other ad, even though it's in a different ad group. The ads have the same ID number, which means that they're essentially the same ad.

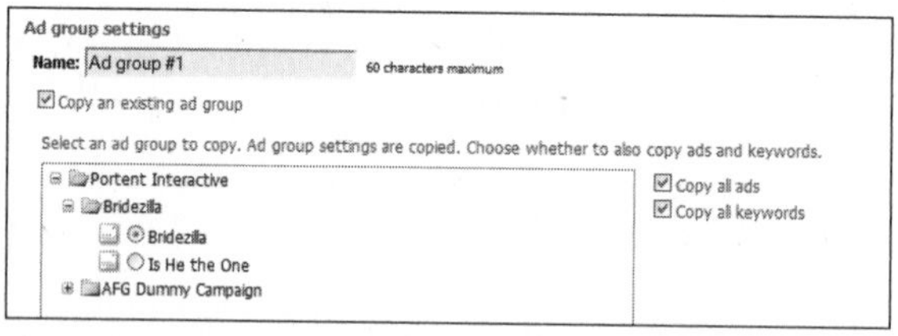

Figure 2-26:
Specify
which ad
group you
want to
copy.

Ad group settings
Name: Ad group #1   60 characters maximum
☑ Copy an existing ad group
Select an ad group to copy. Ad group settings are copied. Choose whether to also copy ads and keywords.

Portent Interactive — Bridezilla — Bridezilla / Is He the One / AFG Dummy Campaign ☑ Copy all ads ☑ Copy all keywords

You may be able to use this feature to your advantage, however, if you have a large campaign with many ad groups and need to make identical changes in all the ads.

6. **If you didn't copy an existing ad group's settings, enter your ad copy in the Create an Ad page; save the ad; and click Continue.**

   The Choose Keywords page opens.

7. **Enter your keyword list for this ad group, and click Add to Keyword List.**

8. **Click Continue.**

   The Pricing page opens.

9. **Set your campaign's budget (on a per-month or per-day basis), and specify how fast you want MSN to spend it (spread out over the month or just spend it until the funds are gone).**

10. **Set your default maximum CPC bid.**

11. **Set up incremental bidding, if you want.**

    For more information, refer to "Adjusting keyword lists and setting incremental bidding," earlier in this chapter.

12. **Click Save and Continue.**

13. **Review your campaign and all its settings.**

    Click Edit if you need to make any changes.

14. **Click Submit to submit the campaign.**

Adding an ad group to an existing campaign

To add an ad group to an existing campaign, follow these steps:

1. **Click the campaign to which you want to add the ad group.**

2. **Click the Create an Ad Group link.**

3. **Follow the steps in the preceding section.**

   You can change the campaign name and budgets as well, even though you're creating only an ad group.

Adding an ad to an existing ad group

To add an ad to an existing ad group, follow these steps:

1. **Click the ad group to which you want to add an ad.**

2. **Click the Ads tab.**

3. **Click the Create an Ad link.**

4. **Add your headline, body, and URLs.**

5. **Click Save.**

Additional MSN adCenter tools

MSN adCenter is very new to the game. Several tools are still in beta development, including an offline editor and an add-in for Microsoft Excel. The add-in works only if you have Microsoft Office 2007. As for the offline editor, I discuss it in Book IV, Chapter 7.

At this writing, you can access these tools only by applying for and being accepted into the beta program.

Chapter 3: Making Keyword Lists That Sell

In This Chapter

✔ Selecting and organizing keywords

✔ Selecting match types

✔ Working with keyword destination URLs

✔ Understanding advanced keyword targeting techniques

✔ Expanding and contracting keyword lists

The *keyword list* is the foundation on which your campaigns are built. A good, well-organized keyword list can make a lot of difference in how your account performs — or doesn't perform.

This chapter shows you how to build, expand, and organize your keyword lists for the most effective return on your investment. It also shows you how to segment individual keywords further to give your site's visitors the best user experience possible.

Choosing Keywords

Generate keywords that describe the product or service being offered, such as colors, styles, sizes, or brands. Depending on how popular these terms are, they might have to be sectioned off into separate ad groups or campaigns.

Also, if you sell a variety of products, you want to have a separate ad group for each product you promote.

Suppose that you sell two different types of pens: ballpoint and gel. Also suppose that you want to promote six kinds of ballpoint pens but only one type of gel pen. Putting the keywords for the gel pen in with those for the ballpoint pens may save you a little time, because you don't have to create a separate ad group for the gel pen, but overall, combining these keywords won't produce your desired pay per click (PPC) result or return on investment (ROI). (See Chapter 1 in this minibook for details on PPC.)

For the same reason, you wouldn't bid on the keyword *pen* in either ad group. The term is too general and *high traffic* (a very popular term likely to generate a lot of impressions and clicks), and it isn't as targeted as *ballpoint pen* or *gel pen*. A high-traffic keyword like *pen* may need to be in its own campaign because it's so broad that it will generate a lot of traffic, much of which could have nothing to do with your pen. Your ad could show up for inquiries having to do with *pig pen*, *pen pal*, *pent up*, and *penny*, for example.

The best practice is to decide the subject of your campaign before you start selecting keywords. Sketch out your subject and keep it in mind while you're building your ad groups and keyword lists.

Organizing Keywords in Ad Groups

Organizing your keywords in ad groups makes the overall management of your campaigns easier and cleaner, and shows much more clearly which keywords are successful and which ones aren't. In this section, I give several examples of just how granular you need to be when you organize your keywords in ad groups.

Suppose that you sell floral wedding invitations. You want to promote the type/brand Flora Wedding Invitations, and you know that rose, lily, and daisy invitations are very popular. To plan your campaign, you might create a table like Table 3-1.

Table 3-1 Ad Groups and Keywords for a Sample Campaign

Ad Group	Keywords
General Floral Wedding Invitations	flower wedding invitations, floral wedding invitations, flower wedding invites, floral wedding invites
Rose Wedding Invitations	rose wedding invitations, rose wedding invites, pink rose wedding invitations, pink rose wedding invites, red rose wedding invitations, red rose wedding invites
Lily Wedding Invitations	lily wedding invitations, lily wedding invites, lily wedding invitations, lily wedding invites, calla lily wedding invitations, calla lily wedding invites
Daisy Wedding Invitations	daisy wedding invitations, daisy wedding invites, yellow daisy wedding invitations, yellow daisy invites, gerber daisy wedding invitations, gerber daisy wedding invites
Flora Wedding Invitation Branded	flora wedding invitations, flora wedding invites, flora company wedding invitations, wedding invitations flora

Make your keyword lists as segmented and relevant as possible from the start. Although it may seem like a lot less work to cram everything into a few ad groups, that practice will actually create more work and headaches for you down the line as the account matures.

The example in Table 3-1 is a highly segmented campaign of several ad groups and keywords. Even though the ad groups are highly targeted, they're within the same campaign which will give you greater control of cost and allow you to add negative keywords easily. (For more information about negative keywords, see "Knowing the match types," later in this chapter.)

The fewer keywords you use in an ad group, the better. A good rule is to have no more than 30 keywords in an ad group. A keyword list of several hundred terms is hard to manage and affects both the ad group and the campaign in many negative ways, including relevancy, quality score, ease of ad-text creation, and bidding. The more targeted and more specific your ad group is, the more benefits you reap from search engines in terms of PPC, relevancy (see Book IV, Chapter 1), and ad position.

Working with Match Types

Match types are what you use to tell the search engine the context in which you want your ads to be shown. A broad match type, for example, tells the search engine that you want the ad to appear more often and in conjunction with keywords that are similar to your keyword, even if they're not exactly the same. A phrase match type is more targeted, allowing other words to appear before and after your keyword, whereas an exact match tells the search engine to display your ad only if the user types the exact keyword. I discuss all these types in detail in the following sections.

Knowing the match types

Most search engines use at least three basic match types: *broad, exact,* and *negative.* If they don't, you don't want to use those search engines. Some engines also have *phrase* matches.

Table 3-2 describes all four match types and gives specific examples of keywords used with those match types.

Table 3-2	Match Types	
Match Type	*Ad Display*	*Example*
Broad	Ads are displayed for keywords in singular, plural, and synonym forms. This option is the most inclusive one and triggers ads more often than the others.	The keyword *bicycle parts* triggers ads for *bike parts, bicycle part, parts for bikes,* and *bicycles.*
Phrase	Ads are displayed for keywords in plural form, and the keywords must be in the same word order as the search term.	The keyword *green tea cups* triggers ads for *green tea* and *cheap green tea cups* but not for *tea green cups.*
Exact	Ads are displayed only if what the user searched on matches a keyword in your list.	The keyword *health care plans* trigger ads only for *health care plans* (plural), not for *health care plan* (singular).
Negative	Ads are not displayed in conjunction with these keywords.	The keyword *glass vases* would have negative keywords to exclude other media, such as *ceramic, porcelain, china,* and *plastic.*

Choosing the match type to use

When you know what the match types are, your next decisions are what match types to use for your situation. The following list outlines the best-case scenarios for the different match types. If you find that your situation falls between two categories, you can use both match types in the same ad group and test them against each other. A phrase match might convert better for you than an exact match, or a broad match might bring you more of what you want than a phrase match.

✦ **Broad:** This match type is best for *long-tail* keywords (three words or more), misspellings, and URLs, and for maximizing the number of times your ad appears.

✦ **Phrase:** This match type is a good place to start if you're not sure what the keyword will do, and if you're very budget conscious. It's also a good choice for keywords that are popular enough that you need to filter out some searches (for items you don't carry, for example). Also, a phrase match often turns up great keywords that you'll want to add or block out as the campaign progresses.

✦ **Exact:** This match type is best for keywords that are popular and short (one to two words) and that rack up several thousand *impressions* (how many times your ad appears to users) very quickly. Exact match is a good way to control costs and targeting, because it cuts down on impressions for broader search inquiries; the typical user is searching for something specific.

✦ **Negative:** This match type is best for keywords that you don't want your ads to appear in conjunction with. Popular negative keywords include *discount* and *used.*

Segmenting Keyword Lists by Destination URLs

When you have a complete keyword list organized by ad groups and match types, you can segment the list even further. This situation applies if you want to drive visitors to a specific product or place, but starting a separate ad group doesn't make sense.

In the example shown in Table 3-1, earlier in this chapter, some of the keywords indicate specific colors for rose wedding invitations: red and pink. Rather than drop visitors off the product page for rose wedding invitations, you can take them one click further by using a keyword destination URL for each color. Select the URL for the product page of the pink rose wedding invitation, for example, and direct visitors there specifically for the keywords *pink rose wedding invitation* and *pink rose wedding invites.* This strategy works especially well if you have only one type of product but still want to have the keyword so that when someone does search on it, your ad appears.

All three of the major search engines — Google, Yahoo!, and MSN — offer keyword destination URL targeting. I cover how the process works in those engines in the following sections.

Applying keyword destinations in Google

To use keyword destination URLs in Google, follow these steps:

1. **Click the ad group's name to open the ad group.**

2. **Select the Keywords tab.**

3. **Select the check box for each keyword to which you want to add the destination URL.**

4. **Click Edit Keyword Settings.**

   You see the keywords you selected and options for changing the bids and destination URL (see Figure 3-1).

Figure 3-1:
Google
keyword
destinations.

5. **Type or paste the destination URL in the Destination URL text box.**

   If you're typing the URL, omit the `http://` or `https://` prefix. If you're pasting the URL into the text box, remove the `http://` or `https://` prefix and instead choose the prefix from the drop-down menu.

6. **Click the Save Changes button.**

If you want to add the same destination URL to more than one keyword, simply select all the keywords in Step 3, paste the URL in the Destination URL box in Step 5, and click the little button with the arrow on it to copy the URL to the other keywords.

Applying keyword destinations in Yahoo!

To use keyword destination URLs in Yahoo!, follow these steps:

1. **Click the ad group's name to open the ad group.**

2. **Select the keyword to which you want to add a destination URL.**

   You can add a keyword destination URL to only one keyword at a time.

3. **Scroll down to the Ads pane, and in the Destination URL section, select the check box labeled Use a Custom Destination URL for This Keyword.**

   Yahoo! asks you for the URL to use.

4. **Type or paste the URL in the text box (see Figure 3-2).**

5. **Click the Save button.**

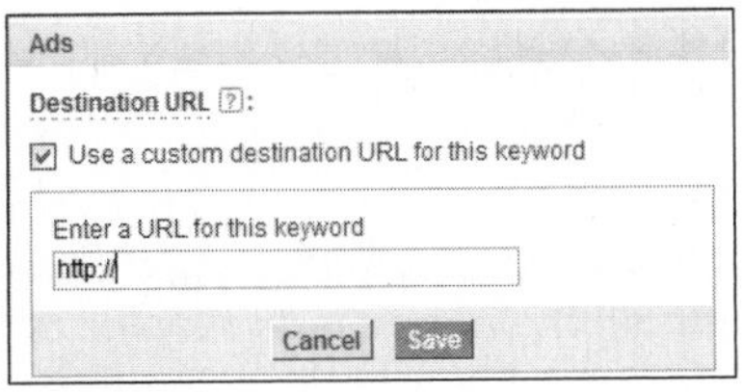

Figure 3-2:
Yahoo!
keyword
destinations.

Applying keyword destinations in MSN

To use keyword destination URLs in MSN, follow these steps:

1. **Click the ad group's name to open the ad group.**

2. **In the Keywords tab, click Edit Keywords.**

   You see your entire list of keywords, with blank form fields for each one: Negative Keywords, Destination URL, and two Placeholder fields (see Figure 3-3).

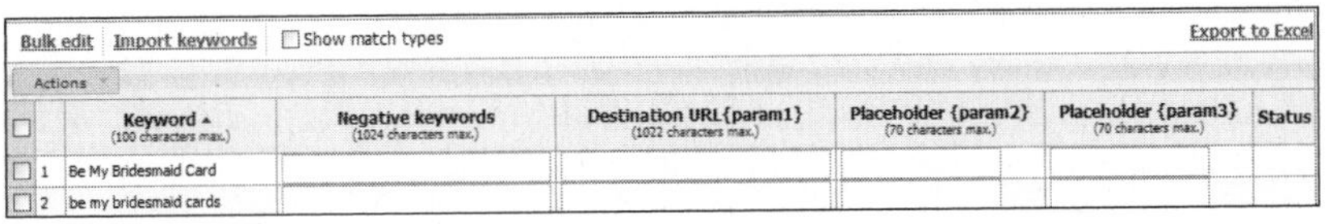

Figure 3-3:
MSN
keyword
destinations.

3. **In the Destination URL {param1} field, type or paste the destination URL for all the keywords to which you want to add it.**

4. **Click Continue.**

   You see a page for editing bids, location targeting, and demographics. In this exercise, you're interested only in destination URLs, so you don't need to take any action here.

5. **Click Save and Continue at the bottom of the page.**

   A pop-up dialog box tells you that your changes have been saved.

6. **Click OK.**

**Book IV
Chapter 3**

Making Keyword
Lists That Sell

Using Advanced Keyword Targeting in Yahoo! and MSN

Both Yahoo! and MSN offer deeper keyword destination URL targeting for those who really want to get into all the nooks and crannies of keyword targeting tools. This level of keyword URL targeting is optional and won't have a major effect on your account. If you've organized and deployed your ad groups and keyword lists as efficiently as you can, with maximum relevancy, you don't need these tools. In fact, using them is overkill unless you have generic ad groups and campaigns, and need to make your ads as dynamic as possible.

Although Google offers many other tools, it currently doesn't offer this one.

Advanced keyword targeting in Yahoo!

Yahoo! offers an Alternate Text option next to the destination URL options for each keyword. Alternate text, which is enabled on a per-keyword basis, applies if you have ads with dynamic parameters within the ad copy.

To use this option, click the keyword you want to use alternate text with. In the Ads section of the keyword detail page, select the Alternate Text check box; the section expands as shown in Figure 3-4. Type a keyword that you want to show in the ad instead of a keyword from the list, and click the Save button.

Figure 3-4:
Advanced
keyword
targeting in
Yahoo!

The best use of this option is for a keyword longer than the maximum number of characters in an ad. Suppose that the keyword is *cheapest Hawaiian vacation flights,* but the dynamic keyword placeholder in the ad is *Hawaii vacation,* which is much shorter. If you want the ad to appear for the keyword *cheapest Hawaiian vacation flights,* use *Hawaiian flights* as the alternate text.

Advanced keyword targeting in MSN

MSN offers a {param} or dynamic text option for ads that contains placeholder text. If the ad copy contains a dynamic keyword or {param} and your keyword list contains keywords that are too long to fit within the {param} parameter of the ad text, you can specify something else to display instead. Suppose that the ad copy reads Save on {param2}, as shown in Figure 3-5, but the keyword that the user searched on is *cheapest Hawaiian vacation packages,* which is too long to display. If you configure {param2} as *Hawaiian vacations,* the ad will display *Hawaiian vacations* instead.

Figure 3-5:
An MSN adCenter ad with {param2} set.

Great Vacation Packages
Save on {param2}! Great Rates &
Great Destinations!
www.Vacations.com

Expanding Keyword Lists

As any PPC campaign progresses, it becomes more and more apparent which keywords are generating the quality of traffic you want and which ones are not. The best way to determine how your keywords are performing is to use an analytics or conversion tracking package (see Book IV, Chapter 4) that can tell you the amount of revenue a keyword has generated, the number of pageviews, the amount of time visitors spend on the site, and how quickly they leave. Depending on your PPC goals (see Book IV, Chapter 1), these stats determine whether a keyword is a keeper.

If you started your campaign with only a few keywords as a test or simply want to increase impressions for your ads, you're ready to expand your initial keyword list to grab additional traffic. The best way to start is to use the search engine's free keyword-generation tool. Often, this tool also estimates the impressions and clicks that those keywords will generate. The tool gives you a few options for generating additional keywords:

+ Selecting keywords in your current list

+ Entering the URL of the site

+ Selecting categories

When you use keyword-generation tools, review the keyword suggestions carefully before adding any of them. Never select Add All; the search engines reach far and wide to come up with keyword suggestions, and accepting all of them will result in a large ad group that's difficult to manage. In addition, you might add keywords that aren't relevant to your ad group.

Adding keywords in Google

Google AdWords offers a free keyword-generation tool to expand your current keyword lists. To use it, follow these steps:

1. **Open the ad group to which you want to add keywords.**

2. **Click the Keywords tab.**

3. **Click the Keyword Tool link.**

   The Keyword Tool page opens.

4. **Choose one of the following options:**

   - *Descriptive Words or Phrases:* Select this radio button; in the text box, type words or phrases that describe the product or service that the ad group targets.

   - *Website Content:* Select this radio button; in the text box, enter the destination URL.

   - *Existing Keyword:* Select this radio button, and choose one of the keywords in the ad group for the tool to use as a baseline for suggestions.

5. **Click the Get Keyword Ideas button.**

   You see a long list of suggestions with estimated search volume, peak times of year, and advertiser competition.

6. **Click the Add link for each keyword that you want to add to your ad group.**

   The selected keywords appear on the right side of the page.

7. **If you think of additional keywords that you don't want to run a search for, click the Add Your Own Keywords link, and type those keywords.**

8. **When you have all the keywords you want, click the Save to Ad Group button.**

Adding keywords in Yahoo!

To add a keyword to an existing ad group, follow these steps:

1. **Open the ad group to which you want to add keywords.**

2. **Click the Add Keywords button.**

3. **Choose one of the following options:**
   - *Quick Add:* Type the keywords to add.
   - *Choose from List:* Yahoo! gives you a list of suggestions based on your current keyword list.
   - *Research Keywords:* You go to Yahoo!'s keyword-generation tool.

Adding keywords in MSN

To add a keyword to an existing ad group, follow these steps:

1. **Open the ad group to which you want to add a keyword.**

2. **Click the Keywords tab, if it isn't already open.**

3. **Click the Edit Keywords link.**

4. **Enter your desired keywords.**

5. **Click the Add to Keyword List button.**

   Your new keywords are added to the existing keyword list.

6. **Click Continue.**

   You see a page that allows you to set bidding options. For this exercise, though, you aren't editing those options.

7. **Click Save and Continue.**

No matter what edits you made — or if you made none — when you click the Save or Save and Continue button in MSN, a message informs you that your changes have been saved. So even if you didn't edit anything, you still see that message.

Contracting Keyword Lists

Just as any keyword list might need expansion, it might need contraction at some point in its career. I discuss how to downsize keyword lists in the following sections.

Analyzing underperforming keywords

Using the statistics from conversion tracking or analytics tools, determine which keywords aren't meeting your goals, and delete any terms that are driving lots of impressions and costs but aren't performing to your expectations.

If you're not sure about a keyword, pause it and watch what happens. (For help with pausing, see Book IV, Chapter 2.) See whether your impressions or traffic decrease while your conversions or other stats improve. Often, a keyword can eat up your budget, leaving little funds for the rest of your keyword list, which would generate more conversions. By removing the budget-eating keyword, you might get your ads to appear more often on better-quality terms, and your money will be better spent.

Deciding when a keyword should be deleted

Deciding when to delete a keyword depends on your industry and goals, but the best approach is the common-sense approach: If a keyword is generating thousands of impressions but no click-throughs, sales, conversions, or good time on site or pageview results, something's wrong.

Check your ad copy first. Is the keyword relevant to the ad, and vice versa? A poor ad click-through rate (CTR) means that people are searching and seeing the ad but not finding what they're looking for. If the keyword and the ad are relevant to each other — particularly if the keyword in question is in the ad copy or headline — the problem is with the keyword.

If you feel that the keyword should still be in your list, try adjusting the match type; you may be going too broad, and irrelevant searches are driving up your impressions. (For details on match types, read "Choosing the match type to use," earlier in this chapter.)

In Google AdWords, you can run a Search Query report, which gives you a good idea of what search terms your ad is appearing for. This report is also a good way to find additional negative keywords (see Table 3-1, earlier in this chapter) to use in your ad groups and campaigns. This option is located on the Reports tab of your account dashboard.

An alternative solution is to turn the term into a *long-tail keyword* (a longer, more specific keyword) to increase relevancy.

At this point, if the keyword still isn't performing, it's time to cut it, despite how much you may want to bid on it. Part of good PPC management is accepting that sometimes a keyword or ad isn't relevant to the search engine or the searchers.

Chapter 4: Writing Ads That Earn Clicks and Pay You Back

In This Chapter

✔ Understanding the structure of ads

✔ Writing compelling ads

✔ Testing ads

✔ Determining which ads are successful

A d copy is a two-second chance to catch a searcher's attention, so clearly, your ads need to grab and keep a reader's attention.

In this chapter, I show you how to create pay per click (PPC) ads that are not only catchy and retain attention, but also catch the attention of the kinds of users you want to bring to your site and cause desired behaviors, such as purchases, downloads, or pageviews. (For more information on PPC in general, refer to Book IV, Chapter 1.)

Working with PPC Ads

A PPC ad is made up of the following elements:

✦ Headline

✦ Body

✦ Display URL

✦ Destination URL

Each component should be constructed carefully and separately, yet all the parts should flow together as a whole. In this section, you find tips for writing each part. (For more details, see "Writing PPC Ad Copy," later in this chapter.)

Creating the headline

Your headline is the most important part of your ad. Most often, searchers don't read whole ads; they scan the headlines to narrow down their choices. Keeping this fact in mind, the best practice for any PPC ad is to use a high-traffic keyword (your most revenue-generating one, if possible) in the headline.

A *revenue-generating keyword* is one that you know brings in results, whether those results are sales, downloads, or signups. A *high-traffic keyword* is one that drives a lot of impressions and clicks but doesn't necessarily result in sales. Some campaigns have a keyword that meets both those criteria. Check your analytics package, if you have one (and if you don't, you should!), or check the past performance of that keyword in the PPC interface to determine what your high-traffic and revenue-generating keywords are. (For details on analytics, see Book III.)

If the keyword you want to use is a longer, more targeted word, simply using the keyword alone as the headline (depending on length) is all you need to do to capture a searcher's attention. Typically, search engines limit a headline to 35 characters although Yahoo! Search Marketing allows 40 characters.

Also, break up your ad groups so that high-traffic keywords are broken up appropriately, making it easier to write new ads and maintain the ad group (see Book IV, Chapter 2).

Figure 4-1 shows an example of an ad with a high-traffic keyword as the headline. In the following sections, I use "*leather dog collars*" as an example of a popular term, assuming that the term is targeted yet popular enough for plenty of searches.

Figure 4-1:
Increase revenue potential with a high-traffic keyword.

Leather Dog Collars
Huge Selection, Great Prices!
Shop Dog Collars Online Now.
www.exampledogcollars.com

Crafting the body

The body of the ad can be two separate phrases, two separate sentences, or one longer sentence that wraps around from the first line of the ad to the second line. The important thing is to get your message in the body of your ad within the normal 70-character limit.

The search engine you use determines the character limits. Typically, the body must be no more than 70 characters long, including spaces and punctuation marks. Be sure to consult the search engine's editorial guide for its character limits. You don't have a lot of space, so make every word count! For more on writing body copy, see "Writing PPC Ad Copy," later in this chapter.

Planning the display URL

Often thought of as the place where you plug in your Web address, the display URL can be useful in ad optimization as well. Consider the following points as you write your ads:

✦ Starting the URL with `http://` and starting it with `www.` can often yield very different results. (See "Testing for Successful Ads," later in this chapter.)

✦ The same goes for beginning the URL with no prefix at all (`leather dogcollars.com`, for example).

✦ It may be worthwhile to test adding a keyword to the display URL. The URL `www.leatherdogcollars.com/studded`, for example, could drive more traffic than `www.leatherdogcollars.com`.

Choosing the best destination URL

The destination URL is the location where the user arrives after clicking your ad. This URL could be the homepage, a product page, or a specially crafted landing page. The choice of a destination URL can affect your visitor's experience, which is why I recommend keeping the following guidelines in mind:

✦ **Deliver on the promise of the display URL.** Most search engines require the destination URL to match the site that's advertised in the display URL. This requirement makes for a much better user experience and prevents advertisers from spamming users. Suppose that you click an ad for women's sandals (`www.womenssandals.com`) but arrive on a site that sells diet pills. Clearly, this site isn't what you were looking for. This practice causes users to distrust PPC ads. (For more on search engines' policies on destination URLs, see Book IV, Chapter 6.)

✦ **Keep in mind your keyword list and ads.** If the ad is promoting leather dog collars — a very specific product — you should direct the user to a product page offering different types of leather dog collars or a product page for a specific leather dog collar.

A highly targeted group of keywords can perform even better with a combination of the two. An ad group targeting the keyword "*studded leather dog collars*", for example, would attract more searchers without selection or color features listed, as the features (*studded* and *leather*) are built into the keyword itself.

✦ **Don't drop users off on the homepage without considering their user experience.** You should direct users to a homepage via a PPC ad only for branded or very general terms. If your keyword is "*dog collars*", and dog collars are the only products you sell, the homepage is an acceptable place to send visitors. If you also sell cat and ferret collars, however, you want to select the dog category or product page as your destination URL.

The more that users have to click around and search on your site for what they're looking for, the more likely they are to click the Back button and look elsewhere. You want to direct people to the item or service they're looking for in the fewest clicks possible.

Writing PPC Ad Copy

You have only a few characters to get your point across, so you have to make every word count! Use the keywords in your ad group, use attention-getting language, and follow the editorial guidelines of the search engine for spelling and grammar, and you'll find that writing ads comes naturally. In this section, I show you a few methods that make the process even easier.

Follow the benefits/features model

Try following the benefits/features model to start with. The *benefits/features model* is a standard PPC ad practice dictating that within the ad, you state both a benefit to the searcher and a feature of the product or service you're promoting. The first line of the ad states a benefit or feature (on sale, free shipping, in stock), and the second line of the ad states the remaining benefit or feature (colors, sizes, quality).

 Traditionally, ads that mention benefits tend to perform better than ads that focus on features. Customers are more drawn to offers of free shipping, in-stock availability, and cash-back offers than they are to ads that focus on selection, styles, and sizes.

Craft the call to action

You also need a clear call to action, such as the two clear calls to action using the *leather dog collars* keyword in Figures 4-2 and 4-3. The ad in Figure 4-2 shows the feature of selection, the benefit of price, and the call to action *Online Now*. Figure 4-3 shows the features of style and color, the benefit of a sale, and the call to action *Shop Now!*.

Figure 4-2:
This ad has
a clear call
to action.

Leather Dog Collars
Huge Selection, Great Prices!
Dog Collars Online Now.
www.exampledogcollars.com

Figure 4-3:
This ad
shows
different
calls to
action.

> Leather Dog Collars
> Sale on Leather Dog Collars.
> Shop Lots of Styles & Colors Now!
> www.exampledogcollars.com

As you write your ads, also keep these points in mind:

✦ If you're writing to attract buyers, drive traffic, or promote a time-sensitive offer, aggressive copy with a clear call to action is your best bet. An exclamation point adds a sense of urgency (*Buy now!* or *On sale!*).

✦ If you're trying to get people to download a white paper or simply to visit your site, you need to be less aggressive and more informative. Give people a reason to visit in your call to action, such as *free download* or *thousands of articles.*

A more aggressive call to action targets an immediate response, such as purchasing a sale item. A more informative call to action is intended for those who are researching or browsing around.

Focus on goals, grammar, and guidelines

You should have a clear picture of what you want your ads to do before you start writing them. For more information on setting PPC goals, refer to Book IV, Chapter 1.

Be sure to use proper grammar, as the search engines' guidelines dictate. Acceptable uses of punctuation, spelling, and abbreviations vary from search engine to engine, but all search engines require a more formal approach.

Keep these points in mind:

✦ **Spelling counts.** Search engines reject misspellings, which are also unprofessional and spammy-looking.

✦ **Editorial guidelines count.** Often, search engines immediately reject ads that don't follow their guidelines, such as using all capitals (*FREE*) or using numbers or letters in place of words (*2* instead of *to*). An ampersand (&) is okay to use in place of *and,* however. I cover editorial guidelines in depth in Book IV, Chapter 6.

Avoid common mistakes

Avoid making these common mistakes in writing PPC ad copy:

✦ **Neglecting to use your keywords, which are the words and phrases that you're bidding on:** Any search terms from your keyword list that the user types will be boldface in the ad, so make sure to use keywords that will make your ad stand out.

✦ **Using too many keywords:** The body of the ad should be populated with keywords but not stuffed to the point where the entire ad would appear in boldface. This situation could cause *ad blindness* — a condition in which the searcher doesn't even see the ad due to its overly zealous approach. Also, ads crammed with keywords look like spam and are less likely to attract the kind of traffic that you seek.

✦ **Using poor grammar or spelling:** Not only does poor grammar or spelling make your ad look unprofessional (or like it could be some sort of scam), but also, the search engines have editorial guidelines in place that reject ads with gross misspellings. Poor grammar is harder for search engines to catch, but grammatical errors make life much more difficult for users if they have to decipher your ad before clicking it.

✦ **Using too much fragmented text:** Use complete sentences whenever you can because this kind of language lends authority and authenticity to your offer.

Testing for Successful Ads

Testing ads is extremely important to any PPC campaign. Different industries have very different keyword lists, and users themselves behave in very different ways when conducting searches and completing actions, such as sales or downloads. The ads and keywords you would use for the wedding industry, for example, attract a certain kind of user who displays specific behavior on a Web site; you'd need to use different ads and keywords for the different type of user in the heavy-machinery industry. To determine which ad will generate the most successful actions for your industry, you need to conduct tests to find your most successful combinations.

Conducting A/B tests

The most basic test and best practice is A/B split testing, in which you create two slightly different ads and run them both at the same time, splitting the traffic between them.

A/B tests range from simple to complex. The best practice is to start simple and work your way up in terms of complexity. The more *variables* (differences) you have in your ads, the harder it will be to track down the most successful variable. If you run two different ads against each other, one will inevitably outperform the other, but you'll have to do some guesswork about the determining variable.

Viewing example tests

Following are examples of tests you can run, starting with a simple A/B test and working up to more complex variations:

Headline
Ads have different headlines but identical body copy.

Women's Shoes on Sale
Save on Hundreds of Styles!
Shop Women's Shoes Online.
www.womensshoes.com

Sale: Women's Shoes
Save on Hundreds of Styles!
Shop Women's Shoes Online.
www.womensshoes.com

Capitalization of body copy
Ads are identical except for capitalization schemes.

Rebuilt Garbage Disposals
Save on Garbage Disposals Rebuilt
By Experts! Don't Pay Full Price.
www.garbagerebuild.com

Rebuilt Garbage Disposals
Save on garbage disposals rebuilt
by experts! Don't pay full price.
www.garbagerebuild.com

Capitalization of display URL
Ads are identical except for the capitalization of the display URL.

Office Supplies
Shop Pens, Paper, Clips & More!
Ships Same Day, Guaranteed.
www.OfficeSuppliesOnline.com

Office Supplies
Shop Pens, Paper, Clips & More!
Ships Same Day, Guaranteed.
www.officesuppliesonline.com

Extended display URL

Ads are identical except that one ad has a longer display URL.

Great Comic Books
Thousands of Back Issues Online!
Shop All Our Comic Books.
`www.joescomicdungeon.com/marvel`

Great Comic Books
Thousands of Back Issues Online!
Shop All Our Comic Books.
`www.joescomicdungeon.com`

Dynamic headline

Ads are identical except that one ad uses a dynamic headline.

`{Keyword: Plant Seeds}`
Hundreds of Flowers, Vegetables &
More! Shop Our Seed Catalog Now.
`www.seedpackets.com`

Plant Seeds
Hundreds of Flowers, Vegetables &
More! Shop Our Seed Catalog Now.
`www.seedpackets.com`

Dynamic ad copy

Ads are identical except that one ad uses dynamic copy.

Organic Makeup
Shop `{Keyword: Organic Lipstick}`
100% Organic & Cruelty Free!

Organic Makeup
Shop Organic Lipstick.
100% Organic & Cruelty Free!

Destination URL

Ads are identical except that the URLs go to different locations. One goes to the homepage and the other to a product page, or one goes to a landing page and the other to a product page.

In the following sections, I show you how to set up an A/B test in the top three search engines' PPC programs: Google AdWords, Yahoo! Search Marketing, and MSN adCenter. (For more information on these programs, refer to Book IV, Chapter 2.)

Setting up an A/B test in Google AdWords

REMEMBER

By default, Google AdWords is set to *optimize,* so it determines which of your ads is best and shows that ad most often. To do an A/B test, you need to set it to *rotate.*

To set up an A/B test in Google AdWords, follow these steps:

1. **Open the desired campaign, and click the Edit Campaign Settings link.**

2. **Scroll down to Advanced Options, and click Rotate.**

3. **Click Save Changes.**

Setting up an A/B test in Yahoo! Search Marketing

By default, Yahoo! has all ad groups set to Optimize Ad Display, which means that Yahoo! determines which ad is best for you and shows that ad most often. To perform an A/B test in Yahoo!, you need to change that setting from Yes to No.

To set up an A/B test in Yahoo! Search Marketing, follow these steps:

1. **Open the ad group, and click the Ad Group Settings link.**

2. **In the Ad Group General Information section, click Edit.**

3. **In the Optimize Ad Display section, select No.**

   This setting is at ad-group level, not campaign level, so if you want all the ads to rotate, you have to go into each ad group and change the settings.

4. **Click Save Changes.**

Setting up an A/B test in MSN adCenter

MSN automatically rotates ads when an ad group contains multiple ads, eventually selecting the ad to show most frequently (based on impressions, clicks, and age of ads). You have no way to change this setting. Every time you change an ad, however, MSN resets the ads to rotate. For more information about changing ads, see "Determining When to Change an Ad," later in this chapter.

Using dynamic keyword insertion

Dynamic keyword insertion (DKI) is a great way to write highly targeted ads with minimal effort. This technique inserts the keyword that the searcher used directly into your ad. The trick is composing your ad so that the text makes sense — grammatically and logically — to the searcher when the keyword pops in.

You can use DKI in both headlines and ad copy as long as the searched term is short enough to fit within the character limits.

Be sure to use a keyword from the ad group as placeholder text. Don't leave *Keyword* in as the default, as shown in the following example. Use a keyword from that ad group's list. If the search term doesn't quite match a keyword in your list, the search engine might show your ad with the placeholder keywords instead.

**Book IV
Chapter 4**

Writing Ads That
Earn Clicks and Pay
You Back

The following two examples illustrate what to do and what not to do. The good example shows *Mother's Day Gifts* as the placeholder keyword, whereas the bad example doesn't have anything after `{Keyword: }`. As a result, the word *Keyword* could appear to users as a headline.

Good example:

`{Keyword:Mother's Day Gifts}`
Mother's Day Gift Sale.
Huge Selection, Free Shipping!
`www.gifthouse.com`

Bad example:

`{Keyword}`
Mother's Day Gift Sale.
Huge Selection, Free Shipping!
`www.gifthouse.com`

Format the placeholder keyword as you want the keyword to appear in the ad:

✦ If you use `{keyword}`, the term appears in lowercase.

✦ If you use `{Keyword}`, the first letter of the word is capitalized.

✦ If you use `{KeyWord}`, all initial letters of the search term are capitalized.

Determining When to Change an Ad

Ad testing is a continual process of trying to find the best combination to bring you the most quality traffic. Because your offers might change, and because product availability, seasonality, and prices might fluctuate, you need to change underperforming ads as often as you can.

Using goals to make changes

The winning ad can be determined by your goals:

✦ If your goal is revenue, the winner is the ad that generated the most revenue.

✦ If your goal is traffic, the winner is the ad that generated the most clicks.

✦ If your goal is downloads . . . well, you get the idea.

For more information on PPC and goals, refer see Book IV, Chapter 1.

Using click-through rate to make changes

Suppose that you're not sure which ad is doing what, and the only statistics you have to go on are clicks, click-through rate (CTR), and cost per click (CPC). In this case, the ad with the better CTR for the lowest CPC is your winner.

Measuring success in 100 clicks

A good rule in determining when to delete, pause, or edit an ad is *100 clicks.* Depending on the industry and search volume, it could take a day to reach that number, or it could take a month. If you have low search volume and won't reach 100 clicks in a month, you have a different kind of problem (see Book IV, Chapter 3).

After you reach the 100-clicks mark, assess your success so far. Is the ad doing what you need it to? Are users clicking through to your site? If not, it's time to change the ad. Add a keyword to the headline or body, change the headline completely, or add a feature or benefit that you didn't use before. (See "Conducting A/B tests," elsewhere in this chapter, for specific examples to test.)

At best, a week is a good minimum test if you want to go by time and not by volume (100 clicks or more), and one month is the longest period you should let a test run. At that point, a clear winner should emerge, and you should edit one of the other ads to begin a new test.

Be sure to compare the *ad-serving percentages* — the amount of time that an ad was shown in comparison with the other ads — to ensure that both ads had a fair amount of time. If one ad runs for a week and another ad runs for two weeks, however, the numbers of times the ads were shown will be different. Take that difference into consideration when making your decision.

Don't make the mistake of not checking on your campaigns at least once per week. An editorial issue, bidding issue, or billing issue could knock your campaigns offline and leave you without any ads! To prevent such issues from going unnoticed, set up notifications in your account so that when something does occur that turns your ads off, you receive an e-mail alerting you to that fact. Look in the account settings section of your search engine for e-mail notification preferences.

Using conversion tracking to make changes

One of the best tools to have in your PPC ad-management toolbox is conversion tracking within the PPC search engine's interface. This tool shows you at a glance which ad caused conversions — the goal of your PPC efforts. A *conversion* is completed when the user goes to a specific URL that you determine. A sales conversion, for example, would be a Thank You or receipt page; a download conversion would be a download-complete page. Knowing how much each conversion costs you, and which keywords and ads contributed to those conversions, greatly reduces the time that you spend digging around in analytics programs.

All three of the major search engines offer this kind of visibility through their PPC interface if you install all the tracking codes on the needed pages. Each set of codes is different, but all three sets are supposed to be able to coexist on one page without breaking or interfering with the others.

You must set up conversion tracking separately in each search engine for the process to work properly. (Each search engine offers implementation guides in its help center if you need additional support.) Following are quick tips on setting up conversion tracking in Google AdWords, Yahoo! Search Marketing, and MSN adCenter:

✦ **Google AdWords:** Conversion tracking is a tool in the Campaign Management tab. Create a new action (such as a sale or purchase), obtain the snippet of code, and place it on the page where completed conversions take place (such as a Thank You page). The code must be inserted between `<card>` and `</card>` tags. See the Google Help Center for a tutorial video and live support via phone and chat.

✦ **Yahoo! Search Marketing:** Your conversion-tracking options are Conversion Only and Full Analytics. The Full Analytics option pulls in much more information, such as specific revenue numbers. Conversion Only shows you which keywords and ads generated conversions, and at what cost.

In the Administration tab, click the Analytics link; choose the desired type and revenue value setting (dynamic or constant average); then click Activate. Yahoo! generates the necessary code.

Full Analytics is a much more involved process that requires universal tags to be placed in the headers of all pages on the site, as well as a prospect tag on the shopping-cart page and a conversion tag on the Thank You page. Live phone support is available for this feature — and it is highly recommended.

✦ **MSN adCenter:** To use conversion tracking in the adCenter interface, you must enroll in Gatineau, MSN's beta analytics package. If you install Gatineau, you can see conversions by ad and keyword within the adCenter interface. The code must be placed on all pages to be tracked, but it can be placed on the conversion page only if you want to see only conversions — not other behavior on other pages of the site. Currently, MSN offers only e-mail support for this program.

Chapter 5: Budgeting and Bidding on Keywords

In This Chapter

✔ Setting your PPC budget

✔ Deciding what to spend per keyword

✔ Managing the bidding process

✔ Targeting your spending by industry and niche

In this chapter, I talk about the most important aspect of your pay per click (PPC) account: money. The amount you spend and how you spend it determine the overall outcome of your campaigns — unless, of course, you have an unlimited budget and don't need to see a positive return on your investment. Very few marketers fall within that category, though.

The very first question you should ask yourself is "How much can I spend?" After you establish how much you can spend, you can really expand and optimize your account.

In this chapter, I help you decide where to set your daily budgets and how much to bid on a per-keyword basis. Depending on your industry, these costs can vary greatly, but if you follow the general rules of thumb in this chapter, you'll be managing your campaign costs like a pro.

Determining Your PPC Budget

Establish your PPC marketing budget with the assumption that you might not make it all back. Any get-rich-quick promises or pitches that guarantee that you'll quadruple your return on investment are just as fishy as they sound. Not all industries, products, or services flourish in PPC. Industries that sell equipment retailing for thousands of dollars might have a much harder time than a site that sells shoes, for example. Those types of industries should consider PPC to be a tool for gathering leads for sales and increasing brand awareness. Building your campaigns smartly and capping the amount you spend per day with careful budgeting, however, ensures that you get the most bang for your buck.

Researching your assets

To determine your PPC marketing budget, you need to do some research on your assets. Decide exactly how much you want to dedicate to PPC marketing, and stick to that budget to start with. If the campaigns are going very successfully for you, reevaluate your budgets and reinvest some of that success, if necessary. If you aren't doing well, consider making edits to your campaigns (such as pausing underperforming ad groups or keywords) before you turn everything off and call it quits. Whichever path you choose, make sure that your business has the money to spend and won't be in dire need if the investment isn't returned.

Deciding the duration and reach of your budget

You need to determine how long you want your budget to run: daily or monthly. You also need to determine how much you want to spend per day and per campaign. The best practice is to set budgets at campaign level per day rather than rely on a monthly budget. If you rely on a monthly budget, the search engine is stretching — and at some points, even stopping — the display of your ads to stay within that monthly budget limit. A daily budget does the same thing, but on a much more granular and flexible level. By budgeting one day at a time, you ensure that your campaign starts each day with the same amount of funds. By contrast, if you're on a monthly budget, depending on how fast clicks accumulate, you could be out of money before the end of the month and have no ads showing at all.

Google AdWords, Yahoo! Search Marketing, and MSN adCenter have both monthly and daily spending limits; you can tell the search engine the absolute most you want to spend per day or per month. If you choose a monthly or account budget, the search engine simply takes the amount you enter and divides it among the days of the month, evenly distributing funds to your campaigns or ad groups. If you choose to do daily budgeting instead, the search engines add up all the campaign budgets and show the total cost of all your campaign budgets combined per day within the dashboard interface.

Plan on setting an overall monthly budget to spend because a month gives you enough time to gather the data you need and buy the necessary ad impressions, but use daily budget features on campaign level.

Whichever style of budget you choose, stick to it across all your campaigns. Setting one campaign to daily and another to monthly is a recipe for confusion, making it very easy for you to overspend.

Considering ad schedules

You want to make sure that your ads are showing on the necessary days and at the necessary times. Your industry might have more actual sales at the end of the month, when potential customers get paid, for example. But earlier in the month, those potential customers were shopping around, saw your ad, and visited your site. They could return to your site later to make a purchase, arriving via a bookmark or a copied link, or they might enter the search term again and look for the ad. For this reason, you want to make sure that your budget fits your ad-serving needs so that when people search for your products or services, your ads are showing for those searches.

Setting and sticking to your budget

After you figure out how much you can spend, stick to that number. PPC is a little like gambling; you shouldn't assume that you're going to "win" big every time. Determine what you can spend, assume that you won't make your investment back — and never go back into your savings for more money you don't! If what you tried didn't work and you want to try again, change your account through optimization techniques (discussed throughout this minibook, such as ad copy edits in Book IV, Chapter 4) before spending more money.

For further help with determining what your marketing budget should be, consult *Small Business For Dummies,* 3rd Edition, by Eric Tyson, MBA, and Jim Schell (Wiley).

Entering Your Budget in the Big Three Search Engines

If you already have an account with Google AdWords, Yahoo! Search Marketing, or MSN adCenter, the search engine should have required you to enter a campaign budget during account setup. (For help with the setup process, see Book IV, Chapter 2.) Just follow the easy steps in the following sections to set or adjust your budget.

Setting a budget in Google AdWords

To set your budget in Google AdWords, follow these steps:

1. **Log in to your AdWords account.**

2. **Click the Edit Campaign Settings link to see all your campaigns in the account.**

3. **Select the campaign for which you want to edit the budget, and click the Edit Campaign Settings link to display the Budget Options settings.**

4. **In the Budget text box, enter your budget amount in U.S. dollars (see Figure 5-1).**

5. **In the Delivery Method section, choose the speed at which you want your ads to appear.**

    If you choose Standard, Google will adjust impressions throughout the day to meet the budget that you just entered. If you choose Accelerated, Google will show your ad continuously until the budget you entered is spent.

**Book IV
Chapter 5**

**Budgeting and
Bidding on
Keywords**

6. **Click the Save Changes button.**

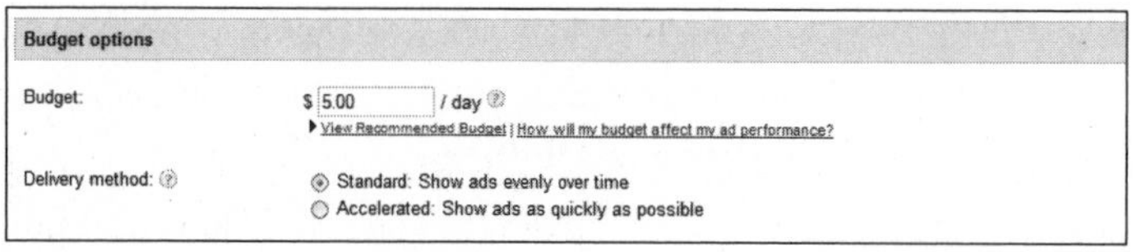

Figure 5-1:
Set a
Google
AdWords
budget.

Budget options	
Budget:	$ 5.00 / day ⑦ ▸ View Recommended Budget	How will my budget affect my ad performance?
Delivery method: ⑦	⦿ Standard: Show ads evenly over time ○ Accelerated: Show ads as quickly as possible

Google also offers a Manager Defined Spend feature, which allows you to set and track a budget efficiently from a dashboard. To use this feature, you must be managing several accounts through My Client Center and must be on invoicing terms with Google; you can't set a monthly budget. For more information on this feature, see the AdWords help center.

Setting a budget in Yahoo! Search Marketing

To set your budget in Yahoo! Search Marketing, follow these steps:

1. **Log in to your Yahoo! Sponsored Search account.**

2. **Select the campaign for which you want to edit the budget.**

The campaign details page opens.

3. **In the Campaign Performance section, click the Change button next to Daily Spending Limit.**

You see the Set Campaign Budget and Schedule section.

4. **If you haven't set a budget before, click the Yes radio button.**

5. **Enter the desired amount in the Campaign Daily Spending Limit text box (see Figure 5-2).**

6. **Click the Save Changes button.**

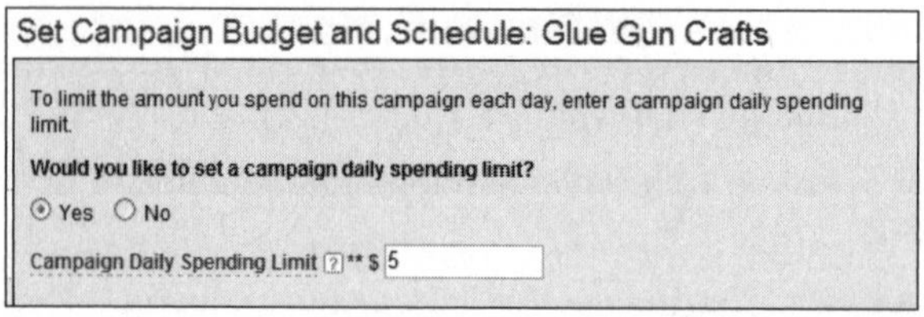

Figure 5-2:
Set a
Yahoo!
Search
Marketing
budget.

Set Campaign Budget and Schedule: Glue Gun Crafts
To limit the amount you spend on this campaign each day, enter a campaign daily spending limit. **Would you like to set a campaign daily spending limit?** ⦿ Yes ○ No Campaign Daily Spending Limit ⑦ ** $ 5

Setting a budget in MSN adCenter

To set your budget in MSN adCenter, follow these steps:

1. **Log in to your MSN adCenter account.**

2. **Select the campaign for which you want to edit the budget, and click the Edit Campaign Settings link.**

3. **In the Budget Settings section of the page, enter the desired budget amount in the Campaign Budget (USD) text box, and choose a duration (Per Day or Per Month) from the drop-down menu.**

4. **Choose a Spend Settings option:**

   - *Divide Budget across the Month* (see Figure 5-3) spreads your budget over the entire month.

   - *Spend Budget until Depleted* shows your ads repeatedly until the ads have gotten enough clicks to eat through the entire budget. This setting means that you could be out of money in two days or not even spend the entire budget, depending on the popularity of your industry.

5. **Click Save.**

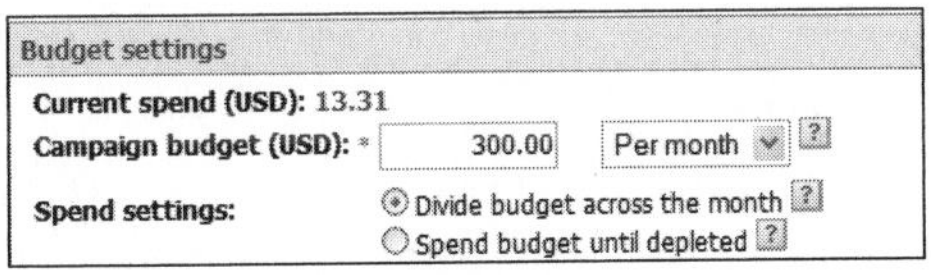

Figure 5-3:
Set an MSN adCenter budget.

Budget settings

Current spend (USD): 13.31
Campaign budget (USD): * [300.00] [Per month ▾] [?]
Spend settings: ⊙ Divide budget across the month [?]
○ Spend budget until depleted [?]

Budgeting by Campaign

Only you can tell a search engine how much per day you want to spend — and where you want to spend it. If you have a budget of $3,000 per month, which works out to $100 per day, you need to divide that $100 among your campaigns.

All campaigns are unique, with different ad groups and different budget requirements. Some just have more expensive keywords, more traffic, or less traffic than others. You need to assess each campaign individually by those same measurements to determine how much to budget for each one.

Estimating traffic

Good old common sense plays a major part in predicting whether a campaign will be a high-traffic campaign. The more generic your keywords are, the more popular they'll be — and the more times your ads will show up. You can find some guidelines in "Deciding what to bid," later in this chapter.

**Book IV
Chapter 5**

**Budgeting and
Bidding on
Keywords**

When you're starting a new campaign, use the search engines' free traffic-estimation tools (see Book IV, Chapter 7) to generate a predicted number of impressions and clicks for the keywords in your ad groups. If the search engine is predicting a lot of clicks for a campaign, you'll want to set a higher budget for it than you would for a campaign that isn't expected to receive a lot of clicks.

Also, run a search for some of your keywords in the search engine and see how many search results and competitor ads appear. If a keyword generates 100 ads, it's popular!

Setting an example campaign budget

Every single campaign has different factors that influence how much it spends and when — and even those factors vary from day to day. Unfortunately, I can't look at your account and tell you where to put your money. But to help you better understand how to set budgets by campaign, I set up an example account to guide you through the process.

In this example, you sell office-cubicle furniture through three campaigns:

+ **Office Furniture:** This campaign is the most generic of the three and is predicted to bring in a lot of traffic. The keyword "*office furniture*" is also highly competitive and is often searched on for related terms such as *desks, chairs,* and *filing cabinets.*

+ **Cubicles:** This campaign also generates a fair share of traffic, but the keyword is more targeted and very relevant to what you're selling.

+ **Panel Systems:** This campaign is a much lower-traffic campaign than the others, but the keyword is very highly targeted. People who are searching for "*panel systems*" are familiar with the fact that this keyword is an industry term and, therefore, are knowledgeable about the product.

If you have $100 per day to spend, here's how much each campaign will receive:

+ **Office Furniture: $15**

    Why: The keyword "*office furniture*", although relevant, isn't as relevant as it could be to what you're selling. Keywords related to this phrase will bring in a lot of searches but not a lot of conversions, as people looking for items other than cubicles will click the ads. This campaign is also more expensive than the others because you don't offer office furniture other than cubicles, and other, more-relevant vendors that also sell office furniture are bidding on these keywords, too.

+ **Cubicles: $60**

Why: The keyword *cubicles* is going to be your No. 1 source of conversions. It describes what you sell, it's highly relevant, and it's in a popular set of search terms. Your ads will show up often, and you'll receive a better cost per click (CPC) price because of the relevancy.

✦ **Panel Systems: $25**

Why: "*Panel systems*" may be a low-volume keyword, but it's highly relevant to your campaign. By targeting searchers who are familiar with industry terms, you're targeting educated customers who already know what they want. You're simply getting your products out in front of them. The clicks you pay for in this campaign are going to be high-quality clicks that create a better return on your investment.

Bidding on Keywords

One of most complex aspects of PPC management is bid management. Most search engines require you to set your bids when you set up an ad group.

Bids are set at two levels:

✦ **Ad-group level:** At ad-group level, you must set a maximum bid — the largest amount that you're willing to pay for a single click. You may not pay that actual amount, but be prepared to do so.

✦ **Keyword level:** A keyword-level bid is the maximum CPC you're willing to pay for that single keyword.

By default, all keywords receive the ad group's maximum CPC. If you want to change the amount you're bidding on a single keyword, see Book IV, Chapter 3 for instructions on editing your keyword bids in the Big Three search engines.

Knowing how CPC is determined

Cost per click (CPC) is determined by the search engines based on their own algorithms. These algorithms calculate various factors to determine the minimum bid for a given keyword, the smallest amount that the search engine will charge for that keyword, and the rate you pay for it.

Search engines keep their algorithms as closely guarded secrets so that advertisers can't exploit or cheat the system. Google, Yahoo!, and MSN, however, use several known factors to calculate CPC:

✦ Relevancy of the keyword to your ad

✦ Relevancy of the search term to your keyword

✦ Destination URL (where the ad takes the searcher)

✦ Daily budget

✦ Keyword bid amount

✦ Amount of competition

✦ Relevancy of the competitors for that keyword compared with you

Deciding what to bid

When you select your keywords or use keyword tools to add new ones (see Book IV, Chapter 3), most search engines show you an estimated number of searches, CPC, and cost per day for each keyword. Those estimates are valuable tools for determining your maximum CPC. For more information on predicting a keyword's CPC through traffic-estimation tools, see Book IV, Chapter 7.

Automated bidding options

Google AdWords has a few automated options that set and adjust bids for you based on performance, click-through rate, budget, and impressions:

🖊 **Maximum CPC Bidding:** This setting (the default) means that you're setting the maximum CPC manually, using the amount that you entered when you set up the ad group.

🖊 **Preferred Cost Bidding:** This setting (see the first figure) bases bidding on the average price that you're willing to pay for each click. You enter your preferred average CPC for that campaign, and Google manages your bids to target that amount. Preferred cost bidding is for those who want more consistency in the cost of their keywords for day-to-day operations, who

have little time to maintain their accounts, or who know how much each click is worth to the overall business and want to pay that amount — and only that amount — for the duration of the campaign.

🖊 **Budget Optimizer:** When you choose this option (see the second figure), you specify the maximum amount that you want to pay over 30 days. Google manages the bids over those 30 days for you, with the goal being to earn you the most clicks possible within that period. The goal of this option is clicks, not conversions. Also, this option isn't compatible with ad scheduling (covered in the following section). This feature is best for those who want to simply drive traffic and spend a specific amount consistently. It's also the lowest-maintenance automated option.

⊙ **Preferred cost bidding**
Average CPC bids
 • Set the average price you want to pay for each click
 • Google will manage your bids to give you a predictable average cost per click
 Learn more

⊙ **Budget Optimizer**
No bids needed
 • Set a 30-day budget
 • Google will manage your bids, trying to earn you the most possible clicks within that budget.
 • Choose this option for the simplest bidding experience. Great for new users
 Learn more

A best practice in setting a maximum bid for an ad group is to start high and lower that bid as necessary. This practice gives you a running start with the search engine. Your ad will appear quickly and often, giving you results much sooner than if you start low and try to work your way up. This technique also places your ads in good positions on the result page; a higher position on the page means increased visibility to searchers.

Bidding by Day and Time

Each industry is unique and has a unique Web-traffic pattern. Some days of the week might be better in one business segment than in another, or some times of day might be better — or a combination of both. For this reason, it might be in your best interest to set your campaigns up to run and spend more or less on specific days of the week or hours of the day.

Suppose that (as in most commercial-goods businesses), your company's traffic and sales are strongest during the week and decrease over the weekend. You want to set up your campaigns to reflect those traffic patterns so that when customers are online looking for you, they can find your ads quickly and easily, and you don't have to stretch your budget over gaps of time that bring you poorer-quality traffic.

In the following sections, I discuss ad scheduling in Google AdWords and MSN adCenter. (Yahoo! Search Marketing currently doesn't offer ad scheduling.)

Scheduling options in Google AdWords

Google AdWords' Ad Scheduling option is the most complex system for adjusting your campaign costs to different traffic patterns. You find this tool in the campaign settings page of each of your campaigns. By default, all campaigns are set to show your ads every day, all day, until the budget is depleted.

Google allows you to choose whether your ads run every day of the week, or just weekdays or weekends. You can also choose the times of day when those ads run.

Basic ad scheduling

To enable basic ad scheduling in Google, follow these steps:

1. **Open the campaign for which you want to enable this feature, and click Edit Campaign Settings.**

2. **Scroll down to the Scheduling and Serving section.**

3. **In the Ad Scheduling section, click Turn on Ad Scheduling.**

   You see a chart that shows when your ads are currently scheduled to run (see Figure 5-4). A dialog box reminds you that any other changes you make on this page won't be saved.

4. **Click OK.**

5. **Select the appropriate day, or click the Bulk Edit link to see the schedule (weekdays, weekends, all days) you want to apply.**

6. **Click the Save Changes button.**

   You return to the Edit Campaign Settings page.

7. **Click the Save Changes button at the bottom of the page.**

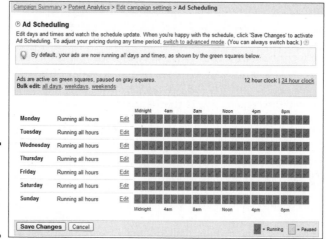

Figure 5-4:
Check when your ads are scheduled to run.

Advanced ad scheduling

Advanced ad scheduling (see Figure 5-5) allows to you set hours of the day and incremental bids for those hours. Incremental bidding is set on a scale of 100 percent; you can raise or lower your bids during different hours of the day.

Suppose that you want your campaigns to run from 8 a.m. to 8 p.m., and you receive most of your traffic between 11 a.m. and 1 p.m. You can set your account so that Google automatically increases the amount that you're bidding between those hours to 115 percent, which means that Google takes all the set bids in that campaign and increases them by 15 percent between 11 a.m. and 1 p.m. You don't see the bids change physically; the amount that you specified as your maximum CPC still appears. The only place you see a difference is in the amount of clicks billed.

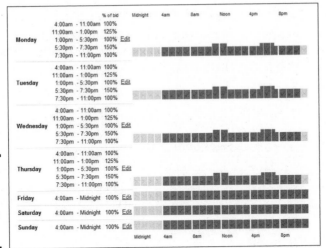

Figure 5-5:
Ad
scheduling
in advanced
mode.

In addition, you can not only set your bids to increase from 11 a.m. to 1 p.m., but you can also determine the days of the week when incremental bidding takes place. If Mondays, Tuesdays, and Thursdays are your best revenue-generating days, you can apply that strategy to only those days, and leave the bid amount for Wednesdays and Fridays from 8 a.m. to 8 p.m. at 100 percent. Or you can decrease the bids for off days or off hours by choosing an amount less than 100 percent. Entering 90 percent, for example, tells Google that during those hours, you want to bid 10 percent less than your maximum CPC setting.

If you edit your maximum CPC setting later, take this feature into account if you have it enabled!

To set up advanced ad scheduling, follow these steps:

1. **Open the campaign for which you want to enable this feature, and click Edit Campaign Settings.**

2. **Scroll down to the Scheduling and Serving section.**

3. **In the Ad Scheduling section, click Turn on Ad Scheduling.**

   A dialog box reminds you that any other changes you make on this page won't be saved.

4. **Click OK.**

5. **Click the Switch to Advanced Mode link.**

6. **Depending on your planned schedule, click the Bulk Edit link or the day of the week that you want to edit.**

7. **Enter the desired times of day and percentages.**

8. **Click Add Another Time Period to enter another block of time and percentages on the same day, or click the Add button to finish.**

9. **Click the Save Changes button.**

   You return to the Edit Campaign Settings page.

10. **Click the Save Changes button at the bottom of the page.**

These settings cannot be copied to other campaigns; you must go into each existing campaign and edit the settings manually.

Know what schedule you want to implement before you get started; the operation may time out on you. Don't dilly-dally when setting up ad scheduling.

Scheduling options in MSN adCenter

MSN allows you to target your customers by days of the week and by specific blocks of time. It also offers demographic bidding, which I talk more about in Book IV, Chapter 7.

To set up ad scheduling in MSN, follow these steps:

1. **Open the ad group, and click Edit Ad Group Settings.**

2. **In the Target Your Customers by Day of Week section, click the Select Specific Days of the Week radio button.**

3. **In the Available list, select the days of the week when you want your ads to appear, and click the Add button to move them to the Selected list.**

   You can't edit days of the week separately. You can't choose just Monday and have ads show only from 7 a.m. to 6 p.m., for example.

4. **In the Target Your Customers by Time of Day section, click the Select Specific Times of the Day radio button.**

5. **In the Available list, select the times of the day when you want your ads to appear, and click the Add button to move them to the Selected list.**

   These times apply to all days of the week you selected in Step 3. Figure 5-6 shows an example schedule.

6. **Click the Save button.**

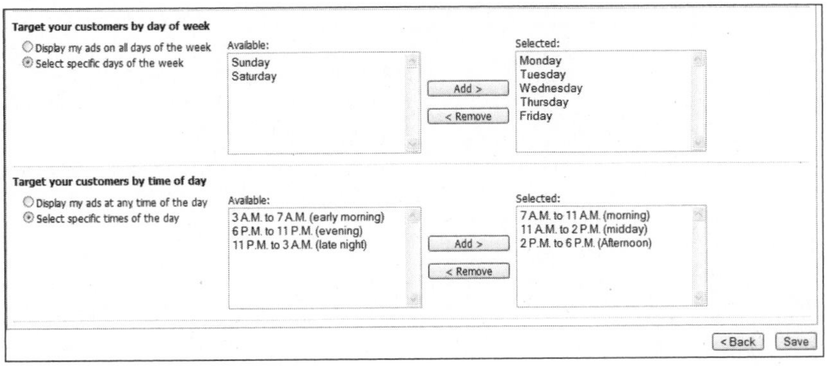

Figure 5-6:
Example of
adCenter ad
scheduling.

Tailoring Your Spending

In this section, I explain a couple of ways in which you can tailor your spending to match your industry or niche. By spending in these areas, you can avoid excess costs and overpopular keywords that might not perform how you'd like them to in your campaigns.

Spending by industry

Some industries have higher traffic than others, and some have a much higher *cost per conversion* (the amount of money you have to spend to get someone to perform the desired action on your site, such as a purchase) than others. A vendor that sells T-shirts online is going to have a much lower cost per conversion for its average $20 sale than a vendor that sells particle size–measuring lasers with an average sale value of $20,000.

Keeping this example in mind, now you have to determine whether PPC is the right way for you to be advertising in your industry. Items or services that have a low cost per conversion and a short buying cycle tend to fare better than industries that are more complex and have a longer buying cycle. Clearly, a T-shirt is a much less complicated investment than a laser, and your budget should reflect that fact.

Spending by niche

You can find the proverbial PPC gold mine if you can carve out a nice niche for yourself. The niche needs to be highly relevant to your keywords, ads, and account structure, and must have low competition — and your site or landing page must exemplify the same niche.

**Book IV
Chapter 5**

Budgeting and
Bidding on
Keywords

Suppose that you sell Christmas ornaments, which are very popular items in general. Think about what kinds of ornaments you sell. Is a type or brand exclusive to your company? Do you sell a style that's unique or unusual?

Perhaps you have a collection of marine mammal Christmas ornaments — in particular, sea otter ornaments. That product is unusual, so related keywords will come up in search queries often, which makes them highly relevant to your product.

To maximize a niche like this, create a separate ad group for keywords associated with *sea otter ornaments* and *sea otter Christmas* in a broad match (refer to Book IV, Chapter 3), create ads that use the same keywords (see Book IV, Chapter 4), and set a modest daily budget — say, $10, with a maximum CPC of 50¢. This daily budget should exceed the amount of clicks that you would accumulate in a day — that is to say, you'll rarely reach the spending limit for this daily budget. The bids should be set high enough that your ads consistently show up in the first two ad positions.

Make your ad's landing page the product page for the sea otter ornaments, and if you don't have a dedicated page for that product, select a product page offering several items related to the niche. This scenario is a great example of creating and exploiting a niche.

For more information on using budget, bidding, and keyword tools, see Book IV, Chapter 7.

Chapter 6: Legally Speaking: PPC and the Law

In This Chapter

✔ Sticking to editorial guidelines for ads and keywords

✔ Following trademark and copyright regulations

✔ Fighting click fraud

*O*ne of the most common pitfalls of pay per click (PPC) management to which new users fall victim is getting ads returned from search engines because of editorial guidelines. Sometimes, the problem is simply a matter of trying to use a shortcut such as an ampersand (&) instead of *and* or *2* instead of *to*. But in some cases, the problem is more serious, such as a copyright or trademark infringement.

In this chapter, I walk through the most common editorial issues you're likely to run into and show you how to avoid copyright or trademark errors. At the end of the chapter, I discuss click fraud.

Understanding Editorial Guidelines

Editorial guidelines are always set forth by the search engine or the distributor of PPC ads, so many variations exist. The major search engines have similar rules and regulations that are fairly easy to follow, but if you run into issues or have questions, consult the help center for that particular engine.

Ad editorial guidelines

Most search engines are similar in their requirements for the format, language, and grammar of an ad. If you're using PPC honestly and writing ads that advertise what you're selling, you shouldn't have a problem.

Here are the most common rules to follow:

✦ **Watch your language.** Don't use sexually explicit or offensive language, such as swearing.

✦ **Don't make false claims.** One example of a false claim is offering a price or promotion in the ad but not making that same offer on the landing page. Another example is saying that you're "No. 1" or "the cheapest" without being able to prove your claim.

Proving your claim requires verification by a third party. See your search engine's help center for its specific policy on this issue. Google AdWords, for example, allows you to make such a statement as long as you can show — through a link to or a direct quote from an independent third party — that your claim is true. This information must be available within one or two clicks of the destination URL for the PPC ad.

✦ **Keep the ad copy clean.** Avoid using all capital letters for anything but acronyms (FREE, BUY NOW), excessive punctuation (Save Now!!!!), or repetition beyond two words (Buy, Buy, Buy!).

✦ **Mind your grammar.** Use proper grammar. Sentences and phrases must be logical and must make sense.

✦ **Use standard typography.** Things *not* to do include using inappropriate spacing (Buy S h o e s!) and using numbers or symbols as words (Deals 4 U here, Not 2 be 4gotten!).

✦ **Don't use generic *click* calls to action.** Examples include text such as *Click here* and *Click this ad.*

If you simply craft your ad to sell what you're selling without trying to be gimmicky or spammy, you'll be just fine. See Figure 6-1 for an example ad with three editorial violations: *4* instead of *for,* all caps (*ONLINE*), and an extra exclamation point.

Figure 6-1:
This ad contains three editorial violations.

All in One Reference
Internet Marketing Desk Reference!!
4 Dummies! Shop ONLINE Now.
aio.marketing.dummies.com

Most search engines will catch a big editorial issue; they display an error message telling you what the issue is and prevent you from saving the ad (see Figure 6-2). If the ad contains multiple or more subtle errors, the search engine allows you to save the ad but rejects it on further review. The engine stops running the ad and sends a notification e-mail to the address associated with the account.

Figure 6-2:
A Google
AdWords
error
message
for an ad
that violates
editorial
guidelines.

Headline:		All in One Reference	Max 25 characters	
Description line 1:	✗	Internet Marketing Desk Reference!!	Max 35 characters	

❶ Punctuation - nonstandard punctuation ⓘ
Google policy does not permit excessive or unnecessary punctuation or symbols, or use of nonstandard punctuation, including tildes (~), asterisks (*),and vertical rules (|). Please see our full policy.
▸ Request an exception

❷ Punctuation - nonstandard punctuation ⓘ
Google policy does not permit excessive or unnecessary punctuation or symbols, or use of nonstandard punctuation, including tildes (~), asterisks (*),and vertical rules (|). Please see our full policy.
▸ Request an exception

Description line 2:	4 Dummies. Shop ONLINE Now.	Max 35 characters
Display URL: ⑦	http:// aio.marketing.dummies.com	Max 35 characters
Destination URL: ⑦	http:// ▾ aio.marketing.dummies.com	Max 1024 characters

If you receive an error message and feel that the ad doesn't contain an error or that the search engine is mistaken, you might be able to request an exception, which allows you to enter a short explanation of the situation and run your ad for the time being. Even though the search engine will review the ad again, it still may reject the ad if it doesn't accept the reason you're requesting the exception.

Keyword list guidelines

Building your keyword list (refer to Book IV, Chapter 3) can be a difficult task, especially because you have to be aware of editorial guidelines as well.

Most of the guidelines apply directly to the ads that you're building with your keywords, so if you follow those guidelines (see the preceding section), you should have minimal issues with your keyword lists.

In keyword lists, you can bid on trademarked and copyrighted terms (see "Trademark and copyright guidelines," later in this chapter), but with some caveats. If you're selling or promoting drugs (prescription or otherwise), pornography, counterfeited items, gambling, fireworks, fake documents, weapons, or scams, you won't be allowed to add those keywords to your keyword list. If you try, an error message should appear, pointing out the specific problem.

The best practice for keyword lists is to follow the general guidelines of the search engine. If you can't sell a product online, you won't be able to purchase keywords for it, either.

Display and destination URL guidelines

The display URL, which is listed inside the ad below your ad copy, usually is just long enough for the main URL of the Web site you're advertising. (See Book IV, Chapter 4 for information on optimizing your display URLs.)

**Book IV
Chapter 6**

**Legally Speaking:
PPC and the Law**

Although it's representative of your site's address, it may not be the same as the destination URL — the address of the page you're sending visitors to. The destination URL, which can be much longer than the display URL, leaves lots of room for you to send visitors deep within your site and even to append a tracking code, if necessary.

A *tracking code* is a piece of code that you can paste onto the end of the destination URL for a PPC ad. This code doesn't hurt or influence anything in the ad, but it helps tell your analytics package (if you have one) where the visitor came from, on what keyword, and on which ad. Depending on the analytics package you selected, this code may not be necessary; consult the software's help system or representative for information about tracking PPC ads in different search engines.

Display URLs

For your display URL to comply with search engine guidelines, it must have a domain extension (such as `.com`, `.net`, or `.edu`) and must be somewhere on the site you're advertising. If you use the display URL `www.shoeson line.com`, for example, users must be taken to that site when they click your ad — not to any other site (such as `www.fraudschemes.com`).

Destination URLs

A destination URL must work; when users click the ad, they should be taken to the listed URL, not to an error or "page not found" page.

The destination can't be under construction; it has to be a Web page with content ready for people to view. It also must be a working Web site — not an image, a video, a document, or an additional URL that requires users to open another application or program to go any farther on your site.

Trademark and copyright guidelines

Before I discuss the guidelines for trademarks and copyrights, you should know the difference between the two:

✦ **Trademarks:** A *trademark* can be a word, logo, phrase, or image that people or companies own to represent themselves or their businesses. Trademarks are owned at country level, so if you want to use a trademarked term to advertise in several countries, you have to get permission for each country. You can get this permission with the help of the search engine you're trying to advertise with. See each search engine's Help Center section on trademarks, which should outline that search engine's process for receiving permission to use trademarked terms.

✦ **Copyrights:** A *copyright* applies to material (such as a book, musical composition, or artwork) that belongs to its creator (such as the author, musician, or artist).

Dynamic keyword insertion with trademarks and copyrights

Dynamic keyword insertion is a great tool — a neat way to generate custom ads based on what the user is searching for. Dynamic insertion involves a placeholder phrase in the headline or ad copy that's populated by the search term that the user typed, provided that the search term matches a keyword in your keyword list. (See Book IV, Chapter 4 for more information on this tool.)

Warning: If you're using dynamic insertion and include copyrighted or trademarked terms in your keyword list, your ad could be populated with those keywords. Unless you have permission from the trademark or copyright owner to use those terms in your ad copy, don't use dynamic insertion in conjunction with trademarked or copyrighted keywords. (Refer to

"Trademark and copyright guidelines," earlier in this chapter.) You can still bid on them as keywords; you just can't have the terms show up within the ad.

Suppose that you're reselling Avon makeup products, and one of your keywords is *avon makeup.*

In this case, the headline would read Avon Makeup, which includes a trademarked term. Unless you are able to get an exception as an authorized reseller, you have to refrain from using dynamic insertion with this particular keyword list. (For information on exceptions, refer to "Ad editorial guidelines," earlier in this chapter.)

You need to know how to work with trademark and copyright issues if you're a reseller of items (shoes, makeup, books, or CDs, for example). Often, resellers can't use the name of the product or service, or the name of the artwork's creator, without showing they are authorized resellers or distributors of the items in question.

If you want to create ads for the vast library of CDs you're selling, for example, you can't use the names of the specific artists in your ad without permission. You can still bid on the artist's name as a keyword, but the name can't appear in the ad. If it does, the search engine could disapprove your ad, and someone could even file a complaint against you.

This restriction works both ways, however. If you find an advertiser using your trademark in an ad without permission, you can file a complaint with the search engine. Often, the search engine will tell you to contact the advertiser directly first; the search engine may not mediate or participate in disputes such as this without the filed complaint. If contacting the person or company that's using your trademark isn't successful, you should file the complaint paperwork. Filing a complaint forces the search engine to look into the issue further and shut down the offending advertiser's ads.

If you have a copyright issue, the same procedure applies. Contact the advertiser directly and ask him or her to cease. Involving the search engine requires you to fill out and mail or fax a copyright claims form. Check the search engine's help center for specific details on filing a copyright or trademark complaint. When the paperwork is on file with the search engine, someone there will look into the issue further and possibly stop the offending advertiser from using your copyright. The search engine will also add you to its ever-growing database of copyrights, and if any future violations occur, you'll already have a history on file.

Dealing with Click Fraud

All PPC search engines have some level of *click fraud,* which occurs when a person, computer, or automated program clicks an ad for malicious purposes. The actual amount that occurs on a day-to-day basis is an ongoing debate in the PPC industry. For the purposes of your campaigns, simply keep an eye out for potential fraud, and call or e-mail the search engine if you suspect that click fraud has occurred so that representatives can look into the situation further.

Recognizing click fraud

Some programs go out on the Internet and click ads repeatedly, eating up advertisers' budgets and driving up their clicks with no intention of being honest users who are searching for or researching something specific. Each search engine has ways of dealing with obvious and/or massive click-fraud issues. A search engine will credit your account for whatever funds it feels were spent on fraudulent clicks.

Detecting click fraud

The best way to detect click fraud is to check your server logs and study IP addresses and patterns in the clicks to your site. If you see several hundred visits coming from the same IP address within a few hours or minutes, you could be experiencing click fraud.

Another way to detect click fraud is to examine where in the world your clicks are coming from. If they're coming from a non–English-speaking country or from a country you don't advertise or sell to, and a lot of activity is going on, click fraud may be going on. If your campaigns are correctly geotargeted (set to display only in specific countries; see Book IV, Chapter 7), this situation shouldn't be much of a problem. You can combat it further by implementing ad scheduling — not showing ads outside the time zones in which you want to advertise. For details on ad scheduling, refer to Book IV, Chapter 5.

All sorts of programs have been developed to detect and prevent click fraud. If you decide to invest in one of these programs, be sure to do a lot of research and participate in live demonstrations before signing up. Click fraud–detection programs can be pricey, but they might be worth the investment if you're working with a large number of keywords and ads. If you're just starting out or dabbling in PPC, you're not likely to need these programs.

Each search engine that serves PPC ads also has some sort of click fraud–detection program in place. Check the line in your billing detail titled something like Service Adjustment or Click Charges Reversed. If you see a credit to your account for a couple of dollars or a few cents, the search engine determined that some of the clicks your ads received were not legitimate clicks.

Search engines are tightening and improving their methods for detecting these activities, even though they report a much lower percentage of fraudulent clicks than the companies that create click fraud–detecting programs do. Each side has a deeply vested interest, and any release of specific detection information would provide assistance to the perpetrators of click fraud.

Reporting click fraud

Call the customer service department of the search engine in which you're experiencing the issue. Be prepared to show your server logs highlighting the activity. If the activity is obviously suspicious, the search engine may simply credit your account the amount it charged you for the clicks.

Suppose that one of your campaigns sees an average of 2,000 impressions per month and gets about 200 clicks. But one day, you log in and find that your campaign generated 2,000 impressions and 85 clicks during a single day. If you haven't made any changes to your account that could generate more clicks, you could be experiencing click fraud. Bring those stats to the attention of your customer service representative. Make sure that the representative takes a close look, and be persistent.

Chapter 7: Using Tools, Tips, and Tricks of the Trade

In This Chapter

✔ **Working with offline editors**

✔ **Managing keyword traffic**

✔ **Placing demographic bids**

✔ **Using geographic targeting**

✔ **Structuring content network campaigns**

✔ **Picking an analytics program**

*E*very industry has insider tips and golden bits of information to make your job either easier or more efficient, and the world of pay per click (PPC) is no different. In fact, because PPC can be so granular and complicated, you can find a lot of tools (some of them free) to make managing a PPC account much easier on yourself.

In this chapter, I introduce some of the most popular tools and practices used by experts in the PPC industry. Not every tool is required for every campaign, but based on your PPC goals, you should be able to determine which of these tools may work for you.

Using Offline Editors

Both Google AdWords and MSN adCenter have offline editors that allow you to see your entire account and all your campaigns, ad groups, and keywords without having to wait for pages to load or multiple screens to click through. (Yahoo! Search Marketing doesn't offer an offline editor at this time.)

The editors are organized a little differently, but they have the same purpose: to enable you to make PPC edits faster and more easily than you could otherwise.

To use an offline editor, you load the program and the account you want to work on. (If you load the account without many of the stats and go for a basic download, the process is even faster.) Then you can go offline, sit at a bus stop or in a lobby, and make the edits you need to make. When you're ready, simply go back online and upload your changes.

These two editors allow you to do the following things:

✦ **Copy entire campaigns, ad groups, ads, and keywords.**

✦ **Add negative keywords and Web sites (content network only).**
Negative Web sites work like negative keywords; they're sites on which your ad will not appear. For more information, see "Managing a Content Network Campaign," later in this chapter.

✦ **Use a keyword suggestion tool and upload the suggested keywords.**

✦ **Change budgets and bids.**

✦ **Target edits for both geography and the content network.**

✦ **Edit languages.**

✦ **Search.**

In the following sections, I dive into a little more detail about each offline editor.

Google AdWords Editor

Google AdWords Editor has been around for a few years now; it continually undergoes upgrades that make it work more smoothly and provide more bells and whistles. You can save a copy of your entire account to upload again later, for example. Suppose that you hire a company or contractor to make some changes in your PPC account, but things don't work out, and you want to go back to your original account. Simply download a copy of your account before granting the company or contractor access, and save the copy. Later, if you need to, upload the old account to replace the new one.

Google AdWords Editor is free. Just download it from `www.google.com/intl/en/adwordseditor/index.html` and then import your AdWords accounts.

Each time you start your work in the editor, click the Get Recent Changes button to get the editor up to date with the most recent stats. A drop-down menu gives you a choice between the basic and minimum cost per click (CPC). If you choose the basic option, you'll be up to date in a jiffy. If you go with the full version, updating takes only a few seconds more (depending on the size of your account) and includes minimum CPC data, which the basic version doesn't provide. Figure 7-1 shows the main dashboard.

Click different tabs to see different parts of your account, such as campaigns and keyword lists. You can also import statistics such as cost and performance; you just have to wait a couple of minutes for those figures to load. Click the View Statistics button in the top navigation bar, and select either the entire account or an ad group for which you want to download statistics.

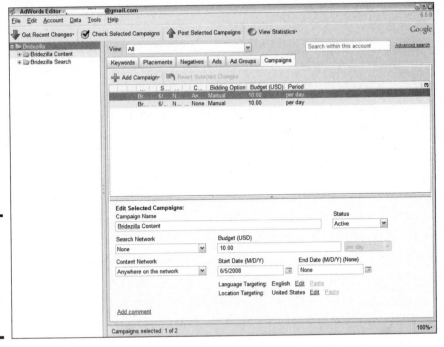

Figure 7-1:
Complete
dashboard
view in
Google
AdWords
Editor 6.5.0.

For more information on using the AdWords Editor, click one of the help links on the main page.

The MSN adCenter editor

MSN adCenter's editor is undergoing beta testing at this writing. You can apply to use the beta version but may not get in. To apply to use the editor, go to

```
http://advertising.microsoft.com/adcenter-beta-pilot-signup
```

Figure 7-2 gives you a look at the Microsoft adCenter Desktop.

In many ways, the Desktop gives you the same capabilities as the Google AdWords Editor. You can download and upload entire campaigns or accounts for storage, change bids, edit ads, create new ad groups, and import statistical information such as click-through rates (CTR) and impressions. Additional features allow you to set alerts that notify you when a campaign or account reaches a certain CPC, use the keyword tool to generate and add keywords, and find and replace text.

The default Desktop view doesn't show all these tools, so to sort through and use all the available tools, you need to customize your view fairly heavily.

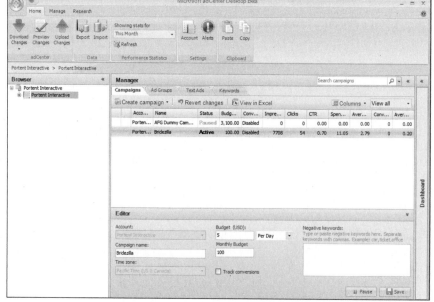

Figure 7-2:
Complete
dashboard
view in the
beta version
of Microsoft
adCenter
Desktop.

The Desktop cuts down significantly on loading time, so if you plan to work in MSN beyond a couple of campaigns, you'll want to apply for the beta; it's a big timesaver.

Using Keyword Traffic Tools

At some point, you'll want to expand your keyword list (see Book IV, Chapter 3). But how do you determine which keywords to add? The search engines offer tools that tell you — based on data from previous searches and related searches — how many impressions and clicks you may receive for your new list of keywords.

In the following sections, I discuss the traffic-estimating keyword tools in Google, Yahoo!, and MSN.

Estimating traffic in Google

Google's free keyword tool predicts — based on the keywords, URLs, or categories you select — how many clicks and searches you'll record for that month. This tool can also show you the amount of competition and peak months of the year for searches on your selections.

To access the keyword tool, follow these steps:

1. **Log in to your AdWords account.**

2. **Select the ad group for which you want to do traffic estimates.**

3. **On the ad group's Keywords tab, click the Keyword Tool link to open the tool.**

4. **Choose how you want to search: by descriptive words and phrases, Web-site content, or existing keywords.**

   For this exercise, search for the number of clicks, the number of searches, and the amount you'll spend for your current keyword list.

5. **Select the Existing Keyword radio button.**

   A list of your highest-traffic-generating keywords appears.

6. **Select the keyword for which you want to generate suggestions.**

   Google shows you a list of the keywords you selected and related terms with all the pertinent information (see Figure 7-3).

   You can filter your results further by changing the match type (see Book IV, Chapter 3), adjust the bid to see what the difference would be, and even add more keywords to your ad groups by making choices from the drop-down menus on this page.

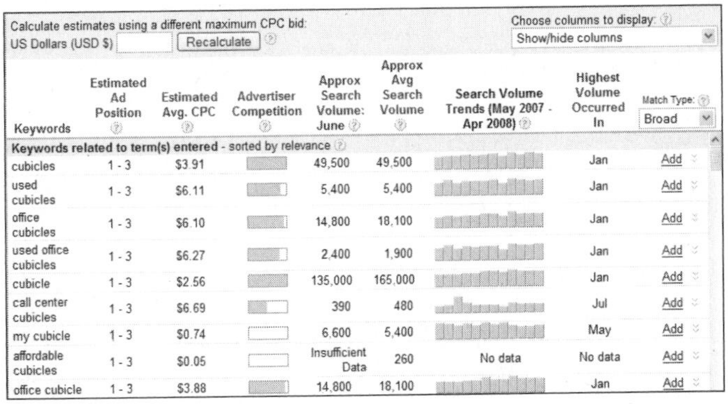

Figure 7-3:
Example estimated-traffic result page for keywords related to *cubicles*.

Keywords	Estimated Ad Position	Estimated Avg. CPC	Advertiser Competition	Approx Search Volume: June	Approx Avg Search Volume	Search Volume Trends (May 2007 - Apr 2008)	Highest Volume Occurred In	Match Type: Broad
Keywords related to term(s) entered - sorted by relevance								
cubicles	1 - 3	$3.91		49,500	49,500		Jan	Add
used cubicles	1 - 3	$6.11		5,400	5,400		Jan	Add
office cubicles	1 - 3	$6.10		14,800	18,100		Jan	Add
used office cubicles	1 - 3	$6.27		2,400	1,900		Jan	Add
cubicle	1 - 3	$2.56		135,000	165,000		Jan	Add
call center cubicles	1 - 3	$6.69		390	480		Jul	Add
my cubicle	1 - 3	$0.74		6,600	5,400		May	Add
affordable cubicles	1 - 3	$0.05		Insufficient Data	260	No data	No data	Add
office cubicle	1 - 3	$3.88		14,800	18,100		Jan	Add

Calculate estimates using a different maximum CPC bid: US Dollars (USD $) [ ] Recalculate
Choose columns to display: Show/hide columns

Google also has a free site that's dedicated to tracking trends on keywords over time. On the Google Insights for Search site (www.google.com/insights/search), you can enter a keyword and see how many searches were made on it over time as far back as 2004. You can filter searches by location worldwide and by time ranges, as well as compare keywords.

Estimating traffic in Yahoo!

To use the free keyword research tool that shows traffic estimates in Yahoo! Search Marketing, follow these steps:

1. **Log in to your account.**

2. **Open the ad group on which you want to do traffic estimates.**

   You must be in an ad group to access this tool.

3. **Click the Add Keywords button.**

4. **From the drop-down menu, choose Research Keywords.**

5. **In the text box titled Words That Describe Your Products and Services, enter the keywords you want to research.**

   You can also search by a specific URL on your site. Yahoo! will crawl the site or page and make suggestions based on the content.

   You can't leave this text box empty, even if you plan to search by URL instead.

   Yahoo! shows you the number of estimated monthly searches for the suggested keywords, but does not show the estimated CPC (see Figure 7-4).

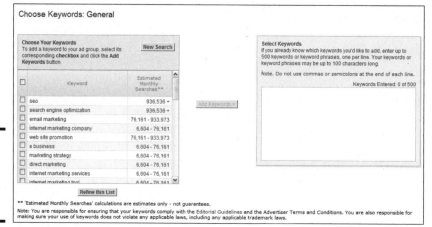

Figure 7-4: Example keywords result page in Yahoo!

Estimating traffic in MSN

To use the free traffic-estimating tool for keywords in MSN adCenter, follow these steps:

1. **Log in to your account.**

2. **Click the Research tab of your adCenter dashboard (see Figure 7-5).**

3. **Enter a URL or keyword to help MSN find the types of keywords you're looking for.**

   MSN displays a list of keywords and, next to them, the number of searches from the previous month, the CTR, and the average CPC for those visits (see Figure 7-6).

Figure 7-5: The Research tab in MSN adCenter.

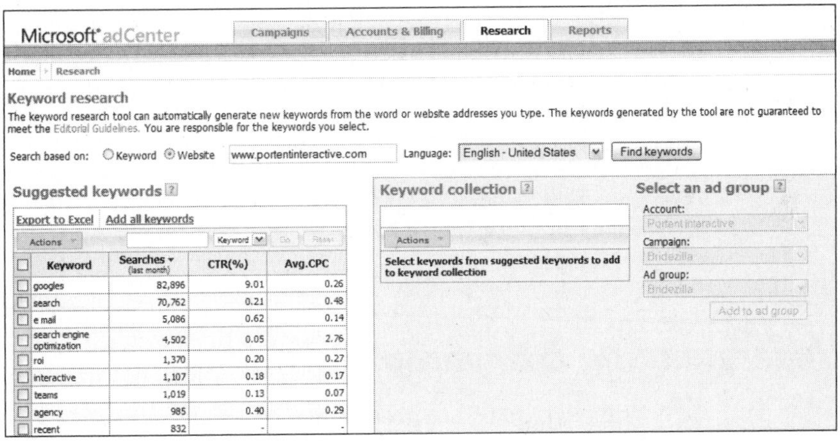

Figure 7-6: Example MSN adCenter keyword research result page.

4. **Select the check boxes next to the keywords that you want to add to your keyword list.**

   When you make selections, the Add to Keyword Collection button becomes active.

5. **When you finish selecting keywords, click the Add to Keyword Collection button.**

Employing Geotargeting

When you set up any new PPC account or campaign, you're asked to select your target market area — a process called *geographic targeting* or *geotargeting*. The countries, states, cities, or ZIP codes you select are the ones where users will see your ads when they search for keywords in your keyword list.

Making sure that your ads are shown in locations appropriate for your business is important. But what if you want to target a specific state more closely, or run ads in just a few states because your company serves only those areas and doesn't have the licenses required to operate elsewhere? From a single dashboard, you can use geotargeting to optimize or filter out certain areas of the country or to run campaigns that serve multiple countries.

If you plan on advertising in multiple countries, you should set up a separate campaign for each country and then use ad scheduling to show those ads during peak hours in that country's time zones — especially because your account is set to run ads based on the time zone you selected during setup. (For more information on ad scheduling, refer to Book IV, Chapter 5.)

Local businesses in particular can benefit greatly from this feature, so that ads for a flower shop in Miami aren't being shown in Denver, for example. When a Miami business chooses to show ads only in the Miami area, the search engine will treat the ad a little differently, giving the ad a higher average position among searches in the Miami area. Also, the search volume for one city will be less than that of an entire country, because it's such a targeted area, so the average daily cost will be significantly lower than that of a campaign that targets the entire United States.

The major search engines' PPC platforms offer slightly different options for geographic targeting. For information on adjusting these settings, refer to Book IV, Chapter 2.

Understanding Demographic Bidding

Demographic bidding is a great tool if you have a certain audience that you're trying to reach. If you know that your product is wildly popular among women 35 to 49 years old, for example, you can increase the amount that you're bidding to increase the chance that women in that age group will see and click your ad.

Demographic bidding in MSN

MSN offers an option that allows you to increase your bid in percentage increments based on the predicted gender or age of the searcher. This option applies to both search and content networks on the ad-group level.

To place a demographic bid in MSN, follow these steps:

1. **Open the ad group you want to use.**

2. **Click the Edit Bids link.**

3. **Scroll down to the Demographics section (see Figure 7-7).**

4. **Set the options you want to use in the Gender and Age Groups sections.**

   Options are set in increments of ten percent and are cumulative. When you choose both Gender and Age Groups options, for example, your choices will be added together for a total percentage increase. If you set your bids at a 10-percent increase for women and a 10-percent increase for the 18–24 age group, for example, your bid is increased by 20 percent when a woman in the 18–24 age group is detected as the user.

5. **Click the Save button.**

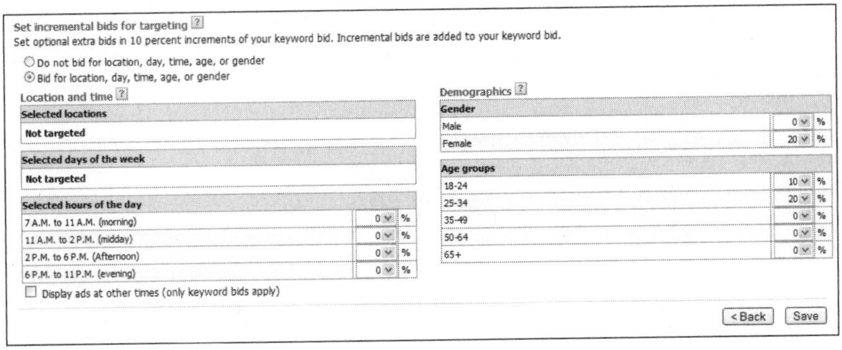

Figure 7-7:
Set bids that increase based on location, time, and demographics.

Demographic bidding in Google

Demographic bidding in Google is new and available only in the content network (see Managing a Content Network Campaign," later in this chapter) and at campaign level. If you're running a content network–only campaign and have a distinct audience you are trying to reach, such as men between the ages of 18 and 34, this tool would be worth a try for you. It takes the percentage that you specify and increases your bids by that amount when someone in the chosen demographic is detected as a user. The only age group you can't target is 17 and younger, because people in that age group are minors.

To place a demographic bid in Google AdWords, follow these steps:

1. **Open the desired content network campaign.**

2. **Click the Edit Campaign Settings link to open the Edit Campaign Settings page.**

3. **Click the Demographics: View and Edit Options link near the bottom of the page.**

   You should see a page that looks like Figure 7-8.

4. **Adjust your settings by clicking the pertinent Edit buttons and increasing or decreasing the bid amounts for the demographics you want to bid on.**

   To exclude a demographic, click the Edit button for that demographic and check the exclusion check box.

5. **Click the Apply Changes button.**

   Google automatically adjusts your content network bids for you.

For more information on content networks, see the next section.

Figure 7-8:
Increase
or exclude
demo-
graphics for
the Google
AdWords
content
network.

Traffic Report by Gender (for last 7 days)	Impr.	Clicks	CTR	Cost	Make Adjustments	
Male	0	0	0.00%	$0.00	Bid + 0%	Edit
Female	0	0	0.00%	$0.00	Bid + 0%	Edit
Unspecified	0	0	0.00%	$0.00		
Total	0	0	0.00%	$0.00		

Traffic Report by Age (for last 7 days)	Impr.	Clicks	CTR	Cost	Make Adjustments	
0-17	0	0	0.00%	$0.00	Bid + 0%	Edit
18-24	0	0	0.00%	$0.00	Bid + 0%	Edit
25-34	0	0	0.00%	$0.00	Bid + 0%	Edit
35-44	0	0	0.00%	$0.00	Bid + 0%	Edit
45-54	0	0	0.00%	$0.00	Bid + 0%	Edit
55-64	0	0	0.00%	$0.00	Bid + 0%	Edit

Combined Demographics Example

Female / 35-44

Females who are 35-44

When two demographics overlap, your increased bids for both are added together.

Resulting Combos
This campaign has no overlapping demographic bids.

Managing a Content Network Campaign

A *content network* (or *partner network,* as it's sometimes called) is a set of Web sites, affiliated with the search engine, that are authorized to show PPC data provided by that search engine. The ads appear on those Web sites alongside their content, not alongside search results. If you're on a Web site about chocolate (see Figure 7-9), and the person who owns the site is serving Google ads, you see ads related to chocolate alongside the article or even in the middle of the article.

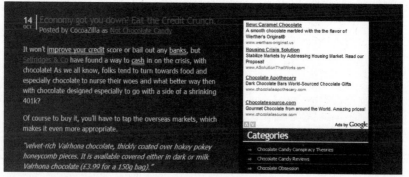

Figure 7-9:
Google
AdWords
content
network
ads,
displayed in
the top-right
corner.

In the Google content network, you can specify which Web sites are authorized to show your ads and which ones aren't. In the Yahoo! network, you can specify only which partner Web sites can't show your ads — a feature called *domain exclusion.* In MSN adCenter, the ads appear only on Microsoft-owned sites. I discuss the nuances of each engine's networks later in the chapter.

Tips for success in content networks

By following these examples, you can avoid costly mistakes and separate out your data (such as CTR) to see more efficiently what is working in your campaigns and what isn't working:

✔ **Create separate campaigns for your search and content networks.** You can use some of the same keywords and ads. They won't overlap or compete, because the networks are different.

✔ **Don't use exactly the same keywords and ads in all your search and content campaigns.** Chances are that you'll use some of the same keywords in both campaigns, but make the ad copy in the content campaign much more aggressive, gimmicky, or attention-getting. Remember, the ad appears amid Web page content.

✔ **Choose a keyword list that describes the sites on which you want your ad to appear.** If you sell an energy-drink powder that's perfect for hikers, bikers, and people on the go, for example, create an ad group around one of those niches, such as hiking, and create a keyword list that will get the ad picked up by sites with similar content. Keywords might include *hiking drinks, hiking sites, places to hike, hiking equipment,* and *hiking supplies.*

✔ **Limit keywords to three words (preferably two).** Long-tail keywords for more targeted searches, such as *pink daisy wedding invitations,* are good for search campaigns. Getting ads with a lot of long-tail terms on content networks is harder.

✔ **Bid lower on the content network than on the search network.** The average CPC is generally lower, and a high maximum CPC can rack up clicks fast. Whatever your search CPC is, slash it in half to start the content campaign, and adjust as needed.

Remember: It's normal to see a lower CTR in a content network–only campaign than in a search campaign. A search result page means that someone was specifically looking for that item; a content ad is trying to persuade someone to leave the page he's looking at now and go to the advertiser's site.

✔ **Keep track of the network sites.** If your content campaign is racking up impressions but no clicks, check which sites your ads are appearing on. You may need to add some sites to your lists of excluded domains.

The No. 1 thing to know about content and partner distribution networks is that you participate in them by default in all three major search engines. If you don't want to participate in a content or partner network, you must opt out at campaign level.

Google's content network

Of the three main search engines, Google's content network gives advertisers by far the most control of where their ads appear, when and to whom, as well as CPC and negative sites. Although total transparency isn't available yet, you can get a much better idea of which sites are working for you and which ones aren't. The Google content network is a busy one, and the best way to manage your account effectively is to separate your content and search campaigns at the start.

Disabling other options

Before you create a Google content network campaign, make sure that all your other campaigns have the content network option turned off. You have to repeat this process for each campaign individually. Follow these steps:

1. **Open a campaign.**

2. **Click the Edit Campaign Settings link to open the Edit Campaign Settings page.**

3. **In the Networks and Bidding section, check the Google Search and Search Partner check boxes, and clear the check box titled The Content Network (see Figure 7-10).**

Google will ask whether you're sure that you want to opt out. You are.

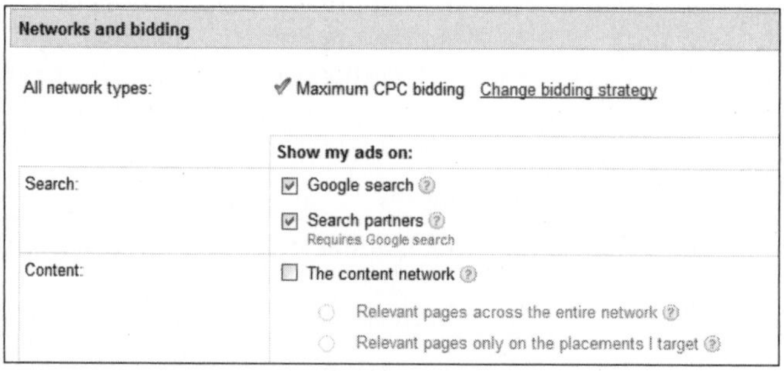

Figure 7-10:
Enable or
disable
the Google
search and
content
networks.

Networks and bidding		
All network types:	✓ Maximum CPC bidding Change bidding strategy	
	Show my ads on:	
Search:	☑ Google search ⑦	
	☑ Search partners ⑦ Requires Google search	
Content:	☐ The content network ⑦	
	○ Relevant pages across the entire network ⑦	
	○ Relevant pages only on the placements I target ⑦	

4. **Click OK.**

The search partner network is made up of sites that work directly with Google to provide Google search results, such as Google Product Search, AOL, and Ask.com. You can opt out of this network as well, but I recommend that you see what your traffic volumes are before opting out.

Enabling a content network campaign

To create a Google content network campaign, follow these steps:

1. **Create and save a new campaign as you normally would.**

For details on setting up a campaign and expanding the keywords list in Google, refer to Book IV, Chapter 3.

2. **Click the Edit Campaign Settings link to open the Edit Campaign Settings page.**

3. **Clear the Google Search and Search Partners check boxes, and select the check box titled The Content Network.**

4. **Click the Save Changes button.**

Yahoo!'s partner network

Yahoo! calls its content network the partner network and enrolls all campaigns in it automatically. A lot less activity goes on in the Yahoo! partner network than in the Google content network, and unfortunately, unless you're up for scouring through your Web logs, you'll have a much harder time finding out which sites are working for you and which ones aren't. It's not unusual to run a campaign in Yahoo! with the partner network enabled and generate almost no impressions.

The best practice is to set a separate bid for the content network and allow it to run in conjunction with your search campaign to start with. Check out the Yahoo! help center or FAQs for more information.

You can opt out of the Yahoo! partner network on both the campaign and the ad-group level. If you don't want any of your ad groups to participate in the partner network, opt out at campaign level; otherwise, go into each ad group individually to opt out. I describe both procedures in the following sections.

Opting out at campaign level

To opt out of the partner network at campaign level, follow these steps:

1. **Open the campaign you want to remove from the partner network.**

2. **Click the Campaign Settings link to display the campaign settings.**

3. **Click the Edit button in the Tactic Settings section to open the Tactic Settings page (see Figure 7-11).**

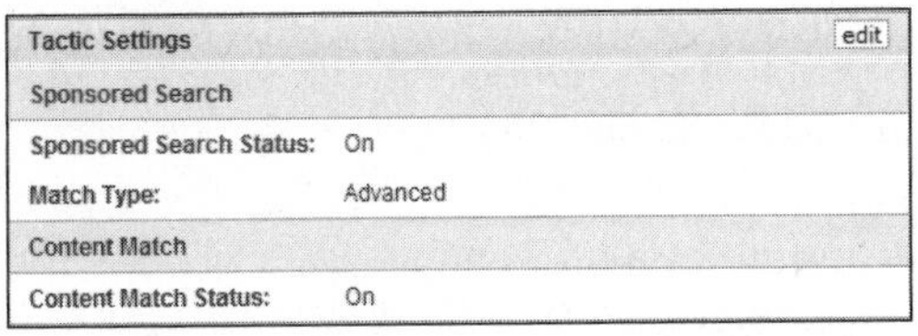

Figure 7-11:
Yahoo!
search-
tactic
settings.

Tactic Settings		edit
Sponsored Search		
Sponsored Search Status:	On	
Match Type:	Advanced	
Content Match		
Content Match Status:	On	

4. **Choose Off from the Content Match Status drop-down menu.**

5. **Click Save Changes.**

Opting out at ad-group level

To opt out of the partner network at ad-group level, follow these steps:

1. **Open the ad group.**
2. **Click the Ad Group Settings link to open the settings page.**
3. **Click the Edit button in the Tactic Settings section to open the Tactic Settings page.**
4. **In the Content Match Status section, choose Off from the drop-down menu.**
5. **In the Set Your Content Match Bid section, adjust the content network bid to 10 percent.**

    A bid of 10 percent is the lowest amount you're allowed to bid. This setting is just for extra measure, in case your changes aren't saved or Yahoo! takes a while to adjust your settings.

6. **Click Save Changes.**

Blocking domains

To block your ad from appearing on certain Web sites, use Yahoo!'s Blocked Domain tool. The domain blocker works at account level, and you can block up to 500 Web sites per account.

To use this tool, follow these steps:

1. **Open the Administration tab**
2. **Click the Submit Domains link in the Account General Information section.**

    The Block Domains option page opens.

3. **Enter the domains you want to block.**

    Read the article "How Blocking Is Applied" to the right of the entry area to make sure that you've entered the right URL to block. This section explains root domains, sub-domains, and directories; what they are; and how many of each kind you can block.

4. **Click Submit.**

MSN's content network

MSN opts all new campaigns into its content network, called Content Ads Beta. This network comprises all Microsoft properties, including MSN Money, MSN Autos, and Windows Marketplace. Other participating partner Web sites are included but remain unnamed at this time. (I called MSN adCenter to ask what these mystery sites are, but the representative I spoke with told me that even the representatives don't know.)

The concept remains the same: Ads appear alongside relevant content on Web pages across these properties at a given CPC. You can set a different maximum CPC for the content network.

Also, you can opt out of the program at ad-group level. To do so, follow these steps:

1. **Open the ad group.**

2. **Click Edit Settings.**

3. **Clear the Content Network check box (see Figure 7-12).**

4. **Click Save Changes.**

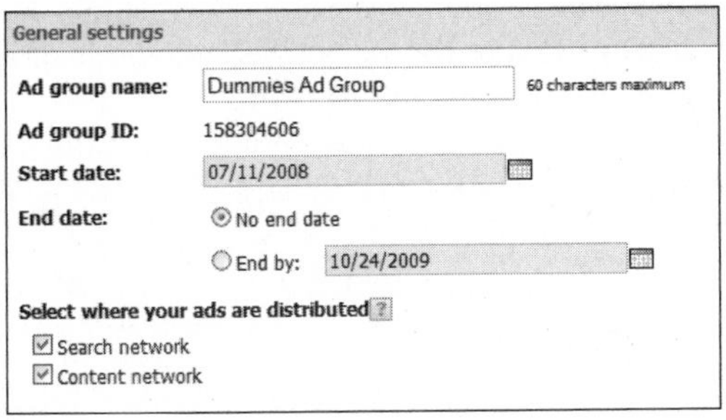

Figure 7-12:
Select or
deselect
search and
content
networks
here.

General settings		
Ad group name:	Dummies Ad Group	60 characters maximum
Ad group ID:	158304606	
Start date:	07/11/2008	
End date:	⊙ No end date	
	○ End by: 10/24/2009	

Select where your ads are distributed ?
☑ Search network
☑ Content network

Any targeting you set in the ad group for geography, demographics, and negative keywords apply on both the search and content network levels.

For MSN adCenter, it really isn't necessary to separate your ad groups into separate search and content targets right away. Because the current inventory of MSN isn't very voluminous, unless you're working in a large industry — automobiles, real estate, or financial advice, for example — it's best to allow the campaigns to run together for a couple of weeks and see what the volumes are for your industry.

The MSN content network is the most expensive, in terms of average CPC, of the three major search engines. Also, you can't block certain Web sites in the network.

Choosing an Analytics Package

The question isn't "Do I need analytics?" Rather, it's "Which analytics do I need?" You need some sort of analytics to give you hard, measurable results besides CTR and guesstimates on your PPC campaigns.

Before you drop dollars on a monthly or annual subscription for an analytics package, be sure to check out the free offerings first. Depending on your situation, you may not need as robust an analytics program as the paid sites offer.

Each of the major search engines offers some sort of integration with conversion tracking. You define a conversion — it could be a sale, a signup, a download, or a filled-out form — and the search engine drops the number of conversions you record into your PPC dashboard.

The following sections describe how the process works in the three major search engines. For more information on analytics, see Book III.

Analytics in Google

Google offers free conversion tracking within AdWords, so you can see which ads and which keywords brought you conversions. It can't tell you how much revenue a conversion generated, though. For that statistic, you need something like Google Analytics, which is also free. You can find it at www.google.com/analytics.

Analytics in Yahoo!

The Conversion Only Analytics tool shows you which ad and keyword generated a conversion. Although you can see how many conversions you have and what ads or keywords produced them, you can't see the amount of revenue generated.

Yahoo! doesn't have a separate analytics program like Google's, but you can use Google Analytics to track your Yahoo! progress fairly well.

To check your campaign performance in Yahoo! Search Marketing, follow these steps:

1. **Click the Administration tab in your Yahoo! PPC account and then click the Analytics link.**

2. **Click the blue Enable Analytics button.**

   The analytics options screen appears.

3. **Choose the Conversion Only Analytics or Full Analytics radio button.**

   Yahoo! generates a block of HTML code for your account and directions for installing it on your site.

4. **Follow the directions to install the code on your Web site.**

   You must be able to edit your site's HTML code or have someone who knows HTML do the work for you. If the code isn't installed properly, the analytics program won't work.

You can also find directions at

`http://help.yahoo.com/l/us/yahoo/ysm/sps/screenref/16877.html`

Analytics in MSN

The adCenter interface doesn't offer conversion tracking unless you're enrolled in beta testing of the Gatineau Analytics program. This program is meant to do what Google Analytics does, in that it doesn't give you just PPC statistics, but also what people searched on to find your site or whether they typed your URL directly in a browser's address bar without using search, as well as any revenue-generation information. The program is fairly compatible with Google Analytics for conversion-tracking purposes.

To register for adCenter analytics, go to

`http://advertising.microsoft.com/advertising/adcenter-analytics-registration`

Book V
E-Mail Marketing

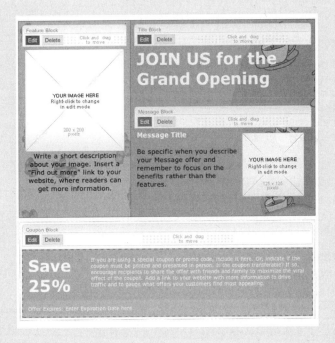

Contents at a Glance

Chapter 1: Adding E-Mail to a Web Marketing Strategy **445**

Understanding the Benefits of E-Mail Marketing 445
Combining E-Mail with Other Media 447
Taking Advantage of E-Mail Service Providers 449

Chapter 2: Becoming a Trusted Sender **453**

Complying with Spam Laws 454
Asking for Permission 457
Minimizing Spam Complaints 463

Chapter 3: Building a Quality E-Mail List. **469**

Preparing Your E-Mail Database 469
Collecting Contact Information 471
Offering Incentives to Increase Signups 480
Building a List with List Brokers 482

Chapter 4: Constructing an Effective Marketing E-Mail **483**

Creating From and Subject Lines That Get Noticed 483
Branding Your E-Mails to Enhance Your Image 491
The ABCs of E-Mail Layout 495
Including Images in Your E-Mails 498
Including Text in Your E-Mails 501
Including Links in Your E-Mails 505

Chapter 5: Making Your E-Mail Content Valuable **517**

Sending Valuable Offers 518
Writing an Effective Call to Action 523
Giving Your E-Mail Content Inherent Value 525
Finding Help with Content Creation 529

Chapter 6: Tracking Your E-Mail Campaign Results **531**

Understanding Basic E-Mail Tracking Data 531
Tracking Non-Click Responses 536
Evaluating E-Mail Click-Through Data 539

Chapter 7: Maximizing E-Mail Deliverability **545**

Managing Bounced and Blocked E-Mail 545
Reducing Filtered E-Mail 552
Understanding E-Mail Authentication 558

Chapter 1: Adding E-Mail to a Web Marketing Strategy

In This Chapter

✔ Discovering the benefits of e-mail marketing

✔ Combining e-mail with other media types

✔ Understanding E-Mail Service Providers

Walking into a business where the first dollar of profit is framed victoriously on the wall always reminds me how important the first customer is to any small business. Your first customer represents validation of your business idea and proof that your products and services are valuable enough to cause someone to part with his money in order to obtain them.

The first dollar of profit is certainly cause for celebration. However, you need a plan to deliver ongoing communications to build a steady influx of customers — or your framed dollar of profit will start feeling lonely.

In this chapter, I show you the benefits of using e-mail in combination with other marketing media to communicate with customers and prospects, and I show you how to take advantage of e-mail marketing services to help you manage your strategy.

Understanding the Benefits of E-Mail Marketing

E-mail might seem like a cost-effective way to deliver your marketing messages. For the most part, it is, because you can send personalized, targeted, and interest-specific messages to a large number of people. The value of e-mail marketing doesn't end with the cost, however. E-mail marketing has certain advantages over other forms of direct marketing for your business and for the people who request and receive your e-mails.

Asking for immediate action

You don't have to wait around too long to determine whether an e-mail message was successful. According to MarketingSherpa (www.marketing sherpa.com) *Email Marketing Benchmark Guide 2007,* 80 percent of the e-mail you send is opened in the first 48 hours after delivery.

After an e-mail is opened, it doesn't take long for your audience to take immediate action because people can take action on an e-mail with one click of the mouse. Immediate actions include

✦ Opening and reading the e-mail

✦ Clicking a link

✦ Clicking the Reply button

✦ Forwarding the e-mail

✦ Printing the e-mail

✦ Saving the e-mail

I cover asking for immediate action in Chapter 5 of this minibook.

Gathering feedback

E-mail is a two-way form of communication, and even commercial e-mail can be used to gather feedback and responses from your audience. People can easily reply to e-mails, and many consumers love to share their opinions when it's easy for them to do so. Feedback from e-mails comes in two basic categories:

✦ **Stated feedback** happens when someone

• Fills out an online form

• Fills out an online survey

• Sends a reply

✦ **Behavioral feedback** happens when you track

• Link clicks

• E-mail open rates

• E-mails forwarded to friends

Generating awareness

When was the last time you mailed thousands of postcards, and your customers began crowding around copy machines trying to duplicate the postcard so they can stick stamps to them and forward the message to their friends? E-mail programs have a Forward button with which users can easily send a copy of your e-mail to one or more people in your recipient's address book. E-Mail Service Providers (ESPs) also provide a trackable Forward link that you can insert in your e-mails so you can find out who is forwarding your e-mails. To find out more about ESPs, flip ahead to the section "Taking Advantage of E-Mail Service Providers," later in this chapter.

Staying top-of-mind

If you send periodic e-mails with valuable content, people who aren't ready to buy right away are more likely to remember you and your business when they become ready to buy. Here are some ways that e-mail can be used for top-of-mind awareness and future reference:

✦ Archive your e-mail newsletters on your Web site.

✦ Ask people to save your e-mails, as shown in Figure 1-1, to a folder in their e-mail program.

✦ Ask people to print your e-mails and post them.

✦ Print your e-mails and place them in a flip book on your counter so you can refer to recent offers and show samples of the value of your e-mail list.

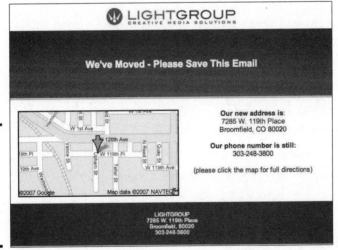

Figure 1-1:
Ask your audience to save your e-mails for future reference.

Combining E-Mail with Other Media

In marketing, you're likely to employ several media and messages over a period of days, weeks, months, and years to communicate everything necessary to attract and retain enough customers.

Delivering your messages by combining different media is an effective way to market your business, but you'll probably find it more affordable to lean heavily on a few communication media where delivering your message results in the highest return. E-mail is one such medium because it's cost-effective and the returns are generally outstanding.

Keeping the design elements and personality of your e-mails and other messages similar or identical over time — *branding* — reinforces each of your messages and makes each successive message more memorable to your audience.

Consumers are more likely to respond positively to your e-mail messages when they can identify your brand and when the content of each message feels familiar to them. Plan all your marketing messages as if they were one unit to ensure that each message contains design elements that become familiar to your audience when multiple messages are delivered.

Here are some branding ideas to help you give all your marketing messages a familiar look and feel:

✦ **Make your logo identifiable and readable in all types of print and digital formats, with color schemes that look good online and in print.**

   In general, your logo and colors should look consistent on

   • Signs

   • Order forms

   • E-mail signup forms

   • Your Web site

   • Receipts

   • Business cards

   • E-mails

✦ **Include your company name in all your marketing.**

   Incorporate you name in

   • E-mail `From` lines

   • E-mail addresses

   • Your e-mail signature

   • Online directories

   • Your blog

✦ **Format your messages consistently across media.**

   When repeating messages in multiple media, make sure the following elements are formatted consistently in your e-mails:

   • Fonts

   • Layouts

   • Images

   • Headlines

- Contact information
- Calls to action

    You can read about calls to action in Chapter 4 of this minibook.

 Sending commercial e-mail to complete strangers is illegal. To keep on the right side of the law, combine at least one other medium with e-mail in order to initiate relationships with prospective customers. For more information about the legalities of sending commercial e-mail, see Chapter 2 of this minibook.

Taking Advantage of E-Mail Service Providers

The days when you could send a single e-mail and *blind-copy* hundreds of other people — by adding e-mail addresses to the BCC field in an e-mail — are over. Spam filters, firewalls, junk folders, and consumer distrust are all reasons to turn to professionals for help with your e-mail strategy. *ESPs* are companies that provide one or more of the following commercial e-mail services:

- ✦ Improved e-mail deliverability
- ✦ Database and list management
- ✦ E-mail template design
- ✦ E-mail message and content creation
- ✦ Tracking reports
- ✦ Advice and consulting

Checking out leading providers

The following is a list of some of the leading ESPs in various niches. To conduct your own ESP investigation, search for *"e-mail marketing solutions"* on Google.

- ✦ **Constant Contact (www.constantcontact.com):** Comprehensive service designed for small businesses offering an easy-to-use graphical user interface, simple list upload, and over 200 templates as well as an integrated e-mail/online survey product. Starts at a $15 flat fee per month and includes unlimited free support and online training.

- ✦ **Microsoft Office 2007 (http://office.microsoft.com):** Offers template creation through Word and Publisher documents and includes a separate e-mail marketing service for bulk sending through Outlook. Watch out for CAN-SPAM compliance issues. (See Chapter 2 of this minibook for additional CAN-SPAM information.) Starts at a $9.95 flat fee per month after purchasing and installing the Office suite. (Suggested Retail Price is $399.99.) Sign up for the e-mail marketing service at http://smallbusiness.officelive.com.

✦ **VerticalResponse (www.verticalresponse.com):** Offers e-mail marketing and postcard marketing integration. The service also includes a survey feature. Fees for e-mail marketing are charged only on a per e-mail–sent basis starting at $15 per thousand with tiered discounts after the first 1,000 sent e-mails.

✦ **1ShoppingCart (www.1shoppingcart.com):** Offers auto-responders and other types of e-mail campaigns along with the ability to integrate opt-in mechanisms with an online shopping cart. Starts at $29 per month.

✦ **ExactTarget (www.exacttarget.com):** Offers an e-mail marketing application with higher-level database integration and advanced features. Schedule a demo for pricing information. An annual contract may be required.

Exploring provider benefits

ESPs allow you to accomplish much more with your e-mail marketing than you otherwise could on your own. Some ESPs even provide various levels of outsourcing for higher prices if you don't want to do your own e-mail marketing. Here are a few examples of the kinds of benefits that ESPs provide:

✦ **Give your business a professional look.** ESPs can help you create great-looking e-mail communications without programming knowledge. Most ESPs provide templates with consumer-friendly layouts to accommodate any type of message. Some ESPs provide template-creation wizards that allow you to control all your own design elements for a low cost, and some ESPs either include professional services to help you with semi-custom designs or allow you to completely outsource and customize your template designs. Here are some of the templates that ESPs usually provide:

- Newsletters

- Promotions

- Announcements

- Press releases

- Event invitations

- Greeting cards

- Business letters

Figure 1-2 shows an e-mail template that an ESP provides.

Figure 1-2:
This e-mail template is ready for content.

Courtesy of Constant Contact

✦ **Keep your marketing legal.** ESPs are required to incorporate current e-mail laws in order for customers to easily comply. Reputable ESPs take compliance a step further than the basic legal requirements and adhere to more professional standards that reflect consumer preferences. Examples of professional standards include the following:

- Safe one-click unsubscribe links

- Privacy statements

- Physical address added to e-mails

- Sending from a verified e-mail address

✦ **Help you with logistics and reporting.** ESPs can help you manage the data and feedback associated with executing your e-mail strategy. Here are some examples of ways ESPs can help you manage your information:

- Storage and retrieval of subscriber information

- Reports on deliverability

- Automated handling of subscribe and unsubscribe requests

- Tracking information on blocked and bounced e-mail

✦ **Help with content.** ESPs want you to be successful because if your e-mail messages are effective, you'll likely reward your ESP by being a loyal customer. Many ESPs have resources available that will help you develop your content and use best practices. Examples include

- Online communities
- Webinars
- Tutorials
- Classroom-style training
- Consultation

✦ **Teach you best practices.** ESPs can give you valuable information on consumer preferences that would be too expensive or impossible for you to obtain on your own. ESPs send a lot of e-mails on behalf of their customers, and they're good at staying up to date on consumer preferences and professional standards. Some ESPs are willing to share their knowledge to make your e-mails more effective. Some things you might find out include

- Best times and days to send
- How to improve your open rates
- How to avoid spam complaints
- What to do when e-mail is blocked or filtered
- How to design and layout your content

Chapter 2: Becoming a Trusted Sender

In This Chapter

✓ Understanding spam laws

✓ Getting permission

✓ Familiarizing yourself with e-mail laws

✓ Minimizing spam complaints

*E*veryone who uses e-mail deals with spam on one level or another. Consumers receive so much spam that they're hesitant to open e-mails unless they know and trust the sender, and they're more than willing to report your e-mails as spam to their Internet service provider (ISP) if your e-mail doesn't appear trustworthy.

Every e-mail marketing strategy is subject to the possibility of consumer spam complaints, and numerous legal and professional standards apply to commercial e-mail. Consumers also expect marketing e-mails to come from a trusted source with just the right frequency and amount of content. Here are the three authoritative benchmarks for determining whether your commercial e-mails are regarded as spam:

✦ **Legal standards,** as outlined in the CAN-SPAM Act of 2003 and the 2008 revisions

✦ **Professional standards,** as outlined by consumer advocates and the e-mail marketing industry

✦ **Consumer preferences,** as dictated by consumers themselves

Adhering to e-mail professionalism keeps your e-mails legally compliant and improves your relationships with the people who receive and open your e-mails. In this chapter, I show you how to become a trusted e-mail sender, minimizing consumer spam complaints while maximizing the trust between your business and your existing and future e-mail list subscribers.

Complying with Spam Laws

Spam is bothersome enough that lawmakers enacted the CAN-SPAM (Controlling the Assault of Non-Solicited Pornography and Marketing) Act of 2003 to help prosecute spammers. Names aside, the law makes certain e-mail marketing practices illegal and gives legal definitions to many best practices.

The following sections summarize the basic tenets of the CAN-SPAM Act of 2003 and revisions made in 2008. You can read the CAN-SPAM Act at

www.ftc.gov/bcp/conline/edcams/spam/rules.htm

and you can access the 2008 revisions at

www.ftc.gov/os/2008/05/R411008frn.pdf

to make sure that your own e-mails comply.

This section is intended to broaden your understanding of industry practices and shouldn't be used to make decisions regarding your own compliance to the law. Contact your attorney if you need more information.

Determining which e-mails have to comply

The CAN-SPAM Act of 2003 applies to commercial e-mail messages, which the law distinguishes from transactional or relationship messages. In general, the CAN-SPAM Act defines the two separate kinds of e-mail messages, as follows:

+ A **commercial e-mail** is basically an e-mail containing an advertisement, promotion, or content from a business' Web site.

+ A **transactional or relationship e-mail** is basically anything other than a commercial e-mail.

Although understanding that some e-mail messages fall outside the definition of commercial e-mail is important, understanding that all e-mails sent in the name of your business can be construed by the recipient as commercial in nature is equally important. Best practice is to make sure that all your business-related e-mails are legally compliant.

The CAN-SPAM 2008 revisions specify that e-mails forwarded to others by a recipient may be subject to all the CAN-SPAM requirements. For example, if you send a coupon to a customer and your customer forwards that coupon to a friend, your customer's forwarded e-mail might be subject to CAN-SPAM rules. Talk to your E-Mail Service Provider (ESP) to make sure your forwarded e-mails are CAN-SPAM compliant.

Collecting e-mail addresses legally

The CAN-SPAM Act makes certain types of e-mail address collection illegal and requires permission from your e-mail list subscribers before you send certain types of content. (The CAN-SPAM Act uses the term *affirmative consent* instead of *permission.*)

Potentially illegal e-mail addresses collection methods aren't always easy to spot, so the best practice is to make sure that you have explicit permission from everyone on your list to send them e-mail. Here are some best practices for steering clear of potentially permission-less e-mail addresses:

+ **Never purchase an e-mail list from a company that allows you to keep the e-mail addresses as a data file.** E-mail addresses kept in a data file are easily bought and sold, and e-mail addresses with explicit permission are too valuable to sell.

+ **Never collect e-mail addresses from Web sites and other online directories.** I advise against this practice because you don't have affirmative consent (or permission) from the owner.

+ **Don't use an e-mail address collection service.** The exception is a service that collects confirmed permission from every subscriber that it obtains.

+ **Don't borrow an e-mail list from another business and send e-mail to that business' e-mail list.** Those subscribers didn't explicitly opt-in to receive your e-mails.

+ **Don't rent an e-mail list unless you're certain that the list rental company's practices are legally compliant.** Most rental companies don't have permission-based lists. (You can read more about list rental in Chapter 3 of this minibook.)

Including required content in your e-mails

The CAN-SPAM Act requires you to include certain content in your e-mails. Include the following in your e-mails to stay CAN-SPAM compliant:

+ **Provide a way for your subscribers to opt-out of receiving future e-mails.**

   You're required to remove anyone who unsubscribes from your e-mail list permanently within ten days of the unsubscribe request, and you can't add that person back without his explicit permission. When providing an opt-out mechanism, remember that it's illegal to charge someone to opt-out or to ask for any information other than an e-mail address and opt-out preferences. Your opt-out process also has to be accomplishable by replying to a single e-mail or by visiting a single Web page. Your ESP can provide you with an opt-out link that automatically unsubscribes in one click.

✦ **Make sure that your e-mail includes your physical address.**

If your business has multiple locations, include your main address or the physical address associated with each e-mail you send, as shown in Figure 2-1.

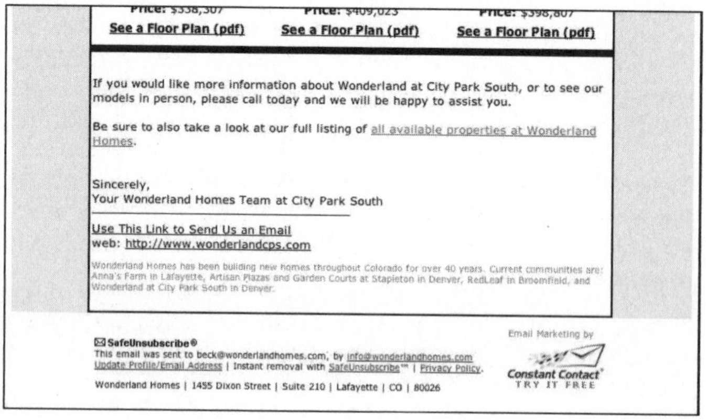

Figure 2-1:
Adding a physical address to your e-mail is required under the CAN-SPAM Act.

> Price: $338,307   Price: $409,023   Price: $398,807
> **See a Floor Plan (pdf)**   **See a Floor Plan (pdf)**   **See a Floor Plan (pdf)**
>
> If you would like more information about Wonderland at City Park South, or to see our models in person, please call today and we will be happy to assist you.
>
> Be sure to also take a look at our full listing of all available properties at Wonderland Homes.
>
> Sincerely,
> Your Wonderland Homes Team at City Park South
>
> Use This Link to Send Us an Email
> web: http://www.wonderlandcps.com
>
> Wonderland Homes has been building new homes throughout Colorado for over 40 years. Current communities are: Anna's Farm in Lafayette, Artisan Plazas and Garden Courts at Stapleton in Denver, RedLeaf in Broomfield, and Wonderland at City Park South in Denver.
>
> ☒ SafeUnsubscribe®   Email Marketing by
> This email was sent to beck@wonderlandhomes.com, by info@wonderlandhomes.com
> Update Profile/Email Address | Instant removal with SafeUnsubscribe™ | Privacy Policy.   Constant Contact®
> Wonderland Homes | 1455 Dixon Street | Suite 210 | Lafayette | CO | 80026   TRY IT FREE

Courtesy of Wonderland Homes and Constant Contact

TIP

If you work from home and don't want your home address in every e-mail, the CAN-SPAM 2008 revisions confirm that you're allowed to include your post office box address as long as the post office or box rental company associates the box to your legitimate business address.

✦ **Make sure that your e-mail header information clearly identifies your business and doesn't mislead your audience in any way.**

Your e-mail header includes your From line, Subject line, and e-mail address. Make that sure your e-mail's From line information clearly and honestly represents your business. The term *misleading* is open to legal interpretation. Speak to your attorney if you have questions.

✦ **Make sure that your e-mail's Subject line isn't misleading.**

Don't use the Subject line to trick your audience into opening your e-mail or to misrepresent the offer contained in your e-mail.

✦ **Make sure that your e-mail clearly states that the e-mail is a solicitation.**

The exception is when you have permission or affirmative consent from every individual on your list to send the solicitation. (Read more about permission later in this chapter.)

✦ **Make sure that your e-mail complies with any applicable guidelines for sexually oriented material.**

If your e-mail contains such material, make sure your e-mail's Subject line complies with the CAN-SPAM Act supplementary guidelines and also clearly states that the content of the e-mail is adult in nature without being explicit in the way you describe the content. You can access the supplementary guidelines on the Federal Trade Commission (FTC) Web site at www.ftc.gov/spam.

Asking for Permission

Collecting information without asking for permission can cause prospective subscribers to hesitate — or worse, they could perceive you as a spammer who abuses their privacy. Obtaining permission also ensures that your list starts out in compliance with the current CAN-SPAM laws.

Taking some time to formulate a professional permission strategy before embarking on e-mail collection tactics can reward your overall e-mail strategy with loyal subscribers who love to open, read, and take action on the e-mails you send.

Deciding on a permission level

When formulating your permission strategy, put yourself in the prospective subscriber's shoes so that you can assess the level of permission necessary to meet individual expectations.

Each type of permission is a two-way notion. You should be able to attest to each subscriber's level of consent, and your subscriber should feel that he did indeed authorize you to send him e-mail. This type of two-way permission comes in three basic levels, each with a higher level of demonstrated consensus: implied, explicit, and confirmed.

Level 1: Implied permission

Implied permission happens when someone shares her e-mail address with you in the course of normal business communications. The transaction implies that the purpose of giving you the e-mail address is to receive e-mails from you in reply. This level of permission isn't recommended as a best practice even though it's sometimes suitable in the recipient's view. (I describe why this isn't a best practice in a bit.)

An example of implied permission is a prospective customer who fills out an online form to obtain a quote for your services. The form includes an E-Mail Address field. The prospect shares her e-mail address within the form, expecting that you'll use that e-mail address to send the quote. If you send the quote and then begin sending weekly promotions without disclosing the fact that sharing an e-mail address on the quote form results in additional e-mails, however, you run the risk that your new subscriber will feel violated.

The main reason why implied permission isn't considered one of e-mail professionalism's best practices is that it doesn't take much extra effort to move from implicit permission to a higher standard. In the previous example, the business owner could easily add a link to his permission policy under the E-Mail Address field. Or, he could insert text that reads

> *By sharing your e-mail address, you'll receive your quote via e-mail along with concise weekly product updates to which you can safely unsubscribe at any time.*

Level 2: Explicit permission

Explicit permission happens when you include text or language disclosing how you plan to use the prospective subscriber's e-mail address. For example, an explicit subscriber might be a Web site visitor who clicks a Sign Up to Receive Our Weekly E-Newsletter link and then clicks another link on the following page to submit additional information that he types into an online form. Explicit permission also happens when prospective subscribers contact you and explicitly ask to be added to your e-mail list.

Explicit permission doesn't have to be a lengthy or complicated process, but the benefits of obtaining explicit permission are worth having a straight-forward process. Here are some examples of explicit permission that you can adapt to your own subscriber situations:

✦ **Verbal:** When someone shares his e-mail address by handing you a business card or dictates an e-mail address to you during a phone conversation, you could query, *Is it alright if I send you my weekly event invitation e-mail?*

✦ **Written:** If a prospective subscriber sends a single e-mail to you and you want to add him to your e-mail list, you could reply to the e-mail and ask, *By the way, may I add your e-mail address to my list so that you can receive my monthly e-newsletter?*

✦ **Physical:** Some subscribers physically add their e-mail address to a guest book or sign up via a paper form. If you have such an arrangement, you could post a professional-looking plaque or sign next to the guest book or signup form that states, *Thank you for giving us permission to send you our weekly e-mail coupons by signing our guest book. We promise never to share your e-mail address with anyone outside the company without your permission.*

✦ **Incidental:** Sometimes, you can ask for explicit permission in the context of a transaction related to your e-mail information. For example, you might want to give online shoppers the ability to receive cross-promotions by selecting a check box during the check-out process. The text describing the check box could read, *Select this check box to receive periodic promotions that enhance the value of your purchase.* Just be sure that the default setting on the check box is deselected (clear), or else it's no longer an example of explicit permission.

Don't mix your list messages

I consulted with a restaurant owner once who also owned a travel agency. He decided to place signup cards on each table in his restaurant so that his restaurant patrons could sign up for his travel newsletter. Lots of restaurant patrons filled out the cards, but they were confused when they began receiving a travel newsletter because they thought they were signing up to receive e-mails from the restaurant.

To ensure that permission is viewed as explicit on both sides of the information exchange, be as clear as possible in your messaging and context. For example, don't send coupons when your subscriber signs up in order to win a prize, unless you clearly state your intentions. When your context and messaging are as clear as possible and you still notice subscriber confusion, consider using an even higher level of permission.

Level 3: Confirmed permission

Confirmed permission happens when someone implicitly or explicitly subscribes to your e-mail list, and you respond to the subscriber with an e-mail requiring the subscriber to confirm his interest by reading your intended usage and then clicking a confirmation link. If the subscriber doesn't confirm, his e-mail address isn't added to your list, even if he explicitly filled out and submitted a form or physically signed your guest book. Figure 2-2 shows an example of a confirmation e-mail.

Figure 2-2:
A prospective subscriber must click an additional link for confirmed permission.

Courtesy of Constant Contact

Although confirmed permission is the most professional form of permission, it's also the most difficult for subscribers to understand. Therefore, confirmed permission isn't always suitable. Generally speaking, confirmed permission should be used when you want to be *absolutely sure* that your subscribers want your e-mail.

Confirmed permission is the appropriate level if

+ You send sensitive information.

+ Your subscribers tend to forget signing up.

+ You want to have a physical record of the subscriber's authorization to send e-mail.

Confirmation e-mails generally have low response rates, so if you're using explicit permission to build your list, you might lose subscribers who really want to be on the list but fail to read the confirmation e-mail and click the required link. The trade-off, however, is that your confirmed subscribers are more likely to receive and open your e-mails.

Inheriting a list: Getting permission after the fact

Sometimes, you might find yourself in possession of an e-mail list with questionable — or even no — permission. This often happens when you obtained your list in one of (or more of, but not limited to) the following scenarios:

+ You purchased an existing business and inherited an e-mail list without knowing the source of the e-mail addresses on the list.

+ Your list contains e-mail addresses collected over a long time period, and you can't identify each type of associated permission.

+ You purchased a list or built your list with low permission standards before you read this chapter — and now you're wondering whether your list is useless.

Sending e-mails to a permission-less list might violate the current CAN-SPAM laws and is likely to result in a high number of spam complaints from recipients.

Follow these steps to determine the permission status of an inherited list with questionable permission:

1. **Sort your list by source.**

If the source doesn't imply a two-way business relationship and the recipient likely won't recognize your e-mail address, discard the e-mail address or set aside the contact info to ask for permission.

Sources can include order forms, business cards, e-mail correspondence, guest books, or purchased lists. Inherited lists rarely detail the source as a field in a database or a note on the back of a business card, so determine the source by matching each record to other clues.

For example, if your list is contained in a customer relationship management system database, you might be able to export all the customers who made a purchase — and assume that names were obtained as the result of a business transaction.

Always discard purchased lists because purchased lists are almost never permission-based to begin with. (See the section on building a list with list brokers in Chapter 3 of this minibook for more information about purchased lists.)

2. **Sort your list by date; discard any addresses belonging to customers who haven't made a purchase in over a year.**

   E-mail addresses belonging to customers who made purchases in years past and haven't returned are unlikely to appreciate your e-mails. Older e-mail addresses should be kept only if the person who owns the e-mail address is a recognizable current customer.

3. **Check your list visually; discard any addresses that begin with ambiguous names or that are part of a distribution list.**

   Ambiguous names include Webmaster@ or Info@. *Distribution lists* (single e-mail addresses that forward the e-mail to multiple addresses behind the scenes) make it impossible to tell whether the underlying e-mail addresses are permission based.

4. **Sort the rest of your list by category.**

   At this point, consider using different messaging, depending on your relationship to the person who owns the e-mail address. If the e-mail address belongs to a prospect, you might want to proceed more cautiously than if the e-mail address belongs to a person who has purchased a product several times.

5. **Confirm permission to send e-mail.**

   If, and only if, an e-mail list passes the preceding four steps and you're certain that the people who own the e-mail addresses on your list will recognize your business and your relationship to them personally, contact them to confirm permission.

   - *If you have a small list:* Confirmation can be verified with a phone call or an e-mail containing a confirmation link.

   - *If you can't contact people personally:* Send a professionally written confirmation e-mail.

Protecting your e-mail list

A quality list of permission-based e-mail subscribers segmented by interest and behavior is something to be proud of. Lists and data are assets and represent a significant competitive advantage to your business.

When it comes to e-mail data, protecting your asset is as important as building it in the first place. Don't violate the trust of your e-mail list subscribers by sharing their e-mail addresses with others who don't have permission to send to your list. Don't abuse your e-mail list subscribers by sending information they didn't ask for or by using their permission as a platform for selling lots of unrelenting banner ads in the body of your e-mail newsletters.

As a general rule, don't do anything with your e-mail list data that isn't explicitly agreed to and expected by your subscribers.

Verifying permission for an old, outdated, or questionable list can prove frustrating even if you follow these steps because people change their e-mail addresses from time to time and because your database might not include the information you need to effectively sort through an inherited list.

If the aforementioned steps seem highly labor intensive or prove to be impossible — or if you can't make a determination because of the organizational state of your database — you should probably bite the bullet and discard the list or attempt to reestablish permission with the people on your inherited list without sending an e-mail.

If your list contains additional contact information other than the e-mail address, consider using direct mail, phone calls, and other advertising methods to drive the prospects through an explicit signup process on your Web site or at a physical location.

Minimizing Spam Complaints

Spam is also known as *unsolicited commercial e-mail.* Although numerous stories, analogies, and myths exist about the origin and meaning of *spam,* one thing is for sure — consumers don't like receiving it.

Even if your e-mail doesn't meet the legal definition of spam, consumers can easily report your e-mail as spam and thus impede your ability to send e-mail in the future. For example, Yahoo! customers can deem your e-mail as spam with a click of a button (see Figure 2-3). Most ISPs (including AOL, Yahoo!, and the new Windows Live Hotmail) give their customers Spam buttons to use to block suspected spammers.

Readers click this button
to report e-mail as spam.

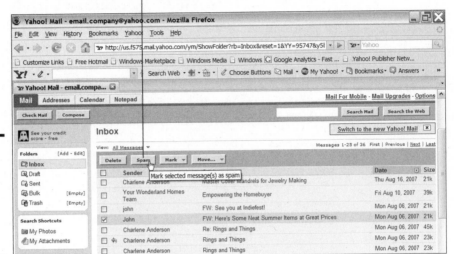

Figure 2-3:
Most ISPs
allow
customers
to report
e-mails as
spam.

If your e-mails are perceived as spam by your audience and you receive too
many spam complaints, ISPs will block your e-mail server from sending
e-mails to their customers. As few as 2 spam complaints per 1,000 e-mails
can block your e-mail server temporarily, and higher percentages can result
in your server being added to a permanent block-list.

Because consumers have control over the Spam button, no e-mail marketing
strategy is immune to complaints. Keeping your e-mails in line with the
following guidelines is the best way to ensure that your spam complaints
remain below industry tolerances.

Allowing your audience to unsubscribe from receiving e-mails

The CAN-SPAM Act requires that you include a way to let your audience
unsubscribe from receiving future e-mails from you, but the law doesn't
specify which mechanisms are appropriate for processing unsubscribe
requests. You can ask your subscribers to reply to your e-mails with their
unsubscribe request and manually keep track of your unsubscribed prospects and customers, but this process can be tedious with larger lists.

The most professional practice, and the most automated, for processing
unsubscribe requests is to use an ESP to automatically and permanently
remove anyone who unsubscribes from all e-mail lists in one click. Figure 2-4
shows a one-click unsubscribe link in the footer of an e-mail.

Spam: Meat(like) or Monty Python mayhem?

According to the Hormel Foods Web site, the luncheon meat SPAM originated in 1937 when the company came up with the recipe. The company held a contest to help name the product and offered $100 as a prize for the winning name. The winner, Kenneth Daigneau, combined the letters *sp* from *spiced* and the letters *am* from *ham* to create the word SPAM — short for *spiced ham.*

In 1975, Monty Python's Flying Circus created the infamous comedy skit wherein Vikings sing, "Spam, spam, spam, spam . . ." in a restaurant that includes SPAM in every menu item.

Not long after the Monty Python skit hit the air, Internet users in Multi-User Dungeons (MUDs; multi-user computer games), bulletin boards, chat rooms, and Usenet (User Network) message boards began using *spam* to refer to annoying postings and unwanted messages. Ultimately, the term was also applied to unwanted e-mail messages. Today, consumers define spam on their own terms and log their complaints accordingly.

Most reputable ESPs automatically insert a one-click unsubscribe link into your e-mails. When a subscriber clicks the link, the ESP automatically removes the subscriber or changes the status of the subscriber in the ESP's database to Unsubscribed so that the subscriber stops receiving e-mails immediately.

Unsubscribe link

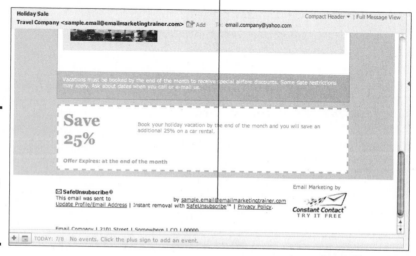

Figure 2-4: E-mail recipients can safely unsubscribe in one click with this link.

Courtesy of Constant Contact

Providing a one-click unsubscribe mechanism gives your potential e-mail list subscribers confidence when subscribing to your e-mail lists and encourages them to differentiate your e-mail from spammers who use dubious opt-out methods, if any.

Keeping your e-mails from looking like spam

To avoid having your e-mails reported as spam, understand how consumers evaluate e-mails. When you think about whether your audience is likely to perceive your e-mail as spam, remember that spam is in the *I* of the receiver:

✦ ***I* don't want it.** Unwanted marketing e-mails are perceived as spam by most consumers, especially if they feel that they didn't authorize the sender to send it. Sometimes, consumers even start to perceive e-mails as spam after they receive them for months just because they no longer want them.

✦ ***I* can't verify it.** If consumers can't tell whether an e-mail came from a legitimate source, they perceive it as spam. Most consumers look at the From line in an e-mail header to determine whether an e-mail is familiar.

✦ ***I* think it's too frequent.** Consumers tend to perceive frequent e-mails as spam when they feel that the content is irrelevant, repetitive, or too long.

Even when consumers don't perceive your e-mail as spam, they might be inclined to click the Spam button on your e-mail for one or more of the following reasons:

✦ They can't figure out how to unsubscribe from your e-mail.

✦ They don't trust the unsubscribe link in your e-mail.

✦ They accidentally click the Spam button while sorting through their e-mail Inbox.

✦ They unintentionally include your e-mail while clicking the Spam button on a large group of other spam e-mails.

Keeping spam complaints to a minimum is a matter of adhering to professional practices and consumer preferences over the course of your entire e-mail marketing strategy.

No matter what the method of accepting permission, always take your prospective subscriber's circumstances into account. Even explicit permission can result in spam complaints or negative emotions if your subscriber doesn't remember subscribing or doesn't recognize the e-mails you send after subscribing.

You can minimize your spam complaints over time by doing the following.

✦ **Say thanks.** Send a welcome e-mail immediately after the subscriber joins the list, as shown in Figure 2-5.

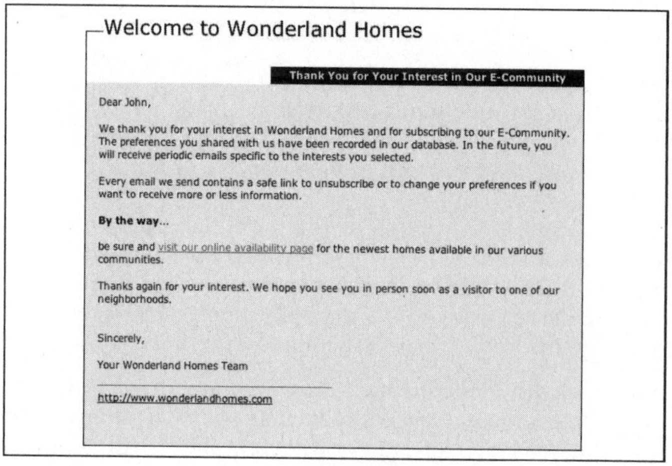

Figure 2-5: This welcome e-mail reinforces permission and helps reduce spam complaints

┌─Welcome to Wonderland Homes

Thank You for Your Interest in Our E-Community

Dear John,

We thank you for your interest in Wonderland Homes and for subscribing to our E-Community. The preferences you shared with us have been recorded in our database. In the future, you will receive periodic emails specific to the interests you selected.

Every email we send contains a safe link to unsubscribe or to change your preferences if you want to receive more or less information.

By the way...

be sure and visit our online availability page for the newest homes available in our various communities.

Thanks again for your interest. We hope you see you in person soon as a visitor to one of our neighborhoods.

Sincerely,

Your Wonderland Homes Team

http://www.wonderlandhomes.com

Courtesy of Wonderland Homes and Constant Contact

✦ **Send e-mail reminders.** Insert a paragraph of text at the top of every e-mail reminding the recipient how you obtained his e-mail address.

✦ **Keep your e-mail frequency in line with your e-mail content and your e-mail list subscribers' expectations.** You can read more about the relationship between frequency and content later in this list.

✦ **Reinforce branding.** Include your logo and colors on your signup form and make sure that future e-mails match your brand. (Read more about this in Chapter 4 of this minibook.)

✦ **Reinforce familiarity.** Make sure that every e-mail's From line is memorable and familiar. (Read more on this in Chapter 4 of this minibook.)

✦ **Send a reminder letter.** Send a permission reminder letter periodically that tells your subscribers exactly how you obtained their e-mail address and gives them links for updating their preferences and unsubscribing.

✦ **Make your e-mail content valuable so your e-mail list subscribers continue to want your e-mails.** You can read more about creating value in your e-mails in Chapter 5 of this minibook.

✦ **Make your signup process memorable for your list subscribers and clearly identify your business in every e-mail's From line so your audience can verify the source of your e-mails.** Ideas for optimizing your e-mail's From line appear in Chapter 4 of this minibook.

✦ **Ask everyone who unsubscribes from your e-mail list to tell you why they don't want your e-mail.** You can then adjust your strategy accordingly.

✦ **Use an ESP that authenticates your e-mails.** You can read more about e-mail authentication in Chapter 7 of this minibook.

✦ **Include a description of your e-mail content and your typical frequency in your signup process.** For example, if you send a monthly e-mail newsletter along with periodic promotions to your e-mail list, your e-mail list signup form might include a sentence that reads

> *Signing up allows you to receive our monthly e-mail newsletter as well as periodic special offers related to our newest products.*

✦ **Send only the content that your e-mail list subscribers expect you to send.** For example, if potential e-mail list subscribers share their e-mail address in order to receive a quote for your services, don't send them offers unless they gave you permission as part of requesting a quote.

✦ **Allow your e-mail list subscribers to choose their own interests.** If you send several distinct types of e-mail content — such as coupons and event invitations — give your e-mail list subscribers a list of categories to choose from when signing up. Make sure to give them a mechanism for changing their interests, such as a link to their profile, in every e-mail.

Chapter 3: Building a Quality E-Mail List

In This Chapter

✓ Getting your e-mail database ready

✓ Gathering valuable contact information

✓ Attracting e-mail subscribers

✓ Obtaining e-mail addresses through list brokers

Collecting e-mail addresses isn't an easy task. Some people are so bothered by unsolicited e-mails that they're willing to share almost anything else with you before they will share their e-mail address. Others might give you their e-mail address, but when the e-mails they receive from you don't meet their expectations, they resort to unsubscribing or marking the e-mails as spam, even if they're loyal customers.

Fortunately, an e-mail list needn't be large to be effective. The best e-mail lists are those that contain the names of loyal repeat customers, referral sources who respect others' privacy, and interested prospects who know you and your business well enough to recognize your e-mails.

This chapter guides you through some of the best tactics for building a permission-based e-mail list with a high number of quality subscribers. This chapter summarizes how and where to collect information, what information to collect, and how to prepare your database. A quality list helps ensure that your e-mail messages are received by the people who are most likely to respond with repeat and referral business.

You need to collect permission in addition to collecting contact information in order to send successful e-mails. I cover the details of collecting permission in Chapter 2 of this minibook.

Preparing Your E-Mail Database

Sending e-mails to your list requires your list data to be stored in a useful electronic format, so take care to enter your data into a database while you collect. Building and maintaining an electronic database allows you to

✦ **Organize and view your list data easily.**

✦ **Sort your list data into categories to send targeted e-mails.** For example, you might use your database to sort your data by ZIP code so you can send a more targeted event invitation to a list of people in a specific ZIP code.

✦ **Process and keep track of unsubscribed contacts.**

✦ **Query your list to extract useful information and reports.**

You don't need a highly sophisticated database for effective e-mail marketing, although additional database features can improve your ability to target your contacts with specific messages. Keep in mind that databases with a lot of complex features are more expensive than simpler applications. Make sure any fancy functionality in your database can return more than a dollar for every dollar you spend to gain that function. You can always upgrade later when your e-mail marketing strategy outgrows your initial functionality.

If you're not sure which database will give you the best results, start with a basic database application or with your E-Mail Service Provider's (ESP) built-in database utility. Figure 3-1 shows an example of an ESP database feature set.

Figure 3-1:
Using an ESP's built-in database makes list management easy.

Courtesy of Constant Contact

If you use an external database, make sure the database you choose can easily transfer data to or synchronize data with your ESP. Doing so allows you to send e-mails without having to maintain two databases.

Whether you use a well-known database application or a customized solution, most databases can export data in one or more compatible formats. Ask your ESP for a list of supported formats and then check the export feature on your database to see whether you have a match. You can read more about what information to put in your database later in this chapter.

I don't recommend storing your data in an ESP database system alone unless the service allows you to access the data belonging to unsubscribed contacts. Just because someone unsubscribes from receiving future e-mails doesn't mean that she isn't a good customer or prospect. Phone numbers, mailing addresses, and behavioral information become even more useful when someone has unsubscribed from your e-mail list.

Collecting Contact Information

The quality of your e-mail list depends greatly on where and how you collect the information in the first place as well as where and how you store and manage the data. The best way to ensure that you collect quality information is to obtain information and permission directly from the person who owns the information in the first place — namely, your prospects and customers.

Your challenge is to provide multiple opportunities and incentives for prospects and customers to share their information as well as to manage the resulting data effectively and efficiently.

If you already have a database of prospective e-mail list subscribers or if you have a lot of contact information from various sources waiting to be entered into a single database, flip to Book IV, Chapter 2 before adding those contacts to your e-mail list. There, you find information about inheriting a list.

Deciding what information to collect

Many businesses have been bought and sold based on the strength of the contact information they possess. Quality list data stored in a useful format is a goldmine for targeting your e-mail marketing messages and converting prospects and customers into steady streams of repeat and referral sales.

The two things you need to collect are an e-mail address and permission to send someone a professional e-mail. Generally speaking, enlisting subscribers is easier if you ask for as little information as possible. You'll improve your results in the long run, however, if you make plans to gather increasing amounts of information over time — such as interests and personal information — as you interact with customers and prospects.

Table 3-1 lists several types of information you can ask prospective e-mail list subscribers for to help you build a valuable list.

Table 3-1	E-Mail List Information Collection		
Category	*Description*	*Use*	*Examples Include*
Essential Information	Information that your customers or prospects expect you to know	Use to personalize your e-mails	Preferred e-mail address First name ZIP code
Behavioral Information	Indicates how your audience is likely to act toward your e-mail content	Use privately to group your list subscribers into categories for targeted messages	Prospects Coupon users Repeat purchasers Advocates Very Important Customers (VICs)
Personal Information	Reveals important details about the person you're sending to	Use to send more relevant information	Gender Marital status Family info Preferences

You don't have to obtain all subscriber information upon the first contact with a prospect or customer. As long as you have a good permission-based e-mail address, you can ask for more information in future e-mails by

✦ Sending short, relevant e-mail surveys

✦ Asking for information in the context of your regular e-mails

✦ Using forms and links on your Web site to collect information from people who are browsing or making purchases

✦ Asking for more information through other marketing media as more trust develops in your relationship

When is essential information essential?

How your prospects and customers view essential information is likely to depend upon how personally you interact with your prospects and customers at the beginning of a relationship. People are also more comfortable sharing information when they understand how you'll use the information.

For example, an online retailer could be viewed as intruding when asking a site visitor for a physical address before he's ready to make a purchase. After the site visitor decides to check out with an item in the shopping cart, collecting a physical address becomes necessary in order to ship the item.

Getting to know your list members better

Believe it or not, most of your prospects aren't interested in everything that you decide to send in the context of an e-mail strategy. When you collect contact information and permission, consider asking your prospective subscribers to share their interests. Using interest information allows you to sort your e-mail lists into categories and send information relevant to that category.

Instead of open-ended questions, come up with some basic list categories and ask your prospective subscribers to self-identify when signing up. Here's an example of an open-ended question and an example of a category-specific question:

+ **Open-ended question:** "Why do you dine with us?"

+ **Revised category-specific question:** "Which answer best describes why you dine with us?"

  • Money-saving offers

  • New menu items

  • Wine recommendations

  • Live music and special events

Some people will tell you what interests them only when they feel that they'll get preferential treatment as a result. Try positioning interest information so that the reward is receiving the information. List ideas include

+ Priority, reserved event tickets

+ Members-only discounts

+ First-to-know product announcements

+ Early bird access to product-specific sales

Figure 3-2 shows a registration form that allows the reader to indicate a variety of interests.

Don't give your subscribers too many choices too early. Ask them to adjust their interests over time and collect information as you interact. You can also collect interest information without asking your subscribers by tracking their click behavior. For more about e-mail tracking, see Book IV, Chapter 6.

Getting personal with demographic interests

Asking for *demographic* information — such as age or income — can prove difficult because people are concerned about privacy and they generally aren't as willing to share demographic information unless they know why you need it and how you use it. To get the information you need, though, try combining demographic and interest questions as one category so that you can make inferences without being too direct. Here's a sample of possible list titles for specific types of businesses:

- Spare-no-expense travel destinations
- Singles-only event invitations
- Golfing with kids younger than 12
- Entertaining with limited space
- Gardening on a budget

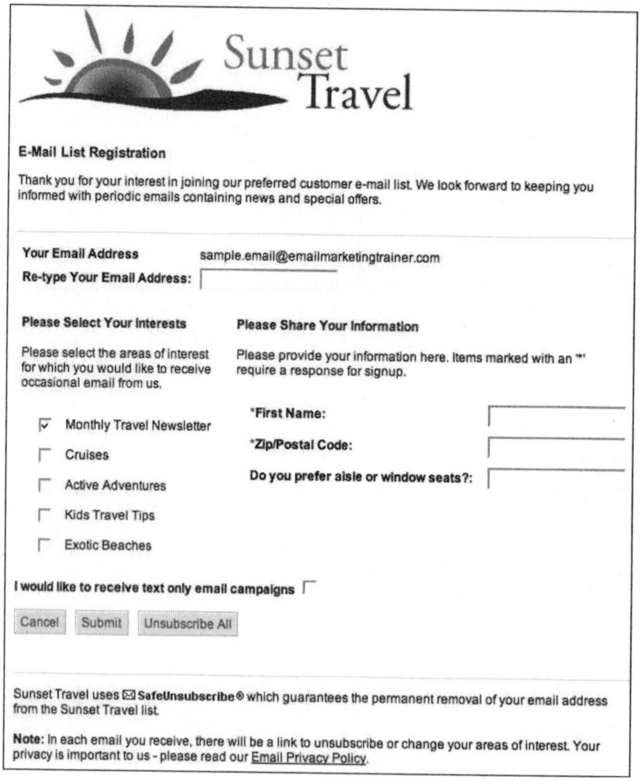

Sunset Travel

E-Mail List Registration

Thank you for your interest in joining our preferred customer e-mail list. We look forward to keeping you informed with periodic emails containing news and special offers.

Your Email Address   sample.email@emailmarketingtrainer.com
Re-type Your Email Address:

Please Select Your Interests

Please select the areas of interest for which you would like to receive occasional email from us.

- ☑ Monthly Travel Newsletter
- ☐ Cruises
- ☐ Active Adventures
- ☐ Kids Travel Tips
- ☐ Exotic Beaches

Please Share Your Information

Please provide your information here. Items marked with an '*' require a response for signup.

*First Name:

*Zip/Postal Code:

Do you prefer aisle or window seats?:

I would like to receive text only email campaigns ☐

[Cancel] [Submit] [Unsubscribe All]

Sunset Travel uses ✉ **SafeUnsubscribe**® which guarantees the permanent removal of your email address from the Sunset Travel list.

Note: In each email you receive, there will be a link to unsubscribe or change your areas of interest. Your privacy is important to us - please read our Email Privacy Policy.

Figure 3-2:
Give your subscribers a selection of interest categories.

Creating a media mailing list

Most media entities accept press releases via e-mail and will post additional e-mail addresses for communicating newsworthy information person to person. If you're planning to send press releases, be sure to keep your media list separate from your customer list so that you can restrict media personnel to newsworthy press release e-mails only. Permission, privacy, and professionalism matter just as much to the media as they do to the consumer, so kindly contact your media professionals and ask them to be on your press release list before you start sending.

Posting signup links online

Placing a signup link in every online presence possible is a great way to collect information with explicit permission. A *signup link* is a text box, button, or text that usually links to a signup form or a confirmation page that allows your subscriber to enter and submit additional information and preferences. Figure 3-3 shows three different types of signups.

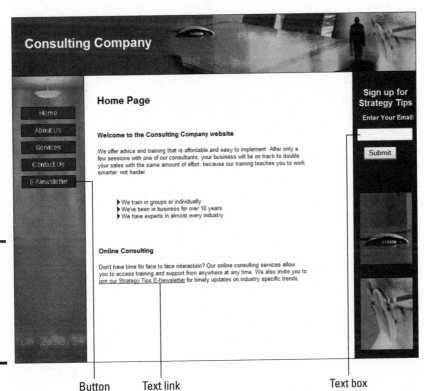

Figure 3-3:
This
Web site
contains a
text box, a
button, and
a text link.

Button   Text link   Text box

Some means of putting signup requests on a site include

✦ **Text boxes:** These allow your subscribers to enter information without clicking-through to an additional signup form. Text boxes can ask for an e-mail address, or they can contain several fields making up an entire form.

✦ **Buttons:** These are graphical representations of links that take the subscriber to a form to complete and submit. Buttons can be images with text, flashing boxes, icons, or other creative graphics.

A signup button should stand out, but don't draw too much attention away from the content of your Web site for visitors who are already subscribers.

✦ **Text links:** These are short headlines of plain text linked to a signup form. Text links are ideal if you want to add an option to subscribe within the context of other information or if you want to put a line of text in your e-mail signature.

✦ **Check boxes:** These are usually employed on multiuse forms to save additional steps. For example, someone who is making an online purchase already has to fill in her name and address, so adding a signup check box to the shipping form is a great way to gain permission to use the information for shipping the item and sending future e-mails. Figure 3-4 shows a shipping form with a simple check box within the text.

Figure 3-4:
Include an opt-in check box within online forms.

If you use check boxes, leave the box deselected (cleared) as the default setting because you don't want people who overlook the box to become disgruntled when they receive future e-mails and feel that they were added to your list without their permission.

Whether you employ forms, buttons, text links, or any other element, experiment with different placement ideas. You can place a signup link almost anywhere HTML (HyperText Markup Language) is possible. Try adding a signup link to the following locations:

✦ **On every page of your Web site.**

✦ **In your e-mail signature, as shown in Figure 3-5.**

✦ **On your blog or personal Web site.** You can read more about blogs in Book VI.

✦ **In banner ads and online advertising.** You can read more about online advertising in Book IV.

✦ **On other Web sites (with permission).**

✦ **In e-mails that your noncompeting colleagues send to their customers (with permission).**

✦ **In online directories.**

Figure 3-5:
Place a
signup link
in your
e-mail
signature.

> Regards,
>
> Peter Smith
> Owner, La Italia
>
> Free lunch when you
> Join Our E-Mail List

Collecting information in person

According to the Ten Foot Rule, whenever anyone is within ten feet of you, ask for her contact information. A warm body or a verbal conversation can equate to a captive audience for communicating the benefits of joining your e-mail list.

Always ask for permission when you collect information in person. Here are some ways to connect and collect without being intrusive:

✦ **Swap business cards.**

Ask whether that person's preferred e-mail address is on the card.

✦ **Place a guest book on the counter in your store or office.** Keep a guest book in your car so you can ask people anywhere to sign it.

✦ **Place a basket for business cards on your table at trade shows and events.** Make sure to place a sign on the basket that states your intent to send e-mails.

✦ **Train your employees to take down customer information.** Ask anyone who answers the phone at your business to ask for e-mail addresses and permission when customers and prospects call.

Collecting information through print

Adding signup information to direct mail and print advertising is a great way to help maximize your advertising dollars. You can use print to drive people to your Web site or store, you can ask them to fill out a paper form and return it, or you can ask them to send you an e-mail requesting to join the list.

Here are some ideas for using print to drive people to a signup process:

✦ **Send a postcard offering an incentive to return the card to the store (such as a free gift or an entry into a drawing) with the recipient's e-mail address filled into a space on the card.** Be sure to explain your intended usage and also ask permission in the text.

✦ **Position your signup incentive to add value to your print offer.** For example, you could print

> *Free child's haircut with subscription to our preferred customer e-mail list.*

✦ **Add your signup incentive to the back of your business cards.** For example, a discount store's business card could include

> *Our e-mail list members save 10% more! Join online, in person, or by phone.*

✦ **Purchase an intuitive domain name and place it in your print advertising to promote signups.** In the preceding example, the discount store could purchase a domain such as www.JoinMyEmailList.com, and point it to the signup form on the company Web site.

Offering Incentives to Increase Signups

Because your e-mail list is an asset — hopefully containing e-mail addresses belonging to loyal customers who spend more money as well as referral sources who love to tell others about you — offering an incentive in exchange for an e-mail subscription is really the least you can do to thank and reward your most valuable contacts.

Offering incentives for joining your e-mail list can reward your business in at least two ways:

✦ **Increased signups:** The number of people willing to share their contact information with you is likely to increase if they feel that they're getting something of value in return.

✦ **Increased loyalty:** An incentive rewards your subscribers and can cause loyalty, repeat business, and referrals to increase.

Giving subscribers immediate incentives

Some incentives, such as ongoing discounts, can be an inherent part of being on the list — and are, therefore, immediate upon the subscription. Immediate incentives abound and could include

✦ Discounts or reward points on every purchase

✦ VIP access to special events, front row seats, and so on

✦ Access to members-only information

✦ Free trials, gifts, or additional services

Giving subscribers future incentives

Some incentives aren't immediate but are instead forthcoming for members of the list. For example, imagine a clothing store that has a 48-hour sale twice per year, and only e-mail list subscribers are invited to save 50 percent if they order within the 48-hour period.

If e-mail list subscribers are the only customers invited to the event, the invitation is the incentive, but it isn't immediate because the subscriber has to wait for an invitation to take advantage of the incentive.

Not all incentives are all-liked

After you determine where and when to ask for e-mail addresses and permission, decide how to ask. For example, if you offer subscribers a link to Join the E-Mail Blast, people who don't want a blast or don't know exactly what they are likely to receive will pass on the opportunity to subscribe.

Find out what motivates your prospects and customers before determining an incentive. For example, some people will join an e-mail list in exchange for a discount on all future purchases. On the other hand, some people associate discounts with words like *cheap, discontinued, last year's model,* or *out of style.*

If your customers aren't motivated by discounts, consider employing a more creative strategy, such as a Very Important Customer (VIC) club, where e-mail subscribers are the first to know about the latest high-tech products available at a prestigious price.

Permission and privacy as incentives

Adding a privacy and permission policy to your data collection forms as well as clearly stating your intended usage up front helps put people more at ease when sharing information. Even if no one reads your privacy and permission policy, the fact that a link to privacy information appears is often reassuring.

Remember that people who share an e-mail address always do so with personal expectations in mind, and sometimes those expectations are hard to determine. As a best practice, make sure that your privacy and permission policy benefits your subscriber more than your business. Keep your privacy and permission statements short, using information in accordance with people's expectations at the time of information exchange.

Because the sale happens only twice per year, the store could send other e-mails between the sales with other offers and information. Imminent incentives are limited only by your own creativity and could include the following promotions:

+ Early shopping hours during the holidays

+ Invitations to periodic private events

+ Random rewards, such as prize drawings

 If you can't think of an incentive to offer your e-mail list subscribers or if the intrinsic value of the content in your e-mails is the incentive, use your messaging to be as clear as possible about what subscribers can expect in place of an incentive.

For example, asking potential subscribers to Sign Up for Friday Quick Tips tells them what to expect. Comparatively, asking a subscriber simply to Sign Up for Our E-Mail List is too generic and might cause prospective subscribers to hesitate — or, worse, disappoint subscribers when their expectations are not met.

Building a List with List Brokers

List brokers are marketing companies that collect and sell contact information. If you decide to build a list with the help of a list broker, recognize the significant differences between obtaining a list of physical addresses or phone numbers and obtaining e-mail addresses.

When you contact a reputable list broker to obtain e-mail addresses, the process isn't as simple as selecting demographic information and paying to receive a data file because the e-mail addresses on a brokered list must, by law, be permission based.

The process of obtaining e-mail addresses from any list broker is full of potential pitfalls because consumers get annoyed by unsolicited mail. If the broker you choose doesn't understand or adhere to permission laws and trends in the consumer landscape, sending e-mail to the list you obtain can damage your image and your future ability to send e-mail.

Because the consumer ultimately decides what *unwanted* e-mail looks like you can do everything right and end up with negative results. Furthermore, most ESPs discourage or disallow using rented lists and almost never allow using purchased lists.

As of this writing, I recommend that you obtain e-mail addresses by using the collect-where-you-connect methods that I discuss earlier in this chapter. If you still feel it's best to proceed with the services of a list broker, however, read on and proceed with caution.

Sticking to quality

Confirmed-permission lists are the only viable option for sending e-mails through list brokers. Confirmed-permission lists can be quite expensive because they are more difficult to obtain and because they contain e-mail addresses belonging to people who (at least for the moment) are interested in receiving specific types of information. You can expect to pay between 10 and 30 cents per e-mail address to send a single e-mail to a confirmed-permission list.

Confirmed-permission lists vary in quality, so remember to ask any broker some tough questions about the process used to obtain permission. The acid test of quality for a confirmed-permission list is whether the subscriber remembers opting-in and also whether members of the list expect an e-mail from you as a result.

Make sure to clarify the following information and use the responses to judge the likelihood of a memorable experience for the list subscriber:

✦ **Where and how the e-mail addresses were obtained:** Make sure that any online forms used to obtain the e-mail addresses ask for explicit permission to share the e-mail address as opposed to stating usage in a separate permission policy.

✦ **When permission was confirmed:** List subscribers might not remember opting-in if permission was confirmed at the onset of the subscription and time has passed between the initial confirmation and the e-mail you intend to send. Ask the list broker to provide the opt-in date with any sample list or count.

✦ **How interests are selected:** Some list brokers make assumptions about their subscribers' interests based on where the information is collected as opposed to brokers who actually ask subscribers to select or state their interests. For example, someone who fills out a survey and indicates that he loves live jazz music is a more valuable list subscriber than someone who purchases a jazz CD from a music Web site and fails to share whether he purchased it as a gift or was motivated by another interest. Make sure that interest information was supplied by the subscriber before paying an additional fee for an interest-based list.

Renting to own

Because quality confirmed-permission lists are so valuable, beware of supposed confirmed-permission lists for sale as a data file. Quality confirmed-permission lists are always rented out because the e-mail addresses are too valuable to sell.

As you might guess, *list rental* means that the list broker will never give you the e-mail addresses used to send your e-mail. Instead, you supply content to the list broker, and the list broker formats and sends your e-mail to the list.

Because list rental buys only one sending opportunity, I recommend that you include a signup link in your brokered e-mail. Simply asking the recipients to Buy It Now is asking for a small percentage of responses.

Including a signup link asking recipients to subscribe to your personal e-mail list can make it possible to own the information provided by people who are interested but who aren't ready to buy the moment they receive your brokered e-mail. If the list broker doesn't allow a subscription link in the e-mail, make sure that any links in your brokered e-mail lead to a *landing page* that includes your signup box, button, or link.

If you can capture sales and information by using a rented list, make sure that your e-mails continue to meet or exceed all possible professional standards to help keep subscribers interested and happy to be on the list after they've confirmed.

For more information about e-mail professionalism standards and best practices, visit the Email Sender and Provider Coalition Web site at www. espcoalition.org and click the Resources link.

Chapter 4: Constructing an Effective Marketing E-Mail

In This Chapter

✔ Creating From and Subject lines

✔ Creating and laying out e-mail content

✔ Branding your e-mails

Deciding how to design and lay out your e-mail content is possibly the most important step in executing your e-mail marketing strategy. Designing your e-mail content entails choosing a format, such as a newsletter or event invitation, that matches your message and placing your content in visually appealing arrangements.

E-mail design is important because consumers tend to scan e-mails instead of reading them in their entirety. If your e-mails aren't easy to scan, no one will pay attention long enough to grasp your message or take action.

In addition to making your e-mails easy to scan, good e-mail designs enhance your business image by giving your e-mails a consistent and professional brand identity. Brand identity makes your e-mails more inviting and recognizable to your audience and tells your audience that your e-mail comes from a trustworthy and familiar source.

In this chapter, I show you how to organize and design your e-mail content so that your audience can easily scan and understand your message. I also cover branding your e-mails to enhance your business image and identity.

 Designing your e-mails to maximize scannability and identity requires HTML. If you aren't an HTML programmer, check out any e-mail templates that your E-Mail Service Provider (ESP) provides. E-mail templates allow you to start with a familiar e-mail format, such as a newsletter or promotion, and then customize the format with your own layout and design elements before inserting your content.

Creating From and Subject Lines That Get Noticed

Creating an effective e-mail begins with placing familiar and motivating information into every e-mail header. The *header* is the portion of your e-mail that contains the following:

   ✦ A From line

   ✦ A From address

   ✦ A Subject line

   ✦ Messages and code inserted by e-mail programs

Individual e-mail programs display portions of your e-mail's header information so users can sort and prioritize their e-mails and decide whether to view and open each e-mail. Figure 4-1 shows how Yahoo! Mail displays headers. When used appropriately, your header information helps your audience to identify you as a trustworthy sender and also helps to determine whether your e-mails are worthy of immediate attention.

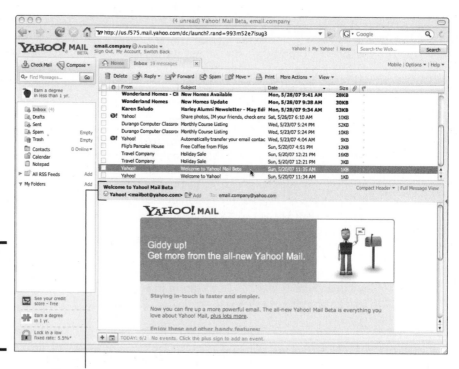

Figure 4-1:
An e-mail header displayed by Yahoo! Mail.

E-mail header

Although you can't control all the information in your e-mail headers, you can control three important pieces of information that are most useful to your audience and to the deliverability of your e-mails:

   ✦ **From line:** Your *From line* is a line of text that tells the recipient of your e-mail whom the e-mail is from. Most e-mail applications and ESPs allow you to add a line of text to the header of your e-mail to identify yourself.

✦ **From address:** Your *From address* is the e-mail address that is associated with you as the sender of the e-mail. Some e-mail programs display your From e-mail address along with your From line, but others display one or the other.

✦ **Your e-mail server's From address:** A *server address,* also known as an *Internet protocol (IP) address,* is a unique number that identifies the server you use to send your e-mail. Most Internet service providers (ISPs) look at your e-mail server address in your header to see whether your server is recognized as a sender of legitimate commercial e-mail or whether your server has been reported as sending unsolicited e-mails. If you send e-mail from your own e-mail server or if your e-mail hosting company sends your e-mails from a server that is unfamiliar to the major ISPs, you can change the servers you send your e-mails from by switching to an ESP with a good reputation. (You can find out more about working with an ESP in Book V, Chapter 1.)

In the following sections, I show you how to create an e-mail header that makes your e-mails more familiar to your audience and prompts your audience to open your e-mails.

Filling out the From line

Altering your From line helps to ensure that most e-mail programs display enough information for your audience to identify and trust you as the source of your e-mails. Changing your From line is usually a matter of typing sender information in your e-mail application's account options as shown in Figure 4-2, but ESPs allow you to create unique header information for each specific e-mail campaign during the campaign-creation process.

Ask yourself how your audience is most likely to recognize you, and then craft your From line to include that information.

Including the following information in your headers keeps your e-mails familiar to your audience:

✦ **Your name:** If you're the only employee for your business or if your audience is most likely to identify with you personally rather than with your business name, use your name.

✦ **The name of your business:** If your audience is likely to recognize the name of your business but won't necessarily know you by name, use your business name. If your business commonly uses initials instead of spelling out the entire business name, make sure that your audience recognizes the abbreviation. For example, if your business is Acme Balloon Consultants, Inc., don't place ABCI in your From line unless you are sure your audience can identify you by your initials.

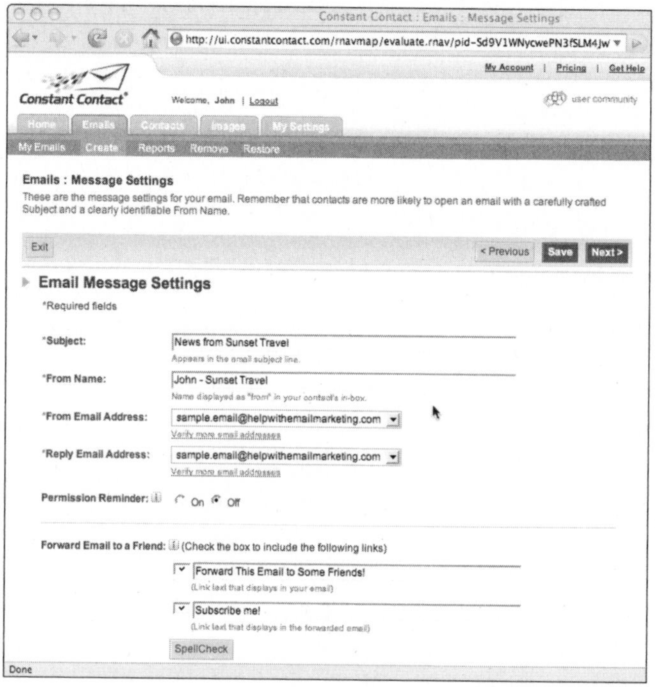

Figure 4-2:
This ESP interface allows you to create header information.

Courtesy of Constant Contact

✦ **Your name and your business name:** If you're a personal representative of a larger well-known business or franchise, use your name along with your business name. For example, you might use your first name followed by your business name, as in

```
Steve - Sunset Travel
```

✦ **Representative name:** If you have multiple representatives in your business whom your customers and prospects know by name, divide your e-mail addresses into separate lists by representative and use the most familiar representative's name for each e-mail list.

✦ **Your location:** If you're part of a large franchise or have multiple locations and your audience isn't likely to recognize the names of individuals within your organization, use geography. For example, you might use your business name followed by the city, as in

```
Sunset Travel, Denver
```

✦ **Your Web site domain:** If your audience is more likely to recognize your Web site domain name over your name or your business name, use your Web site domain name. If your domain uses an abbreviation, initials, or an alternate spelling of your entire business name, you might still want to use your business' full name in the From line for brand clarity.

Does this header look familiar?

E-mail applications usually display only the portions of the e-mail header that are useful to their users. An entire e-mail header actually contains code and data that help e-mail applications to identify, sort, and deliver e-mails. E-mail programs also use the entire header to filter and block certain senders, so using an ESP with a good reputation and close relationships with ISPs and e-mail programs ensures that your e-mail header is familiar and identified as friendly to the programs that consumers use to read their e-mail.

Here's an example of an entire e-mail header. The portions that most e-mail applications display to their users by default are in bold print:

```
Microsoft Mail Internet Headers Version 2.0
Received: from edgemail1.roving.com ([192.168.254.99]) by svrmail.roving.com with
         Microsoft SMTPSVC(6.0.3790.1830);
Thu, 24 May 2007 15:07:10 -0400
Received: from ccm06.constantcontact.com (ccm06.constantcontact.com [63.251.135.98])
         by edgemail1.roving.com (Postfix) with ESMTP id 968167C0001 for <test-email@
         constantcontact.com>; Thu, 24 May 2007 15:07:13 -0400 (EDT) Received: from
         ws019 (unknown [10.250.0.101]) by ccm06.constantcontact.com (Postfix) with
         ESMTP id 5FD3211AEC0 for <test-email@constantcontact.com>; Thu, 24 May 2007
         15:07:13 -0400 (EDT)
Message-ID: <2002007742.1180033638314.JavaMail.prodadmin@ws019>
Date: Thu, 24 May 2007 15:07:18 -0400 (EDT)
From: Zak <zb.baron@constantcontact.com>
Reply-To: zb.baron@constantcontact.com
To: test_email@constantcontact.com
Subject: FW: Volunteers Needed For Sat. June 2nd
Mime-Version: 1.0
Content-Type: multipart/alternative;boundary="
----
=_Part_381273_1572255422.1180033638314"
X-Mailer: Roving Constant Contact 0 (http://www.constantcontact.com)
X-Lumos-SenderID: 1101539495996
Return-Path: ccbounce+zbbaron=constantcontact.com@in.constantcontact.com
X-OriginalArrivalTime: 24 May 2007 19:07:10.0436 (UTC) FILETIME=[BAE54A40:01C79E36]
------
=_Part_381273_1572255422.1180033638314
Content-Type: text/plain; charset=iso-8859-1
Content-Transfer-Encoding: 7bit
------
=_Part_381273_1572255422.1180033638314
Content-Type: text/html; charset=iso-8859-1
Content-Transfer-Encoding: quoted-printable
------
=_Part_381273_1572255422.1180033638314--
```

✦ **Your e-mail address:** In addition to making sure your `From` line identifies you and your business, you can create an e-mail address that serves as your `From` address. I recommend creating an e-mail address that identifies who you are and what you're sending. Here are some examples:

- *If you're sending a newsletter and your audience recognizes your personal name:* Send your e-mail newsletter by using

    `newsletter@`*yourname*`.com`

- *If you're sending coupons and your audience recognizes your business name:* Send your e-mail coupons by using

    `coupons@`*yourbusinessname*`.com`

- *If you're sending an event invitation and your audience recognizes a personal representative as well as your business name:* Send your e-mail invitation by using

    `event_invitation@`*repname.businessname*`.com`

- *If you're sending an announcement and your audience recognizes your Web site's domain name:* Send your e-mail announcement by using

    `announcement@`*yourdomain*`.com`

Current CAN-SPAM laws prohibit you from misrepresenting your `From` line and your `From` address. Make sure the information in your `From` line honestly represents you and your business and also make sure you send your e-mails from a real, working e-mail address. For example, if you're a member of the local Chamber of Commerce, don't send the other Chamber members e-mail using the name of the Chamber in the `From` line. Reputable ESPs require you to send e-mails from a verified e-mail address to ensure your e-mails are CAN-SPAM compliant. For more information about professional standards and the CAN-SPAM laws, see Book V, Chapter 2.

Writing a Subject line

Your e-mail *Subject line* is a line of text that gives your audience a hint at the content in your e-mail. The most effective `Subject` lines are those that prompt your audience to open your e-mails to look for specific information.

Consistently coming up with good `Subject` lines is tough because most e-mail programs display only the first 30 to 50 characters, which gives you a limited amount of text to get your point across. Figure 4-3 shows how Microsoft Outlook displays `Subject` lines.

Save the information highlighting the benefits of your products or services for the body of your e-mail and use your `Subject` line to tell your audience why to open your e-mail immediately. Stating the immediate benefit of opening the e-mail creates a sense of urgency and tells your audience that your e-mail is important.

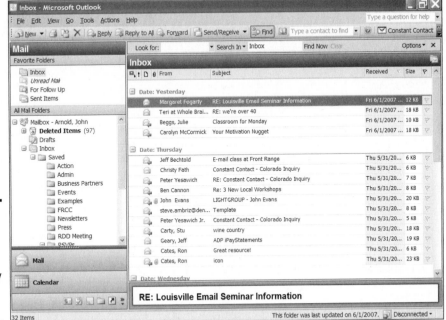

Figure 4-3:
E-mail
`Subject`
lines
displayed by
Microsoft
Outlook.

Creating a sense of urgency with your text helps to increase viewer opens, but urgency can easily wear off if your `Subject` lines make urgent statements without hinting at the content in your e-mail. For example, `Subject` lines such as `Only 10 left` or `Sale ends soon` don't communicate the main subject of your e-mail — and are urgent only when they are used infrequently.

The following examples show how you can create urgency while still hinting at the main idea of the message. In each example pair, the first is a `Subject` line without urgency, and its mate is a revised `Subject` line with added urgency.

Not so good: What you need to know about Denver real estate

Better: What you need to know *now* about Denver real estate

Not so good: Flower sale

Better: Flower sale – early entry information

Not so good: Seminar invitation

Better: Last chance to register

Not so good: Tips for remodeling your kitchen

Better: Tomorrow's tips for remodeling your kitchen today

Baiting your audience with your Subject lines

I'm a lousy fisherman, but I like to go catch-and-release fishing now and then, so I decided to subscribe to a fishing tips e-mail newsletter written by the owner of a local fly fishing shop. One of the e-mail issues I received read, See huge trout caught in Colorado in the Subject line. I opened the e-mail. The picture of the trout was right at the top of the preview pane, but it was too small to see. The caption under the picture read, Click to see full picture, so I clicked and was immediately taken to the shop owner's fly fishing Web site where there was a larger picture of a father and his very happy son holding a

huge trout. Right next to the picture was a picture of the fly that was used to catch the trout and the shop owner's offer to tie several of the flies and take eight lucky people on his next guided fishing trip to the exact same place where the father and son team had caught the huge fish. The main point of the shop owner's e-mail was communicated so well that by the time I called, the guided tour was already full. The rest of the e-mail newsletter contained the shop owner's valuable fishing tips and his guided trip schedule in order to deepen his relationship with anyone who wasn't ready or able to purchase a guided trip immediately.

Test your Subject lines by sending the same e-mail with different Subject lines to a small sample of your list to determine whether a Subject line is going to result in the most opens. For example, if you have a list of 1,000 subscribers, send your e-mail to 100 list subscribers with one Subject line and to a different 100 list subscribers with another Subject line. Wait a day or two, and then send your e-mail to the remaining 800 with the Subject line that received the highest number of opens.

You might want to look at your junk folder occasionally to see what the spammers are up to so you don't inadvertently copy some of their Subject line techniques. Here are some Subject line mistakes to avoid:

✦ Excessive punctuation, such as lots of exclamation points or question marks

✦ Symbols, such as dollar signs and asterisks

✦ Words with all capital letters (usually perceived as yelling)

✦ Your recipient's first name in the Subject line

✦ Using RE: unless the e-mail is really a response to a previous e-mail Subject line

✦ A blank Subject line

✦ Vague Subject lines that attempt to trick the reader into opening your e-mail. For example

- Hey you

- Check this out

- RE:
- Personal information
- Hi!

The current CAN-SPAM laws prohibit Subject lines that are "likely to mislead a recipient, acting reasonably under the circumstances, about a material fact regarding the contents or subject matter of the message," so make sure your Subject lines clearly and honestly represent the content in every e-mail. For more information about Subject line compliance, see Book V, Chapter 2.

Branding Your E-Mails to Enhance Your Image

Branding is the use of graphic design elements to give your business a consistent and unique identity while forming a mental image of your business' personality. Examples include

- ✦ Graphics and logos unique to your business
- ✦ Text and fonts that differentiate your business
- ✦ Colors used consistently to give your business an identity

Branding your e-mails helps your audience to immediately recognize and differentiate your e-mails from the unfamiliar e-mails they receive. Keeping your e-mail branding consistent over time allows your audience to become familiar with you and your e-mails as they receive multiple e-mails from you.

The following sections show how you can brand your e-mails to match your identity and the expectations of your audience.

Branding your e-mails with colors and design elements requires using HTML. If you don't know HTML, look to your ESP. Most ESPs allow you to customize your e-mail templates with your branding elements. If you aren't using an ESP to send your e-mails, a Web designer can help you create a custom look and feel for your e-mail templates.

Matching your e-mails to your brand

All your business communications should contain consistent branding elements, and your e-mails are no exception. Matching every e-mail to your brand gives your audience confidence and makes your business more memorable every time your audience clicks to access your Web site or walks into your store and sees the same branding elements.

You can design your e-mails to match your brand in the following ways:

- ✦ **Include your logo in your e-mails, as shown in Figure 4-4.**

Position your logo in the upper left or top center of your e-mail where readers are most likely to see it.

Using a company logo along with identifiable design elements brands your e-mail and reinforces your company's image.

Figure 4-4:
Use a
company
logo.

Courtesy of Avalon Photography

+ **Use the colors from your logo in your e-mails.**

  If your logo has multiple colors, pull the colors from your logo and use them for the borders, backgrounds, and fonts in your e-mails. If your logo uses only one color, you can use a graphic design program to create a palette of colors that work well with the color in your logo. You can find a list of helpful color-matching tools at www.EmailTrainer.com.

+ **Use the colors from your Web site in your e-mails.**

  When readers click from your e-mail to your Web site, they might hesitate if your Web site looks different from your e-mail. When you design your e-mails, use the colors in your Web site in a similar fashion. For example, if your Web site uses a gray background with black text, use the same colors for those elements in your e-mails.

+ **Match your Web site offers with your e-mail offers.**

  If your e-mail includes an offer with a specific design, make sure that your Web site uses the same design elements in the offer if you're directing people to your Web site to complete a purchase or to read more information about the offer in your e-mail.

+ **Match your print communications to your e-mails.** If you're sending direct mail or printing ads to follow up or reinforce your e-mail messages, make sure that your print communications match your e-mails as well as the rest of your communications.

✦ **Use fonts that match your brand in your e-mails.**

Consistent fonts add to the overall look and feel of your e-mails as well as adding emotion behind the text. Keep your fonts consistent in all your communications and use the same fonts for similar visual anchors. For example, if your e-mail contains three articles with three headlines in one column, use the same font for each headline in the column. The benefits of font consistency are negated if you use too many different kinds of fonts in one e-mail. Stick with two or three different fonts in each e-mail to avoid heaping visual distractions on your audience.

✦ **Make sure your e-mails reflect your business' personality.**

Just as you want design elements that match your brand, your writing should match your business's personality, too. Show your e-mails to a few trustworthy friends or advisors and ask them to tell you whether your writing style is a good match for your image. If you aren't a good writer, consider using a copywriter to help you maintain your image using the text of your articles and offers. Tell your copywriter whether you want the text in your e-mail to make your business seem

- Serious or humorous
- Professional or casual
- Formal or friendly
- Exclusive or universal
- Urgent or customary
- Insistent or politely persuasive

Maintaining brand consistency with multiple e-mail formats

If you use multiple formats and each format doesn't match your brand with enough consistency, your audience might not recognize every e-mail you send. At the same time, if your audience can't tell the difference between your formats, you lose your ability to effectively communicate the appropriate amount of urgency in each of your e-mail formats. For example, if your readers recognize your e-mail as a lengthy newsletter format, they might be inclined to read it later. If your audience recognizes your e-mail as an event invitation, they might be inclined to take immediate action by responding with a reservation.

The best way to brand multiple e-mail formats is to match your brand identity in each format while keeping your e-mails just different enough for people to know that each e-mail is unique. Figures 4-5 and 4-6 show two distinct e-mail formats with similar brand identity.

Making the difference just noticeable

If you look at a 1950s Coca-Cola bottle and a Coca-Cola bottle produced today, you'll notice a significant difference. Big companies (such as Coca-Cola) continuously research their branding elements to keep them up to date with consumer preferences. Still, Coca-Cola wouldn't dare to change the branding on its cans and bottles too rapidly, or consumers might have a hard time identifying them on the store shelves. Marketing experts use a concept known as *the just-noticeable difference* to change brand identities over time: That is, you change the brand just enough to be noticeable but not enough to be unrecognizable. If you need to change your e-mail branding elements, such as when your Web site gets a new face lift, make sure you change your branding elements slowly over time so your audience still recognizes your e-mails while the changes are taking place.

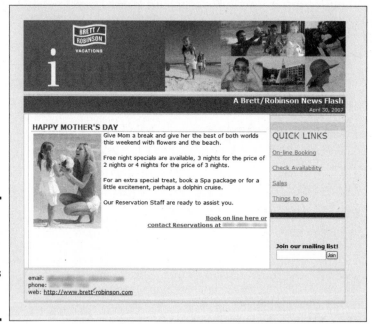

Figure 4-5:
This e-mail is branded to identify the business and offer a news flash.

Courtesy of Brett/Robinson Vacations

Here are some ways you can brand multiple e-mail formats with consistency while giving each format a unique identity:

✦ Use the same top-bar image with slightly different colors for each format.

✦ Change the colors in your logo slightly for each format.

✦ Use slightly different colors for backgrounds and borders in each format.

✦ Use graphical text to create a unique title for the top of each format.

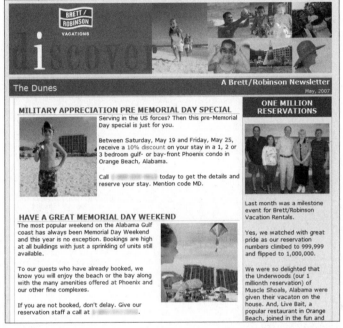

Figure 4-6:
This e-mail is branded to identify the business and reinforce its newsletter content.

Courtesy of Brett/Robinson Vacations

The ABCs of E-Mail Layout

Consumers tend to focus their attention on your e-mail content by using the layout in the e-mail as a guide for their eyes. E-mail marketing experts often use e-mail heat maps to determine which areas of an e-mail are likely to draw the most attention. An e-mail *heat map* is an image generated by a special device that tracks eye movement when someone looks at an e-mail. You can see several examples of e-mail heat maps at www.eyetools.com.

Heat maps use different colors and shading to illustrate which parts of an e-mail draw the most attention. Data gathered by using heat maps and testing various e-mail designs helps to shed light on the e-mail designs and layouts that are most likely to get your content noticed.

A good way to visualize your content positioning is to mentally divide each of your e-mail templates into quadrants and then position your visual anchors and related content according to the order in which consumers tend to focus their attention on each quadrant.

Figure 4-7 shows how the majority of consumers scan e-mails. Most consumers begin reading in the upper left and then continue in one of two directions, depending on the strength of the visual anchors in the adjacent quadrants: down the page (the figure on the right) or across the page (the figure on the left).

Figure 4-7: Most consumers focus their attention on the upper left of an e-mail and then scan across down the page (right) or across the page (left).

Courtesy of Constant Contact

Because the upper left tends to get the most attention from consumers, position your most important content there in your e-mail.

And although you don't have to divide your content into quadrants visually, you should emphasize important content in the upper left. Here are some examples of positioning e-mail content in the upper-left quadrant:

✦ **Display your brand.**

Your audience is more likely to read your e-mail when they recognize the source of the e-mail. Make sure that your business name, logo, and other brand-identifying design elements appear somewhere in the upper left.

✦ **Begin your e-mail message with a main headline.**

A main headline doesn't have to reside completely within the upper left, but main headlines get more attention if they begin there.

✦ **Include your e-mail's main call to action.**

A *call to action* is a statement that asks your audience to do something specific, such as purchasing a specific item, clicking a link, or dialing a phone number. If your e-mail contains valuable offers, make sure your main offer is contained — or at least referenced — in the upper left. If your e-mail's main intent is to get your audience to read a specific section of your e-mail that contains your main call to action along with supporting information, make sure you use the upper left to prompt your audience where to look.

✦ **Place the strongest visual anchors.**

Visual anchors — such as images, links, headlines, icons, bullets, and graphics — can reinforce your audience's perception of your most important content. Strong visual anchors used in the upper left help minimize how long your audience spends trying to figure out what content is important enough to read. Figure 4-8 shows how an arrow, as a visual anchor, reinforces information.

Figure 4-8:
Use an
arrow as
a visual
anchor to
emphasize
content.

Thank you for placing an order with us!
We appreciate your business.

Other items you'd enjoy...

Please contact us with
any questions at the
email address or phone
number listed below.

Promotion Name
Try phrases like: dramatic savings,
clearance, overstocked, reduced rates, buy 1
get 1 free, treat yourself, you deserve it, and
don't miss out. Add a "Learn More" link at the
bottom of your promotion to drive traffic to
your website.

YOUR IMAGE HERE
Right-click to change
in edit mode

150 x 150
pixels

Courtesy of Constant Contact

✦ **Limit the size of images.**

Images draw attention, but if you include an image in your e-mail that takes up most of the upper-left quadrant, your audience might miss the text associated with that image. If you decide to use an image in the upper left, use one small enough to allow the inclusion of the first few words of a text headline. You can read more details about images later in this chapter.

✦ **Show your audience where to look next.**

If your e-mail includes important content in different quadrants, use navigation links and directions in the upper left to help your audience navigate the e-mail. For example, the e-mail's upper-left quadrant might contain a table of contents with navigation links. You can read more about navigation links later in this chapter.

Using columns to organize your content

Positioning visual anchors in quadrants is a fine way to attract attention to multiple groups of content, but unless you organize your visual anchors and related content into patterns, your audience won't be able to effectively prioritize the additional content that your visual anchors are trying to emphasize.

Using columns to organize your visual anchors and related content allows your audience to locate different groups of content as they scan through your e-mail. Most ESPs provide e-mail templates with lots of column-based layouts, and Web designers and some ESPs can assist you in creating more customized column-based layouts.

Including Images in Your E-Mails

Images can enhance the look and feel of your e-mails and help to reinforce the messages contained in the body of your e-mails. Images are strong visual anchors that help to communicate your main message and divide your text into more-easily scanned sections.

Proper image positioning makes your e-mail appear inviting and easy to read. Arbitrarily positioned images are cumbersome to scan and can cause your e-mail to appear cluttered.

Placing images in your e-mails requires more than an eye for design, however, because images and e-mail browsers don't always play well together. Embedding images into the body of your e-mail can cause deliverability issues and make your e-mail slow to download, so you need to employ a few extra steps to ensure your images are ready to include.

The next sections cover what kinds of images you can include in your e-mails and how to effectively place them in your e-mails.

Choosing a file format for your images

Images are graphic files that graphics programs can read and display on a computer screen. Whether you obtain your images with a digital camera or buy them online from a provider of royalty-free stock photography, make sure that your images are formatted for use in e-mail:

✦ **Use a file format that e-mail browsers can read.** An *image file format* is the type of compression used on an image in order to limit the amount of data required to store the image on a computer. *Compression* changes the amount of space the image takes up when stored on a computer, and image compression causes the graphics to display differently (especially when you reduce or enlarge the dimensions of the image). The three best file formats to use in e-mail browsers are

  • *JPG or JPEG (Joint Pictures Expert Group):* This format is a standard for Internet and e-mail images, and works well for most images.

  • *GIF (Graphic Interchange Format):* This format is best for images with only a few colors.

  • *PNG (Portable Network Graphics):* This format is similar to GIF compression but has the ability to display colors more effectively.

If your image isn't already in one of these three formats, use a graphic design application or image editor to save the image as a JPG file.

✦ **Check your file size.** The *file size* of your image refers to the amount of data your image contains measured in kilobytes (K). Images should be less than 50K to download quickly enough for most e-mail users. If an image you want to use in your e-mail is more than 50K, you can change the file size in a graphic design or image editing application.

  • *Reduce the dimensions of the image.* Smaller images contain less data.

  • *Reduce the image resolution to 72 dpi. Image resolution,* also known as dots per inch (dpi) or pixels per inch (ppi), refers to how many dots (or pixels) are in each inch of your image. The more dots per inch, the more detail your image is capable of displaying. More dots require more data, however, so images with higher resolutions download and display more slowly than images with lower resolutions.

72 dpi has enough resolution to appear properly on a computer screen, but images printed at 72 dpi are likely to appear fuzzy. If your audience is likely to print your e-mail and it's important that your images are printed with more definition, link your audience to a PDF version of your e-mail containing print-quality images that are 300 dpi or higher.

Don't embed: Referencing your images

Never embed images in your e-mail as a file or attached to your e-mail because embedded and attached images usually cause a higher percentage of your e-mails to be filtered into junk folders.

Instead of embedding or attaching images, use image references that point to images stored in a public folder on your Web site server. An *image reference* is a line of HTML that tells your computer to display an image that's located in a folder on a remote server. Here's an example:

```
<img src="http://www.yourwebsite.com/public/imagefolder/imagename.jpg">
```

If you aren't comfortable using HTML to create image references in your e-mails, you can use an ESP to help you reference images. If you can't store images on your Web site server or if you don't have a Web site, you can use an ESP with an image-hosting feature. That way, you can store your images on that server and automatically create image references to insert the images you upload to your e-mails. Figure 4-9 shows an ESP interface that allows you to reference images in a folder on your server or images that you upload to the ESP's server.

Figure 4-9:
Use an ESP
to insert
image tags
in HTML
to avoid
attaching
images to
your e-mail.

Courtesy of Constant Contact

Whether you code your own image references or use an ESP, you need to know the URL of the image you're referencing.

To find the URL of an image that's on your Web site, follow these steps:

1. **Open your Web browser.**

2. **Navigate to the page that contains the image you want to include in your e-mail.**

3. **View the image properties by right-clicking (Windows) and choosing Properties; or by Control-clicking (Mac) the image and choosing Copy Image Location.**

Some browsers allow you to view the URL by selecting image properties, and other browsers require you to open the image in a new browser window to view the image URL.

With Internet Explorer, you can find the URL in the Address (URL) field of the Properties dialog box. With Firefox, you can copy the URL directly or view the image by itself and copy the URL that appears in your navigation bar.

If your image isn't already on your Web site, follow these steps to find the location of your image file:

1. **Upload the image file to a public folder on your server.**

2. **Go to your Web site server's file manager and find the folder that contains your image.**

   The image URL is the folder location followed by the image filename. For example

   ```
   http://www.yourdomain.com/public/site/image_files/filename.jpg
   ```

When you reference image locations, you must have permission to use the images if you don't own them, even if they're publicly accessible on a Web site. Also keep in mind that you can't determine the location of background images and images that appear in Flash Web sites by clicking the image. You have to find the image location by using the folder address on your server or by finding the reference in your Web site's HTML.

Including Text in Your E-Mails

Text is mandatory in e-mail marketing messages. Plain, text-only e-mails significantly underperform compared with e-mails that include HTML design elements along with the text in the message, so applying design elements to your text is a balance. Too much plain text can make your e-mails appear unapproachable and difficult to read. Comparatively, too many design elements can cause distractions and make your messages more difficult to understand.

When used correctly, different fonts and text styles can create moods in your e-mails and change the tone of the words that you use:

✦ *Headlines* can help to entice your audience to read longer sections of text or take action on your e-mail content.

✦ *Paragraphs of text* can give your audience important information, help them form opinions, and give them compelling reasons to purchase your products or services.

✦ *Links* in your e-mails let your audience click keywords and phrases to take action on the content of your e-mails without having to use another medium. (I talk about using links in the upcoming section, "Including Links in Your E-Mails.")

It's important to choose fitting text elements for your e-mails to enrich your e-mail's meaning as well as ensure that your text communicates the main idea of your e-mail quickly and effectively. To accomplish greater success with text, apply deliberate use of fonts and styles instead of opting for plain text.

Fonts are graphical representations of letters in the alphabet. Fonts are useful for

✦ Making your words more legible

✦ Giving your words more emphasis

✦ Suggesting moods and emotions to reinforce your words

✦ Branding your e-mails and making your e-mails look more professional

In addition to applying different fonts to your text, you can also alter your fonts by applying different style elements to the font. This section includes tips for choosing fonts and applying stylistic changes to them so that the appearance of your text matches your e-mail's theme and message.

Because most e-mail programs use HTML to display e-mails to their users, you need to apply fonts and styles to your e-mail text by using the HTML code that tells the e-mail program which fonts and styles to apply when it displays your text to the user. Here's an example of a line of HTML code that defines various font elements for a headline:

```
<font color="#FFFFFF" face="Arial, Verdana, Helvetica, sans-
    serif" size="5" style="FONT-FAMILY: Arial, Verdana,
    Helvetica, sans-serif;FONT-SIZE:18pt; FONT-WEIGHT:bold;
    COLOR:#FFFFFF;">
    Headline Here</font>
```

A good rule is to make your headlines 2 to 4 point (pt) sizes larger than your paragraph text. For example, if your paragraph text is 12pt, use 14pt or 16pt for your headline.

To avoid the HTML hassle, most ESPs allow you to specify fonts and apply style elements to your fonts by using font tools in a special user interface. Figure 4-10 shows a font and style toolbar in an ESP interface.

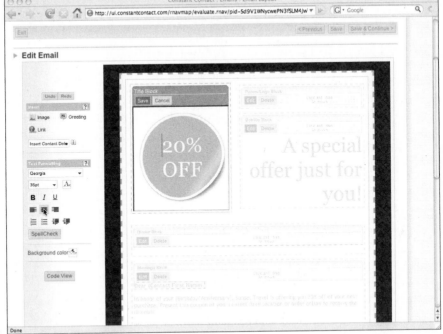

Figure 4-10:
Use an ESP user interface to apply font and style changes to your e-mail text.

Courtesy of Constant Contact

Fonts specified in HTML tell the user's computer to display the applicable text, using the specified font. Any font specified in the HTML code has to be available on the user's computer to display properly.

Because most people don't go to the trouble of installing the latest fonts on their computers, formatting e-mail text by using fonts that are common to the majority of computers helps ensure that your text looks the same on your audience's computers as it does on yours. Figure 4-11 shows a list of fonts that are commonly available on default operating systems.

If you want to use text in a font or style that's not commonly available or one that's not possible with HTML, you can use graphic design software to create an image of the text you want to use. Use this option sparingly, however, because images take longer to download than text, and e-mail programs don't usually display the images in an e-mail until the recipient enables them. You can read more about image blocking in Chapter 6 of this minibook.

Making your e-mails accessible

People with disabilities and physical challenges need to be able to read your e-mail content and respond accordingly. Some disabled and aging e-mail users can read and respond to your e-mails only if you design your e-mails with their challenges in mind. And some disabled people, such as those with visual impairments, have special tools that verbally read your e-mail or otherwise help them comprehend e-mail and other online content. Some e-mail designs make such tools cumbersome to use, so design your e-mails accordingly — or provide two versions of your e-mail.

Visual impairments aren't the only disabilities that might make your e-mail difficult to understand. Here are some tips for making your e-mails accessible to many types of disabled and aging subscribers. If you use an ESP to design your e-mails, talk to those folks about accessibility requirements. You can read more about making all your Internet marketing efforts accessible at www. w3.org/WAI.

✔ **Provide a link to a text-only version of your e-mail** to allow text-reading devices to easily read your content to people with visual impairments. Make sure your e-mail begins with the link and a summary of your e-mail content so that visually impaired subscribers can tell whether your e-mail is worth listening to in its entirety. Also make sure your text version adequately describes any video, images, charts, and graphics in your e-mail.

✔ **Use image descriptions,** also known as *alt text,* when including images in your e-mail. Reading devices read alt text so that a visually impaired person knows what images are in the e-mail. This is especially important when you use images that contain text.

✔ **Use fonts and point sizes that are easy to read** so that people with diminished vision can interpret them. Make sure the text version of your e-mail avoids using absolute font sizes in your HTML; otherwise, your fonts can't be enlarged (not good).

✔ **Use text and background colors with sufficient contrast** so that words are easy to read.

✔ **Provide a link to a text-only transcript** of any audio used in your e-mail.

✔ **Make sure any forms you ask your subscribers to fill in** can be tabbed through in a logical order. Along the same line, design your forms to minimize the number of keystrokes necessary to complete the form.

✔ **Keep your e-mail designs short, concise, and easy to scan.** Avoid distracting design elements — such as blinking text, flashing images, or audio and video streams — that can't easily be turned off.

Including too many different fonts in a single e-mail can make your text look disorderly and cluttered, so make sure you limit your e-mail's text to only two or three different fonts. Using one font for all headlines and another font for all body text is an acceptable standard.

Figure 4-11:
Use
commonly
available
fonts to
ensure that
text displays
properly
on your
audience's
computers.

Arial

Arial Narrow

Comic Sans MS

Courier New

Garamond

Georgia

Impact

Lucida Console

System

Tahoma

Times New Roman

Trebuchet MS

Verdana

Including Links in Your E-Mails

Your e-mail isn't going to sell anything to your audience if you don't make it easy for your audience to take action on your message. Placing links in the body of your e-mails gives your audience easy ways to

✦ Visit specific pages on your Web site.

✦ Download files and additional information.

✦ Order your products or services by clicking through from your e-mail to an online shopping cart.

✦ Jump to specific sections of your e-mail by clicking instead of scrolling.

In the following sections, I explain how to include the most effective links in your e-mails so you can drive your audience toward actions that benefit your business objectives.

E-mail links can be tracked back to the clicker when you use an ESP. You can read more about link tracking in Book V, Chapter 6.

Using text links

Text links are clickable words or phrases that result in certain actions when clicked. Links use HTML to tell the computer what to do when someone clicks the link, so your e-mail links need to contain HTML to work in e-mail programs.

If you're using raw HTML to create links for your e-mails, a simple link to a Web site looks like this:

```
<a href="http://www.yourwebsite.com">Link Text Here</a>
```

Most ESPs and e-mail applications allow you to add a link without typing in the HTML code by highlighting the text you want to turn into a link and then typing the address of the Web page or file you want the text to link to. Figure 4-12 shows an ESP interface that allows you to create text links in your e-mails.

Figure 4-12: This ESP interface allows you to create links using any text.

Courtesy of Constant Contact

Most e-mail programs and ESPs allow you to enter a URL into a user interface, and the program then takes care of adding the HTML behind the scenes to turn your text into a link that points to the URL you entered. Follow these steps for finding a URL for the most common types of linked content.

To link to a landing page on your Web site (HTML Web sites only), follow these steps:

1. **Open your Web browser and navigate to the page where you want your link to point.**

2. **Highlight all the text in your browser's address bar (including the `http` part).**

3. **Copy the text:**

   • *Windows:* Right-click the selected text and choose Copy.

   • *Mac:* Control-click the selected text and choose Copy.

Linking to an e-mail address

Instead of linking text to another Web page, you might want to link text to an e-mail address. This type of link opens a new message in your visitor's default e-mail program, often with the To text box filled with an e-mail address you designate in the link. To link to an e-mail address, type **mailto:**, followed by the e-mail address you want to link to into your e-mail program's link-creation user interface. For example

```
mailto:email.company@test-
    email.com
```

If you want an e-mail link to pre-fill the Subject line or From line, or if you want to use an e-mail link to include several e-mail addresses, you can find a free, e-mail link

encoder that automatically generates the code you need at the following Web site:

```
http://email.about.com/
    library/misc/blmailto_
    encoder.htm
```

E-mail links tell the user's computer to open the default e-mail program on the user's computer. If the person clicking your link uses a Web-based e-mail program (such as AOL or Yahoo!) instead of a desktop e-mail program (such as Outlook or Outlook Express), the link won't allow them to use their Web-based application. To eliminate confusion for Web-based e-mail users, spell out the e-mail address in your link so that folks can type it in their preferred e-mail program when necessary.

---

4. **Paste the URL into your e-mail program's link-creation user interface.**

   • *Windows:* Right-click and choose Paste.

   • *Mac:* Control-click and choose Paste.

One of the most important things about text links is choosing the appropriate words to name the link. Although you can't employ every tip for every link you name, you can apply these tips to links throughout your e-mails as appropriate:

✦ **Name your links intuitively.**

A good rule for naming links is "what you click is what you get." In other words, name your links to tell your audience exactly what is going to happen when they click the link. Here are some examples:

• *If your link downloads a file:* Include the file type in parentheses. For example, a link that downloads a portable document format file could read

```
More Info On This Product(PDF)
```

• *If your link takes the reader to a Web site where he might have to search or scroll to view information:* Include the directions in your link. For example, if a link takes your audience to your blog, your link could read

```
Details on my blog (scroll to article 5)
```

- *If your link requires additional clicks or actions after the initial click:* Name your link describing the first step in the process. For example, a link that reads `Donate Your Car` isn't as clear as a link that reads

  `Read 3 steps to donating your car`

- *If you're linking to an e-mail address:* Include the e-mail address in the link because e-mail links open the resident e-mail program on the user's computer, and users who use a Web-based e-mail program won't be able to use the link. (See the nearby sidebar for more on linking to an e-mail address.) For example, instead of using a link that reads `E-Mail Us`, your link should read

  `E-mail us at company@yourdomain.com`

✦ **Name links using the text in your articles and headlines.**

Link names, such as `Click Here`, should be avoided because links attract attention and your audience won't be able to identify interesting text links if you give them generic names. Figure 4-13 shows an example of text links within the body of a paragraph.

Figure 4-13: This e-mail uses text links in the body text.

Membership Renewal Offer - A $300 value!
Free Networking for a Year!

Renew your chamber membership this month and you'll receive free admission to every networking event for an entire year.

If your membership isn't up for renewal, you can still take advantage of this special offer with our new 3-year membership. Read More

✦ **Name links to give you information about the clicker.**

Because e-mail links are trackable back to the clicker, naming your links in ways that give you insight into the motivations of the clicker makes your click reports more meaningful. For example, if your e-mail newsletter contains an article that includes three of the best places to golf with kids and you provide your readers with a link to view more information about family golf vacations, getting a group of people to click a `Read More` link isn't as valuable as getting a group of people to click a link that reads

  `Are your kids under 12? Read about best places to golf for
  younger kids.`

✦ **Name links by describing the immediate benefits of clicking the link.**

You're likely to get more clicks when you give your audience good reasons to click. Instead of naming links by highlighting the mechanics of the click — as in, `Go to Our Web Site` — include the benefits in the link. For example, try

  `Shop on our website and receive an additional 10% off
  and free shipping.`

Text only, please

Text-only e-mails are a reality for people who check their e-mail on portable devices. Some people also install e-mail filters and firewalls on their computers to convert HTML e-mails into text to protect their systems from malicious programs and files. When a device or filter converts an HTML e-mail into text, the e-mail can become garbled and confusing for the recipient. Some conversions result in displaying the entire HTML code; and others show the text along with long lines of code for links, images, and other design elements.

Because sending text-only e-mails to everyone eliminates links and tracking altogether, you might want to use an ESP that allows your e-mail list subscribers to choose a preformatted, text-only version of your HTML e-mails. That way, your e-mail is converted before it's sent and formatted to look good to the recipient. Some services even allow you to create and edit text-only versions of your HTML e-mails so you can control the content of the text version completely.

Making your images into links

Consumers like to click images, so making your images clickable gives your audience more opportunities to engage in your information. Making images into links requires using an image tag `<src>` combined with a URL link tag `<href>` in HTML. Here's an example:

```
<a href="http://www.yourwebsite.com">
    <img src="http://www.yourwebsite.com/filename/imagename.jpg/></a>
```

If you aren't familiar with coding your own image links, use an ESP with a user interface for creating image links. Figure 4-14 shows an ESP interface that allows you to insert a URL to add a link to an image.

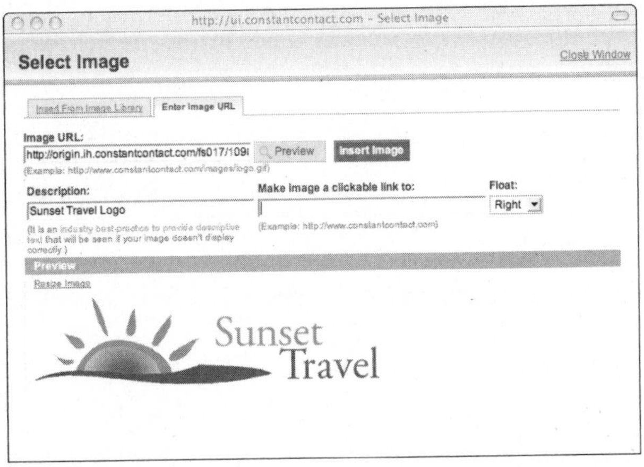

Figure 4-14: This ESP interface allows you to insert a URL to make an image into a link.

Courtesy of Constant Contact

Here are some tips for making your image links more effective when you include them in your e-mails:

✦ **Make your image links intuitive.** If your image doesn't make the destination of your link clear to your audience, you're probably better off with a text link or using text to tell your audience what will happen when they click the image.

✦ **Link logos to your Web site.** Most people expect your logo to link to your Web site's homepage, so including link functionality in every logo allows your audience to easily access your homepage information.

✦ **Link single images to more images or larger images.** When space allows for only one image or for smaller-size images, you can link your images to Web pages that contain more images and images with higher resolutions. Remember to make sure the content related to the image states or implies that the image links to more images.

Adding navigation links

Navigation links are HTML links that allow your audience to jump to visual anchors within the body of your e-mail. If your e-mails have one or more headlines or bodies of content that your audience has to scroll to for viewing, you can include navigation links in your e-mail to

✦ Highlight the content that your audience can't see immediately.

✦ Allow your audience to access the information by clicking a link instead of scrolling.

You can also include links to your Web site to allow your audience to jump from your e-mail to specific content on your Web site.

Navigation links are actually anchor links in HTML. *Anchor links* are HTML tags that reference a specific portion of content within an HTML document and automatically scroll the browser to the top of the referenced content when clicked. To create an anchor link, you have to create a name for the anchor using an anchor tag and place the anchor in your Web site code at the beginning of the content you want to link to. Then you add a link in your e-mail text that points to the anchor. Using your HTML or Web site editor of choice, follow these basic steps (the specifics depend on the editor you're using):

1. **Use an anchor tag to place your anchor, and include the name attribute to identify the anchor's name.**

Use the first word of the headline or section of content for the anchor name so you can remember how to name your anchor link later.

- *To set the anchor in text,* include an <a> anchor tag with a name attribute within your paragraph tags:

```
<p><a name="anchorname">headline or title</p>
```

- *To name an image as an anchor,* include the name attribute within the image tag:

```
<img name="anchorname" src="http://www.emailtrainer.com/
     sample/image_file/imagename.jpg">
```

If you're new to HTML, note that you should replace `anchorname` in the preceding examples with whatever name you'd like to use. Also, `headline or title` stands in for the text that actually appears on your site, and the URL in the preceding image tag also stands in for the location and filename of the image you actually want to use.

2. **Create your anchor link by inserting the <a> anchor tag in your HTML e-mail text, with the `href` attribute pointing to the anchor name you specify in Step 1, and preceded by a # character.**

    - *To create a TOC link that scrolls to your anchor tag,* use the following:

    ```
    <a href="#anchorname">TOC link text</a>
    ```

    Details on TOC links appear in the next section.

    - *To create a navigation link that scrolls to an anchor link on your Web site,* use the following:

    ```
    <a href="http://www.yourwebsite.com/page.html#anchorname>
         navigation link text</a>
    ```

Most ESPs allow you to create navigation links in your e-mails, and many include navigation links in basic e-mail template designs.

Including a table of contents in your e-mails

An e-mail *table of contents* (TOC) is a special group of navigation links that lists headlines; each headline is linked to a different section of content within your e-mail. Figure 4-15 shows an e-mail that includes a TOC in the upper-left quadrant.

TOCs are necessary only when your e-mail has lots of content that your audience has to scroll to view. If you decide you need a TOC in your e-mail because of the amount of content in your e-mail, take a moment to think about whether you're sending too much information in a single e-mail. Cutting down on your content and increasing your frequency might be a better solution to making your e-mails easier to scan.

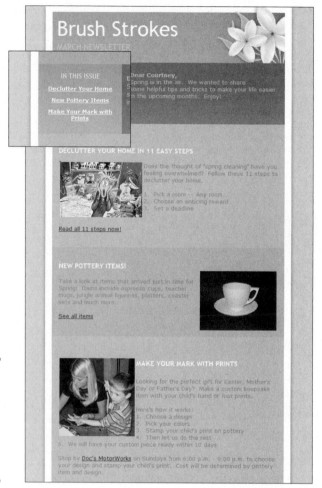

Figure 4-15:
This e-mail includes a TOC to help readers find information quickly.

If you can't cut down your content, using a TOC is a great way to summarize your content and allow your audience to find and access the content that interests them most. Here are some tips for including a TOC in your e-mails:

✦ **Include a heading above your table of contents.** Use wording, such as `Quick Links` or `Find It Fast`.

✦ **Keep your link headlines short.** You can use the first few words of the article headlines to which you're linking, or you can repeat short headlines as your main headlines and then use subheadings in your articles to expand on main headlines.

✦ **Make your link headlines clear.** Links should clearly communicate the content readers will see when they click. Clever links that intend to generate curiosity are generally harder to understand than clear link headlines and might cause disappointment if the linked message doesn't meet the clicker's expectations.

✦ **Keep your TOC above the scroll line.** The *scroll line* is the point at the bottom of your audience's screen where the e-mail content is no longer visible in the preview pane without scrolling. The whole point of a TOC is to keep people from scrolling. Thus, if your TOC is so long that it stretches beyond the preview pane, your e-mail probably has too much content.

Linking to files in your e-mails

E-mail can deliver attached files of all sorts, but attaching files should be reserved for sending personal e-mails to a small number of people at a time. Most e-mail programs and e-mail servers have security settings that send e-mails with attached files to a junk folder when the program suspects that the e-mail is commercial in nature.

Even though file attachments are e-mail delivery killers, you can still use files by linking to them within the content of your e-mails.

To link to a downloadable file (if your file is already accessible with a link on your Web site), follow these steps:

1. **Open your Web browser and navigate to the page that contains the link to your file.**

2. **Copy the link:**

   • *Windows:* Right-click and choose Copy Shortcut.

   • *Mac:* Control-click and choose Copy Link Location.

3. **Paste the shortcut into your e-mail program's link-creation user interface.**

   • *Windows:* Right-click and choose Paste.

   • *Mac:* Control-click and choose Paste.

If your file isn't already on your Web site, use the following steps instead:

1. **Upload the file to a public folder on your server.**

2. **Type the location of the file into your e-mail program's link-creation user interface.**

   For example

   ```
   http://www.yourdomain.com/public/site/public_files/filename.pdf
   ```

The next section describes some of the files that you might want to include in your e-mails along with tips on how to link to them.

Linking to video files

Video can be a powerful selling tool for some businesses, but deliverability is a challenge if you try to send an entire video file in an e-mail. Instead of delivering a video in its entirety — embedded in the content of an e-mail — insert a screen-shot image of your video and include a link to play the video on your Web site, as shown in Figure 4-16.

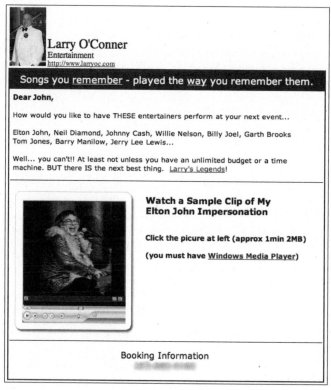

Figure 4-16: Host videos on your Web site and link them to your e-mail content by using a screen shot of the video.

Courtesy of Larry O'Conner Entertainment

TIP

If your video has sound, warn people before they click in case they're reading your e-mail at the office or in a place where sound might cause a distraction.

Linking to sound files

Sound files can allow your audience to multitask by listening to information while they scan and click the links in your e-mail. Like other files, sound files should be hosted on your Web site and linked to text or images in your

Book V
Chapter 4

Constructing an
Effective Marketing
E-Mail

e-mail. Links to sound files that contain soothing music or other mood elements can distract your recipient from more important clicks, so make sure that sound helps to communicate your main message.

If the message itself is your sound file — say, you're announcing your latest podcast or an archived radio show appearance — link the user to your Web site to play the sound file so he can surf all your valuable information while listening. Figure 4-17 shows an e-mail with a link to a sound file. For more on podcasting, see Book VI, Chapter 7.

Figure 4-17:
This e-mail uses an image of playback controls to link to an audio file.

Courtesy of The Mark Crowley Radio Show

Linking to document files

Portable Document Format files (PDFs) are the most popular files for e-mail delivery. Like with other files, don't attach PDF files to your marketing e-mails. Instead, link to their location on your Web site. When linking to a file, make sure you tell your clickers that their click will result in a download.

For example, if a short, summarized article in your newsletter ends with a link to the entire article in PDF format, make sure the link includes (PDF) in the text of the link or use an icon to indicate that clicking will result in a document download. If the document is long and the information the clicker wants to obtain isn't on one page, make sure you tell the clicker where to find the information. For example, your link might read

```
Read entire article (PDF page 3)
```

Chapter 5: Making Your E-Mail Content Valuable

In This Chapter

✔ Determining the value of your e-mail content

✔ Including valuable offers in your e-mails

✔ Coming up with a strong call to action

✔ Making your e-mails inherently valuable

✔ Giving your e-mails relevance over time

When people subscribe to your e-mail list, they share personal information with the expectation of receiving something valuable. Consumers aren't likely to value multiple e-mails that highlight only the distinguishing characteristics of your business. Repetitive e-mail content results in subscriber boredom. And boring your audience leads to low open rates, lost clicks, and unsubscribe requests.

Keeping your e-mail content valuable over time helps ensure that your list subscribers keep their attention and their subscription active while you attempt to capture purchases from them throughout the course of each buying cycle. The two basic types of value when it comes to e-mail content are

✦ An offer that is valuable when acted upon

✦ An *inherent* value: that is, content that's valuable in and of itself

Valuable content won't automatically make your audience rush to your business to part with their money. Your e-mail also needs to have a strong call to action to give your content a purpose and prompt your audience to help you meet your objectives.

This chapter covers some fundamental guidelines for including value in your e-mail strategy to deliver important information about your business while giving your audience continued reasons to open, read, and take action on your e-mails, no matter which stage of the buying cycle they're in.

Sending Valuable Offers

Offers are conditional statements that give your audience one or more reasons to make an immediate decision instead of postponing a decision.

Offers don't necessarily have to require a purchase decision to have value. Sometimes offers are necessary just to motivate your audience to consider all the information related to making a purchase decision. Whether your offers ask for an immediate purchase or just a visit to your Web site, your offers have to be valuable, or your audience won't take action on them.

Because the value in postponing a decision almost always has to do with the fact that people prefer to hold on to their money, offers usually take the form of discounts and savings. However, some people value other types of offers. The following sections describe money saving offers as well as other types of offers.

Creating content to promote something

When the main idea of your e-mail is to promote your products or services, your e-mails need to include descriptions and images that support your promotion. Here are some ideas and sources for creating promotional content to include in your e-mails:

✦ **Ask manufacturers for content.**

Companies that manufacture your products are great sources for product descriptions, images, and headlines.

✦ **Take digital photos.**

Use a digital camera to create product photos and show your services in action.

✦ **Ask your customers for descriptions.**

Sometimes your customers can describe your products or services in ways that speak to your audience better than you can.

✦ **Ask people to write testimonials.**

Asking people to tell you about their experiences can be interesting and relevant to your audience as well as powerful motivators. Testimonials don't have to come from your customers. Sometimes you can find examples of other people who have used products and services like yours and demonstrate how their testimonial applies to your business.

Make sure you have permission to use testimonials.

✦ **Check your e-mail.**

Keeping track of the types of e-mails your customers and prospects send to you can give you insight into the topics that interest your audience. When your customers and prospects ask questions and make inquiries about your business, use your answers to help you develop content that promotes how your products or services help solve their problems. For example, a business consultant who gets several e-mails asking about the impact of mobile marketing is wise to create an e-mail addressing the most common questions or concerns related to mobile marketing and the services provided by the consultant.

Cashing in on coupons

Coupons are traditionally printed on paper and redeemed in person, but e-mail coupons can take many forms, such as

✦ Printable HTML designs on a Web page or in an e-mail for use in a brick-and-mortar store

✦ Codes that customers enter into a form field when making an online purchase

✦ Links that include special HTML code that applies a change to the price field of a product database when someone clicks to view the product or add it to an online shopping cart

Most ESPs allow you to create dotted-line borders to give your coupon content the appearance of being clippable. If you format your coupons to have a traditional cut-out look onscreen, make sure that your coupons include redemption directions because consumers need to know how to redeem your coupon. (After all, they can't just cut it out of the computer screen.) For example, if you intend for your consumers to print the coupon, cut it out, and come to your store for redemption, include those instructions in your e-mail. Figure 5-1 shows an e-mail that includes traditional-looking coupons as well as directions for using the coupons.

Coupons contained in the body of your e-mail can be forwarded to anyone, so make sure you're ready to honor the unlimited use of your coupon by individuals who aren't on your e-mail list. If you want to make sure your coupon is used only by a few selected individuals, you can ask your audience to request an official copy of the coupon; or, give every coupon a unique code and tell your audience that you will allow only one use per coupon code. Some ESPs allow you to merge database fields into your e-mail so you can assign unique numbers to each customer's printable coupon. If your coupon is redeemable online, you can use the same code on every coupon and require your audience to create an account or log in before using the coupon code so you can keep track of unique redemptions.

Figure 5-1:
Include
redemption
directions
with
coupons.

Courtesy of Fajita Grill

You should also think through the financial implications that your coupon might create if someone tries to abuse your offer. Including an expiration date and limiting the number of redemptions per product or customer can help to limit any attempts to maliciously exploit your coupon's basic intentions.

Including incentives

Incentives are limited-time offers that reward a specific action. Incentives differ from coupons in that no physical redemption process is involved to take advantage of an incentive. Incentives are highly flexible; they can take the form of financial savings or special privileges. For example, a low financing rate might be the initial incentive to purchase a particular car, but membership to an exclusive automobile club is an additional incentive for purchasing the same car.

Incentives are particularly useful when you can identify your audience's specific interests and then match your audience's interests with your incentive. For example, if you know that your audience likes baseball, you might include two free tickets to a baseball game as an incentive for making an immediate purchase.

Using giveaways

Giveaways are complimentary products or services that are awarded to a single winner or a limited number of participants who take a specific action. Giveaways allow you to offer your audience a chance at a valuable prize or special privileges without having to worry about meeting the demand for a high number of requests for freebies. In addition to rewarding purchases, using giveaways can motivate your audience to

✦ Share more of their interests and contact information

✦ Respond to surveys and polls

✦ Forward your e-mails to friends and colleagues

Figure 5-2 shows an e-mail that offers a giveaway to reward a visit to the store.

 When your giveaway involves a prize drawing or contest, make sure that your giveaway complies with all applicable laws in your area. In the United States, you can usually find your local contest laws online at your state's Secretary of State Web site.

Making gains with loss leaders

A *loss leader* is an offer to purchase a product or service that results in a financial loss to your business to gain a new customer who represents more profitable revenue in the future. For example, a camera store might be willing to sell a specific type of camera for far less than all its competitors to obtain highly profitable printing and accessory sales from those customers.

Figure 5-2:
This e-mail offers a giveaway to a limited number of people who visit the store.

Courtesy of Abode

Loss leaders are useful when some of the people on your e-mail list have to experience the quality of your products or services firsthand before they can understand the true value inherent in your regular prices. Because loss leaders represent a customer acquisition cost, reserve them for obtaining customers who have never purchased from you before.

Extending urgent offers

Sometimes, products or services are valuable enough to cause an immediate purchase decision all by themselves because they fulfill a need that your audience perceives as an emergency. For example, a landscaping company might offer to blow out sprinkler systems for their audience because a cold front is moving in that has the potential to freeze pipes and cause serious water damage.

E-mail offers that highlight urgent needs are most effective when used sparingly.

Writing an Effective Call to Action

Even when your content is valuable, most consumers simply scan and delete your e-mails unless you prompt them with alternatives. If decreasing your deletion rate is one of your objectives, every e-mail you send needs to include a strong call to action. A *call to action* is a statement that prompts your audience to complete one or more specific tasks in favor of your objectives.

Calling your audience to action isn't as simple as including your phone number in the body of your e-mail or giving your audience lots of links to click. Consumers need directions and compelling reasons for taking specific actions, especially when their actions require spending time or money.

Anyone who reads e-mail is familiar with the stalwart phrase `Click Here`, but such generic phrases are not necessarily models for writing an effective call to action. An effective call to action acts like a little sign that allows your audience to visualize the steps involved to take advantage of your e-mail's content. Figure 5-3 shows an e-mail offer that includes the call to action, `Contact Us Today!`.

Words are the building blocks of a strong call to action, and the quality and the number of words that you choose significantly affects how many responses your call to action receives. The most effective way to write a call to action is to begin with one or more *action* words: verbs that propose a specific task to your audience. Here are some examples of actions and action words that are useful for calling your audience to action.

In the following, I list calls to action, paired with strong verbs you could choose to help motivate a reader to act. If you want your audience to take a certain action, here are some action-word suggestions you could work into your e-mail:

- ✦ **Read your e-mail:** Read, look, consider, notice, scroll
- ✦ **Fill out a form:** Contact, respond, comment, advise
- ✦ **Save your e-mail:** Save, keep, store, file, move
- ✦ **Request information:** Download, request, learn, e-mail, compare
- ✦ **Print your e-mail:** Print, post, bring, hang
- ✦ **Visit a physical location:** Drive, come, park, attend
- ✦ **Forward your e-mail:** Forward, share, send, refer
- ✦ **Visit a Web page:** Visit, view, go, navigate
- ✦ **Make a purchase:** Buy, add, purchase, own, order

✦ **Register for an event:** Register, reserve, sign up, R.S.V.P.

✦ **Phone your business:** Call, phone, dial

✦ **Make an appointment:** Schedule, arrange, meet, set up

Figure 5-3:
This e-mail includes an offer and a call to action.

Here's how you can build on action words to create a strong call to action. You can see the progression of the call to action as you make it stronger and stronger:

1. **Combine your action word with the subject of the action word.**

Order *this item*.

2. **Include the place where the action happens.**

Order this item *online*.

3. **Add the urgency of the action.**

Order this item online *before Friday*.

4. **Finish with an adjective to underscore the value inherent in the action.**

   Order this *hilarious* item online before Friday.

The combination of one or more action words along with your supplementary words makes a complete call to action. Writing an effective call to action can become more of an art than a science, but becoming a good call to action writer is just a matter of practice.

Turning your action words into links is a great way to prompt your audience to click to take action. (You can read about creating links in Book V, Chapter 4.)

Giving Your E-Mail Content Inherent Value

E-mails containing valuable information based on your knowledge and experience are generally more effective over long periods of time than e-mails that repeatedly contain only offers. Even when your offers are compelling, people aren't always ready to take action right away.

The longer your sales cycle and average time between repeat purchases, the more you need to include inherently valuable content in your e-mails to keep your audience subscribed and interested. Figure 5-4 shows an e-mail that contains an offer with a "quick tip" section included as inherently valuable content to enhance the overall value of the e-mail.

Inherently valuable content is most valuable when your content is relevant to your audience's stage in the buying cycle and targeted to your audience's interests. To make sure your content is appreciated, ask your customers what they're interested in before you start creating inherently valuable content.

The following sections detail how you can create inherently valuable content or combine it with various related offers.

Creating content to inform your audience

When the main objective of your e-mail is to deliver information, you might find yourself looking for facts, data, and expert opinions to help you make your case and add an element of authority to your information. Here are some ideas and sources for creating informative content to include in your e-mails:

✦ **Be an aggregator.** Sometimes the best way to tell your story is to let someone else tell it. Information abounds on the Internet, and the chances that your audience is going to find exactly what you want them to read are relatively low. Aggregating information from the Internet is a great way to generate content and inform your audience with the information you want them to see.

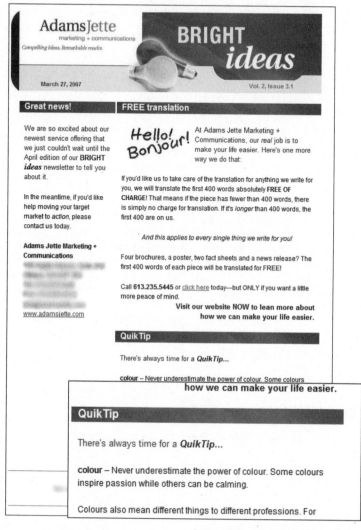

Figure 5-4:
This e-mail uses a QuikTip section for inherently valuable content.

Courtesy of Adams Jette Marketing & Communications

Make sure you have permission to include excerpts of other people's online information in your e-mails before you include them. Also, ask whether you can post the content on your Web site with a link to the outside source so that people who click links in your e-mail are sent to your Web site before they have the opportunity to link to someone else's Web site.

+ **Have an opinion.** If you don't have time to search for outside content and ask for permission in order to aggregate information, you can save yourself and your audience a lot of time by summarizing outside information for your audience. For example, a fashion designer who reads a lot of fashion magazines could create an e-mail that summarizes the two most stylish ways to tie a scarf so that the audience doesn't have to read all the scarf-tying articles in all the fashion magazines.

+ **Be an expert interviewer.** If you find yourself running out of opinions, you can usually find someone with expert information and advice for your audience. Instead of borrowing content, ask someone whether you can interview him about his expertise and share it with your audience. Interviews can also be broken up into themes or individual questions and included in a series of e-mails.

+ **Find a story teller.** People love to tell stories, and some of them can help you to inform your audience. Start by asking your current customers to tell you stories about their experiences with your business and your products or services.

Adding tips and advice

If your products or services require special knowledge for customers to use them, or if your audience needs a trusted opinion to buy your products in the first place, including tips and advice in your e-mails can reinforce your expertise.

Here are some ideas for including tips and advice in your e-mails:

+ **Start a tips and advice e-mail newsletter where the bulk of your content is informative.**

   For example, a gardening center might send an e-mail newsletter with tips for keeping gardens alive with less effort, or advice on plants that thrive with little or no attention. The gardening newsletter could include related offers for plants mentioned in the newsletter, or separate offers could be sent after their audience has enough information to engage in the buying cycle.

+ **Include one tip in each promotional e-mail you send with a link to additional tips on your Web site.**

   For example, a shoe store could include the location of a secret hiking trail in every e-mail with a link to an archive of hiking trails featured in the past. If you include single tips in your e-mails, make sure that your Web site's tips page includes related offers.

+ **Share your opinion.**

If you and your audience have the same beliefs, sharing your opinion can strengthen your customer relationships. For example, a store that sells recycled products might have a customer base that's more likely to be concerned about the environment. Such a customer base might be more loyal to a company that includes opinions concerning recycling issues along with offers to purchase recycled products.

✦ **Share another opinion.**

If your audience doesn't perceive you as an expert in your field, find an expert who is willing to share an opinion. You can ask permission to include opinions in your e-mails or interview an opinionated expert and include the highlights of the interview in your e-mail.

✦ **Dedicate a section of your e-mail newsletter to answering customer questions.**

For example, a Web site designer could answer a different customer question related to search engine optimization in every e-mail.

Providing instructions and directions

If your products or services require your customers to follow detailed instructions, include information that gives your audience timesaving shortcuts. For example, an e-mail promotion from an online auction might include steps for setting up account options. Here are some ways you can include instructions and directions in your e-mails:

✦ **Ask your customers to submit creative shortcuts.**

You can then feature the shortcuts in your e-mails.

✦ **If your directions involve several detailed steps, include one step with details in each e-mail.**

For example, a hobby store could include instructions for building a great model airplane, beginning with choosing a model and ending with painting and displaying the model.

✦ **Include instructions that are valuable for reference and ask your audience to save them in their e-mail Inboxes.**

For example, a promotion for a product that includes a one-year warranty could include return and refund instructions along with instructions for saving the information in case there is a problem with a recent or future purchase.

Putting in entertaining content

Some audiences value e-mail content that gives them a good laugh or diverts their attention with an interesting story. If your products or services are related to entertaining content and your audience values diversion, the following examples of entertaining content might be appropriate:

+ **Retell the stories you hear from your customers that relate to using your products and services.**

For example, a business that sells boats might include interesting stories about customers who live on the ocean or use boats to help people in the community.

If you include such stories, make sure you have permission from your customers before you send such stories to your list.

+ **Include links to online videos that are related to your products or services.**

For example, a guitar store might include a link to a video showing a different guitar hero who plays the guitars that the store sells.

Like with any link to content you don't own, make sure you have permission to include the link, and also make sure that the content you're linking to is legally obtained.

+ **Write your own stories about your experiences or knowledge relating to your products or services.**

For example, the owner of a restaurant might include stories about her trips to the French vineyards that inspire the wines featured in the restaurant.

Including facts and research

If you sell products or services that are enhanced by helpful facts and research, you can include them in your e-mails in order to add value to related offers. Here are a few possibilities:

+ **Conduct your own research and publish your findings in your e-mails.**

For example, a men's clothing store could conduct a poll and find out how many women think it's fashionable for men to wear pink shirts. The results of the poll could be included along with a pink shirt sale if the results support wearing pink shirts — or blue shirts if the results indicate that pink is out of favor.

+ **Include facts and research through external sources.**

Facts and research abound on the Internet, and the people who publish them are usually willing to share their findings with proper attribution to the source. If you locate facts and research that interest your audience, ask the source whether you can include them in your e-mails.

Finding Help with Content Creation

You can turn to many sources for help creating interesting and relevant content for your e-mails. Marketing companies and content providers can help you when

✦ You don't have time to create e-mail content.

✦ Your content isn't giving you the results you want.

✦ You don't like creating your own content for your e-mails.

Marketing companies and content providers often have services that range from small amounts of copywriting to fully outsourced, turnkey solutions. Most companies that provide content creation for e-mail marketing provide one or more of the following services:

✦ Copywriting, using themes and ideas you provide

✦ Formatting content that you provide into HTML for e-mail

✦ Custom e-mail template design

✦ Advice and consulting

✦ Image creation, design, and licensing

✦ Matching your Web site content to your e-mails

✦ Archiving e-mail campaigns to your Web site

For a list of marketing companies and content providers that can help you with e-mail content design and creation, ask for a list of business partners, education partners, or professional services at

www.constantcontact.com

Chapter 6: Tracking Your E-Mail Campaign Results

In This Chapter

✔ **Navigating e-mail tracking reports**

✔ **Understanding e-mail statistics**

✔ **Tracking other responses**

*O*ne of the most practical and valuable features of using e-mail to market your business is using e-mail tracking reports to find out what your audience is doing with your e-mails after you send them.

Most E-Mail Service Providers (ESPs) can track your e-mails and allow you to view the results in an e-mail tracking report. In this chapter, you find out how to make sense of the data in an e-mail tracking report as well as other creative ways to track responses not captured in a tracking report.

Understanding Basic E-Mail Tracking Data

You have to be an advanced HTML and database programmer to track e-mails on your own, so I recommend using an ESP to track your e-mails for you. ESPs automatically add special tracking code to the links you include in your e-mails. The tracking code is unique to each individual on your e-mail list and is also tied to each e-mail campaign. ESPs also have programs that automatically read the code from other e-mail servers when they return undeliverable e-mail so you don't have to do the hard work to determine why a particular e-mail wasn't delivered.

E-mail tracking reports are analytical summaries of the results of a given e-mail campaign that can tell you

+ Which e-mails bounced

+ Why they bounced

+ Who opened your e-mails

+ What links they clicked

+ Who unsubscribed from your e-mails

+ Who forwarded your e-mails

Figure 6-1 shows a summary e-mail tracking report, generated by an ESP, that allows access to the report details when the user clicks the summary statistics. Making sense of the data in an e-mail tracking report takes a little getting used to because the technology involved in the e-mail tracking process causes the data to take on a slightly different meaning than you might expect.

This section explains the origins of the data found in a typical e-mail tracking report so you can interpret the true meaning of each number being reported. This section also includes references to current industry statistics so you can decide whether your data warrants any action to refine your strategy.

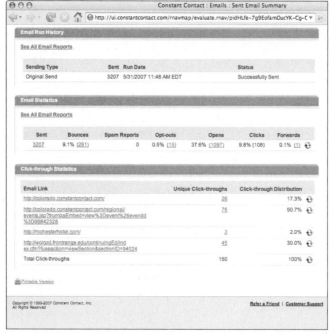

Figure 6-1:
Use an
e-mail
tracking
report
to view
summary
statistics.

Courtesy of Constant Contact

Calculating your bounce rate

Bounce rate is the number of e-mails that were returned as undeliverable, expressed as a percentage of total e-mails sent. ESPs calculate bounce rate by taking the total number of bounced e-mails and dividing by the number of e-mails sent. You can calculate your own bounce rate as follows:

1. **Divide the total number of e-mails that bounced by the total number of e-mails sent to get the total number of bounces per e-mail.**

For example, if you send 100 e-mails and 20 of them bounce, you bounced 0.2 e-mails for every e-mail sent.

2. **Take your bounces per e-mail and multiply by 100 to get your bounce rate as a percentage.**

   For example, the bounce rate for 0.2 bounces per e-mail is 20%.

According to a study conducted by ReturnPath (www.returnpath.com), the average bounce rate for commercial e-mails is 19.2. (For more information about why e-mails bounce and how to lower your bounce rate, read the next chapter in this minibook.)

Calculating your non-bounce total

Non-bounce total is the number of e-mails that were not bounced and therefore assumed delivered. ESPs calculate non-bounce total by subtracting your total number of bounced e-mails from the total number of e-mails sent. You can calculate your own non-bounce total as follows:

> Total e-mails sent
> –Total bounced e-mails
>
> Non-bounce total

For example, if you send 100 e-mails and 20 of them bounce, your non-bounce total is 80.

Non-bounce total is sometimes expressed as a percentage, but the non-bounce total is more useful as a real number because e-mail open rates are actually based on your non-bounce total instead of the total number of e-mails sent. (I explain open rate in more detail in the following section, "Calculating your open rate.")

Your non-bounce total isn't the same as the total number of e-mails delivered. Some e-mails aren't reported as bounced because software on the user's computer or a portable device — not an e-mail server — bounced it, and some e-mail servers falsely deliver your e-mail to a junk folder that users can't access. (For more information about e-mail filters and other non-delivery issues, read the next chapter in this minibook.)

Even though you can't be sure whether your non-bounced e-mails are being delivered, you can assume that your non-bounced e-mails are reaching your audience until you have good reasons to believe otherwise. Because non-bounce total is basically the converse of the bounce rate, the average non-bounce rate is approximately 80.8%, according to ReturnPath.

Calculating your open rate

Open rate is the number of specific interactions with an e-mail server after the e-mail is sent expressed as a percentage of non-bounce total. Your e-mail isn't counted as open until one of the following interactions occurs.

✦ The recipient enables the images in your e-mail to display either in the preview pane or in a full view of the e-mail.

✦ The recipient clicks a link in the e-mail.

ESPs calculate open rate by taking the number of tracked opens and dividing it by your non-bounce total. Here are the steps involved in calculating open rate:

1. **Take the total number of tracked opens and divide it by the non-bounce total to get opens per e-mail assumed delivered.**

   For example, if 80 of 100 e-mails you send don't bounce, and 20 of them are tracked as opened, you received 0.25 opens per e-mail.

2. **Multiply the number of opens per e-mail by 100 to get the open rate as a percentage.**

   For example, the open rate for 0.25 opens per e-mail is 25%.

You calculate your open rate by using your non-bounce rate instead of the total e-mails sent because your open rate indicates the strength of your e-mail's identity and content apart from the strength of its deliverability. Because e-mails that aren't delivered can't possibly be opened, they are excluded from your open rate calculation.

According to a 2007 study by Bronto Software (http://bronto.com), the average, tracked open rate for all industries is 23.6%. Open rates depend highly on industry, as you can see in Figure 6-2.

Figure 6-2:
The average open rate depends on the industry.

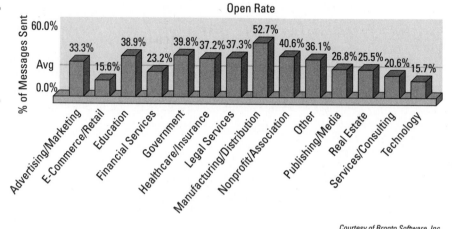

Courtesy of Bronto Software, Inc.

Because the default setting on an increasing number of e-mail programs is to block images until the user clicks to enable them, some people scan through e-mails without enabling images at all. In such cases, the true number of e-mails that your audience views is probably higher than your e-mail tracking report's open rate indicates.

Plain, text-only e-mails without any links or images are not trackable unless your audience replies to them directly. Make sure your ESP inserts a blank image in every e-mail to ensure that open tracking is possible.

Calculating your click-through rate

Your *click-through rate* is the number of unique individuals who click on one or more links in your e-mail, expressed as a percentage of total tracked opens. ESPs calculate click-through rate by taking the total number of unique individuals who click a link in your e-mail and dividing by the total number of tracked opens. Here are the steps for calculating click-through rate:

1. **Take the total number of clicks on all links in the e-mail and subtract any multiple clicks attributed to a single subscriber to get total unique clicks.**

    For example, if your e-mail contains two links and ten people clicked both links or clicked the same link multiple times, subtract ten from the total number of clicks.

2. **Take the total number of tracked opens and divide by the total number of unique clicks to get clicks per open.**

    For example, if 30 of your e-mails track as opened and you receive 3 unique clicks, your e-mail received 0.1 clicks per open.

3. **Multiply clicks per open by 100 to get click-through rate.**

    For example, the click-through rate for 0.1 clicks per open is 10%.

Because clicking a link in your e-mail causes the e-mail to track as an open, your click-through rate never exceeds the number of tracked opens. Your e-mail might receive more total clicks than tracked opens, however, because some people click a single link multiple times or click more than one link in your e-mail.

Even if your audience clicks multiple times, your click-through rate represents only the number of unique individuals who click one or more links. Most e-mail tracking reports also allow you to view the total number of clicks attributed to each unique individual as well as show you exactly which links are clicked.

Average click-through rates vary widely by industry. Figure 6-3 shows an ESP report that includes comparative tracking information along with e-mail tracking reports to compare results with ongoing averages.

Figure 6-3: Compare click-through rates with larger groups to gauge your results.

Tracking Non-Click Responses

Some e-mail marketing objectives can't be accomplished through a click. For example, if your goal is to increase the number of phone calls to your sales representatives to increase appointments — and, ultimately, closed sales — your e-mail requires an approach to tracking and evaluation apart from click-through reports and Web analytics.

This section explains how you can track non-click responses and calculate return on investment (ROI) so you can measure your effectiveness in converting customers outside the realm of your Web site.

Tracking in-store purchases

If the goal of your e-mail is to generate purchases in a brick-and-mortar store, you need to find a way to track the foot traffic that results from your e-mails and also compare any increase in foot traffic against any increase in sales. Here are some ideas for tracking your in-store visitors and linking them to your e-mail marketing efforts:

✦ **Ask your e-mail audience to print the e-mail and bring it with them when they visit your store.**

Count the number of e-mails you receive over a fair test of time (such as one month) or over the course of a series of e-mail campaigns.

✦ **Ask your e-mail audience to mention your e-mail when they visit your store.**

Offer your audience a gift so they have an incentive to mention your e-mail — even if they don't walk up to the counter to buy something. Count the number of gifts you give away to determine how many visitors result from your e-mails.

✦ **Have your sales staff ask all store visitors whether they received your e-mail.**

Count the number of visitors who say that they remember receiving it.

✦ **Promote a specific product or service and a specific offer in your e-mail.**

Count everyone who visits the store in search of the offer. Figure 6-4 shows an offer that only appears in the e-mail so that all inquiries can be attributed to the e-mail.

Figure 6-4:
Mentioning a special in your e-mail (and nowhere else) allows you to track inquiries.

Courtesy of McDonald Garden Center

Tracking phone calls

If the goal of your e-mail is to increase the number of inbound phone calls, your e-mail needs to include a method for tracking which phone calls result from your e-mail. Here are some ideas for tracking your phone calls and linking them to your e-mail marketing efforts:

✦ **Ask your e-mail audience to mention your e-mail when calling.**

Count the number of callers who mention it.

✦ **Set up a special phone number to accept calls from your e-mails and publish that number in your e-mails.**

Every time a call comes to that number, you can count the call as coming from one of your e-mails.

✦ **Promote a specific product or service in your e-mail.**

Count each call related to that product or service.

✦ **Ask your e-mail audience to request a specific person in your organization when they call.**

Count the increase in the number of calls that person receives.

✦ **Tell your sales staff to ask callers how they found your phone number.**

Count every caller who references your e-mail.

Tracking event attendance

If the goal of your e-mail is to increase event attendance, your e-mail needs to include a method for tracking how many event attendees resulted from sending your e-mail. Here are some ideas for tracking your event attendance and linking attendance to your e-mail marketing efforts:

✦ **Ask your e-mail audience to bring your e-mail to the event.**

Count the number of attendees who bring the e-mail.

✦ **Ask your e-mail audience to mention your e-mail or include a code in the e-mail that gets them into the event.**

Count the number of attendees who mention the e-mail or code.

✦ **Ask your e-mail audience to preregister by calling or replying to your e-mail.**

Count the number of attendees who preregistered.

Tracking e-mail replies

Sometimes, asking people to reply to your e-mails is enough to meet your ultimate objectives. An ESP can't track a reply to your e-mail, but you receive an e-mail from your list subscriber with a `Subject` line that reveals the source of the reply. For example, say you send an e-mail with a `Subject` line that reads, `Last chance to register`. When someone replies to your e-mail, the `Subject` line reads, `RE: Last chance to register`.

Counting the number of replies you receive from your e-mails isn't particularly useful, but replies can be very useful when you track the qualitative information inherent in your replies. Here are two ideas for tracking replies and putting the information to good use:

✦ **Keep track of the nature of each reply.**

Record whether your reply contained a complaint, suggestion, or inquiry and then track the reply to its source. For example, if you receive enough replies from people who want to know your hours of operation, you might include a link to your normal business hours in your future e-mails or make the information easier to find on your Web site.

✦ **Keep track of your response to each reply and the result.**

For example, if your response to a complaint results in a resolution or an order fulfillment, make a note of the situation so you can address anyone with a similar complaint using your Web site, Help files, or blog. You can also share the information with everyone on your sales team so they can address future complaints successfully.

Evaluating E-Mail Click-Through Data

Every time someone clicks a link in your e-mail, you have the opportunity to track the click back to the individual and use the information to accomplish more meaningful objectives and increase the value of your e-mail list.

You have to be an advanced HTML and database programmer to write your own link-tracking code, so I recommend that you use an ESP that can generate link-tracking code automatically for you. An ESP also provides a click-through report for each e-mail campaign. Figure 6-5 shows a detailed click-through report, generated by an ESP, that shows each link in the tracked e-mail and allows the user to view the individuals behind each click.

The next sections include tips and techniques for extracting practical meaning from your click-through data and for acting on your click-through data to make your e-mail marketing efforts more effective over time.

Using click-through data to target your e-mail offers

Someone clicking an e-mail link in response to an article or offer allows you to make assumptions about your clicker's interests. For example, a bookstore that receives 100 link clicks leading to information about a guitar book can assume that those 100 subscribers are interested in guitars.

Emails : Reports : Click-through Statistics

Click-through Statistics

Here you can compare the effectiveness of each link in this email by viewing the click-through statistic. For recent emails, you can click on the unique click-through number to see the contacts who clicked on a link.

You may save the contacts who clicked on this email as a new list - the new list will not be displayed on your Visitor Signup Form as a default. Contact click-through data is maintained for 90 days from the day of the email.

< Back   🖨 Printable Version

Email Name: New Workshop Calendar 3-06-07

Date Sent: 3/7/2007

Email Link	Unique Click-throughs	Click-through Distribution
http://colorado.constantcontact.com/	34	9.9%
http://colorado.constantcontact.com/learning-center/books/index.jsp	4	1.2%
http://colorado.constantcontact.com/regional/bio.jsp	8	2.3%
http://colorado.constantcontact.com/regional/bio.jsphttp://colorado.constantcontact.com/regional/bio.jsp	3	0.9%
http://colorado.constantcontact.com/regional/events.jsp?trumbaEmbed=view%3Devent%26eventid%3D59678132	52	15.2%
http://colorado.constantcontact.com/regional/events.jsp?trumbaEmbed=view%3Devent%26eventid%3D64116411	159	46.4%
http://colorado.constantcontact.com/services/index.jsp	4	1.2%
http://community.constantcontact.com/	2	0.6%
http://www.bouldersbdc.com/?site_id=167&id_sub=7726&page_id=4724&productgallery_id=1	77	22.4%
Total Click-throughs	343	100%

Save as List

Figure 6-5: Click-through reports show links in tracked e-mails.

Courtesy of Constant Contact

REAL WORLD

Simple event registration

Asking people to tell you in advance whether they're coming to your event is a great way to make room arrangements and prepare enough materials. However, asking people to fill out a long online registration form or take multiple steps to preregister before making a commitment might create a barrier to preregistration, especially if your event is free. Because you can track e-mail links to the clicker, you can create two links for each event and ask your audience to click one of them to indicate their intentions. For example, your two links might read, `I'd like to attend` and `No, thanks`.

After you create the links, you can point one link to a landing page that reads, `Thanks for confirming your attendance`, and you can point the other link to a landing page that reads, `Thanks for giving up your seat`.

Make sure your that landing page also has additional links, such as maps, directions, and other important event information. After you count the number of unique clicks on each link, you can plan for the appropriate number of visitors and send a follow-up e-mail that delivers more event information and asks your preregistered guests to confirm their attendance or purchase their tickets.

Placing your clickers into different e-mail lists based on their interests allows you to send future e-mails with more-targeted offers. For example, if a bookstore compiles its 100 guitar book clickers in a guitar-interest list, the bookstore could include offers and information related to guitars in every e-mail sent to that specific list. Figure 6-6 shows an ESP interface that allows you to save clickers to a list.

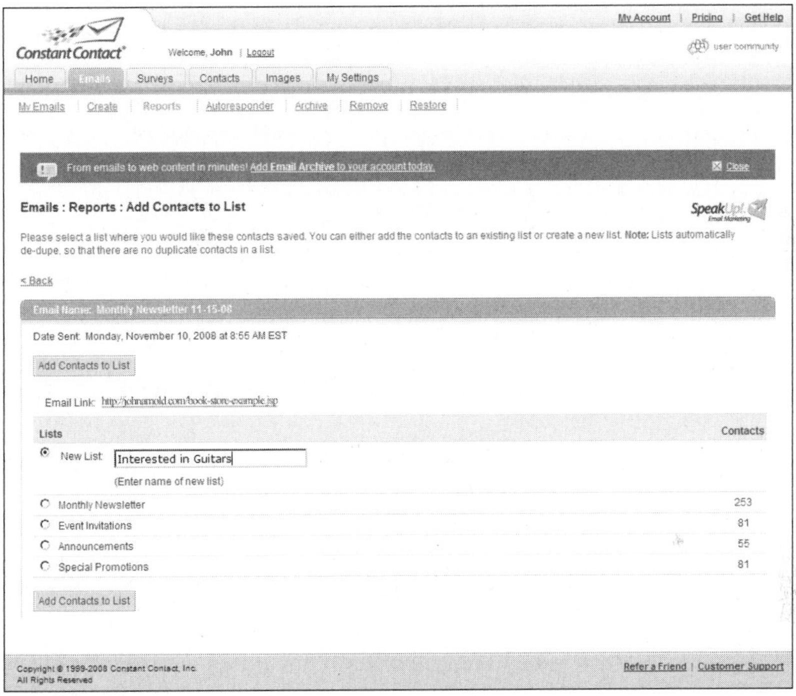

Figure 6-6:
Save your
clickers
as a list to
target future
e-mails by
interest.

Courtesy of Constant Contact

Here are some tips to help you determine your audience's interests and for dividing your e-mail list by using click-through interests:

✦ **Turn your links into data mines.** Clicks are much more meaningful when you write them in ways that affirm the clicker's personal information. For example, if a golf store sells kids' golf equipment as well as adult golf equipment, the store might include a link that points to kids' golfing tips:

```
Do you have kids under 12 who golf? Read our latest kids
    golfing tips.
```

The golf store can save the names of those who click the kids' tips link as a list and then target their kids' equipment offers to those clickers because they are more likely to value them.

✦ **Rearrange your e-mails by interest.** You don't need to send a completely different e-mail to each subscriber with a different interest. Instead, you can make small changes to your e-mail content based on the interest list you're targeting. For example, you can send the same e-mail newsletter to all your lists while changing the `Subject` line or rearranging the order of your articles to highlight the most interesting content for each of your interest lists.

✦ **Change your offers by interest.** People often respond to calls to action in your e-mails based on the strength of your offers. When you send offers to different interest lists, keep your call to action the same but change your offer according to each interest. For example, if your e-mail contains a call to action asking your audience to take a survey, you might offer one interest list a discount for taking the survey while offering another interest list special privileges. (You can read more about creating valuable offers in Book V, Chapter 5.)

Using click-through data for intelligent follow up

When someone clicks an e-mail link but doesn't follow through with a purchase or other commitment, you can use your click-through report to follow up with your clicker and find out what might have caused him or her to abandon the conversion process.

Following up with e-mail can be effective, but it's also a good idea to collect phone numbers and mailing addresses from your subscribers in case you need to follow up outside the inbox. For example, a consultant who sends an event invitation with a registration link could compare the list of subscribers who click the registration link with the number of completed registrations and then call each person who clicked *without* registering. Such follow-up can help you determine what might have prevented the registration from going through. The phone calls might reveal that those who didn't register had questions that your Web site didn't answer or felt uncomfortable typing a credit card number into the registration form.

Here are some tips for following up on the data in your click-through reports using e-mail as well as other forms of communication:

✦ **Send a second-chance offer** to those clickers who did not follow through by making a purchase or other commitment. You can use another e-mail or a postcard highlighting a more compelling second-chance offer.

✦ **Send a postcard thanking your clickers** for considering your offer and asking them to consider an alternative product or service.

✦ **Call your clickers** and ask them whether they have any questions.

✦ **Send a survey to your clickers** asking them about any interests that the link seems to have uncovered. (You can read more about e-mail surveys later in this chapter.)

✦ **Thank your subscribers** who forward your e-mails.

✦ **Send a postcard to clickers who unsubscribe** from your e-mail list telling them that they are still valued and thanking them for considering your products and services.

Using click-through data for testing your offers and calls to action

A spike or a decline in your click-through rate usually means that your offers or calls to action aren't compelling. Sending your offers and calls to action to a small and random portion of your e-mail list and tracking your click-through rate allow you to test your offers and calls to action before sending them to your entire e-mail list. Here's how you can create and execute your own click-through test:

1. Randomly select 10 percent of your e-mail list subscribers from your database and copy them to a new database or category in your database.

2. Create two versions of your e-mail and send each one to half of your test list.

3. Wait 48 hours and compare each e-mail's click-through report to see which links received the most clicks.

4. Create a final version of your e-mail using the elements that produced the most clicks and send it to your entire e-mail list.

If your sample click-through rates are lower than you expect in both versions of your e-mail, you can adjust your offers or calls to action accordingly and test again using a different test list. You can improve a low click-through rate with these simple techniques:

✦ Rewriting your headlines to attract more attention to your offer

✦ Adjusting your offer to deliver more value

✦ Moving your call to action to a more visible location

✦ Rearranging your layout to make your offer easier to scan

Chapter 7: Maximizing E-Mail Deliverability

In This Chapter

✔ **Dealing with bounced and blocked e-mail**

✔ **Understanding e-mail content filters**

✔ **Maximizing delivery rates**

✔ **Working with emerging delivery technology**

Thinking about the early days of postal mail delivery conjures up images of Pony Express riders traveling long distances and risking their lives to get mail delivered, proudly in the name of the United States of America. Although sticking a stamp on a letter or postcard and dropping it off at a U.S. Postal Service office doesn't necessarily assure its delivery to someone's mailbox, mail carriers most often do succeed in delivering your mail to the mailbox of the intended addressee; or return your mail to the mailbox specified in the return address, along with a clear reason for the failed delivery.

E-mail delivery, though, isn't quite as trustworthy as the U.S. Postal Service. Even e-mail sent to a correct e-mail address doesn't always reach the Inbox, and returned e-mail doesn't always include unmistakable reasons for the failed delivery.

However, the good news is that the positives of e-mail marketing greatly outweigh the deliverability issues inherent to sending commercial e-mail. This chapter uncovers the various reasons why some e-mail fails to reach an Inbox. Then I offer solutions for maximizing your e-mail delivery rates.

Managing Bounced and Blocked E-Mail

Sometimes, e-mail is simply returned to the sender either by the e-mail server or by a software application, such as an e-mail program or delivery control system. You hear the terms *bounced* and *blocked* applied to returned e-mail somewhat interchangeably, but the two have some slight differences:

✦ **Bounced:** A *bounced e-mail* happens on a per–e-mail basis when an e-mail is returned because of conditions that make a particular e-mail undeliverable, such as a full e-mail Inbox or an e-mail address that is misspelled or doesn't exist. Bounces can be hard or soft, which I talk about in a bit.

✦ **Blocked:** A *blocked e-mail* happens on an all-inclusive basis when an e-mail is returned because of characteristics that make a particular type of e-mail unwanted, such as when a systems administrator decides to refuse all e-mails with attachments or all e-mails from a particular sender.

E-mail is usually returned with code that indicates the reason for the bounce or the block. Most of the time, the code is unintelligible to the average human. Figure 7-1 shows an example of an e-mail returned to the sender with bounce code.

When you team with an E-Mail Service Provider (ESP), you don't have to spend time scanning through lines of HTML because most ESPs automatically file bounced and blocked e-mails into a bounce report. A *bounce report* shows how many of your e-mails bounced and were blocked as well as the plain-English reason for the bounce or block response.

Figure 7-2 shows a bounce report generated by an ESP. You can see the number of bounced e-mails by category as well as individual bounced e-mails and associated database records.

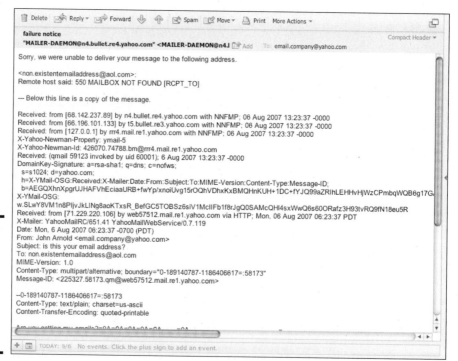

Figure 7-1: Bounce code can be difficult to interpret without the help of an ESP.

Figure 7-2:
Use a
summary
bounce
report to
see the
number of
bounced
e-mails by
category.

Courtesy Constant Contact

Although some bounced or blocked e-mails will never get delivered, some bounced and blocked e-mails are *temporary:* that is, the e-mails might be delivered if you try sending again later. The following sections explain how to take the appropriate action on each type of bounced and blocked e-mail so you can refine your e-mail list — and get your e-mails delivered to more of your list subscribers.

Taking action on bounced e-mail

Bounced e-mails are generally unavoidable because the causes of bounced e-mail fall outside your direct control. You can take, however, some reasonably effective methods for minimizing bounced e-mail.

The following sections show you how to deal with bounces and when to take corrective action.

Dealing with hard bounces

A *hard bounce* is an e-mail that's returned because a permanent condition makes delivering the e-mail impossible. When your ESP's bounce report shows e-mails delivered to nonexistent addresses, your e-mail can't be delivered to that address no matter what action you take. *Nonexistent* e-mail addresses are either

✦ Misspelled (for example, *name*@hotmai.1com)

✦ Invalid (such as when your subscriber changes her e-mail address)

Keeping up with e-mail address changes

According to a study conducted by ReturnPath, more than 30 percent of your e-mail list addressees are likely to change their e-mail address each year. Because losing your entire e-mail list every three to four years isn't going to help improve repeat business, periodically remind your list subscribers to update their e-mail addresses.

Because most people keep their old e-mail address active for a short period of time between changes, sending a subscription reminder every two to three months is a good way to ask your list subscribers to share their new e-mail address before their old e-mail address is completely deactivated. If you have a large e-mail list, make sure that your subscription reminder links your audience to a secure, online form where they can update their own information and save you from replacing your selling time with data entry. Here's an example of text you might use in your subscription reminder:

```
Subject Line: Subscription
    Reminder

Body: This e-mail is sent every
    other month to remind you
    that you are subscribed to
    the ABC Company e-mail list.
    If your contact informa-
    tion or interests should
    changed at any time, please
    select your interests (link
    to interests form) or update
    your contact information
    (link to secure profile
    form) so we can continue to
    send you valuable offers and
    information.
```

You can check your hard-bounce report for obviously misspelled e-mail addresses and correct them in your database. Most of the time, though, you can't tell whether an e-mail address is misspelled or invalid. In those cases, you need to obtain a new e-mail address.

If your hard-bounce list is too large to contact each individual to obtain a new e-mail address, or if you don't have any alternative contact information for the subscribers, remove those e-mail addresses from your e-mail list.

Dealing with soft bounces

A *soft bounce* happens when the delivery of an e-mail is delayed temporarily. Soft bounces happen because of technical conditions inherent in the technology that makes e-mail delivery possible. Examples include

- ✦ A full mailbox
- ✦ A server that's temporarily down
- ✦ A software application that can't accept the e-mail

When an e-mail address bounces for a reason that's temporary in nature, try resending your e-mail later or simply wait until your next e-mail campaign to see whether the same address still bounces. If an e-mail address bounces repeatedly for temporary reasons, contact the subscriber for a more reliable e-mail address.

Reducing blocked e-mails

Blocked e-mails are sometimes temporary and sometimes permanent, depending on whether the server or software blocking the e-mail does so in response to the content of a single e-mail or the characteristics of a specific type of e-mail. The following sections show how you can keep from being blocked by someone on your e-mail list.

Responding to a challenge response system

A *challenge response system* is a software program that returns all unrecognized e-mail to the sender with instructions for getting the e-mail delivered that only a live person is capable of following, in order to verify that the sender is a real human being — not a computer generating e-mail addresses. Figure 7-3 shows an e-mail returned by a challenge response system that asks the sender to click a link and fill out a form.

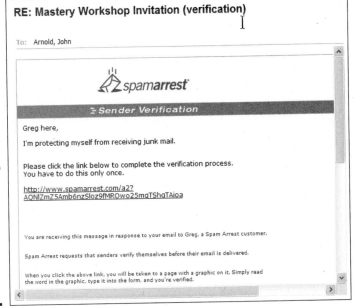

Figure 7-3:
This challenge response e-mail asks the sender to verify its legitimacy.

Courtesy of SpamArrest

Challenge responses are generated by third-party applications that integrate into e-mail applications. For example, someone who wants to eliminate computer-generated spam might purchase a challenge response application to verify all e-mails sent to his AOL e-mail address. If you send e-mail to someone with a challenge response system, the returned e-mail might ask you to click a link and enter specific characters in a form field or reply to the e-mail with a specific subject line. Following the instructions in the returned e-mail adds your server address or e-mail address to the subscriber's friends list or address book so that future e-mails are delivered without a challenge.

Keeping your e-mail address or server off a block list

A *block list* (also known as a *blacklist*) is a database that contains the domain names and server addresses of suspected spammers. Block lists are maintained by Internet service providers (ISPs) and other companies that monitor spam complaints across the Internet. Server addresses and domain names are added to block lists based on the number of spam complaints logged by consumers.

If you send an e-mail that gets too many spam complaints, the server you use to send your e-mail might be added to one or more block lists. (You can read more about avoiding spam complaints in Book V, Chapter 2.)

Avoiding spam trap e-mail addresses

A *spam trap* is a false e-mail address placed on the Internet by a company with an interest in reducing spam. When spammers using Web crawlers to capture e-mail addresses try to send an e-mail to the spam trap e-mail address, the sender's domain and server address are automatically added to the block list. (A *Web crawler* is a computer program that searches the Internet for specific types of content, such as lines of text that look like an e-mail address.) Many companies share their spam trap block lists. If you happen to send e-mail to a spam trap address, your deliverability could be doomed.

Here are some ways to avoid spam trap e-mail addresses:

✦ **Don't surf the Internet to obtain e-mail addresses.**

Besides risking your deliverability, this behavior is also illegal.

✦ **Don't send e-mail to a purchased list.**

Purchased lists are often collected without permission and can contain spam trap addresses.

✦ **Send a welcome e-mail to every new list subscriber and immediately remove e-mail addresses that return your welcome e-mail.**

That way, you can weed out anyone who tries to maliciously join your e-mail list by using a known spam trap address.

Getting past e-mail firewalls

An *e-mail firewall* is a piece of hardware or a software application programmed to identify and block e-mails that appear untrustworthy. Firewalls can be customized and configured to block almost any e-mail element. For example, a system administrator at one company might configure a firewall to block e-mails with certain types of content, and another system administrator might configure a firewall to block e-mails from certain senders while gnoring the content altogether.

Because firewalls have so many variables, telling whether your e-mail is being blocked by a firewall is usually impossible. If you use an ESP that provides blocked e-mail addresses in its bounced report, however, you can at least find out which e-mail addresses are being blocked and then take action to try to get the e-mail delivered.

Changing your tactics to get e-mail delivered to a blocked address is difficult, but the following remedies might prove effective:

✦ **Ask your audience to add your e-mail address to their address book or contacts list when they sign up for your e-mail list.**

Some content-blocking systems allow e-mail to go through if the sender's e-mail address is in the recipient's address book.

In your welcome letter and subscription reminders, give your audience instructions for adding your e-mail address, as shown in Figure 7-4. This e-mail asks the reader to help ensure delivery by adding the sender's e-mail address to the reader's address book.

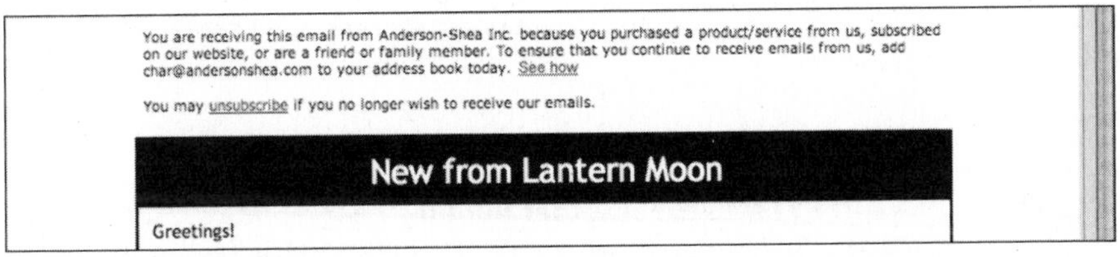

Figure 7-4:
Help ensure
delivery.

> You are receiving this email from Anderson-Shea Inc. because you purchased a product/service from us, subscribed on our website, or are a friend or family member. To ensure that you continue to receive emails from us, add char@andersonshea.com to your address book today. See how
>
> You may unsubscribe if you no longer wish to receive our emails.
>
> **New from Lantern Moon**
>
> Greetings!

Courtesy of Anderson-Shea, Inc.

✦ **Obtain an alternative e-mail address from each of your blocked subscribers.**

Sometimes, half the battle with blocked e-mail is knowing that a particular e-mail address is being blocked. When your ESP's bounce report shows a particular blocked e-mail address, you can ask your subscriber to provide a different address.

✦ **If the blocked e-mail address is a work address, ask the IT expert at your subscriber's company to add your ESP's e-mail server address to the friends list on the company's e-mail server.**

A *friends list* (also known as a *white list*) is a database containing e-mail addresses from welcome senders. Some firewalls ignore their blocking instructions when the sender's e-mail address exists in the friends list.

Reducing Filtered E-Mail

An *e-mail filter* is a program that scans the content of your e-mail to identify whether your e-mail contains unwanted content. If your e-mail contains content that's identified as potentially unwanted, the program places the e-mail into a holding place (such as a junk folder) or tags the e-mail with a message to identify it as potentially unwanted.

Filters are different from programs that block and bounce e-mails because filters don't return the e-mail to the sender.

Sometimes an e-mail is filtered even though the recipient wants the e-mail. Desirable e-mail content that still gets filtered is a *false positive.* False positives are all too common because of the enormous amount of spam e-mail content that's similar in nature to legitimate e-mail content. Some e-mail filters result in more false positives than others because the people behind the filters get to decide what kinds of content are considered unwanted. For example, an e-mail that contains the word *drug* might be filtered by a systems administrator who believes that certain prescription drug advertisements are spam even if the word is being used by a bookstore to describe a book.

Unfortunately, you can't tell whether your e-mail is filtered unless the recipient notifies you that your e-mail landed in the junk folder or that your e-mail is being delivered with a filter tag. The following sections explain how you can get a higher percentage of your e-mail through the most common types of filters.

Establish your sender reputation

Getting more e-mail delivered starts with sending your e-mail from a reputable e-mail server. According to a recent study conducted by ReturnPath (www. returnpath.com), 77 percent of e-mail delivery issues occur because of the sender's reputation. Most companies that provide e-mail delivery for their customers consider the reputation of the sender when filtering e-mail.

Because your own e-mail server isn't likely to have a reputation, delivering your mail through an ESP with a respectable and well-known reputation is one of the most important steps you can take to maximize your e-mail deliverability. Make sure you choose an ESP that can

✦ **Authenticate your e-mail:** *Authentication* allows e-mail servers to identify the sender of an e-mail. (I cover authentication later in this chapter.)

✦ **Eliminate customers with high spam complaints:** ESPs send e-mails from their own servers on behalf of their customers even though the e-mails appear to come from their customers. Because too many spam complaints might cause the ESP's servers to become block listed, I recommend associating with an ESP that takes action when one of its customers receives too many spam complaints. Reputable ESPs keep their overall complaint rates low — and your sender reputation as clean as possible.

✦ **Affirm the quality of their customers' e-mail lists:** Although ESPs can't guarantee or predetermine the quality of their customers' e-mail lists, reputable ESPs require customers to adhere to strict permission policies to caution their customers when attempting to use e-mail addresses that could generate a high number of complaints.

✦ **Confirm permission from their customers' list subscribers when necessary:** Some businesses, such as those in the financial industry, inherently receive a lot of spam complaints because their legitimate e-mail content looks similar to a lot of spam e-mails. Use an ESP that either has options for such businesses or has a policy to recommend such businesses to another service that specializes in working with e-mail senders that have the potential for generating a lot of spam complaints.

✦ **Keep customers from sending repeated e-mails to unknown users:** Spammers send billions of e-mails to every possible e-mail address hoping to uncover real addresses. Because ISPs (such as AOL, Yahoo!, and Hotmail) spend a lot of money bouncing e-mails sent by spammers, they aren't appreciative of e-mails sent to nonexistent addresses. As a result, your deliverability could suffer if your e-mail server is labeled as a nuisance. To help protect your sender reputation (as well as that of the ESP), most reputable ESPs stop sending your e-mail to nonexistent e-mail addresses after two or three attempts even if you don't remove the e-mail addresses yourself.

E-mail filters often rely on sender reputation before content filters, so make sure to put your ESP to the test. You can check your ESP's sender reputation against the competition by signing up for a free account at SenderScore (www.senderscore.org). Type the domain name of the company and then click each of their listed e-mail servers to see the sender score for each server used to send e-mail on behalf of the ESP's customers. A score of 0 on a particular e-mail server is the worst, and a score of 100 is the best. After you feel comfortable that you're sending e-mail via a reputable ESP, you can be sure that your efforts to optimize your e-mail content won't be wasted.

Understand automatic content filtering

A small percentage of e-mail content filters are controlled completely by e-mail system administrators to keep their users from administering their own filter settings. The e-mail system administrator (usually IT personnel at a company, or an ISP) sets up the automatic filter with specific global parameters that apply to all e-mail users in the same way.

Because automatic e-mail filtering is generally controlled by technically knowledgeable people with all kinds of backgrounds, the types of e-mail content that get filtered through automatic filtering vary widely. For example, one system administrator might decide to filter HTML e-mails, but another might decide to filter e-mails with attachments. If someone on your e-mail list wants your e-mail and his or her system administrator has strict filter settings, your e-mail has a greater chance of false positive identification. (You can read about false positives earlier in this chapter.)

Automatic filtering affects a relatively small percentage of your e-mails. You can't do much about it unless you happen to know the system administrator and you can coax him or her into relaxing a particular company's filtering standards.

Understand user-controlled content filtering

The majority of e-mail filters are included within e-mail programs and written with broad consumer preferences in mind to filter e-mail content that has spam-like characteristics. E-mail filters within e-mail programs almost always allow the user to access the default filter settings and alter them according to user preferences.

Filters often look for spam-like content, so avoid simulating spammer techniques. Recent examples include

✦ Generic Subject lines and anonymous From lines

✦ PDF attachments containing advertisements

✦ Images of entire advertisements without any plain text

✦ Excessive promotional phrases and words

Most consumers don't alter their default e-mail filter settings manually, so avoiding false positive filtering by the most common e-mail filters is partly a matter of building your e-mails to exclude the most commonly filtered content. Figure 7-5 shows a sample of the headers in a junk e-mail folder.

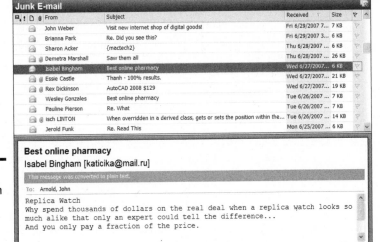

Figure 7-5:
Filters often
look for
spam-like
content.

Read some of the e-mails in your own junk folder to see examples of what to avoid: namely, the most common types of content that spammers include in their e-mails.

You can prevent your e-mails looking like spam if you do the following:

✦ **Don't include your subscriber's first name in the `Subject` line of your e-mails.**

The practice is common among spammers because most consumers can't understand how a complete stranger could know their first name. (Spammers use Web crawler programs to pull the information out of your e-mail headers.) After being tricked a few times, most consumers associate this technique with spam.

✦ **Always include a `From` line in your e-mail header.**

Excluding the `From` line is an attempt by spammers to trick people into opening e-mails in the hope that the consumers are curious to find out who the e-mail is from. Most filters automatically identify e-mails with no `From` line as untrustworthy.

✦ **Avoid excessive punctuation (such as strings of exclamation points!!!!!) and "crafty" symbols (such as ¢ents or dollar ign).**

Spammers often use strings of punctuation to make their offers more eye-catching, and the practice is just as attention-catching to e-mail filters.

✦ **Don't send marketing e-mails with attachments.**

Consumers are understandably nervous about e-mail with unfamiliar attachments, and e-mails sent to more than a few people with attachments are usually filtered.

✦ **DON'T WRITE SENTENCES IN ALL CAPITAL LETTERS.**

Writing in all capital letters draws attention to e-mail headlines, and this tack is as annoying to consumers as it is noticeable to e-mail filters.

Building your e-mail content with the most common filter settings gets more of your e-mail delivered to the inbox, but several types of user-controlled filters aren't so simple to sidestep.

Individual filters

A small percentage of consumers do access their filter settings to make changes. Figure 7-6 shows some of the individual filter settings available in Yahoo! Mail.

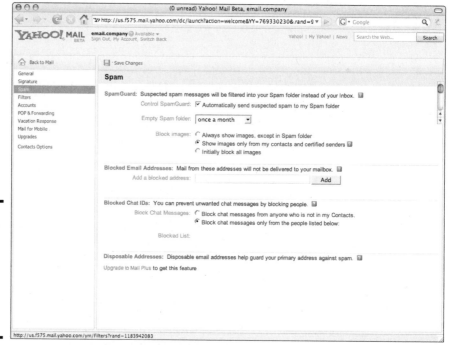

Figure 7-6:
Yahoo! Mail allows users to access and personalize filter settings.

What's your spam score?

Instead of filtering specific types of content on an individual basis, some companies choose to score every e-mail by comparing the content in the e-mail with the content in known spam e-mails. These companies compare e-mails to lists of keywords, HTML structure, attachments, published block lists, and domain names to determine how closely the e-mail resembles a typical spam e-mail. The more each e-mail's content resembles the content in spam, the higher the e-mail's spam score. The company sets a limit for the spam score and then tags, filters, or returns those e-mails that exceed the score. Some ESPs help you score your own e-mails before you send them, as shown in the following figure. If you use such a service, make sure that your spam score is 0 before you send.

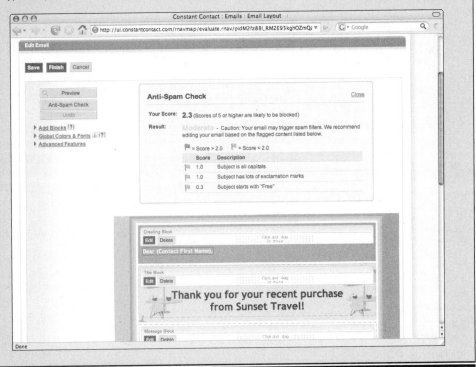

If someone on your e-mail list accesses his personal filter settings to set up a filter, your e-mail content is obviously subject to being filtered based on the personal settings for that user. Because you can't know every personal setting in an individual filter, there is little you can do to get your e-mail through. Accessing filter settings allows the user to personally filter one or more of the following e-mails.

✦ From specific senders

✦ Containing specific words or phrases

✦ With links or images (usually converted to plain text only)

✦ From senders not in the user's address book

✦ With certain domain extensions, such as `.biz` or `.info`

✦ With certain types of encoding, such as international languages

✦ With attachments

Trained content filters

Some filters begin with broad default settings and are automatically updated based on whether the user identifies certain e-mails as unwanted. The most common example is the Spam button (as you can read about in Book V, Chapter 2), which is a clickable link in an e-mail program that reports the e-mail as spam to the e-mail system administrator. Clicking a Spam button not only reports an e-mail as unwanted but also scans the content to identify content that recurs frequently in the reported e-mails.

When a user clicks a Spam button, a filter scans the e-mail to look for words, phrases, and other types of content to determine whether there is a pattern to the types of content being reported as spam by the user. For example, if a user continues to click the Spam button on multiple e-mails containing the phrase *discount meds,* the filter begins to learn that phrase and automatically filters any e-mails containing that phrase to a junk folder.

Trained content filters work fairly well, but a filter can't distinguish between wanted words and unwanted words in an e-mail that is marked as spam. Because spam e-mails share many common characteristics with legitimate e-mails — such as the phrase Click Here — some legitimate e-mails are identified as false positives.

Understanding E-Mail Authentication

Filtering and blocking technologies are constantly improving. Although it might seem as if spammers are always one step ahead of the game, several promising technologies are emerging to help reduce spam.

Keeping up with emerging technology is important so that your e-mails are optimized for current deliverability standards as well as poised to comply with emerging technology that might cause your e-mails to go undelivered.

Spammers forge the e-mail addresses they send e-mails from by using technical tricks to replace the legitimate header information in an e-mail with false information. Several major ISPs have developed technology to validate the `From` information in an e-mail. The following is a list of the most popular sender authentication methods. The list also represents the most likely technology to emerge as standards for your own deliverability.

✦ **Sender ID:** This technology developed by Microsoft uses an algorithm to select a header field containing the e-mail address responsible for sending the e-mail. The sending e-mail address is then checked against a list of authorized e-mail servers for that e-mail address.

✦ **DomainKeys:** This technology developed by Yahoo! uses cryptography to generate a set of unique public and private encryption keys. All outgoing messages are digitally signed by the sender using the *private key* (known only to authorized senders), and the public key is published with the sender's Domain Name Service (DNS) so that recipients can use the public key to validate that the correct private key was used by the sender.

✦ **Sender Policy Framework (SPF):** SPF is similar to Sender ID in that the technology validates the sender's `From` information by allowing the owner of a specific domain to specify his or her e-mail sending policy or SPF. When someone receives an e-mail that appears to originate from the specified domain, the e-mail server receiving the message can check the SPF record to see whether the e-mail complies with that domain's specific policy.

Self-publishing your own authentication information is beyond the scope of this book, but you can easily employ authentication technology in your e-mails by using a reputable ESP that complies with current authentication standards to send your e-mails. You can find ESP recommendations at www.johnarnold.com.

Book VI

Blogging and Podcasting

The 5th Wave   By Rich Tennant

"I'm sorry. I'm answering email right now. And since when does the Taco Bell Chihuahua have a blog anyway?"

Contents at a Glance

Chapter 1: Picking Your Blog Topic **563**

Choosing a Blog Topic 563

Thinking about Your Blog Goals 566

Sizing Up Your Space 568

Chapter 2: Getting Yer Blog On **571**

Choosing Your Blog Platform 571

Getting Your Blog Set Up 577

Writing Your First Post 584

Chapter 3: Writing Like a Blogger **585**

Following the Three Blog S's 585

Clearing Bloggage 590

Chapter 4: Tracking Other Blogs **593**

Understanding Feeds and Feed Readers 594

Setting Up Google Reader 595

Using Folders and Tags to Organize Your Feeds 597

Reviewing Feeds Fast with Hot Keys 602

Creating a Shared Items Page 603

Chapter 5: Getting Involved on Other Blogs **605**

Connecting with Other Bloggers 605

Leaving Great Comments 606

Linking to Other Blog Posts 609

Giving Credit Where Credit Is Due 610

Writing a Guest Post 610

Joining Blog Carnivals 611

Chapter 6: Promoting Your Posts **615**

Publishing Your Post 615

Letting the World Know: Using Pinging 616

Submitting Your Post to StumbleUpon 616

Submitting Your Post on Digg (Once in a While) 618

Submitting Your Post to Bookmarking Sites 620

Chapter 7: Introducing Podcasting **623**

Podcasting 101 623

Setting Up Your Podcasting Studio 624

Setting Up Your Studio 627

Testing Your Setup 628

Supporting Podcasting on Your Blog 629

Preparing Your Podcast Script 630

Chapter 1: Picking Your Blog Topic

In This Chapter

✔ **Finding a blog topic you care about**

✔ **Creating goals for your blog**

✔ **Calculating the size of your audience**

*B*logs sound faintly, well, magical. After all, they're everywhere. They're not necessarily mystical, though. A *blog* is simply a toolset with which you write and publish entries *(posts),* and then visitors can comment on those posts.

To have a blog — and use it for Web marketing — you need a solid topic upfront. Choose something about which you're passionate and knowledgeable. That way, you can build a base of followers, which in turn drives traffic to your site (or sites) — and ultimately, your endeavor.

Choosing a Blog Topic

If you're going to write a blog, you need a topic: a *focus.* Without one, you have a tough time attracting an audience. Your goal is to reach the point where your audience seeks you out because you consistently offer information that they find helpful in light of their interests.

No focus means no consistency, which means no audience.

Picking that topic can be tougher than you might think. Common questions and concerns that I hear are

I don't want to pick a narrow topic. I'll be stuck writing about it forever.

No wants want to hear what I have to say.

My topic is so boring. Why would anyone read it?

I can't think of anything.

All the preceding questions translate to one issue: fear. We're all trained to be terrified of writing. Starting in grade school, we're told that we'll lose two points for a missing comma or four points for an incomplete sentence, and we'll flunk the class if we use *than* when we should use *then.* I don't know why, but that's how it's done.

Well, you can let go of that fear now. Blogging is the best form of writing therapy on the planet. People read blogs for content, not for grammatical perfection. Of course, you should strive to write grammatically correct language lest your readers think that you're not well educated or that your work is sloppy in general. But one misplaced punctuation mark doesn't mean that you get an F.

Before you read the rest of this chapter, just *relax*. Take a breath. Smile. You're among friends.

If you read nothing else in this chapter, read these key tips:

◆ Write about something that excites you.

◆ Write about something you know.

You're probably thinking, "But I'm doing this to grow my business!" If you're blogging for your business, I hope that you're enthusiastic about it, too.

Think about it, and find the one or two or many things you care about in your career. For example, if you're a passionate collector of bottle tops, that's your blog topic. If you're an Internet marketer and truly care about the profession, write about it.

Don't select a topic simply because you think that a lot of people search for it, or because you think that it would have a big audience. Here's why:

◆ **Blogging requires a long-term commitment.** You can more easily write regularly on a topic in which you're interested. And, you can more easily write regularly if you know a lot about the subject material.

◆ **Your audience won't hesitate to point out subject matter mistakes.** That's not a big deal: Mistakes happen. But make sure that you're right more often than not. Knowing the topic is important.

◆ **Your audience knows if you're not passionate.** You won't attract as many dedicated readers.

◆ **It's no fun if you write about a topic with which you're unfamiliar.** Writing about a familiar topic is much more fun than struggling to write about an unfamiliar topic.

"What if no one is interested in my topic?" Many folks ask that question. In my experience, someone is always interested. If you have a business and you're selling products successfully, chances are good that you have an audience.

Narrow blog topics work

The blog Glue Gun Crafts, shown in the figure, covers crafts made with glue guns. That's a narrow topic. Still, the blog receives a healthy number of visitors and even earns a little money.

Consider what you do and then ask yourself these questions:

✦ How can I make this topic funny?

✦ How can I make this topic fascinating?

✦ What can I say about this topic that will prompt discussion?

✦ Which questions are asked repeatedly?

Here are a few examples:

+ **If you sell cash registers,** you could blog about the coolest-looking cash registers.

+ **If you're a management consultant,** write a blog about applying your favorite time-management technique to midsize companies.

+ **If you're a roofer,** create a question-and-answer blog for homeowners.

+ **If you're a real estate agent,** blog about your favorite staging techniques.

+ **If you're a chef,** write about the best frozen foods with taste testing.

+ **If you're a teacher,** come up with a daily list of homework tips.

You have dozens of possibilities. *Never* start by telling yourself, "What I do is boring." It's not!

Thinking about Your Blog Goals

After you decide on a topic, determine what you're trying to achieve by writing this blog. When you answer, keep the following concepts in mind:

+ **Few blogs succeed in the first six months of life.** Whatever your goal is, give yourself at least 6 to 12 months to reach it.

+ **For the first six months, you almost certainly will "speak to an empty room."**

+ **Only a handful of blogs generate appreciable direct income through advertising or other cash generators. Most are marketing tools with indirect benefit for your business.**

If you're blogging for your business, your first priority should be the business, not your online ego. (I'm not trying to discourage you. I just want you to set achievable goals.)

I try to set my goals in six-month cycles. That timeframe gives me enough time to work but gives me something to work toward.

Set a six-month goal for your blossoming blog. Consider the following goals as a starting point:

+ Answer the top 20 questions asked by customers.

+ Write 42 posts.

+ Send 20 potential clients to read the blog.

+ Find two potential clients on the Web.

If you're feeling truly ambitious, strive for these results:

✦ Use my blog to write a book.

✦ Sign up at least 300 subscribers.

✦ Get at least half my traffic from search engines.

All these goals are attainable and provide a substantial boost for your business.

Bad goals include

✦ Earn a five-figure income.

✦ Rank No. 1 for a competitive phrase in the search engines.

These two goals, although attainable, are quite difficult to reach. Plus, they don't necessarily help your business. Earning $10,000 from your blog, for example, doesn't help if you spend the equivalent of $20,000 worth of time to do it. And, ranking No. 1 for a relevant phrase *might* help, but you need to do a lot of research first. See Book II for more on search engine optimization (SEO).

When I started writing my blog, Conversation Marketing, I had only one goal: to create a place I could send clients to figure out how I think. That goal kept me focused. I answered common client questions, introduced my own (sometimes bizarre) sense of humor, and introduced my company's marketing method. See Figure 1-1 for an example of my blog the way it looked a *long* time ago (left) — and how it looks now (right), as it's matured.

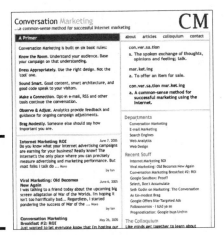

Figure 1-1:
My blog, back in the day, and now.

Sizing Up Your Space

After you pick a blog topic and create goals for your blog, it's time to figure out who else is writing about your topic and how big your audience might be.

Using Technorati

Technorati.com is a blog search engine. When you visit it and search on your topic, you find a list of blogs written about your subject or a related topic. Even better, you see them ranked according to the number of other blogs linking to each of the listed blogs.

Be sure to click the Posts tab so that you see results only from blogs.

In Figure 1-2, you can see a search for the term "*internet marketing*".

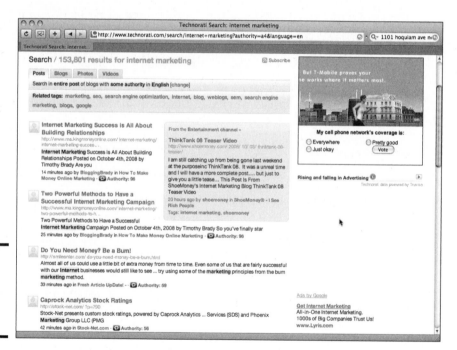

Figure 1-2:
A
Technorati
search
result.

Using Google Trends

Google Trends shows you changes in search volume for different terms over time. Using this information is a good way to figure out whether your blog topic is on the upswing.

Visit `www.google.com/trends` and search for a key phrase. You see changes over time in both search volume and news references, as shown in Figure 1-3.

If you see a `Not Enough Search Volume` message as a result, it doesn't mean that your topic is never searched. It means only that people haven't searched for the phrase the number of times (potentially thousands) that are required in order to show up in Google Trends.

If a phrase **does** show up in Trends, though, you know it's very, very hot — and it's worth pursuing the topic.

**Book VI
Chapter 1**

**Picking Your
Blog Topic**

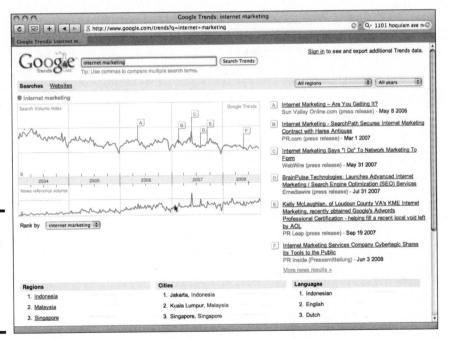

Figure 1-3:
Use Google
Trends
to see
changes
in search
volume.

Using search engines

Go to your favorite search engine and search for your chosen topic. Use the Blog Search option, if your search engine has one. Google Blog Search is shown in Figure 1-4.

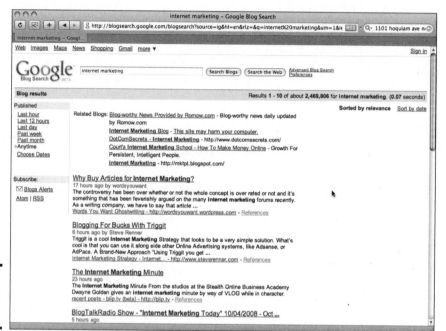

Figure 1-4:
Google Blog
Search.

Check for the following:

+ **How many other bloggers write about your topic?** If there are millions, you may have a hard time standing out.

+ **What do other bloggers say about your topic?** You might have a valuable counterpoint.

+ **Are there any gaps in their knowledge that you can fill?**

+ **What kinds of comments do those bloggers get?** Comments can give you insight into unanswered questions that you can answer.

The key here is to figure out where you can offer the most value to readers. That's your opportunity to turn your blog into a valuable marketing platform.

Chapter 2: Getting Yer Blog On

In This Chapter

✔ **Choosing a blogging tool**

✔ **Setting up your blog**

✔ **Changing the look of your blog**

✔ **Putting your first post in print**

Blogging is defined, in part, by the tools you use to publish the words you write. These tools tend to be extremely easy to set up, but you still have to do a little work.

This chapter helps you select the best tool for your purpose and then set up the tool and perhaps customize it. After you accomplish all those tasks, I walk you through writing your first post.

Choosing Your Blog Platform

First things first: Choose your tool. All blogging tools have certain characteristics in common:

✦ They work in your Web browser.

✦ They publish your written material on a Web site.

✦ They enable site visitors to then write comments in response to your entries (called *blog posts*).

✦ They include a way for visitors to subscribe to your blog by using the *RSS* feature. (I tell you more about that later.)

Apart from those similarities, though, the various blogging platforms differ widely. In the following sections, I describe four of the most popular ones in detail and then list a few others that you might want to investigate.

Blogger and WordPress.org: Easy and free

Blogger.com is a basic blogging service owned by Google. You can sign up in a few quick steps and start publishing your first posts in a few minutes. Figure 2-1 shows the Blogger authoring tools.

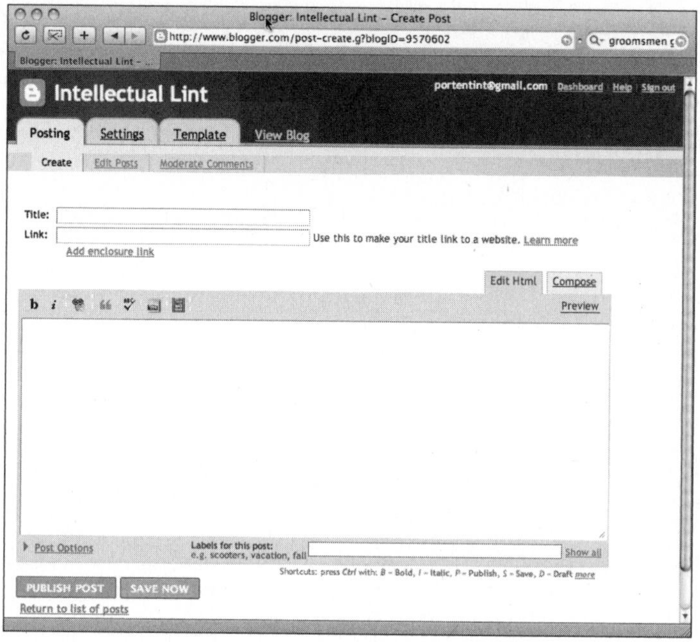

Figure 2-1:
Writing
a post in
Blogger.

WordPress.com is a hosted version of the now ubiquitous WordPress blogging toolset. In this sense, *hosted* means that WordPress has its own Web servers, with WordPress already set up, so you don't have to install anything. Like Blogger, it's easy to use and offers a helpful, prebuilt solution. You can see what a WordPress.org blog looks like in Figure 2-2.

WordPress.com and Blogger's strengths are listed here:

✦ **They're easy to use.** They're *really* easy to use. The moment you set up your blog, you have commenting and subscriptions and all the other basic features of a successful blog.

✦ **You don't have to install any software.**

✦ **They're free.**

✦ **You can use lots of prebuilt designs.**

✦ **You're not responsible for maintaining the code that powers the site, because upgrades happen automatically.**

Figure 2-2:
A blog
hosted on
WordPress.
com.

However, both WordPress.com and Blogger have some drawbacks, too:

+ **No customization:** If either of these blogging platforms were a car, the hood would be welded shut. You can't customize either one to any great degree. Even WordPress.com Premium, which allows you to modify the look and feel a bit, won't let you add plug-ins or make changes to the underlying blogging software.

+ **SEO weakness:** Both systems have some drawbacks from a search engine optimization (SEO) standpoint. Because your blog isn't part of your Web site, it doesn't help you add useful content to your site. See Book II for more information about SEO.

+ **No quick updates:** Someone else is responsible for maintaining the code. You get the idea: If something goes wrong, it may be a little while before it gets fixed.

Blogger and WordPress.com are helpful places to start. If you later decide to make blogging part of your Internet marketing strategy, you'll probably move to a more customizable solution.

TypePad is another hosted blogging solution with features similar to WordPress.com and Blogger. Although TypePad isn't as popular as Blogger or WordPress.com, it's worth a careful look if you want to set up a blog quickly. *Note:* TypePad is not free.

WordPress installed: A sports car

WordPress also offers its blogging platform in a software program you can install on your own Web site. And that means you can run WordPress on your own server. Some businesses even use WordPress to drive their entire Web site. You can find it at `www.wordpress.org`.

The software's free. If you know your way around a Web server, you can install it in about ten minutes. If not, many Web hosts are willing to set up a WordPress blog for you.

WordPress installed looks and works like WordPress.com, with a few critical differences:

✦ **You can customize WordPress installed.** The entire blog is built on PHP, a common Web programming language.

✦ **You can take advantage of how other folks have already customized WordPress installed.** Hundreds of *plug-ins* (extensions built to add new capabilities to WordPress) are all available on the WordPress.org Web site.

✦ **You can maximize SEO with WordPress installed.** By using a few plug-ins, you can make WordPress an SEO powerhouse. Don't worry about this concept yet; just understand that the option exists later on, if you want it.

✦ **You can make your WordPress installed blog part of your Web site.** If you install WordPress on the same server that hosts your Web site, your blog can live at `www.yoursite.com/blog` or a similar URL, as shown in Figure 2-3.

WordPress installed has some challenges, though:

✦ **You're totally responsible for your installation.** If you want an upgrade, you have to do it. If something goes wrong, you have to either fix it or pay someone else to fix it.

✦ **You need to know a bit about installing software on a server.** Or, you have to hire someone else who knows about it or pay your hosting provider a fee to get you set up. The cost is low, but it's still a cost.

✦ **The basic installation can run only a single blog.** If you want to run multiple blogs, you need multiple WordPress installations. That can become a challenge if you have to maintain them all yourself.

Figure 2-3:
Neat! A blog
that's on my
Web site!

WordPress is like a popular sports car: It is by far the most-often-used installed blogging platform on the planet. A huge community helps support you if you decide to use it, but it's not intended for the Web novice. You need to either gain expertise or hire someone with that expertise. Otherwise, you end up in a ditch.

For all the ins and outs on WordPress installed, check out *WordPress For Dummies,* 2nd Edition, by Lisa Sabin-Wilson (Wiley).

Movable Type: A racing car

If WordPress is a nice little sports car, Movable Type is the one you can race at the Indianapolis Motor Speedway. Find it at `www.movabletype.com`.

Out of the box, Movable Type gives you

+ **A customizable blogging platform**

+ **A library of plug-ins you can use to add capabilities**

+ **An extremely SEO-friendly blogging platform**

+ **Its own handy template language so that you can create custom designs relatively easily**

✦ **The capability to manage multiple blogs**

This difference is *critical:* With Movable Type, you can write, publish, and manage as many blogs as you want.

Alas, like a racing car, Movable Type offers some trade-offs:

✦ **Cost:** You can get the personal edition for free, but if you're going to put Movable Type to commercial use of any kind, you have to pay based on the number of blogs you'll write and authors to whom you provide access.

✦ **Difficulty:** Movable Type is challenging to install and customize. It's far more complex than WordPress. I've personally done more damage to Web sites with Movable Type in five minutes than I can do in a month with WordPress.

✦ **More cost:** Upgrades might cost more. If Six Apart (the company that builds Movable Type) makes major improvements, you'll probably be charged for the upgrade.

Movable Type is a fantastic solution if your company launches and maintains multiple blogs. It's the hands-down winner for large organizations, too. Just understand that you need a fair amount of expertise to take full advantage of it.

Other blog options

You have (at least) dozens of other options for blogs or blog-style sites. I'm inevitably leaving some out, which will lead to a storm of indignant e-mail from fans of those blogging tools, but here are a few:

✦ **Joomla!** (available at `www.joomla.org`) is a free, PHP-driven blogging and content management system (CMS) that offers an amazing array of tools in a single package.

✦ **ExpressionEngine** (`www.expressionengine.com`) is a CMS and blogging tool in one.

✦ **Textpattern** (`www.textpattern.com`) is a flexible, textile-based content manager that's PHP driven and open source.

✦ **LiveJournal** (`www.livejournal.com`) is a hosted blogging system that you don't have to install, much like WordPress hosted and Blogger.

✦ **Drupal** (`www.drupal.org`) is a broader social "plumbing" system — a CMS plus comments, membership, accounts, and messaging — that includes blog features.

If you're like me, you'll start with a hosted system like Blogger and then move to a custom system. When you make that change, a little research pays off.

Getting Your Blog Set Up

After you choose your blog tool, you need to take the next steps: First set up an account. Then design your blog's look and feel, configure comments, set up pinging, and create your RSS feed.

Blog account setup

Depending on the platform you choose, you might need to simply set up an account, as shown in Figure 2-4. In that case, you just need to visit the blogging site and enter some basic information.

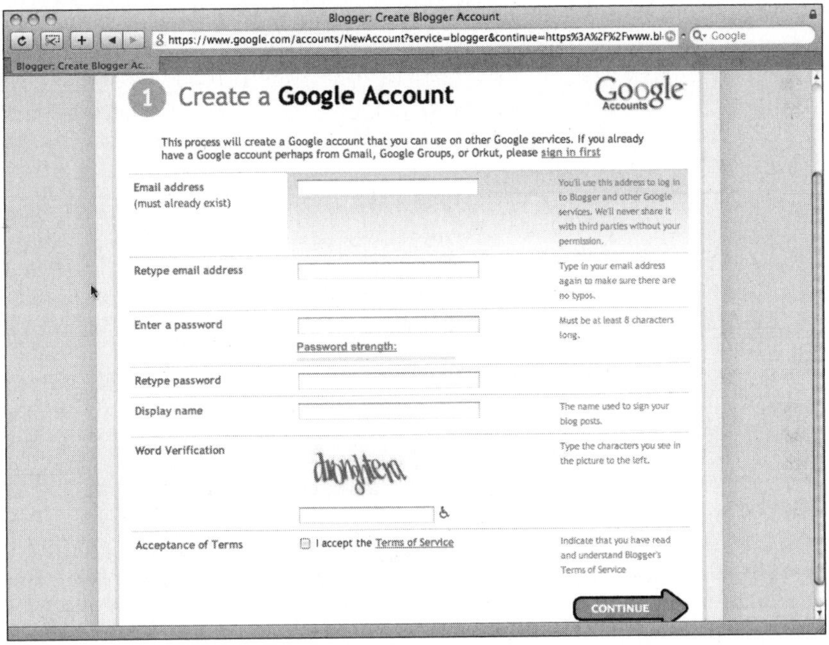

Figure 2-4:
Setting up a blog on Blogger doesn't take much.

If you're using an installed blogging tool, you need to

1. Download the required software and install it (or pay someone else to do it for you).

2. Configure it for your server and Web site.

3. Set up your login and password.

4. Make a short post and comment to ensure that everything is working properly.

Picking your blog look

After the basic setup is complete, make your blog look just the way you want. You have a few options, which I describe here, from the easiest to the most difficult.

Easy: Use a preinstalled template

Most blogging systems come with a set of templates that you can easily select. If you're happy using one of these templates, changing the look of your blog is as easy as choosing from a group, as shown in Figure 2-5.

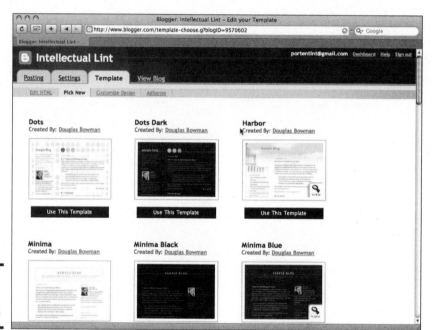

Figure 2-5:
Choosing a blog design.

Installed platforms such as WordPress and Movable Type are supplied with a few templates, too.

Intermediate: Download a new template and install it

Hundreds of free blog templates are available. You just have to download and install them on your blog.

On most hosted blog systems, this task is a relatively straightforward cut-and-paste operation. On an installed blog, you might have to download some files and then upload them to your server.

Whatever you do, if you use a free template, *provide a credit to the author.* The author gave you a great design for free — give him something in return.

Hard: Download a new template, install it, and customize it

You can also find a template that's close to what you want, install it on your blog, and then tweak it until it's just right.

In most cases, completing this task requires a solid knowledge of HTML and style sheets.

Superhard: Create your own

If you're truly determined, you can create your own fully customized template. Every blogging platform, from Blogger to WordPress, offers ways to customize the look and feel of your blog.

So, you can create your own, perfect look and then use the blogging platform's special template language or system to build the look into your site.

Creating your own template requires a lot of HTML expertise and the patience of a saint. It's challenging; however, it can also be a heck of a lot of fun and an excellent way to learn your way around your own site. Just realize that you might spend days creating a template. Having the perfect look (perfect in my eyes, anyway), as shown in Figure 2-6, might be worth your while.

Book VI
Chapter 2

Getting Yer Blog On

Figure 2-6:
The author's
blog design.

Many qualified professionals can help you with this type of customization. Check your blogging platform's site for a list of specialists. Chances are good that one of them can refer you to a developer.

Configuring comments

After your blog looks the way you want, make sure that you're handling comments the way you want. The key is moderation. I'm talking not about "all good things in moderation," but rather the controls that let you review comments before they're published.

Most blogs provide a few options for comment moderation:

✦ **Don't**

- *Let anyone publish a comment with no moderation.* Bad idea. Don't use this option unless you want your blog stuffed with links to sites hawking pharmaceuticals.

- *Refuse to allow anyone to publish comments.* That's also a bad idea. A blog without comments isn't really a blog.

✦ **Do**

- *Review all comments before publishing.* This option keeps things simple. You review every comment before you click Publish, which helps you learn the process.

- *Allow trusted commenters to publish without approval.* If you set a specific commenter as Trusted, your blog publishes that person's comments without moderation. As your site receives increasingly more visitors — and more folks writing comments — this option might make your life a lot easier.

Pick the option that makes the most sense for you. I strongly recommend that you enable Review All Comments Before Publishing because it gives you the most flexibility at the start.

Setting up pinging

When you write a new post on your blog, your blogging software can send out a ping. A *ping* is a short message sent out to major blogging search engines and directories that says, "Hey, I have a new story here!"

A timely ping sends the basic information about your new post to sites such as Technorati and Weblogs.com. Those sites then publish the post title and a short snippet from the post itself.

Pings can be an effective traffic generator, and they involve zero effort after you set them up.

Your blogging software probably includes a ping configuration page, such as the one shown in Figure 2-7. Note that it might be called Web Services Settings, or Pinging, depending on the blog software.

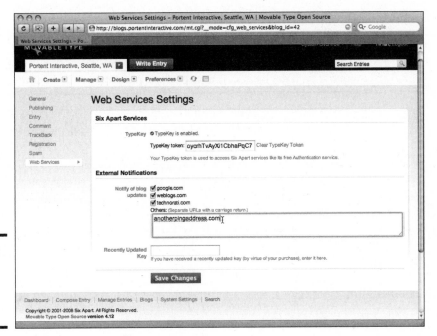

Figure 2-7:
Setting up pinging in Movable Type.

Paste in the pinging service addresses you want included. From then on, your blog automatically pings those services when you publish. Here's a good starting list of pinging services:

```
http://rpc.pingomatic.com

http://ping.blo.gs

http://ping.feedburner.com

http://ping.syndic8.com/xmlrpc.php

http://ping.weblogalot.com/rpc.php

http://rpc.blogrolling.com/pinger

http://rpc.technorati.com/rpc/ping

http://rpc.weblogs.com/RPC2

http://topicexchange.com/RPC2

http://rpc.icerocket.com:10080
```

If you don't have a pinging tool built into your blog, that's okay. Visit www.pingomatic.com and use its simple form to ping new posts. It takes only a moment, and the instant exposure is an excellent traffic generator.

Creating your RSS feed

Every blog should have at least one RSS feed.

RSS stands for (among other things) really simple syndication. It's not a technology. It's a format: a common way to publish the headlines and a summary of each post on your blog or the complete post. If you looked at an RSS feed in the raw text format, it would look like the nonsense shown in Figure 2-8.

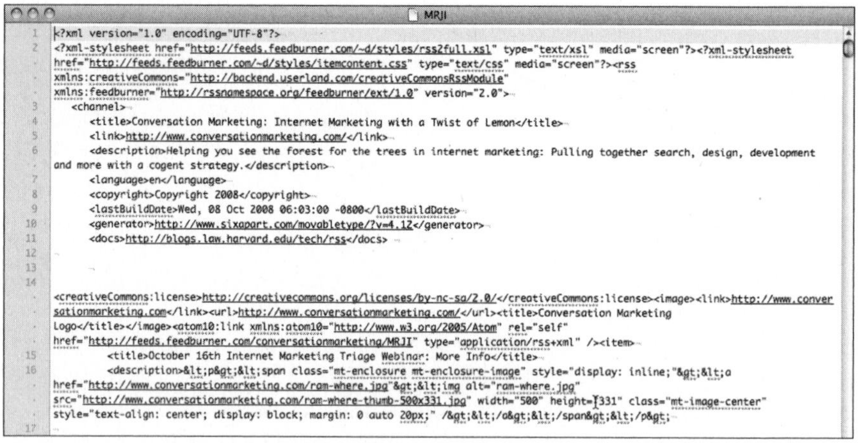

Figure 2-8: An RSS feed — not pretty.

Look at the same text with any standard RSS feed reader, and — *voilà!* — you see what's shown in Figure 2-9.

Figure 2-9: Ah, that makes more sense.

Visitors can subscribe to your RSS feed by using one of hundreds of easy-to-use RSS feed readers, including Google Reader (www.google.com/reader) and Microsoft Outlook. They then see an updated list of recent articles on your blog, without having to visit the blog. It's a helpful way for visitors to keep track of lots of blogs at one time.

You *can* use your blog's built-in RSS generation to provide the RSS feed. That strategy works fine. But the FeedBurner service (now owned by Google) lets you take it a step further. FeedBurner lets you turn your single simple feed into a marketing tool. Using FeedBurner, you can

+ Add advertising to your RSS feed.

+ Deliver your feed in multiple formats for best compatibility.

+ Track subscriptions.

+ Add nifty features, such as E-mail a Friend, directly in your feed.

+ Add e-mail subscriptions.

+ Leap tall buildings in a single bound.

Okay, I made that last one up.

But FeedBurner can truly make your life easier. And, it's free.

To burn your feed, using FeedBurner, follow these steps:

1. **Visit www.feedburner.com.**

2. **Create an account and log in.**

3. **Find your blog's feed address.**

   Check your blog documentation if you're stumped.

4. **Paste that address into the Burn a Feed Right This Instant field and then click Next.**

   FeedBurner provides a new address for your feed.

5. **In your blog, replace the old feed address with the new FeedBurner address.**

   Your blogging tool now points subscribers to the FeedBurner feed instead.

Writing Your First Post

Pshew. The blog is set up. Your RSS feed is set up. It's time to take a break!

Not so fast. Didn't you forget something? Oh, yeah — a post!

Writing your first post can be difficult. You want it to be perfect, of course. You want to explode onto the blogging scene and into stardom.

But, because that's not going to happen (sorry, it's just not), you should have some fun instead and have a stress-free launch. Here are my tips for a first post:

✦ **Don't aim for perfection.** Aim for from-the-heart writing instead. Just say what your aspirations are for your blog.

✦ **Don't write about how you don't know what to write.** Everyone knows what writer's block is like. You don't need to remind us.

✦ **Do create a time capsule.** Write a first post that you can look back on later to create a sense of why you started this project in the first place.

✦ **Do publish it right away.** It's always good to edit. But don't spend days or even weeks trying to make that post *just right.* You have to go live sometime.

The most important thing about that first post, though, is getting it done. It won't be your best, and that's totally okay. Blogging is about practice and improvement. Get started!

Chapter 3: Writing Like a Blogger

In This Chapter

✔ **Blog writing style and structure**

✔ **Writing content for online readers**

✔ **Setting a blogging schedule (and sticking to it)**

✔ **Battling bloggage**

*N*o single *blog style* of writing exists. However, you can try out different techniques to make your blog easier to read (and write), such as using bullets to make more scannable pages, and using images to grab the reader's attention.

For most people, reading online is hard — far harder than reading a print page. You need to take that into account when you write your blog posts. And that's what this chapter is about: how to write posts that are easy for your readers to scan and read, write posts that they'll love, and write consistently over a long period of time.

All these efforts add up to a blog that firmly connects readers to your blog and your business. That, in turn, translates to a better connection with potential customers, and a more successful Internet marketing campaign.

Following the Three Blog S's

The ideal blog post (and blog) creates an image of you, the writer, in the reader's mind. That image is consistent, and it's one with which the reader can identify.

To reach that point, though, you have to know how to structure your posts, eliminate roadblocks to readers, and make sure they get your point. If you want to achieve that, all blog posts you write must follow the three S's:

✦ **Simplicity:** Your writing should be clear and easy to read. Flowery language is a helpful way to show off your vocabulary, but it doesn't necessarily communicate. Keep your writing simple. For example:

- *Okay:* The steak was the epitome of flavor and texture.

- *Better:* The steak was delicious.

✦ **Scannability:** People don't read online: They scan. Use bullets, photos, and other techniques to break up your writing and make it easy to skim. For example:

- *Okay:* You'll love this Web site because it has simple lessons, great tips you can act on right away, and no sales pitch.

- *Better:* You'll love this Web site because it has
  Simple lessons
  Great tips you can act on right away
  No sales pitch

✦ **Sharpness:** Your writing should get to the point — right away. For example:

- *Okay:* I wrote for hours. Then I pondered a bit. And wondered some more. And then I realized that 1 + 1 = 2.

- *Better:* 1 + 1 = 2. I realized this after I wrote for hours, pondered a bit, and then wondered some more.

In the rest of this chapter, I review techniques for following the three S's and then describe the logistics of consistently publishing a blog.

Writing for simplicity

Mark Twain once wrote, "If I had more time, I would have written a shorter letter." You would think that writing simple prose would be the easiest method, but it takes practice. Follow these ten tips every time you write, though, and you'll be off to a good start:

✦ **Shred the thesaurus.** Nothing breeds complex writing like a thesaurus. Throw it away. Use a dictionary if you need better words. And, never replace a perfectly appropriate two-syllable word with a four-syllable one. For example, "melancholy" is a great word, but if "sad" will work just as well, why not use it instead?

✦ **Write, think, revise.** Don't try to produce the perfect sentence in your head before you write. Just write down what you're trying to say. You can always improve it later.

✦ **Count syllables.** Make a game for yourself. Read a sentence in your post and see whether you can reduce the number of syllables by 20 percent without changing its impact or meaning. Do this for at least four sentences per day. The practice will help you write shorter, clearer prose. For example:

- *Okay:* I pedaled my bicycle to the grocery store.

- *Better:* I rode my bike to the store.

✦ **Minimize prepositions.** Prepositions, or words such as *about* and *in* and *from,* can give readers headaches (see the third bullet in this list):

- *Okay:* If you end *up with* a sentence that has too many prepositions *in* it, it might be *from* overediting.

- *Better:* Overediting often creates sentences *with* too many prepositions.

✦ **Use active voice, not passive.** If you find yourself using *was* or *have been* or similar wording, you might be using passive voice. Grammatically, it's okay, but it's more difficult to read and leads to overly complex sentences:

- *Okay (passive):* The boy was bitten by the dog.

- *Better (active):* The dog bit the boy.

✦ **Minimize parentheticals.** If you use parentheses or an em dash (—), you're creating a *parenthetical,* which can be a handy literary tool that helps you explain something. I use parentheticals far too much, myself — I'm attached to them — and I have a hard time getting rid of them. There — see that? Just keep them to a minimum.

✦ **Break up compound sentences.** Whenever you combine sentences using conjunctions, commas, and such, you create a sentence that's hard to read online.

- *Okay:* Writing simply is a must, because it invites readers in, while complex writing, though fancier, drives readers away.

- *Better:* Writing simply is a must. It invites readers in. Complex writing, though fancier, drives them away.

✦ **Blow away fluff.** It's hard to resist adding words such as *really* or *extremely.* Resist anyway.

✦ **Be confident.** Make your statement with authority. Don't dilute it with "I think" and "I feel." Obviously, this blog should offer your take on the topic at hand.

- *Okay:* I think simple writing is best.

- *Better:* Simple writing is best.

✦ **Don't get cute.** It's hard to resist writing "$ave dollar$ and ¢ent$". It's also hard to read it. Don't use cutesy punctuation. Don't use texting shorthand like LOL, either, unless it fits your audience.

✦ **Don't! Use! Too! Many! Exclamation! Points!!!!!** Hopefully, I don't need to say any more on that subject.

✦ **Practice!** Writing is not a talent. It's a skill. The more you write, the better you get. Practice doesn't help you only with blogging. The work you put in on your blog pays off anytime you sit down to write.

Writing for scannability

Online, people don't read. They scan. Typical readers rapidly scroll down the page, looking for words, pictures, and ideas that catch their attention.

Change makes the eye pause: Paragraph breaks, photos, and bold or italicized text all draw attention. Used properly, these devices help readers get your point before they dive into reading every word of your post.

Before people read your article from start to finish, they want content that

✦ **Has no paragraphs longer than four or five lines**

✦ **Lists important points in numbered or bulleted lists**

✦ **Breaks up major points with headlines**

✦ **Includes images to emphasize points and give the eye a break**

✦ **Includes only one idea per paragraph**

✦ **Is short and concise**

   See the section "Writing for simplicity," earlier in this chapter.

✦ **Includes headlines that explain the subsequent copy on their own**

   You should be able to write a headline on a blank sheet of paper and immediately understand it:

   • *Okay:* Overview

   • *Better:* Overview of Online Writing

✦ **Includes links that follow the same rule**

✦ **Uses line spacing of at least 1.5 lines**

✦ **Places headlines closer to the paragraphs that come after them than to the paragraphs that come before**

Figure 3-1 shows an example of a blog post I wrote that uses at least a few of these principles: I used images to break up the page, added subheadings and numbered lists, and kept my paragraphs short.

Here's an another advantage to scannable posts: Many readers skim through countless posts from multiple blogs using their RSS feed readers. When they do, elements such as headlines and images catch their eyes.

In the example shown in Figure 3-2, you can see a couple of differences in the posts:

✦ **First post:** It's more scannable and therefore catches your eye. You're more likely to read it.

✦ **Second post:** The lines in this post run together somewhat and are less likely to draw the reader's eye.

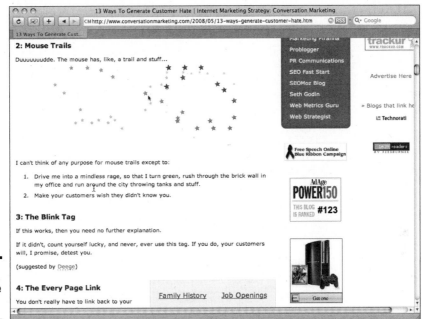

Figure 3-1:
A scannable
blog post.

Scannable

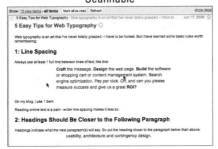

Not Scannable

Figure 3-2:
If you prefer
the first
post, you're
a typical
reader.

Scannable content gets a chance to be read: The text you write is more likely to be read by visitors to your site.

Writing sharp

Get to the point!

In grammar school, we're taught the funnel writing style: Start broad and then narrow your focus until you draw a conclusion at the end of your essay.

Forget that method. Instead, adopt a more journalistic, *upside down* style. Lead with your conclusion. Tell readers why they should continue reading, and tell them what benefits they'll see if they do.

The first paragraph (or paragraphs) of your blog post should include

✦ What the reader will learn

✦ Why they need to learn it

✦ How it will benefit them

This isn't a hard-and-fast rule. (No rule ever is.) You can always add a little extra introduction for entertainment value. If you start by writing the sharpest possible text and get to the point, however, the result is always a more readable post.

Clearing Bloggage

If you're avoiding writing on your blog, or staring at your computer screen for an hour without writing a word, you have blogger's block. I call it *bloggage*.

Here are a few ways to clear bloggage:

✦ **Read instead of write.** Find something that someone else wrote, said, or did that makes you laugh, scream, or cry. Responding is sometimes easier than writing from scratch.

✦ **Request ideas.** Ask your audience what they want to read. They may give you some helpful ideas.

✦ **Go wild.** Write something in a tone that's nothing like your normal style. Pretend that you're a new guest author on your blog and write under a pseudonym. It's fun!

✦ **Take a break.** If you're jammed up, it may be your brain's way of saying, "I need a vacation." Walk away from your blog for a few hours or days. Read a book. Come back refreshed and see whether the ideas flow more easily.

✦ **Start talking.** Rather than write, start talking about your subject matter. Use a recording device and pretend that you're teaching a class. Transcribe what you said after five or ten minutes, and you'll likely have some interesting ideas for a post.

Keep reading for more on bloggage-blockage removal techniques that I find helpful.

Setting your editorial calendar

Using — and sticking to — an editorial calendar can help you avoid bloggage. Dedicate a few days each week to a specific type of article.

For example, Monday might be book review day. Or, Wednesday might be list-of-photos day. On my blog, I have site review day, when I ask readers to submit their sites for review and I write my recommendations as a post.

I don't always follow my editorial calendar. I do, however, use it when I'm running low on ideas.

Keeping an idea list

Always keep a pad or file on your computer where you can compile a list of potential blog posts. This idea list is your resource when you're running out of ideas. It also ensures that you don't forget any outstanding ideas when they pop into your head.

Here are some types of information you can keep on your list:

✦ Interesting Web sites that inspire you

✦ Ideas that just pop into your head

✦ Questions your clients or customers ask

✦ The title of a book or magazine article that made you think

✦ A quote or comment from you or someone else that might make an interesting topic

✦ Anything else that occurs to you

I keep a small notebook with me at all times (even on my nightstand). I also keep a list of ideas on my computer and transcribe any new ideas from my notebook to my computer.

Note that I don't keep many details. I can fill them in later. This list becomes a sort of "tickler" for me. If I'm short on ideas, I review the list for extra inspiration. And, I don't have to worry about forgetting a particular site or idea, because I already wrote it down.

Writing ahead

No rule stipulates that you must write one complete blog post, publish it, and then move on to the next.

If you have a half-formed idea, start writing. Save it as a draft in your blogging software. That way, you can return to it later.

If you're inspired and suddenly want to write a series of related blog posts, all at one time, do it! Publish the first one and save the rest to publish later. Writing ahead in this way creates a library of material that you can publish at any time.

Finding guest bloggers

Letting another blogger write on your blog can give you a break when you need it. It can also attract attention (if the blogger is well known) and bring that blogger's audience to your blog. And, it can get you invited to post as a guest on that person's blog, too.

If you know of a blog that complements yours, or if you comment regularly on a particular blog, consider contacting that blog's author. Ask that person whether she's interested in guest-posting on your blog.

Your invitee doesn't need to guest-post right away. Just keep a list of bloggers who indicate an interest in guest-posting. If you're stumped for an idea or you're going on vacation or you have an interesting idea that requires guest posts, contact a potential contributor.

Chapter 4: Tracking Other Blogs

In This Chapter

✔ **Understanding RSS and feed readers**

✔ **Setting up Google Reader or Netvibes**

✔ **Reviewing your feeds fast with hotkeys**

✔ **Getting organized with folders and tags**

Two things power the blogging world: writers and the community in which they function. In earlier chapters of this minibook, I talk about you, the writer. But that's only half the equation.

Somehow, you need to get involved with the larger community: that is, the many bloggers and readers out there already talking about your subject. That involvement leads to links and references to you by other, more influential bloggers. If you want that kind of involvement, want to be noticed, and want to become a respected member of the community, you need to do one of the following:

✦ Leave a pithy comment on an influential blog.

✦ Reference another blogger's post in one of your own and link to that post.

✦ Write something highly relevant to current events.

All these methods require that you know what's going on in your industry or community, as well as related news. To that end, you need to know how to track blogs. With that knowledge, you can then "listen" to the conversation that's going on amongst related blogs and join in with useful information in the form of blog posts of your own. That's what this chapter holds.

Note: This chapter is very similar to Book VII, Chapter 2. If you've already read that chapter, you can skim through this one. This chapter might also seem similar to Chapter 1 of this minibook, but it's not. That chapter shows you how to find the right topic. This chapter focuses on how to track relevant blogs on an ongoing basis.

Understanding Feeds and Feed Readers

Geekery ahead! This section is filled with terms like *RSS* and *XML*. These terms will help you understand how this stuff all works. If you got hives in computer class in high school, I fully understand that you might want to skip ahead.

All blogs (at least within my definition of a blog) generate a list of updates in an *RSS feed.* RSS stands for really simple syndication, which is a standard way of delivering a list of headlines and articles or article summaries as a streamlined text file.

RSS is built using XML, if you care about that sort of thing.

The raw content of an RSS feed looks like what you see in Figure 4-1.

Figure 4-1:
Raw RSS.
Blech.

Information in this format isn't very useful, is it? Well, not for the average humanoid, at least. However, this format allows a type of computer software — *feed readers* — to retrieve headlines and summaries from just about every blog on the Internet, and deliver them to you in a pretty, easy-to-read format, as shown in Figure 4-2. Much better!

Every time a blogger publishes a new post, the blogging software adds that post to the RSS feed. When you sign into your feed reader, it goes and checks the RSS feed for updates. Your feed reader then alerts you to the new post.

Here's the first takeaway for convenience and expediency: When you use an RSS feed reader, you can subscribe to the RSS feeds from Web sites you like and review the latest headlines in the reader instead of having to visit the Web site itself.

Show: 15 new items - all items	Mark all as read	Refresh		show details
☆ October 16th Internet Marketing Triage Webinar: More Info - Sign ups for my October 16th Internet			Oct 8, 2008	⊙
☆ Nah, You Don't Need A Blog - You don't need to tell the public about your product and why it inspires			Oct 6, 2008	⊙
☆ 59 Things Webinar, October 16th - Sign Ups Open - I'm starting a webinar series on Internet marketing.			Oct 3, 2008	⊙
☆ 14 Instant Landing Page Upgrades - Landing pages are a great way to generate sales from			Oct 1, 2008	⊙
☆ 3 Things Your Description Tag Must Contain - The description META tag won't do much to improve your			Sep 30, 2008	⊙
☆ 5 Tips To Make Sure You're Speaking to the Right Audience: Congress Bails on the Bailout -			Sep 29, 2008	⊙
☆ Google Analytics Tip: Learn How They Found That 1 Page. - You can use Google Analytics to figure out			Sep 27, 2008	⊙
☆ Test Drive: Evri Search and Discovery Tools - Evri doesn't bill itself as a search engine. Their motto is			Sep 26, 2008	⊙
☆ 5 Tips for Crisis Marketing: The Perils of Being McCain - John McCain took a big gamble yesterday,			Sep 25, 2008	⊙
☆ Create Better Slide Presentations: slide:ology - At conferences, three things are a constant: Lack of			Sep 25, 2008	⊙
☆ 5 Tips for Generating 10,000 Links Overnight - Don't No, really, don't. Are you listening? If you get them			Sep 24, 2008	⊙
☆ 10 SEO and Marketing-Friendly Title Tag Formulas - You want keywords in the title tag. Your marketing			Sep 23, 2008	⊙
☆ U-Haul: Fire Your Lawyer (and Your Marketer) - Sarah over at SEOMOZ outlined U-Haul's ridiculous			Sep 23, 2008	⊙
☆ 4 Metrics for Analyzing SEO Traffic (and one to ignore) - I have a defense mechanism: When			Sep 22, 2008	⊙
☆ 5 Daily Social Media Builders In Less Than 10 Minutes (Total!) - I am sick of social media. Social this.			Sep 19, 2008	⊙

Figure 4-2:
The same
RSS feed,
in Google
Reader.

**Book VI
Chapter 4**

**Tracking Other
Blogs**

Here's a bigger takeaway, which explains the power of feed readers: They enable you to collect information from many different Web sites, blogs, and other news sources (many non-blog sites publish RSS feeds, too). Then you can sort through it all, keep and organize the information you need, and ignore the rest.

Setting Up Google Reader

One of my favorite feed readers (and one of the most popular) is Google Reader. It's easy to use but includes powerful features for reviewing and organizing lots of information at once.

Although I focus on Google Reader here, many other great tools are available. Whatever feed reader you use, though, the basic principles I talk about in this chapter are the same, and you should be able to transfer the lessons from one feed reader to another.

If you have a Google account, you already have a Google Reader account, too. Visit www.google.com/reader and log in using your username and password.

If you don't already have a Google account, set one up and then visit www.google.com/reader. See Book VII, Chapter 2, for more about setting up a Google account.

You see the Google Reader welcome page, as shown in upcoming Figure 4-3.

Subscribing to feeds in Google Reader is easy:

1. **Click the Add Subscription link, as shown in Figure 4-3.**

A small box opens right below the link.

2. **Type the Web address of the blog to which you want to subscribe.**

Click to subscribe

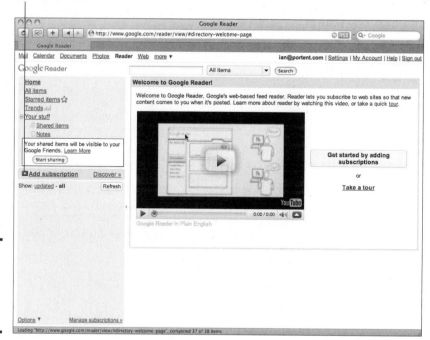

Figure 4-3:
Google
Reader, the
first time
you log in.

3. Click Add.

Google Reader detects the blog's RSS feed and subscribes to it.

If a blog's RSS feed isn't set up correctly, Google Reader might not find the feed. No problem. Move on to the following set of steps where I show you how to subscribe to a blog's RSS feed from the blog's homepage.

First, look for the RSS subscription icon or link. It'll look something like the link in Figure 4-4.

RSS subscription icon

Figure 4-4:
Try
subscribing
from a blog
homepage.

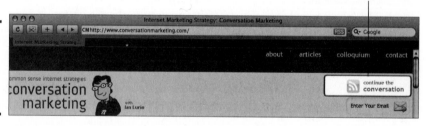

After you find the RSS subscription link or icon

1. **Click the link or icon.**
2. **Choose Google Reader.**
3. **Click OK.**

   Google Reader adds the feed.

If a blog's RSS feed is *really* stubborn, you might have to add it to Google Reader manually. Don't worry! It's not as difficult as it sounds.

1. **On the blog's homepage, find the RSS link or icon; refer to Figure 4-4.**
2. **Right-click the link.**
3. **From the menu that appears, choose Copy Link or whatever similar option your browser shows you.**
4. **Log into Google Reader.**
5. **Click Add Subscription; refer to Figure 4-3.**
6. **Paste the link into the subscription field and then click Add.**

   Google Reader grabs the feed and adds it to your subscriptions.

**Book VI
Chapter 4**

If these methods don't work, contact the blog author. Something's wrong, and chances are that the author will appreciate the note (because he's losing subscribers).

Go ahead and subscribe to a few of your favorite blogs and news sites using Google Reader. Then come back. I'll wait right here, don't worry.

Google Reader saves all those subscriptions in your account. When you next log into Google Reader, you'll see those feeds, updated with the latest headlines from those sites and blogs.

Using Folders and Tags to Organize Your Feeds

If you have only five or six feeds to review, you can keep them all lumped together in a single folder, with no categorization. If you're like me, though, you're going to end up maintaining a list of more than 100 feeds. When that happens, I seriously recommend keeping your feeds organized. Otherwise, you'll rapidly lose track of different feeds. The best tools for that, in any feed reader, are

✦ **Folders:** Use folders to group content into broad topics, such as *search engine optimization* or *local news.*

✦ **Tags:** Use tags to group articles even if they're in different folders.

Using folders to organize feeds

I read about 50 different feeds about search engine optimization. I *could* leave those feeds mashed into all of my various advertising information. But that'll make one heck of a mess, as you can see in Figure 4-5.

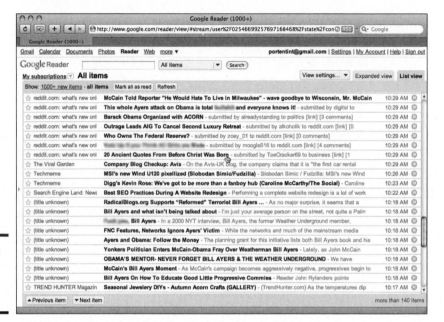

Figure 4-5:
Total feed higgledy-piggledy.

I can't find a thing in there! So, to be neat, tidy, and organized, I can file this feed in a folder.

When you organize all your feeds like this — grouping them into relevant folders — you get a much more usable feed environment, as you can see in Figure 4-6.

Wait a minute. On second thought, I don't want that feed in that folder. For feeds like this, I want a new folder, named SEO.

Guess I have to create a new folder. It's a snap, though. Here's how to create a folder — and then add a feed to that folder:

1. **Log into Google Reader.**

   If you don't have a Google Reader account, see the earlier section, "Setting Up Google Reader."

2. **Click the feed that you want to place in a folder.**

3. **At the upper right, open the Feed Settings drop-down, as shown in Figure 4-7.**

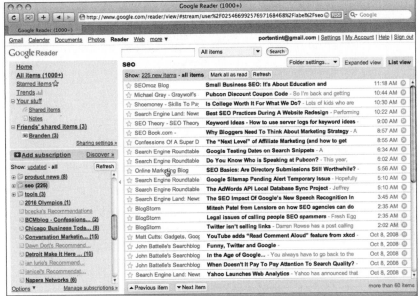

Figure 4-6:
A more
organized
set of
feeds, using
folders.

Click to create a folder

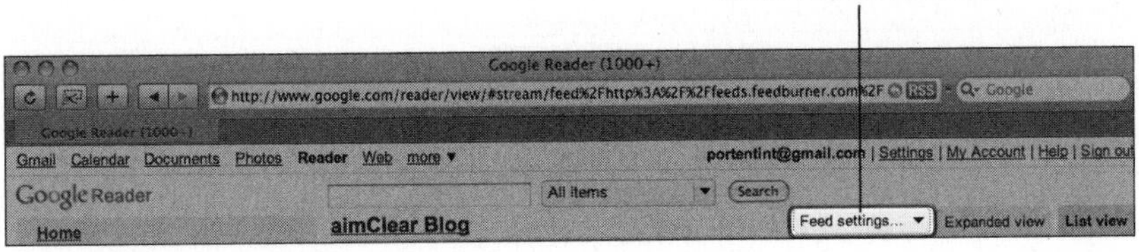

Figure 4-7:
Open Feed
Settings to
create a
folder.

4. Click New Folder.

Speed demon that you are now, you can also create many folders at once:

1. **Log into Google Reader.**

2. **At the bottom left, click Manage Subscriptions. See Figure 4-8.**

You see a list of every feed you have as well as the feed's folder
assignment. Each feed that's assigned to a folder shows the folder name
on the right, as shown in Figure 4-9. You can add, change, or delete
folders as desired.

Folders are indeed fantastic tools, getting you halfway to a totally organized
blogging radar screen, as it were. Do try to use simple, clear folder names
you'll recognize later. It's tempting to just type in **New Folder** for now, thinking you'll come back and fix it later on. Trust me, you won't. Use a good label
now and you'll be happier for it.

Figure 4-8:
Manage
sub-
scriptions
from here.

Click to create many folders at once

Figure 4-9:
The Manage
Subscrip-
tions page.

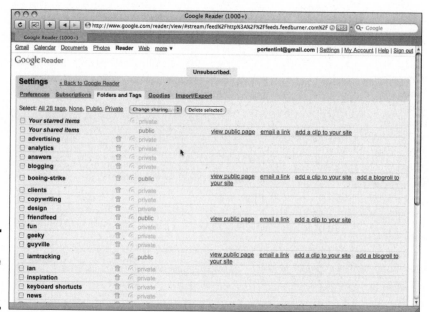

Here's where the real world bumps heads a little with your new organizational system. What if you store two different articles in two categories, but those articles are still related? Say I have a newspaper article about search engine optimization that ends up in my News folder, and a blog post with a great SEO tip that's related to the newspaper article. I want to link the two somehow so that I can see them in the same "bucket" and remind myself that they're related. However, I don't want to put their feeds in the same folder. The business section of the newspaper doesn't always talk SEO. The SEO blog doesn't always talk news.

This is where tags can be a great tool.

Using tags to organize feeds

Tags are keywords or phrases you assign to a single post instead of an entire feed. Using the preceding example, I could tag both the newspaper article and the blog post with *SEO*. Then I'd see both articles when I view the hits on my SEO tag.

Here's how you add a tag to a post:

1. **Click the post you want to tag.**

2. **Click Edit Tags at the bottom of the post, as shown in Figure 4-10.**

The Add Tags box will appear right above the link.

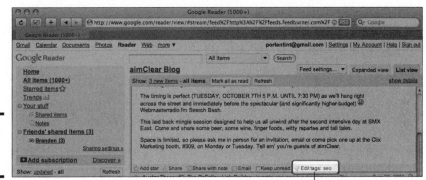

Figure 4-10:
Add tags
from here.

Click to add a tag

3. **Type the tags you want, separated by commas, and then click Save.**

That's it! You tagged your post.

Here's how to tag posts without touching your mouse. While viewing the post in Google Reader, press T on your keyboard. You enter your tags in the Edit Tags field that appears.

You can view all articles with a given tag by either

✦ **Clicking that tag at the bottom of the article.**

✦ **Clicking the tag name on the lower left side of your Google Reader window.**

See Figure 4-11.

Figure 4-11:
Tags listed
in Google
Reader.

When you use tags and folders together, you can save and organize a lot of information — fast.

Reviewing Feeds Fast with Hot Keys

Pshew. All that tedious housekeeping is done (for now, at least). The question before you is how to skim through more than 100 feeds every day. Answer: With hot keys!

Google Reader and most standard feed readers include hot keys, which allow you to use your mouse to rapidly view, tag, or manipulate each post.

In Google Reader, you want to know six critical hot keys:

Pressing This	Does This
J	Moves you down to the next item.
K	Moves you up to the previous item.
Shift+N	Moves you to the next folder.
Shift+P	Moves you up to the previous folder.
T	Opens the tagging menu.
Shift+S	Shares an item on your Shared Items page.

More on the Shared Items page in a bit.

To find many other hot keys, look in the Google Reader Help center by searching for "*keyboard shortcuts*".

I press the J hot key to zip down through my unread items. Then

✦ **If I see a headline that catches my eye,** I stop to read it.

✦ **If it looks really interesting,** I tag it.

I have tags like *tools* and *tips,* so I can return later to see all the tips on a given subject.

If I want to share it with my team, I press Shift+S. That puts it on my Shared Items page (more on that in the next section).

The most important thing to remember is that you're not here to read the details on every item. You're here to build a reference library. More on that in the upcoming section, "Avoiding Information Insanity."

Creating a Shared Items Page

If you work on a team, you might want to make interesting items available to them. Google Reader allows you to do this via its Shared Items page.

As I mention earlier, the easiest way to share items is to click the Share icon or press Shift+S. That adds the item to your general shared items feed.

And to refine your shared posts, you might want use tags just like how you tag what you file in your own post folder structure. That way, you can separate the cute pictures of cuddly animals with *Aunt Myrtle* tags (wink) and the articles about investment banking with *corporate board of directors* tags.

Here's how you create a custom shared feed:

1. **Create a tag and tag a few items.**

   See the earlier section, "Using tags to organize feeds," to see how.

2. **Click Manage Subscriptions at the lower left of the Reader window; refer to Figure 4-8.**

3. **Click the Folders and Tags tab.**

4. **Click the Share icon next to the tag you want made public.**

   This makes every item you tag with that tag public.

   See Figure 4-12 for an example.

**Book VI
Chapter 4**

Tracking Other Blogs

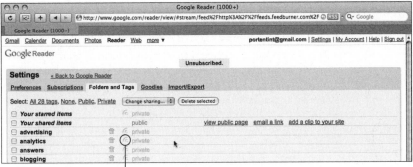

Figure 4-12:
Make a tag
public here.

Click to make this tag public

5. **Click View Public Page next to the tag you just made public.**

   E-mail that link to those with whom you want to share posts, and they'll be able to subscribe to all of the items to which you add this now-public tag.

Shared feeds are doubly handy because they

✦ Create a page that folks can visit to see items you consider important

✦ Create an RSS feed

Now your team has two options for finding what they want.

Avoiding Information Insanity

You can easily get buried in articles, posts, and random information. You don't want to end up with a pile of hundreds or thousands of items that's so huge you throw up your hands and give up.

To avoid information insanity, try these rules:

✦ **Organize; don't read.** The most important thing you can do is find interesting stuff and organize it for later. If you want to read a full article, go ahead! But don't force yourself. Tag it and file it. That way, you can retrieve it later.

✦ **Declare bankruptcy.** Every now and then, if you're so hopelessly behind in reviewing your feeds, you can just declare feed bankruptcy. Mark everything as read and start over. Something really compelling will likely be mentioned in future articles, so don't worry about missing anything.

✦ **Be picky.** Don't keep any feed subscriptions that you never read. Clean out your feed reader ruthlessly at least once per month.

With these tips and Google Reader in hand, you're now armed and ready to start getting involved in the blogging world.

Chapter 5: Getting Involved on Other Blogs

In This Chapter

✔ Why connecting with other bloggers is important

✔ Seeing how to connect with other bloggers

✔ Minding your manners

✔ Blog carnivals: The good and the bad

*Y*our blog will grow if more people find it and like it. But, for your blog to grow, more people will have to find it and like it. An Internet marketing Catch-22, if you will.

There is a pretty simple solution, though. Other bloggers have already gone through this process. They've attracted the readers and have a loyal audience. If you strike up a conversation with them and they like what you have to say, they'll pass you along to their audience. Instant publicity.

This approach might sound manipulative or cynical, but it's not. Established bloggers keep their audience by presenting great information. Some of that information is stuff they write on their own; some of it, though, is new stuff — quite possibly your stuff — they find in day-to-day research. (See Chapter 4 of this minibook to read about tracking other blogs.)

So, think of this progression as a kind of online social compact: You present content with great value. Other bloggers find it and pass it along to their audience by writing about it and linking to your post. They get some credit for finding what you wrote. In exchange, you get more visitors and more links.

Your job, then, when you first launch your blog, is to connect with some of those bloggers.

Connecting with Other Bloggers

Step 1: Find the bloggers with whom you want to connect. You might have already done this, or put some thought to it, if you've been through Chapter 4 of this minibook. If you haven't, use a Google blog search, Technorati. com, or the search engine of your choice to locate a few really authoritative blogs.

Step 2: Make contact. However, you can't just start sending those bloggers unsolicited e-mails in hopes that one of them will respond. They might, but I'm predicting that you probably won't like their reply of *Stop e-mailing me.*

Instead, have a quick look at Book VII, which covers social media marketing. Set up a Twitter account and "follow" bloggers there. (No, I'm not proposing any type of lurid stalking. *Following* has a very legit meaning in the world of social media, so read all about it in Book VII.) Write about their posts on your blog and link to them. Introduce yourself with your content and your comments on their content.

Take your time with this. No blogger (even an unknown "C List"-er like me) likes to be harassed with, "Hey, link to me!" e-mails and comments.

Leaving Great Comments

The best way to first introduce yourself to a blogger is by contributing to her posts. The easiest way to do that is through comments. A well-written, well thought–out comment can lend a lot to a blog post. It prompts discussion in a way that only audience participation can, and bloggers appreciate it. I once wrote a post that listed Internet marketing tips. The tips themselves were pretty good (if I do say so). But readers left comments that were so good they made the post into something more: a public discussion of the value of Internet marketing, with a live, growing list of tips and details about the topic.

Here are a few tips for writing a good comment:

✦ **Read the whole post first.** Otherwise, you might jump to incorrect conclusions.

✦ **Read all the other comments left before yours.** See whether you want to reply to those.

✦ **Don't be afraid to bring up a conflicting viewpoint.** Just make sure you present it well. Being ornery won't make you any friends.

✦ **Don't link to your site unless there's truly something relevant there.**

And, a few ideas for responses to a post:

✦ Agreeing and adding another idea/point/tip

   I totally agree with your post. You might also want to consider flipping the pancakes right before you serve them.

✦ Agreeing, but with a qualification about one tip or another

   I totally agree with your post. But regarding butter in the pan: Folks can use a little nonstick cooking spray, instead, if they're calorie conscious.

✦ Politely disagreeing with one point, and offering an alternative

> *Great post. One other viewpoint, though: Buckwheat pancakes can taste just as good if they're not over mixed.*

✦ Following up to someone else's comment

> *Frank's point about chocolate chips is a good one. I'd add that you can use dark chocolate chips and make your pancakes a good cough suppressant, too.*

Come back to the same blog and comment on different posts, too. The blog author will notice that you're a contributor.

Tracking replies to your comments

If you're commenting on two or three blogs every week, keeping track of them all can be hard. I recommend using a tool called Commentful to keep track of what folks say in response to your comments. It's easy to use, and it's free.

After you make a comment on a blog post, copy the Web address of that page. You'll add that address to Commentful. You can set up Commentful in a few steps:

1. **Go to www.blogflux.com.**

2. **Set up an account.**

3. **Under Select Blogflux Services, choose Commentful.**

4. **Click the Add URL to My Watchlist button, as shown in Figure 5-1.**

Click to track comments

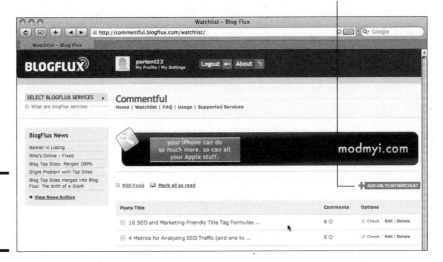

Figure 5-1:
Track
comments
from here.

5. **In the URL field of the Add URL to My Watchlist window, paste the address of the blog post on which you commented.**

6. **Click Add.**

7. **(Optional) If you want to receive updates regarding new comments via e-mail, select the Subscribe to Daily Updates via E-Mail check box. See Figure 5-2.**

Figure 5-2:
Add a URL
to your
watchlist.

Check to receive updates

Commentful will keep track of new comments on that post. If you sign up for e-mail updates, you'll receive those updates every day. Otherwise, check in on your Commentful page to see new comments as they're made.

You can also subscribe to Commentful updates via RSS. Then you can review it in your feed reader.

I don't generally subscribe to every blog page on which I comment. Instead, I keep track of the pages where

✦ I know there might be a discussion.

✦ There are already a lot of comments.

✦ I've had a lot of folks respond to my comments before.

Avoiding foot-in-mouth syndrome

When you're speaking to someone in person, your body language, tone of voice, and expression tell her whether you're kidding, angry, or trying to be nice. When you type a comment on a blog, though, there's no way to communicate those emotions.

Thus, a comment that seems innocent to you could offend the blog author, or another commenter, or every single person who happens to read what you wrote. That's a big deal.

Here are a few famous examples from my checkered commenting career:

✦ I wrote, "You're too dang smart, and I hate that," meaning it as a compliment. Instead, I greatly offended the author and had to apologize, profusely.

✦ I used the phrase *higgledy-piggledy*. Another commenter didn't know what the phrase meant and thought I was insulting the author. That person wrote about my nastiness on another blog. Suddenly, I had dozens of angry e-mails in my Inbox.

✦ I complimented a blogger who thought I was being sarcastic about a cool hat. Sigh.

You can't avoid every misunderstanding. However, you can minimize the risks. Here are some pointers on how to stay out of the doghouse:

✦ **Don't be sarcastic.** Sarcasm relies on tone of voice. A 50-word comment can't communicate it.

✦ **Don't be nasty.** Ever. If you have nothing nice or helpful to say, don't say anything. It's okay to disagree, but you can do that without being nasty.

✦ **Don't make jokes** unless they're really clear.

Make smart, polite, and helpful comments, and you've taken the first step toward building a blogging relationship.

Linking to Other Blog Posts

The next step is linking to other bloggers. Links are the lifeblood of the blogging world. When you link to someone's post, she will appreciate it.

If a post really catches your attention, you can post to your own blog in response. Here are a few styles of response posts.

✦ **Use the link list.** Pick three or four related posts that impressed you and write a short summary of each post, why you like it, and a link.

✦ **Cite another post as support for an argument** you're making in your post, and use a link.

✦ **Cite another post as an additional resource** and link to it.

✦ **Use the step-by-step review and critique.** Write a post reviewing each point in another blogger's piece. Add your own clarifications, changes, and additions.

Most bloggers are obsessive. They check their Web analytics reports to see which sites are sending them visitors. If they see you're one of those sites, they'll look at your blog. If they like what you're saying, they'll reciprocate. Those links help you move up in the search engines. More importantly, links are like a reference: The blogger who links to you is saying you've made an impact with him. That will get you visitors.

Giving Credit Where Credit Is Due

One quick note: You must always give credit! If you reference another post, link to it and give the author's name.

That's a given, I know — or, it should be a given. But plagiarism is common online, and bloggers are always on the lookout for it. So never quote a blog without giving a link and a reference.

Also, don't use `nofollow` to deny links from your blog to another. Many blogging tools will automatically have `nofollow` links in comments. That means search engines will ignore those links. You're using `nofollow` if your links look like this:

```
<a href=http://www.mysite.com rel="nofollow">link here</a>
```

You're denying the other blogger the search engine optimization benefits of the link. So give credit where credit is due: Remove the `nofollow`.

Writing a Guest Post

One great, great way to build traffic to your blog is to guest-post on another. In essence, you can offer to write a piece for another person's blog. Bloggers want great content. Guest posts help them build that content, even if they're on vacation, taking a break, or are too busy writing a book to post to their blog. While you build relationships with other bloggers, be on the lookout for guest-posting opportunities.

Bloggers look for guest authors to cover when they go on vacation, to help expand their coverage, or to lend extra expertise.

You can't really invite yourself to guest-post, but you can offer to trade guest posts with another blogger. He writes a post on your site, and you write a post on his.

Here are a few points to remember when guest-posting:

✦ **The blog owner gets some control over what you write.** The blog owner will review what you write, and he'll probably suggest a few ideas that he'd like you to write about. That's his right.

✦ **Put in extra time on the writing.** I'm not saying you don't do your best on your blog, but when you're posting to another blog, it's like you're going to a car show. A little extra polish never hurts.

✦ **Be clear with the blog owner about linking.** Is it okay to link back to your own site? Will he likewise do it for you?

✦ **Provide a little biography of yourself.** Chances are that the blog owner will want to include it with your post.

Joining Blog Carnivals

Blog carnivals are scheduled events where a single author or editor solicits posts on a specific topic. Carnivals are usually scheduled and managed through a central site, such as Blog Carnival (see Figure 5-3).

The carnival host collects the posts and publishes them, with links, on the host's blog. The result usually looks similar to Figure 5-4.

Carnivals usually travel, with different hosts, editors, or authors each time. The *host* is the blogger who publishes the posts on his blog.

Getting involved in a blog carnival is easy. Do a quick search on Google for *"blog carnivals"*, or for *"[topic] blog carnivals"*. Find a few carnivals and read the submission requirements. If you have a great post idea that can contribute to the carnival, go ahead and submit it.

Here are a few things to look for when you submit to a blog carnival:

✦ **Check the history of the carnival.** Make sure that the editor doesn't have a history of stealing content. It doesn't happen often, but it does happen. It's easy to check: Just do a search on the carnival host's name and make sure there are no complaints.

Figure 5-3:
Look for central sites that manage blog carnivals.

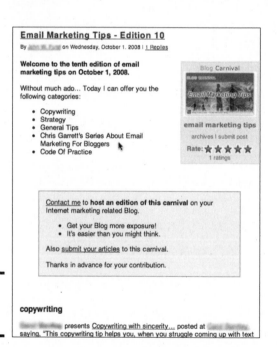

Figure 5-4:
A blog carnival.

✦ **Think about whether you'd want to host the carnival at some point.** You'll want to participate if you submit content more than once.

✦ **Check linking policies.** Is it okay to link to your blog in the posts? Or will the host link to you as part of the carnival?

✦ **Similar to guest-posting, be sure to submit your most-polished, highest-quality content.** You're in front of a larger audience, and you're part of a team. It's your responsibility to put your best content out there.

The Art of Asking Nicely

You undoubtedly hate it when your neighbor starts using his turbo-charged leaf blower at 8 a.m. on Sunday. That's just bad manners. Blogging communities dislike those kinds of disruptions, too. If you want to become a valued member of the community, you need to mind your manners. Ultimately, that's great for your blog and your company's image.

✦ **Never**

- Ask a blogger for a link more than once.

- Ask a blogger for a link if you haven't already corresponded with him.

✦ **Always**

- Say please.

- Say thank you.

- Reciprocate. If a blogger links to you, link back at some point. If the blogger comments on your blog, check in on his blog once in a while and see whether you can comment there, too.

Chapter 6: Promoting Your Posts

In This Chapter

✔ Publishing your post

✔ Using pinging to let the world know about a new post

✔ Submitting your posts to social media sites

✔ Letting other bloggers know when you write a new post

You spent hours writing that perfect post. Or you got inspired and hammered one out in a few minutes. Either way, you want to let the world know there's something new on your blog.

Closing that loop and promoting yourself is that essential last step that turns your blog from a collection of great writing to a real Internet marketing tool.

Just clicking that Publish button in WordPress isn't enough. A whole online ecosystem has sprung up to help spread the word about new blog posts. This chapter will introduce you to it.

Publishing Your Post

In most blogging software, when you click Publish, a lot more happens than you might think. The blog software

✦ **Publishes your post on the blog**

✦ **Updates the blog RSS feed to show the new post**

✦ *Pings* **(alerts) relevant sites**

See Chapter 2 of this minibook for more information on how to set up pinging.

Publishing is really more like "pushing." When you publish, your blog alerts many other blogs and Web sites about the new post. So, publishing a new post affects more than your own blog. It potentially alerts many, many other Web sites, as well as everyone who subscribes to your blog's RSS feed.

I'm not telling you that you're alerting thousands (or more) people about a new post when you publish to give you stage fright. I just want you to understand this because it helps you also understand the real, underlying power of blogging: The connection to a vast network of other blogs and sites.

You *can* accomplish the same thing on a standard Web site by going to each Web site and manually pinging it. Ugh. However, blogging evolved in a way that makes this process far easier. That's why I often recommend making a blog part of your Internet marketing strategy.

Letting the World Know: Using Pinging

I talk about pinging quite a bit in Chapter 2 of this miniboook, but there I focus on how you configure your blog to ping relevant sites and services. Now I want to talk more about what pinging can do for your blog.

In case you didn't read Chapter 2 (I'll wait), a *ping* is a short message, typically sent automatically by your blogging software. When a blog sends out a ping, here's what happens:

1. When you publish a new post, your blog sends the ping to specific sites, such as Technorati.

2. Technorati receives the ping, and its software retrieves the new post.

3. Technorati adds the new post to its index.

4. Technorati users have access to your new post, minutes after you publish it.

You can't take back a ping. After you publish and ping, the sites you ping retrieve your post. If you made a horrific typo, it's published for all to see. *Some* services update retrieved posts when you re-ping, but not all. So it pays to proofread a bit before you publish.

Because pinging is such a powerful way to keep the rest of the Internet up to date about your blog, make sure your ping list is up to date. See Chapter 2 for detailed instructions on setting up pinging as well as what to do if your blog software doesn't support pinging.

Submitting Your Post to StumbleUpon

StumbleUpon is a huge, addictive bookmarking service. Members can install a toolbar in their browser and simply click a Stumble button. The toolbar then takes them to a site selected based on the member's previous thumbs-up or thumbs-down preferences (also handled in the toolbar). See Book VII, Chapter 4 for more about StumbleUpon.

You need to have the StumbleUpon toolbar installed, and have a StumbleUpon account set up, to follow this section. See Book VII, Chapter 2 for instructions. Or just visit www.stumbleupon.com and follow the directions there. It's an easy setup.

Members can also submit new content to the StumbleUpon directory. That content is then added to the available sites, and users have a chance of, um, stumbling upon it.

The more folks stumble and give a thumbs-up to a particular page, the more often the page is sent to other stumblers with related interests. So a well-written blog post can generate an unbelievable number of visits, in a very short time. Figure 6-1 shows what happened with one post I wrote: I received more than 10,000 visits from StumbleUpon in just a day.

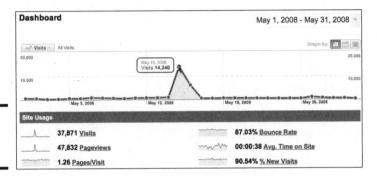

Figure 6-1: A Stumble Fest!

Do not treat StumbleUpon as a PR service! It's tempting to submit your own blog posts to the service and do nothing else. Don't. You need to build a solid profile by stumbling other content from other sites, too. When you're a good citizen and contribute to the community, StumbleUpon will reward you. If you don't contribute, StumbleUpon might penalize or even ban your account. See Book VII, on social media marketing, to learn more.

When you submit any new content to StumbleUpon, you'll get a pop-up window — the Discovery dialog box — as shown in Figure 6-2. There, you can type in the title of the content, a description, and relevant keywords.

When you complete that form, follow a few basic rules:

✦ **Use a good, descriptive title.** Another reader should be able to easily figure out what the post is about by reading the title.

✦ **Write a good description, too.** I suspect StumbleUpon uses the description when it decides what your post is about.

✦ **Use good tags.** Tags are just keywords. Use words and phrases that describe the content you're adding to StumbleUpon, as shown in Figure 6-2.

✦ **Pick your first tag from the Topic list.** Then add more specific ones after that.

✦ **Send your post to StumbleUpon friends if you think they'll like it.** Don't abuse this, or you'll lose your friends.

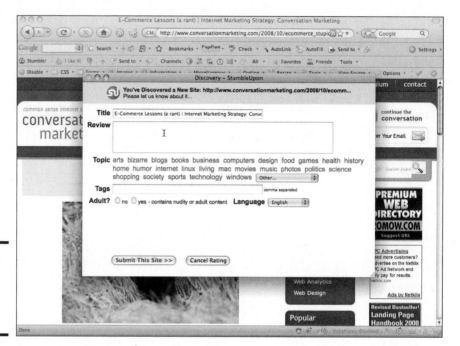

Figure 6-2:
Submit
content to
Stumble
Upon.

Don't expect StumbleUpon to generate scads of traffic every time. Building your profile takes a while. Plus, not every submission will become popular. However, StumbleUpon is a great community, and you never know when a new post will get huge coverage across the network.

Also, sometimes a post you submitted a year ago will be discovered by an influential stumbler. So your effort might pay off later.

Submitting Your Post on Digg (Once in a While)

Digg is the Gold Rush of traffic. If you can hit it big, you'll end up with a *lot* of traffic. Just realize that the chances of success are slim. Digg can deliver server-crushing traffic in a matter of hours. See Figure 6-3 for the kind of traffic a front-page Digg story can produce.

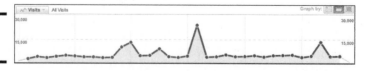

Figure 6-3:
Digg this!

For more about how Digg works, read Book VII.

The madness of Digg

Digg is about getting on the front page. If you reach the front page of Digg.com, you'll get that burst of traffic.

If you don't get on the front page, you'll remain in obscurity. You reach the front page if enough folks vote for (*Digg*) your content.

The problem with Digg and similar social content sites, though, is that even when you *do* get lots of traffic, there's no guarantee that traffic will lead to long-term growth for your blog.

I still think it's worth it to keep trying on Digg. Trust me. If you get 30,000 visitors in a few hours, it's bound to boost your rankings.

Knowing when you're Digg-worthy

You need to be picky about what you submit to Digg. Your post has the best chance of competing on Digg.com if it

+ **Covers a current topic, a bizarre topic, or something funny**

+ **Has high production standards**

    Put in the time to write super-scannable content (see Chapter 4 of this minibook), and don't forget to include lots of images.

+ **Has a high sneeze factor**

    See Book VII, Chapter 1 to read about this.

+ **Has high geek value**

    If it's content that'll make someone like me say, "Ooooh, aaaaah," good choice. News about a newly discovered solar system is good. News about the weekend football game is not.

Other social voting sites

You can find other sites similar to Digg. Here are a few, and why or when you might choose them:

+ **Reddit.com (`www.reddit.com`):** More news-focused

+ **Yahoo! Buzz (`http://buzz.yahoo.com`):** A slightly newer site, and a little less techie-focused

+ **Sphinn (`http://sphinn.com`):** A social voting site that's focused purely on Internet marketing

+ **Mixx (`www.mixx.com`):** Very similar to Digg

+ **Newsvine (`www.newsvine.com`):** In decline but still a good source of links and traffic

✦ **Fark (www.fark.com):** Fun for bizarre stories

✦ **Plime (www.plime.com):** Another social news site similar to Digg but again, may offer some niche opportunities

Submitting Your Post to Bookmarking Sites

Another promotion resource you can use is bookmarking sites. Sites like del.icio.us, Diigo, and Ma.gnolia all offer you a way to get your blog posts noticed.

Here are a few tips for submitting your posts to these sites:

✦ **Like StumbleUpon, these sites reward good citizenship.** Don't just bookmark your own posts. Bookmark other useful content, too.

✦ **Accurately and completely tag your bookmarks.** That way, other users can more easily find relevant content on your blog.

✦ **Connect with other users on these sites and share bookmarks.** That kind of networking can spread your posts more rapidly, as some might follow what you bookmark.

Sending a Polite E-Mail

There's nothing wrong with sending a polite e-mail asking folks to take a look at your new post.

You can send an e-mail to

✦ **Other bloggers:** If you think a fellow blogger might want to follow up on your post with one of his own, or if you cited his post in yours, send him a note.

✦ **Subscribers:** Many blogs have e-mail signup as well as RSS subscriptions. Notify those folks via e-mail.

✦ **Other contacts:** If you've been in contact with reporters, clients, or others who might be interested in this post, notify them, too.

Be conservative. Send e-mails regarding posts that are only directly relevant to the recipient's interests. For example, if I read a post about guinea pigs that I really like, and write a review with a link back to that post, I might e-mail the author. Or, if I chat with someone at a conference about SEO and I write a post about SEO, I might e-mail that person, too.

Participating in Online Communities

Finally, don't rule out sites like Facebook and microblogging communities like Twitter. A simple announcement similar to the one shown in Figure 6-4 can generate an initial burst of interest that leads to StumbleUpon traffic, Diggs, or just lots of readers.

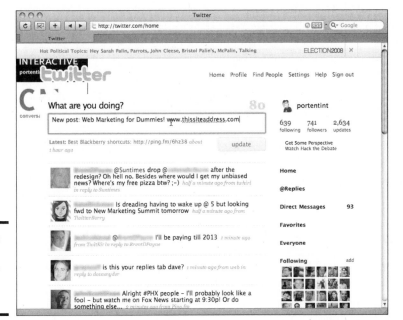

Figure 6-4:
A Twitter announce-
ment of a
new post.

You can be a little freer with your announcements in these communities. When I write a new post, I almost always announce it on Twitter, Plurk, and Facebook. I once stopped announcing posts in Facebook because I felt I was being too pushy, only to receive a few notes in my Inbox from readers asking, "Hey, why did you stop writing?"

Chapter 7: Introducing Podcasting

In This Chapter

✔ **Setting up an inexpensive production studio**

✔ **Preparing a podcast**

✔ **Recording a podcast**

✔ **Distributing your creation**

*B*logging puts words on a page. Podcasting puts your voice directly on the Web in the form of audio files that your readers can download and play back at their leisure. That creates a kind of direct connection with your audience, as they hear your tone and inflection.

Because of that, podcasting is a great supplement to your blogging strategy as part of your Internet marketing campaign.

This chapter is a *very* high-level view of podcasting. If you're going to try it once or twice, the information here will get you through the initial throes. If you're going to get serious, though, read *Podcasting For Dummies,* 2nd Edition, by Tee Morris, Chuck Tomasi, Evo Terra, and Kreg Steppe (Wiley). It covers everything from using special mics to advanced promotion techniques.

Podcasts do require some extra technology as well as a few extra steps on your part. That's what this chapter is about: getting your blog to a podcast.

Podcasting 101

Podcasting is no longer the realm of audiophiles and sound engineers. Recording, producing, and distributing your very own online audio show has become relatively easy.

A *podcast* is an audio or video recording you make and then distribute by using a special RSS feed. Don't let the word *special* scare you. I'll get to that later in the section, "Supporting Podcasting on Your Blog."

Podcasts are always fun to produce, but they're best when used to deliver

+ Training or tutorials

+ Interviews

✦ Any topic where you need to communicate more subtly than you can with writing

✦ A blog entry when you're sick of writing

Podcast listeners can then subscribe to your podcast via their favorite RSS feed reader, or such audio software as Windows Media Player or iTunes. That software then downloads the audio files and transfers them to listeners' iPod or other MP3 player, so they can listen to them on the go.

So, obviously, because podcasts are portable, folks can listen to them when and how they like. And because they're audio (compared with print, a visual medium), they provide another way for readers to connect to you, by becoming listeners.

Setting Up Your Podcasting Studio

Setting up a podcasting studio is remarkably similar to setting up a home recording studio. (Go figure.) Think recording device, software, input device, and then (of course) some vehicle for broadcasting. For podcasting, my studio consists of

✦ **Recording device:** A laptop or desktop computer

You can use any newer PC or Mac to record and edit your podcast. Chances are that if you're reading this book, you already have one of those. So the most expensive tool you need is already all set.

You *will* want a computer with a fair amount of hard drive space (at least 20 gigabytes) and enough processor oomph to edit audio files. You'll also likely need an available USB port for your microphone. If your computer is a creaky 8-year-old machine, it probably can't handle podcasting. But any computer made in the last few years can do the job.

✦ **Software:** A copy of GarageBand (or Audacity)

You use this to record and edit the cast. You can read more about these in the following section.

✦ **Input device:** Um, a microphone

Read more about your options in "Getting a good microphone."

✦ **Broadcasting vehicle:** A FeedBurner account with a SmartCast (www. feedburner.com)

Oh, and you need a place to record and work. I cover that later, too.

Getting the right recording software

You can find many software options for podcasting. Search for *podcasting software* on your favorite search engine to see what I mean.

You can, of course, use higher-end audio software, such as Adobe Audition or Logic Studio Pro. Feel free. But I'm starting with the simple stuff. Here are my recommendations, per OS platform.

If you're on a Mac running OS X

✦ **GarageBand** (www.apple.com/ilife/garageband) comes with everything you need to record, edit, and distribute a podcast. It also allows you to do quite a bit of post-recording editing as well as set up your podcast feed. GarageBand costs $80 or so as part of Apple iLife.

✦ **Übercaster** (www.ubercaster.com) is the easiest-to-use podcasting program on the planet. See Figure 7-1 for the Übercaster recording screen. It doesn't offer the same post-recording editing features as GarageBand, but it's very streamlined for podcasting. It has exactly the features you need, and it's easier to figure out. Übercaster costs $80 or so.

I tend to prefer GarageBand, myself, because I'm more familiar with it. But I've never been sorry when using Übercaster, either.

✦ **Audacity** (http://audacity.sourceforge.net) is free and straightforward. Did I mention it's free?

Book VI Chapter 7

Introducing Podcasting

Figure 7-1:
Übercaster offers a nice, intuitive interface.

If you're on a Windows PC running either Windows XP or Vista

✦ **Audacity** is your first choice. See Figure 7-2 for a look at Audacity in action. If you're a Windows snob and hopped here instead of reading my Mac recommendations, let me repeat that Audacity is free (in life, as well as this software). It's also easy to use and a very refined tool for podcasters.

✦ **PodProducer** (www.podproducer.net) is a more sophisticated tool for sound editing. It's free, too.

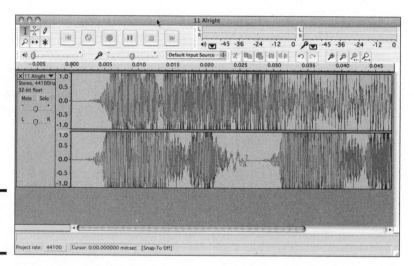

Figure 7-2:
Audacity in
action.

Pick one program and stick with it for a while. Get comfortable with the ins and outs of audio editing.

Read. The. Documentation. Sure, you *can* record audio by pushing a button and talking, but just a little time spent learning how to tune and tweak your microphone and software will make a huge difference in quality.

Getting a good microphone

The microphone makes or breaks the podcast. The better the mic, the better the audio quality. No software on earth can improve a recording if it was recorded with a lousy mic.

The real problem with choosing a microphone, though, is the thousands of options. To simplify things a bit, I'll list the ones I've tried, and the pluses and minuses of each. Search for *podcasting microphones* on your favorite search engine if you want to get the whole story.

Beyond the basics

You might want to invest in a USB mixing board, too. I don't have one, but I've heard they're very, very helpful if you're combining many different audio sources. Also, if you're doing phone interviews, invest in a quality phone.

✦ **Internal:** If you use a laptop, your laptop's internal mic *might* be okay to start. It's free, and it's already configured. But the sound quality will be tinny at best, and you'll sound like you're talking through a paper cup.

✦ **A USB headset:** Headset mics — like the many made by Plantronics (www.plantronics.com) are great. They're inexpensive (they start at less than $30) and easy to set up. However, they won't work if you're interviewing someone, or if you want more radio-style sound.

✦ **The Blue Snowball** (www.bluemic.com) is a fantastic USB microphone for about $120. It can work as a unidirectional or omnidirectional mic (omnidirectional is great for interviews), produces great sound quality, and looks cool to boot. But, it does cost $120.

✦ **The Zoom H2** (www.samsontech.com) can function as a USB microphone or as a stand-alone audio recorder. That makes it very, very flexible. It's also the best omnidirectional microphone I've seen for less than $300. But it costs the most of any microphone in this category, and you'll want to read the manual before you start recording.

I use the Blue Snowball at home and the Zoom H2 when I'm at work or traveling.

✦ **The Griffin iMic** (www.griffintechnology.com) isn't actually a mic but rather a device with which you can connect most microphones to your computer. It filters out a lot of the noise that a computer might add to your recording. It costs $49.95, and despite the "I" notation, it works on both Mac and PC.

When setting up your mic, follow the instructions that come with your microphone. And read the entire manual! The manual contains tips for getting the best quality sound.

Setting Up Your Studio

You need a quiet place to record: your studio. A room where the dog isn't barking doesn't count. Background noise — such as appliances, noisy air-conditioning, or ticking clocks — will leap out in a recording. And pay attention to how the room is configured and dressed: A room with bare walls or floors might produce echoes.

If you're really concerned about echoes and other acoustics, you can buy damping tiles. Or, do what I do, and hang a few blankets on the walls. I'm sure every audiophile reading this just cringed, but it worked for me.

Here are a few tips for setting up a quiet recording space:

✦ **Close the windows.** It never fails. If you leave the windows open, then ten minutes into your recording, a train, garbage truck, car with no muffler, or murder of crows will position itself right outside and start rumbling, honking, roaring, or cawing away. Trust me on this. Close the windows.

✦ **Stay away from appliances.** Even a small office refrigerator produces a *lot* of noise.

✦ **Unplug the phone.**

✦ **Turn off your cellphone and/or PDA.**

✦ **Move your microphone as far away from the computer as possible.** Your computer's fans, hard drives, and such can produce quite a racket.

✦ **Exit any instant messaging or other software that produces bells, whistles, or other sound effects.**

✦ **Put your microphone** *at eye level.* Use a stack of books, if nothing else. When you look up when you speak, your voice has a much clearer quality. Looking down when you speak makes you mutter.

Most important, stay sane. It's easy to spend a lot of money setting up a room in your house to be the perfect sound studio. Remember, the audio you record will be compressed and sent over the Web. So a professional studio isn't necessary. Some people record their podcasts in their living room, their car, or the middle of crowded airports.

Testing Your Setup

Before you spend an hour scripting and recording your first podcast, test your setup! Here's how you do it:

1. **Get a passage of text as a test.**

   Make sure the sentence mixes in most of the typical consonant and vowel sounds, so you get a good sample.

2. **Record the passage a few times using different microphone positions (at eye level, sitting on the desk, held in your hand) and software configurations as suggested by your software's documentation.**

Eye level is almost always best, but it's possible that your mic works better in a different position.

You *did* read the documentation, right?!

3. **Encode the audio as you will when you upload your podcast to the Web.**

   You can read more about this in the upcoming section, "Encoding and Uploading Your Podcast."

4. **Listen to each version and choose the best combination of settings and microphone position and setup.**

   Listen for background noise, volume, clarity of speech, and overall quality.

A little advance work like this will save you from the heartbreak I've had: I once recorded a 20-minute interview using two Blue Snowball microphones, only to discover that I'd left one of the microphones off. Sigh.

Supporting Podcasting on Your Blog

As I mention earlier, podcasting works because the audio you create is inserted right into an RSS feed.

You can set up and edit a separate, custom podcasting RSS feed from your blog and group all your podcasts. If you want to do that, look at programs such as Podcast Maker (for Mac; www.lemonzdream.com/podcastmaker) or PodProducer (for PC; www.podproducer.net), or using your audio editor to generate the RSS. If you're really a glutton for punishment, you can generate the feed by hand. Don't.

Creating a separate podcast feed has advantages. If, for example, you want to add your podcast to iTunes or other major podcast directories, it's best to have a separate feed. Remember, though, you can always do this later.

You can also keep it simpler by attaching the audio file directly to a blog post, and then making sure your blog's RSS feed supports *enclosures,* which are file attachments that are embedded in the feed. When feed subscribers open a post that includes an enclosure, they'll see a link to download the file. That will create the podcast automatically.

Movable Type 4 (www.movabletype.com) includes built-in support for podcasting, and so do WordPress.com and WordPress installed (http://wordpress.org).

Or you can enable SmartCast in FeedBurner and get the same result on any blogging platform.

Preparing Your Podcast Script

Writing for a podcast is a little different than writing a blog post. You'll almost never write down, word for word, what you're going to say in your podcast. Instead, you'll make a list of the items for discussion with an opening sentence or two and then a list of *talking points* — stuff you absolutely want to mention.

 Write out at least an outline of your podcast. Going one step further, I often write down a rough draft of everything I'll say as a blog post. That way, I've rehearsed at least once, have all my thoughts organized, and can post the rough draft as a transcript.

If you're comfortable going the outline route, include — at a minimum — the following:

+ **Your introduction:** "Hi, I'm Harrison and you're listening to The Sci-Fi Kids' Podcast. Today is September 20th. . . ."

+ **The topics you'll be discussing**

+ **Your closing:** "You've been listening to The Sci-Fi Kids' Podcast. I'm Harrison, and I'll see you next week. . . ."

If you're doing an interview, write down the questions you'll ask, as well as follow-up questions if you think you know what the answers will be to the first questions.

Try to aim for a 10- to 20-minute podcast. Scripts tend to expand after you start recording. Unless you have a really dense topic, 30 minutes will be your audience's maximum attention span.

Recording Your First Podcast

You're ready to go! Time to record your first podcast. Before the rubber really hits the road, though (or, your dulcet tones tickle the airwaves), make sure you take care of the following nuts and bolts:

1. **Do a test.**

   Yes, do it again! Check sound levels and make sure everything's working.

2. **Double-check that your phone's unplugged, all noisy appliances are squelched, the neighbor's dog has a mouth full of peanut butter, and so on.**

3. **Make sure your notes are easily visible.**

It's now time to click Record and start speaking.

You might feel a little nervous. It happens. Just relax and focus on your topic. Be sure to speak slowly and clearly, and remember to look up while speaking so you don't start mumbling.

If you can, keep one eye on your recording levels, just in case something goes wrong. Better to find out halfway through the podcast than when you're done.

After you're done, save the recording. Then listen through the podcast to check for sound quality and such. If you find any places where you stumbled or stuttered and don't like how it sounds, you can use your sound editor to literally select and cut out the guilty seconds, as shown in Figure 7-3.

Finally, add a title and other information to your podcast. Many podcasting programs, such as GarageBand or Podcast Maker, let you add artwork as well as the date, author name, and title. Artwork is a chance for you to include your logo or otherwise reinforce your brand in the podcast; that artwork will appear in the listener's media player and on any podcast directories that support it. See Figures 7-4 and 7-5 for examples.

Book VI Chapter 7

Introducing Podcasting

Figure 7-3: Using GarageBand to erase a sneeze.

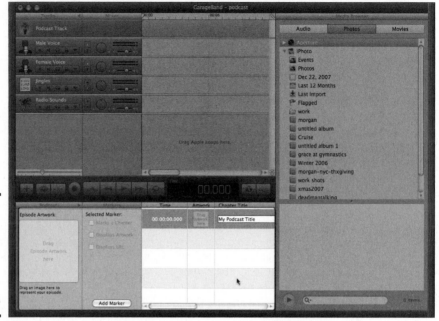

Figure 7-4:
Adding
descriptive
information
to my
podcast in
GarageBand.

Figure 7-5:
Manually
adding
information
in Podcast
Maker.

After you're happy with the audio and the podcast description, it's time to encode and upload it.

Encoding and Uploading Your Podcast

Whatever software you use, you have to *encode* your recording. The audio you just recorded is stored on your computer in an uncompressed format. It's a huge file. By encoding it, you store it in (encoded) MP3 format, which is the standard for audio delivery over the Internet. In Figure 7-6, I'm encoding my edited podcast in GarageBand.

After you encode your podcast, listen to it again. Whenever you compress an audio file, you're reducing the quality. The sacrifice you make for the file size reduction is worth it. Just watch that you don't overdo it, or it will sound awful: Try encoding a bit of the podcast and listening to it first. Make sure you've used the right balance of sound quality and faster downloading.

Most audio software comes with default podcast encoding settings now. Use those and you should be just fine.

The final result of your encoding process will be an MP3 file. That's your podcast.

One step left: Upload the podcast. If you're including it in a blog post, attach the file to the post itself using your blog editor, as in Figure 7-7.

Figure 7-6:
Encoding
my podcast.

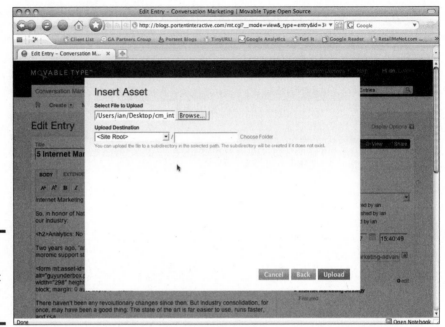

Figure 7-7:
Uploading
my podcast
in Movable
Type 4.

If you're doing a manual upload, you'll need to use some kind of file transfer software, such as an FTP client, to upload your MP3 file. On a Mac, I recommend Transmit. On a PC, I like CuteFTP, but FileZilla is great, too.

If what I just said was total nonsense, use your blogging software to upload your podcast. Don't start messing with manual upload.

Promoting Your Podcast

Now your podcast is live. How do you get people to listen to it?

You can promote your podcast the same way you promote blog posts (see Chapter 6 of this minibook) by using pinging, blogger networking, and social media sites.

And here are a few additional (free) opportunities:

✦ **Add your podcast to iTunes.** Visit the iTunes Store via your iTunes software (it's free) and then find Submit Podcasts to the iTunes Directory.

✦ **Add your podcast to PodcastDirectory.com.**

✦ **Look for other podcasting sites like PodcastAlley.com and add your podcast there, too.**

Book VII
Social Media Marketing

"So far our web presence has been pretty good.
We've gotten some orders, a few inquiries,
and nine guys who want to date our logo."

Contents at a Glance

Chapter 1: Understanding Social Media 637

Marketing, Social Media Style 637
Exploring Social Media 638

Chapter 2: Creating Your Social Media Desktop 651

Setting Up Your Social Media Desktop with RSS 651
Setting Up Your Social Media Desktop in iGoogle 653
Creating Your Social Media Desktop on Netvibes 658
Creating Your Social Media Desktop on My Yahoo! 661
Deciding What to Track 663

Chapter 3: Creating Your Social Media Plan .665

Researching Your Audience 665
Crafting Your Social Media Message 674
Setting Your Social Media Style 675
Preparing Your Social Media Profile 676
Choosing Your Target Social Media Sites 677
Reviewing Your Site for Social Skills 678
Setting Your Social Media Marketing Routine 681
Planning for the Long Social Media Marketing Haul 682

Chapter 4: Navigating Top Social Media Sites 683

Making Friends on Facebook 684
Socializing on MySpace 693
Networking for Business on LinkedIn 697
Bookmarking Your Way to the Top 699
Playing the Social News Game 701
Growing Your Business with Media Sharing 703
Talking in Discussion Forums 706
Using Microblogs as a Launchpad 708

Chapter 5: Building Your Network 713

Finding Friends 713
Keeping Friends 715
Expanding Your Network with Questions and Answers 715
Obeying the (Unspoken) Rules 717
Knowing When to Stop 718

Chapter 6: Creating a Winning Social Media Campaign 721

The Importance of Creating a Winning Social Media Campaign 721
Marketing by Providing Tools 722
Social Media Marketing with Content 725
Leveraging Networks to Create a Winning Social Media Campaign 728
Addressing Harm to Your Reputation 728
Applying These Lessons Everywhere 729

Chapter 1: Understanding Social Media

In This Chapter

✔ Discovering what social media is

✔ Checking out key social media sites

✔ Adding social media to your Web-marketing strategy

What in the world is social media (as opposed to "antisocial" media) — and what's it got to do with Web marketing? Good questions. Social media (as a concept) traces its roots back to the first bulletin board systems, discussion forums, IRC (Internet Relay Chat), and news groups. (It might also trace its roots back to the first time when two particularly advanced apes grunted at each other. But for Internet marketing purposes, you can ignore the animal world.)

Today, social media is a complex web of sites and software that allows you bookmark, discuss, vent, and then share with other people. Social media users represent an enormous market. Facebook alone has over 80 million active users. That number is according to Facebook, but hey! — even if it's exaggerated and you divide that number in half, it's still a lot of people.

You need to understand this space of social media. Even if you're not doing any social media marketing, your customers are there, talking about you. Knowing where they talk and how to answer them is critical.

In this chapter, I introduce you to popular social media sites and terminology. I explain how you can use social media to grow your business, build an interested audience, and keep in touch with your customers in a way that everyone appreciates.

Marketing, Social Media Style

Social media sites and tools enable you to build your reputation and audience over time. Every friend you add on Facebook, every bookmark you add to StumbleUpon, and every post you make on a microblog increases your profile. You can read more about bookmarking in the later section, "Bookmarking sites."

Why social media is so important: The sneeze principle

Here's one critical lesson of social media: the *sneeze principle*. Any social media allows a visitor to watch a video, read an article, or see some other content. Then it lets the visitor *sneeze:* That is, a visitor can somehow indicate he agrees (or disagrees) with that content by leaving a comment, posting a bookmark, checking an I'm a Fan check box, or doing something else.

That's the sneeze effect: When that first visitor sneezes, others see it. They go and look at the same content. Then they might sneeze, too. So *their* circle of friends sees the same thing, and has the option of transmitting the message even further.

Here's an example:

I read a funny blog post and give it a thumbs-up on StumbleUpon. I also have about 50 fans on StumbleUpon, and they all see that I liked that post. They go and read it, too. A few of them really like it, too, so they give it a thumbs-up. They each have 40–400 fans, who then see that someone they follow liked the post. In a matter of hours, this one blog post has been sneezed to thousands of visitors.

It's not as easy as it sounds, but if you understand the sneeze principle, you understand why social media can be so powerful.

If you spend this capital wisely, you can use it to

✦ Announce a new product.

✦ Ask everyone for feedback about a new idea or blog post.

✦ Build some buzz and get others talking about you — and your online presence.

The catch? If the networks or their members think you're abusing them to promote yourself, they'll penalize you or ban you altogether.

I dedicate the remainder of this minibook to dealing with walking that fine line between market research and promotion and self-aggrandizement to help you learn your way around — and exploit — this diverse and expanding marketing medium.

Exploring Social Media

Social media umbrellas any Web site or Web application that allows your audience to interact with your site and each other, directly or indirectly. Table 1-1 shows the seven basic categories of social media sites.

Table 1-1	Social Media Sites by Category	
Social Media Type	*Description*	*Examples*
Blogs	Allow you to write, journal-style, and then invite comments from your readers	Blogger WordPress
Social networks	Where people can interact and connect online	Facebook MySpace
Bookmarking sites	Allow you to save bookmarks, just like you would in your browser, but on a site you can access from any computer	Delicious Ma.gnolia StumbleUpon
Microblogging sites	Allow you to blog one or two sentences at a time	Twitter Plurk
Media sharing sites	Where you can upload and share video, audio, and photographs	YouTube Flickr
Popularity sites	Where you can collect bookmarks and then let visitors vote on them	Digg Reddit
Aggregators	Help the truly social and connected keep up with all this stuff	FriendFeed

All seven categories are important for you to explore because they're all interconnected: A Facebook member may also have a YouTube account. If someone forwards her a funny video via Facebook, she can zip over to YouTube to review it. Then, she might tell her Facebook friends. If one of those friends has a Twitter account and posts, his 540 Twitter friends might see it, too.

Social media, more than any other vehicle, has the potential to spread a message far and fast.

You also need to know what sites are social media hot spots and what each site's specialty is so you can successfully use social media to spread the word about your products or services online.

In the following sections, I explain each category and explore the benefits so you can begin to formulate your social media strategy.

Beware of social network spam

Social network operators do not like spammers! Don't use a social network to make friends with hundreds of strangers and then start sending them coupons or other offers. Chances are you'll end up getting kicked off the network. Instead, approach them like you would a party. Say hello. Shake hands. Chat a bit. Make your sales pitch only when someone states he's looking for the product or service you provide.

Posting and commenting on blogs

Blogs are probably the first thing you think of when you think of social media. A *blog* (short for *weblog*) is a set of regularly published entries by one or more authors that allows visitors to post their comments on each entry. The word *blog* can refer to

+ **The software that's used to publish a Web site:** For example, WordPress is a blogging software.

+ **A writing and publishing style:** For example, blog *posts* (the articles on a blog) typically appear in chronological order, and the tone is usually very casual compared with, say, a business report.

+ **Something as simple as a set of journal entries on a Web page:** For example, someone who writes a daily memoir.

 Most blogs are social media sites. Note that I said *most* blogs are social media sites. Not all. If a site calls itself a blog but doesn't allow comments, it's not a social media site. Think about it: How can you be social if you're the only one talking? You can read more about effective blogging in Book VI.

For the purposes of this discussion, a blog includes regularly published entries by one or more authors and also allows visitors to post their comments on each entry.

 Regularly published can mean once per day, once per month, or even once per year. Generally, though, a blog is viable only if the author(s) publish at least once weekly.

Folks write blogs for a lot of reasons: to promote a business, talk about a hobby, keep friends up to date on their world travels, or espouse a political viewpoint. The possibilities are endless.

And some blogs are major businesses. For example, Engadget (www. engadget.com) and Gizmodo (http://gizmodo.com) — blogs catering to gadget geeks worldwide — are big business. They publish many posts per day, have multiple editors, and support themselves based on considerable advertising income. Figure 1-1 shows just how polished some of the big blog sites look.

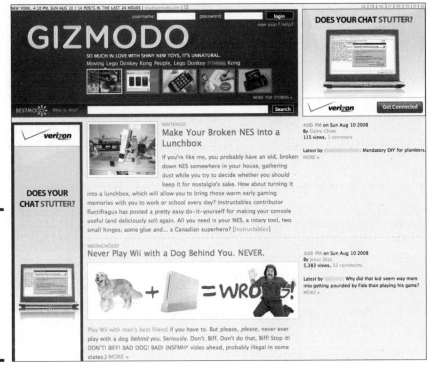

**Book VII
Chapter 1**

**Understanding
Social Media**

Figure 1-1:
Major
blogs have
a polished
look and
a huge
number of
posts in a
single day.

Big or small, though, all blogs have these two standard hallmarks:

✦ Comments

✦ A serial publishing style, where posts are shown sequentially.

To see examples of the many blogs on the Internet, visit Technorati
(http://technorati.com) and look through its top 100 or 200 blogs. It's a
great set of examples.

If you're looking to make that first step in social marketing, a blog is the
place to start. Blogs offer a terrific way to

✦ Talk directly to your customers by posting and commenting on
your blog.

✦ Explain your business philosophy by writing in your own style and
exposing your ideas to the public at large.

✦ Demonstrate your expertise by commenting on other blogs or creating
your own expert blog.

✦ Win over potential customers by driving the people who read your blog
toward your business.

Blogs are your most powerful social marketing tool. The rest of the social media world has grown up around blogs to help bloggers get the word out: Bookmarking sites, social networks, and all their derivatives draw from thousands of blog entries, authors, and discussions. You can use that infrastructure to find the right readers and grow your online presence.

Finally, using a blog can help you move up in the search engine rankings. A blog's text-focused style, regular publishing, and capability to attract links can give you a much-needed boost by building your authority in the search engines. See Book II, which covers search engine optimization (SEO), for more about that.

For the ins and outs of writing a successful blog, see Book VI.

Connecting via social networks

Social networks are sites that let you create your own profile, seek out and connect with other members, and talk to your friends from a single profile page. Social networks also let you share photos, images, links, and other tidbits of information within your circle of friends.

Facebook, MySpace, and hundreds (if not thousands) of other sites all qualify as social networks.

At their simplest, they offer you — and your online presence — a great opportunity to

+ **Get a feel for your potential customers.** Social networks help you find friends and users by interests, geography, and hobbies.

+ **Get advice from colleagues.** Services like LinkedIn offer special Answers networks where you can ask and answer questions from other members.

+ **Demonstrate your expertise.** You can tell your social network friends about recent accomplishments, answer their questions, and provide the occasional tip.

After you start using the more advanced features on the major social networks, you can also

+ **Distribute custom tools** by using these networks' special development kits.

+ **Create targeted discussion groups** by using features like Facebook Groups.

Here is a list of social networks that you should be familiar with. They've been around for a while, have thousands or millions of users, and offer access to the widest audience:

✦ **Facebook:** One of the dominant sites, Facebook (www.facebook.com) allows you to create your own profile pages, as shown in Figure 1-2. You can send messages to other members and make friends with them by adding fellow members to your Friends lists. Facebook also allows custom applications: games, puzzles, utilities, and other little widgets created by third-party developers. You can join for free by creating an account in just a few minutes.

✦ **MySpace:** Another dominant site, MySpace (www.myspace.com) pre-dates Facebook, offering much of the same toolset and features. The site also allows custom *skins* (designs) for your profile page and has served as a launchpad for up-and-coming performers. As with Facebook, you can join MySpace for free in just a few minutes.

✦ **LinkedIn:** A members-only, pay-to-register network for businesspeople, LinkedIn (www.linkedin.com) is business networking on steroids. After you pay a fee and create a detailed profile, other businesspeople worldwide can connect with you based on common interests, previous work together, or networking groups. Members can create networks of literally hundreds of people.

✦ **Yahoo! Answers:** Have a question? Visit http://answers.yahoo.com. Thousands of helpful members offer answers to questions on topics ranging from Internet marketing to wedding planning to pet care. It's free to join, and answering questions is easy. Plus there's a nice ego boost when someone picks your answer as best.

Figure 1-2:
Use
Facebook
to create
a profile
page and
share it with
millions.

✦ **Discussion forums:** Forums are still out there. Sites like Webmaster World.com (`www.webmasterworld.com`) and Google Groups (`http://groups.google.com`) are basically enormous collections of discussion threads where you create your membership and then join the fray. Most discussion forums are free to join.

All social networking sites offer a rare opportunity to spread the word about yourself or your company to thousands or even millions of people. The trick is doing it politely. See Chapter 5 and Chapter 6 of this minibook for advice on doing just that.

Bookmarking sites

Bookmarking sites are applications that let you move your bookmarks from your computer to a single, central account that you can access from any Internet connection. Members of bookmarking sites get convenience. Instead of storing their bookmarks on a single computer, they store them in a central location. They can access their bookmarks from any other computer, and don't have to worry about losing them in a computer crash.

Bookmarking sites are a handy utility and a community at the same time. Members can connect with other members who have similar interests and share bookmark recommendations. You can use bookmarking sites to

✦ Share bookmarks with others.

✦ Review each other's choices.

✦ Generally gossip about your most recent finds.

Examples of bookmarking sites that are worth exploring include

✦ **StumbleUpon:** Install the StumbleUpon toolbar on your computer and then click a button. StumbleUpon (`www.stumbleupon.com`) takes you to sites marked as thumbs-up by folks who share your interests. You can submit additional pages, review them, and follow other members as they bookmark sites. Warning: Highly addictive!

✦ **Delicious:** Clever name, huh? Use Delicious (`http://delicious.com`) to save bookmarks on its server instead of on your browser, so you can access them from any computer. You can also add notes, automatically publish your bookmarks to your blog, and subscribe to other members' bookmark lists. Figure 1-3 shows the unique Delicious homepage.

Some sites, such as StumbleUpon, even recommend bookmarks based on their popularity, as shown in Figure 1-4. So, if many StumbleUpon users all "stumble" onto your site in a short period of time, you can get thousands or even hundreds of thousands of visitors.

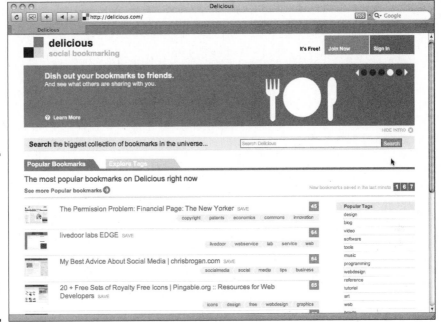

Figure 1-3:
The Delicious homepage has a "hotlist" that shows the most-bookmarked items.

Figure 1-4:
Stumble Upon uses a toolbar installed in your Web browser.

As an Internet marketer, you can also use bookmarking sites to drive traffic toward your business. If you or someone else bookmarks an article or page on your Web site with one of these services, and then others do the same, you can gain a lot of traffic from people who *want* what you're offering.

Plus, search engines often *crawl* — read through all the content — these sites looking for important, relevant content. Again, bookmarking sites offer a great benefit for your search engine optimization efforts. See Book II for more about SEO.

Beware of social network spam

It needs repeating: Social network operators do not like spammers! Don't use a social network to make friends with hundreds of strangers and then start sending them coupons or other offers. Chances are you'll end up getting kicked off the network. Instead, approach them like you would a party. Say hello. Shake hands. Chat a bit. Get to business when everyone's ready.

Microblogging

Microblog sites allow members to make lots of short blog posts. And by *short*, I mean **short** — often less than 140 characters. Microblogs are fast, easy, and can be updated from a cellphone, computer, or even via voice mail.

Microblogs look and feel more like old-fashioned chat rooms than blogs. Participants post statements, which are visible in a common *public timeline,* which everyone can see and read. See Figure 1-5.

You might think that microblogging is just like a social network, but microblogs tend to be more "real time," with some participants posting every few minutes. So they allow for more of an ongoing conversation. But yes, the lines do get blurry at times.

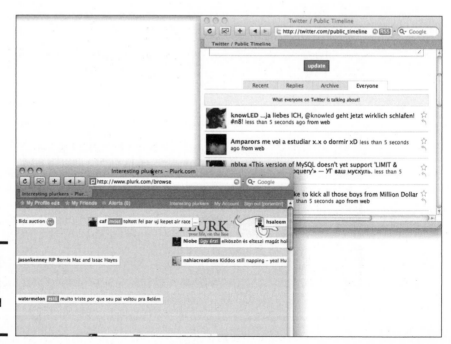

Figure 1-5:
The public timeline on Twitter and Plurk.

More importantly, participants can follow fellow microbloggers whom they find interesting. After you make friends on a microblog, you follow them, and they follow you. Then their friends see you and follow you, and so on. On most microblogs, you mark people as friends by clicking Friend, or Follow. Then they confirm, and you're friends. It's that easy.

Therefore, microblogging is a great way to build a focused audience to which you can pose questions, make suggestions, or announce a new blog post.

There aren't many microblogs out there, yet, but here are two examples:

✦ **Twitter.com:** Half addiction, half publicity platform, Twitter (`http://twitter.com`) is a microblogging tool with which you can enter 140-character messages. By following other people you find interesting, you'll receive their messages. Think of it as a huge chat room that remembers what you said. It's free to join. Like most social networks, you create a simple identity and can start posting right away.

   In Figure 1-6, notice that Twitter allows you to see the most recent posts on the network and statistics regarding who's following you. The 400 or so followers in this example are mine and they are happy to hear from me. When I post, their Twitter timeline automatically updates to show my post. If I announce a new blog post, many of them will read it right away.

✦ **Plurk.com:** Like Twitter, but with an even odder name, Plurk (`www.plurk.com`) provides the same kind of microblogging but adds a funky, fun interface. If Twitter is the U.N., Plurk is a disco. Signup is free and just as simple as Twitter.

Book VII Chapter 1

Understanding Social Media

Figure 1-6:
A typical Twitter page allows people to follow you.

The real power of microblogging lies in your ability to get many followers and then announce things to them. Because the entire purpose of microblogs is to make short announcements, try using the following examples as a guide:

>   **Announcement:** You just finished writing a new book or white paper.
>
>   **Post:** "Just finished writing my new book!"
>
>   **Announcement:** You just got home from a business trip to New York
>
>   **Post:** "Just got home from New York."
>
>   **Announcement:** I have a new product.
>
>   **Post:** "Check out this new product I'm selling." (Be sure to add a link to your product.)

Media sharing sites

Media sharing sites allow you to upload videos, photographs, and audio to a single directory. Then visitors can browse through and see your masterpiece. If you've been online in the last four years, you know a few of these sites. Examples include

+   **YouTube:** This is the biggest video-sharing site out there. Upload your video (ten minutes or less), and visitors can view and comment on it. Garnering more views and favorites ratings moves you up in the directory. Whole careers have been launched on YouTube (www.youtube.com). YouTube is free and lets you upload video in a wide array of formats.

+   **Flickr:** Use Flickr (www.flickr.com) to upload and manage photographs. You can divide them into groups, organize them by tags, and restrict access as desired. Flickr also lets you publish your photos individually or as a "stream" on other Web sites. Flickr just started supporting video, as well.

As an Internet marketer, you can post your videos, photos, and illustrations on these sites. It's hardly a sure thing, but the right content at the right time can get you hundreds, thousands, or even hundreds of thousands of new visitors. That's why you want to put your photos and videos on third-party sites: They get a lot of traffic and put you in front of an enormous audience.

Popularity sites

Half-social network, half-bookmarking sites, *popularity sites* allow members to submit new content and then vote on other submissions. Items that get enough votes move up in the listings and get more traffic. Popularity sites include

✦ **Digg:** A front-page listing on Digg (`http://digg.com`) has been known to crash servers and bring Web sites to their knees. Digg is a *very* busy site focusing on technology and the funny/odd/bizarre. Members vote on items. If an item gets enough votes in a short time, it moves to the front page, and a flood of traffic ensues. In Figure 1-7, you can see that the Diggs badges show the number of votes about each article. The left side shows the most recent items to get significant votes.

Figure 1-7:
The Digg homepage is total chaos, and a lot of fun.

✦ **Reddit:** Very similar to Digg, but more focused on news, Reddit members place news items of all kind on the network. Browse Reddit at www.reddit.com.

Posting on popularity sites is a gamble. You can't ignore them because a front-page listing on a site like Digg can bring you the biggest possible burst of new visitors. But that kind of listing can prove very, very difficult to achieve.

Aggregators

Say you jumped on the social networking bandwagon, and now you're a member on a photo-sharing site, a social network, a bookmarking service, and two popularity sites. How do you keep track of it all? Enter the aggregators.

Aggregators allow you to publish the stream of information from all these sites in a single location. Two examples are FriendFeed.com (shown in Figure 1-8) and Secondbrain.com. Note how the FriendFeed.com example shows all my Twitter, rich media (video, animation, or audio), and other posts in one place.

Most aggregators are free. They require a little bit of work because you have to set them up to work with your current social media profiles on other networks. But once they're set up, you can post and review content from all your social networks in one place.

This integration matters to you because it offers links the search engines can crawl and also serves as yet another place where you can build an audience. The best part is that you don't have to write or publish anything new. Create your account, add the feeds from your other social media sites, and you're set.

Figure 1-8:
A typical
FriendFeed
aggregator
page.

Chapter 2: Creating Your Social Media Desktop

In This Chapter

✔ Setting up your social media desktop

✔ Adding updates to your tracking center

✔ Deciding which information to track

*O*ne of the first problems you encounter in any social media campaign is information overload, or how to keep track of what people are saying on dozens of different sites.

If you create and use a *social media desktop,* however, you have one central place where you can easily monitor

✦ The things that people say about you or your organization

✦ Any stories or themes you want to track

The best part of having a social media desktop is that you don't have to type the Web address for every site and search result you're trying to track, because it's all in one place.

In this chapter, I show you how to build your social media desktop. Note: If you haven't read Chapter 1 of this minibook, hop over there and check out my discussion on the sneeze principle. (Gesundheit.) You need a social media desktop so that you can know when other people, um, *"sneeze"* (spread along) your content. You also need a social media desktop so that you can find and pass along other people's great content. That makes you a more valuable member of the community — giving you more authority and making your messages more contagious. Being contagious, so to speak, can boost all your Internet marketing efforts — you'll get more links (which helps search engine optimization), get more fans (which helps in blogging), and build your brand (which helps with everything).

Setting Up Your Social Media Desktop with RSS

Take a deep breath. Relax. Dry your palms. Setting up your social media desktop is easy — honest!

Your *social media desktop* is just an account you set up, using one of many services that let you track various search results, blogs, and news stories with a few clicks of the mouse. Check out the iGoogle example shown in Figure 2-1. At a glance, I can see what folks are saying about my company and what my favorite blogs are talking about.

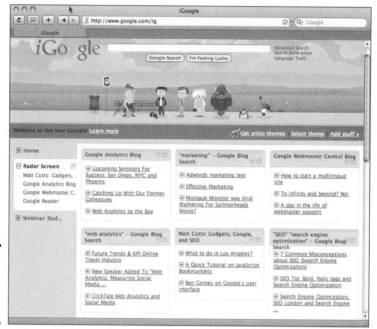

Figure 2-1:
A sample social media desktop.

The key to your social media desktop is *really simple syndication,* or *RSS,* in which you build your desktop by subscribing to several RSS feeds for Web sites, blogs, or search results. That way, you can stay up to date without visiting the site, blog, or search result. By putting all those subscriptions in one place, you create your social media desktop: a single place where you can keep an eye on what folks are saying about you, your company, and your competitors.

RSS is a simple way for Web sites to deliver a list of the latest headlines, articles, or content. An RSS feed is the actual list of headlines. You don't need to worry about the technical details.

You can use any RSS feed reader or organizing service you like, but in this chapter, I talk about using iGoogle, Yahoo!, and Netvibes. All three of these are free, and offer a broad feature set.

Setting Up Your Social Media Desktop in iGoogle

iGoogle is one of the simplest social media desktop tools. If you already have Gmail or use another Google service, then you can simply add it to your existing account. Plus, it integrates with Google's various other services.

My only complaint about iGoogle: Sometimes I'd like a little more control over how my page looks. I'm not a fan of the Google aesthetic for pages that have a lot of text on them. And, as you'll soon see, your social media desktop will have a lot of text on it.

Setting up an iGoogle homepage

You can set up an iGoogle homepage as your social media desktop in just a few simple steps:

1. **In your Web browser, go to `www.google.com/ig`.**

2. **If you already have a Google account**

   - *But you aren't logged in:* Sign in, and then skip to Step 4.

   - *And you're already logged in:* Accept the offer on the iGoogle splash page to make it your homepage, and then skip to Step 4.

   If you have a Gmail account, you already have a Google account. Sign in, using your Gmail address and password.

3. **If you don't have a Google account, follow these steps:**

   a. *Click Get Started.*

   b. *Enter your e-mail address and password; see Figure 2-2.*

      If you don't want Google to remember your login, clear that check box.

      And, if you don't want Google to store your *Web history* (a record of your searches), clear that check box, too.

4. **Select a theme, but leave your interests blank.**

   You'll fill your page with other widgets that bring you news feeds, headlines, and content related to your interests, from blogs, news Web sites, and search engines.

5. **When your iGoogle homepage appears (see Figure 2-3), with a bunch of preselected items (such as Google News, weather, and the current time), you can remove all of them, too.**

   You're ready to start adding items, such as search results and your favorite blogs.

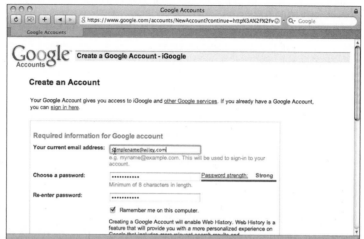

Figure 2-2:
Creating
your iGoogle
homepage.

Figure 2-3:
Your
iGoogle
homepage.

Adding a Web site or blog feed to iGoogle

After you create your iGoogle homepage, you can start tracking news feeds
and getting up-to-date information. You might already have a few blogs or
Web sites that you read regularly. If you do, you can watch their updates on
your iGoogle homepage. Here's how:

1. **Go to the Web site or blog.**

2. **Click the RSS subscription button or link; see an example in
   Figure 2-4.**

Figure 2-4:
Typical RSS
subscription
options on a
Web site.

The Add to Google page appears. If your Web browser is set up to add RSS feeds to a different program, the Google page may not appear — your browser will open a different Web page, instead. If that happens, skip to the later section "Adding feeds to iGoogle manually" to work around this issue.

3. **Click the Add to Google Homepage button.**

You see the latest headlines from that Web site or blog, as shown in Figure 2-5.

From now on, when the Web site to which you just subscribed updates, the widget on your iGoogle homepage will immediately update.

Figure 2-5:
See updated
headlines.

Adding a blog search result to iGoogle

Rather than follow just one specific blog, you can track what most blogs are saying, all at one time, by using Google Blog Search. Running a search for your company name, for example, shows every blog entry mentioning your company. Here's how to subscribe:

1. Go to www.google.com.

2. Click the More link at the top of the page and then choose Blogs from the drop-down menu; see Figure 2-6.

Click

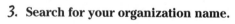
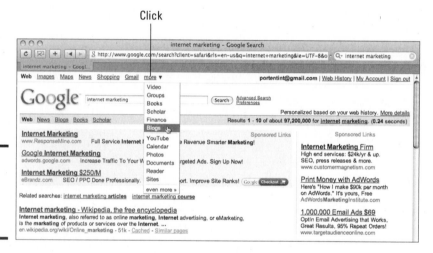

Figure 2-6: The Blogs search option on Google.

3. Search for your organization name.

   Enclose the name in double quotes. Using quotes narrows your search result to include all words in your company name, whether you have a one-word or a ten-word name.

4. Click Search Blogs.

   To see the most recent results first, click the Sort by Date link, in the upper-right corner. See Figure 2-7.

5. Click the RSS link (in the Subscribe section on the left side of the screen), and then select Add to Google Homepage. See Figure 2-7.

6. Go back to your iGoogle homepage.

   You see the search result in a nice, neat box. When iGoogle adds a new blog post to this search result, you see it there, as shown in Figure 2-8.

Click to subscribe   Sort

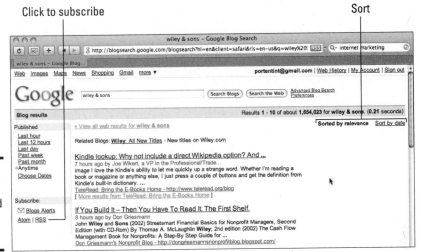

Figure 2-7:
Subscribe
to feeds and
sort results
here.

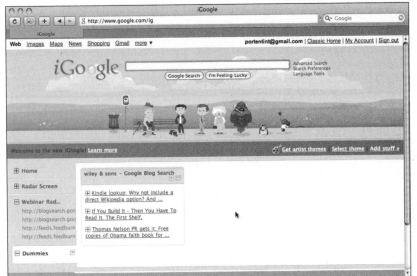

Figure 2-8:
The search
result,
added to
your iGoogle
homepage.

You can add other search results, too. Examples include

✦ Competitor names

✦ Names of individuals in your company

✦ Names of individuals at competitors

✦ Product names

✦ Your Web address

✦ Common typographical errors for all elements in this list

Adding feeds to iGoogle manually

I mention earlier in this chapter that clicking the Subscribe link or the RSS link might open a page other than the Add to Google page — and that you'll need to add the feed to iGoogle by hand. This occurs when your browser is set up to use a different RSS reader by default. Only a few steps are added, though, so don't worry:

1. **Right-click the link.**

2. **From the shortcut menu that appears, choose the Copy Link Location command (or a similar one).**

3. **Go to your iGoogle homepage and click the Add Stuff link.**

4. **In the lower-left corner of the Add Stuff page, click Add Feed or Gadget.**

5. **In the box that appears right below the Add Feed or Gadget link, paste the feed URL.**

6. **Click Add.**

You're done — you added a feed by hand.

You can try a shortcut for adding feeds to iGoogle: Type the Web address of the site to which you want to subscribe. If it has a correctly configured feed, Google detects and adds it.

To see more or fewer results in a specific content box on the iGoogle home-page, click Edit Settings and select the number of items you want to see.

Creating Your Social Media Desktop on Netvibes

If you like a slightly more polished interface, want more customization options, or aren't comfortable using Google because of privacy concerns (some folks just aren't), Netvibes is an excellent choice. Don't worry: It works similarly to iGoogle.

Setting up a Netvibes homepage

Setting up a Netvibes homepage takes only five steps:

1. **In your Web browser, go to www.netvibes.com.**

2. **Click Sign In and then click Sign Up.**

3. **Enter your e-mail address and password.**

4. **Agree to the terms of service and then click Sign Up.**

You're logged in to your new account; see Figure 2-9.

Click to add content

Figure 2-9:
Your new
Netvibes
homepage.

5. **Delete all the widgets that are already on the page; Click the X at the upper-right corner of each widget, then select Delete Forever.**

In Netvibes, you have two pages: Your public page and your private page. I don't recommend making your public page your social media desktop, unless you want the entire world to know what you're following. To make sure you're on your private page when adding widgets, look at the upper-left corner of the Netvibes page. There should be a Go to My Public Page button. That means you're on your private page, and all is well. If the button reads, "Go to My Private Page," click that button to go to your private page and start adding stuff there.

You're now ready to start adding widgets that display RSS feeds and other content.

Adding content to a Netvibes homepage

Adding content to Netvibes is similar to adding content to iGoogle by hand. See the earlier section, "Adding feeds to iGoogle manually."

1. **Go to the site, blog search, or other page to which you want to subscribe.**

2. **Right-click the RSS or Subscribe to RSS link.**

3. **From the shortcut menu that appears, choose the Copy Link Location command (or a similar one).**

4. **Go to Netvibes and log in (if you aren't already logged in).**

5. **Click the Add Content button; refer to Figure 2-9.**

6. **In the page that opens, click the Add a Feed button; see Figure 2-10.**

7. **Paste in the feed URL and then click Add Feed.**

   Netvibes presents options, if necessary. Options are determined by the specific widget. The kind of content you want or don't want, whether to include photographs, or whether to play video automatically are possible options.

8. **Click the Add to My Page button.**

Here are a couple of shortcuts for adding feeds to Netvibes:

✦ **Simply click Add Feed and then, in the field that appears, type the Web address of a site.** If the site has a feed, Netvibes finds and adds it automatically.

✦ **Use a Firefox plug-in** (if you use Firefox as your Web browser). Be sure to read about those items when you start using Netvibes. Plug-ins are great and easy to install, but do a little research to find the ones that have been around a while and are proven to work.

Click to add a feed

Figure 2-10:
The Add a Feed button and menu on Netvibes.

The feed is now on your Netvibes homepage. Netvibes offers a few additional options with which you can

✦ **Change the number of items shown in the feed box.**

✦ **Color-code the content boxes; see Figure 2-11.**

Color-coding might seem silly at first, but it can make your social media desktop much easier to review.

✦ **Show more information about each post.**

To access these options and others, click Edit or the Options button at the top of each content box.

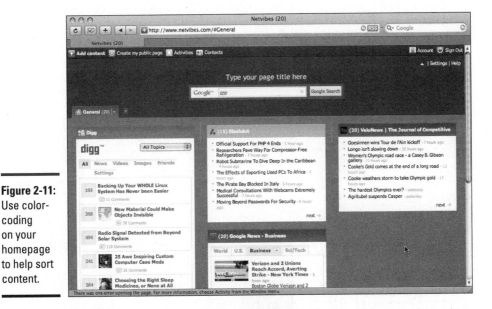

Figure 2-11: Use color-coding on your homepage to help sort content.

Creating Your Social Media Desktop on My Yahoo!

My Yahoo! has a lot of the same features as iGoogle and Netvibes. (Tell me whether you detect a theme here.) Consider using My Yahoo! if you

✦ **Already have a Yahoo! account**

✦ **Use Yahoo! as your search engine**

✦ **Use the Yahoo! social media properties often**

Yahoo! has many social media properties: Flickr, del.icio.us, Answers, and MyBlogLog are just four of them.

✦ **Want to read full articles directly on your social media desktop**

Setting up a My Yahoo! homepage

Here's how to set up a My Yahoo! homepage:

1. **In your Web browser, go to** my.yahoo.com.

2. **Sign in.**

   - *If you already have an account,* click Sign In and then log in.

   - *If you don't already have an account,* click Sign Up and then complete the signup form.

3. **Remove all widgets on the homepage; or create a new, empty tab.**

   Read more about tabs in the sidebar, "Using tabs to stay organized."

   You're now ready to start adding items. See Figure 2-12.

Figure 2-12:
Your new
My Yahoo!
homepage.

Adding content to you're My Yahoo! homepage

Adding content to My Yahoo! works much like Netvibes:

1. **Go to the site, blog search, or other page to which you want to subscribe.**

2. **Right-click the RSS or Subscribe to RSS link.**

3. **From the shortcut menu that appears, choose the Copy Link Location command (or a similar one).**

4. **Go to My Yahoo! and log in (if you aren't already logged in).**

5. **Click the Add Content button.**

6. **Click the Add RSS Feed button.**

7. **Paste the feed URL into the field marked Type or Paste the URL Below, and then click Add.**

If you use Yahoo! as your primary search engine, you can easily add Yahoo! search results — including information from the Yahoo! social media sites Flickr, del.icio.us, and Yahoo! Answers — to you're My Yahoo! homepage. Click the Add to My Yahoo! button on those pages.

See Figure 2-13 for a completed My Yahoo! homepage.

Figure 2-13: My completed My Yahoo! homepage.

Book VII Chapter 2

Creating Your Social Media Desktop

Deciding What to Track

You can start adding content to your social media desktop by tracking a few blog search results and Web sites or blogs of interest. Later, you might want to add

✦ Twitter feeds or search results

✦ News search results from Google, MSN, or Yahoo!

✦ Stock data

✦ A FriendFeed page

✦ A Flickr or YouTube channel

Using tabs to stay organized

When you start tracking innumerable different searches and sites, you might find that your social media desktop can get a bit out of control, not unlike a cluttered closet. You can see what I mean in the figure here. (Talk about info overload!)

When that happens, organize your home-page by creating separate tabs and using them to divide your content accordingly. Netvibes, iGoogle, and My Yahoo! all have an Add Tab (or New Tab) link you can use.

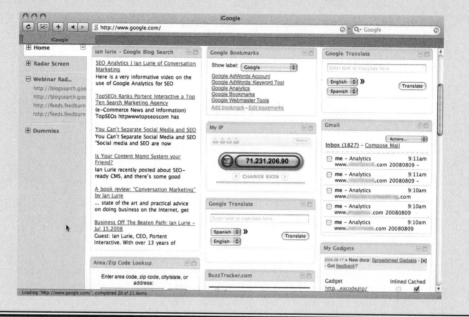

The sky's the limit. As you get comfortable using the tools, you might want to add all manner of feeds and information to the page. Some truly advanced marketers even create tools that generate their own readouts of search rankings and other data.

You need to be judicious — okay, picky — though. Otherwise, your social media desktop will leave you just as buried in information as you were before you created it. As a rule, add a feed only if

✦ You need to check it daily or more often.

✦ The information doesn't show up in another feed.

✦ You can skim it.

That last requirement is particularly important. Your social media desktop should be something you can quickly skim in a matter of minutes. Anything that can't be digested in a list doesn't belong there.

Chapter 3: Creating Your Social Media Plan

In This Chapter

✔ Researching your audience

✔ Reviewing your site for social skills

✔ Preparing for social media greatness

✔ Finding your message

✔ Setting your routine

In this chapter, you find out how to research your audience and pick the message and style that work for you. I also show you how to select target sites accordingly as well as prepare a profile that you can use repeatedly. After you make those decisions, it's time to set your social media schedule.

Researching Your Audience

Social media is unique enough that you'll want to analyze your audience there separately from other vehicles, such as search engines. For example, you might expect instant sales from a paid search ad or an e-mail marketing campaign. But when it comes to social media, you're looking for evidence of steady inroads with your audience, such as increased blog mentions about your company, which won't lead to sales for weeks or months. When you research your audience, you need to answer five basic questions:

✦ **What kinds of people are in your audience?** You need to know whom you're speaking to.

✦ **Why are they participating in the community?** What do they want from it? If they're participating so they can trade pictures of their pet bunny rabbit with friends and you suddenly show up selling hunting rifles, they won't appreciate it.

✦ **What communities and sites do they most often use?** Best to focus your efforts where your audience goes.

✦ **How big is this audience?** If a social media campaign on Facebook is going to reach 20 people in six months, for example, Facebook might not be your ideal venue.

✦ **How often do they participate?** This, combined with audience size, helps you determine how often you need to participate. It lets you be more efficient.

Write all five questions down so that you can take notes while you research. I usually use a spreadsheet similar to the one shown in Figure 3-1.

Figure 3-1: Start with a social media research worksheet.

The worksheet is your central storage for research, so keep it handy.

Now I want to talk about how you can find this information. The Internet offers some great resources.

Starting with online communities

Most important, you have to spend some time exploring a few communities to see what your potential audience is saying and doing. I recommend looking at

✦ **Google Groups:** Visit `http://groups.google.com`. Search for your product or service and then look around some of the discussions that you find. What are people asking? See whether you could contribute to the discussion. How active are the discussions? If participants are posting every hour, this is a very active community — you'll need to follow closely if you're going to participate. Make sure you're receiving updates via e-mail so that you can respond quickly.

✦ **Yahoo! Groups:** Search and review Yahoo! Groups for the same kinds of information as Google Groups.

✦ **Facebook:** Facebook.com is so big, and so busy, that groups exist for nearly every imaginable interest. Search Facebook Groups for the topics that relate to your business. See how many members these groups have: More members mean a bigger audience for you. And don't forget to look at how often participants post to groups because frequent posts mean a more active community.

✦ **Digg:** Search Digg.com for topics, products, people, or ideas related to your business. If people are submitting relevant stories, how are they received? If relevant stories get a lot of votes, social news sites are a potential venue for you, and there's an interested community of readers. If relevant stories are received with sarcastic comments and a handful of votes, you'll want to avoid social news sites — or find a different way to approach the topic. The now-famous Will it Blend? YouTube videos are a great example of this: Blenders don't make good Digg material. But shoving an iPod into a blender? Pure Digg gold!

✦ **Blogs:** Use Google Blog Search (`http://blogsearch.google.com`), Technorati.com, and Icerocket.com. Search again for topics relevant to your business. How many bloggers are writing about the topic? The more bloggers, and the more often they're posting, the larger and potentially receptive your audience. What do the bloggers focus on? Their interests may indicate your audience's interests, too.

Audience research is the most important research you can do. Data is great; and the hard numbers I provide in the next few sections will be tremendously helpful, too. But social media marketing is not easily quantified — the general feel you get by checking out the communities is essential, too.

When you look at each community, note what you find on your social media research worksheet.

Researching with adCenter Labs

adCenter Labs, from Microsoft, is a fantastic free tool that lets you research your audience based on the search keywords they use and the sites they frequent. You can find the site at `http://adlab.msn.com`.

The tools adCenter Labs offers are experimental. That is, they come and go, and they change periodically. For this discussion, I'm focusing on two tools that haven't changed much. New tools spring up all the time, though, so it's worth keeping an eye on things.

adCenter Labs is a particularly good tool for you if

✦ You run an online store.

✦ Your audience is likely to use Hotmail or other Microsoft sites.

✦ You can easily define your audience by the search keywords they use and the sites they visit. If you sell a common product or provide a common service, then your audience uses phrases you can easily find with the methods outlined in Book II, Chapter 2.

✦ You're on a tight budget. (It's free, after all.)

To research your audience on adCenter Labs, start by using the Detecting Online Commercial Intention tool, which shows the probability that someone who searches on a particular phrase or visits a particular site is really going to buy something. Use this tool if

✦ You run an online store.

✦ You send traffic to another online store.

✦ Your site or strategy is built around reviewing products.

To open the Detecting Online Commercial Intention tool, choose Tools⇨ Audience Intelligence⇨Online Commercial Intention. Then try various types of searches:

✦ **Search for non-branded names of products or services you offer.**

For example, search for *accounting* or *tires.*

✦ **Search for brand names of the products you carry, review, or discuss.**

For example, search for *"Jane's track shoes."*

You need to search for branded and non-branded traffic separately because people searching on branded terms will generally have far higher commercial intent numbers, and can throw off your research.

✦ **Try entering the Web address for relevant informational sites.**

Try a product review site or a how-to site related to your industry or business.

✦ **Enter the Web address of various social media sites.**

Try Facebook.com, MySpace.com, LinkedIn.com, and any other sites you feel might be relevant to your campaign.

In each case, note the Probability for Commercial Query on your social media worksheet. The higher the number, the more likely that query is going to generate a purchase. The best possible score is a 1. If your end goal is a sale, you want to favor focus on terms with a higher probability in the next step. If you're running an online store and a particular site shows a very low commercial probability, you might want to cross it off your list.

A sample search for bicycles is shown in Figure 3-2.

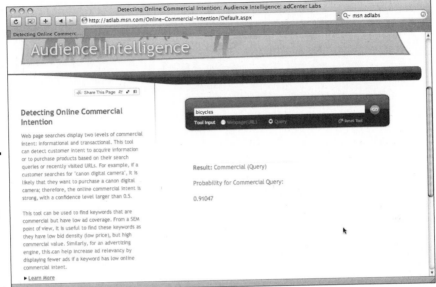

Figure 3-2:
Run an
Online
Commercial
Intention
search on
adCenter
Labs.

Figure 3-3 shows that LinkedIn visitors are very unlikely to make an immediate purchase. That makes sense because most visitors to LinkedIn are networking. They might be looking for services but not products they can buy online.

**Book VII
Chapter 3**

Creating Your
Social Media Plan

✦ **Noncommercial:** These visitors are not going to make an online purchase in the near future. They're looking for information.

✦ **Commercial-Informational:** These visitors may make a purchase but at this point they're just browsing. What you show them now may affect their interest later.

✦ **Commercial-Transactional:** These visitors are looking to buy right now. Give them what they want and you're set.

If you're running an online store and use the Online Commercial Intention tool, focus your research on the keywords and sites that show the highest commercial intent.

You can also help define your audience by using the Demographics Prediction tool (also found at Tools⇨Audience Intelligence). Use this tool to help predict age, gender, and other attributes based on the keywords they use on Live.com and the sites they visit. You can see a sample of this kind of search in Figure 3-4.

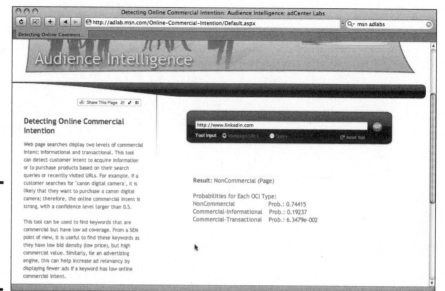

Figure 3-3:
Running a
search for
LinkedIn
commercial
intent.

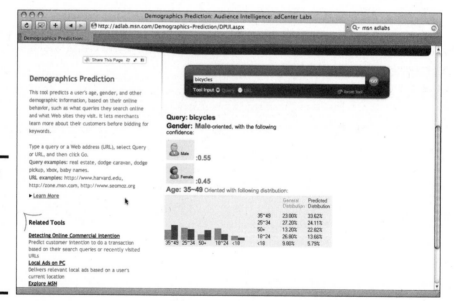

Figure 3-4:
A demo-
graphics
prediction
based on
a keyword
search for
bicycles.

To use the Demographics Prediction tool:

✦ **Search for the non-branded names of your products or services.**

For example, search for *"internet marketing books"* and not *"internet marketing for dummies."* Note the age and gender distribution.

✦ **Search for the brand names of your closest competitors, or of the products or services you sell. If there's data, note the age and gender distributions for those, too.**

For example, if you sell Joe's Widgets in your store, use that phrase.

✦ **Select the Webpage(URL) radio button and enter the Web addresses for your site, your competitors, and any major authority sites in your industry.**

For example, if you're a lean manufacturing consultant, enter the Web address of the top online resource site you know of.

✦ **Enter the addresses of any social media sites you think you might want to include in your campaign.**

- *If their demographics match up with the data you found in the first three bullets of this list,* keep those sites on your list.

- *If not,* consider whether you should skip them, or at least make them a lower priority.

In each case, note the relevant data and the keyword or site on your worksheet. (Refer to Figure 3-1.) If you already input data for that keyword or site, add another column and insert it there.

In Figure 3-5, the demographics for *"math tutors"* show you the gender breakdown and age distribution among Microsoft Live Search users who search using that phrase.

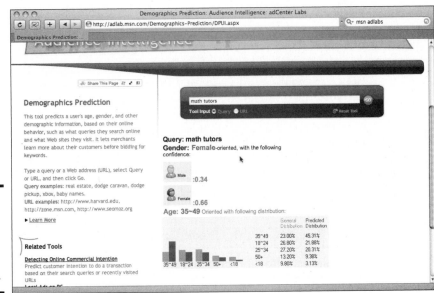

Figure 3-5: Running a demographics search for math tutors.

Why isn't this site showing up?

Some sites don't get enough traffic to register in the Quantcast database. Well, those sites *can* get into Quantcast data, but the site owner has to add a special snippet of code to his site. You can find the code and instructions on the Quantcast Web site. Site owners also need to permit Quantcast to collect some statistics, such as lifestyle or geographic information. You may also want to disclose that you're using the code snippet in your privacy statement on your site.

Getting more data with Quantcast

Microsoft adCenter Labs is great for getting basic demographics based on keyword searches. If you want demographic data on a site-by-site basis that's more detailed, though, Quantcast is a great free resource.

On Quantcast, you can get site demographics, including:

✦ Visitors by age group

✦ Visitor ethnicity

✦ Household income

✦ Children in household

✦ Visitor education level

✦ Gender

✦ Other sites and categories of sites visited by a site's typical user

Using Quantcast is easy. Go to www.quantcast.com, type the Web address of the site you want to check, and click the Find Profile button. You should see something similar to Figure 3-6.

Ever hear the expression that 50 percent of statistics are true and 60 percent are lies? Yeah. Be careful when you use any data collected by sites like Quantcast. They're great resources, but we humans have a funny way of screwing up carefully written measurement tools. If the data makes zero sense based on your gut instinct, listen to your gut, at least a little.

Again, add this data to your social media worksheet. (Refer to Figure 3-1.) Supplement what you already have for each of these sites. By now, your worksheet should have a solid picture of each site, like in Figure 3-7.

Figure 3-6:
A sample
Quantcast
report.

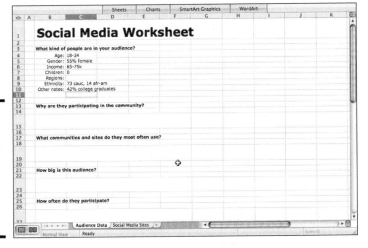

Figure 3-7:
Social
media
research
worksheet
with
Quantcast
data.

Getting fancy with paid data services

So far, all the data I've showed you how to collect came from free sources. If you have some dollars to spend on research, though, a number of services can give you far more detail.

✦ **Nielsen Online (`http://www.nielsen-online.com`) NetView** lets you create custom reports based on demographics and online viewing habits. Reports are incredibly detailed comparisons between your audience and the entire Internet population.

✦ **Hitwise (`www.hitwise.com`)** provides in-depth reporting on entire industries or online categories, or specific sites.

✦ **Compete (`http://compete.com`)** delivers search and site-usage analytics. Site data is free, but the search reports are not.

✦ **comScore (`www.comscore.com`)** provides a wide range of advertising and site-usage analysis tools.

Expect Nielsen Online and comScore to require an ongoing subscription. Hitwise offers individual reports or an ongoing subscription. Compete.com lets you buy credits you can use to generate reports.

I recommend purchasing one or more of these services if you

✦ **Have a large social media budget and want to make sure you allocate it effectively.** If spending a few thousand dollars on reports will mean you can better spend tens of thousands of dollars later, it's worth it.

✦ **Can't afford to spend a month or two testing your campaign.** The detail you get from these paid services can eliminate a lot of trial and error.

✦ **Have other uses for this data.** If you're also doing a pay per click (PPC) campaign and a banner ad buy, you might need this data anyway.

✦ **Have the time and interest to dig deep into statistics and create an ultra-detailed picture of your audience.**

Social media marketing is an emerging field. No one has the ideal toolset for campaign planning, so you end up engaging in some trial-and-error no matter how much data you get. Invest in paid reports to paint a more complete picture, but don't expect a photograph.

Crafting Your Social Media Message

You need a message for your social media campaign. Yes, social media is informal. And yes, it's supposed to be spontaneous. But social media is also like standing in front of 50 million reporters. It's best to have some guidelines to prevent foot-in-mouth syndrome.

Your social media marketing message is a little different, though, insofar as it's more about the kind of person or organization you are than it is about the benefits of a particular product or service. It's not so much a message as a guide: A Jiminy Cricket for your social media participation.

Keep it real

Don't forget Sony!

Right now, you're rolling your eyes. There goes Ian on his hand-waving, New Age marketing stuff. But I'm not. This is practical advice. You might remember that Sony got caught publishing fake blogs by supposed fans of its new PS3 gaming console. I'm guessing that "oops" wasn't one of the words Sony had in its social media message.

Here's how you set your message: Take a piece of paper and write down three or four words you want to associate with you and your company — words like *honest, funny, annoying* (hopefully not), and *smart*.

Those words are your message. Mine have always been *smart, funny,* and *honest*. That doesn't mean every word I write on a social network has to fit all three characteristics. But any time I'm about to post anything, anywhere, I think of those three words and consider whether I'm about to do the opposite.

Write down the message on your social media worksheet, too. Compare it against the sites, audiences, and keyword data you already have. Does your message fit the audience to which each site caters? Use this comparison to further narrow where you're going to concentrate your efforts.

Book VII
Chapter 3

Creating Your
Social Media Plan

Setting Your Social Media Style

Style is different from message. Here are a few archetypal social media styles. You won't fit totally into any of them, but you can probably find a few favorites. Your style can really guide where and how you participate in social media.

✦ The **troublemaker** loves to poke people a little bit, all the time. She's not mean or evil. She's just working to make sure everyone questions assumptions. Opt to be a troublemaker *only if you know for certain* that you know a *lot* about the topic about which you're going to stir up trouble. Troublemakers can get a lot of attention and admiration. Always be courteous, and poke a little fun at yourself. Troublemakers end up spending a lot of time on microblogging networks and discussion forums, as well commenting on blogs.

✦ The **maven** is an expert who loves to help others, thereby demonstrating her knowledge and expertise. You'll seek out folks who are asking questions. If you're a consultant, it's great to be a maven. Spend a lot of time on Yahoo! Answers, LinkedIn, and your blog. Use microblogs to let folks know when and how you're providing information.

✦ The **new kid** is polite and tends to keep a low profile, learning his way around. If you're the new kid, you're not necessarily silent, but you're definitely self-effacing. You're getting to know everyone. Be the new kid if you're striking out in a new industry, or if you're going into a social network where the demographic is totally different from your own. Be sure to tell folks why you're there: "I want to help," or "I'm starting a business," or "I want to learn." Focus on big social networks like Facebook, as well as microblogs like Twitter. Stay away from answers networks unless you know enough to separate good answers from bad.

✦ Everyone knows the **rock star.** If his name shows up on a social network, he instantly attracts dozens or even hundreds of friends and followers. If you're not a rock star, you're jealous. (I am, anyway.) Be the rock star if you're well known in your industry or field. Use Facebook Groups, microblogs, your blog, and any niche sites to keep in touch.

I'm not suggesting you don a fake persona when you start a social media campaign. Far from it. What I am suggesting, though, is that you put serious thought into your strengths and weaknesses as a member of the community. Then play to your strengths.

Preparing Your Social Media Profile

Every social media site asks you to create a *profile* that includes basic information, such as your name, your Web site (if you have one), and the like.

Every social media site also asks for info that's harder for you to come by, so you might as well collect it all now.

Open your social media worksheet. Then add the following:

✦ **Your avatar:** Just about every social media site will want a photo of you, or a symbol, or some graphic to represent yourself. This is your *avatar.* (Skip ahead to upcoming Figure 3-9 to see mine.) Find an image or graphic you like (it doesn't have to be a photo of you) and save it. Most services will resize it automatically, but if you know how, you can resize the image to about 200 x 200 pixels to save yourself some time later.

✦ **A short description of yourself:** This can be funny, serious, or anything in between. Write three to four sentences and save it to re-use. You might want to write more than one for different purposes. For example, I have a serious bio, a funny one, and a few others.

✦ **Separate, short lists of activities and interests:** Also write down your favorite books, foods, TV shows, and music. Sites like Facebook will ask for this info again and again.

+ **(Optional) Basic contact information:** Gather your e-mail address, mailing address (if you want to share), and any instant messaging (IM) addresses. It's easier to cut and paste this static info than it is to rewrite it every time.

Now it's time to figure out where to put all this information.

Choosing Your Target Social Media Sites

When attempting to do a quick count of social media sites, I gave up at 152. Chances are you don't have 20 hours per day to spend patrolling social media sites for new connections.

So you need to make a few choices. I can't do that for you, but here are a few guidelines:

+ **Check the logic:** Go to your social media worksheet. While you select sites, check the answers you wrote to each of the five questions. Do the sites you're picking make sense?

+ **Think big:** If you need to reach consumers, look at the big social networking sites: Facebook and MySpace. These are big, big sites and it's hard to stand out, but they're your best potential venue.

+ **Think business:** If you're more business-to-business (B2B), look at business-focused social networks, such as LinkedIn. Also look at microblogs, such as Twitter and Plurk.

+ **Think media:** If you have video, PowerPoint, or photos to post and you want lots of folks to see them, you're definitely going to need the big media sharing sites: YouTube, Flickr, SlideShare and iTunes. (Yes, iTunes lets you upload your own media.)

+ **Remember bookmarking:** If you care about search engine rankings (and you'd better), put the major social bookmarking sites on your list: Delicious, Ma.gnolia, and StumbleUpon, to name a few.

+ **Make the news — maybe:** If you have something that could be Really Big News, consider the social news sites like Digg and Reddit. Otherwise, don't waste your time on these networks. The audiences on these sites are big, noisy, and very difficult to win over.

+ **Find your niche:** Consider whether any niche social sites cater directly to your audience. Sites like Gooruze.com (marketing), Autospies.com (cars), and QoolSqool.com (education) offer focused audiences. See Figure 3-8 for a great example of a niche social media site.

Figure 3-8:
Don't
overlook
a niche
audience.

While you create your list of target sites, remember to keep asking yourself: Will this site help you realize your marketing goals? That doesn't mean the site has to generate sales or leads directly. It may just offer you a chance to improve your brand, talk to customers, or learn what your customers want. But make sure the site will help somehow.

After you pick your sites, set up your accounts. Be sure to subscribe to each one and put it on your social media desktop.

Reviewing Your Site for Social Skills

Now it's time to determine whether your site is ready to get social. Here are some things you need to line up before you're good to go for any social media–ready site:

✦ **Great bait:** At least some of the content on your site should be the kind that gets folks talking and passing the page to their friends.

✦ **RSS (really simple syndication) subscriptions:** Visitors must be able to subscribe to an RSS feed for your site! Without this, you're shouting from a soundproof room. See Book VI, Chapter 2, for more information.

✦ **Easy sharing:** Visitors should also be able to bookmark, digg (okay, use Digg), and otherwise link or pass your pages to their favorite social networks.

Creating great bait

You don't need yet another book telling you to "write compelling content." If it were as easy as saying that, everyone would write it. Here are a few specific ways to write content that attracts readers:

✦ **Answer specific questions:** If one question pops up again and again in discussions, answer it in an article.

✦ **Write lists:** I don't know why, but lists always get attention.

✦ **Use graphics:** Great photography and informational images will always attract attention.

✦ **Write about things that make you angry:** A little passion never hurt a writer.

✦ **Write about things that make you laugh:** It's a great way to entertain and bring back visitors.

✦ **Write for scannability:** Use bullets, short paragraphs of no more than three lines, and subheadings so that a reader can quickly scan the page.

Put all these tips together, and you can get great results. The page in Figure 3-9 generated 22,000 pageviews in two days, and continues to attract comments and attention. That kind of anchor content makes a site social-friendly.

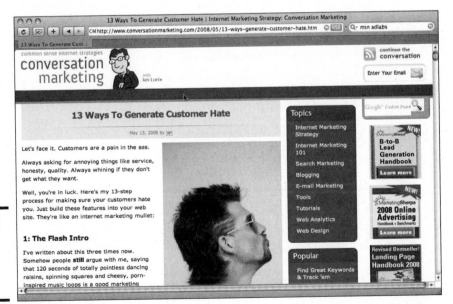

Figure 3-9:
Generate
traffic by
creating
great bait.

You can find more about writing great content in Book II, Chapter 7. The same techniques that work for search engine optimization work for social media. Bonus!

Employing RSS subscriptions

RSS (really simple syndication) is a standard way to deliver the latest headlines from your Web site to any browser, software, or device that's set up to read it. *RSS feeds* drive much of the social media world, and any functional blog has one. They're a wonderful tool. With a *feed reader* — such as Google Reader — Web surfers can subscribe to dozens of blogs and sites and then quickly skim down the latest headlines, reading what they find interesting.

Think of an RSS feed as a kind of news ticker that you deliver to anyone who wants it. Your audience can check this ticker any time they want. Many users prefer this to e-mail updates because they don't want to give you their e-mail address or deal with the hassle of finding your e-mail in their spam folder.

Remember all the talk about headlines in the preceding section? RSS feeds are part of the reason why they're so important. The headline is usually what visitors see when they skim through their RSS feed reader. I'll say it again: Write a good headline.

But RSS feeds aren't just for blogs. You can and should use them anywhere you have content that updates. For example:

✦ A Special Offers page in your store

✦ A News page on your site

✦ A Tips or Advice section

✦ Any part of your site that includes articles or other serial content

You can tell whether a site has an RSS feed by looking for the well-known RSS chicklet. The RSS button is known as a chicklet because it's shaped like the gum of the same name.

Make sure your site has at least one RSS feed available and is *auto-discoverable*. When a site is auto-discoverable, a visiting Web browser, search engine, or other software can automatically find the RSS feed and tell a visitor that he can subscribe to the feed. The technical details of doing this are beyond the scope of this book.

Let folks subscribe via e-mail, too, if they want to. Send them updates just how you always have.

Make sharing easy

Sharing is the essence of social media. Your ultimate goal is to have visitors to your site grab links and pass them along to friends and connections in their favorite communities. With that in mind, make this task easy for them:

✦ **Easy buttons:** Make sure the most popular pages on your site have buttons that let visitors post the page on their favorite social networks. Services such as AddThis (`www.addthis.com`) provide easy, reusable buttons you can cut and paste onto your site.

✦ **Easy address:** If possible, keep your page addresses as simple as possible. For example, you can see how much easier it is to remember

```
MySite.com/shoes
```

than

```
MySite.com/index.aspx?product=2&category=321
```

Which one would you rather cut and paste to your Facebook page?

✦ **Easy contact info:** If you have a Twitter or other microblogging account, or accounts on other social networks, make sure you list your contact information for those networks on your site. Visitors might pass those around, too.

Setting Your Social Media Marketing Routine

Three-quarters of social media marketing is consistency. You need to set a routine and stick with it. Your routine centers around the social media desktop. You need to regularly check the desktop and respond to messages, react to posts, or just keep track of what's going on.

How you define *regularly* depends on your time and your goals.

✦ **If you're being aggressive and looking to become a major authority in your space,** spend five minutes scanning and responding via your social media desktop every hour.

✦ **If you're looking to maintain your reputation and gain some authority over time,** spend five minutes two or three times per day.

✦ **If you're just getting your feet wet,** spend five minutes once per day.

Schedule this time! I actually have a timer running on my desktop. It goes off every hour. When it does, I check my e-mail for five minutes and spend another five minutes doing my social media chores. Then I go back to whatever else I was doing.

Keeping to a schedule helps you keep to a social media routine without distracting you from all the other requirements of your day.

Planning for the Long Social Media Marketing Haul

Big caveat here: Social media marketing is *not a quick thing.* It takes a long time to gain the trust of a community, and even longer to parlay that trust into an asset for your business. Your time and effort spent are worth it because you'll get the best customers you've ever had. But it does take a long time.

Therefore, you need to plan for the long haul. Make sure that you consider the following:

✦ **Substitutes:** Do you need someone to stand in for you while you're on vacation or away on business? They don't need to pretend they're you. But if you're blogging, for instance, it's great to have a guest keep things going while you're offline.

✦ **Convenience:** For this to become part of your daily routine, it needs to be convenient. Use a browser, such as Firefox, and have it memorize your various logins. Bookmark all the social media sites you need to visit.

✦ **Fun:** Make sure it stays fun! If one network or another becomes a pain in the neck, take a vacation from it. Go where there are people you enjoy talking to. Those are who will be your best audience anyway.

✦ **Promotions:** Plan a few special promotions that you'll offer just to your social media audience.

✦ **Measure:** Make sure you have a solid Web analytics plan in place, so you can measure whether these efforts are paying off. See Book III to read more about Web analytics.

If you haven't already, go to Chapter 1 of this minibook and read (and re-read) about the sneeze principle. Your social media plan should put you amidst the most susceptible audience so that your content passes from person to person.

Chapter 4: Navigating Top Social Media Sites

In This Chapter

✔ Networking with Facebook, MySpace, and more

✔ Bookmarking with Delicious, Ma.gnolia.com, and others

✔ Growing your business with multimedia

✔ Talking in discussion forums

✔ Using Twitter as a launchpad

✔ Building your reputation with Yahoo! Answers

✔ Using the power of niche sites

From earlier chapters of this minibook, you set the foundation for a social media campaign that will attract the right audience to your site: You profiled your audience, set up your profiles, and targeted your sites. Now it's time to get to work — *net*work, that is.

In this chapter, I walk you through specific examples of networking on each of the major social networks, as well as using bookmarking sites, microblogs, and other social media centers. I also show you a few examples of niche sites and discussion forums. And don't skip over the information about how to build your reputation on Yahoo! Answers.

Chapters 5 and 6 of the minibook go into more detail on these topics. The most important thing you need to understand at the end of this chapter is how the various social media sites fit: say, how you can use Twitter to announce a new video on YouTube and then have the video direct folks to a blog. That's the real gold in social media.

The major social networks are a great starting point. Facebook, MySpace, and LinkedIn can help you find your audience and let them know you're available.

You can apply what you learn on the big networks to the small, niche ones, too. I offer more information in the upcoming section, "Unleashing the Power of Niche Sites."

Making Friends on Facebook

Facebook is the current social networking leader. With tens of millions of users, Facebook offers an audience for nearly any business.

Read this section even if you're going to focus on using MySpace. Many similarities exist between the two services.

Use Facebook if any of the following are true:

✦ Your audience is mostly consumers.

✦ You have a marketing message or tool people will find fun.

✦ You have an online store or product.

✦ You already have a group of customers that you know is on Facebook.

✦ You're going to use Twitter and/or write a blog.

That last item is a no-brainer because you can set Facebook to automatically publish your latest Twitter or blog post to your Facebook profile — even when you don't log in for a few days.

Don't rule out Facebook if your audience is older than 40. Facebook membership covers ages 15–55 and older.

If you haven't read Chapter 1 of this minibook, go there to check out my discussion of the sneeze principle. Facebook is particularly good at spreading a message like a virus. Any two connected Facebook users know whether their friend posted something, joined a new group, became a fan of a page, installed a new Facebook application, or otherwise acted within the community. Word can spread fast.

From a marketing perspective, you can break up Facebook into three types of tools:

✦ Networking

✦ Branding and publicity

✦ Custom applications

Using the Facebook networking tools

Networking tools let you find and make friends with similar interests, post messages on friends' *walls* (the central location for all the stories about a user), and send private messages back and forth. The two basic networking tools on Facebook are profile pages and groups.

The *profile page* is your home address on Facebook. Here, you post notes, update your status, share photos, and otherwise keep in touch.

Creating a great Facebook profile page

Here are five ways to create a great profile page on Facebook:

✦ **Use your avatar as your picture!** Nothing says "outsider" like a profile with no image. Plus, your avatar is your social media brand. Use it everywhere you go. I have a fun avatar that Chris Furniss drew for me:

✦ **Keep your profile up to date.** Use automatic updates from Twitter or your blog if you need to, but keep it up to date. If you never update your profile, people assume you're not really part of the community and ignore you. That's not the objective.

✦ **Update your status, too.** That's the little phrase that shows up after your name. I try to have fun with it, as you'll see in Figure 4-1.

✦ **Post something new on your wall every now and then.** If you can, include a relevant link. Your wall posts show in your Facebook friends' news feeds, remind them you're there, and invite them to keep in touch.

✦ **Fill in as much detail as you can.** The more you include about yourself, the more easily folks with similar interests can find you, and the more you look like a good citizen in the community.

To see a very simple example, take a look at my Facebook profile page in Figure 4-1.

Book VII
Chapter 4

Navigating Top Social Media Sites

Your status   Update your status here

Figure 4-1: My Facebook profile page. C'mon in! Make friends!

After you set up your profile page, it's time to make friends. Start by contacting people you already know. (I guarantee some of them are on Facebook!) Visit their profile pages and click the Add as Friend link. It's that simple.

You have several ways to find and make friends, but these two methods will get you started.

✦ **Look through your friends' lists of friends.**

Don't worry; it's okay to do that. Go ahead and invite other folks to be your friend.

✦ **Find friends through relevant groups.**

See the next section about groups.

Launching a Facebook group

If you think of your profile page as your home on Facebook, then *groups* are networking and social events. Create your own group based on interests, location, or any other criteria, and then invite others. Or join other people's groups. They're a great way to meet people, make friends, and build an audience. A few examples of groups include

✦ 1,000,000 Strong for Stephen Colbert

✦ Web 2.0 Entrepreneurs

✦ Proud Military Wives

✦ Giants Fans

Groups are about to become even more important as Facebook phases out networks. *Networks* (in Facebook) used to link people who lived in similar places, went to the same schools, or were otherwise connected by geography or history. Without networks, groups will be your main way to link up.

Here's how we created the Facebook group *Conversation Marketing*, as shown in Figure 4-2:

1. **Log into your Facebook account.**

2. **Click Groups in the Applications section of your homepage.**

3. **Click the Create New Group button.**

4. **Enter the group name, description, and category.**

5. **Complete the rest of the fields on the form if you can.**

The more information you provide, the easier it will be for interested Facebookers to find you.

Why not a wiki?

If you're a Web veteran, then you know you could use a *wiki* (a Web site that visitors can edit) or a discussion forum to accomplish the same thing. However, seeing as how Facebook already has millions of members — millions of potential community members for you — why fight it?

6. **Click the Create Group button.**

7. **On the next page, upload a picture, enter a Web site address if you already have a related Web site, and set up permissions for the group.**

8. **Click the Save button. Note that you can always change this stuff later.**

9. **Finally, invite any friends you think might be interested in the group.**

Book VII
Chapter 4

Navigating Top
Social Media Sites

Figure 4-2:
The Conversation Marketing Facebook group.

Participating in groups

When it comes to "group" behavior in Facebook, here are three broad and simple things I recommend:

✦ **Seek, find, and join.** Look at your friends' groups. In the Applications area on the right side of your homepage, click the More link. Click

Groups in the list of applications that appear. The left-hand column is a list of groups joined recently by your friends. Look there first for groups you might find useful.

✦ **Be discerning.** You're going to be inundated with group invitations. You don't have to join every single one, nor should you. Your time is limited, so stick with groups you really think might prove helpful.

✦ **Participate!** It's easy to just glance at the groups list every few months and otherwise ignore them. Instead, post to group discussions occasionally, or share a link on the group's wall.

You can create your own group, too. Well, you *can* — just keep in mind that there are already a *lot* of groups on Facebook. If you're creating a group, make sure it'll be useful.

Creating a great group

If creating your own group — a great group — fits the bill, keep the following in mind:

✦ **Be unique.** If you're just copying another group so you can grab the glory, stop. You can gain more by participating in and growing other, relevant groups than by getting into a tug-of-war with someone else.

✦ **Update.** If you let a group lie silent for weeks, it'll stop growing. Trust me, I know.

✦ **Invite officers.** If you have friends who are influential on Facebook, invite them to be officers in your group. Officers don't have to do anything if they don't want to, but are called out as leaders within the group and can contribute.

Branding and publicity: Facebook Pages and Facebook Events

Facebook offers two other kinds of community builders: Pages and Events. If Groups are gathering places, Pages are trade show booths, and Events are invitations handed out to everyone. You can use the two to announce new products or services, solicit questions from your loyal customers, or provide special incentives.

Building a company presence with Pages

The primary branding and publicity tool on Facebook (if you don't want to spend money) is *Facebook Pages*. Don't confuse these with a standard profile page. Facebook Pages provides a customizable page where you can add your own Flash animations, Facebook applications, images, and text. Take a look at the examples in Figure 4-3, and you'll see how unique they can be:

Figure 4-3:
Two
Facebook
pages.
See how
different
they are?

If visitors like the page, they can become a fan. When visitors do that, their friends will see it, and then go and look at the page, too. And so on.

Here's how to create a great Facebook Page:

✦ **Develop an idea that's more than advertising.** Don't just create a billboard. Design a page that teaches visitors something new every day, offers them access to a special tool, or entertains them.

✦ **Write well.** If you're not a professional copywriter, hire one. It's worth it. You don't have much time to convince the visitor that they should stay and become a fan of the page.

✦ **Have great graphics.** If you don't have professional-looking illustrations or photos, don't use any at all.

✦ **Make the page "sneezable"** with photos and short, punchy messages that visitors can quickly scan, read, and pass along.

Read about the sneeze principle in Chapter 1 of this minibook.

✦ **Update it!**

Announcing cool stuff with Facebook Events

Facebook Events is another great publicity tool. When you create an event, you can invite any of your Facebook friends, as well as non-Facebook members.

Facebook Events is a great tool *if you don't abuse it.* However, the more events you announce, the less folks will read them. Be sure to read the rules for Facebook Events, too.

Use Facebook Events if

✦ **You have a specific event you want to promote.** The event can be online or at a real location, or just be a silly made-up occasion that you think might be fun.

✦ **You want to build some buzz around that event.**

✦ **You have specific people on Facebook you want to invite or otherwise inform about the event.**

Here are four things to always include on a Facebook Events page:

✦ **A great event name:** Using something akin to "Tour our store" is fine, but using "Store Sale & Tour at Widgets R Us" might garner more interest.

✦ **A great image:** Again, a great graphic will go a long way toward making folks stick around and read about your event.

✦ **A great guest list:** If you can get some well-known folks on the guest list *and* have a public guest list so folks can see it, others are more likely to sign up. Same goes for the number of guests. Social proof is very compelling.

✦ **Updates:** And yes, once again, periodic updates are essential. Don't forget about the event page after you're done. Post photos, video, and other notes about the event. Then you can use that page to boost your next event by saying, "Look at how much fun the last event was."

If you're hosting an event at a physical location, try to have a laptop and an Internet connection. Posting an occasional note, photo, or video might create an impromptu audience on Facebook.

Creating your own audience with Facebook applications

Facebook also lets you create custom applications, using a toolbox that Facebook provides. You can then make those applications available via the Applications area.

Examples of applications include

+ To-do list managers

+ Trivia tests and quizzes where you compete against other members

+ Photo-display tools

+ Widgets that display your latest blog or Twitter post

+ Games where you virtually bite other members who then have to virtually bite someone else. (I'm not making this up.)

You can also find recipe collections, music listings, travel maps, file sharing, and applications for just about any other purpose you can think of.

Here's the gold to pan: If you can create a really fun or useful application — and then get a lot of people to use it — you can build a huge audience quickly. Successful applications can accrue 300,000 users and more. And, because you're permitted to link to your own Web site or Facebook page in the application itself, the marketing opportunity is big. Sweet!

Facebook holds thousands of applications. Don't expect overnight success. It'll take persistence and a really cool little program to get the attention you want.

Again, the sneeze principle is important. If one user selects a Facebook application for her homepage, her Facebook friends will know and might look, too. A successful application spreads fast.

If you have a yen to create your own Facebook app, here are six tips:

+ **Hire a developer!** Unless you're a programmer yourself, you'll end up tearing your hair out using the Facebook toolset. It's good, but you need to understand basic programming to use it.

+ **Don't imitate.** You need to come up with something really unique if you're going to succeed.

+ **Test some ideas.** If you have a few close friends on Facebook, test your application out with them first. If you launch it system-wide, only to discover it doesn't work or drives users nuts, it'll be too late to recover.

✦ **Include your brand.** There is nothing wrong with including your logo and a link back to your site.

✦ **Integrate with your brand.** The application you build should somehow relate to your business. If you make wagons, create a little wagon wheel game. If you make telescopes, make a constellation flashcard game.

✦ **Integrate sneezability.** Include something in your application that entices users to send their score or something else to their friends. Some applications are built purely to send around (like the bite-style application I mention earlier).

✦ **Market it.** If you have close friends on Facebook, send them a message letting them know about the new application. Install it on your profile page. And announce it on your Facebook Pages page. Finally, have a launch Event! (Read about Facebook Events earlier in this chapter.)

Facebook is a very complex world with a lot of ways to network. This section gives you the basics. Take a look at *Facebook For Dummies* by Carolyn Abram and Leah Pearlman (Wiley) if you want a more detailed tour.

Socializing on MySpace

MySpace was one of the first of a new crop of social networking sites. Facebook followed soon after, but MySpace still caters to a very active membership. (Yes, I know Friendster started it all. But it's relatively quiet these days, so I recommend MySpace.)

A lot of folks think MySpace is focused on teenagers. However, it's more focused on the "trendy" types than any specific age group. Don't rule it out just because your audience is 30.

Use MySpace if

✦ **You're pursuing a younger age group or are going for the "cool factor" with your product or service.**

✦ **You're a band:** MySpace has become *the* launchpad for bands.

✦ **You want to build traffic to your site from a huge audience.**

✦ **Your business is connected to entertainment in any way.**

✦ **You have a product to promote to the trendy audience.**

MySpace has the same types of opportunities as Facebook: namely, networking, publicity, and custom applications. However, MySpace also incorporates a few other social media tools, including blogs, discussion forums, and video and music sharing.

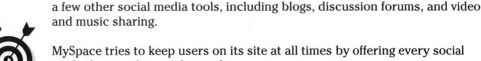

MySpace tries to keep users on its site at all times by offering every social media feature they might need.

Getting started on MySpace

Everything you do on MySpace centers around your profile page: That's your home base.

Here's how I recommend you work toward creating a great MySpace profile page.

- ✦ **Choose your username wisely.** It becomes part of your MySpace address. For example, my username is portentint, so my MySpace address is `myspace.com/portentint`. Keep your username clean and free from misinterpreted innuendo. You can't change this later.

- ✦ **Link to your Web site from your profile.** MySpace warns users when they're about to leave the site, but it's still worth it. If you gain a lot of friends, those links could send you a fair bit of traffic. Unlike Facebook, MySpace doesn't provide a place to type your Web address, so you'll want to add it to your profile description.

- ✦ **Customize it.** If you know a little HTML, you can customize how text and images look on the page. That can be a huge help for visitors, and lets you emphasize the important stuff.

- ✦ **Hire a designer.** If you really want to create a great MySpace page, consider hiring someone to design a *skin* (a custom look for your MySpace page) for you. There are professionals who do nothing but design great MySpace pages.

- ✦ **Complete it!** Don't leave any information areas blank.

- ✦ **Don't go gadget-happy.** Plenty of MySpace pages cover every square pixel with hopping/flashing/blinking graphics. You don't need to add to the pile.

- ✦ **Design for sneezability.** Even more than Facebook, MySpace has huge viral potential. Design your profile page to be something folks will want to pass along. It'll pay off.

Take a look at my MySpace page in Figure 4-4. I actually spend more time on Facebook, but found that investing a little bit in a custom MySpace look was worth it. The MySpace page brings additional traffic from folks who may not use Facebook.

**Book VII
Chapter 4**

Navigating Top
Social Media Sites

Figure 4-4:
My
MySpace
page, with
custom
design.

Understanding what's different about MySpace

Because Facebook and MySpace profiles, groups, and events are so similar, I'm not going to repeat them here. (You can read about this earlier in the chapter, in the sections on Facebook.) And, most of the basic principles of marketing on MySpace are similar to Facebook. Making friends, joining groups, and marketing with events and applications work much the same way. Be sure to read the previous sections about Facebook.

Having said that, MySpace is different from Facebook in a few critical ways:

First, MySpace doesn't have a separate type of page for marketing. Therefore, you want to create a unique profile page to promote your company, products, or services. See what Aquafina did in Figure 4-5. Aquafina completely customized its page, branded it heavily for its product, and provided calls to action that are relevant to MySpace: Make friends, view pictures, view videos, and so on.

Also, MySpace audiences have an even lower tolerance for in-your-face promotion than their Facebook counterparts. Don't go into the forums hawking products, and don't make 10,000 friends so you can bury them in company news. You're going to need to work your way into the community; provide some eye candy; and then attract traffic through custom applications, links, and other devices.

And, multimedia plays a bigger role on MySpace than Facebook. With its music library and built-in video streaming, MySpace offers more opportunities to grab the user's attention. Use your judgment, though: Don't load up your page with multiple videos. As I said earlier, MySpace has plenty of cluttered pages. You don't need to add one.

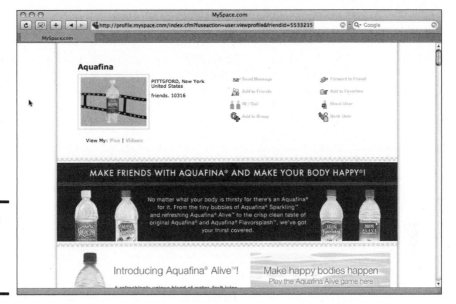

Figure 4-5: The Aquafina MySpace page.

The sneeze principle, revisited

MySpace might be the single most infectious piece of Web real estate. If you add an application, vote for a piece of music, or give a thumbs-up to a blog post or discussion forum message, your friends will know.

Because you can do so many things on MySpace, you can broadcast your message a lot of different ways.

✦ **Write a blog.** Even if you write only once per month, do an occasional post on MySpace. The updates will show in all your friends' notification lists. And they can subscribe to your blog, too.

✦ **Make friends.** Don't be shy. Go out and find users with similar interests; then make friends with them. Every friend you add gives you access to a broader and broader network.

✦ **Be professional.** Many MySpace users behave like they're in a food fight. Don't take the bait.

✦ **Participate in the forums.** Find a relevant discussion forum and contribute. You'll find a lot of friends that way.

✦ **Check out the classifieds.** Depending on your business, this forum might hold an opportunity to reach more visitors.

✦ **Be consistent.** Make sure you update regularly, and that you add friends at a steady pace. It takes a **lot** of work to reach a nice critical mass of friends and attention on MySpace.

✦ **Build an application.** If you operate a blog, consider building a simple widget folks can add to their MySpace profile pages that provides a news feed. *Note:* This will work only if you're providing really useful content, of course — but if you do, this can generate a lot of traffic.

✦ **Don't believe the naysayers.** A lot of folks have written off MySpace as a marketing opportunity. But it still works.

✦ **Plan for the future.** That said, MySpace marketing takes a looong time, so don't expect overnight results.

Networking for Business on LinkedIn

LinkedIn is an entirely different kind of social network. Built entirely as a vehicle with which businesspeople connect and interact, it functions based on connections rather than friends. Although this might sound like a purely semantic difference, it's not, and here's why:

✦ **LinkedIn restricts whom you can add as a connection.** You need to be able to indicate how you know that person before you can even attempt to connect.

✦ **LinkedIn includes recommendations that you can get from colleagues and clients.** Those recommendations show on your profile page.

✦ **Your profile includes your work history.**

✦ **People are automatically grouped by company.**

✦ **You can't contact people who aren't in your network directly except through InMail,** for which LinkedIn charges a fee.

✦ **Companies can get their own separate profile pages** (a new feature).

Use LinkedIn if

✦ Your company provides professional services.

✦ Your clients are other companies.

✦ You're a consultant of almost any kind.

✦ You want to focus on quality connections, not quantity.

You can't customize the look and feel of your profile page on LinkedIn. However, completeness is important — even more important than on Facebook and MySpace — because LinkedIn is driven by one-to-one connections between individuals, and those connections are typically formed based on work history, location, and so on. It's a pure business networking environment.

Figure 4-6 shows my LinkedIn page, completed.

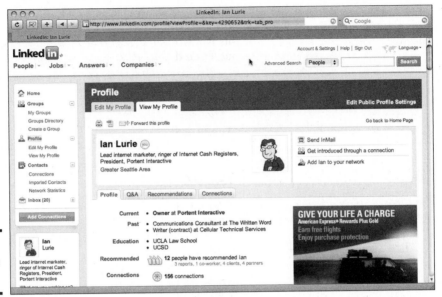

Figure 4-6:
My LinkedIn
page.

To give yourself the best chance of succeeding on LinkedIn, heed these four things:

✦ **Quality:** A few quality connections will take you a lot farther than dozens of lousy ones. Connect with folks you already know, or have someone else introduce you using the introduction feature on LinkedIn.

✦ **Recommendations:** Get recommendations when you can. They look great on your profile page, and many potential clients will research you via LinkedIn.

✦ **Groups:** The LinkedIn groups feature works much like MySpace and Facebook, but LinkedIn groups focus entirely on professional networking.

✦ **Answers:** Use LinkedIn Answers to provide or seek advice. If you provide great information, folks will mark your answer as "best." Get enough of those, and you'll be tagged as having expertise in a particular subject.

LinkedIn is a very specialized network. Don't go in there expecting to sell 400 insurance policies. Set up your profile with the expectation that you can make valuable, long-lasting business connections.

Bookmarking Your Way to the Top

Bookmarking sites let you save links to sites you like and share those links with other site users. All bookmarking sites share some common features:

+ They let you save bookmarks in an account on a server.

+ You can make friends or follow other members.

+ Bookmarks are ranked, either according to the number of times they're bookmarked or according to votes by members. A top-ranking bookmark is worth a veritable swarm of visitors.

+ Every major bookmarking site offers a toolbar or other gadget you can add to your Firefox Web browser (and, in some cases, Internet Explorer) so you can quickly and easily add bookmarks.

Every business that has a Web site should belong to at least one of the major bookmarking services. Four services you should definitely consider are

+ StumbleUpon

+ Delicious

+ Ma.gnolia

+ Diigo

Bookmarking sites spread your message when other site members bookmark the same stuff you do or vote for your bookmarks.

The number of friends you have doesn't matter as much as their ability to spread the word about your bookmarks. Yes, having 100,000 friends can help, but having 10 friends who are well known on the bookmarking site is better. Their vote or bookmark will spread the word network-wide.

Bookmark-driven "sneezes" can happen right after you post something new, or weeks or months later. If your post doesn't get any attention, don't lose heart. Keep posting and bookmarking good stuff.

Your success in the bookmarking world depends on

+ **Your influence on the network:** The more content you bookmark that others like, the more influential you'll become, and the more weight the network will assign to your bookmarks.

+ **Your connections:** As I said earlier, the quality of your friends is more important than the quantity. Influential friends who spread the word for you will give you a huge boost.

+ **Proper tagging of bookmarks:** I talk more about this in a moment.

Building your bookmarking reputation

Building your reputation on a social bookmarking site is fairly straightforward. Bookmark good content, consistently. You don't need to work miracles.

Keeping your bookmarking tool at your fingertips

Whenever you join a new bookmarking site, install the toolbar widget or quick-bookmarking tool provided. That tool will allow you bookmark to new content you find when you find it. Now bookmarking is far easier, and you don't have to go to the bookmarking site, log in, fill out the submission form, and so on.

The figure here shows Firefox with Digg, Delicious, and StumbleUpon toolbar buttons installed. With these loaded, I can easily bookmark content with just a few clicks.

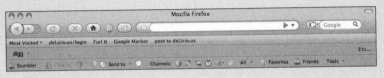

If you bookmark consistently, you'll occasionally add something completely new to the site. That will lift your influence. It will also attract more fans/friends/followers who will keep track of what you bookmark. Over time, you'll build a little following. When they see you post something, they'll take a look, share with *their* friends, and spread the word.

**Book VII
Chapter 4**

Navigating Top
Social Media Sites

Making bookmark connections

When you first sign up for a bookmarking service, start following the top five to ten people who bookmark content you might like. You can find those people by searching for the top bookmarks from topics you like. Then find the people who submitted those bookmarks.

Follow those folks. Vote on or bookmark their submissions if you like them. Comment when you can. Then add them to your network or contact list on the bookmarking site. Chances are they'll reciprocate.

Keep repeating this process, and you'll steadily grow your circle of friends on bookmarking sites.

Tagging bookmarks properly

Tags are keyword labels that you assign to a bookmark. In Figure 4-7, I assigned tags to a bookmark about my favorite car.

Good tags should make it easy for others to find your bookmark if they're interested. They should be descriptive. And they should be thorough. Always use more than one tag!

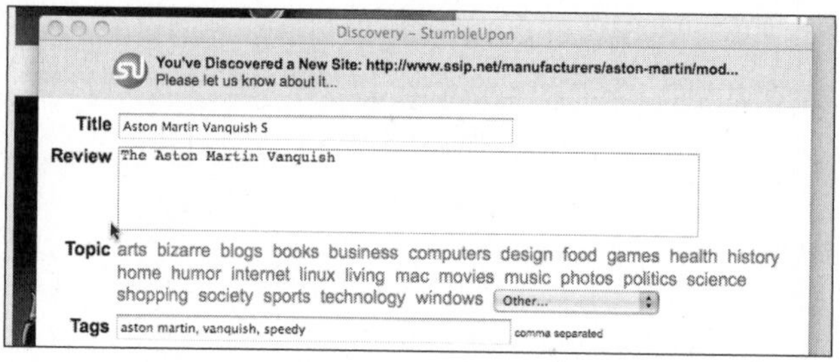

Figure 4-7:
Use good
tags.

Playing the Social News Game

If any social media makes you grind your teeth down to nubs, social news sites are the ones. Sites such as Digg and Reddit can generate an avalanche of visitors. Stories that make the first page on social news sites aren't just sneezed: They become a full-on epidemic.

Great, you say. Sign me up!

Not so fast. *Everyone* knows the power these sites have. When you submit a story to a social news site, you're joining thousands of others who, at that very moment, are taking their shot at social media stardom, too.

If you're going to try to get a hit in social news, bear in mind the following tenets:

✦ **Assume you're going to fail.** A lot. You need to keep trying.

✦ **Commit the time.** Count on spending at least a half-hour per day, for at least a few weeks, just submitting content you find. By submitting lots of content, you can build your reputation on the network, just like on book-marking sites.

✦ **Build a very complete profile page.** When you submit content, other site participants might want to check you out to make sure you're a real person. Spammers abound on social news sites, so folks are bound to be suspicious. A complete profile puts their minds at ease.

✦ **Build a network of friends** whom you can directly contact when you submit something new to say, "Hey, what do you think?"

Getting "Dugg"

Digg.com is a phenomenon all its own. The *Digg effect* — what happens if your site gets onto the first page of the Digg — can send floods of traffic that literally crash servers. That's a good thing, trust me.

Making a hit on Digg requires special care:

✦ **Reputation first.** Spend a *lot* of time building your reputation first. Seek out and submit new news, hilarious videos, and other content the community will appreciate.

✦ **Get some friends.** Build a good circle of fans to whom you can shout when you submit something really juicy.

✦ **Copywrite creatively.** Write a great title for your Digg submission. *Bicycle breaks 60 mph* isn't as good as *Flaming Tires: A really fast bike.*

✦ **Use link bait.** Write content that's so compelling folks feel they have to link to it and share it. Obey all the rules of link bait as described in Book II, Chapter 7.

Even if you do everything right, Digg's first page might prove impossible to crack. After all, it is one of the busiest social sites on the Web. However, the potential traffic often makes trying worth it.

Submit your content to Digg if any of the following are true:

✦ You have truly newsworthy content.

✦ You have truly funny content.

✦ The story you're submitting is breaking news.

If you want examples of successful stories, look no further than the Digg home page.

Behaving yourself

Try to fool the social news sites by having everyone in your office vote at once or by setting up 20 different accounts so you can vote for yourself more than once is tempting. Believe it or not, though, you're not the first person to have thought of that. Not a smooth move, and here's why.

Avoid doing anything that seems like cheating. These sites are very, very savvy and will likely ban you the moment you misbehave.

Social news is all about the sneeze principle. You don't have to do any additional work: The whole point of social news sites is to separate the sneezable from the not-so-contagious content.

Growing Your Business with Media Sharing

Media-sharing sites allow you to upload videos, photos, or audio files to a single location where others can see them. These sites offer a chance to put your work in front of large audiences, prompt discussion, and drive traffic to your business.

Use media-sharing sites if

+ You create any form of video or shoot photos in the course of your business.

+ You're comfortable putting that content in front of hundreds, thousands, or hundreds of thousands of viewers.

+ You don't mind that content being reused or redistributed. Although you can control this to some extent, it's bound to happen.

Using Flickr as a networking tool

Flickr is a photo-sharing service. The site, owned by Yahoo!, offers a suite of tools you can use to upload, edit, and organize photos. Flickr is also a social media site. You can share photos with friends, comment on others' photography, and form groups around specific topics. One of my favorite groups on Flickr is Ridiculous Marketing Nonsense because it often provides a much-needed laugh.

With Flickr, you can

+ Invite other members to be your contacts.

+ Comment on and discuss others' photos.

+ Join groups built around events or topics.

Here are my recommendations for success on Flickr:

+ **Be picky.** Don't just upload every photo you have. Upload only the best.

+ **Annotate.** Write complete descriptions, tag your photos with relevant keywords, and write good titles.

+ **Organize.** Keep your photos grouped in a way that your audience will find useful. Using a title like *Photo shoot 123* might help you, but it doesn't tell me much about the content.

Other photo-sharing sites

Other photo-sharing sites include 23hq.com and Zooomr.com. Flickr is the big player right now, but always look for other, smaller sites where you might have a better chance of getting some attention.

✦ **Discuss.** Join groups, comment on others' photos, and make a few connections.

✦ **Publicize.** If you post a photo you really think is great, let folks know through other channels, too, such as Twitter or your blog.

Flickr now supports short snippets of video, too. To date, that hasn't had much of an impact, though. I recommend sticking with video-sharing services for your video content.

Spreading the word on YouTube

YouTube works a lot like Flickr, only for video. You upload a video to the site, give it a description and tag it with keywords, and then the rest of the community gets to take a look.

A popular video on YouTube can get tens of thousands of views (or even hundreds of thousands). But, as you've likely figured out by now, getting a big hit on any social network, YouTube included, takes a lot of work.

Use YouTube if you

✦ Have pre-existing video content, and all you have to do is upload it

✦ Have entertainment-based content

✦ Want to introduce a wide audience to training, branding, or other video

✦ Are going to produce a series of short videos

YouTube has a few rules you should know about, too:

✦ Videos must be ten minutes or shorter.

✦ Videos must be 100MB or smaller.

✦ You must have permission to publish the video on YouTube!

Here are some tips I recommend for YouTube success:

✦ **Keep it short.** The most successful videos on YouTube are two to three minutes long. Obviously, if you're doing a training piece, your video might have to be longer, but try to create a series of short videos instead if you can.

✦ **Make friends.** It's easy to forget YouTube is a social network and just start uploading videos. Find folks who create great content, make friends with them, and comment on their videos. They'll reciprocate.

✦ **Complete your profile.** Just like on any other social network, a complete profile will establish trust when other users come looking.

✦ **Respond to comments!** If someone comments on your video, reply. Say, "Thanks" or "Good point" or whatever's relevant. There's a reason it's called *social* media.

✦ **Write a good title for your video.** The title is what gets folks to watch. *My road trip* isn't as good as *Pulled Over In Louisiana.*

✦ **Write a good description.** A keyword-rich description increases your chance of a good ranking in Google's blended search results. See Book II, Chapter 5 for more about keywords and blended search.

✦ **When you post a new video, let your friends know.** YouTube partly ranks videos according to the number of views and view *velocity* (the rate at which you're getting those views). If you can get a little mob watching the video, it'll give you a boost.

Reaching more folks with TubeMogul

Many other video-sharing sites are out there. I can't possibly cover them all in one short section, but getting your video on multiple networks at once can be a huge boost.

One service, called TubeMogul, allows you to upload and then track videos on over a dozen of the biggest video sites, including YouTube. (For what it's worth, I have no connection whatsoever with TubeMogul.)

The free version lets you deploy up to 150 videos per month. One video uploaded to one site is one deployment, so figure 10 to 20 videos per month. TubeMogul also includes cross-site analytics and automated submission to social bookmarking sites. The paid versions allow you to add more videos, and they boast faster deployment and a little more analytics data.

The service handles a lot of the grunt work of sending a video to many services. In my experience, you'll get about 30 to 40 percent higher viewership, on average, if you use it.

You can sign up at www.tubemogul.com.

Talking in Discussion Forums

Discussion forums have been around a long, long time. They predate the Internet, in fact, forming the backbone of many bulletin board services (BBS) that geeks like me connected to using a phone modem that looked like two huge suction cups.

Smaller is sometimes better

Forums don't have the same sneeze potential that Facebook or MySpace might. That's okay.

To their advantage, forums let you talk one on one with your most interested audience.

Include discussion forums in your marketing plan if

✦ You have a small, concentrated niche audience.

✦ You're a leading expert and want to demonstrate that fact.

✦ You want to reach and contact individuals based on their questions.

Forums are versatile, cover a huge array of topics, and often offer the most receptive audience. Sites like WebmasterWorld.com (in Figure 4-8) focus on Internet topics. Others, like CyclingForums.com (in Figure 4-9), focus on a single sport or hobby.

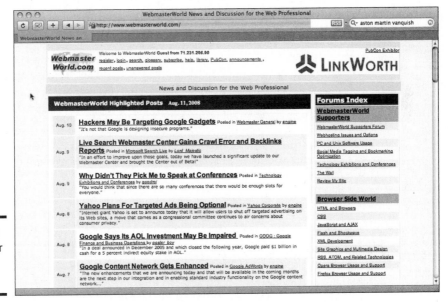

Figure 4-8: Webmaster World forums.

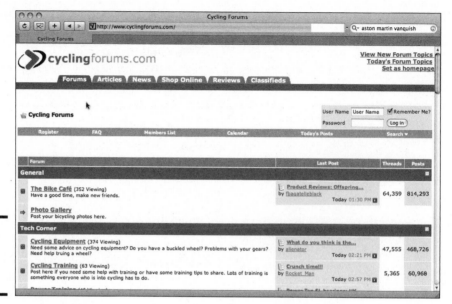

Figure 4-9:
Cycling
Forums.
com.

Finally, such forums as Google and Yahoo! Groups cater to every imaginable topic.

Forums are also very tight communities. If you barge in and start promoting your product or service, you'll receive a healthy serving of scorn and dislike.

You can succeed, though, if you follow a few basic rules.

+ **Choose relevant forums.** Don't select a discussion forum based on traffic potential or page rank. Pick one in which you'll enjoy participating.

+ **Contribute; don't spam.** You need to spend some time *lurking;* that is, seeing what folks are saying and what's okay or not okay behavior on that forum. Then you can post messages other members will appreciate.

+ **Include your Web address and information in your signature line.** Also include your Facebook, MySpace, Twitter, or other addresses if permitted. That way, every post will provide a way for readers to contact you.

+ **Start by replying to existing threads,** not creating new ones. It's a good way to get introduced to the community.

✦ **Research your answers.** If you're not sure about the answer to a question you find on the forum, do a little research first.

✦ **Link to supporting information.** If there are other sites, forums, or pages where you found good information, provide the address. It's like having a citation in a report: It supports your statement.

Using Microblogs as a Launchpad

Microblogs are a social media vehicle by which you can post lots of short (usually a 140-character limit) statements about what you're doing, interesting links, and other trivia as you go about your day.

Typical microblogs support posting from your cellphone or your computer, so it's easy to send an occasional message.

Twitter, shown in Figure 4-10, is currently the best-known microblogging platform.

Other microblogs include Plurk (`www.plurk.com`), FriendFeed (`http://friendfeed.com`), and Identi.ca (`http://identi.ca`).

**Book VII
Chapter 4**

**Navigating Top
Social Media Sites**

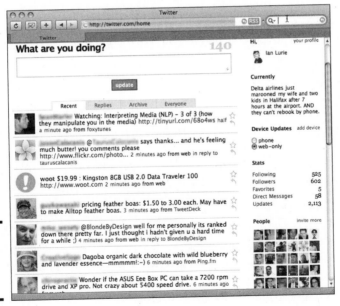

Figure 4-10:
A typical
Twitter
page.

Should I start my own forum?

Many marketers want to start their own forums, which can have advantages. Namely, you can add content to your site and brand it as desired. However, starting a forum from scratch is a **lot** of work. If another, more active forum already exists on the same topic, try that first. You can always start your own later.

Understanding microblogging

Most marketers look at microblogs the first time and walk away, shaking their heads. These sites look like a huge time-waster, but that's about it. But look closer and you'll see thousands of users talking to each other in a dynamic, ongoing chat.

Microblogging success is all about followers. People who follow you will see every post you make — and they're your potential sneezers. If they like something you post, they might blog about it, pass it along to their other microblogging friends, or talk about it at their next meeting.

Building a microblog following

You need to accumulate a lot of followers. Then you can capitalize on that to launch a new product, blog post, or site if you follow a few basic steps:

✦ **Set up a complete profile.** The more detail, the more easily others can decide whether they want to keep in touch.

✦ **Follow others.** Look around. Who are some of the biggest participants in the community? Follow them by clicking Follow or the similar button in their profile. They'll likely follow you, too, at some point.

✦ **Announce that you joined.** If you have a blog, let everyone know you just joined the microblog and provide your account name. Existing members who see that will probably follow you, too.

✦ **Contribute.** If you find an interesting link, have a bit of trivia or just a funny observation, post it! Microblogs are very informal. Make sure that if your cellphone has a Web browser, you set up mobile access as well.

✦ **Reply.** If someone you're following posts something that catches your attention, let him know.

✦ **Be consistent.** I set a goal for myself of making four to six microblog posts daily. This takes about two minutes, *total*. That's accumulated a nice following.

After you accumulate a following, make sure you announce new blog posts or other important news — and don't forget to include a link. If you announce one or two items per day, the community won't just respond — they'll appreciate it!

Avoiding microblogging overload

Microblogging *can* become a huge time-waster. I've often found myself drifting back to Twitter or Plurk, idly flipping through posts.

Avoid this kind of overload by disciplining yourself to stick with the routine you set. (Read about this in Chapter 3 of this minibook.) Set times when you'll post. Then keep Twitter (or whatever other site you're using) closed the rest of the time.

If you find you post a lot, try a tool that lets you post without logging into the microblog. Ping.fm, for instance, will let you post to multiple microblogs from your instant messaging program or the Ping.fm site. Figure 4-11 shows Ping, as well as an example of sending a post to Twitter and Plurk using Ping.

Don't let microblogging disrupt the rest of your work. It's exactly the kind of small task that can really sap your efficiency if you let it. Try to be efficient.

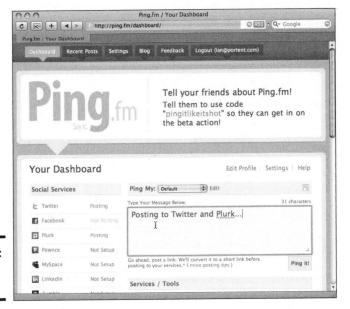

Figure 4-11:
Using Ping.
fm to post.

Building a Good Reputation in Yahoo! Answers

Yahoo! Answers is a unique phenomenon. It's a free, open community where users can post questions, and other users can post answers. The questioner can then indicate which answer is best. The answerer gets points based on the number of answers he has posted and the number of best answers.

Figure 4-12 shows a typical Yahoo! Answers page, with a list of questions begging for answers.

Include Yahoo! Answers in your social media marketing plan if you

✦ **Like answering questions.** Sounds painfully obvious, but that's all you'll do on Yahoo! Answers, so make sure you're going to enjoy it.

✦ **Have expertise to offer.**

✦ **Have an hour a week to dedicate to answering questions.**

✦ **Want to help your search rankings, too.** Yahoo! Answers allows links to your site. Those links can help you with your search rankings. See Book II, Chapter 7, for more about links.

Figure 4-12: Yahoo! Answers.

Yahoo! Answers will keep score, so first and foremost, make sure you have a good, informative profile page that points people to your Web site and/ or blog. My profile page, in Figure 4-13, includes a little blurb about me, two links, and information Yahoo! automatically collects based on my answers and other users' responses.

Here are some tips for Yahoo! Answers success:

+ **Set an hour a week to answer questions.** This seems like a lot, but you'll need the time if you're going to build a good profile.

+ **Vary the topics where you answer questions.** If you're a consultant, you can answer questions in your area of expertise. But you can also offer advice about owning your own business, or about your favorite sport. Mix things up a bit.

+ **When relevant, include a link to relevant resources.** Try to reference your own content occasionally if it will really help the reader. Those links will drive traffic, support your statements, and add authority to your answers.

+ **Ask questions, too!** It's always a good idea to ask an occasional question. If nothing else, you experience the other side of Yahoo! Answers, and those lessons can be valuable when you're answering.

+ **Add contacts.** If someone marks your answer as *best,* add him to your contacts. That's the real sneeze potential of Yahoo! Answers because your contacts might pass along your answers to *their* contacts, and so on.

+ **Don't be glib or nasty.** If someone asks a question and you think it's silly, *don't answer it.* Too, don't be nasty. Bad social media karma will come back around on you.

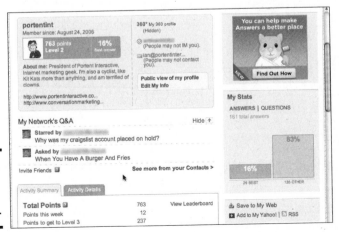

Figure 4-13:
My Yahoo!
Answers
profile page.

Unleashing the Power of Niche Sites

In this chapter, I cover some of the major social media sites. Don't overlook, though, the many, many sites devoted to individual professions, hobbies, sports, and lifestyles.

Use the search engines to track down other niche sites: Type your topic, followed by *social network, bookmarking,* or *forums,* and you'll probably find quite a few sites.

Although I focus on the major players in this chapter, you might find that niche sites are a better use of your time. Apply what you read in this chapter to those sites, and you'll reach a smaller but more focused audience.

How do you know whether to use niche sites? Ask yourself

+ Is my market very small? If yes, check for niche sites.

+ Am I finding my audience on major social media sites? If no, start looking to see whether there's a relevant niche site somewhere.

+ Is my time really tight? If you can't even find a few minutes a day for social media marketing, a niche site might let you make efficient use of your limited time.

Don't neglect the major sites if you don't have to. But keep in mind you always have options, and remember that new social media sites are springing up every day.

Chapter 5: Building Your Network

In This Chapter

✔ **Finding and keeping friends**

✔ **Expanding your network with questions and answers**

✔ **Behaving yourself in social media**

To this point in this minibook, I've talked a lot about the mechanics of social media: setting up profiles, talking to your friends and followers, and posting new items. In this chapter, you see how to actually meet and keep friends — and how to deal with the occasional foot-in-mouth incident.

Finding Friends

All social media Web sites work on the principle of friends. In social media, a *friend* is someone who keeps tabs on what you're doing on that particular site. The mechanism might vary, as you can see in Figure 5-1, but the principle remains the same: More friends means a bigger network, which means more people to pass your message along. That means more people to sell to, of course. But more important, it means you have a larger audience of potential fans of you and your brand. They can tell other folks about you and multiply the number of people you can reach directly and indirectly.

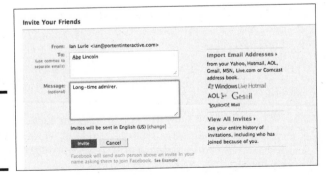

Figure 5-1: Adding friends on Facebook.

✦ **On social networks, such as Facebook or MySpace,** friends receive updates when their friends write a note, make a blog post, or take some other action. They can also send messages to each other.

+ **On bookmarking sites, such as StumbleUpon or Delicious,** friends can share bookmarks and pass really interesting bookmarks to each other.

+ **On social news sites, such as Digg,** friends can "shout" to each other about interesting stories.

+ **On microblogs, such as Twitter or Plurk,** friends *(followers)* see other friends' posts.

+ **On media sharing sites, such as YouTube and Flickr,** friends can send each other videos.

You can read about all the preceding sites in Chapter 1 of this minibook.

Having a network of friends is how you really make social media marketing work. Friends are your "sneezers," which you can also read about in Chapter 1 of this minibook: They pass along your message. Here's how you find friends on any social media site:

+ **After you set up your profile, search for groups or content on the site that matches your interests or marketing goals.** For example, when I signed up on Facebook, I looked for Internet marketing groups. On Twitter, I searched for posts about advertising and marketing.

+ **Invite the people participating in groups of interest to be your friends.** On microblogs, follow the people you find interesting.

+ **Check your social media desktop.** When stories, articles, or posts catch your eye, see whether the authors are members of the social media sites that you work on. If they are, invite them to be your friends or follow them.

+ **Get used to asking people you meet, "Are you on ___?" and then connecting with them online.**

+ **Post early, post often.** I'm sure you're tired of hearing "write interesting stuff," but it's true. When you post great photos, video, and thoughts, you get friends and followers.

+ **Join groups.** On sites that have groups, join. For example, on Facebook, I joined the Search Engine Optimization group. On LinkedIn, I joined a group devoted to Web analytics.

+ **Latch on.** You *can* find the biggest contributors on a given network and try to friend or follow them, too. But they will likely have thousands, if not tens of thousands, of messages and friends. You'll have to get through the clutter.

How many friends do I need?

There's no way of knowing how many friends you need to accumulate before you can really spread a message. One friend who has 1,200 other friends might have more than enough. Just take it a step at a time, and try to accumulate and keep friends who'll stick around.

Keeping Friends

After you have friends, how do you keep them? Some friends might stay with you because they're simply too busy to remove you from their list. But there are positive steps you can take to keep friends around:

✦ **Update.** Remember your social media routine? Stick to it. Make a post, even if it's just a sentence or two, or a link you happened on. Those contributions will show up in your friends' updates, and they'll remember who you are. And of course, they might pass them along, getting you even more friends.

✦ **Reply.** If friends send you something — a link, a note, a photo, or something else — reply to them. Make sure they know you received it, and what you thought.

✦ **Remember.** If you're on a social network, you likely have tools that report others' birthdays and other special dates. A quick Happy Birthday note can go a long way to cementing a social media friendship.

✦ **Behave.** Read the rest of this chapter for more information about this, but you must respect others.

Expanding Your Network with Questions and Answers

You can attract a lot of followers and friends by asking the right questions. Sites and services (such as LinkedIn, Twitter, Plurk, and Yahoo! Answers) are particularly good places to try this strategy. A good question can be as interesting as a good answer. Just remember the sneeze principle; hop to Chapter 1 of this minibook if you haven't read about this yet. You need to write the question in such a way that it encourages folks to pass it along.

Sniffle. "Does anyone know about Internet marketing?"

A-CHOO! "I own a bicycle shop and want to market it online. Anyone have advice, or know someone who does?"

Suddenly you have a winner. This question is crafted well because it

✦ **Is specific to an interest**

   Cyclists, other shop owners, and even other small business owners will pay attention.

✦ **Invites others to respond**

✦ **Invites others to pass it along**

By hitting these three points, you're enhancing the community *and* attracting others at the same time. Win-win.

Don't become a question machine. Ask questions when you have them, rather than from some need to attract attention. Remember what it's like when a little kid keeps asking, "Why?" every time you speak? That's how other users feel when you start deluging them with questions.

Of course, another great way to grow your network is to provide answers to some of those great questions. You have to accomplish two things if you're going to answer questions and win friends:

✦ **Find questions that need answering,** even if the questioner isn't your friend. Yahoo! Answers and LinkedIn do this for you. Other sites, such as Twitter and Facebook, aren't as easy.

✦ **Provide a really great answer.** I also recommend providing a way for the questioner to follow up if necessary.

Finding questions

Sites that aren't specifically designed for question-and-answer don't necessarily hide questions, but they can make them hard to find. Here are a few tips for finding questions:

✦ **Facebook:** Join groups and look in the discussions for each group. That's where most will go looking for answers.

✦ **Twitter:** Use Twitter's search service, search.twitter.com, to search for key terms. For example, searching for *"seo question"* got me 10 to 20 good questions right away.

✦ **YouTube:** Search the comments on the site by using YouTube's built-in search tool. Then answer questions with another comment.

Make great answers

Your answer should be very clear, offer steps to a solution, and/or invite the questioner to contact you directly if you can't easily answer the question without more information or without more room for text. Twitter, for example, allows only 140 characters per post. Here's a good example of an answer that has a good chance of gaining you a friend:

> *Hi John – I suggest starting out with a Kevlar-belted road tire first. They're a little slower, but they're nearly flat-proof. Try the Armadillo, or maybe the ReallyFlatProof106. If you have other questions, let me know: Bikerguy123*

Don't take it personally when someone doesn't say, "Thanks." It's okay, in terms of Internet etiquette; accept the answer and move on.

Obeying the (Unspoken) Rules

Here are a few unspoken social media rules I've learned:

Crass Promotion Is Never Okay

If you find yourself writing something like "10% off sale on my site! Come now!" then pinch yourself and delete your post. This kind of thing will only alienate your friends. It might even lead to penalties from the site owners.

Promoting yourself is okay. Just keep it a bit lower-key. Something like the following is generally acceptable:

> *Shameless plug: I just published a new book about Internet marketing. Please have a look at www.mybookwebsite.com.*

The following is not acceptable, especially if you repeat it ten times per day:

> *Buy my new book! Learn how to earn millions online! www.mybooksite.com.*

Don't Post Angry

No one can follow this rule 100 percent of the time. Eventually, someone will say something that really makes you angry, and you'll retort and click Submit before you can stop yourself.

If you snap back at someone, *everyone sees it*. It can reflect on you, your company, and your entire online identity.

But wherever possible, avoid the angry post. If you're inexorably drawn into an online shouting match, try these strategies:

✦ **Take 5. Take 10. Take 100.** Turn off the computer. Go outside. You'll be surprised how minor the offending post or comment seems later.

✦ **Go to the source.** Contact the person via private or direct message. Instead of a slap fight, try asking, "Hey, did I just misunderstand?" or "What'd I do?"

✦ **Vent in private.** Get it out of your system by first writing any angry reply in a word processor. Then step back, take a breath, and edit it to be more diplomatic. Only then, post it.

Do Apologize

No matter what you do, at some point, you're going to shove your foot firmly into your mouth. Social media is still *social* — you're often talking to people all over the planet, and misunderstandings happen. If you offend, overreact, or just forget about a request someone made, just let him know you're sorry. Social media is all about online karma: The community will generally remember how you behave, but no one expects perfection. A little humility goes a long way.

Do Be a Good Citizen

Help others if they have questions about how to use the site or network. Lend a hand, just as others probably helped you when you signed up.

Do Add Value

Contribute to the community. If you're microblogging, contribution can be as simple as an interesting link or video. On social networks, support the groups to which you belong by answering questions and inviting others to join. You don't have to be the top expert in your field to add value. Value can mean humor, a sympathetic ear, an interesting link, or just pointing a few people in the right direction.

Knowing When to Stop

Sometimes you can overstay your welcome. Here are a few sure signs that you should take a break and stop sending a specific person or group messages:

✦ **The individual stops replying.** Don't take it personally, but do leave that person be for a few days.

+ **A lot of friends or followers start unsubscribing or otherwise going away.** Again, take a break. Look at what you're writing. Any chance a change is in order?

+ **You get a warning.** This *should* be obvious: If a site moderator or other person in authority says, "Cool it!", listen.

+ **You feel like you're working really hard to come up with something to say.** Conversations can get strained and uncomfortable online, too. But you can walk away without offending anyone.

Social media communities are very tolerant. It's unlikely you'll ever overstay your welcome. Just try to be somewhat self-aware, and take a break when you need it.

Chapter 6: Creating a Winning Social Media Campaign

In This Chapter

✔ Marketing by providing tools

✔ Marketing by providing content

✔ Marketing by providing entertainment

✔ Leveraging your network

✔ Addressing harm to your reputation

Social media marketing is more than making friends and expanding your network. At some point, you need to get your message out.

I hint a few times in this minibook that the balance between marketing and not alienating the community can be tricky. Social network participants don't like it when one of their supposed friends suddenly starts hawking items for sale or charging for answers to questions.

The key to social media marketing success is to treat the social network how you would any other community. To that end, you need to

✦ Provide compelling tools, content, and entertainment that entice others to spread the word.

✦ Use your existing network to help kick-start your efforts.

✦ Correct false rumors or statements about your company, without getting defensive.

And that's what I cover in this chapter.

The Importance of Creating a Winning Social Media Campaign

Compare these two scenarios. Think about what kind of Web marketer you want to be — and which results you want.

Scenario 1

You're walking down the street. Someone wearing a sandwich board steps in front of you and shoves a flyer in your face, advertising a new *a cappella* singing group that's just released a CD.

There you were, walking along and minding your own business, and now this stranger is trying to pressure you into buying a CD or going to a performance. You were just walking down the street, enjoying a nice day. So, how do you feel? Intruded upon, probably.

Scenario 2

You're walking down the same street, enjoying the weather. A small knot of people ahead catches your interest. You walk up. In the middle of the crowd, you see three performers singing *a cappella.* They're brilliant. You listen, and more people show up because of the growing crowd. The group has its CD on display, right there. Even though you don't buy a copy, you walk away smiling, and you might even mention the group to your friends later that day.

Scenario 1 is, in many ways, traditional interruption-based marketing, which works to a point but generally alienates those who aren't really in buying mode. Even worse, this type of marketing especially alienates folks who feel they're part of a community that doesn't include any agreement to buy.

Scenario 2 is the classic social media–marketing technique. The *a cappella* trio gave a free performance. Passersby could stop and listen or ignore them. Those who enjoyed the music stuck around, which caught the attention of others. The crowd that grew enjoyed the music without obligation. *Some* of the crowd certainly bought the CD. And others told their friends about the group. That's social media marketing at its best.

Social media marketing has been around a lot longer than the Internet. Scenario 2 really is social media, which has been around since we could speak to each other in grunts.

Marketing by Providing Tools

Social media is the perfect place to help your company by helping others. Say there's a bicycle shop in your community called Harrison's Bikes. In the summer, the bike shop does a brisk business selling bikes and helmets, and doing repairs. As fall approaches, though, business slows. People are still riding their bikes, but they don't think the bike shop has anything to offer them when they get ready for the long, cold winter.

Harrison could stand out on the street, stapling flyers to telephone poles. He could also buy an ad in the local newspaper advertising a sale on rain fenders (with free installation, even!).

Instead, Harrison starts riding with a few of the local bicycle clubs. He puts his best rain fender on his bike. He doesn't blurt out, "Hey! Look at my cool rain fender!" But other riders see the fender, which really is pretty cool looking. They ask him about it. They already know who he is, and that he owns a bike shop. He explains that this new fender is for serious riders (like them) who don't want to look ridiculous, but also don't want to commute to work and end up splattered with mud. He lets them know he's installing them for free this week.

The next day, a few riders show up at Harrison's shop. They buy the new fenders and let him install them. While they're there, they notice some good rain gear and buy that, too. (Trust me: We cyclists are like that.) More important, when they ride into work that Monday, their cycling co-workers ask about the fender. Harrison's new customers spread the word.

This is a perfect example of marketing by providing tools. Although providing free tools sometimes helps, you can do just fine by providing solutions and tools that cost money, if you make the offer compelling enough.

What's important here is that Harrison didn't push his product. He simply went into the community and *used* the product.

A successful tools-based campaign should

✦ **Offer a tool that's simple to use:** The whole community should be able to understand the value and use it. That's why Harrison installed the fenders for his customers.

✦ **Have very few barriers to entry:** Having few barriers might mean the tool's free, or that it's immediately available. Just don't make the community work for it. Again, Harrison installed the fenders for customers. That eliminated any excuse for not participating.

✦ **Be contagious:** If you haven't been there already, skip to Chapter 1 of this minibook to read about the sneeze principle. Something about the tool must be spread (disseminated) easily. In Harrison's case, every customer who bought the fenders became an advertisement. Other cyclists saw them, and when asked, the new fender owner told them to go to Harrison's shop.

✦ **Be honest and straightforward:** Any tools that appear to have an ulterior motive — such as harvesting e-mails for an unrelated campaign, or getting people's contact information when it's not necessary — will fail.

Here's a real-world example of a free tool that actually helped me launch my blog to a large community: In a nutshell, I created a simple calculator, on the Web, that lets visitors figure the value of a click to their Web site. It's pictured in Figure 6-1.

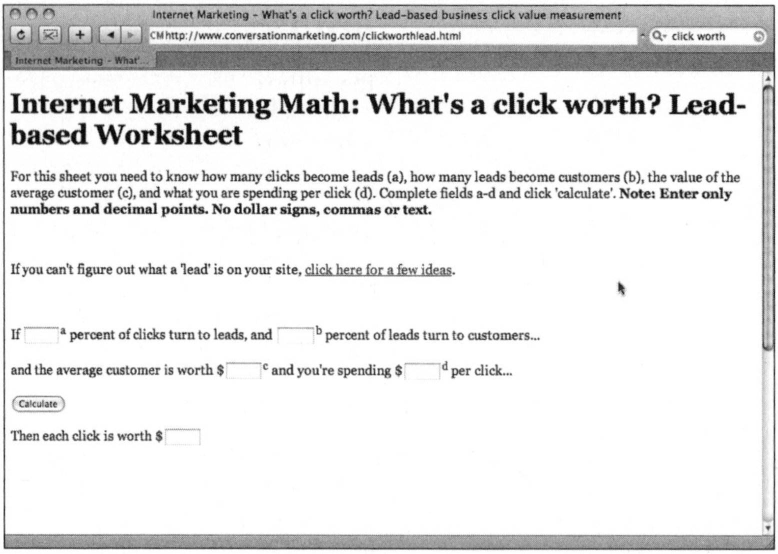

CM http://www.conversationmarketing.com/clickworthlead.html — click worth

Internet Marketing - What'...

Internet Marketing Math: What's a click worth? Lead-based Worksheet

For this sheet you need to know how many clicks become leads (a), how many leads become customers (b), the value of the average customer (c), and what you are spending per click (d). Complete fields a-d and click 'calculate'. **Note: Enter only numbers and decimal points. No dollar signs, commas or text.**

If you can't figure out what a 'lead' is on your site, click here for a few ideas.

If ☐ [a] percent of clicks turn to leads, and ☐ [b] percent of leads turn to customers...

and the average customer is worth $ ☐ [c] and you're spending $ ☐ [d] per click...

(Calculate)

Then each click is worth $ ☐

Figure 6-1:
My click-
worth
calculator.

Notice a few things about this tool:

+ **It's very simple.** Plug in a few numbers, and you're all set.

+ **It has no barriers to entry.** The user doesn't have to log in, provide any information, or do anything else to use this tool.

+ **It's contagious (in a good way).** It's easy to forward a link to this page, and it offers a tool (albeit simple) that's something every online marketer needs.

+ **It's straightforward.** No tricks here. Plug in your data and get the result. Come back as often as you want.

After I completed the tool, I contacted a few friends and colleagues and then also politely e-mailed five or ten well-known bloggers. Within a few weeks, three major bloggers linked to this tool from their blogs. Within a few days of that, traffic to my blog had tripled. When more and more people came to see the click calculator, a few of them recommended it to friends using their own blogs, StumbleUpon, or Digg.

That simple tool, which took about two hours to create, built traffic to my blog, and generated additional clients for my company. All that, and the tool's page doesn't even have a logo!

Don't have any tools in mind? If not, that's okay. You can do the same thing with content. Keep reading.

Social Media Marketing with Content

The *a cappella* singers I describe at the beginning of the chapter didn't offer any tools, per se. Instead, they put their content in front of the audience. You can do the same thing: Create informative or entertaining content, put it in front of a community, and then let those folks spread the word.

If you haven't read about Harrison and his bike shop, hop back to the preceding section and then come back here. I want to talk about that same story in terms of marketing with content.

The fender installations campaign (via a tool) was successful, but a lot of cyclists simply pack up their bicycles for the winter. They don't need fenders. Their primary concern is staying in shape during the winter.

So, Harrison creates a small booklet entitled, "Summer Fitness, Winter Months," that tells cyclists how they can stay in shape during the winter by doing a few simple exercises and also by buying a stationary trainer. (The stationary trainer turns a regular bicycle into a stationary bike, so you can ride your bike indoors.)

He sets a small stack of the booklets next to the cash register in his store. He also attends the monthly meetings of a few local bicycle clubs, and does a few free lunch-hour classes at his shop. Harrison tells the community members how they can stay in shape during the winter, points out the equipment they need, and explains why this is a good alternative to the gym for those who don't like lifting weights.

As a result, he sells stationary trainers. He also gets a reputation among local cyclists as someone who genuinely knows them and helps out.

All this without creating a tool. All Harrison did was deliver some useful content.

The hallmarks of a successful content campaign

Not all content is made for social media. In the preceding example of Harrison and his booklet, Harrison stuck to some basic principles:

✦ **Don't sell!** Your content shouldn't be an overt advertisement for one product or your services. Inform and teach, but don't advertise. Harrison demonstrated relevant equipment, but he never told folks where or how to buy.

✦ **Be relevant.** Focus on your audience's immediate needs. Harrison focused on indoor training because winter is coming. In May, this training won't help.

**Book VII
Chapter 6**

**Creating a Winning
Social Media
Campaign**

✦ **Be available.** Your content has to be easy to find and access. Harrison went to other people's places of work and bicycle clubs. He offered training at his shop during lunch.

✦ **Don't try tricks.** Similar to the earlier tools example, don't try to get information that's not required. I know it's tempting to collect e-mail addresses, but that's not your mission here.

A bike shop's great, you say, but we're talking about the Internet. Fair enough. Here's another real-world example — online.

I despise *plagiarists* (folks who steal your content without asking and without attribution). So, I wrote a blog post about a sneaky way to trap thieves; you can see it in Figure 6-2.

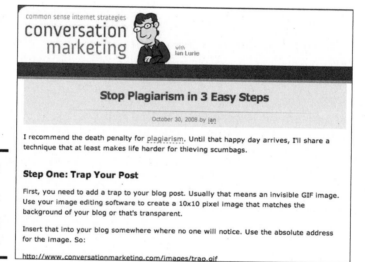

Figure 6-2:
I posted a blog about setting a trap to nab plagiarists.

I posted this on my blog. (See Book VI for more about blogging.) Then, I alerted a few friends via Twitter.

A few days later, I woke up to alarms from my blog host telling me that the site was being overloaded. Word of the plagiarism post had spread. A few people added it to Digg, and within a few hours, more than 2,000 people had "Dugg" the article. (See Chapter 2 of this minibook for more about Digg.)

Traffic to my blog erupted, as you can see in Figure 6-3.

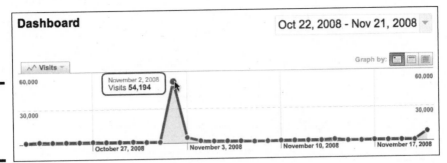

Figure 6-3:
Whoa.
That's a lot
of traffic.

I didn't continue to get 60,000 visits per day. However, since then, my blog has had 30 percent more subscribers and daily visitors.

This post stuck to the rules:

+ **There was no sales pitch.** It was, in fact, 100 percent pure rant.

+ **It was very relevant.** Any blogger, writer, or other content producer hates plagiarism. It's enormously frustrating. So any example of someone putting one over on the thieves is going to be popular.

+ **The article was easily available.** It's just a blog post. No login or purchase required.

+ **I didn't do anything tricky.** Readers could go straight to the content without any hurdles, such as e-mail signups.

Providing entertainment with a content campaign

Including some entertainment in your content has value. Whether you're using written text, video, or photos, your chances of producing truly sneezable content are far higher when you can teach and entertain at the same time.

Sometimes, the entertainment value is built in: Inserting ridiculous photos into the Web sites of unwitting thieves is *funny*. Sometimes, you'll want to add entertainment value to subjects that aren't overtly fun or funny. For example, I often use photos of animals with thought bubbles, as shown in Figure 6-4.

Humor increases the chances that someone will carry your content to her friends.

Figure 6-4:
That bird
has nothing
to do with
marketing.

Leveraging Networks to Create a Winning Social Media Campaign

You can produce the coolest tool or the best content on the planet. If no one knows about it, though, it won't help.

In earlier chapters of this minibook, I talk a lot about building your network. Now is the time to use it. After you post your article or tool, send a quick note to your Twitter followers, your Facebook friends, and your other audiences in the social media world. Don't push it: Just a single note will do.

Try to write a note that will catch attention. This probably won't help:

> *New blog post about plagiarism.*

This approach is better because it catches folks' attention:

> *I wreak horrific vengeance upon plagiarists. Mwahahahahaha.*

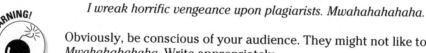

Obviously, be conscious of your audience. They might not like to read *Mwahahahahaha.* Write appropriately.

Addressing Harm to Your Reputation

Sometimes, folks will misinterpret what you write, disagree with you, or resort to plain ol' name calling. That's the nature of any community.

If readers misinterpret what you write, *don't snap at them.* Reply to them via whatever network they're using and explain what you meant. Even better, thank them for pointing out something that wasn't clear about your content or tool and then explain how you fixed it. For example, when I wrote a blog post about overuse of Flash on Web pages, one contributor made a great point: My post could've been taken as an extreme — remove all Flash no matter what — and that wasn't what I meant. So I responded to the contributor with an apology and a clarification.

If readers disagree, just grin and bear it. If you want everyone to agree with you, don't publish anything online. Disagreements are in the nature of any community. Tastes and opinions vary. Don't take it personally, and again, don't snap at anyone.

Finally, if someone just starts calling you names (trust me, it happens), don't take the bait. Sure signs you shouldn't bother replying are when folks call you an idiot or a cretin, or say you're clueless. Ignore such taunts, respond with humor, or let your community handle it for you.

In all these cases, responding in anger or pointing out that the dissident is dumb, wrong, or silly will only serve to pour gas on the fire. That's the most important lesson in managing your reputation: Respond only when you can do so in a positive manner.

By the way, no one's perfect. I've lost my temper a few times and published things I regretted. The best thing you can do then is admit you're human, apologize to the community, and move on.

Applying These Lessons Everywhere

Compelling social media marketing campaigns succeed because you show genuine interest in helping the community. Help might mean providing a tool, or valuable information, or a laugh. Help does not mean a sales pitch.

It also requires patience and a little faith in your community. You have to trust that they have the judgment to know what's legitimate and good and what's not.

And, it requires persistence. If you're lucky, one in ten of your social media marketing campaigns will succeed when you start.

All these lessons hold true in all Internet marketing. Deliver value, be patient, trust your community, and be persistent. Success is nearly inevitable if you do.

Book VIII

Mobile Marketing

Contents at a Glance

Chapter 1: Getting Started with Mobile Marketing **733**
Understanding and Weaving Mobile into Marketing.............................. 734
Adding Mobile to Your Marketing Strategy... 736
Understanding the Many Paths within the Mobile Channel 741

Chapter 2: Planning a Mobile Marketing Campaign **759**
Setting Up a Plan... 759
Understanding the Costs of Mobile Marketing 762
Working with Common Short Codes 765
Managing Opt-Ins 769
Handling Opt-Outs 774

Chapter 3: Running Mobile Communication Campaigns **775**
Planning Your Communication Flow.. 775
Providing Text Promotions 781
Calling People to Action: Polling 786
Offering Incentives: Gifts, Freebies, Samples, and Coupons................ 789
Applying User-Generated Content... 793

Chapter 4: Launching a Mobile Advertising Campaign. **797**
Reviewing the Mobile Ad Players 798
Placing Ads on Mobile Internet Sites 800
Placing Ads in Mobile Messages.. 804
Going Local with Location-Based and On-Package Advertising............ 806

Chapter 5: Delivering Valuable Mobile Content. **815**
Sourcing Your Mobile Content 815
Sending Content via Messaging 816
Providing Mobile Enhancements and Applications 820
Making Marketing Fun with Mobile Games and Applications................ 824
Serving Up Mobile Web Sites 826

Chapter 6: Getting Paid for Your Mobile Marketing Efforts **831**
Methods of Monetizing the Mobile Channel 831
Offering Your Content through a Carrier's Portal.................................. 832
Making Money through Premium Text Messaging.................................. 834
Selling Your Content and Services via the Mobile Internet 838

Chapter 7: Tracking a Mobile Marketing Campaign **841**
Building Your Marketing Database.. 841
Creating Consumer Profiles 842
Populating a Marketing Database... 846
Using Your Database to Deliver Targeted Programs 849
Managing Feedback.. 850

Chapter 1: Getting Started with Mobile Marketing

In This Chapter

✔ Seeing how mobile marketing fits into your marketing plans

✔ Understanding the technologies behind mobile marketing

✔ Determining which services you need

✔ Complying with rules, regulations, and best practices

*Y*ou've probably heard about mobile marketing. Maybe you've even thought about using it — sticking your toe in the water or taking it for a spin, as they say. But you also might have heard the following things (or even said them yourself):

✦ "I wouldn't want to receive spam on my phone, and my customers certainly wouldn't either."

✦ "Mobile text messaging . . . well, it's just for kids. Certainly, I'm not going to get any value from it."

✦ "It has to be too expensive, too complicated, and way too difficult for me to employ. Only big companies like Coca-Cola, ESPN, and McDonald's can do it."

If you've heard or had these thoughts, don't be discouraged. This chapter explains why mobile marketing, done properly, isn't spam; isn't "just for kids"; and certainly doesn't need to be expensive, complicated, difficult, and only for the benefit of Fortune 500 companies. In fact, it can be an effective channel for increasing customer brand awareness, responses, interactions, and satisfaction.

When you're done reading this chapter, you'll have a clear understanding of exactly what mobile marketing is, how it can fit into your marketing strategy, and how you can use it.

Understanding and Weaving Mobile into Marketing

Many people are mystified by the term *mobile marketing.* They see the word *mobile* in front of the word *marketing,* and they suffer a palpable sense of the unknown — in many cases, fear. Well, I'm here to tell you that mobile marketing is not an arcane, mysterious, alchemical process. Rather, it simply is one of the many practices of marketing, such as retail, direct mail, Internet, e-mail, TV, radio, and advertising.

The following sections review the definition of marketing and discuss how *mobile* fits into this definition.

Reviewing marketing and its elements

Marketing is a critical function for any business. According to a 2007 statement by the American Marketing Association (AMA; see `www.marketing power.com`), marketing is

> *the activity, set of institutions, and processes for creating, communicating, delivering, and exchanging offerings that have value for customers, clients, partners, and society at large.*

In the following list, I deconstruct the elements of this definition:

✦ **Communicating:** *Communicating* means imparting information and news about your offerings and related activities to your audience members — customers, clients, partners, prospects, leads, employees, advisors, investors, the press, and all the other people and organizations that play a role in your business, as well as society at large — so that they find out what your organization does and the value it has to offer.

You probably use any number of traditional and new-media channels (TV, radio, print, live events, outdoor media, point-of-sale displays in stores, the Internet, e-mail, telemarketing, and so on) to communicate indirectly or directly with members of your audience. *Direct* communication occurs when you initiate contact directly with individual members of your audience, as in the case of sending an e-mail or initiating a call to a specific person. *Indirect* communication happens when you advertise or present some other form of promotional message through mass-media channels (such as TV, radio, or print) to expose members of your audience to your communication, but leave it up to individual audience members to initiate direct contact with you.

✦ **Delivering:** *Delivering* means providing your products or services and exceptional customer service to members of your audience.

✦ **Exchanging:** *Exchanging* means swapping value (which I define later in this list). Often, you exchange your goods and services for money, but you can determine for yourself what to take in exchange.

✦ **Offerings:** *Offerings* are simply the products and services produced by your organization.

✦ **Value:** *Value* refers to a sense of worth. People value something when they perceive that the item's worth exceeds what it costs them to obtain, consume, or use it.

The days of mass market–marketing are waning. We've entered an age of connectedness — an age of hyperfragmentation of communication/media channels and market segmentation down to individual members of the audience. With mobile marketing, you're not broadcasting messages to the masses. Rather, you use mass media and the mobile channel to engage individuals in a one-to-one interactive exchange.

Defining mobile marketing and its elements

Now that I've reviewed marketing, I'm ready to weave mobile into it. As I note earlier in this chapter, mobile marketing isn't mystical; neither does it falls outside the practice of marketing. Therefore, the definition of *mobile marketing* mirrors the definition of marketing. I define *mobile marketing* as

> *the set of activities, institutions, and processes that supports marketers in their pursuit to communicate, deliver, and exchange offerings that have value for customers, clients, partners, and society at large by way of the mobile and mobile-enhanced traditional and new-media channels.*

This definition differs from the AMA's definition in that I introduce two new terms:

✦ **Mobile channel:** *Mobile channel* refers to the collection of companies and systems — wireless networks, mobile phones, application providers, marketers, and so on — that make it possible for a marketer to interact with an individual audience member directly through a mobile phone or wirelessly enabled *terminal* (a mobile device that doesn't have voice capabilities, such as a Sony PlayStation Portable or Apple iPod Touch). You can use many paths within the mobile channel to engage members of your audience; see "Understanding the Many Paths within the Mobile Channel," later in this chapter.

✦ **Mobile-enhanced traditional and new-media channels:** Marketers rely heavily on traditional and new media to build awareness among members of their audience and to promote their offerings. A *mobile-enhanced* traditional or new-media channel is one that has been mobilized by having a mobile marketing call to action introduced in it.

A mobile marketing *call to action* is a set of instructions promoted in the media that shows someone how to use his phone or mobile terminal to participate in the marketer's mobile marketing program. (For details on mobile marketing calls to action, see Book VIII, Chapter 2.)

**Book VIII
Chapter 1**

**Getting Started with
Mobile Marketing**

In the following sections, I address the two main types of mobile marketing: direct and indirect.

Direct mobile marketing

Direct mobile marketing refers to the practice of proactively reaching out and engaging individual members of your audience via the mobile channel on their mobile phones. As I discuss in Book VIII, Chapter 2, direct mobile marketing may take place only if customers have given you explicit consent (permission) for you to proactively engage them — that is, text-message and/or call them.

Indirect mobile marketing

Because mobile marketing requires that individual customers give you permission to interact with them on their mobile phones directly and proactively, you can use indirect mobile marketing to expose people to your offerings and invite them to give you permission to contact them directly. Therefore, *indirect mobile marketing* refers to the practice of mobile-enhancing your traditional and new-media programs (TV, radio, print, outdoor media, Internet, e-mail, voice, and so on) and inviting individual members of your audience to pull out a phone or mobile terminal and respond to your mobile call to action. On television, for example, your call to action may ask viewers to text a keyword to a short code to cast a vote. Or, you may ask them to fill out a form on the Web or mobile Internet, including their mobile phone number, to participate in the program. For more information about managing opt-ins and about using short codes and keywords, see Book VIII, Chapter 2.

Adding Mobile to Your Marketing Strategy

It's no mistake that the definition of mobile marketing in the preceding section mirrors the AMA's definition of marketing (see "Reviewing marketing and its elements," earlier in this chapter). You should not consider mobile marketing to be separate from your other marketing activities; rather, you can and should integrate it with those activities. You can use mobile marketing both directly and indirectly to enhance all your marketing activities.

The following sections explain the key resources you need to weave mobile marketing into your overall strategic marketing plan.

Planning for the complexities of the mobile channel

Marketing to people through the mobile channel and through mobile-enhanced traditional and new-media is unlike any other marketing practice you'll face. Mobile marketing has several characteristics that set it apart from other marketing channels and practices.

First and foremost, mobile phones today are more than just telephones; they're also rich computing platforms capable of consuming all forms of media. Moreover, mobile phones come in myriad shapes and sizes, and run on a plethora of networks and operating systems that support a wide range of capabilities.

In the following sections, I discuss both the challenges and the payoffs of marketing through the mobile channel.

Complexities of mobile technology and channel

Before you begin integrating mobile marketing into your marketing programs, you need to grasp the complexities of the mobile phone and the mobile channel, including the following:

✦ Mobile phone screens are smaller than computer screens.

✦ Mobile phones have no mice or printers, and the keyboards on some models are limited.

✦ Mobile phones use numerous operating systems, networks, and Web browsers with broadly different requirements.

✦ Bandwidth may be restricted. (*Bandwidth* is the size of the pipe regulating how quickly data can be sent to a phone — to display a mobile Web page, for example.)

✦ Data connections and messaging cost money — in some cases, a lot of money.

These situations are just a few of the many complexities you'll need to contend with. I realize that they sound daunting, but don't get discouraged; you can overcome these challenges. See the next section for the advantages.

Benefits of mobile capabilities

You and your audience can take advantage of myriad capabilities that are unique to the mobile phone:

✦ Send and receive messages.

✦ Take, display, and exchange photos.

✦ Take, play, and exchange videos.

✦ Record, play, and exchange music.

✦ Ensure that your marketing is relevant to your audience members' surroundings.

✦ Facilitate commerce.

✦ Browse and connect to the Internet.

✦ Oh, yeah — and make calls, too.

Partnering with mobile service providers

To take advantage of the capabilities of the mobile channel for your marketing, you need to be able to adjust, in real time, to the diversity of the mobile channel and its complexities.

Addressing the complexities of the mobile channel can be daunting if you attempt to go it alone. To get your mobile marketing practice started, you should consider looking for help. Luckily, help is right around the corner, in the form of mobile service providers. The following sections provide an overview of the various mobile service providers and how they can assist you in getting your mobile practice off the ground.

What mobile service providers do

Mobile service providers enable mobile marketing on technical- and professional-services levels. These providers are people, companies, business practices, and marketers that help you leverage the mobile channel to engage your customers with compelling mobile and mobile-enhanced marketing programs.

Types of mobile service providers

To launch a mobile marketing campaign successfully, consider working with one or more of the following types of mobile service providers:

✦ **Traditional and new-media providers:** You need traditional media to start the direct mobile marketing engine, because you must have explicit permission to contact people directly on their mobile phones. The way to go about getting this consent is to introduce people to your mobile program by mobile-enhancing a traditional and new-media campaign. In fact, mobile marketing takes inert passive media and makes it interactive (see Figure 1-1). You can read more about obtaining consumer opt-in in Book VIII, Chapter 2.

✦ **Wireless carriers:** *Wireless carriers* (also commonly referred to as *mobile operators, wireless networks,* and *wireless operators*) provide the piping, towers, billing systems, support, outlets, and more so that you can engage your customers via the mobile channel. You may be surprised to find that hundreds of wireless carriers operate around the world. The United States has about 50 of these carriers, although the market is dominated by AT&T Mobility, Sprint, T-Mobile, and Verizon Wireless, which support about 93 percent of all the mobile subscribers in the country.

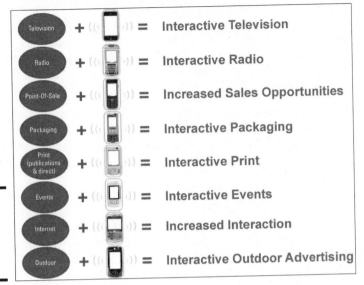

Figure 1-1:
Mobile-
enhancing
traditional
media.

+ **Connection aggregators:** You aren't likely to work directly with wireless carriers unless you work for a very large brand. *Connection aggregators* are the bridges that connect you, application providers, and wireless carriers. With one connection aggregator, you can gain access to hundreds of wireless-carrier networks around the world. Leading connection aggregators include VeriSign, Sybase 365, mBlox, OpenMarket, SinglePoint, MX Telecom, and Ericsson IPX.

For a complete list, visit the connection-aggregator page of the Common Short Code Administration Web site at

```
www.usshortcodes.com/csc_aggregators.html
```

I discuss short codes in detail in Book VIII, Chapter 2.

+ **Application providers:** These companies furnish the software and support services you need to manage your mobile marketing campaigns and your interactions with members of your audience through the numerous paths of the mobile channel. A host of important mobile services and applications are related to mobile marketing, and you should consider including some of the following in your marketing plan: messaging, mobile Internet, mobile applications, mobile video, interactive voice response (IVR), Bluecasting, content management, content production and licensing, advertising, search solutions, and mobile commerce. A handful of application providers will aggregate many of these services, but most specialize in just one.

There are all kinds of application provides out there: Those that have the capability but don't actually have any software written, those that have some technical elements built but require a rocket-scientist to use their solution, and a handful that have developed really easy, templated solutions. When talking with your prospective application provider, be sure to have them show you what they have to offer. If you can, ask them to give you a login so that you can try their service yourself. This is the true test of a self-administrable mobile marketing application provider.

The rest of this minibook is dedicated to helping you understand how to integrate all these players and the many paths of the mobile channel into your marketing. In the following sections, I explain each path in detail.

Aligning all the players in the mobile marketing ecosystem

Now that you know a bit about mobile marketing, I can show you how all the players in the mobile marketing ecosystem fit together. Figure 1-2 shows the strategic mobile marketing ecosystem. When you look at this figure, think about where you fit in.

Note that the ecosystem is segmented into five spheres:

✦ **Product and services sphere:** Brands, content owners, and marketing agencies

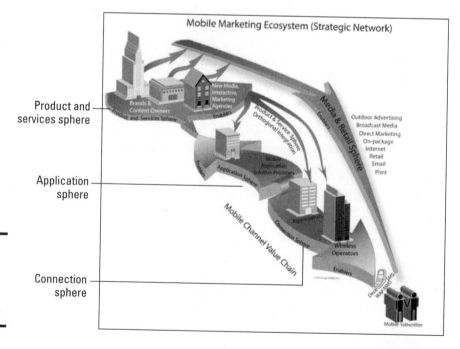

Figure 1-2: Strategic mobile marketing ecosystem.

✦ **Traditional, new media and retail sphere:** All the media players

✦ **Application sphere:** The realm of the application provider

✦ **Connection sphere:** The realm of the wireless carrier and connection aggregator

✦ **Mobile subscriber:** The individual with a mobile phone in her hands

Note the arrows pointing from the players in the product and services sphere to each of the other spheres. These arrows indicate that each of these players may choose to work with any number of the mobile service providers and traditional/new-media and retail players described earlier in this chapter. They choose to work with one or more of these players based on their selected strategic approach to mobile marketing. You'll need to decide for yourself what your approach will be. For more information, see Book VIII, Chapter 2.

Understanding the Many Paths within the Mobile Channel

It's easy to look at a mobile phone and think, "It's just a phone." But it really isn't a phone anymore. Sure, you can make voice calls with it, but that function is just the tip of the iceberg. Today's mobile phones are also newspapers, maps, cameras, radios, stores, game consoles, video music players, calculators, calendars, address books, stereos, TVs, movie theaters, and concert halls. These devices can be much more than most people expect. You can make them what you want them to be by creating rich, interactive experiences with the many interactive paths to mobile phones, shown in Figure 1-3.

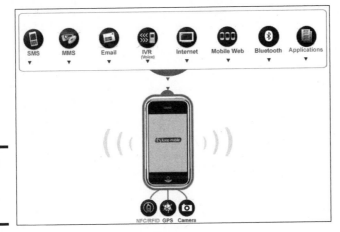

Figure 1-3:
Paths to a mobile phone.

This section explains the various mobile paths and applications you can employ to reach your customers via the mobile channel and mobile-enhanced traditional media.

Understanding SMS capabilities

Short Message Service (SMS), commonly referred to as *text messaging* or just *text,* is an incredibly versatile path to nearly all mobile phones on the planet. An SMS is a 160-character alphanumeric digital message that can be sent to and from a mobile phone — that is, it consists of letters (A, B, C, D, a, b, c, d . . .) and numbers and symbols (1, 2, 3, 4, !, @, #, $ . . .) that can be exchanged among mobile phones.

Text messaging is an extremely popular service that caught on in the United States via TV shows such as "American Idol" and "Deal or No Deal," which asked people to text in to cast votes or try to win prizes. From these basic roots, text messaging has blossomed into a rich interactive medium. In the United States, billions of text messages are sent every day. In fact, text messaging has become the primary mobile communications medium. As of October 2008, according to Nielsen Mobile, U.S. mobile subscribers sent an average 357 text messages per month compared with 204 voice minutes used during the same period. Collectively, we're sending more than 2 billion text messages a day in the United States alone!

More than just a person-to-person channel now, text messaging is the cornerstone of mobile marketing. In addition to offering voting services, you can launch trivia programs, provide search capability, send information and text alerts, trigger interactive calls, deliver content, operate coupon programs (see Figure 1-4), and even charge people for content and services consumed on the phone (such as ringtones and television subscriptions).

Figure 1-4:
Text
coupon.

You can do many things with the SMS path, including the following common SMS applications:

+ **Quiz/trivia/survey:** Random delivery of both structured and unstructured questions sent to the phone, including limiting how many times someone can participate during a given period (once a day, twice a week, once in the entire program), billing options (per interaction, per series), and clue management (whether subscribers can get hints on how to answer a question).

+ **Reverse auction:** SMS-based auctions in which the lowest bidder rather than the highest bidder wins.

+ **Polling/voting:** Real-time polling/voting of consumer response to media, with live results being sent immediately to consumers' phones or made available via XML and/or screen-ready charts (pie charts, bar charts, and so on).

+ **Text alert/mobile CRM (mCRM):** Permission-based marketing that targets lists and alert messaging. You can collect information on your clients, which is where mobile customer relationship management (mCRM) comes into play. Then you can filter this data based on criteria you apply (people in the Los Angeles region 18 to 25 years old who like shoes and sports, for example) and broadcast alerts to these people: news, coupons, sports scores, whatever you think they'll value.

+ **Viral marketing:** Personalization of messaging (name, number, message, and so on) triggered by consumers through virally promoted marketing initiatives. (For more information on viral marketing, see Book VIII, Chapter 4.)

+ **Moderated Text2Screen and Picture2Screen:** A service that allows you to moderate user-generated text and picture messages and display them on a screen during a live event, on television, on a Web or mobile Internet site, or on a related promotional channel.

+ **On-package promotions:** Instant-win programs in which consumers message promotion codes from product packages for prizes. These promotions also generate participation in loyalty programs.

+ **Mobile sweepstakes:** Use of the SMS channel to encourage people to participate in marketing programs through promotional incentives such as sweepstakes.

+ **Text2Give:** Use of SMS to enable people to make micro donations (such as $1, $5, or $10) to their favorite charities, with the donations being added to their mobile phone bills and the proceeds being sent to the charity. (For more information on SMS with a billing twist, see Book VIII, Chapter 6.)

**Book VIII
Chapter 1**

**Getting Started with
Mobile Marketing**

✦ **Commerce and sampling:** Programs in which you bill for digital goods transactions and physical purchases and requests for samples to be shipped to customers' physical location. See Book VIII, Chapter 6 for more information on sampling programs.

✦ **Mobile couponing:** Programs that use SMS to deliver coupons to mobile phones (refer to Figure 1-4, earlier in this section).

Leading companies specializing in SMS-based applications include iLoop Mobile (www.iloopmobile.com), ipsh! (www.ipsh.com), Vibes Media (www.vibesmedia.com), and Limbo (www.limbo.com).

The preceding list contains just a few of the nearly infinite things you can do with the mobile channel. Let your imagination go wild and then validate the mass versus niche and future market practicality of your ideas with your mobile application partner.

Enhancing your messages with MMS

Multimedia Messaging Service (MMS) is sometimes referred to as *picture messaging* to help differentiate it from SMS, which is text messaging. MMS is delivered almost the same way as text messaging but can include multimedia objects (images, audio, video, and/or rich text), often in a slideshow format.

Internationally, MMS and SMS are free for end users to receive on their phones and cost a premium to send. In the United States, end users are charged for both sending and receiving SMS and MMS messages if they don't have a messaging plan. Service providers pay a fee to deliver SMS or MMS messages to end users. MMS messages are more expensive than SMS because they're larger.

Two important features of MMS make it ideal for mobile marketing and content delivery:

✦ **Direct delivery to Inbox:** The message content is delivered directly to a recipient's messaging Inbox in the same way that SMS messages are. This system increases the likelihood that the recipient will actually see the message; he knows where to look for it and doesn't have to complete any additional steps to retrieve it or find it on the mobile Internet.

✦ **End-user flexibility:** The content can be saved to the recipient's handset and (unless it's forward-locked) forwarded to family members and friends.

Creating and delivering MMS content require a significant investment in technology. Most mobile marketers, service providers, and content providers opt to use a hosted MMS delivery platform such as Cellyspace, offered by Skycore (www.skycore.com). Other leading multimedia service providers include iLoop Mobile (www.iloopmobile.com), Comverse (www.comverse.com), and Acision (www.acision.com).

E-mailing your messages

The e-mail path is just what you think. An e-mail message can be originated and delivered from any standard e-mail system or through mobile carrier networks. E-mail can be an effective means of delivering messages to a mobile phone or mobile-enabled terminal. Messages are accessed on the phone via the mobile Internet browser or e-mail application installed on the phone.

Mobile e-mail is most popular on a class of mobile phones referred to as *smartphones,* including Research In Motion's BlackBerry, Apple's iPhone, and phones running Google's Android software or Symbian and/or Microsoft mobile operating systems. E-mail is rarely used for mobile marketing; controlling the user experience is difficult, and many technical hurdles and legal landmines still need to be overcome.

Leading companies that specialize in e-mail marketing services include Constant Contact (www.constantcontact.com) and mobileStorm (www.mobilestorm.com). E-mail marketing is the focus of Book V.

Humanizing your messages with IVR

The voice path refers to your phone's standard telephone capability — the means by which you make and receive phone calls. In addition to talking with a live person, a very popular use of the voice channel is interactive voice response (IVR). You're probably familiar with IVR, which is a common prompting system used in automated customer support. When you call most businesses today, you reach an automated prompt that tells you to say or press 1 to get this, or to say or press 2 to get that. That's IVR.

IVR can be a power mechanism for marketing activities beyond support. Sony Pictures, for example, used IVR in the spring of 2007 to promote the horror movie *Vacancy* by mobile-enhancing its television advertising. The TV ad encouraged people to call a toll-free number. When they did, they were greeted by an auditory extravaganza of screams and other sounds from the movie. When the cacophony quieted, the listener was asked to choose among various prompts to get movie listings, join a text-alert service, participate in a poll or sweepstakes, and so on.

Another example of using voice for mobile marketing is streaming audio via the voice channel. National Public Radio (NPR) uses the voice channel to stream live and recorded radio broadcasts via the voice channel of mobile phones. You can dial a toll-free number and start listening to an NPR show. Or you can send a text message or click a link on a mobile Web site, and suddenly, your phone rings. When you pick up, you'll find the live or recorded broadcast piping through the phone.

Leading IVR mobile services providers include Aptera, Angel.com, CommerceTel, and SmartReply.

Working the mobile Internet

The term *mobile Internet* is used primarily to refer to browsing Web sites on a mobile phone. The Internet connection on a phone, however, can also be used to power the data connection for installable applications (see "Building installed applications," later in this chapter). For the purposes of this mini-book, when I refer to the mobile Internet, I'm referring primarily to mobile browsing.

With the mobile Internet, you can create rich and compelling mobile experiences filled with text, colors, and images. Leading brands that are leveraging the mobile Internet include The Weather Channel, World Wrestling Entertainment, E!, NBC, and others.

You don't need to create an entire Web site for a mobile campaign, though. You can create a *microsite* or *landing page* — a smaller version of a mobile Internet site. The difference between a microsite and a mobile Internet site is that the mobile Internet site is designed to be persistent — to hang around for a while — whereas a microsite or landing page tends to be designed for a specific marketing promotion. A site of this sort may hang around for a few months, but at the end of the promotion, the marketer turns it off. Also, unlike persistent mobile sites, microsites tend to have very few pages, with content limited strictly to the promotion. Figure 1-5 shows an example of a promotional microsite.

Figure 1-5: Mobile Internet microsite.

Leading mobile Internet service providers include iLoop Mobile (`www.iloopmobile.com`), Crisp Wireless (`www.crispwireless.com`), StarCut (`www.starcut.com`), MAXX Wireless (`www.maxxwireless.tv`), Netbiscuits (`www.netbiscuits.com`), and dotMobi (`www.dotmobi.mobi`).

Building installed applications

Installed applications — such as games, messaging (SMS, MMS, e-mail, instant messaging, or picture messaging), audio and video players, and browsers — may be preinstalled on the mobile phone by the manufacturer or wireless carrier. Alternatively, they may be installed by mobile subscribers who download them via the mobile Internet; embedded links in received text messages; or a process called *side loading,* in which the phone is connected to a computer and the applications are sent from the computer to the phone.

Applications can provide a rich interactive experience beyond the limitations of the mobile browser. Special applications can be installed on a phone to serve streaming video (TV) and audio (radio), social networking services, and a wide range of other services.

Not all phones support installable applications, and some wireless carriers don't allow these applications to connect to the Internet after they've been installed. See Book VIII, Chapter 5 for details on delivering valuable content via installed applications.

Leading providers of installable mobile applications include Nellymoser, Action Engine, Cascada Mobile, Lightpole (location-aware content services), Cellfire (mobile couponing), Google (Google Maps), MobiTV (mobile television), and Zannel (social networking).

Making connections through Bluetooth

The *Bluetooth path* refers to the use of the Bluetooth communication channel on the phone. *Bluetooth* is a low-bandwidth radio spectrum that has a reach of about 1 to 109 yards, depending on the power of the device.

That little blue icon on your phone represents Bluetooth capability. If you use Bluetooth, you probably use it to pair your phone with a peripheral device such as a wireless headset or hands-free car kit. You also may use it to sync your phone with your laptop computer or to send pictures from your phone to your printer.

In addition to working with peripheral devices, Bluetooth can be used for mobile marketing — a practice called *Bluecasting.* A marketer places Bluetooth access points and a Bluetooth transmitter in a public area (such as a mall, airport lounge, bus stop, or movie theater) or at a live event. When a consumer walks by the access point, if his phone is set to receive

Bluetooth requests automatically, his phone beeps, and he's asked to accept a pairing request from the Bluetooth access point. If he accepts the request, the Bluetooth access point sends an image, ringtone, game, or other communication to his phone.

Leading Bluecasting providers include Qwikker (`www.qwikker.com`), BLIP Systems (`www.blipsystems.com`), and Proximity Marketing (`www.proximitymarketing.com`).

Examining Key Mobile Channel Enablers

In addition to the mobile paths described in the preceding sections, you can use a few capabilities of the mobile phone to enhance your mobile marketing programs, including location, the camera, Near Field Communication, and Radio Frequency Identification chips. I discuss them all in the following sections.

It's a snap: Using the camera

Most mobile phones today come with a camera. For this reason, Nokia, the world's leading phone manufacturer, is one of the leading camera manufacturers and distributors as well. A consumer can use the camera in her phone to opt into a mobile marketing campaign by taking a picture of an ad in a magazine, a bar code, a physical product (such as a DVD or soda can), herself, or any number of other things. See Book VIII, Chapter 2 for details on opt-in methods.

Finding the way with location

Location is a very powerful tool and one of the unique features of mobile marketing. When mobile subscribers are out and about, they *usually* know where they are, but their phones *always* know. Location information can make your programs more contextually relevant to a user's location.

You can identify a mobile subscriber's location in several ways:

✦ **User-provided information:** The consumer can provide the ZIP code, address, or phone number of his current location. (If he provides a landline number, you can look up the address in a publicly accessible database.)

✦ **CellID triangulation:** Every cellular tower is in a fixed location (big steel towers tend not to move around a lot), and each tower has an identification number, commonly referred to as CellID (cellular tower ID). If you know the IDs of the towers that a mobile phone has in range, you can triangulate the mobile subscriber's location with reasonable accuracy. (This system is how Google Maps works.) High-end phones such as iPhones, BlackBerry models, and Nokia- and Microsoft-powered smartphones can tell your application the CellIDs of the towers they're connected to. Then your mobile application provider can look up the towers' Global Positioning System (GPS) coordinates in publicly accessible databases such as OpenCellID (www.opencellid.org).

✦ **GPS:** The Global Positioning System relies on a constellation of satellites surrounding the planet. The location of a mobile phone equipped with GPS can be determined down to a few yards anywhere on the planet. If the wireless carrier and phone permit this function, an application provider can access the phone's GPS data to enhance the application you're offering.

✦ **A-GPS:** Some phones are equipped with Assisted GPS (A-GPS), which combines GPS, CellID, and other enhanced network capabilities to refine the location of the mobile subscriber.

✦ **Local access points:** Low-bandwidth transmitter/receivers, such as Bluetooth and Wi-Fi, can be used to approximate a mobile subscriber's location, because the access-point transmitters are in fixed locations. When a mobile phone connects to an access point, you can approximate the mobile subscriber's location.

✦ **Fem2Cells:** The emerging minitower cellphone technology called Fem2Cells has no practical marketing use today, but I'm noting it here because some applications should be available soon, given all the creative minds out there.

With location, you can create context-sensitive experiences. When a consumer opts in to your mobile marketing campaign, you can send a location-relevant coupon, not just some generic discount for a store halfway around the country from where the consumer is currently located, or you can serve up advertising that's relevant to a nearby establishment.

Many companies, such as Yahoo!, use search terms and proximity access point data to determine a user's location. The main purpose of this type of location detection is serving location-relevant advertising.

Unfortunately, location-enabled phones are still quite limited in the market-place. Not many people have them, and it's difficult for marketers to get access to this location data. Although location-enabled services are great ideas, we still have some time to wait before location services are ready for use by the average marketer.

Many marketers will try to build location services in which the location is the primary value proposition. Location by itself has little value, however; location is an enabling feature that gives value to other services, such as mapping, search, and advertising.

Ticketing and identification with NFC and RFID

Although the technologies are far from mainstream at this point, some phones are being equipped with Radio Frequency Identification (RFID) and Near Field Communication (NFC) chips. These systems are similar in concept to Bluetooth in that they're both short-range communication systems, but they have unique identification and commerce capabilities.

In Germany, for example, NFC-enabled phones are used to purchase train tickets. A user simply swipes the phone past an NFC reader, and the reader charges her linked billing account (a credit card) for the purchase of the ticket.

No commercialized version of RFID has been developed yet. But RFID chips can be used to identify you and can even personalize signs as you walk by. (Did you see the scene in *Minority Report* in which Tom Cruise walks by a sign and the sign talks to him? That's what I'm talking about.)

Deciding How and When to Use a Particular Mobile Path

It truly is amazing to think about all the capabilities the mobile channel has to offer — how much reach it provides and what diverse interactions you can conduct over it. Not every mobile path, feature, and function is ready or applicable for mass marketing use, however — or even for niche marketing use.

In this section, I review the various factors you should consider when you're thinking about integrating mobile marketing into your marketing plans.

Six considerations for mobile marketers

Here are six things to consider when choosing a mobile path for your marketing programs.

Interoperability

Interoperability means that the mobile channel, feature, or function works across all networks (mobile operator and/or Internet) and geographies that you'll be launching your programs in. This factor is important, because in many cases you won't know what mobile carrier or network your audience is using. Especially in mass marketing programs, you don't want to miss out on a big portion of the market because your program doesn't work on one or more mobile phone brands, carriers, or networks.

Standards

You need to consider whether industry technical and business standards have been put in place to ensure the reliability, repeatability, supportability, and sustainability of the particular path, feature, or function you want to use. Text messaging, for example, was a big technological leap forward, and standards had to be developed for the proper creation and delivery of text messages. As text messaging matured, so did the commercial models: how marketers charge and get paid when they use the service. (See Book VIII, Chapter 6 for information on making money with mobile marketing.)

Device and capability proliferation

Just because a new phone and mobile terminal has been released doesn't mean that everyone has one. The iPhone is a perfect example. There are more than 3 billion mobile phone subscribers worldwide, but only 10 million or so iPhones are in use as of this writing. The iPhone is important because it demonstrates the power and potential of the mobile channel, but from a mass market mobile-marketing perspective, its impact is limited because relatively few people have iPhones compared with all the phones that are out there.

Moreover, not all phones are created equal, and not all capabilities are on all phones. Marketers should consider a particular mobile capability as applicable for mass market use only if a feature is on most phones (SMS for example) and consumers both know about it and choose to use it. For example, the average consumer changes his phone every 18 to 36 months, so even if a new capability is built into every new phone that's released, it will take years for that capability to propagate through the market enough to be considered appropriate for mass market use by marketers.

Device and capability adoption

Just because a phone has a particular capability doesn't mean that everyone knows how to or chooses to use it. Just look at SMS. SMS has been on the market for more than 17 years worldwide (7 years in the United States), but only about 60 percent of U.S. mobile subscribers use it (versus 90 percent of 18- to 25-year-olds). SMS is just now being adopted enough to be considered for mass-market mobile marketing use.

Ecosystem and player health

When you choose the capability that you want to launch, you need to take into account the health of the overall mobile ecosystem and the health of the specific mobile service provider you'll be working with. If the ecosystem as a whole, for a particular capability or service provider, is unstable because of immaturity or poor health, this instability could affect the success of your campaign.

Geography

You must understand the country and/or region in which you'll be launching your programs. All countries are different, so you may need to find one or more different service providers in each country, tailor your applications to meet local regulations, or localize the language of your programs. If you plan to launch programs in multiple regions at the same time, you need to consider this issue in your plan and make sure that you find the right partner.

Ratings for mobile technologies

Taking into account all the variables in the preceding section, you can rate the mass-market applicability of each mobile path by using a rough criteria — for example, whether a path meets the factor for mass market applicability (can it reach 80 percent of the audience?). Table 1-1 scores each mobile channel and how it rates on the six mass marketing applicability criteria.

Table 1-1	Mobile Path Marketing Applicability Rating						
	Voice	*SMS*	*Mobile Internet*	*MMS*	*E-Mail*	*Bluetooth*	*Installed Application*
Inter-operability	X	X	X				
Standards	X	X	X		X		
Device and capability pro-liferation	X	X	X				
Device and capability adoption	X	X		X			
Ecosystem and player health	X	X	X				
Geography	X		X				
Score	6/6	5/6	5/6	1/6	1/6	0/6	0/6

Figure 1-6 depicts channel-marketing applicability visually and shows that the IVR, SMS, and mobile Internet channels are the most applicable for mass-market programs, whereas all other channels and various content types are more appropriate for niche marketing programs or simple experimentation at this point. See the nearby sidebar "Focus on your target market" for a discussion about how to adjust your perspective of these different channels.

Focus on your target market

Even if a particular mobile path isn't applicable for mass marketing use, you shouldn't ignore it. Services such as video delivery through MMS or applications are perfect for niche markets — markets in which you can be fairly sure that your audience members have mobile phones capable of accessing the mobile Internet, that they have data plans (they're paying their wireless carriers for data services such as mobile Internet), and that they know how to use the feature.

Business market segments, iPhone users, and high-end niche consumer markets are perfect candidates for a rich mobile experience, such as iPhone-specific application downloads. You can be widely successfully with this path, and many players are seeing their applications downloaded hundreds of thousands of times a month via iPhones, whereas they're not seeing these numbers on a mass market level because the application doesn't meet the mass market criteria. In short, you'll want to rely on voice and text messaging, and then start introducing the mobile Internet, and then other services until you better understand the members of your target market and the phones and services they use. Then, after you know what phone they use, you can focus on the services that these people have. For example, 85 percent of iPhone users regularly use the mobile Internet and download applications.

Figure 1-6:
Mobile technology applicability for marketing.

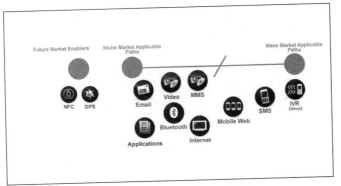

Complying with Regulations and Guidelines

Like in any industry, you must follow numerous regulations and best practices to stay in compliance with the rules of the industry, protect consumers, and ensure the best possible user experience:

✦ **Regulations** are government-mandated rules and laws that must be followed on the state and federal levels in the United States or throughout a particular region in other parts of the world.

✦ **Best practices and guidelines** are compilations of accepted industry practices, wireless carrier policies, and regulatory guidelines that have been agreed on by representative members of a particular industry.

In the following sections, I provide the industry's best practices, guidelines, rules, and regulations so that you can stay on the right side of the law and practices.

Adhering to industry standards and best practices

Every industry needs to have rules; otherwise, you'd simply have chaos. Chaos leads to costly inefficiencies that eat up a lot of time and money and that affect consumers adversely. Moreover, many industries find that some methods work better than others. These methods rise to the top and are referred to as *best practices* — the best, most efficient ways to get the job done and stay in compliance with the rules.

Balancing the demands of consumer protection and openness is difficult, but experienced representatives of every sphere of the industry ecosystem developed the mobile marketing industry's best practices; they know what is effective and what is ineffective with consumers.

Moreover, as is the case with the mobile marketing Consumer Best Practices Guidelines published by the Mobile Marketing Association (MMA), following the guidelines is mandatory. Each wireless carrier and messaging aggregator in the United States requires marketers to follow the practices outlined in this document, which provides detailed implementation guidelines for text messaging, IVR, and mobile Internet programs for the U.S. market. The guidelines are updated twice a year (in January and June), and sections are refined and added as the industry matures. You can download the MMA Consumer Best Practices Guidelines at `www.mmaglobal.com/best practices.pdf`.

Steering clear of mobile spam

Spam is unsolicited, unwanted communications — e-mail, text messages, multimedia messages, and so on — sent to a mobile phone user. Spam is regulated, however. The U.S. CAN-SPAM Act of 2003 (Controlling the Assault of Non-Solicited Pornography & Marketing Act) and European Union Directive 2002/58/EC explicitly prohibit spam, as do other regional directives and industry best practices and guidelines.

Each directive has different rules about what constitutes spam. The mobile channel is recognized as requiring explicit consent from mobile subscribers before you can message them, for example, but with e-mail, typical regulations allow you to e-mail anyone without consent as long as you provide a clear and conspicuous way of opting out (telling you not to contact them).

Other trade association guidelines

Several industry organizations produce guidelines that are applicable to mobile marketing:

✔ **Mobile Marketing Association (MMA):** In addition to its Consumer Best Practices Guidelines, the MMA publishes a global code of conduct; regional and global mobile advertising guidelines; and educational materials on topics such as IVR, Bluecasting, mobile Internet, sweepstakes, and couponing. For more information, visit the organization's Web site at www. mmaglobal.com.

✔ **Direct Marketing Association (DMA):** The DMA is a leading trade organization in both the United States and the United Kingdom that focuses on direct marketing practices, including mobile marketing. The UK organization's mobile council has produced several guidelines that can help you execute your mobile marketing programs properly; you can find them at http://mobile.dma.org.uk/content/Inf-Case.asp.

In the United States, the DMA has formed a mobile advisory board, mobile council, and a series of mobile committees to develop best practices for mobile marketing. For more information, visit www.the-DMA.org.

✔ **Interactive Advertising Bureau (IAB):** The IAB's mobile committee produces best practices and mobile advertising guidelines, which are available at www.iab.net/iab_ products_and_industry_services/1421/1488/mobileplatform.

✔ **dotMobi:** This organization, which runs the .mobi top-level domain, also creates best practices and guidelines for the mobile Internet and offers a wide range of services. See http://mtld.mobi for more information.

You can read the rules and figure out exactly what is allowed and what isn't, but the easiest way to stay clear of problems is to avoid sending unsolicited messages to anyone. Get permission first. (For details on obtaining an opt-in, see Book VIII, Chapter 2.)

Checking mobile SMS and content program certification

Marketers may want to run a nearly infinite number of mobile programs through the mobile channel and the many paths through it. If these programs have SMS, premium SMS, or mobile content elements associated with them, they must be precertified by the U.S. mobile carriers, especially premium programs.

Each country has different rules about what needs to be precertified and what doesn't. Contact your application provider or connection aggregator for assistance.

The wireless carriers create the rules for certification, with input and program auditing from leading trade associations. In the United States, the wireless carrier and connection aggregator agreements require all marketers to obtain preapproval certification from wireless carriers before running a program. You can obtain this certification with the assistance of your connection aggregator and/or application provider partners.

The guidelines you must follow are detailed in the MMA's Consumer Best Practices Guidelines (refer to "Adhering to industry standards and best practices," earlier in this chapter), as well as in frequently asked questions and carrier-playbook documentation published by connection aggregators. Your application provider can provide you with a summary of these rules — if you use an application provider, that is. If you don't, you'll have to dig through the rules yourself.

Avoiding contact with the National Do Not Call Registry

On October 1, 2003, the U.S. Federal Trade Commission (FTC) gave consumers a choice about receiving most telemarketing calls by developing the National Do Not Call Registry. Consumers can register their home and mobile phone numbers with the Do Not Call Registry at `https://www.donotcall.gov`. Most marketers are forbidden to place telemarketing calls to any phone number listed in the registry, but some exceptions exist, such as political organizations, charities, telephone surveyors, and companies that have preestablished business relationships with a consumer. Marketers are required to check the registry at least once every 31 days to clean their internal lists.

The FTC considers text messaging and e-mail to fall under the umbrella of the Do Not Call Registry. Make sure that you get consumers' consent before you contact them through these channels.

Safeguarding the privacy of children

Children (13 years old and younger) use mobile phones, too, and you must be very careful when marketing to them. In the United States, rules for marketing to children are clearly spelled out in the Children's Online Privacy Protection Act of 1998 (COPPA), which you can find at `www.ftc.gov/ogc/coppa1.htm`. The act clearly outlines how and when you can engage children, as well as rules about gathering their personal information and gaining parental consent.

In addition to COPPA, you should pay close attention to Section 4 of the MMA's Consumer Best Practices Guidelines (refer to "Adhering to industry standards and best practices," earlier in this chapter), which details the industry-accepted methods for marketing to children via the mobile channel.

Protecting personal information

You should take the security of consumers' personal information very seriously. If you don't, at best you may simply ruin any possible future relationship with a consumer; at worst you could pay a severe fine and even end up in jail (especially in Europe, which has incredibly stringent consumer protection laws).

Personal information can take many forms, including a consumer's mobile phone number, address, health and financial data, and behavioral data. (For a review of various data types, see Book VIII, Chapter 7.) In marketing, personal information is divided into two classes:

+ **Personally identifiable information (PII):** *PII* is any and all information that can be used to identify a person.

+ **Non-personally identifiable information (Non-PII):** *Non-PII* is information collected through the course of the marketing process, such as clicks on a Web site, that can't immediately be linked to a specific person.

Both PII and Non-PII are collected in mobile marketing interactions. The information may simply be a person's phone number, as when someone text-messages into a program, or it may include additional details such as age, name, and address. The information may be provided by the consumer during the course of his interaction with you or obtained later by combining data from multiple public and private data sources. (See Book VIII, Chapter 2 for details on collecting and using data.)

Regardless of how the information is collected, it's critical that you protect and safeguard all information that you collect during your interactions with consumers. Frankly, it's prudent to collect only information that you really need. Why assume the liability of having it if you don't have to?

Staying compliant in special cases

You should take great care with a few special types of programs, including sweepstakes, contests, giveaways, and premium billing programs. You not only have to make sure that you have these programs precertified by the wireless carriers, but you also have to ensure that you're in compliance with local, state, and federal laws. If you don't, you may find yourself not getting paid and possibly getting sued. The best practice is to consult an expert; your application provider and connection aggregator can help.

You may want to consult a specialty marketing firm to handle your sweepstakes and contests. Detroit-based ePrize (www.eprize.com) is an interactive agency that has expertise in this area.

Chapter 2: Planning a Mobile Marketing Campaign

In This Chapter

✔ Setting goals and strategies for mobile marketing

✔ Counting the costs

✔ Understanding Common Short Codes (CSCs)

✔ Handling opt-ins and opt-outs

*P*lanning leads to success. Why? Because planning is the process of thinking things through before you act. You need to set objectives, and you need to calculate the costs of achieving them so that you can decide whether your ideas are financially feasible and achievable before you spend money and time on them.

You also need a plan to reach the members of your audience — both before you contact them using mobile, because of legal issues with permission, and after you have their permission, because of the wide variety of mobile marketing solutions and communication methods available.

The chapter provides strategies for planning your objectives, estimating your financial and time investments, coordinating your use of short codes, and inviting people to participate in your mobile marketing programs.

Setting Up a Plan

You should list all your marketing objectives in a written plan that provides a complete 360-degree view of your marketing efforts. You should start your plan by listing your goals, taking an in-depth look at all the elements that will influence your ability to achieve your goals, and choosing an approach for handling those elements. The following sections address these topics.

Starting with a goal

When planning, you need to think through what you want to accomplish — that is, start with your goal in mind. Following are some common objectives for mobile marketing plans:

✦ **Increase brand awareness and recall.** Increase the number of potential customers who know about you, the number of news stories or blog posts written about you, click-through rates (CTRs) on a Web site, and consumer recall of your marketing programs and brand.

✦ **Generate leads and identify new prospects.** The objective is to fill the opt-in database so that you have qualified, interested people to market to in the future. (For details, see "Managing Opt-Ins," later in this chapter.)

✦ **Acquire new customers.** Generate initial transactions from first-time buyers or drive first-time attendance to events or traffic to retail stores.

✦ **Increase revenue and profits from customer base.** Generate repeat purchases from customers for both existing and new products at sustainable profit levels.

✦ **Enhance customer loyalty and activity.** Increase loyalty-point redemption; stimulate word-of-mouth activities; and increase customer participation in programs, such as driving attendance to an event, store, or Web site.

✦ **Improve resolution time for customer inquiries and complaints.** Make people happier by addressing their questions, issues, and problems in a cost-effective, low-stress, timely manner.

✦ **Stimulate word-of-mouth/viral marketing activities.** Get your audience talking about you in a positive way.

I hope you aren't surprised that these objectives aren't objectives just for mobile marketing, but also for all types of marketing. Mobile marketing is simply a tool to help you market and achieve your company's objectives.

Instead of focusing on a specific tactical initiative, weave mobile marketing into your entire marketing plan (read Book VIII, Chapter 1).

Planning your coverage

Your marketing plan should cover the following elements:

✦ **Your target audience:** The plan should specifically call out the audience you want to reach: prospects, customers, partners, society at large, and so on.

✦ **Your offerings:** The plan should detail exactly what you offer and the value your customers will get from your offerings — in other words, how your offers will fulfill customers' needs, alleviate their pains, and/or meet their capability demands. In addition, you should think about how your offerings will change over time.

✦ **Your quantified objectives:** The plan should detail what you want to accomplish, such as increasing brand awareness, improving sales in a particular region by X percent, becoming the No. 1 player in your market within Y years by holding Z percent of the market, and so on.

✦ **Resources:** The plan should detail all the resources (such as people, partners, money, technology, and services) you'll need to accomplish your objectives.

✦ **Your communication efforts:** Your plan should be very specific about what you want to say to the market, as well as the channels — including mobile — that you'll use to communicate your message. You should also consider how this message and your communications will change through every stage of the customer life cycle.

✦ **Delivery channels:** Your plan should detail how you'll get your offerings out to the market.

✦ **Exchange:** Finally, your plan needs to state specifically how you'll exchange value with your audience.

Deciding who handles what

When you plan your mobile marketing program, whether you're creating individual campaigns or complete strategic initiatives, your program must be founded on four key building blocks:

✦ Strategy

✦ Creative elements

✦ Tactical planning and execution

✦ Platform/technology choices

Consider which of these four areas you want to handle yourself and which ones you want selected mobile service and marketing providers to assist you with. (For information on choosing mobile service providers, refer to Book VIII, Chapter 1.) Your decision about who handles what determines your approach to mobile marketing, which I discuss in the following section.

Choosing an approach

You have four basic approaches to choose among when you want to launch a mobile marketing program:

✦ **Agency approach:** You contract with one or more general marketing agencies or mobile service providers to handle everything for you.

✦ **Do-it-yourself approach:** You do everything yourself, asking for help from no one.

✦ **Platform approach:** You handle the strategy, creative elements, and tactical execution, and you use a mobile service provider's licensed software application or platform to handle all the technical elements of your program, including relationships with connection aggregators. (For more information about connection aggregators, see Book VIII, Chapter 1.)

> ✦ **Hybrid approach:** You pick elements of the aforementioned approaches. You may outsource creative elements to a mobile service provider or agency, keep strategy for yourself, and license a platform for one part of a campaign, for example.

The approach you select depends on how much of the overall mobile marketing process you want to take on personally, as well as what pieces you see as being critical to your company's competitive advantage and core business offerings.

Your approach can vary over time. You might use the agency approach when you launch your mobile marketing program, for example, if you're unsure whether mobile marketing is going to be a one-off activity for you. Over time, as you become more confident and competent with mobile marketing, and as mobile marketing becomes a cornerstone of your marketing, you might want to take on more responsibility for other activities.

Understanding the Costs of Mobile Marketing

Mobile marketing involves both up-front and variable costs that you need to be aware of before you plan and eventually execute your strategy. This section explains how to include costs in your plan.

How you absorb these costs depends on the approach you take to executing your mobile marketing program (refer to "Choosing an approach," earlier in this chapter). If you're simply going to run one-off campaigns and don't plan to invest in mobile marketing, you need to consider only the variable costs. If you plan to strategically integrate mobile marketing into your business, however, you want to consider the up-front costs as well.

Calculating up-front costs and estimated timelines

Some mobile marketing costs apply at the outset of your mobile marketing practice. Following are some common up-front costs to consider:

✦ **Strategy and resources:** You need to estimate the costs for your team members and their training, as well as the costs for the development and maintenance of your strategy. This activity can take as little or as much time to complete as you want, depending on the nature of your program and your partners.

✦ **Mobile marking application fees:** You pay these fees to gain access to the application software that powers your mobile marketing programs. (Trying to build the mobile marketing applications yourself could become quite expensive and time consuming.) On average, depending on the functionality you license, mobile marketing application fees range from a few hundred to thousands of dollars per month. Licensing access to a mobile marketing application can take a few minutes to many weeks — or even longer, depending on your licensing and procurement procedures and on the number of providers you evaluate and ultimately select.

In addition to monthly fees, you should budget for account setup and training fees when you sign up with an application provider.

✦ **Connection aggregator fees:** These fees apply if you decide to go it alone and build your own application software. You need to connect your application to a connection aggregator, and this setup will cost you between $1,000 and many thousands of dollars per month, depending on the aggregator you use. Connection aggregators' fees typically are included in mobile marketing application fees (discussed earlier in this section), which is one of the many benefits of working with an application provider. (You can read more about connection aggregators in Book VIII, Chapter 1.) Like working with an application provider, contracting with a connection aggregator can take a few days to weeks.

If you have *high-throughput* requirements — that is, you need to send and receive hundreds or thousands of messages per second — you should expect to pay extra to the connection aggregator or application provider for this higher-than-average throughput.

✦ **Short-code leases:** A Common Short Code (CSC) is a phone number that is only five to six digits long. If you're going to run any text-messaging mobile marketing programs, you must lease a CSC. In the United States, short-code leases cost $500 to $1,000 per month and are billed quarterly. You may be able to rent a short code from your application provider or connection aggregator, but you'll probably pay a similar fee.

Leasing a CSC takes about an hour, but then you must work with your application provider to have the short code activated and approved for use. It takes 8 to 15 weeks (or more) to obtain approval across all participating wireless carriers. You can read more about short codes in "Working with Common Short Codes," later in this chapter.

Accounting for variable costs

Following are the variable costs of a typical mobile marketing program:

✦ **Program strategy development:** These costs include all the activities needed to conceive your campaign and lay out the plan. This activity can take as little or as much time to complete as you want, depending on the nature of your program and your partners.

✦ **Creative concept development:** These costs include all the design activities associated with your campaign. This activity can take as little or as much time to complete as you want, depending on the nature of your program and your partners.

✦ **Content licensing and/or creation:** These costs include licensing fees or design fees for any content you may use for the campaign (such as images, ringtones, videos, or newsfeeds). This activity can take anywhere from a few minutes to a few weeks, depending on the type of content and who you're working with.

✦ **Mobile marketing application fees:** These costs are the fees you pay a service provider for hosting and reporting on your campaign — that is, if you're not already licensing an application or haven't built it yourself. (Refer to "Calculating up-front costs and estimated timelines," earlier in this chapter, for additional explanation.)

✦ **Tactical execution of program:** These costs include creative, program certifications (as needed), technical implementation, legal fees (if you're running a sweepstakes program, for example), and any custom nonrecurring software development that may be needed to tailor the application(s) to your specific campaign. This activity can take as little or as much time to complete as you want, depending on the nature of your program and your partners.

✦ **Transactional items:** These costs include messaging traffic — via Short Message Service (SMS), Multimedia Messaging Service (MMS), or e-mail; Internet and mobile Internet pageviews, advertising pageviews and click-throughs, content downloads, interactive voice response (IVR) minutes, content royalties, images recognized, and individual wireless-carrier tariffs. (For more information on messaging and IVR, see Book VIII, Chapter 1.)

✦ **Program certification:** In the United States, all mobile marketing programs must be precertified by the wireless carriers. An application form must be completed and submitted through your application provider or connection aggregator to each carrier. Costs for this activity vary (free to thousands of dollars), as does the timing (typically, 8 to 15 weeks or more, depending on the nature of the program).

✦ **Campaign auditing:** Wireless carriers in the United States regularly audit mobile marketing programs running over their networks. Although no up-front cost is involved when a carrier audits your program, you may incur a cost for updating your program if, after an audit, a carrier finds that your program doesn't comply with current industry guidelines.

✦ **Traditional media and retail channels:** These costs are the fees you pay to promote the program in any traditional media, new-mediator retail channel.

Depending on the provider you're working with, you might be quoted a single price for your entire mobile marketing program plus fees for traditional media buys and retail promotions. Or you may get a detailed breakdown of the costs. Often, it's helpful to ask for the breakdown if you're not provided one so that you can adjust your plans and strategies accordingly.

Often, you can reuse portions of your strategy, creative elements, and any custom software and content development in future campaigns, as well as in your broader strategic mobile marketing program. This multiple-use strategy can end up saving you quite a bit of money and time down the road.

Estimating your timeline

Finally, you need to plan your timeline. As I discuss in the preceding sections, you have to consider several activities when you develop your program, and each of these activities takes time. Some activities can be done in parallel; others need to be done in a serial manner. The time you actually need depends on the nature of your program and the partners you're working with. Typically, however, obtaining certification for and launching a typical mobile marketing program take 8 to 15 weeks, in addition to the time required to design the program, develop its creative elements, and coordinate media channels. The process takes longer for an atypical program.

You may be able to speed your timeline if you're working with an application provider that takes care of precertified programs and other elements, in addition to having templated services that streamline the setup of your programs. Consult your application provider or connection aggregator to see what can be done if you're on a tight timeline.

Working with Common Short Codes

Regardless of which approach you employ to launch and run your mobile marketing program (refer to "Choosing an approach," earlier in this chapter), one of the most important elements to plan is how you'll manage your short codes.

A *Common Short Code (CSC)* is simply a short (five or six digits) phone number used to address and route commercial text messages through wireless-operator networks. CSCs are critical because nearly all effective mobile marketing programs leverage text messaging in one way or another, and you need a CSC to launch and run a commercial text-messaging program.

Given the importance of CSCs, you don't want to leave CSC planning to the last minute or put it into someone else's hands, because if your CSC has problems, so does your mobile marketing.

Knowing what CSCs do

CSCs are effective for mobile marketing because they're all of the following things:

+ **Bidirectional:** Messaging traffic can be addressed both ways with CSCs, both to and from the mobile subscriber and you.

✦ **Cross-carrier enabled:** After they're activated on a carrier network, CSCs work across most of the leading U.S. carriers, extending a marketer's reach to more than 200 million mobile subscribers in the United States.

CSCs are country-specific, unlike Internet domains, which work worldwide. You need to lease a CSC in each country you want to run your mobile marketing in (see "Renting access to a CSC," later in this chapter).

✦ **Billing engines:** You can use premium Short Message Service (SMS) messages and charge people for participation in your programs. (For more information about premium SMS, also called PSMS, see Book VIII, Chapter 6.)

✦ **Effective mechanisms for permissions marketing:** CSCs are the primary means of obtaining opt-ins in mobile marketing (see "Managing Opt-Ins," later in this chapter).

✦ **Useful:** CSCs are useful for a wide range of marketing campaigns and services.

Acquiring a CSC

You have two ways to gain access to a CSC for your mobile marketing program: lease one or rent access to one. The following sections describe both methods.

Leasing a CSC

If you'd like to lease your own CSC directly, you can obtain it from one of the few short-code administration bodies:

✦ **United Kingdom:** UK Mobile Network Operators (www.short-codes.com)

✦ **United States:** Common Short Code Administration (www.usshort codes.com; see Figure 2-1)

✦ **Canada:** Common Codes Administration (www.txt.ca/common.htm)

✦ **France:** SMS+ (www.smsplus.org/index.php)

✦ **China:** Ministry of Information Industry Short Code Administration Group (www.miit.gov.cn)

Many countries don't have a centralized short-code administration body, however, in which case you must rent access to a short code (see the following section).

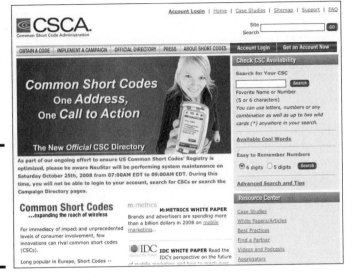

Figure 2-1:
U.S.
Common
Short Code
Admini-
stration
Web site.

Renting access to a CSC

If you're not prepared to get your own short code — due to the expense or time it takes to activate one — you can ask an application provider or connection aggregator to rent you access to a short code and run it under a shared or dedicated schema (see "Going dedicated or shared," later in this chapter).

Deciding what type of CSC to use

When you lease or rent access to your CSC, you must make a few choices. Are you going to get a vanity or random short code? How many digits long will your code be? Will you use the code in a shared or dedicated model? If you don't know what these terms mean, don't worry; I explain them in the following sections.

Choosing random or vanity code

You'll need to choose between two short-code schemas:

+ **Random short code:** A short code is considered to be *random* when the code-administration body assigns a random number sequence to the company leasing the code.

**Book VIII
Chapter 2**

**Planning a
Mobile Marketing
Campaign**

✦ **Vanity short code:** A short code is considered to be *vanity* when the code-administration body allows the company leasing the code to pick the numbers. An example of a vanity short code would be 46645, purchased specifically to spell *googl*. A company may choose to lease a vanity code to facilitate easy recall (77777) or to build its brand (57238 = *kraft*).

Rarely, if ever, will you rent a vanity short code from an application provider.

Deciding on five or six digits

In addition to choosing a random or vanity short-code schema, you need to pick how many digits you want to use in your code: five or six. In the United States, you can lease five-digit codes as either random or vanity short codes, but six-digit codes can be leased only as vanity codes.

You might see four-digit short codes, but these codes tend to be reserved for the sole use of wireless carriers. Codes longer than six digits are called *long codes,* and they're primarily used when running cross-border (international) programs.

Going dedicated or shared

Finally, you can choose to run multiple mobile initiatives on a single short code simultaneously or to run only one at any given time. When multiple mobile marketing campaigns are run on a single short code, the code is referred to as *shared.* When only one service is running on the code at any given time, the code is referred to as *dedicated.*

In short-code terms, *dedicated* and *shared* have nothing to do with who owns or leases the short code; they apply solely to how the short code is being used. Therefore, you can use your own dedicated code, rent a dedicated code, use your own short code in a shared model, or rent access to a shared code.

Both dedicated and shared short-code models have pros and cons, as you see in Table 2-1.

Table 2-1	Short-Code Models	
Model	*Pros*	*Cons*
Shared	Multiple initiatives can be run under one short code for a lower cost per initiative.	You need to include keywords in SMS messages to identify the initiative. User flow and instructions for initiatives are more complex. One noncertified "outlaw" initiative could shut down all other initiatives on a shared short code.
Dedicated	End-user task flow is easy. End users can text without having to include keywords to identify the initiative. You have more flexibility in initiative tactics. Reporting is easier.	The company is not amortizing short-code costs over multiple initiatives. All metric data can belong only to the initiative on the dedicated short code. Dedicated short code is more expensive than shared.

The shared and dedicated models are not cast in stone. As part of a company's CSC strategy, a short code can be used as dedicated for a certain period and then used as shared with multiple initiatives running on it. Consult your application or connection-aggregator partner for details.

Managing Opt-Ins

Mobile marketing is about establishing a dialogue with the members of your audience via the mobile channel. Sometimes, this interaction occurs only one time: A customer reaches out to you to request some information, you send the information, and the interaction ends. At other times, you invite a customer to receive ongoing communication from you via the phone channel, and if that customer gives you consent to contact him in the future, you have the right to contact him again via the same channel. This process is often referred to as *obtaining an opt-in*. As a result, the process of obtaining opt-ins is crucial to your long-term success in mobile marketing.

The following sections help you determine how to obtain opt-ins. You can read more about the legalities of obtaining permissions in Book VIII, Chapter 1.

Industry best practices and regulations require all text messages to contain opt-out instructions, such as a *stop* keyword. For more information about opt-out instructions, see "Handling Opt-Outs," later in this chapter.

Placing an opt-in call to action in media

A request for an opt-in is called an *opt-in call to action*. You can place an opt-in call to action in any traditional, new, and mobile media channel, including the following:

✦ Television

✦ Print

✦ Radio

✦ Point-of-sale displays

✦ Face-to-face encounters

✦ Outdoor advertising

✦ A Web or mobile Internet site

✦ An e-mail

✦ A customer-care call

✦ Online advertising

When you place a call to action in media, you're asking the members of your audience to pull out their phones, respond to your offer (opt in to the campaign), and receive the benefits of your offer.

Figure 2-2 shows the seven primary calls to action you can use to enhance your media. The following sections explain these calls to action in more detail.

Figure 2-2: Multiple methods of opt-in and interaction with mobile marketing applications.

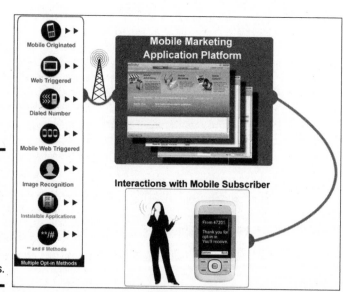

All the following opt-in methods can be monetized. For details, see Book VIII, Chapter 6.

Dialing and pressing

Dialing and pressing is all about using the voice channel of the mobile phone. You can encourage people to call a phone number by asking them to "Dial 1-800-XXX-XXXX to experience the sounds of the movie" or "Call 408-XXX-XXXX to listen in on the game," for example.

You don't have to answer the calls yourself; you can use an IVR system to ask the caller to make selections. Selection options in an IVR session could be "Press 1 to receive a ringtone," "Press 2 to get your last five transactions," or "Press 3 to get the movie listings sent to your phone." You can read more about IVR in Book VIII, Chapter 1.

Texting

Texting simply means sending and replying to text messages. You can place the call to action in traditional, new, and mobile media by saying something like "Text *win* to 12345 to enter the sweepstakes." You can also obtain a mobile subscriber's opt-in via texting.

Mobile marketing programs and any other programs that use text messaging (such as IVR, Internet, or mobile Internet) must use a CSC to address and route the message traffic. For details on CSCs, refer to "Working with Common Short Codes," earlier in this chapter.

Snapping and scanning

Snapping and scanning means taking a picture and scanning a bar code. More and more phones have high-resolution internal cameras.

The camera is a wonderful tool for gathering opt-ins. You can instruct audience members to take a picture of an object — a soft-drink can, a magazine ad, a movie poster, or almost anything else that has clearly defined edges — and then instruct them to e-mail or text (via MMS) the picture to your mobile marketing program. When your program receives a picture, it processes the picture and then opts the mobile subscriber in to the program.

Two companies lead the pack in this field: Snaptell (www.snaptell.com), based in Palo Alto, California, and Los Angeles–based SnapNow (www.snapnow.com). See Figure 2-3 for an example of opting in with a camera phone.

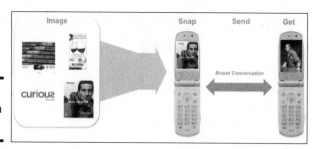

Figure 2-3:
Opting in via
the camera.

Submitting

Another great way to invite someone into your mobile marketing program is to present a form on an Internet page or a mobile Internet page, or in an installed application. A customer can opt in to receive text alerts from Sony, for example, regarding its minisode program via the mobile Internet (`http://mini4sony.mobi`).

Star and pound

Two companies — Zoove (`www.zoove.com`) and Singletouch (`www.singletouch.com`) — have developed two alternative opt-in channels.

Zoove's method uses the star (*) key on the mobile phone. A mobile subscriber on the Sprint network, for example, can press **267 — that is, **AOL — and the Send/Talk button on his phone (typically, the green button). In return, an AOL promotional mobile Internet site is sent to the phone. Singletouch's solution works the same way but uses the pound (#) key instead.

Both services are still limited in their deployment across wireless carriers, but you can see the possibilities of these methods of opt-in.

Executing opt-ins

In all the opt-in methods discussed in the preceding section, several messages are required to execute the opt-in completely. In the following sections, I discuss the three types of opt-ins: single, double, and multistep.

Understanding MOs and MTs

First, however, you need to be familiar with two important text-messaging classifications:

✦ **Mobile originated (MO):** A mobile subscriber composes *(originates)* a message on her phone and sends it to you.

✦ **Mobile terminated (MT):** A message goes from an application provider's service to a mobile phone, so the message ends *(terminates)* on the phone.

Bar codes and other uses for the camera

Another way to leverage the camera phone is to have it interact with an installed or embedded application on the phone.

In Japan, phones have bar-code readers (or QR code readers, a common form of bar code) embedded in their operating systems. When a consumer takes a picture of the bar code in a magazine, for example, the phone automatically recognizes the code and processes the command buried within the bar code, which may instruct the phone to open a mobile Internet browser, go to the restaurant related to the bar code, and then display how many seats are available at the restaurant. The mobile Internet page may even include functions that allow the mobile subscriber to reserve a table.

When someone opts in to your mobile campaign with an MO message, you return an MT, as I discuss in the following sections.

Executing a single opt-in

In a *single opt-in,* someone sends in an MO, and you send an MT back confirming the opt-in. For subscription alerts or ongoing programs, very few carriers support single opt-ins. Mostly, this process is used for one-time interactions; when the initial interaction is done, no future interactions will occur.

Executing a double opt-in

A *double opt-in* typically is used to gather an individual's confirmation. The flow is straightforward:

1. The user opts in to the program.

2. The mobile marketing application responds with a text message that asks for confirmation ("Reply *y* to 12345," for example).

3. The user sends the confirmation.

4. The mobile marketing application processes the request and sends back a welcome message (such as "Thank you. You're now in the group. To opt out reply *stop,* or for help reply *help*").

Executing a multistep opt-in

You use *multistep opt-in* when you want to challenge consumers with additional questions before they can participate in your program. You may ask users for their ages if you're running a program suitable only for users 17 and older, or you may ask a series of questions to collect additional *metadata* (data about themselves). After a user responds to the additional challenges, the interaction may end, or you may follow up by triggering a double opt-in as well to get expressed consent for future marketing. (See the preceding section for details on double opt-ins.)

Handling Opt-Outs

I know that you don't want to hear it, but sometimes people just want to leave; they want to opt out and stop interacting with you. Maybe they'll come back, and maybe they won't, but you need to handle their requests with grace. Accept each request, reply politely, and *never contact the person again.* Otherwise, you'll become a spammer, and you don't want that.

Every best-practices guideline on calls to action covers opt-outs. You'll want to include opt-out instructions in your media and in the legal terms and conditions that explain your program.

You can use any of the opt-in methods discussed earlier in this chapter to capture opt-outs. But the most convenient way to gather an opt-out is simply to have the mobile subscriber send the mobile marketing application a text message that includes the keyword *stop* (or any other reserved opt-out keyword, such as *end, quit,* or *cancel*). When you receive the opt-out request, you'll want to send a final reply, such as this: "Thank you. Your opt-out request has been processed. We'll miss you. If you'd like to join again, reply *join* to 12345." Figure 2-4 shows an example.

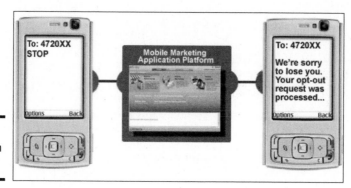

Figure 2-4:
Handling an
opt-out.

Chapter 3: Running Mobile Communication Campaigns

In This Chapter

✔ Setting up mobile communication user flows

✔ Interacting with users through quizzes, surveys, and polls

✔ Giving users incentives

✔ Encouraging user-generated content

The first mandate of marketing is to communicate — and oh, boy, can you communicate with mobile marketing. You can use mobile marketing to generate consumer responses to your queries, disseminate information, collect information, entertain your audience, and conduct commerce.

In this chapter, I focus on showing you how to set up and run interactive communications via text messaging — including promotion services, quizzes, polls, and surveys — as well as the various ways you can get consumers into the game by generating and sharing their own content.

In the following pages, you discover how to create program user flows, documenting all the steps of communication between your company and the mobile subscriber so that you can significantly enhance your marketing programs. You find out about the common elements of mobile marketing communication programs (such as opt-in/opt-out management and error/response messaging) and about the unique elements of common mobile marketing communication programs (such as trivia games, polls, and surveys).

When you're done with this chapter, you'll have a clear, concise picture of exactly what it takes to run a mobile marketing communication program.

Planning Your Communication Flow

Launching a mobile communication campaign takes more planning than you may expect. One of the most important aspects of planning is creating *user flows* — documents that show as thoroughly as possible how your users engage in your campaign. User flows are critically important for two reasons:

✦ **They help you design and execute your program.** You'll save time and money by planning early in the program-development process instead of fixing mistakes later. Moreover, a detailed user flow clarifies any ambiguity about interactions between mobile subscribers and your program. Finally, it helps streamline communication among members of your marketing team and any partners and vendors you may be working with to launch the program.

✦ **They're required for certification of your program.** As part of the certification process (see Book VIII, Chapter 1), you're required to submit your program's user flows to your mobile marketing application provider or connection aggregator. Wireless carriers test your program against these user flows. If the program works as described in the user flows, the carrier should certify the program; if not, the carrier will reject it. Also, carriers use submitted user flows for future campaign audits to make sure that your program still meets the original certification criteria.

Creating a user-flow diagram

The best way to plan your communication campaign flow is to use *a user-flow diagram* — an image that outlines the user flow (just described) and details all the interactions that may occur between a mobile subscriber and your mobile marketing program (see Figure 3-1).

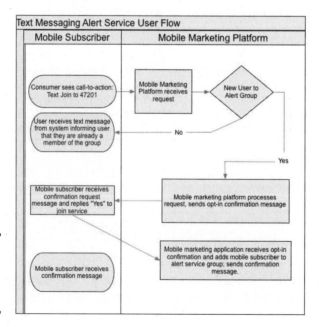

Figure 3-1:
Example
user-flow
diagram.

User-flow diagrams typically are created with software applications such as Microsoft Word, Excel, PowerPoint, or Visio. Some people use standard flow-charting techniques; others use images of phones to map the user flow. Figure 3-1 shows an example of a flow-chart method; Figure 3-2, in the following section, shows the phone method. The method you choose depends on which one is more useful for documenting all the possible interactions that a mobile subscriber may have with your program.

Your application provider or connection aggregator typically has the most common user flows already designed — as well as the not-so-common ones. Rather than start with a blank piece of paper, ask the provider to give you a few examples. Then you can tailor an existing user-flow diagram to your individual needs, as you see in the following sections.

Customizing a user-flow diagram

To customize a user-flow diagram for your mobile marketing campaign, start with the user flow provided by your application provider, and envision all possible scenarios and interactions between mobile subscribers and your mobile marketing program. Then write down what you envision, using the following sections as a guide.

Step 1: Paint a positive picture

Start by imagining what you want to have happen when everything works flawlessly. Picture what you want the perfect consumer experience to be. How do you want the opt-in flow to work, for example? What will the content-download experience look like?

Step 2: Map your opt-in flow

List the steps that a mobile subscriber must take to opt in to your program. Single opt-in is appropriate for programs that don't charge the consumer for participation or programs in which you're picking up the user's share of the text-messaging costs. These programs typically are called *free to the end user (FTEU)* or standard-rate, text-messaging programs.

If you're going to have ongoing interactions with mobile subscribers, however, or plan to charge them a premium for participation, the industry's consumer best practices and regulations require you to get a double opt-in from all subscribers, so you need to include that requirement in your user flow. (See Figure 3-2 for an example.) You can read more about managing opt-ins in Book VIII, Chapter 2. For more information about industry best practices and regulations, turn to Book VIII, Chapter 1.

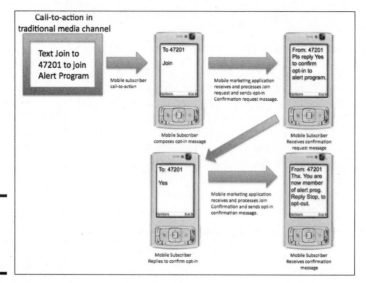

Figure 3-2:
Double
opt-in user
flow.

Step 3: Map your opt-out flow

List the steps a mobile subscriber must take to opt out of your program. At any time, a subscriber should be able to send *stop, end, quit,* or any related reserved keyword to your program to opt out of it. *Reserved keywords* are keywords reserved by industry best practices, meaning that they're designated to perform a specific function. The reserved keyword *stop* must opt someone out, for example, and *help* must elicit a help message.

After you receive an opt-out request from a mobile subscriber, you must cease all interactions with the mobile subscriber with regard to the specific program. If you don't, you run the risk of being fined by the wireless carrier (at best) or being fined *and* having your programs shut down.

You can read more about managing opt-outs in Book VIII, Chapter 2.

Step 4: Map your help user flow

How will participants in your program get help if they have a question? At minimum, according to the Mobile Marketing Association's Consumer Best Practices Guidelines (www.mmaglobal.com/bestpractices.pdf), if a user needs help and sends the text *help* to your program, the program must respond accordingly.

If your program's keyword is *win* and its short code is 12345, for example, anyone who's interested in getting help with your program should be able to text *win help* or *help win* to 12345. Your mobile marketing application must respond by returning a text message that includes information about the campaign's terms and conditions, along with details on how to get help. (For more information about short codes, refer to Book VIII, Chapter 2.)

Considering what could go wrong

In addition to mapping out the best-case inter-action scenarios for your program, you want to map out the worst-case scenarios and edge cases for your program — that is, try to think through all the things that could go wrong with your program, even the most outlandish possi-bilities (the edge cases), and then map them in your user-flow diagram.

Document how both you and your mobile marketing application will react if one or more

of these scenarios comes to pass. What if some of your potential customers speak French instead of English, for example? Your mobile subscriber may respond to your program's opt-in call to action by sending *oui* instead of *yes* as instructed. To prepare for that possi-bility, you need to configure your mobile marketing application to accept *oui, si, yup, ok, yse, yes, y,* and so on as synonyms of *yes.*

You might want to include in this message a link to a Web or mobile Internet site where the user can get detailed program terms and conditions, as well as a phone number that the user can call to talk to someone or interact with your automated customer-care system. (In the United Kingdom, this number must be a toll-free number.)

Step 5: Map your error response

How will your mobile marketing application respond if the mobile subscriber does something wrong, and what instructions will the application provide automatically to help the subscriber? If the program requires the subscriber to submit a redemption code *(abc123)* along with the program keyword *(win),* and the mobile subscriber text-messages only *win* to the short code, the mobile marketing application should reply automatically with a help message (such as "Sorry, we did not understand. Pls txt *win* to *<your code>* to opt in to this program").

Step 6: Map your final message

When the mobile subscriber is done interacting with your program, what will you say in the final message? Common final messages include "Thank you" (or "Thx") and an invitation to participate and opt in to other pro-grams. You could send a final message like this one: "Thx. The survey is complete. To join our messaging alert service pls reply *join* to 12345."

Considering optional user flows

You also might want to consider several common optional user flows that don't apply to all mobile communication campaigns:

✦ **Age verification:** To augment the opt-in process, you may provide the mobile subscriber an age-verification challenge — that is, require him to reply with his birth date before he can move on to the next step of the program. If you're promoting an R-rated movie or have other content that's not suitable for children, you may want to make sure that you have the mobile subscriber's proffered birth date in your campaign's customer database. Figure 3-3 shows a typical age-verification challenge that you can send to a mobile phone.

✦ **Instant win:** You may want to award loyalty points, free content, a coupon, or some other form of incentive to participants. You could configure your mobile marketing application to award an instant prize to every third participant in the program, for example, or set it so that one in three participants wins. Ask your application provider how to configure this user flow in your system.

✦ **Grand prize:** A grand-prize winner is selected from the pool of participants at the end of the campaign. The mobile marketing application can be set up to draw the specified number of grand-prize winners automatically at the end of the campaign, or you can make the drawing manually from the list of participants, based on whatever selection criteria you choose.

Make sure that your rules are in line with both state and federal regulations.

✦ **Couponing:** Couponing is a very powerful incentive for participation in mobile programs. You may consider adding coupons within any message in your user flow to encourage continued participation in your programs as well as to encourage users to purchase your offerings.

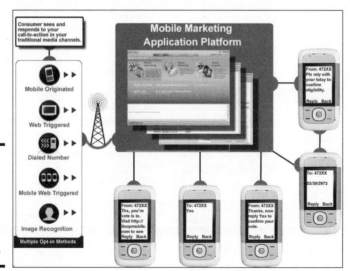

Figure 3-3:
Typical
multistep
opt-in
user flow
with age
verification.

When you send out a message, a coupon — either generated by the mobile marketing application or supplied by you to the application — can be appended to or inserted into the message.

✦ **Personalization:** If your mobile marketing program is integrated with an internal or external customer relationship management (CRM) system (see Book VIII, Chapter 7 for information on user customer data), you may be able to pull data from this system to personalize the messages in the program. You could insert a participant's first name in a message, such as "Hi, Mike. Pls reply *yes* to confirm."

Providing Text Promotions

One of the most basic mobile marketing communication programs you may want to run is a text promotion. In a *text promotion,* a mobile subscriber sends a text message to a mobile marketing application, and the application sends a message back. The content of the message depends on the nature of your program, but it may include details about a new movie or a recipe and coupon.

Setting up a text promotion service in your mobile marketing application can be as straightforward as filling out a form on the Web. Figure 3-4 shows an example of how to do this in the iLoop Mobile mFinity platform (a mobile marketing application furnished by a mobile service provider).

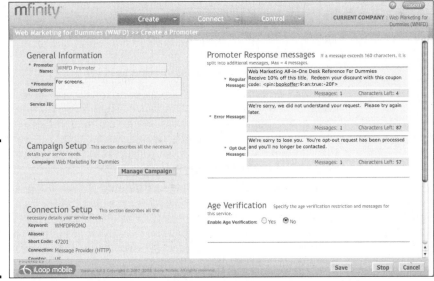

Figure 3-4: Configuring a text promotion service in a mobile marketing application.

Using quizzes to gather information and entertain

Mobile subscribers interact with quizzes by responding to questions sent to their phones. You can use text messaging in quiz programs to gather feedback, consumer opinions, or votes, as well as to inform and entertain. Your customers can have a great time with trivia programs, for example.

A *closed-ended* quiz is a program that gives mobile subscribers a fixed set of response options, such as *a, b, c,* and *d* or *true* and *false*. If a user gets the answer right, you can send a response message saying "You're correct" or "You win." But if the user sends an answer that doesn't match any of the predefined answers, you should send back an error-response message with instructions for answering the question correctly. If the user tries to answer a question twice, you could send a reply like "I'm sorry, you've already answered that question" or "We did not understand your answer."

Setting quiz options

In addition to the typical user-flow program elements listed in "Planning Your Communication Flow," earlier in this chapter, your mobile marketing application provider should be able to provide the following configurable options for a quiz program:

✦ **Question-response format:** Decide which format you'll use for user responses, such as alphanumeric selection (*a, b, c,* and *d* or *1, 2, 3,* and *4*), binary choice (*true* and *false* or *yes* and *no*), or individual items (*red, green, blue,* and so on).

✦ **Question order:** Decide whether questions should be delivered in fixed linear order or pulled randomly from a pool of questions. You may want your audience to answer the same five questions in a specific order, or you may have the service pull five questions randomly from a pool of 500, generating a random set of questions for each participant.

✦ **Question count:** Decide how many questions a user must answer to complete the program. If the quiz is configured so that the user has to answer five questions, for example, the mobile marketing application will send the next question in the sequence or pull one randomly (see the preceding item) until all the questions in the campaign sequence are sent and/or the user opts out of the service.

✦ **Auto-response format:** Decide whether each question has a correct answer or is simply being used to collect user input (see the next section, "Setting response options"). In either case, you also need to decide when to send an individual text message to the mobile subscriber: after each answer (correct or incorrect) or upon completion of the quiz, for example.

Ratings by the pint: An interactive Guinness program

The Great Guinness Pint contest is an example of an interactive program. The program, which ran in 2008, allowed consumers to rate their pints of Guinness directly via mobile phone. Each time a consumer rated a pint, she was entered for a chance to win a trip to the Guinness brewery in Dublin, Ireland, for the company's 250th anniversary celebration. Participating accounts received recognition for the quality of pints they served. Each account owner, along with the Guinness team, tracked ratings in real time directly on a mobile phone as well as online. In addition to tracking progress, the Guinness team added or edited an account on the fly. When a new account was added, a keyword was generated automatically, allowing consumers to participate immediately.

Here's how the program worked: Throughout a participating account's bar, various point-of-sale (POS) materials were displayed, such as coasters, table tents, posters, and custom pint-rating cards. These POS materials encouraged customers to help Guinness find the greatest pint in America. Consumers were directed to text the word *great* (or a unique keyword assigned to each account) to 88500; when they did, they were prompted to rate the pint of Guinness that they were just served. Each POS material educated consumers on what makes a pint great, above and beyond taste.

In developing this program, John Lim, chief executive officer of Mobile Card Cast, knew that its success would be driven by the competitive nature of Guinness accounts and by high participation levels among consumers. Therefore, he used simple Short Message Service (SMS) technology to create ease of use for consumers and to allow account owners to access rankings through a simple mobile landing page. The following figure shows an example of the marketing materials used to promote the program within an establishment.

Setting response options

You may run a quiz that doesn't have correct or incorrect answers; you just want a response. In this case, you don't have to specify the response options as being correct or incorrect. All responses are simply accepted and recorded. Following are a few examples of response options you can set:

✦ **Clue:** If your program supports a clue element, users can request a clue to answer a question. Suppose that a user is stuck on question 3. If he texts *clue* or *hint* to the mobile marketing application, the application sends back a clue for the question — in this case, question 3.

✦ **Action on incorrect response:** Decide what happens when users give incorrect responses. If a user gets question 3 wrong, for example, does she simply start over or move on to the next question until the campaign question count is reached? (For more information about question count, refer to "Setting quiz options," earlier in this chapter.)

✦ **Response timing:** You can choose to run a speed quiz that measures the speed of user responses. The fastest responder may win, for example.

✦ **Participation cap:** You may want to set a participation cap to limit how many times users can participate in the program during a given period — one to ten times a day, once a week, once a month, one time only, or unlimited times through the entire program, for example.

✦ **Repeat questions:** Decide whether to configure the service so that users receive some questions more than once or whether they always get different questions.

✦ **Premium billing:** Decide whether to bill mobile subscribers for participation in the program. (For details on making money with your mobile marketing programs, see Book VIII, Chapter 6.)

Figure 3-5 shows some example quiz-response settings.

You can also use the application for quizzes to direct mobile subscribers to a particular next step in an application's user flow, such as a product offering (a content storefront, for example) or another text-messaging campaign or service. You can use the response to a question to initiate a mobile subscriber into a horoscope program, for example. When the subscriber answers the question, his response is used to configure the next question to be sent to his phone.

Gathering input with open-ended survey questions

You can use open-ended, text-messaging survey programs to gather information such as consumer, candidate, or employee feedback. After a job interview, for example, you could send the candidate a text message like this: "Please give us your feedback on the interview process. Reply to this message with your feedback."

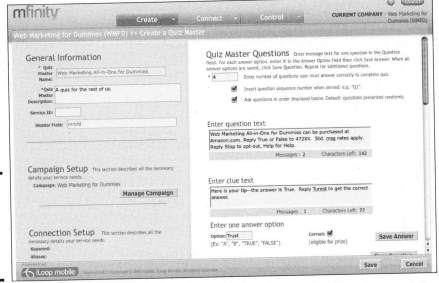

Figure 3-5:
Quiz
template
in a mobile
marketing
application.

Unlike questions in quizzes (refer to "Using quizzes to gather information and entertain," earlier in this chapter), survey questions sent to mobile subscribers' phones don't have preconfigured response options, such as multiple choice or true/false. Rather, subscribers are asked a question and invited to send free-form responses. You may ask a mobile subscriber "What's your e-mail address?" for example. When he answers this question, the mobile marketing application automatically sends out the next question, and the process repeats until all the required questions have been sent and answered.

Ask your mobile marketing application provider whether you can chain your survey program, or even your quiz programs, with any other mobile marketing programs you're running. When you chain one program to another, you can do really cool things. Suppose that a user is opting in to your couponing program. If you chain a survey template to the coupon service, you can collect the user's preferences and other personal information before you allow her to opt in and get the coupon.

Planning the survey

In planning a survey program, you need to consider the following points:

✦ **How many questions to ask:** Don't go overboard. If you ask too many questions, people will simply drop out without completing their participation in your program.

**Book VIII
Chapter 3**

**Running Mobile
Communication
Campaigns**

+ **The order in which questions will be asked:** Think about the order in which you ask the questions. Does some flow make particular sense?

+ **The required length of answers:** Remember that most people don't have mobile phones with full keyboards, and pecking out long messages can be tedious for them. Try to limit the information you need to short responses.

Setting survey options

In addition to the typical user-flow program elements listed in "Planning Your Communication Flow," earlier in this chapter, your mobile marketing application provider should be able to provide the following configurable options for your survey program:

+ **Question count:** Decide how many questions a user must answer to complete the program.

+ **Question order:** Decide whether questions are always delivered in fixed linear order or pulled randomly from a pool of questions.

+ **Question labels:** Make sure that your mobile marketing application allows you to use a configuration tool to label your survey questions. Later, when you data-mine and report on the survey responses, the labels will help you sort and organize the data. (For details on reporting on your programs, see Book VIII, Chapter 7.)

Calling People to Action: Polling

In *polls* (also referred to as *votes*), unlike quizzes and surveys, the questions you want your audience members to answer are placed in traditional or new media: billboards; in-store end caps; newspapers; television, e-mail, and radio programs; and so on. Like quizzes and surveys, however, polling allows you to gather audience members' opinions and feedback as well as to inform and entertain.

In mobile marketing, a poll poses questions not in a text message but in traditional media. Mobile subscribers see or hear the call to action (such as "Text *a* or *b* to cast your vote"), and when they respond, the mobile marketing application sends a reply (such as "Thanks. You voted *a*. Total tally: *a* 35%, *b* 6%, *c* 59%"). See Figure 3-6 for an example poll user flow and Figure 3-7 for a dynamic poll report.

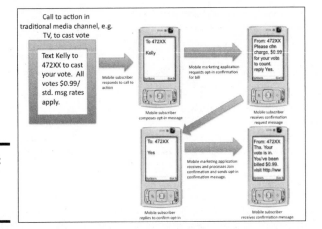

Figure 3-6:
Standard
poll user
flow.

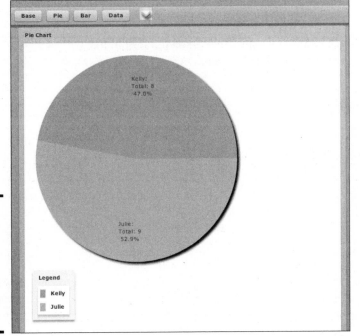

Figure 3-7:
Dynamic
chart for
polling,
displayed
on the Web
or on public
screens.

**Book VIII
Chapter 3**

**Running Mobile
Communication
Campaigns**

Choosing a poll type

Following are some of the most common uses of mobile polling and voting:

◆ **Television voting/polling:** During the 2008 "American Idol" season, the show's exclusive mobile-carrier sponsor, AT&T, reported that more than 78 million votes were submitted over its network. Another popular show, "Deal or No Deal," uses voting for mobile sweepstakes campaigns, and sports and news shows use polls to discern the opinions of audience members.

◆ **Live-event polling and voting:** Increasingly, polling and voting are being used in live events such as sporting events, keynote speeches, and radio broadcasts. The call to action for the poll is placed in traditional media, and people respond. Then the results of the poll are displayed on the stadium's in-venue display screens, on a screen behind the speaker, or on the radio station's Web site.

If you expect high-volume interactions — hundreds of thousands or even millions of messages in just a few hours — be sure to consult your mobile marketing application provider and connection aggregator. They can fine-tune their systems to ensure that high-volume traffic is processed efficiently. Often, in the case of high-volume programs, the marketer opts to turn off the poll's immediate-message-response feature so that the mobile marketing application can spend all its time processing poll responses. Responses can be sent after all the poll responses are processed.

Be sure to take time zones into account when you decide when the delayed responses should be sent. You don't want to wake people up in the middle of the night.

Setting poll options

In addition to the typical user-flow program elements listed in "Planning Your Communication Flow," earlier in this chapter, your mobile marketing application provider should be able to provide the following configurable options for your poll program:

◆ **Question-response format:** Decide which format you'll use for user responses, such as alphanumeric selection (*a, b, c,* and *d* or *1, 2, 3,* and *4*), binary choice (*true* and *false* or *yes* and *no*), or individual items (*red, green, blue,* and so on).

◆ **Response message:** Decide whether you want to include poll statistics in your response message (such as "Thank you. You voted *a*, and so did 60% of the other participants"). Ask your mobile marketing application provider whether it can support real-time results in your response messages.

Offering Incentives: Gifts, Freebies, Samples, and Coupons

It should come as no surprise to you that people respond to incentives. Offer them something of value, and they'll be more inclined to participate in your program and initiate communication with you. Continue offering them value, and they may become customers. Keep offering them value, and they'll become loyal customers. Keep offering them value after that, and you'll turn them into evangelists who'll start doing your marketing for you. This process starts with the first engagement, and an incentive is a great way to kick-start the interaction.

The most common forms of incentives are

✦ **Money:** Coupons, discounts on services, or even hard cash

✦ **Content:** Free ringtones, wallpapers, images, and so on

✦ **Free stuff and experiences:** Tickets for trial and sample products, free movie admission, a chance to go backstage and meet the star, and so on

In the United States, wireless carriers tend to frown on your offering free content such as ringtones and wallpapers, especially if they're selling the same content via their branded content storefronts on the phone. Free content programs must be preapproved and certified with the wireless carriers, and your best shot at getting approval is offering content that isn't available anywhere else.

Not surprisingly, offering this type of content is also your best shot at getting mobile subscriber participation; many subscribers value unique and/or personalized content.

Managing prize promos, contests, and giveaways

It's common practice in marketing to offer prize promotions, run contests, and give stuff away as incentives to encourage people to participate in marketing programs. You could run a program that gives out small prizes instantly throughout the campaign period and ends by awarding one lucky participant a grand prize, such as a new car or a vacation trip. This format works well in traditional marketing programs, and it works well in mobile marketing programs too.

You can enhance any of your mobile marketing promotions — text-based communication programs, voice programs, mobile Internet programs, and so on — with incentives. The process is simple:

**Book VIII
Chapter 3**

**Running Mobile
Communication
Campaigns**

1. **Promote the incentive along with the call to action to participate.**

2. **Set the odds of winning (often a configurable element) in the mobile marketing application.**

   If you're going to have an instant-win component or a grand prize, configure the odds for that too.

3. **Coordinate with your prize fulfillment house if you're going to be giving away physical goods or services, or configure your mobile marketing application to award content (such as a ringtone) to be consumed on a mobile phone.**

When you run any type of contest, sweepstakes, or giveaway program, you absolutely must work with your legal team to document the rules and the related terms and conditions of your program. The law requires you to provide this documentation. Every state has its own laws about these types of programs, so if you're running a campaign, make sure that you're compliant with all the individual state laws. You can read more about legalities of mobile campaigns in Book VIII, Chapter 1.

Offering mobile coupons

Coupons are very effective tools for driving participation in mobile marketing. In the following sections, I discuss three common ways to deliver coupons to a mobile phone: text messaging, installable applications, and bar codes.

Giving people a taste: Product-sampling programs

Sampling is another fantastic tool you should consider using in your marketing communications programs. For many products, all it takes to get a consumer hooked is that first use. Mobile marketing is a good vehicle for sampling. For digital content, you can deliver a clipped version of the song, a photo with *Preview* stamped on it, and so on. You can't get physical goods (such as a new sports drink) into a phone, however, so your best bet is to mail product samples to program participants or mail them a card that they can use to get the samples free at a local store.

To run a sampling program, promote it in traditional media. When a mobile subscriber responds, you can query him for his address via interactive voice response (IVR; see Book VIII, Chapter 6) or text messaging. (You could use a survey for this purpose.) When you have all the information, you can thank the user and send him a text message saying that he'll get his sample in a few days (barring any delays in shipping).

The mobile marketing company ShopText (www.shoptext.com) has refined this process to an art. With ShopText, you can set up not only sampling programs, but also commerce programs.

Coupons by text messaging

Text messaging (see Figure 3-8) is by far the most ubiquitous way to deliver coupons to mobile phones. As in any mobile marketing program, users can request the coupons by responding to your promos in traditional media, or if they've given you consent, you can push a coupon to them.

Text coupons are alphanumeric codes consisting of letters, symbols, and/or numbers (*a23bcs-win,* for example). Your mobile marketing application can generate the coupon codes automatically. Alternatively, the application can generate the codes from a spreadsheet containing your own coupons — coupons that are compatible with your POS system or Web site. All the mobile subscriber needs to do to redeem the coupon is show the coupon code to a store employee (if you're using a POS system) or complete a form on your Web site.

The most challenging part of closing the loop of coupon marketing is POS redemptions. Make sure that you train your people, or your client's people, so that they know what to do when a mobile subscriber brings a mobile coupon into the store.

From: 472XX

Booty Call! Take 20% all boots @ Shops Shoes for Less now through Sunday, 10/05/08. show your phone in-store to save on fall's most fabulous footwear!

Options   Back

Figure 3-8:
Coupon
in text
message.

Coupons from installable applications

Another way to deliver coupons is to work with a couponing wallet company such as CellFire (see Figure 3-9). Couponing wallet companies offer an application that can be downloaded to a mobile subscriber's phone. The application maintains all the coupons locally on the phone and continuously reaches out to the coupon server via an Internet connection on the phone to update itself automatically.

Figure 3-9:
CellFire
couponing.

As with a text coupon, the user simply needs to enter the code in a form on your Web site or show the coupon code on the phone to a store employee.

This method of coupon delivery can be very effective, but it isn't as universally applicable as text messaging for delivering coupons, for several reasons:

✦ The mobile subscriber has to have a phone that supports applications.

✦ The subscriber has to want to install the application.

✦ The subscriber has to know how to use the application.

✦ The subscriber has to be on a data services (Internet) plan with the mobile operator.

These limitations are disappearing fast, however, as mobile subscribers continue to adopt more advanced phones and services.

Coupons through bar codes

Another emerging method of couponing (and ticketing, by the way) is the use of bar codes or QR Codes (another form of bar code). When you use this method, you deliver a 2D or 3D bar code to a user's phone; a special POS scanner scans the bar code and starts the coupon/ticket redemption process. (Traditional in-store scanners can't read a mobile phone's screen reliably, and phone screens are very small, so bar-code data footprints are limited.)

One challenge with this method, however, is that the 2D and 3D scanners can be quite expensive. Although they're common in some countries, such as Japan, they're not widely deployed in the United States. Another challenge is that mobile phones and networks must be configured to support 2D and 3D bar codes. We have a way to go in the United States before this method becomes popular.

One mobile couponing company, bCODE (www.bcode.com), combines text and scanning. The company sends you the coupon via text and gives you a scanner that you can put in your store to scan phones and redeem the coupons.

Applying User-Generated Content

The mobile phone is an extremely personal device for communicating, gathering information, and conducting commerce and exchange, as well as for personal expression. Over the past few years, we've seen a groundswell of user-generated content (UGC, for short). *UGC* is any type of content — videos, pictures, text, news, stories, and so on — that people create and share with their own communities and society at large.

Mobile is a perfect tool for UGC. In fact, some people refer to mobile as the second mouse (the first mouse being the device used with a computer). People use mobile phones to send text messages, take videos, place calls, snap pictures, send e-mail, and so on. Mobile subscribers also use every one of these capabilities to create content.

The following sections provide an overview of some of the most common forms of UGC.

Mobile blogging

Blogging is the practice of maintaining or contributing to a *blog,* which is a Web site (a traditional or mobile Internet site) that features consistently updated commentary on any number of topics, event descriptions, and UGC (videos, pictures, and so on). People commonly use mobile phones for blogging.

From a marketing prospective, you can take advantage of blogging practices by creating a blog and encouraging mobile subscribers to contribute to it, thereby creating a self-sustaining community around your offerings. Your blog can allow users to do the following things:

✦ Send comments, notes, thoughts, and observations to your blog via text messaging, e-mail, or Multimedia Messaging Service (MMS)

✦ Send pictures and videos to the blog

✦ Send audio post to the blog

All you need to do is connect your mobile marketing application with your blogging service, and you're good to go. As your audience members submit content, the content is sent to the blogging service.

It's a really good idea — if not imperative — to have a moderation step between UGC submission and UGC display on the site. In other words, you should use both an automated filter system and a real person to look at all user-submitted content and evaluate its suitability. If the moderator accepts the content, it gets posted on the site immediately. If the moderator deems the content to be unsuitable, she can reject it, and the content isn't displayed.

You can create your own blog or partner with mobile blogging services such as Moblog (www.moblog.net), Watchee (www.watchee.net), and ZapFrog (www.zapfrog.com).

Social networking

Social networking refers to the practice of people interacting with one another, typically on the Internet, about common interests, thoughts, ideas, and activities. In the mobile world, social networking is becoming very popular, because people can use the mobile Web site or installable application to tap into, and communicate with, the network. Depending on your business, mobile social networking also can be an extremely effective marketing channel.

One New York City–based mobile social networking service, buzzd (www. buzzd.com), creates portals to help people find out what's going on around them: local events, concerts, good deals, and so on. Other social networking sites, such as San Francisco–based Zannel (www.zannel.com) and Lightpole (www.lightpole.net), create portal services that allow consumers to interact. Alternatively, you can build your own social network specifically related to your brand and then encourage people to participate in it. Examples include Disney's Club Penguin, a social network for kids (www.clubpenguin.com), and Kodak Gallery, a social network for photography enthusiasts (www.kodakgallery.com).

Many companies can help you build an integrated broadband Internet and mobile social networking service to augment your marketing program. Just peruse the Web, and you'll find a business that can help you.

Text-to-screen and experiential campaigns

Another popular form of UGC is text-to-screen, a simple idea that can create a lot of interaction with live audiences at sporting events, concerts, television broadcasts, and the like. In a text-to-screen program, you place a call to action in traditional media (the giant video screens at a sporting event, a public-address announcement at a concert, or a ticker at the bottom of the TV screen, for example), inviting mobile subscribers to send a text message (such as encouragement for the team or a shout-out to a friend), a photo (such as a picture of a group of friends watching the event), or some other content. When it receives a message of this type, the mobile marketing application places the message in a moderation queue. Then, after the message has been moderated by an automated system and/or live person, it's displayed onscreen at the event for a few seconds.

When U2 toured the United States in 2005, for example, the band used text-to-screen during shows to support the Live 8 antipoverty initiative. U2 asked audience members to text their names to a short code. (For information on short codes, see Book VIII, Chapter 2.) The mobile subscribers' names, along with thousands of other participants' names, were displayed onscreen at the concerts. Later, U2 added up all the names and total participants recorded at all its events and used these figures to show the world that people care about poverty issues.

Another useful application of text-to-screen is to poll audience members during live presentations. Unlike mobile polls (refer to "Calling People to Action: Polling," earlier in this chapter), in which mobile subscribers answer questions, in text-to-screen programs, mobile subscribers ask the questions. You present the call to action during the event, and subscribers text in their question, which you moderate and display onscreen. Then the presenter can look at the screen and provide answers to the audience. This same capability has been used in live events to provide real-time feedback to speakers, but as you might expect, feedback sometimes distracts the speaker, especially if the feedback is negative.

Text-to-screen programs can support interactions with almost anyone. During its annual conference in 2008, for example, the Direct Marketing Association offered a mobile concierge service. Attendees could text in their questions (such as "When will the exhibits close?"), and a person in the information booth would text back the answers via a Web browser.

Tell-a-friend (word-of-mouth) programs

It's generally understood that we're more likely to accept a message coming from a friend, a colleague, or someone we know and trust than from an anonymous person or group. In a *tell-a-friend* program (also referred to as *word of mouth* and *viral marketing*), you can have people share your message with friends rather than communicate it yourself, thereby leveraging existing bonds of trust. You may want to encourage your subscribers to forward mobile coupons or Web site links to their friends in the hope that the community will help you get out your message about your offerings.

Most of the time, people will forward your message simply for the love of sharing interesting things with their friends. If you're running a loyalty program, however, you may want to offer loyalty points or some other form of incentive each time a user forwards a message.

Barack Obama's mobile Web site during the 2008 presidential campaign is a good example. The campaign encouraged site visitors to "share the hope." The call to action asked each site visitor to fill out a form with her name and phone number as well as a friend's name and phone number. (The site could also have asked visitors to enter personal messages, but it didn't.) Soon after the site visitor submitted the form, the friend received a personalized text message including his name, the site visitor's name and phone number, and a list of the "hope" message.

Chapter 4: Launching a Mobile Advertising Campaign

In This Chapter

✔ Recognizing the players in mobile advertising

✔ Placing ads on mobile Internet sites, in the voice channel, and in messaging

✔ Checking out proximity and product-package ads

✔ Adding viral, social, vanity, and charitable elements to mobile marketing

Within the practice of mobile marketing, *mobile advertising* is the paid placement of your marketing messages within mobile media properties. A *mobile media property* is a branded service that uses any of the many mobile paths to reach subscribers and deliver content and services through the mobile channel. (For a review of the mobile paths, see Book VIII, Chapter 1.) A mobile media property could be a classified text-messaging alert service owned and managed by a newspaper, a mobile Web site owned by a movie studio, your own mobile Web site or text-messaging service, or any number of other mobile programs.

Mobile advertising is really no different from any other form of advertising you may conduct in traditional and new media. Its purpose — and the reason you should care about it — is that you can use it to get your message out in the marketplace and in front of members of your target audience so that they know you exist, know what you have to offer, and know what you stand for. If the marketing message that consumers see in your mobile advertising resonates with them, they'll respond to your advertisement and engage in your marketing — participate in your sweepstakes promotion, redeem your coupon, request a product sample, test-drive the car, and so on. In addition, you can make money with mobile advertising.

In this chapter, I review the practice of mobile advertising, starting with an overview of mobile advertising players and their roles. I discuss in detail how to place advertising in the various mobile paths to promote your offerings or to make money. In addition, I discuss how you can use alternative marketing methods such as social, viral, and on-package promotions to get your message into the marketplace.

Reviewing the Mobile Ad Players

Mobile advertising involves two primary players: the buyer and the publisher. You can take on either role or both of these roles. When you take on the first role, you employ mobile advertising by paying to place your marketing message in a mobile media property to generate awareness among members of your audience about your products and services. In the second role, you manage and/or own a mobile media property and sell advertising space — *inventory* — in this property to the buyer. I discuss both roles in more detail in the following sections.

In addition to mobile buyers and mobile publishers, two players are very important and worth mentioning: mobile advertising network aggregators and mobile search providers. Both roles are important in the mobile marketing ecosystem because they bring mobile buyers and publishers together. The section on mobile advertising enablers introduces you to their roles in mobile marketing.

Playing the role of mobile buyer

When you play the role of mobile buyer, you're looking to buy space for your ad in someone else's media property.

A newspaper such as *USA Today,* for example, may have an opt-in database of mobile messaging subscribers for its market-news media property, and its list of subscribers might fit the profile of your target audience. So, if you want to reach these people, you can decide to advertise with the newspaper by buying a certain number of ad *impressions* — the number of times the publisher shows or includes your ad in the alert service.

Mobile advertising, like other advertising media, is often sold through one of the following business models:

✦ **CPM (cost per thousand):** You buy your advertising based on blocks of 1,000 impressions, such as $15 to $25 for every 1,000 people exposed to your ad.

✦ **CPC (cost per click):** You pay for your advertising only if someone clicks the ad.

✦ **CPA (cost per acquisition):** You pay for your advertising only if you acquire a consumer. *Acquiring* a consumer means that the person becomes a lead, buys something, and so on.

Mobile advertising rates vary greatly by brand, media property, and frequency and length of your purchase (the more you buy, the better price you get). In December 2008, *Advertising Age* reported that mobile advertising had a response rate of 1.5 percent compared to 0.5 percent for other media. Many brands report significantly higher rates.

Playing the role of mobile publisher

A *mobile publisher* is someone who owns and controls a mobile media property. A good example of a media property is the mobile Web site operated by The Weather Channel Interactive (TWCI; `http://weather.mobi`). TWCI sells ads on this site, which happens to be one of the most popular mobile Internet sites in the United States. (For more information, see the sidebar "TWCI and Hampton Inn," later in this chapter.)

You can be a mobile publisher yourself if you have a mobile property — such as a mobile Internet site, Short Message Service (SMS) subscriber list, Bluetooth, or other mobile media property that leverages the various mobile paths and is used by a target audience that a buyer is interested in reaching.

As a publisher, you can sell ad inventory on your mobile Internet site. You could sell 500,000 ad banner impressions on your site's homepage (assuming that it generates this volume of traffic), for example. A mobile buyer would purchase this ad inventory from you because your site's visitors meet its target audience profile. As publisher, you would ensure that the ad is placed on the homepage of your site and displayed at least 500,000 times over a specified period (which you negotiated with the mobile buyer) and in rotation alongside other ads you've already sold or will sell.

If you have a well-trafficked site and are willing to place advertising on it, you can make money directly from mobile advertising by selling your inventory to a buyer under one of the business models (CPM, CPC, or CPA) discussed in "Playing the role of mobile buyer," earlier in this chapter. You can do the same for your messaging, e-mail, and other mobile properties.

Understanding the role of mobile advertising enablers

Advertising is a means of getting your message out to the market. It is a tool to let your audience know about your offerings and the value you add. It can also be used as a monetization vehicle to compensate you for your content as you provide it free to users or as you sell space in your media properties. In mobile marketing, mobile advertising network aggregators and mobile search providers fulfill this role of advertising by bringing mobile buyers and publishers together.

✦ **Mobile Advertising Network Aggregators** are companies that align advertising buyers with publishers and provide mobile advertising management applications. There are literally hundreds of them. The leading players in the mobile field include Google/DoubleClick, Yahoo!, Third Screen Media, Ringleader Digital, Millennial Media, JumpTap, 4Info, Quattro Wireless, and others.

✦ **Mobile Search Providers** are companies that enable both paid placement and organic search services for mobile networks. Mobile search provides yet another means for the mobile subscriber to find out about you and your offerings. Leading providers include Google, Yahoo!, JumpTap, Medio Systems, MCN, and others.

Placing Ads on Mobile Internet Sites

Ads on mobile Internet sites are among the most common types of mobile advertising. Mobile Internet-site ads come in two forms:

✦ **Image banners:** Images of varying sizes that depict the ad and its call to action

✦ **Text banners:** Text blocks of varying sizes that depict the ad and its call to action

Figure 4-1 provides examples of both image and text banners.

For a detailed review of creating and managing mobile advertising, see the Mobile Marketing Association's Mobile Advertising Guidelines at `www.mmaglobal.com/mobileadvertising.pdf`.

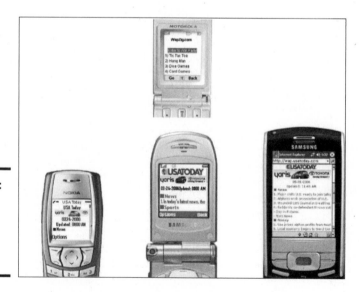

Figure 4-1:
Example mobile-ad image and text banners.

Placing ads on your own site

Integrating advertising into your own mobile Internet site is relatively easy. As I discuss in Book VIII, Chapter 1, you can take many approaches to implementing mobile marketing programs, including building a mobile Internet site.

You can use either of two methods to include advertising in your mobile Web Internet sites and pages:

✦ **Use a mobile Internet visual editor.** Mobile Internet visual editors make placing ads on your mobile Internet site a snap. These editors are integrated with the leading mobile advertising networks. You simply need to get your account credentials (such as user name and password) from the mobile advertising aggregator, paste this information into the editor, and click Save to insert an ad placeholder into your site. When a mobile subscriber visits your site, the mobile marketing application reaches out to the aggregator's system, requests an ad, places the ad on the site, and displays it to the mobile subscriber — all in a matter of seconds. See Figure 4-2 for an example of a mobile Internet site visual editor.

✦ **Paste code into your pages.** If you're not using a visual editor but are simply working in code, getting an ad onto your mobile Internet site may take a few more steps but is definitely doable.

First, you need to verify that your mobile marketing application is integrated with one or more mobile advertising networks. If not, have a member of your technical team or your mobile applications provider contact a mobile advertising network aggregator to ask what it will take to integrate your application(s) with the ad network. Then you can paste the ad-insertion code (supplied by the mobile advertising network provider) into your mobile Internet page. When the code is inserted, the ad is pulled into the mobile Internet site and displayed in the same manner as an ad inserted with a visual editor.

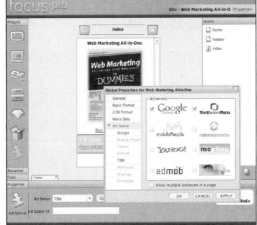

Figure 4-2:
Inserting ads into a mobile Internet site with a visual editor.

**Book VIII
Chapter 4**

Launching a
Mobile Advertising
Campaign

Placing ads on a branded site

Placing ads on a promotional mobile Internet site can be a very effective way to create a presence and boost brand recognition for your programs. Figure 4-3 shows an example: the promotional mobile Internet site for Jaguar XF.

dotMobi (`www.dotmobi.mobi`), the organization that oversees the `.mobi` top-level domain, reported during the Direct Marketing Association's October 2008 conference in Las Vegas, Nevada, that the Jaguar XF branded mobile content site drew more than 85,000 unique visitors from 15 million mobile ad units placed on a variety of mobile Internet sites — a 0.57 percent click-through rate. These unique visitors downloaded more than 12,000 videos and more than 16,000 wallpapers from the site. In addition, 2.6 percent of the visitors requested test drives, and 1.6 percent requested physical brochures. All in all, these results are impressive for a high-end luxury product advertised through the mobile Internet.

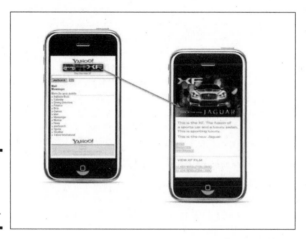

Figure 4-3: Jaguar XF branded content site.

Advertising during page loads and downloads

Another form of mobile advertising is displaying image and text banners on a mobile Internet site during the dead time while pages are loading or content is being downloaded to the phone. This method of mobile advertising is referred to as *bumper screen* advertising. (You may also hear it referred to as *splash, jump-page,* or *interstitial* advertising.) Bumper ads are unobtrusive, and when implemented effectively, they provide information that is both useful and immediately actionable for the mobile subscriber. If someone is downloading a movie trailer, for example, you could show her an ad listing showtimes and locations for every movie in her town.

Figure 4-4 shows an example of bumper advertising. This image would be displayed on the phone while a page is loading or an application is downloading.

Figure 4-4:
Bumper
advertising.

Advertising on a network of mobile Internet sites

Yet another way to get your message into the market is to work with a mobile advertising network aggregator that will syndicate your ad across a network of mobile Internet sites. The value of this type of ad buy is that you can increase the acreage of sites on which your ads are seen during a short period. The downside is that you lose some control of where your ads go. They might end up on sites, or near other ads, that you don't want your brand to be associated with.

You can instruct your mobile ad network partner on your ad placement preferences, and your partner should do its best to follow them. Given the fact that ad network systems are automated, however, you have no guarantee of strict adherence to your preferences.

Placing outside ads on your mobile Internet site

As I discuss in "Playing the role of mobile publisher," earlier in this chapter, you can also play the role of mobile publisher, selling space on your site to marketers who want to gain access to your audience. Selling inventory on your site is a great way to make some money as well as to generate affinity with the brands you're working with.

Many mobile advertising network providers have formed partnerships with mobile application providers or have developed a services arm to help you build a mobile Web site. Also, many mobile application providers have developed relationships with mobile advertising network providers. If you're struggling with getting started, contact your partner of choice and ask for help.

TWCI and Hampton Inn

In 2007, Hampton Inn was looking for new ways to reach its ideal target audience: people who have traveled for business or leisure in the past year. The Weather Channel Interactive (TWCI) serves exactly this demographic. TWCI's mobile Internet site, The Weather Channel Mobile (`http://weather.mobi`), gives users access to hourly forecasts, current conditions, severe-weather warnings, and radar maps for thousands of cities worldwide. The site also offers innovative ad products, including geotargeting and weather-triggered ads. (For more information on geotargeting, see Book IV, Chapter 7.)

Given the perfect fit between its desired target audience and the visitor profile on TWCI's mobile Internet site, Hampton Inn decided to run a mobile advertising campaign, placing banners on TWCI's site. According to TWCI, the program raised message association with Hampton Inn versus other hotel brands and produced the following results:

✔ Respondents' overall favorable impression of Hampton Inn was higher among those who were exposed to the mobile ads (62 percent) than among those who weren't exposed to the ads (48 percent).

✔ Respondents who were exposed to the ads were 11.4 percent more likely to stay at a Hampton Inn during their next trip.

As this case shows, mobile advertising can pay and show demonstrable results. See the following figure for an example of the TWCI mobile Internet site.

Placing Ads in Mobile Messages

You can place ads in text messages to offset the costs of messaging or to generate advertising revenue. You might want to broadcast 1 million messages, for example, but don't want to incur the application or messaging costs associated with such a campaign. In that case, you can partner with a messaging mobile ad network aggregator, which will manage the transmission of the messages and cover some or all of the messaging costs in exchange for placing advertisements in the messages. That is, the aggregator will use the money made from the advertising as both an offset for its costs and as a revenue source. Similarly, you can take in advertising revenue for including ads in your messaging.

Advertising is commonly used in two types of mobile messaging: Short Message Service (SMS) and Multimedia Messaging Service (MMS). I cover both types in the following sections. Also see Book VIII, Chapter 1 for more information about mobile messaging technology.

Combining advertising and SMS

You can combine advertising with SMS messaging in two ways:

✦ Make the entire message an ad or incentive (such as a mobile coupon).

✦ Place the ad at the beginning of the message (*prepend* it) or at the end of the message (*append* it).

The first method of mobile advertising is self-explanatory, but an example can help explain the latter method.

A text message consists of a plain-text, alphanumeric message consisting of no more than 160 characters. When advertising is sold in SMS text messaging alongside content, the 35 to 40 characters at the end typically are reserved for the ad. If you're offering a horoscope service, for example, you make money on the messaging through advertising rather than charging the consumer via premium Short Message Service (PSMS). (For details on making money with mobile marketing, see Book VIII, Chapter 6.)

Figure 4-5 shows an example of a text-message advertisement.

Figure 4-5:
Mobile
advertising
inserted
into an SMS
message.

To see earn how to deliver full-ad SMS messages, ad-enhanced SMS messages, or both, see the sections on alert messaging in Chapter 5 of this minibook.

Displaying ads with MMS

MMS messages are delivered in the same way as SMS messages, but when they're opened, the user's experience is different. An MMS message can be anything from static text or a static picture to an animated picture with text, or it can provide a rich multimedia experience including text, images, and sound. When you place advertising in an MMS message, then, it could be presented as text; as a banner image; as an audio effect; or as a combination of media, either static or animated.

The challenge is that very few phones and networks currently support this type of messaging. This type of advertising really isn't practical today, but it will be common soon.

Going Local with Location-Based and On-Package Advertising

Location plays a critical role in successful mobile marketing because location is a significant element of marketing relevancy and context. If you can combine location with other information about a mobile subscriber, you can generate extremely targeted and contextually relevant engagements. Making your marketing *relevant* means that you're providing an experience that is appropriate for the individual subscriber. *Context* is a key to relevance, which means taking into account many factors — including setting, time, and location — to tailor the message you send to an individual subscriber.

We are far from being able to use location for mobile marketing universally and ubiquitously, but some early options are available. In the following sections, I discuss a few ways that you can use location to enhance your mobile marketing and advertising.

Proximity advertising

Proximity advertising (or *proximity marketing*) is a form of marketing in which mobile marketing and advertising are conducted in a specific location, such as a mall or a movie theater.

In proximity marketing, you have to be able to detect the presence of a wireless device within, at, or near a specific location — a *proximity*. Book VIII, Chapter 1 describes many methods that you can use to identify a mobile subscriber's location; the most common today (besides those employed with installable applications) are Bluetooth and Wi-Fi. I discuss both methods in the following sections.

Bluetooth proximity marketing

Bluetooth proximity marketing uses Bluetooth technology: a low-bandwidth radio frequency that is used to *pair* (connect) a mobile phone with another device. In the case of Bluetooth proximity marketing, that other device is a Bluetooth *access point:* a small Internet-enabled transmitter that can detect a nearby Bluetooth-enabled device, such as a mobile phone.

You need consistent power and a hard-wired or wireless Internet connection for the access point so that you can update it with new content remotely and don't have to visit it every few days to change the batteries.

To practice Bluetooth proximity marketing, you install and activate an access point in a public area, such as a mall, bus stop, movie theater, airport, or park. When a mobile subscriber walks by your access point, if his phone is set to receive Bluetooth requests automatically, his phone will beep, and he'll be given the option to accept or reject the connection request from your access point. If he accepts the request, the Bluetooth access point sends your advertising message or content — such as text, image, ringtone, game, installable application, or MMS message — to his phone.

Wi-Fi proximity marketing

Wi-Fi proximity marketing is very similar to Bluetooth proximity marketing except that the Wi-Fi version is passive rather than active. That is, Wi-Fi access-point broadcasts are passive and don't send connection requests to nearby mobile devices.

For Wi-Fi proximity marketing to work, you have to have traditional media signage to inform mobile subscribers that a Wi-Fi access point is nearby and to ask them to look for and connect to it.

This type of proximity marketing has limited applicability today. Although nearly all new mobile phones sold today support Bluetooth, Wi-Fi features are limited to high-end smartphones, such as Apple's iPhone, Google's Android, and the Nokia E71.

Packaging and point-of-sale advertising and promotion

Advertising your services on product packaging and at point of sale (POS) are great ways to get someone's attention. The following sections describe both methods.

Advertising on product packaging

In packaging-related mobile advertising, you need to decide where to place your call to action: on the package or inside the package.

If the call to action is on the package, mobile subscribers can participate in your program without buying the product. You can assume that the mobile subscriber is in a store and may be interested in buying the product or finding out more about it. In that case, you can use one of the opt-in methods discussed in Book VIII, Chapter 2 to invite a mobile subscriber to get a coupon, join an alert service, take a poll, or participate in any number of mobile marketing campaigns discussed throughout this minibook.

If the call to action is inside the package, the mobile subscriber must buy the product to get details on how to participate in the program.

Even if the call to action is inside the package, you should include a call to action on the package to inform mobile subscribers that details on the promotion are inside.

You can use package-based promotions for any number of campaigns, including the following:

✦ **Content promotions:** You may want to give away some content (such as a ringtone, wallpaper, or video), but consumers have to buy the product to get that content. One example is a 2007 Burger King program that placed a redemption code on Whopper wrappers. Customers could text in the code to receive promotional content, including ringtones.

✦ **Loyalty points:** Mobile subscribers can obtain and redeem loyalty points if they buy the product. You could place a redemption code under the label or cap of a drink bottle, for example. Consumers could take off the label or cap to find the code and text in that code to obtain their points.

Point-of-sale advertising

Point-of-sale (also referred to as *point-of-purchase*) advertising occurs at the physical locations where you display and sell your products and services. A POS location may be at a store you own, at one of the distribution and retail sites you work with, or on the Internet. Based on this physical location, you can discern some level of local context. The mobile subscriber could be at a supermarket and may want some milk, for example, or she could be at a movie theater and may be interested in wolfing down a bag of popcorn and a megasize soft drink.

Mobile marketing and mobile advertising at POS are similar to on-package promotions (discussed in the preceding section), but rather than placing ads on products, you place ads within the store: on cash registers, on refrigerator doors, on floors, on shelves, or any other places where members of your target audience may see them.

Effective POS promotions include coupons, redemption and loyalty programs, and related incentives that may encourage consumers to frequent the establishment or draw attention to your products and services. These programs also focus on the use of mass market paths rather than niche-market paths (see Book VIII, Chapter 1).

Speaking to Your Audience through Voice-Call Ads

Another emerging mobile advertising medium is voice calls. Although piping advertising announcements into integrated voice response (IVR) systems isn't new (see Chapter 1 of this minibook for details on IVR), what *is* new is the ability to detect that the caller is on a mobile phone. You can take advantage of this information to leverage the rich, interactive, multimodal capability of the mobile phone.

When a mobile subscriber hears an ad during a voice call, the ad typically includes prompts instructing the listener to press or say a number. If the mobile subscriber responds to a prompt, your IVR system and mobile marketing application, working in tandem, can interpret the subscriber's action as an initial opt-in and trigger various messaging and content-delivery processes. If you play an ad for a new car, for example, the audio prompt could say something like this: "To get more details on this car via the mobile Internet, say or press 1, and we'll text-message you a link."

This simple example is just the beginning. You can use the same response structure to initiate any of the following:

✦ Mobile communication programs, such as trivia, quizzes, polls, and sampling (Book VIII, Chapter 3)

✦ Mobile couponing programs (Book VIII, Chapter 3)

✦ Mobile content-delivery programs (Book VIII, Chapter 5)

✦ Mobile commerce (Book VIII, Chapter 6)

✦ Mobile customer care (Book VIII, Chapter 2)

You can work with several mobile voice advertising networks, including Jingle Networks (www.jinglenetworks.com), Unwired Nation (www.unwirednation.com), and Pudding Media (www.puddingmedia.com). For details on one network's service, see the nearby sidebar, "FREE411: Advertising at your fingertips."

FREE411: Advertising at your fingertips

FREE411, offered by Jingle Networks, is an advertising-sponsored telephone directory service. Mobile subscribers can call 1-800-FREE411 to receive both residential and business phone numbers and addresses, as in any other voice-enabled directory service. What makes this service different is that it's free (at least monetarily) to mobile subscribers. Subscribers need to listen to a couple of ads, but they pay no surcharges — which often are $1.50 or more per call — to obtain a directory listing.

FREE411 directory listings are voice enabled and default to live agents if necessary, and all the ads are interactive. If a subscriber chooses to receive an ad, he just presses the prompted key.

Adding Viral and Cause Elements to Mobile Advertising Campaigns

Cause and viral marketing and activities can provide a significant boost to any of your mobile marketing programs. *Cause marketing* refers to the association of your brand with a cause, such as the fight against cancer, whereas *viral marketing* refers to the phenomenon of members of your audience sharing your marketing among themselves.

Both types of marketing practices are extremely effective in generating awareness for you and your brand in the early stages of customer acquisition and relationship building.

The following sections review a variety of cause and viral marketing elements that you can use to enhance your mobile marketing and advertising programs.

Managing viral marketing elements

Viral marketing (also called *word-of-mouth* or *tell-a-friend* marketing; see Chapter 1 of this minibook) encourages members of your audience to spread your message among themselves. This type of marketing can reduce your marketing costs significantly and get your message to the market quickly. To use viral marketing effectively, however, you have to run a program that people can become passionate about: a cause, a vanity program, a social program, a charitable program, or something that is simply humorous and fun. (I discuss all these types of programs later in the chapter.)

Viral marketing works because people are more likely to accept and trust a message that comes from someone they know — such as a friend, a colleague, or a family member — than they are to trust a message from an anonymous person or group. In viral marketing, you can ask your audience members to share your message rather than distribute the message yourself. In other words, you can leverage social bonds of trust to get your message out.

You could encourage members of your audience to forward mobile coupons or mobile Web-site links to their friends. Or you could create a series of viral videos, such as the "Will It Blend?" series on YouTube (`www.youtube.com/user/Blendtec`), that people will find funny and send on to their friends. Again, you do this in the hope that people will share your message with their communities.

Setting up a viral marketing program requires only a few simple steps:

1. **Find a mobile application provider that supports viral marketing within its application, or build the application yourself.**

2. **Create your program.**

   If you're working with a mobile marketing application provider, you create a form on your Web or mobile Internet site, with spaces for the names and phone numbers of both the sender and the recipient of the message. (Use either a visual editor or code for this purpose, as described in "Placing ads on your own site," earlier in this chapter.)

3. **Set up the service to respond to the form after a visitor fills it out.**

   When a site visitor submits her forward request on the site you've set up, the mobile marketing application configures the personalized message and sends it out (see Figure 4-6).

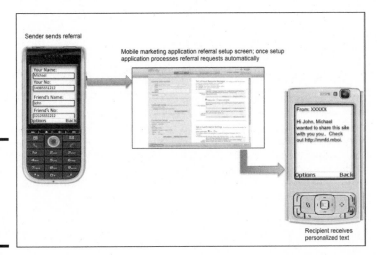

Figure 4-6: Example of viral marketing setup and user flow.

Using mobile marketing to keep kids in school

With four of every ten students dropping out of high school in the United States every year, the Ad Council's BoostUp program (see www.boostup.org) is an important social-marketing initiative, because it focuses on changing a damaging social trend. Early in the development of the program, the Ad Council and the program sponsors recognized that to reach their target audience — struggling teenagers — they needed to go where the teenagers are. Consequently, they deployed Internet, social networking, widgets, and mobile marketing to grab and retain the attention of their audience members and of society at large.

Viral marketing can happen with any form of mobile marketing, not just personalized messaging. You can encourage participants in your programs to forward text messages, IVR dial codes, pictures, and so on. The key is to be creative with the content and build incentives that encourage people to forward your material.

Leaning on vanity marketing

Vanity marketing involves marketing to mobile subscribers' self-interest and desire for intimacy and real-time interaction. It gives subscribers a sense of being part of an exclusive club and having access to something special. Examples of vanity marketing include the following:

✦ Allowing subscribers to associate themselves with celebrities by including widgets or links to stories about the celebrities within the subscribers' own sites

✦ Using a social network to feature subscribers who respond to some loyalty or incentive program

✦ Bringing subscribers onstage during a live event and awarding them a prize, or bringing them backstage to meet celebrities

By combining vanity marketing with mobile marketing, you acquire powerful tools for developing relationships with your customers.

Stimulating social interactions

Social marketing is marketing that strives to achieve changes in specific social behavior for the betterment of society. Like all the other forms of marketing discussed in this chapter, social marketing can apply to all marketing and advertising campaigns.

Changing the world with your fingertips

Jim Manis, one of the mobile industry's most influential players, founded the Mobile Giving Foundation (MGF) after the sale of his company m-Qube to VeriSign in 2007. Manis and the team at MGF have set up a program in which MGF-certified charities, partners, and participating carriers can organize charitable-donation programs using PSMS as the means of capturing mobile subscribers' donations. As in any PSMS program, you promote the call to action; people respond to it and donate; and

nearly 100 percent of the donation makes its way to the MGF-certified charity.

A 501(c)3 or related charity can contact the MGF to go through the certification process and use the mobile channel to make money. A company that wants to make a difference and be socially responsible can use the mobile channel to promote an MGF-certified program. For more information, visit `www.mobilegiving.org`.

Many of the most influential social-marketing programs in the United States are set up and run by the Ad Council on behalf of specific organizations. Following are some of the best-known programs:

+ **Smokey the Bear:** A program that builds awareness about the dangers of forest fires

+ **Feed the Pig:** A program that encourages responsible personal financial management

+ **BoostUp:** A program designed to prevent high-school students from dropping out (see the nearby sidebar "Using mobile marketing to keep kids in school")

These programs are perfect examples of social marketing, because each one has both a mobile marketing element and a mobile advertising element. For more information, visit the Ad Council Web site at `www.adcouncil.org`.

Supporting a cause

Cause marketing is the cooperative use of marketing by a for-profit business and a nonprofit organization for mutual benefit. The business gets to align itself with the value of the nonprofit organization, and the nonprofit organization gets the opportunity to draw attention to its activities and possibly recruit new volunteers and donors.

The mobile channel is ideal for capturing charitable donations. You can mobile-enhance any marketing program and put a call to action in this marketing to elicit a response from your audience. In the case of mobile charitable-donation programs, the response you're looking for is a financial contribution.

Book VIII Chapter 4

Launching a Mobile Advertising Campaign

The most effective of these channels for charitable donations is PSMS, because mobile subscribers don't need to register for a service or use a credit card; the donation can go straight to a subscriber's mobile phone bill, and nearly 100 percent of the donation can be passed to the participating charity. (A small percentage of the donation is reserved for administration fees.) Organizations that use PSMS for this purpose include the American Red Cross (`www.redcross.org`) and Susan G. Komen for the Cure (`http://ww3.komen.org/home`). For more information on using PSMS for charitable donations, see the nearby sidebar, "Changing the world with your fingertips."

Chapter 5: Delivering Valuable Mobile Content

In This Chapter

✔ Developing and distributing mobile content

✔ Adding value with mobile applications, enhancements, and games

✔ Setting up a mobile Internet site

✔ Broadcasting your message in audio and video

✔ Providing branded utility services

Customers are looking for value — that is, they want to acquire content and goods, as well as engage in experiences that they find to be genuinely useful, informative, educational, enriching, delightful, or entertaining. The mobile channel is an ideal medium for value exchange.

Perhaps you want to send content produced by your business; use content as a promotional offer to create awareness for your business; or offer points and coupons that can be redeemed for content, experiences, or products and services. Or maybe you want to generate brand utility by offering store locators, nutrition or financial calculators, shopping-comparison widgets, and similar services. If so, you've come to the right chapter.

When you're done with this chapter, you'll understand what it takes to create, manage, and deliver content to mobile subscribers via mobile marketing services: alerts, installed applications, Web sites, the mobile Internet, loyalty programs, and so on.

Sourcing Your Mobile Content

You can create your own content, or you can license it from third-party content providers and/or content aggregators. For details on working with content providers, see Chapter 1 of this minibook.

Before you use content created by someone else as the basis of your own mobile content, be sure to check with the content rights holder about any licensing or use restrictions. Don't get yourself into trouble by using someone else's content without all the necessary rights and licenses. Just because the content is out on the Web doesn't mean that you have the right to use it or create a derivative work from it (change and/or rebrand someone else's content for your own purposes).

The safest, but not necessarily easiest, way to obtain mobile content is to create it yourself or contract someone to do it for you.

Here are some tips to remember before you create your content or prepare to use someone's third-party content:

✦ **Get permission.** You must always have permission (also referred to as *expressed* or *prior consent*) from mobile subscribers before you can send them a text message. See Book VIII, Chapter 1 for details on industry best practices and regulations.

✦ **Be relevant.** Send your audience members only information that is relevant to them. The mobile phone is a very personal device. If customers find that you're abusing their trust — such as sending them messages about some new hot product when the subscribers didn't opt in for that information — they're likely to perceive your message as irrelevant at best or spam at worst and to opt out of our program faster than you can text *stop*.

Relevance involves many factors. Don't look just at audience demographics, but also look at subscriber preferences, the times when messages are sent, subscribers' locations when receiving messages, and so on. Relevance is about taking the time to understand your customers and their needs and wants.

Sending Content via Messaging

Using the messaging paths, including Short Message Service (SMS), can be a very effective means of delivering content. This section describes how you can use text-messaging alert services to send content.

Sending text alerts to a group

Mobile text alerts are very common content programs, broadcasting SMS or Multimedia Messaging Service (MMS) text messages to subscribers who have given the marketers permission to send those messages. (For details about these technologies, see o Book VIII, Chapter 1.) You can send the same content to an entire group or a tailored message to each person. I discuss both methods in the following sections.

Sourcing text content

To send text alerts as content, you need to create or acquire your text content and ensure that it's formatted properly for text messaging.

Creating text content is easy. All you need are a text editor (such as Notepad or Microsoft Word), your computer keyboard, and some creativity to create compelling messages of no more than 160 characters — the maximum number you can use in a single text message. Remember that spaces and carriage returns count as characters.

You can try to spread your alerts across multiple text messages, but don't exceed two or three messages; otherwise, you'll simply annoy your audience.

Alternatively, you can purchase commercial content or hire a firm such as Washington, D.C.–based Distributive Networks (`www.distributive networks.com`) to write custom content for you.

Make sure that you have the right compliance language, you don't use special characters, the content is encoded properly in your messages, and you maintain alignment with the best practices and regulations of each country you'll be delivering messages to. See Book VIII, Chapter 1 for details. Ask your application provider for help with this.

Setting up the service

After you amass the ingredients of your messaging campaign, the next step is setting up your messaging service. Figure 5-1 shows the application interface of the mFinity platform, a mobile marketing solution from iLoop Mobile. You can use this application to set up and configure your text-messaging alert service, including the opt-in, opt-out, help, and privacy elements. (If you're not doing the work yourself, your agency or partner will use an application like this one to run your messaging campaign.)

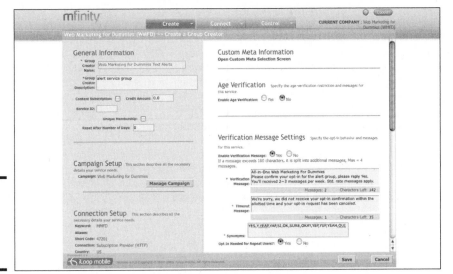

Figure 5-1:
Alert-
service
setup
screen.

Mind your timing

Taking time zones into consideration when sending or scheduling your messages is important. You don't want to wake someone up at 3 a.m.

Also, if you're sending a lot of messages, processing all of them may take time, so you'll want to know the *throughput* of the application you're using — that is, how many messages it can process per second. Add up the total messages you want to send, divide that total by the application throughput, and multiply the result by 60 to find out many minutes it will take to process and send all your messages.

To set up your program, simply fill out the form and click Save. Then you're ready to start promoting your program in traditional media and messaging the subscribers who have opted into your programs. See Book VIII, Chapter 2 for information on gathering opt-ins. For details on setting up communication-program user flows, refer to Book VIII, Chapter 3.

Sending the content

You typically have two ways to send a message to your opt-in list:

✦ **Manually:** To publish your message(s) manually, log in to your mobile marketing application and select the groups to which you want to send the message. Filter the selected groups, if you want, by age, location, carrier, preferences, and other criteria (see Figure 5-2), and then enter the message.

You can send the message immediately or schedule it so that the mobile marketing application sends it later. (See Figure 5-3 for an example of setting up an alert message in the mFinity platform.) You can schedule messages hours, days, weeks, or months in advance. If you have a horoscope service, for example, you can queue up six months' worth of horoscope messages before they're due to be sent.

Figure 5-2:
Group
filtering.

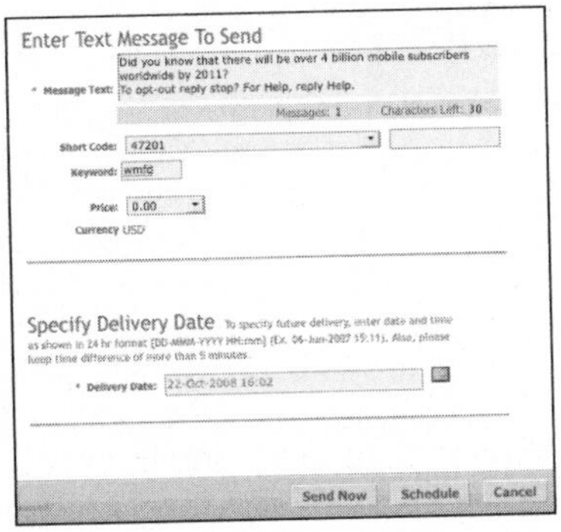

Enter Text Message To Send

Message Text: Did you know that there will be over 4 billion mobile subscribers worldwide by 2011? To opt-out reply stop? For Help, reply Help.

Messages: 1   Characters Left: 30

Short Code: 47201

Keyword: amds

Price: 0.00

Currency USD

Specify Delivery Date To specify future delivery, enter date and time as shown in 24 hr format [DD-MMM-YYYY HH:mm] (Ex. 06-Jun-2007 15:11). Also, phone keep time difference of more than 5 minutes.

Delivery Date: 22-Oct-2008 16:02

Send Now   Schedule   Cancel

Figure 5-3:
Alert-
service
publisher
screen.

✦ **Via an automated data feed:** Instead of, or in addition to, sending or scheduling messages manually, you may want to have messages sent to your audience automatically on a regular basis. Typically, you work with a content provider (such as a news vendor or weather service) and your mobile marketing application provider to set up and schedule automatic alert programs. (I could throw out a bunch of technical jargon on exactly how to do this, but I'd just bore you.) Then you set up a messaging alert schedule. When the content management system is ready to publish a message, it simply pushes the message to the mobile marketing application, which sends the message out.

Be sure to test content feeds coming from a content management system before launching your service commercially. You need to check the feeds to make sure that the messages are within the character limit specified by your service (135 to 160 characters per text message, depending on carrier and country) and that the feeds don't contain special characters or encoding that won't display properly on mobile phones.

Sending personalized text alerts

You may want to deliver a tailored message to an individual customer. You may want to remind him that his car payment is due or that he has a dentist appointment tomorrow, for example, or to provide a coupon tailored to him.

To send personalized text alerts, you use all the systems and processes listed in "Sending text alerts to a group," earlier in this chapter. The only difference is that instead of messaging a large group of people, you're messaging a single person. You can message the person manually, schedule message delivery, or have your content management system prepare a personalized message and send it to that person's phone number.

E-mailing informative messages

E-mail can be an effective way to deliver information to consumers, but it isn't necessarily the best way to reach the mass market. At this writing (August 2008), only about ten percent of consumers can access e-mail on mobile phones, although more and more people are adopting e-mail–capable phones.

For mobile marketing purposes, e-mail isn't always reliable. You have little control of how your content is viewed; e-mail services often reformat content to optimize its readability on mobile phones, and much of your message can be lost in translation. Also, many e-mail clients for mobile phones don't support attachments, and many types of data files are difficult to render on mobile phones, so e-mail attachments are unreliable means of broadcasting your marketing content to a mass audience.

You can use either of two methods to deliver e-mail to a phone (but keep in mind that they're not viable for mobile marketing):

✦ **Traditional e-mail:** The traditional e-mail route is simple. You send a message to an e-mail address (such as XYZ@gmail.com) just as you would in any traditional e-mail marketing program. Alternatively, you may want to consider using a service such as Constant Contact (www.constantcontact.com) or mobileStorm (www.mobilestorm.com). If your mobile subscribers have access to e-mail on their phones, and if they've opted into your campaign, they'll get the message.

✦ **Mobile-phone e-mail:** This method uses the e-mail channels provided by mobile carriers (such as 555-555-5555@t-mobile) to send short bursts of text, similar to text messaging. This system is designed for personal use, not for commercial use, and shouldn't be used for commercial mobile marketing. You can find a list of restricted mobile e-mail domains at www.fcc.gov/cgb/policy/DomainNameDownload.html.

Providing Mobile Enhancements and Applications

Mobile enhancements (also referred to as *personalization content*) are extremely common types of mobile content, as are mobile games and applications. This section describes how to create your own branded wallpapers, screen savers, and ringtones, as well as games and applications. In addition, it reviews various content-distribution strategies.

If you lack artistic talent and can't create compelling wallpapers, screen savers, or ringtones on your own, don't lose heart. You can always hire someone else to create the content or tap your friends and family members to do it. Outsourcing content development to a third party is common and needn't cost much. A professional marketing agency can help you and probably will provide great service, but you can also go to a local art school college, or high school — or even an elementary school — and ask a student to produce your artwork. You can find a lot of talented people out there!

Providing branded wallpapers and screen savers

Mobile wallpapers and screen savers are wonderful ways to personalize mobile phones and are conceptually identical to personal-computer wallpapers and screen savers. A *mobile wallpaper* is the still image displayed on a mobile phone's main screen, and a *mobile screen saver* is the still and/or animated image that's displayed on the mobile phone's screen when the phone is idle.

The image you use for wallpapers and screen savers can be your company's logo or any other image that represents your business or the objectives of your marketing campaign: a character, artistic scene, cityscape, landscape, and so on.

Finding a graphics application

Creating your own branded wallpapers and screen savers is easy. You just need a graphics application, some artistic talent, a mobile marketing application, and a marketing plan to promote your content or one that uses the content as an incentive to promote another offering.

You can use a variety of graphics applications to create your content, ranging from free and low-cost applications to professional packages such as Adobe Photoshop.

Search the Download.com Web site (www.download.com) for graphics software (available for both Microsoft Windows and Macintosh computers), or visit a local software store to find an application that suits your needs and skill level.

Creating wallpapers and screen savers

When you create your mobile wallpapers and screen savers, make sure that you create an array of images with the right resolution and file format:

✦ **Image resolution:** Currently, you need to configure your images for ten common mobile-phone screen sizes. A screen size typically is measured as number of pixels wide by number of pixels high. The most common screen sizes are

- 96 x 65
- 101 x 80
- 120 x 160

- 128 x 128
- 132 x 176
- 175 x 130
- 176 x 208
- 176 x 220
- 240 x 320 (the size of most BlackBerry devices)
- 480 x 320 (the size of the Apple iPhone)

Your images should be designed to fit each screen size. Typical phones support 72 dots per square inch *(dpi),* but newer phones like the iPhone support 163 dpi. The higher the dpi, the more detail you can support in an image and the clearer it is.

Both dpi and image dimensions add to the image file size and thereby affect download speeds. You want the files to be as small as possible.

✦ **File format:** Most mobile phones support JPEG, GIF, and PNG file types. Consult your content management system provider about which file type to use.

If you're creating an animated screen saver, you must save it as a GIF file, because the other image-file formats don't support animation.

Figure 5-4 shows content hosted in a mobile content management system.

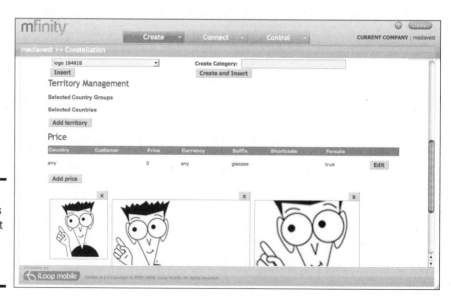

Figure 5-4:
Wallpapers in a content management system.

You may choose to create a single image and rely on the mobile marketing application's content management system to scale it for you automatically. If you use this method, however, the quality of the image may be impaired, especially if the image contains text. Text in an image that looks great on a display 320 pixels wide may be unreadable when automatically resized to 65 pixels wide. A quality mobile content management system will use the appropriate image for the phone and reduce the image size dynamically only as a last resort.

Delivering ringtones and other system sounds

The term *ringtone* refers to the sound a mobile phone makes when it is being called. Ringtones are immensely popular with all consumer segments and can be a great way to offer value to customers. Your subscribers can get ringtones from many places, including their mobile carriers, sounds built into their phones, and third parties like you.

Like wallpapers (which I discuss in the preceding section), ringtones help personalize a user's phone. Unlike wallpapers, however, ringtones are public, because everyone around can hear them when the phone rings. Therefore, ringtones are a great way for a mobile subscriber to demonstrate affinity for a brand, campaign, or cause.

During the 2008 presidential campaign, for example, Democratic Party nominee Barack Obama provided ringtones that let people show their support for his candidacy every time their phones rang. One of the most popular tones was this message: "This is Barack Obama. It's time to change America. Answer the call."

Creating a ringtone

A ringtone is simply a properly formatted audio file associated with a mobile phone's ringer preferences so that the audio file plays when the phone rings.

You can use a variety of audio mixing applications to create your ringtones. You can find a free or inexpensive application on the Internet, or you can purchase one. The audio application you use must be able to save your ringtone in an appropriate file format (see the list later in this section).

When you create your audio file, keep the following parameters in mind:

✦ **Length:** A typical ringtone is 20 to 30 seconds long.

✦ **File format:** Most modern phones support the MP3 audio-file format, but many older phones don't. Also, some carriers (including Sprint and Verizon Wireless) have special formatting requirements.

To support the widest range of mobile phones, keep your ringtones to 128 kilobits mono, and produce them in the following formats and sizes:

- **MP3:** 200 kilobits or less
- **WAV:** 200 kilobits or less
- **AMR:** 45 kilobits or less
- **AMRWB:** 90 kilobits or less
- **MMF:** 100 kilobits or less
- **QCP:** 60 kilobits or less
- **MIDI:** 100 kilobits or less

The files can be bigger, but if they are, they take longer to download and take up more space on consumers' phones.

Distributing a ringtone

After you create your ringtones, you can upload them to your mobile marketing application, which delivers them when a user downloads them from the server. Additionally, the ringtone can be delivered automatically to mobile subscribers who have opted into your content.

You can give your marketing campaign flair by providing unique content for specific events. Before a live concert in 2007, Black Eyed Peas recorded ringtones and uploaded them to their partner's content management system. When they went onstage, they gave the audience the opportunity to download ringtones that were available only for that night. That's adding value.

Making Marketing Fun with Mobile Games and Applications

Given the right conditions, delivering content via applications can be extremely effective. In the context of mobile marketing, an *application* is a piece of software that is downloaded and installed on a mobile phone to perform a specific function. Following are a few examples:

- ✦ **CBS Sports** offers a fantasy-sports application that lets players check in on their teams, update their teams' rosters, and view game results (www.sportsline.com).
- ✦ The **Weather Channel Mobile** has an application that people can download to keep up to date with weather-related news and services (www.weather.mobi).

✦ **Greystripe,** a San Francisco–based mobile "advergaming" company (www.greystripe.com), provides mobile games interlaced with advertising. The advertising is part of the game's content and user experience; when it's missing, the experience is affected in a negative way.

✦ **Cellfire** (www.cellfire.com), a mobile couponing provider, offers an application for managing coupons.

✦ **Lightpole** (www.lightpole.net), which provides location-relevant content services, has an application that tailors content delivery to a customer's location.

Considering the challenges

If you decide to go the route of delivering your content via an application, you should be prepared for challenges. You need to consider all the following points:

✦ **Purpose:** What the application is supposed to do.

✦ **Audience:** Who the members of your target audience are.

✦ **Phones:** What kinds of phones your audience members have.

✦ **Mobile operating systems:** Which mobile phone operating systems you'll support. Your options include Java, Microsoft Windows, Brew, Symbian, Palm, Android, iPhone, and Sony Ericsson.

✦ **Carriers:** Which wireless carriers the application will work on. Carriers often tweak a phone's capabilities, so even if you build the application for a specific operating system, the carrier may have changed the way that the phone works, affecting your application's performance.

Given all these considerations, if you want to build an application that will work on all phones, you could end up creating hundreds of versions of your application, and you'd need to support and maintain them all.

Focus your development only on the phones that the key members of your target audience use. Don't try to "boil the ocean" as they say; focus is the key to optimizing your marketing dollars and your available time.

Creating a mobile application or game

Designing and developing a mobile application or game are tasks that you should leave to experts. Consult your local developer communities for references to people who develop programs for specific platforms.

You can also find firms that specialize in developing mobile applications and games, including Hands-On Mobile (www.handson.com), UIEvolution (www.uievolution.com), SurfKitchen (www.surfkitchen.com), Cascada Mobile (www.cascadamobile.com), and Nellymoser (www.nellymoser.com).

Serving Up Mobile Web Sites

The mobile Internet offers several advantages over simple text messaging and multimedia messaging, in that you can deliver more than just 160 characters of alphanumeric text or simple media files.

With the mobile Internet, you can serve rich content with formatted text (colors, fonts, bullets, and so on), images, video clips, banner ads, and links. See Figure 5-5 for some example mobile Internet sites.

Figure 5-5:
Mobile
Internet
sites.

Employing the mobile Internet

For many marketers, the mobile Internet is becoming a primary channel for distributing snippets of information to users wherever and whenever they go. The medium is great for occupying personal downtime (such as waiting in line) and for providing on-the-spot information to a mobile audience (such as flight schedules and updates). The fundamental value of the mobile Internet is quick access to small nuggets of information and for specific mobile relevant actions, such as local search, purchases, entertainment, and so on — appealingly presented and appropriately targeted, of course.

You can create a *persistent* mobile Internet site (one that stays up all the time) or one that's set up for a short-term marketing promotion, such as a movie launch or advertising *landing page* (a one-page site that's displayed when a user clicks an advertisement). For a discussion of mobile advertising, refer to Book VIII, Chapter 4.

You can deliver all kinds of content via the mobile Internet: articles and stories, pictures, ringtones, videos, audio, applications, games, and more. You can even have people complete forms to request that content be delivered to them via SMS, e-mail, or some other method. Depending on how you set up your site and the kind of content you're working with, the content can be consumed on the screen or downloaded to the phone.

In addition to static content that rarely, if ever, needs to be changed (your address, product descriptions, promotional copy, company description, and so on), you can create links to dynamic content that changes each time the site is visited or the mobile Internet page is refreshed. Content for dynamic pages, such as articles, typically is pulled and updated from a content management system, most often via standard RSS and XML data feeds. If your content is stored in a content management system that doesn't support data-feed access, consider working with a company such as kapow (`www.kapow.com`) or Lightpole (`www.lightpole.net`) that can convert your data to standard RSS and/or XML, which in turn can be streamed to your site.

Don't be lulled into offering on your mobile Internet site the same content and experience that you offer on the traditional Internet. Although mobile phones today are nearly as powerful as many early computers, they're still phones, not computers. Their device profiles are different; their browsers handle content differently (you can't streamline embedded content such as video or audio, for example); and consumers use them differently. Instead, you should consider the mobile phone to be a new medium. See the mobiThinking Web site (`www.mobithinking.com`) for more information about how to think mobile.

Creating a mobile Web site

Building a simple version of a mobile Web site isn't hard. Building a mobile Internet site that will look good on thousands of mobile-phone models and hundreds of mobile browsers, however, is an entirely different story. You can hire any number of companies to build your site (for descriptions of mobile application providers, refer to Book VIII, Chapter 1), or you can use a mobile Internet site-building application to handle all the complexities.

Figure 5-6 shows one of the leading tools for building mobile Internet sites.

On the mobile Internet, design considerations vary significantly from those of broadband sites, as mobile Internet sites need to accommodate various data network speeds, as well as myriad browsers and display sizes. For this reason, mobile sites should be fairly lightweight, featuring bite-size chunks of information and judicious use of images. You need to take care to place featured content so that it appears high on the screen and to minimize slow-loading, bulky images and tricky formatting.

Clean mobile Internet-site designs (such as E!Online at `http://eonline.mobi`) typically render well across a variety of devices, without heavy data-use charges that create "sticker shock" for new mobile Internet users or customer-service headaches for network operators.

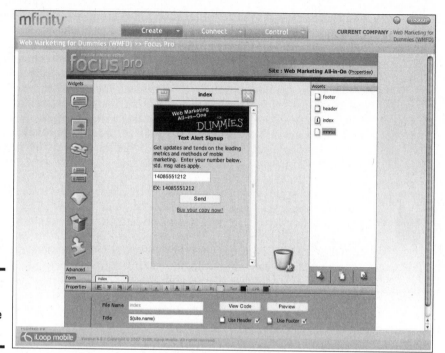

Figure 5-6:
Mobile
Internet site
builder.

Here are some guiding principles for designing a mobile Internet site:

✦ Insert key branding into the header.

✦ Place important content high on the page. (The user's screen may be small.)

✦ Use images and other visual elements only when necessary.

✦ Use short phrases and short blocks of text. If you do use long text, such as an extended article, ensure that the page design is clear, that the user is being taken to an extended story, and that the pages are divided in a way that improves readability on small phone screens.

✦ Don't fall into the trap of designing for the lowest common denominator. Design for both the high and low ends, and let your mobile application provider handle the chore of serving the appropriate experience to the visiting phone.

If you use images and want to control the user experience, consider designing various versions for different screen sizes. Otherwise, let your provider autoscale images. (For more information about scaling images, refer to "Creating wallpapers and screen savers," earlier in this chapter.)

Testing your mobile site

After you create a site, it's a good idea to test it on the top handsets used by your target demographic. Check with M:Metrics (www.mmetrics.com) and Nielsen (www.nielsen.com), two commercial mobile research firms that maintain a monthly record of the top handsets used by mobile subscribers throughout North America and Europe. You also may want to view AdMob (www.admob.com/metrics), which provides a free report of top mobile handsets being used on its global network.

In addition, you can try testing your site with dotMobi's mobile-site readiness tool, ready.mobi, which is available at www.ready.mobi. This tool gives you a free evaluation of your site for mobile friendliness, checking everything against industry best practices and mobile Web standards.

Alternatively, you can subscribe to a commercial service such as Mobile Complete's DeviceAnywhere (www.deviceanywhere.com), which allows you to test your site on real phones via the Internet, or a testing service offered by Keynote (www.keynote.com), another mobile test and measurement solution provider.

Broadcasting Audio and Video Content

Audio and video content are emerging concepts on the mobile horizon, showing significant promise for enriching user experience and demonstrating value.

Creating audio and video content

Creating audio and video content for mobile phones is easy enough. You can use a variety of video-capturing and audio-recording methods, and everything from high-end video production tools all the way down to the phone itself can create video and audio content.

After you capture the content, you need to convert it to a file format that mobile phones can use. For video, the most common formats are 3GPP, MPEG4, MOV, and WMV. For audio, the most common formats are WAV and MP3.

Delivering audio and video content

As for delivering the content, you can use these methods:

✦ **Download and play:** You place the audio and video content in your mobile marketing application's content management system. When a mobile phone requests audio or video files, the content management system sends it the version of the content that's most suitable for the phone (the 3GPP or MOV version, for example). The content is fully downloaded to the phone and then played on a resident player on the device.

✦ **Stream:** With streaming audio and video, the content isn't fully downloaded to the phone before it's played back; instead, the content is streamed to the phone and begins to play back before download is complete. One of the most common applications for video streaming is mobile television; for audio content, the most common applications are radio and sports broadcasts.

Audio and video streamlining are very specialized services that don't work across all carriers and handsets. Moreover, the data charges for these services can be quite high if a mobile subscriber is not on an unlimited data plan. Take special care in launching these services, and take heed that they're not ready for use in mass mobile marketing.

Offering Branded Utility Services

You may also want to offer value to members of your audience by offering *branded utilities:* services carrying your brand that members of your audience will find valuable. You might consider providing a store locator, shopping-comparison service, weather service, consolidated news and information service, or other utilities in your mobile marketing program to add value for members of your audience.

These services can be deployed over and through any of the mobile paths, such as SMS, mobile Internet site, and downloadable applications. The key is to consider the content format and the most appropriate path for delivering the content to mobile subscribers. Numerous marketing agencies, mobile application providers, and consultants can help you build branded utility services.

Chapter 6: Getting Paid for Your Mobile Marketing Efforts

In This Chapter

✔ **Making money through the mobile channel**

✔ **Distinguishing among mobile business models**

✔ **Cashing in on bill-to-phone and alternative billing methods**

The mobile channel is unique. It is a personal, location- and time-independent, interactive marketing channel, and it can be used to enable commerce. With it, you can turn your once-inert print, television, radio, outdoor, Web, and related marketing media into interactive, money-making storefronts. You can also use the mobile channel as a one-to-one engagement medium, assuming that you have express permission and consent from each person you're engaging. (For more information about privacy and permission rules, refer to Book VIII, Chapter 1.)

This chapter reviews the many ways you can use the mobile phone as a medium for commerce. It explains how you can sell content, use Short Message Service (SMS) as a billing mechanism, and mobile-enhance other elements of your mobile offerings for purchases and sampling of physical goods.

Methods of Monetizing the Mobile Channel

Suppose that you're promoting a new product, service, or event. You want people to try it or find out about it; you want to give out samples or coupons, or give people the chance to buy tickets to the show so that it doesn't go on with empty seats. You want to do everything with minimal cost or effort on your part . . . and you can. All you need to do is place a mobile call to action in your media and marketing materials, or send a text message to the mobile subscribers in your permission-based database, and you have a fighting chance of engaging your audience and making some money.

You can run all kinds of promotions on the mobile channel to make money. Following are a few examples:

✦ Mobile subscribers can text *sample* to your short code, such as 12345 (see Book VIII, Chapter 2 for details on short codes), to get a free sample of your product shipped right to their homes. That sample can be a can of soft drink, a bar of soap, a book, or even a pharmaceutical trial kit. (If you think that mobile is only for the young-consumer market, you're wrong.)

✦ Mobile subscribers can take pictures of a specific page in a magazine and/or book with their phone cameras and e-mail those pictures from their phones to your mobile e-mail address (such as `promo@mmfd.mobi`). In return, you text them a coupon for 25 percent off your product or service.

✦ Mobile subscribers can call, text, or visit a Web site to donate $5 to a charity, with 100 percent of the proceeds going to the charity, not to some administration body.

✦ You can promote digital content that can be purchased and consumed on mobile phones: music, news broadcasts, games, applications, ringtones, images, movies, television, text, and so on.

✦ You can sell advertising space in your media properties (see Book VIII, Chapter 4).

These examples just scratch the surface of what you can do with the mobile channel. All you need to do is keep reading.

Offering Your Content through a Carrier's Portal

Every mobile carrier offers its own branded portal on the mobile phone. This portal features content and services created by the carrier and its partners. You too can offer content through a carrier portal, but the process isn't as easy as you may think. To offer your content and services for sale through a carrier's portal and ensure that you ultimately get paid, you must follow one or more of the paths described in the following sections.

Developing a direct relationship

Many companies establish a direct relationship with each individual carrier for the purposes of promoting their content and services directly on the carrier's portal. The deals that you can strike can vary greatly, but here are some common ways to develop revenue opportunities with a carrier:

✦ The carrier gives you a lump-sum payment for access to your content for a certain period.

✦ The carrier provides you minimum sales guarantees.

✦ You and the carrier enter into a revenue-sharing relationship in which you share the revenue (often not equally).

Direct carrier relationships take time to develop and negotiate — often, 12 to 18 months or more, and this time frame assumes that you already have a head start and generally know who to talk to.

Entering into a channel relationship

Many carriers offer developer and content-channel relationship portals that you can sign up for on the Internet. The channel relationship business model differs from the direct carrier relationship discussed in the preceding section, in that you're not negotiating a direct deal. Instead, with a channel relationship you get access to the carrier portal, business terms that are easy to adopt and employ, royalty payments for the sale of your content, access to the carrier's marketing education materials, and more. Table 6-1 lists various carrier content and developer programs.

Table 6-1	Carrier Developer Programs
Name of Carrier	*Contact Information*
Sprint	http://developer.sprint.com
Verizon	www.vzwdevelopers.com/aims
T-Mobile	http://developer.t-mobile.com
AT&T Wireless	http://developer.att.com

Here's how to get started with channel relationships:

1. **Go to the carrier's Web site, and sign up for a standard third-party service program.**

2. **Have your content or service certified.**

This step is important, because you must be certified before the carrier puts your content on its portal. Every carrier's certification process is different, based on the type of content or service you're offering. You'll need to review the details of the process on the carrier's Web site.

3. **Accept the terms and conditions of the program.**

The terms include how much and when you get paid for your services. In very rare situations, you may be able to obtain minor adjustments in the standard program terms.

Contracting with an intermediate company

Some intermediary companies have direct relationships with mobile carriers that have been forged over many years. The intermediary firms sublicense your content to get it on a mobile carrier's portal.

Intermediaries are great channels because they enjoy economies of scale and greater reach than you could get on your own by going to each carrier individually.

Examples of intermediaries include Airborne Mobile (www.airborne mobile.com), Thumbplay (www.thumbplay.com), Zed (formerly 9 Squared; www.9squared.com), and Mobile Streams (www.mobile streams.com). Each company has its own business model, but you make money from every sale of your content and service, minus any revenue splits, transaction fees, setup fees, and maintenance fees charged by the intermediary.

Making Money through Premium Text Messaging

Premium text messaging, or PSMS (*P* for *premium* and *SMS* for *Short Message Service,* or text messaging — yes, all the jargon can be confusing), is an extremely common, fast, and versatile way to monetize a mobile marketing campaign by charging mobile subscribers for content you sell via the mobile channel. When you employ PSMS, the price you charge for access to your content — 99¢, $1.99, $9.99, and so on — is billed to the consumer's mobile phone bill, and after carrier collection of payments and deduction of carrier fees, you get a check.

PSMS can be used only for content and services that can be consumed (read, viewed, played, and so on) on a mobile phone, such as a text message, wallpaper, or ringtone. You can't charge for physical goods or nonmobile services by using PSMS.

PSMS charges are billed in the mobile subscriber's local currency. In the United States, for example, numerous fixed price points between 10¢ and $29 are available for charging mobile subscribers via PSMS. A *price point* means that you can't make up a price; you have to choose among the various price tiers that are available for you to use. Contact your application provider or messaging aggregator for a list of all the PSMS price points that you can use in each country.

You might consider using PSMS to charge your subscribers for the following:

✦ Entering a sweepstakes

✦ Voting in a poll, quiz, or survey

✦ Purchasing your content, such as text (news, horoscopes, sports alerts, and so on), wallpapers, screen savers, ringtones, applications, and games

See Figure 6-1 for an example of a PSMS charge on a mobile phone bill.

Figure 6-1:
PSMS
charge on
a Verizon
Wireless
bill.

Description	Date	Time	Usage Type	Application Price	Total
Prem_sms 76278 Papa ver 2	06/11	02:58P	Q2	$.99	$.99

PSMS can be used for one-time purchases and donations as well as for recurring (weekly or monthly) billing. The versatility of this method comes from the fact that you can initiate the PSMS billing process from any marketing channel, including the following:

✦ Mobile-originated (MO) text messaging — that is, a message originated by consumers and sent from their mobile phones. MO messaging is used in all programs in which you're mobile-enhancing traditional media and retail with a text-messaging call to action (see Book VIII, Chapter 2).

✦ A Web site or mobile Internet site.

✦ A widget, such as a plug-in for use on a social networking site.

✦ An interactive voice response (IVR) session. (See Book VIII, Chapter 1 for more details on IVR.)

Putting PSMS to work: An example campaign

Suppose that you're trying to sell a ringtone called BestSong and want to let everyone know about it. If you use PSMS, the process works as follows:

1. You promote the ringtone in various media:

• **Traditional media:** In flyers, on billboards, in store displays, and so on, you place a call to action like this one: "Text *tone* to 12345 to buy BestSong for $1.99. Standard messaging and other data rates apply."

• **Digital media:** On a Web or mobile Web site, in a widget, or in other digital media, you place a message like this one: "Enter your mobile number in the field below and click Submit to buy BestSong for $1.99. You'll receive a text message asking you to confirm your purchase. Standard messaging and other data rates apply."

• **IVR:** In an IVR session, the singer records a sultry prompt such as this one: "Preview and get the latest track I've laid down, BestSong, for $1.99. Say or press 1. You'll get to hear the preview and then receive a text to confirm your purchase. Standard messaging and other data rates apply."

2. The consumer responds to your call to action.

3. You send a text message to the consumer's phone, asking him to confirm his purchase request. Your message might say something like this: "Please confirm your purchase of BestSong for $1.99 by replying *yes*. Standard messaging and other data rates apply. Reply *help* and/or *stop*."

4. The consumer responds to your purchase request.

5. You send a text message with a download link to the consumer's phone. Your message might say something like this: "Thanks. To download BestSong, click `http://c4d.com/1212fas`."

6. The consumer downloads the ringtone.

7. You send the consumer a final text message to initiate billing (see Figure 6-2).

The actual billing event happens after the content or service has been delivered — not before. Make sure that your application provider is handling this step properly.

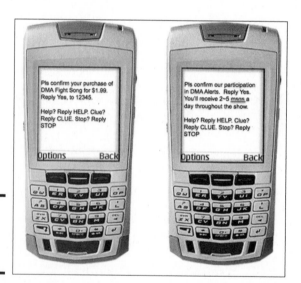

Figure 6-2:
Initiating billing via PSMS.

Setting up a premium messaging program

Setting up a PSMS program is similar to setting up an SMS program (which I discuss in Book VIII, Chapter 3), but you need to complete a few extra steps. To set up and run a PSMS program, you need the following elements:

✦ **A Common Short Code (CSC) approved to run your premium program:** This code must be certified for each price point you want to use it for. (For details on CSCs, flip to Book VIII, Chapter 2, and for more information about price points, refer to "Making Money through Premium Text Messaging," earlier in this chapter.)

✦ **A mobile marketing messaging application solution:** You need a solution that's compliant with carrier and messaging aggregator requirements in each country in which you plan to run the PSMS program.

If you want to bill through PSMS, make sure that you work with an experienced mobile services application provider. You must meet many rules, regulations, and technical requirements before mobile carriers allow you to bill via their networks using PSMS.

✦ **Campaign approval:** The carrier has to review and approve your program and all its user flows, including ensuring that you receive text-message purchase confirmation from the consumer — known as a double opt-in. The carrier also must determine that your program meets all other requirements, such as opt-out, help, and privacy. (For more details on best practices and guidelines, refer to Book VIII, Chapter 1.)

If your program isn't preapproved, the carriers won't turn on billing support. If you have an active short code, your unapproved program may run, but either of two things will happen: (1) You won't get paid, or (2) your CSCs will be shut off, and you'll be blacklisted.

Don't skip the approval process, which takes 8 to 15 weeks. Ask your application or messaging aggregator provider (see Book VIII, Chapter 1 for details on providers) to help you get certification.

Determining how much you'll get paid and when

When you have your program up and running, you can start getting paid for your content and services. Typically, PSMS revenue is split among the following parties:

✦ **Carrier and aggregator:** Messaging aggregators and carriers retain a percentage of the gross receipts from PSMS billing events — combined, typically 40 percent to 60 percent. The percentage depends on the price points of the transactions, the total volume of transactions, and the carriers that the mobile subscribers are using. Payouts typically are made 12 to 15 weeks after the sale.

✦ **Application and billing providers:** Some application and billing providers will negotiate with you to share in a percentage of the revenue in lieu of or in addition to software licensing fees, download fees, or messaging transaction fees.

✦ **Content rights holder:** If you've licensed content from a third party, or if you're using content licensed by your application provider, the content rights holder must be paid from the proceeds of the sale.

Processing PSMS refunds

Refunds are tricky things to manage in the world of PSMS. If you have a customer who calls to complain, you can give her a refund by cutting her a check, but you may be losing out. The customer may already have requested and received a refund from the mobile carrier, in which case the carrier will deduct this refund from your payout. Alternatively, if the consumer went to you for the refund, not to the carrier, you'll refund the entire amount to the consumer; but you'll receive only that amount less any carrier, aggregator, and application provider fees. You'll probably owe the content rights holder a royalty, too, because the content was delivered and can't be revoked.

Be sure to get a rate card from the content rights holder before selling the content. You need to make sure how much you can expect to earn — which may be less than you think. Suppose that you're selling — in moderate volume — a ringtone for $1.99. The mobile carrier and aggregator retain 50 percent of the sale price, leaving 99.5¢. If you have a 20 percent revenue share with the application provider, and the cost of the ringtone from the content rights owner is 50¢, you'll receive a payout of 29.6¢ per sale. And if you're reselling leading-artist ringtones (referred to as master tones), you'll receive 1 percent to 3 percent of the gross receipts after all the fees are deducted. Furthermore, carriers reserve the right to provide credit to customers who complain about a premium charge. Any such credits will be deducted from your receivables before they are paid.

Selling Your Content and Services via the Mobile Internet

The mobile phone is an incredible payment platform, because mobile subscribers almost always have their phones with them. A few years ago, Nokia ran a study asking people which item they'd go back home for: their keys, wallet, or mobile phone. Respondents said that they could live without their keys and wallet, but they'd go back for their phone.

Entire industries are looking to use the mobile phone for payment — not just for mobile-consumable goods and services, as discussed in the preceding sections, but also for physical goods and services to be processed via alternative billing methods. The following sections discuss the most common alternative billing methods you can use to get paid via the mobile phone.

Using mobile Internet link billing

One alternative method of promoting and selling mobile-consumable content and services is the mobile Internet. In industry jargon, this practice is often referred to as Wireless Application Protocol (WAP) billing. To continue the example from "Putting PSMS to work: An example campaign," earlier in this chapter, you can promote your Hot New Ringtone track with a Purchase link on a mobile Internet page. But instead of using the PSMS channel, which uses text messaging to capture consumers' consent to the charge, you can employ mobile Internet link billing.

In mobile Internet link billing, mobile subscribers click a link on a mobile Internet page to initiate and then confirm their purchase of the content or service.

Billing via mobile Internet links is not something anyone can do; it requires special relationships with wireless carriers. If you want to use this method of billing on your mobile Internet site, you need to make sure that you're working with a mobile application service provider that has mobile Internet link billing relationships with the connection aggregators, such as MX Telecom (www.mxtelecom.com) or Ericsson IPX (www.ericsson.com/solutions/ipx), or with mobile billing firms such as Bango (www.bango.com) or Billing Revolution (www.billingrevolution.com).

Mobile Internet billing isn't as universal as PSMS, because not all wireless carriers support this feature. When you deploy mobile Internet billing in your mobile Internet site, make sure that your site is capable of adjusting the wireless carrier dynamically. Be sure to ask your mobile application provider how this adjustment is made in its system.

Collecting credit card payments

A variety of mobile services — including SMS, mobile Internet, and IVR — can be integrated with credit card billing systems for the purpose of initiating credit card transactions from mobile phones. Most mobile application providers can integrate with credit card services, but two firms have complete solutions that you could use immediately: Bango (www.bango.com; see Figure 6-3) for the mobile Internet and ShopText (www.shoptext.com) for SMS.

The ShopText solution can also be used for product sampling — not just for credit card billing for physical goods and services.

Your mobile commerce solution doesn't have to be sexy; it simply needs to add value — and it needs to work. Papa John's International, for example, reported in December 2008 that within five months of launching its mobile Web site (http://mobile.papajohns.com), the pizza chain made more than $1 million in sales from it. That's a lot of dough.

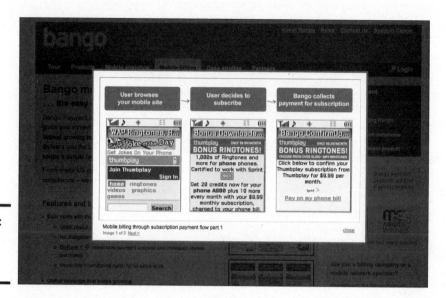

Figure 6-3:
Bango
billing
example.

Getting paid through PayPal

PayPal offers a service called PayPal Mobile (www.paypal.com/mobile), which can be integrated with SMS, the Internet, the mobile Internet, and voice/IVR services. A registered PayPal Mobile subscriber can use her mobile phone to initiate and confirm purchases from participating vendors. The charges for the goods and services are deducted from the subscriber's PayPal account.

Chapter 7: Tracking a Mobile Marketing Campaign

In This Chapter

✔ Creating and populating a marketing database

✔ Profiling your audience

✔ Delivering programs through a database

✔ Gathering feedback

✔ Analyzing customer interactions

✔ Keeping track of purchases

*O*ver the past few years, marketers have been under a significant amount of pressure to demonstrate a return on investment for the organizational resources they consume. In other words, as a marketer you need to show the value of your efforts and how they help the company meet its goals — achieve its bottom line, as the saying goes.

In this chapter, I show you how to document your efforts, starting with collecting data and building a mobile marketing database. You can use this database to report on the success or failure of your campaigns, to respond to customer inquiries and feedback, and to track both passive and active interactions with members of your audience through the mobile channel.

When you finish this chapter, you'll have a good understanding of how you can report back to your boss and say, "Yes, we're contributing, and here are the numbers to show for it."

Building Your Marketing Database

You'll find data all over the place. Getting access to the data isn't the challenge. Rather, one of the biggest challenges you'll encounter in running your marketing programs is combining the data you've amassed into a database to create an actionable view of your business and its interactions with members of its audience.

A *database* is a software application that hosts information. To build your marketing database, consider all the types of information you'll need so that you can better understand the members of your audience and the value they're searching for (see "Creating Consumer Profiles," later in this chapter).

The keys to building a marketing database are

+ Understand what you want to know.

+ Know what kinds of data you need to help you know it.

+ Find the right software application to store the data and gain easy access to it (see the following sections).

Creating the database

After you've considered the types of information you want to capture, you're ready to build your marketing database. Depending on the size and scale of your business, you can start small by using a simple database program like Microsoft Excel, Microsoft Access, or FileMaker Pro; use a more advanced program such as Crystal Reports; or obtain a database solution from an organization such as Oracle.

Accessing your mobile marketing data

Your mobile marketing application service provider captures and stores all kinds of data, including all the interactions and information that members of your audience contribute during their participation in your mobile marketing program.

For basic reporting purposes (such as number of votes, opt-ins, opt-outs, purchases, content downloads, or mobile Internet pageviews), you can access this information in the mobile marketing application's database via standard reporting tools in the application provider's software. For advanced reporting and data analysis, and to build your marketing database, most mobile application service providers allow you to export the information from your account in their systems.

After you've exported all the information from the mobile marketing application, you can combine it with other data you've collected on individual members of your audience or on your audience in general (see the following section). In other words, you can use your mobile marketing data to enhance the profile of your audience as a whole as well as profiles of individual members of your audience.

Creating Consumer Profiles

An important aspect of marketing is developing profiles of the members of your audience. You develop these profiles by amassing several types of data from a wide range of sources:

+ Demographic data

+ Psychographic data

+ Preference data

+ Behavioral data

+ Location data

+ Syndicated data

In tech speak, all this data is commonly called *metadata* — data about something. If a database engineer asks, "What kind of metadata do you want to capture?" you can answer, "I need demographic metadata: age, geography, psychographic data, and so on." Now you're cooking.

Amassing all these data types helps you develop a clear picture of the needs, wants, and desires of your target audience; thus, you have a better chance of giving your customers excellent service and providing them value.

The following sections provide an overview of each data type.

Outlining demographic data

Demography is the study of populations; consequently, *demographic data* consists of the data points that detail a population's characteristics. Think about the demographic data that would be most helpful for your business (every business is different). You may want to consider including the following data in your database:

+ **Age:** Birth date or age range (such as 14–24)

+ **Gender:** Male or female

+ **Race/ethnicity:** Caucasian, African American, Asian, Hispanic, biracial, multicultural, and so on

+ **Religion:** Catholic, Muslim, atheist, and so on

+ **Marital status:** Single, married, divorced, domestic partnership, and so on

+ **Number of children:** Zero, one, two, three, and so on

+ **Level of education:** None, high school, some college, college graduate, doctorate, life experience, and so on

+ **Occupation:** Simply too many options to list individually (isn't that great?)

+ **Income:** Monetary range (such as $50,000–$75,000 per year)

+ **Nationality:** American, French, British, Chinese, and so on

+ **Geography:** Residence, place of work (if you're a road warrior, American Airlines seat B17, for example), and so on

Keeping track of demographic data is very important. Non-Caucasian mobile subscribers are heavy mobile marketing users, for example.

Organizing psychographic data

You may also want to capture and organize psychographic data about members of your audience. *Psychographic data* is qualitative data that measures aspects of a consumer's life, such as the following:

+ **Lifestyle:** Frequent traveler, parent with young children, empty-nester, and so on

+ **Attitudes:** Political and other views

+ **Interests:** Hobbies and pastimes (such as music)

+ **Purchasing motives:** Purchasing for self or as a gift, for entertainment, for utility, and so on

+ **Frequency of product use:** Daily, weekly, as needed, and so on

You can use this information to describe and identify customers and prospective customers, as well as to develop promotional strategies that appeal to specific psychographic segments of the market for your product or service.

Planning for preference data

Preference data is data volunteered by a member of your audience regarding his likes and dislikes, such as favorite food or least-favorite music. Other preference criteria you may consider including are

+ Days of the week and times when the consumer will allow you to message or call him

+ How many times the consumer will allow you to contact him within a particular time frame (perhaps ten times a month but no more than three times a week, for example)

+ The consumer's preferred mode of communication (mobile, e-mail, voice, instant messaging, and so on)

+ The consumer's preferred mobile device

By collecting information on a person's preferences and using it appropriately, you'll have a much better chance of meeting that consumer's needs.

Other important preference data types are presence and availability. *Presence* data tells members of an audience (connected to a network or community) whether someone is online. When a consumer is logged in to an instant-messaging application or a social networking service, for example, he may be listed as present. *Availability* data indicates whether the person is able and willing to be engaged. Presence and availability data points are important for real-time social and marketing interaction services.

Benefiting from behavioral data

Recently, marketers have begun exploring how to capture and leverage consumer behavior data: purchasing history, criteria for choosing products, effect of the environment (location, culture, family, media exposure, and so on) on their choices, Internet sites visited, ads and links clicked, customer-support interactions, and so on. Capturing this data allows you to improve your marketing programs so that you reach and interact with members of your audience more effectively.

Behavioral marketing is an emerging field. Talk to your application provider and connection aggregator to get a sense of what they're doing in this area.

You can get some great mobile subscriber demographic and behavior data from M:Metrics (www.mmetrics.com) and Nielsen (www.nielsen.com), two research firms that track user behavior on mobile phones.

Looking out for location data

Location is a dynamic data point that you can use to adjust your interaction with an audience member in real time so that your interaction with her is relevant to her location. If a mobile subscriber is browsing a mobile Internet site, for example, and you detect her current location, you can display location-relevant advertising. See Book VIII, Chapter 1, for details on how location data is captured.

Aligning with syndicated data

Syndicated data is consumer purchasing data compiled from individually scanned consumer transactions at thousands of locations. The data is collected by market research firms, cleansed, and generalized so that a specific person can't be identified from the data but groups of similar people can. Then this data is studied by marketers who want to understand consumers' purchasing behavior.

Marketers use syndicated data to do the following things:

✦ Improve sales tracking of their products and competitors' products

✦ Monitor marketing promotions and merchandising for their products and competitors' products

✦ Determine which distributors are using their products

✦ Segment customers effectively, identifying their best and worst prospects

✦ Perform market-basket analysis to find out what other products people typically purchase at the same time as theirs

Syndicated data can be very useful. In fact, it can be better than data you collect yourself because it also amasses information about your competitors' client interactions.

Scanning for context

Another data point that is emerging in marketing is automated content tagging. Developers are creating systems that read a document that you're looking at online or on the mobile Internet, *tag* the content (classify it based on what it's about), and use the tag to serve contextually relevant advertising and related marketing calls to action. If you're reading an article about fishing, for example, the system may combine the *fishing* tag with location data to serve up an ad for the nearest seafood restaurant or bait-and-tackle shop.

Populating a Marketing Database

After you build a database that can store the data you collect and make it accessible, you're ready to start populating the database.

One of the most common questions I hear from marketers is "Where do I buy or rent a list of mobile phone numbers so that I can broadcast a message to them and do mobile marketing?" This question is a very natural one to ask, because in nearly all other direct marketing practices, you can use established lists (e-mail, direct mail, telemarketing, and so on) to reach out and engage people proactively without falling afoul of marketing best practices and regulations, such as antispam laws. (For details on regulations pertaining to opt-ins, refer to Book VIII, Chapter 1.) You can purchase some types of data, such as syndicated data (refer to "Aligning with syndicated data," earlier in this chapter), but you must collect most of it over time as you interact with members of your audience.

After people have opted in to your mobile marketing programs, you can collect additional data to enhance your mobile and general marketing activities. If it's properly managed and maintained, the data you collect will become a significant and valuable asset for your firm.

Collecting data through SMS

With Short Message Service (SMS) text messaging, your mobile marketing application service provider's solution may collect additional data by virtue of having access to the mobile phone. This information ensures that you can maintain high-quality service in ongoing interactions with your audience members. In this section, I discuss data collection via SMS in detail.

Collecting data automatically

When a consumer opts into your campaign via SMS, the mobile marketing application captures his mobile phone number. From this mobile phone number, your application provider captures the following data points, all of which you need to support the interaction with the subscriber and analyze your programs:

✦ **Previous participation in other programs you've run:** You can match the number to see whether it has been used in other campaigns.

✦ **Wireless carrier:** The number can identify the wireless carrier that the subscriber is using.

✦ **Crude location:** From the number's country and area codes, you can make a crude estimate of the subscriber's location: country, state, city, time zone, and so on.

You can't use this method for real-time location detection, however, because it doesn't tell you where the person is at any given time — just where his phone is registered.

✦ **Porting status:** You can find out whether the number has ever been moved from one wireless carrier to another.

✦ **Technical information:** You can find out whether the subscriber's phone supports binary data (such as pictures and video).

Asking subscribers for data

You can also ask campaign participants to submit any number of data points via SMS, including demographic, physiographic, and preference data. You may ask a user to submit her birth date as an opt-in challenge, for example, if you're marketing a program that isn't suitable for children, such as an R-rated movie. You simply need to make sure that your text messaging application allows you to collect the data appropriately. Figure 7-1 shows details on collecting consumer information via SMS.

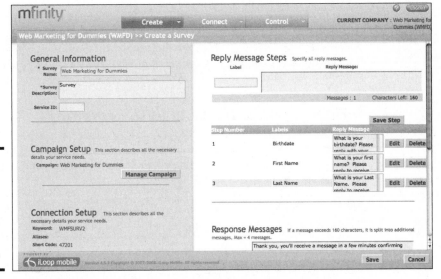

Figure 7-1:
Setting up an SMS survey in a mobile marketing application.

**Book VIII
Chapter 7**

**Tracking a
Mobile Marketing
Campaign**

Connecting through the Web

Collecting data through Web-based applications is a cinch, but you collect data on the Internet and on the mobile Internet in different ways:

+ **On the Internet:** Several rich, technically advanced tools are available for tracking user behavior such as sites visited, links clicked, and search engine terms used. A key component of this technology is the *cookie* — a small piece of code that's stored on the computer to help with tracking. Although this feature works fine on Web sites, most mobile phones (with the exception of a few smartphones) currently don't support cookies.

+ **On the mobile Internet:** On mobile phones, you can capture a limited amount of data from consumers, and you must capture it manually. Wireless carriers don't disclose a user's phone number via a mobile Internet page or application, and because most phones don't support cookies, tracking unique visitors is difficult.

  From a mobile Internet browser, however, a mobile application provider can capture the make and model of the phone, as well as the browser. With this information, the provider can tailor the display of the mobile Internet site and any content that it delivers to the specific requirements of the phone.

As for consumer-proffered data, you can use forms in Internet and mobile Internet browsers or in installed applications. Ask visitors to your site to complete a form, and when they submit it, you can capture the requested data.

If you use forms on mobile Internet sites, be sure to keep them short. Mobile subscribers may not have the patience to complete long forms via their phones, so ask for only basic information. If you need more data, augment the experience with another mobile or traditional method (such as a voice system or the Internet).

Integrating CRM and mobile campaigns

Someday — maybe even today — you'll want to merge your mobile campaign data with the data stored in your company's customer relationship management (CRM) system. This process is easy enough and typically can be handled in any of three ways:

+ **Manually:** You can ask your mobile marketing application provider to give you a report (in an Excel worksheet or an XML data structure, for example) so that you can combine your data with that of the CRM database manually.

+ **Via data feed:** Your mobile marketing application provider should be able to give you access to an XML data feed. Then you can pull data from this feed on a regular basis (such as once a day or every five minutes) so that you can combine your data with that of the CRM database automatically, on the set schedule.

✦ **In real time:** You can ask your mobile marking application provider to send you real-time data as your participants interact with the system. Perhaps you need to know immediately if someone opts out of your campaign so that you can update permission marketing management systems in other parts of your company.

Using Your Database to Deliver Targeted Programs

After you've set up your database, gathered and cleansed the data, and collected all the appropriate consumer and legal permissions to use the data, you're ready to deliver programs (see Book VIII, Chapter 5 for more information).

Delivering targeted messages to your opt-in database is only one piece of the very large universe known as mobile marketing. It's an incredibly important piece, because this database represents extremely qualified people who have demonstrated interest in your products and services by opting in to your campaign — but don't get hung up on blasting content to a list. You can also use mobile marketing to enhance customer care, generate loyalty, and mobile-enhance your other programs.

Protecting list members

You need to protect the trust of the members of your list. Do whatever it takes to protect their trust. To begin with, engage them in marketing campaigns based only on the parameters of the message they responded to. To this end, you should make sure that your database tracks not only opt-ins, but also the parameters of those opt-ins (such as what each consumer agreed to receive).

Tracking opt-ins and opt-outs

You must track all opt-ins and opt-outs, as I discuss in the best practices and regulations section of Book VIII, Chapter 1 and in the opt-in/opt-out sections of Book VIII, Chapter 2. *Opt-in* refers to explicit consent — the permission a mobile subscriber gives you that allows you to interact with him — whereas an *opt-out* is an explicit instruction from a mobile subscriber to stop contacting him.

Your mobile marketing application will not only track all opt-in and opt-out requests, but also take immediate action upon receipt. The application can send a confirmation request; add the subscriber to (or remove the subscriber from) an alert service group; or send a bill, depending on the nature of the service the subscriber was opting into or out of.

**Book VIII
Chapter 7**

**Tracking a
Mobile Marketing
Campaign**

Managing Feedback

You shouldn't simply track communication between you and your audience; you should also manage it actively, because consumers often respond to mobile marketing interactions in unexpected ways. Perhaps they made a mistake in responding to your call to action and want to opt out; they may be reaching out to you to offer feedback (ideally, to tell you how great their experience was); or they may be posing a question, asking for help, or giving a shout-out to the celebrity sponsor of your program. You'll be surprised what some people say.

In this section, I discuss how you can use your mobile marketing application to respond to customer feedback.

Responding to feedback

When you gather and respond to customer feedback, make a point of trying to use the same channel that the mobile subscriber used to contact you. If someone uses SMS to contact you, for example, reply with an SMS. If a consumer leaves you a voice-mail message, call back or leave a voice-mail message in response.

Mobile subscribers, however, may contact you via the mobile Internet, through a form you provide on the page. In this case, you can't follow up via the mobile Internet, which doesn't have real-time communication support. Make sure that you capture the mobile subscriber's preferred mobile path for future communications (ask her whether she wants to receive an SMS message, e-mail, or phone call, for example), and then follow up via her preferred method.

To administer your responses to customer feedback, you can use your mobile marketing application, which is often administered through the Internet. Figure 7-2 shows an example of a text-messaging moderation screen that you could use to receive, review, and reply to mobile subscribers' comments.

Figure 7-2: Example moderation screen for managing customer feedback via SMS.

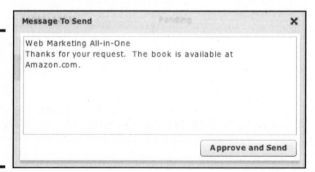

Message To Send   *Pending*   ✕

Web Marketing All-in-One
Thanks for your request. The book is available at
Amazon.com.

Approve and Send

Reporting on feedback

Work with your mobile marketing application provider so that you can label or code each message that comes in: positive feedback, negative feedback, product question, and so on. Later, you can use these labels or code to report on the types of feedback you've received. If you received helpful product feedback, give it to your product team; if customers have a lot of complaints, let your customer-service team know.

Furthermore, you should report the times when questions came in and how long it took you to respond to them. This report is another good measure of your feedback channel.

Finally, if at all possible, report whether your interactions with mobile subscribers were resolved (if resolution was necessary), what percentage of problems was resolved, how the problems were resolved, and how quickly they were resolved.

Tracking and Measuring Interactions: Clicks, Calls, Votes, and More

Your mobile marketing application is capable of tracking most, if not all, interactions a mobile subscriber has with it: calls, text clicks, snaps, scans, StarStars (**), pounds (#), presses, pictures taken, votes, requests, replies, and so on. When you combine this data with data from your traditional media, you can measure the following things and more (it all depends on your program):

✦ Unique and repeat campaign participation

✦ Response rates

✦ Messages delivered and received

✦ Mobile Internet site visits and pageviews

✦ Coupons delivered and redeemed

✦ Prizes awarded and collected

✦ Types of phones and networks your participants are using

✦ Advertising clicks and actions taken

How you track and report on information will vary significantly by the type of mobile method you're using (see the following section).

Tracking methods

Each mobile technology — voice, SMS, mobile Internet, and so on — leaves a unique fingerprint in a mobile marketing application. A voice service, for example, can capture a mobile subscriber's phone number with the help of Caller ID. The same applies to SMS, Multimedia Messaging Service (MMS), and mobile e-mail (an e-mail address going through the wireless-carrier domain, such as `4155551212@t-mobile.net`).

On the mobile Internet, however, carriers rarely provide mobile phone numbers, so you can't capture that information automatically. You need to ask the consumer to provide it via a form. Also, the application provider may be able to see that a visitor is unique but not be able to track who that visitor is. Before running your campaign, ask your mobile application provider to ensure that the necessary data can be tracked and retained.

Data storage and analysis

You'd be amazed how quickly data can be amassed as mobile subscribers interact with a mobile marketing application. Nearly every click, snap, and call can be tracked.

Data storage

Transaction data is stored in the mobile marketing application's database and *log files* (files that record all transactions and that are stored on the server computer's hard drive). During an SMS interaction, for example, the mobile marketing application may record the following transaction: *abcvote yes* 4085551212 543221. Here's the translation of this transaction:

✦ *abcvote* is the keyword associated with a text-messaging voting campaign.

✦ *yes* is the subscriber's response.

✦ 4085551212 is the subscriber's mobile phone number.

✦ 543221 is the wireless *Carrier ID* — a number that tells the mobile marketing application which wireless network the phone number is on (T-Mobile, Sprint, and so on).

This example, however, is the simplest of all possible examples. Log files include a great deal more data, including success and error codes, server IDs, and time stamps. Converting log-file data, which is unintelligible to most readers (log files are written in engineering speak), to actionable results is another matter entirely. Your mobile marketing application provider will need to map the log-file codes to a series of database tables for use in translating the numbers in the log file. Then the provider will map the data in reports (see the following section).

Data analysis

Transaction reports come in two flavors:

+ **Raw data dumps:** A *raw data dump* is a report that provides a line item for every transaction. You can use tools like Excel to analyze and report on the raw data.

+ **Analysis reports:** The mobile application provider can list calculated statistics in an analysis report. If the report is on a voting campaign, for example, the report will display not just the total votes, but also which option received the most votes. Figure 7-3 shows a sample report.

Analyzing data takes a lot of computer power, so a mobile marketing application may not have all current and historical data available in real time. Be sure to ask your mobile marketing application provider what data is available in real time and what data is processed later. Also ask what data is available upon request — data that's in the log files but not readily available in the system for general consumption, for example.

Your application provider will have a lot of experience in collecting and analyzing transaction data. More often than not, however, the provider isn't in *your* business, so it doesn't know exactly how you want to look at the data or what analysis you'll find meaningful. Rather than assume that the provider will know what you need, state clearly the types of results and data you want to see in the transaction reports.

You should have this discussion before your campaign launches; otherwise, you may have some late nights slogging through log files to get the answers you need. By contrast, if you planned and coordinated with your application provider before the launch of your program, the application provider can give you the answers you seek in a perfectly packaged report, often in real time.

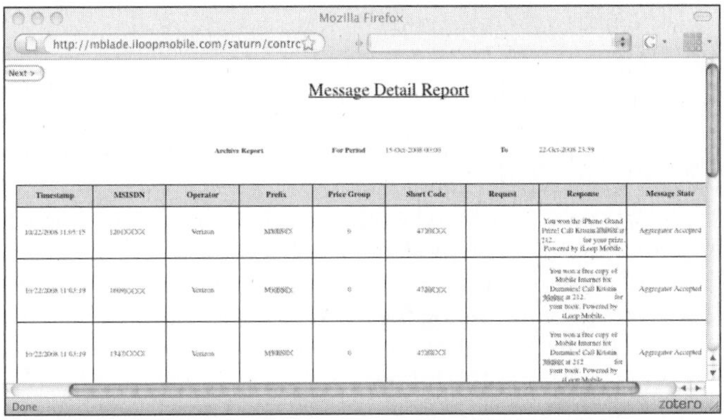

Figure 7-3:
Example
SMS
transaction
report.

**Book VIII
Chapter 7**

Tracking a
Mobile Marketing
Campaign

Tracking and Measuring Purchases

In addition to communication and delivery, mobile marketing is used for *exchange* — for the sale of digital goods and services to be consumed on the mobile phone, as well for physical goods and services. To track purchases via the mobile channel, all you need to do is report on each step of the transaction by pulling the transaction reports from the various systems being used and then reconcile those reports (refer to "Data analysis," earlier in this chapter).

The mobile channel offers different methods for initiating a purchase, capturing the purchase confirmation from the mobile subscriber, completing the transaction, and delivering a receipt. A ringtone purchase, for example, can be initiated via SMS, interactive voice response (IVR), or the Internet.

In the United States, you must use premium SMS (PSMS) or mobile Internet billing for this purpose, so you'll want to track the keywords used in the PSMS and confirm that the billing transaction doesn't occur until the content is actually downloaded by the mobile subscriber. (For more details regarding making money through mobile marketing, refer to Book VIII, Chapter 6.)

Tracking transactions

Make sure that your mobile marketing application tracks each of the four phases of the purchase flow:

1. Purchase initiation (including the channel from which the transaction was initiated)
2. Purchase confirmation
3. Billing
4. Receipt/confirmation message

In addition, make sure that your mobile marketing application can provide easily accessible reports that you can use to track user interactions in each phase (refer to "Data analysis," earlier in this chapter).

Reconciling reports

When you're tracking purchases, you may need to combine data from multiple sources. If your mobile marketing application is managing the interaction with the mobile subscriber, and in the background is using a third-party billing service (such as ShopText, PayPal Mobile, or Bango), you'll want to reconcile the reports from your mobile marketing application and from the billing vendor, just to make sure that all the handoffs between the mobile marketing application and the billing system go smoothly.

Digital services billed to a mobile subscriber's phone bill can be credited back to the mobile subscriber at the discretion of the wireless carrier, and the carrier will deduct this credit from any money it owes you. (For more information, refer to Book VIII, Chapter 6.) Take this fact into account when you reconcile the *payout* (the money you receive for the sale of your content) from the wireless carrier with what you may have expected, based on the reports of your mobile marketing application and billing provider.

Index

Numerics

1ShoppingCart, 33–34, 88, 124, 450
2D codes, 792–793
3D codes, 792–793
100 Clicks, 401
301 redirect, 195, 209
99designs, 52–53
1800MyLogo, 53

A

A/B tests, 396–399
abandonment point, goal funnels, 333–334
About Us/About the Author, blog page, 81
Abram, Carolyn (author) Facebook For Dummies, 692
absolute URLs, 239
access point, 807
accessibility, e-mail, 504
access-point transmitters, local, 749
Account Tactic Settings, 364–365
accounting, as marketing task, 22
accounts
  creating, 347–349, 358–362, 370–375, 577
  Google AdWords, 347–349
  Microsoft adCenter, 370–375
  settings, 364–365, 372–373
  Yahoo! Search Marketing, 358–362, 364–365
Acision, 744
Action Headline Creator, 98–99
action words, in calls to action, 523–525
active voice, 224–225, 587

activity reports from ISPs, 149
ad blindness, 396
Ad Council, 812, 813
ad groups
  adding new, 355–356
  adding to existing campaign, 368–369, 377
  bidding at ad-group level, 409
  defined, 340
  Google AdWords, 355–356, 357
  keywords lists, 380–381
  Microsoft adCenter, 377
  naming, 362
  segmented keywords lists, 380–381
  Yahoo! Search Marketing, 362, 368–369
ad players, mobile, 798–800
adaptation of device, mobile path, 751, 752
add-ons to Firefox browser, 159–168
addresses, e-mail
  From address, 485, 488
  changing, 548
  collecting legally, 455
  on forms, 122
  linking to, 507
  permission to e-mail, 457–462
AddThis, 681
administrative bodies, CSC, 766
AdMob, 829
Adobe Contribute, 91, 94
Adobe Dreamweaver, 94
Adobe Photoshop, 58, 94
ad-serving percentages, 401
advanced keyword targeting, 386–387

advanced scheduling, 412–414
advertising
  about, 3–4
  analytic package choices, 439–441
  budgeting, 403–416
  content network, managing, 434–439
  demographic bidding, 432–434
  geotargeting, 349, 359, 431–432
  Google AdWords, 347–358
    A/B test, 398–399
    accounts, activating, 354–355
    accounts, creating, 347–349
    ad changing, determining when, 402
    ad groups, 355–357
    adding new campaigns, 355–356
    additional settings, 358
    analytic package choices, 440
    bidding, 350–352
    billing, setting up, 352–355
    budgeting, 350–352, 405–406
    budgets and bids, setting up daily, 350–352
    comparing search engines, 346
    content network campaign, managing, 434–437
    cost per click (CPC), 351–352
    daily budgets and bids, 350–352
    deleting keywords, 390
    demographic bidding, 433–434

advertising *(continued)*
  expanding, 355–357
  first campaigns,
    349–350
  keywords, 171–174,
    388, 411–414, 428–429
  PPC budget, 404
  scheduling, 411–414
  Standard Edition,
    347–349
  writing copy that earn
    clicks, 402
keywords
  bidding, 409–415
  budgeting, 403–407
  keyword lists, 379–390
  keyword traffic tools,
    428–431
Microsoft adCenter,
    370–378
  A/B test, 399
  account settings,
    372–373
  accounts, creating,
    370–375
  ad changing,
    determining when, 402
  ad groups, 377
  adding tools, 378
  advanced keyword
    targeting, 386, 387
  analytic package
    choices, 441
  bidding, setting
    incremental, 374–375
  billing, 372
  budgeting for keywords,
    407
  campaign, adding,
    376–377
  comparing search
    engines, 346
  content network
    campaign, managing,
    438–439
  cost per click (CPC),
    371, 374–375

demographic bidding,
    432–433
  expanding, 375–377
  keyword lists, adjusting,
    374–375
  keyword traffic tools,
    430–431
  scheduling, 414–415
  spending limits, PPC
    budget, 404
mobile
  common short codes
    (CSC), 763, 766–767,
    837
  costs and budgeting,
    762–765
  coupons, 789, 790–793
  coverage, 760–761
  defined, 797
  elements and
    approaches, 761–762
  giveaways, 789
  goal setting, 759–760
  incentives and
    giveaways, 789–793
  integrated voice
    response (IVR), 745,
    809
  location-based, 806–807
  mobile ad players,
    798–800
  mobile Internet,
    746–747, 800–804,
    826–829
  mobile media property,
    797
  opt-ins, 769–773
  opt-outs, 774
  package-based, 807–809
  placing ads in mobile
    messages, 804–806
  planning for, 759–774
  point-of-sale (POS),
    783, 808–809
  polling, 786–788
  proximity advertising/
    marketing, 806–807

social marketing,
    812–813
  target-market focus, 753
  text promotions,
    781–786
  tracking results,
    841–855
  user (communication)
    flows, 775–781
  user-generated content
    (UGC), 793–796
  vanity marketing, 812
  viral marketing, 760,
    810–812
  voice-call ads, 809
mobile channel, 797–814
offline editors, 425–428
performance analysis, 265,
    268, 282, 283, 284, 286,
    289, 291
PPC. *See* pay per click
    (PPC)
regulations. *See* legal and
    regulatory compliance
writing copy, 391–402
Yahoo! Search Marketing,
    358–369
  A/B test, 399
  account creating and
    configuring, 358–362,
    364–365
  Account Tactic Settings,
    364–365
  ad changing,
    determining when, 402
  ad groups, 362, 368–369
  adding campaign,
    366–368
  adding tools, 369
  advanced keyword
    targeting, 386–387
  advertising, 358–369
  analytic package
    choices, 440–441
  billing, setting up,
    362–364

budgeting for keywords, 406

comparing search engines, 346

content network campaign, 437–438

cost per click (CPC), 367

expanding, 365–369

first campaigns, 358–362

keyword match types, 365

keyword traffic tools, 429–430

spending limits, PPC budget, 404

writing copy that earn clicks, 402

Advertising Age, 798

advertising campaigns

adding ad group to existing, 357, 368–369, 377

adding campaigns, 355–356, 366–368, 376–377

adding new campaign, 355–356

budgeting for, 407–409

defined, 340

first campaigns, 349–350, 358–362

Google AdWords, 349–350, 355–356, 357, 434–437

managing content network, 434–439

Microsoft adCenter, 376–377, 438–439

mobile channel. _See_ mobile advertising

social media, 721–729

Yahoo! Search Marketing, 358–362, 366–369, 437–438

advice as valuable e-mail content, 527–528

AdWords. _See_ Google AdWords

affiliate aggregators, 24

affiliate link URL, 2

affiliates and affiliate programs

creating, for profit, 40–42

JV hosting, 43–44

1ShoppingCart advantages, 34

product promoting, 24–26

promoting products, for profit, 24–26

tracking, 41

as virtual sales force, 14

affirmative consent, e-mail, 455

age verification, mobile user flows, 780

agency approach, mobile marketing, 761

aggregators

connection aggregators, 739, 763

of content, 525–526

mobile connections and networks, 739, 799

mobile marketing feed, 763

mobile monetization, 837

as social media, 639, 649–650

A-GPS (Assisted GPS), 749

Airborne Mobile, 834

AJAX (Asynchronous JavaScript and XML), 188, 331

allowance per visitor, 21

Amazon.com, 301

aMember, 87

American Marketing Association (AMA), 734, 735, 736

American Red Cross, 814

analysis reports, 853

analyst Web sites, 257

analytic package choices, 439–441

anchor links, 510

anchoring membership sites, 88–89

anger, 248, 679, 717–718

Animal Behavior Associates, 101

annual gross revenue as goal, 18

Apache Server, 195

appearance of blog, 578–580

application fees, mobile, 762–763, 764

applications

Facebook, 691–692

heat map, 59–62

interactive mobile paths, 747

mobile content delivery, 824–825

mobile coupons, 791

mobile graphics applications, 821–822

mobile marketing ecosystem, 740

mobile monetization, 837

mobile providers, 739–740

MySpace, 696

visit quality analysis, 307–309

Arial font, 54

arrows in layout, 67

article pages, 109

Ask Marty About Website Design, 86

Ask sites, 85–86

asking for links, 241–242

assets, setting PPC budget, 404

Assisted GPS (A-GPS), 749

ASV (average sales value), 18

Asynchronous JavaScript and XML (AJAX), 188, 331

AT&T Wireless, 833

auctions, SMS application, 743
Audacity, 624, 625–626
audible, video editing, 133
audience
  audience-driven terms, 169–170
  e-mail information for, 525–527
  horizontal navigation bar, 64
  mobile marketing, 760
  research, and social media plan, 665–674
  size analysis, 282, 283, 568–570
audio
  creating and adding, 129–131
  delivering mobile, 830
  equipment, 129–130, 627
  file format, 130
  to introduce self, 101–102
  media-sharing sites, 639, 648
  mobile content delivery, 829–830
  podcasting, 624–634
    about, 4
    blog support, 629
    defined, 623
    encoding, 633–634
    listening to, 624
    promoting, 634
    recording first, 630–632
    script preparation, 630
    studio setup, 624–629
    testing studio setup, 628–629
    uploading, 633–634
  sales of audio products, 29
AudioTechnica Pro microphone, 132
authentication, e-mail, 553, 558–559
Authorize.Net, 32, 88
auto-discoverable RSS feed, 680

automated content tagging, 846
automated data feed, mobile, 819
automated keyword bidding option, 410
automatic content filtering, 554
automatic data collection, mobile, 846–847
auto-responder linking, mini-sites, 84
auto-responders, 34
Autospies, 677
availability data, 844
avatar, social media profile, 676, 685
average sales value (ASV), 18
AVI files, 134–135
awareness, generating, e-mail marketing, 446
AWeber Communications, 124

B

back-end selling, 38
backup, 11–12, 123
bad neighborhoods, 245
baiting with e-mail subject lines, 490
bandwidth, 737
Bango, 839
Banner Ad Exits, Google Analytics, 27
banner advertising, 27–28, 800, 802
bar code readers, 773
bar codes, mobile coupons, 792–793
Basecamp, 149
BBB (U.S. Better Business Bureau), 209
bCODE, 793
behavioral data, 845
behavioral feedback, e-mail, 446

behavioral information, e-mail, 472
benefits/features model, PPC ad copy, 394
Best Domain Place, 24, 25
Best Hosting Place, 78
Best of the Web (BOTW), 240
best practices, 452, 754, 756–757
bidding on keywords
  automated bidding option, 410
  budgeting for keywords, 409–415
  cost per click (CPC), 409–410
  by day and time, 411–415
  Google AdWords, 349, 350–352, 411–414
  how much to bid, 410–411
  incremental bidding, 374–375
  Microsoft adCenter, 374–375, 414–415
  scheduling, 411–415
  search engine relevance determination, 341
  setting up daily, 350–352
  Yahoo! Search Marketing, 366–368
bidirectional CSC, 765
big picture, tracking SEO results, 252
billing
  Google AdWords, 352–355
  Microsoft adCenter, 371–372
  mobile, 837, 839, 854
  payment options, 1ShoppingCart, 33
  thresholds for, 354
  Yahoo! Search Marketing, 362–364
billing engine, CSC, 766
Billing Revolution, 839

Bitterroot Ranch, Wyoming, 57
black hat SEO, 154, 157–158
Blackberry, 745, 749
blacklist e-mail, 550
blended (universal) search, SEO, 211–219
blind-copy e-mail, 449
BlinkList, 80
BLIP Systems, 748
block list (blacklist), 550
blocked e-mail, 546–547, 549–552
blocking domains, 438
blog, 550, 563
blog carnivals, 611–613
blog posts, 77, 571, 640
Blog Setup Secrets, 84
Blogflux Services, 607–608
bloggage, 590–592
Blogger, 78, 571–574, 577, 639
blogging tools, 78–79
blogs and blogging
  about, 4
  to become recognized expert in field, 14
  blogging tools, 78–79
  commenting, and easy links, 240–241
  creating, 77–81
  design and implementing, 571–574
  e-mail marketing, 448
  guest blog post, 592, 610–611, 682
  hiring professional SEO help, 258
  involvement with other blogs, 605–613
  microblogs, 639, 646–648, 707–709, 714
  mobile, 793–794
  platform and tools, 571–574
  podcasting, 623–634

posting and commenting, 640–642
promoting, 615–621
RSS feed readers, 583, 595–602, 680
RSS feeds, 593–604
  as social media, 639, 640–642
topic selection, 563–570
unique visitors metric for measuring, 283
WordPress installation, 79–81
writing style, 585–592
Blue Snowball microphone, 627
Bluecasting, 747
Bluetooth, 747–748, 807
body, 392, 397
bolded key phrases, relevance, 156
bookmakers, local search optimization, 218
bookmarking sites
  for blog promotion, 616–620
  defined, 644
  Delicious, 639, 644, 645, 698, 699
  Digg, 247, 618–620, 639, 649, 667, 699–701
  friends, 714
  social media, 639, 644–646, 697–700
  social media site targeting, 677
  StumbleUpon, 616–618, 639, 644–645, 698–699
BOTW (Best of the Web), 240
bounce rates
  bottleneck detection from, 312
  defined, 310
  e-mail deliverability, 532–533, 545, 547–549

homepage analysis, 311
  as referring data, 294
  visit quality, 309–312
bounce report, 546, 547
brainstorming, 222, 347–348
branded utilities, 830
branding
  defined, 448
  e-mail, 448, 491–495
  Facebook, 692
  links, 244
  marketing expert for, 138
  mobile marketing, 760
  title tags, 227–228
  Web site design, 49–54
broad keyword match types, 381–383
broadcasting vehicle, podcast, 624
broken links, SEO, 195
Bronto, 534
browsers, 53–54, 500–501, 827
browsing database via links, SEO, 187–188
budget optimizer bidding, 410
budgeting
  Google AdWords, 350–352
  hiring professional SEO help, 260
  membership Web sites, 89–91
  Microsoft adCenter, 371–372
  mobile channel campaign, 762–765
  pay per click (PPC), 342–343, 403–416
  templates, 76
  traffic analysis and reporting, 19–21
  Web site development, 17–22
Yahoo! Search Marketing, 366–368

Building Web Sites All in One For Dummies, 2e (Sahlin and Snell), 30, 54
bullets, Web site relevance, 156
bumper screen advertising, 802–803
business cards, 477–478
business name, e-mail From line, 485–486
business owner, on marketing team, 138
business social media, 80, 643, 669–670, 677
buttons, 65, 127, 476
buying
  credit card transactions Google AdWords, 353–354
  merchant account, 31–32
  mobile content, 839
  1ShoppingCart advantages, 33
  questions to answer before checkout, 35–36
  Yahoo! Search Marketing, 362–364
  high-impact photos, 58
  link for SEO, 245–246
  mobile, 798, 854–855
buzzed, 794

C

call per action (CPA), 28
call to action
  elements of effective, 106
  e-mail, 445–446, 449, 497, 523–525
  meta description tag, 230–231
  mobile, 735, 770–773
  testing, with click-through data, 543
  writing PPC ad copy, 394–395
camera phone, 748, 773

campaigns. *See* advertising campaigns
Canada Common Codes Administration, 766
CAN-SPAM Act, 449, 454–457, 460, 463, 488, 491, 754
capabilities, interactive mobile paths, 750–753
capital letters, avoiding sentences of, 55, 556
capitalization, A/B tests, 397
captivate visitors, C.O.N.V.E.R.T. M.E., 113, 114–115
Carpet Exchange, 50
carrier developer programs, 833
Carrier ID, 852
carriers, mobile channel, 825, 832–834, 837
Cascada Mobile, 825
Cascading Style Sheets (CSS), 53–54, 190, 196
CasinoSoftwareSolutions, 74–75
categories of need, defining, 16
cause mobile marketing, 810, 813–814
CBS Sports, 824
CellFire, 791, 825
CellID triangulation, 748–749
Cellular Telephone Industries Association (CITIA), 5
Cellyspace, 744
centering image, video editing, 133
certification, mobile campaign, 755–756, 764, 776
challenge response systems, e-mail, 549–550
changing ad, determining when, 400–402

channel relationships, mobile, 833
charitable giving, mobile channel, 813–814
chat, live online, 102, 126–129
check boxes, e-mail signup links, 476–477
checkout, 35–36
Chiff, 240
Children's Online Privacy Protection Act (COPPA), 756–757
China Ministry of Information Industry Short Code Administration, 766
CITIA (Cellular Telephone Industries Association), 5
CitySearch, 218
Clark, Brian (author) *Ogilvy on Advertising*, 232
ClickBank, 24
clicks
  click fraud, 422–423
  Crazy Egg utility, 65
  Web site relevance, 157
click-through, e-mail, 28, 535–536, 539–543
click-through rate (CTR), 390, 400, 435
ClickTracks, 271
client-side redirects, SEO, 190–191
Clipart, 58
Club Penguin, 794
CMS (content management system), 91–93, 576
coaching, 37, 138
Coca-Cola, 494
code bloat, SEO, 195–197
coding, with standards, 196
collections, Web site for, 10
color
  as call to action, 106
  e-mail marketing, 448, 492, 494–495
  Web site design, 55–57, 100

Color Calculator tool, 57
color wheel, 57
color-blind sensitivity, 56
columns, e-mail, 498
combinations
  of colors, 57
  e-mail with other media,
    447–449
Comic Sans font, 54
comments
  blog configuration, 580
  on blogs, and easy links,
    240–241
  on other blogs, 606–609
commercial e-mail, as
  spam, 454
Commission Junction, 24
commission payments, JV
  host agreement, 46
commitment, by bloggers,
  564
Common Codes
  Administration, U.S.,
  766
common short codes
  (CSC), 763, 766–767,
  837
communication
  with advertising. *See*
    advertising
  with audio. *See* audio
  with blogs. *See* blogs and
    blogging
  with forms, 121–125
  to introduce self, 100–102
  ISPs, 148–149, 150
  live online chat, 126–129
  as marketing element, 734
  mobile marketing, 761
  with seller, before
    checkout, 36
  telephone
    communication, 34,
    102, 106
  with video. *See* video
  Web site for, 10
company name, e-mail
  marketing, 448

Compete, 674
competition
  copy effectiveness,
    104–105
  identifying and spying on,
    10, 16
  keyword, 176–177,
    180–181
  researching links, 250
  SEO, 180–181
  Web site strategy, 15–17
complaints, minimizing
  spam, 462–467, 553
components, control of,
  Internet marketing
  process, 11–12
compound sentences, blog
  writing, 587
compression, images, 499
computer type
  mobile, 745, 825
  Web design, 53–54
comScore, 674
concept shots, high-impact
  photos, 58
condenser aid, 129
conference call for affiliate
  training, 42
confidence, simplicity in
  blog writing, 587
confidentiality, 35, 47
confirmed-permission lists,
  458–459, 481–482, 553
connection
  connection aggregators,
    739, 763
  main Web site to
    mini-sites, 82–84
  mobile marketing
    ecosystem, 740
  with other blogs, 605–606
Constant Contact, 126, 530,
  745, 820
consumers
  defining target, 15–16
  descriptions, promotional
    content from, 518
  mobile marketing, 760

profile
  mobile channel,
    842–846
  social media, 676–677,
    684–686, 694
  spam perception, 465–466
  standards for trusted
    e-mail, 453
  Web site strategy, 10,
    15–16
contact information,
  472–478, 677
contact list, asking for
  links, 242
content
  backup controls, 11–12
  creating valuable e-mail,
    518–530
  delivery, mobile channel,
    815–830
  duplicate content, SEO,
    191–194
  e-mail filtering, 554–558
  e-mail required content,
    455–457
  E-Mail Service Providers
    (ESPs), 452
  HTML editors, 94–95
  licensing, mobile costs,
    764
  link bait, 248
  list of, in shopping cart, 36
  location, and SEO,
    204–205
  managing, 91–95
  mobile channel
    monetization, 838–840
  mobile Internet, 746–747,
    800–804, 826–829
  package promotions, 808
  program certification,
    mobile,
    755–756, 764, 776
  social media campaign
    creation, 725–728
  supplying, generating
    traffic, 40

content *(continued)*
top content report, 285, 307–308, 312, 324–326
user-generated content (UGC), 554–556, 793–796
writing, 22, 237–238, 523–525
content clusters, 199–203
content management system (CMS), 91–93, 576
content manager, 138
content network, 364–365, 434–439
content sites, for driving traffic, 84–85
contest to design logo, 52–53
context and relevance, 806
ContractorsAccess, 52
contracts, 147, 389–390
controversy, link bait, 248
Conversation Marketing, 567
Converse, 744
conversion
ad changing, determining when to, 401–402
defined, 13, 313, 401
goals for, 313–327
consistency, 315–316
defining, 315–319
goal funnels, 329–335
goal pages for, 316
hidden, 318–319
interpreting data on, 324–327
key performance indicators (KPIs), 264, 313–315, 317, 319
lifetime value of, 319–320
setting, 263–278
soft, 320–321
tracking, 265, 272, 321–324
valuing, 319–321
tracking SEO results, 253

conversion rates, 13, 20, 43–44, 98
C.O.N.V.E.R.T. M.E. formula, 113–120
Convio, 34
cookies, 848
COPPA (Children's Online Privacy Protection Act), 756–757
copy, writing
for advertising and sales
changing ad, determining when, 400–402
C.O.N.V.E.R.T. M.E. formula, 113–120
elements of effective, 97–106
landing pages, 106–113
as marketing task, 22
pay-per-click (PPC), 391–396
testing ads, 396–400
for SEO, 221–233
Copyblogger, 232
copyright, 58, 420–422
Copyscape, 254–255
Core FTP, 13, 94, 95
cost. *See also* budgeting
hiring professional SEO help, 260
membership Web sites, 90–91
mobile channel campaign, 762–765
templates, 76
cost per acquisition (CPA), 798
cost per click (CPC). *See also* pay per click (PPC)
ad changing, determining when, 400
bidding on keywords, 409–410
described, 27–28, 339
Google AdWords, 351–352
Microsoft adCenter, 371, 374–375
mobile buyers, 798

search engine comparison, 346
Yahoo! Search Marketing, 367
cost per conversion, 415
cost per 1,000 page views (CPM), 28, 798
coupons
e-mail, 34, 519–520
mobile channel campaign, 789, 790–793
mobile user flows, 780–781
SMS application, 744
coverage, mobile channel campaign, 760–761
CPA (call per action), 28
CPA (cost per acquisition), 798
CPC. *See* cost per click (CPC)
CPM (cost per 1,000 page views), 28, 798
Craigslist, 143, 144
crawl, 154
Crazy Egg utility, 65
creative concept development, mobile marketing, 763
creative elements, mobile marketing, 761
credit card transactions
Google AdWords, 353–354
merchant account, 31–32
mobile content, 839
1ShoppingCart advantages, 33
questions to answer before checkout, 35–36
Yahoo! Search Marketing, 362–364
Crisp Wireless, 747
CRM (Customer Relationship Management), 34, 743, 848–849

cross-carrier enabled CSC, 766

cross-selling, 37–38, 39

Crown Peak, 34

Crystal Reports, 842

CSC (common short codes), 763, 766–767, 837

CSS (Cascading Style Sheets), 53–54, 190, 196

CSS Web Design For Dummies (Mansfield), 54, 190

CTR (click-through rate), 390, 400, 435

custom purchase form, transaction page, 31

Customer Relationship Management (CRM), 34, 743, 848–849

customers. *See* consumers

customers per month, 17

customizability
blogging platforms, 573, 574, 575, 579
form-processing program, 123
MySpace, 693–694
1ShoppingCart advantages, 33, 34
of templates, 76
traditional Web sites, 74–75
user-flow diagram, 777–778

Cyberduck, 13

CyclingForums, 705

D

dashboard, 281, 293

data. *See also* demographic data; Web analytics
collection through the Web, 848
data mines, e-mail responses, 541–542

on goal funnels, 333–335
mobile storage, 852–853

database
e-mail lists, 469–471
in mobile campaign, 841–842, 846–849

day, bidding on keywords, 411–415

dedicated short code models, 768–769

deep linking, 199, 204

degrading gracefully, 188–189

deleting keywords from lists, 390

Delicious, 639, 644, 645, 698, 699

delivery
defined, 734
e-mail bounce rate, 532–533
mobile marketing, 761
of products, at checkout, 10, 35

demographic data
defined, 843
demographic bidding, 432–434
demographics prediction tool, 669–671
e-mail information, 474
keywords, 177
mobile channel, 843

demography, 843

description page, online chat, 126

design expert, on marketing team, 138

design galleries, 240

design issues
blogs and blogging, 571–574
as marketing task, 22
mobile campaign user flows, 776
mobile Internet site, 828
SEO tracking, 255–256

Web sites
branding, 49–54
checklist, 69–70
color choices, 55–57, 100
font choice, 54–55
layout, 59–69
original Web site design files, 11, 13
pay per click (PPC) drawbacks, 343
photos, high-impact, 57–59
style of text, 54–55
template for, 75–76
usability, 70–72

designers, for traditional Web sites, 74

desired revenue (DR), 18

destination URLs
A/B tests, 398
editorial guidelines, 420
PPC ad copy, 339, 393–394
segmented keywords lists, 383–385

dialing and pressing, mobile call to action, 771

Digg, 247, 618–620, 639, 649, 667, 699–701

Digital Photography For Dummies, 6e (King and Timacheff), 58

digits in short codes, 768

Diigo, 698

direct carrier relationships, mobile channel, 832

direct communication, 734

Direct Debit, Google AdWords, 353–354

direct item, as non-referred source, 294

Direct Marketing Association (DMA), 755, 802

direct mobile marketing, 736

directions, as valuable
e-mail content, 528
directories, 80, 87, 240
discussion forums, 644,
704–707
display URL
A/B tests, 397–398
editorial guidelines,
419–420
PPC ad copy, 393
dispute resolution, JV host
agreement, 47
Distributive Networks, 817
DKI (dynamic keyword
insertion), 399–400, 421
DMA (Direct Marketing
Association), 755, 802
DMOZ, 240
Do Not Call Registry, 756
do-it-yourself approach,
mobile marketing, 761
document files, e-mail links
to, 515
domain exclusion, 434
domain names
affiliation program
forwarding, 26
e-mail From line, 486
logins, control of, 12
mobile-phone e-mail, 820
registrations, control of, 12
DomainKeys, 559
dotMobi, 747, 755, 802, 829
DotProject, 149
downloadable files, e-mail
links to, 513–515
downloads
bumper screen
advertising, 802–803
as conversion goal, 318
mobile audio/video, 830
1ShoppingCart
advantages, 34
dpi, image resolution, 499
DR (desired revenue), 18
dress, appropriate, to meet
JV host, 48
Drupal, 92–93, 576

Dummies, 79
duplicate content, SEO,
191–194
dynamic ad copy, 398
dynamic headlines, 398
dynamic keyword insertion
(DKI), 399–400, 421
dynamic text options, 387

E

easy links, SEO, 238–241
e-books, 29, 37
e-commerce. *See also*
shopping cart
conversion goals, 318–320
funnels in, 329, 330,
331–333
tracking, 265, 272, 322–323
ecosystem, mobile path,
751, 752
e-course registration forms,
124
editing
audio and video, 130,
132–136
writing. *See* writing copy
editorial calendar for
writing blogs, 591
editorial guidelines, 395,
417–420
education and training, 37,
42, 44, 124
educational content pages,
107–109
Elance, 142, 233
elevator pitch, 44
e-mail
about, 4
accessibility of, 504
addresses
From address, 485, 488
changing, 548
collecting legally, 455
on forms, 122
linking to, 507
permission to e-mail,
457–462

authentication of, 553,
558–559
awareness, generating,
446
becoming memorable, 447
benefits of, 445–447
blocked, 546–547, 549–552
bounce rate of, 310
call to action, immediate,
445–446
combined with other
media, 447–449
constructing effective
e-mails, 483–515
content, creating valuable,
517–530
deliverability, 545–559
encouraging visitor
contact, 102
feedback, gathering, 446
filtered, 552–558
firewalls, 551
fonts, 448, 493, 495,
502–503, 505
images in
file format for, 498–499
file size, 499
as links, 509–510
for marketing, 448, 535
referencing, 499–501
interactive mobile paths,
745
legal issues, 449, 451
From lines
addresses, 485, 488
creating effective,
483–485
defined, 484
in effective e-mails,
483–488
filtered e-mail, 555
name, 485–486
lists
brokers, 458–459,
480–482, 553
building quality,
469–482

collecting addresses, and spam, 455
contact information, collecting, 471–478
database preparation, 469–471
inherited lists, 460–462
list brokers, 458–459, 480–482, 553
permissions, 457–462, 480
privacy, 480
protecting, 462
signup incentives, 473, 478–480
Web site as, 10
loss leaders, 521–522
mobile content delivery, 745, 820
mobile messaging, 745, 820, 852
newsletters, 316, 318
non-click responses, 536–539
1ShoppingCart
advantages, 34
permission to e-mail, 457–462
replies and non-click responses, 538–539
scanning, 496–497
Subject lines
creating effective, 483–485, 488–491
filtered e-mail, 555
misleading, 456
tracking results, 531–543
trusted sender reputation, 453–467. *See also* spam
in Web marketing strategy, 445–452
Email Marketing Benchmark Guide (MarketingShepa), 445
Email Sender and Provider Coalition, 482

E-Mail Service Providers (ESPs)
benefits of, 450–452
CAN-SPAM compliance, 454
Constant Content, 449
coupons via e-mail, 519–520
deliverability, 545–559
e-mail database management, 470–471
e-mail marketing, 449–452
Exact Target, 450
fonts in e-mail text, 502–503
to generate awareness, 446
legal issues, 451
Microsoft Office 2007, 449
1ShoppingCart, 450
text links, 505–506
tracking results, 531–543
VerticalResponse, 450
enablers, mobile channel, 748–750
encoding for podcasting, 633–634
encouragement of ISPs, 148–149
energize visitors, C.O.N.V.E.R.T. M.E., 114, 119–120
Engadget, 640
entertainment, content as, 528–529, 727
entity (special character), 224
entry point, goal funnels, 334–335
E!Online, 827
ePrize, 757
Ericsson IPX, 839
error response, user-flow diagram, 779
ESPs. *See* E-Mail Service Providers (ESPs)
essential contact information, e-mail, 472

ethics, in SEO, 157–158
etiquette
asking for links, 242
blogging, 613
social media, 717–718
European Directive 2002/58/EC, 754
evaluating
layout, with heat map application, 59–62
membership sites, 87–89
trust and security, 209
events, 538, 540, 690
exact keyword match types, 381–383
Exact Target, 450
exchange
defined, 734, 854
mobile marketing, 761
tracking mobile campaign, 854–855
excluded words, Yahoo! Search Marketing, 364
execution
mobile campaign user flows, 776
mobile marketing, 761, 764
opt-in mobile call to action, 772–773
expanding
Google AdWords, 355–357, 388
keywords lists, 387–389
Microsoft adCenter, 375–377
MSN (search engine), 389
Yahoo! (search engine), 388–389
Yahoo! Search Marketing, 365–369
expectations
JV host agreement, 46
link bait, 250
Expedient Financial Services, Inc., 31–32
expense allowance per visitor, 21

expert
  become recognized as, 4
  interviews as content, 527
explicit permission to
    e-mail, 458, 465
expose your solution,
    C.O.N.V.E.R.T. M.E., 113,
    117
expressed consent, mobile,
    816
ExpressionEngine, 576
extended display URL, 398
extensions, Joomla!, 91
external drive for video
    editing, 133
EyeTools, 495

F

Facebook
  applications, 691–692
  blog promotion, 621, 667
  described, 684
  Facebook Events, 690
  Facebook Pages, 688–690
  finding questions, 716
  friends, 713
  groups, 686–688
  media-sharing sites, 639,
    648
  networking tools, 684–688
  networks, 686
  profile page, 684–686
  as social media, 684–692
Facebook For Dummies
    (Abram and Pearlman),
    692
facts, as valuable e-mail
    content, 529
fallout report builder, goal
    funnel tracking, 331
false positive, filtered
    e-mail, 552
familiarity with topic, by
    bloggers, 564
Fark, 620

Federal Trade Commission
    (FTC), 454, 457, 756
feedback, 446, 850–851
FeedBurner, 80, 81, 624
FeedBurner RSS tool, 583
Fem2Cells, 749
Feng-GUI, 60
file formats
  audio, 130
  images, 215, 489–499, 822,
    829
  Portable Document
    Format (PDF), 29, 515
  video, 134–135, 215,
    489–499, 829
file names, Web site
    relevance, 157
file size, 499
File Transfer Protocol
    (FTP), 13, 94–95, 136
file transfer via FTP, 13,
    94–95, 136
FileMaker Pro, 842
files, moving with FTP, 13,
    94–95, 136
filter words, SEO copy,
    223–224
filtering
  e-mail, 552–558
  mobile messaging, 818
financial goals for Web
    sites, 18–19
Finkelstein, Ellen (author)
  *Syndicating Sites with RSS
    Feeds For Dummies*, 216
Firefox browser, 159–168,
    258
firewalls, blocked e-mail,
    551
Flash pages, 189–190
Flash Video (FLV), 134–136
Flickr, 215, 639, 648,
    702–703
fluid elements, video
    editing, 134
FLV (Flash Video), 134–136
FLV Producer, 134–136

focus, blog topic selection,
    563–566
folders to organize RSS
    feeds, 597, 598–600
followers, 714
follow-up, e-mail tracking,
    542–543
fonts
  e-mail, 448, 493, 495,
    502–503, 505
  headlines, 100
  Web site design, 54–55
form fields, 122
format
  e-mail
    brand consistency
      across, 493–495
    images, 498–499
  file
    audio, 130
    images, 215, 489–499,
      822, 829
    video, 134–135, 215,
      489–499, 829
  headlines, 100
form-processing program,
    123
forms, for communication,
    121–125
forums
  discussion forums, 644,
    704–707
  horizontal navigation bar
    design, 64
  JV host, finding, 44–45
Forward to Friend link,
    319, 331
forwarding e-mail and
    CAN-SPAM, 454
fragmented text, PPC ad
    copy, 396
France SMS+, 766
FREE, 810
Free Audio Conferencing
    (Web sites), 42

free elements, squeeze page, 111

free search, 39

free to the end user (FTEU), 777

freeware form-processing program, 123

FreeWebsiteTemplates, 76

FreeWebTemplates, 76

FriendFeed, 639, 649, 650, 707

friends
  defined, 713
  Facebook, 685–686
  social media network, 713–719
  tell-a-friend marketing, 125–126, 743, 760, 795–796, 810–812
  white list, e-mail, 552

Fripp, 102

From lines, e-mail
  addresses, 485, 488
  creating effective, 483–485
  defined, 484
  in effective e-mails, 483–488
  filtered e-mail, 555
  name, 485–486

FTC (Federal Trade Commission), 454, 457, 756

FTEU (free to the end user), 777

FTP (File Transfer Protocol), 13, 94–95, 136

fulfillment, JV host, 44

full-time soloist ISP, 139

fun, social media, 682

functional components, layout evaluation, 62

funnel writing style, avoiding, 225–226, 590

funnels, conversion goal, 329–335

G

games, mobile delivery, 824–825

GarageBand, 624, 625, 631, 632, 633

Gatineau Analytics, 370, 441

geographic targeting, 349, 359, 431–432

geography, mobile path, 752

Georgia font, 54

geotagging, local search optimization, 218–219

geotargeting, 349, 359, 431–432

GIF images, 499

GIMP, 58, 94

giveaways, 521, 522, 789–793

Gizmodo, 640–641

Global Positioning System (GPS), 749

Glue Gun Crafts, 565

goal funnels, 329–335

goal pages
  conversions indicated by, 316
  defining, 317
  in goal tracking process, 321, 322, 324

goals
  advertising, 395, 400
  blog topic selection, 566–567
  mobile channel, 759–760
  for Web sites, development of, 17–22

Google (iGoogle), 564–565, 653–658

Google AdSense, 27, 84

Google Advertising Professionals Program, 347

Google AdWords
  A/B test, 398–399
  accounts, activating, 354–355
  accounts, creating, 347–349
  ad changing, determining when, 402
  ad groups, 355–357
    adding ad to existing, 357
    adding new, 355–356
    adding to existing campaign, 357
  adding new campaigns, 355–356
  additional settings, 358
  advertising campaign
    adding ad group to existing, 357
    adding new, 355–356
    setting up first, 349–350
  analytic package choices, 440
  bidding, 350–352
  billing, setting up, 352–355
  budgeting, 350–352, 405–406
  budgets and bids, setting up daily, 350–352
  comparing search engines, 346
  content network campaign, managing, 434–437
  cost per click (CPC), 351–352
  daily budgets and bids, 350–352
  deleting keywords, 390
  demographic bidding, 433–434
  expanding, 355–357
  first campaigns, 349–350

Google AdWords *(continued)*
  keywords
    bidding scheduling,
      411–414
    expanding lists, 388
    research on, 171–174
    traffic tools, 428–429
  PPC budget, 404
  scheduling, 411–414
  Standard Edition, 347–349
  writing copy that earn
    clicks, 402
Google AdWords Editor,
  426–427
Google Analytics
  content report with dollar
    index in, 325–326
  e-commerce tracking by,
    272, 322–323
  goal funnel tracking,
    331–334
  goal tracking, 272, 313,
    322–324
  keywords report, 325
  landing page report,
    326–327
  loyalty benchmark,
    305–306
  reputation of, 266
  SEO results tracking,
    252–253
  top content report,
    307–308
  traffic analysis
    capabilities of, 270
    filter for, 277–278
    five metrics in, 281
    keyword analysis by,
      299–300
    monetization, 27
  Pageviews report by,
    286
  referring data from,
    293–298
  reporting tools used by,
    267
  setting up, 272–278

Time On Site report by,
  288–289
Unique Visitors report
  by, 284
Visits report by, 282
visit quality analysis,
  303–308, 310
Web site, 270, 272
Google Android, 745
Google Blog Search, 258,
  667
Google Docs, 19
Google Groups, 644, 666,
  706
Google Image Search,
  296–298
Google Insights, 178, 429
Google Local, 218–219
Google Maps, 748
Google PageRank, 235
Google Reader, 583, 595–602
Google search engine
  Blogger, 571–574, 577
  for competition research,
    16
  competitor links, 250
  cost per click (CPC),
    409–410
  duplicate content, 192
  FeedBurner RSS tool, 583
  image optimization,
    214–215
  link buying/selling,
    245–246
  multiple PPC accounts,
    347
  news optimization,
    213–214
  product optimization, 212
  as referrer, 295
  segmented keywords lists,
    383–384
Google Sitemap, 109
Google Toolbar, 159, 163
Google Trends, 174–175,
  569

Google Webmaster tools,
  165, 166
GoogleBase, 213
Gooruze, 677
GPS (Global Positioning
  System), 749
Graham, Eric (conversion
  expert), 106
grammar, writing PPC ad
  copy, 395–396
grand-prize winner, mobile
  user flows, 780
graphics, 1ShoppingCart
  advantages, 33
green links, 68
Greystripe, 825
Griffin iMic, 627
Groomstand, 202–203
groups
  Facebook, 686–688
  friends, 714
  LinkedIn, 697
  mobile text alerts, 816–819
guarantee graphic, layout,
  68
guarantees, and checkout,
  35
guest blog post, 592,
  610–611, 682
guest books, 477
guidelines
  editorial, 395, 417–420
  MMA Consumer Best
    Practices Guidelines,
    754
Guinea Pig Olympics, 247
Guinness contest, 783

H

Hampton Inn, 804
Hands-On Mobile, 825
hard bounce e-mail,
  547–548

headers
  defined, 483
  e-mail, 483–484, 487
  online chat, 126–127
headings
  e-mail TOCs, 512
  on forms, 122
  semantic outline, 207–208
  Web site relevance, 156
headlines
  A/B tests, 397, 398
  C.O.N.V.E.R.T. M.E.
    formula, 113, 114–115
  elements of effective,
    98–100
  e-mail, 448, 501, 512–513
  formatting, 100
  link-worthy content, 238
  online tools to generate,
    98–99
  PPC ad copy, 391–392
  SEO copy, 231–232
  squeeze page, 110
  Yahoo! Search Marketing,
    392
headset microphones, 627
heat map, 495
heat map application, to
    evaluate layout, 59–62
hidden text, Web site
    relevance, 156
hierarchical ordering,
    search engine, 155–157
high-throughput,
    connection aggregator,
    763
high-traffic keywords, 392
hiring professional help
  ISP, choosing, 139–150
  marketing team, 138
  for SEO, 233, 257–260
  for valuable e-mail
    content, 529–530
hits
  defined, 279
  as marketing metric,
    279–280
  usefulness of tracking, 280

Hitwise, 674
hobbyist ISP, 139
homepages, 193–194, 311,
    393
horizontal navigation bar,
    layout, 64–66
Hormel Foods, 464
hosting
  blog carnivals, 611–613
  domain name registration
    and controls, 12
  joint venture (JV) hosting,
    14, 43–48
  logins, control of, 11
hot keys, review RSS feeds
    with, 602
HTML
  backup controls, 11–12
  editors, 94–95
  e-mail, 491, 501–505
  fonts in e-mail text,
    502–503
  navigation links, 510–511
  text links, 505–506
*HTML, XHTML & CSS For
    Dummies*, 6e (Tittel and
    Noble), 196
hub pages, 199, 200, 202
human factor, elements of
    effective, 100–102
humor as bait, 247, 679
hybrid approach, mobile
    marketing, 762
hyperlinks, 68

I

IAB (Interactive Advertising
    Bureau), 28, 755
idea list for writing blogs,
    591
Identi.ca, 707
iGoogle, 564–565, 653–658
iLoop Mobile, 744, 747, 781,
    817
image reference, 500–501

images. *See also* photos
  banners for mobile ads,
    800, 802
  captions, Web site
    relevance, 156
  defined, 498
  in e-mail
    file format for, 498–499
    file size, 499
    as links, 509–510
    for marketing, 448, 535
    referencing, 499–501
  file format, 215, 489–499,
    822, 829
  link bait, 248–249
  link-worthy content, 238
  mobile devices, 821–822
  optimization, blended
    search, 214–215
  product optimization, 213
implied permission to
    e-mail, 457–458
incentives, 473, 478–480,
    789–793
incidental permission, to
    receive e-mail, 458
incoming links, tracking
    SEO results, 253
incremental bidding/
    targeting, 374–375
indexed pages, 168, 200,
    253
indirect communication,
    734
indirect mobile marketing,
    736
individual e-mail filters,
    556–558
industry, PPC spending by,
    415
industry associations, 240,
    257
industry commitment,
    effective copy, 102, 103
industry keywords, 178
information products, sales
    of, 29

Infusionsoft, 34
Ingenio Pay Per Call, 28
inherent value, 517. *See also*
content
inherently valuable content,
e-mail, 525–529
inherited lists, e-mail,
460–462
inline text links, 68
in-person contact
information, e-mail,
477–478
instant win, mobile user
flows, 780
in-store purchases, 536–537
instructions, as valuable
e-mail content, 528
integrated voice response
(IVR), 745, 809
Integrity, 195
intellectual property rights,
JV host, 47
Interactive Advertising
Bureau (IAB), 28
interactive paths, mobile,
741–748, 750–753
interest, e-mail, 473–474,
542
intermediate relationships,
mobile, 833–834
internal microphone, 627
Internet Information Server,
195
Internet marketing process,
11–14. *See also* specific
topics
Internet protocol (IP)
address, 485
Internet service provider
(ISP)
attracting, 146–147
choosing, 139–150
contracts, 147
defined, 137, 139
Internet protocol (IP)
address, 485
measuring results,
148–150

nurturing the relationship,
150
outsourcing, 148
possible positions for, 138
referrals to, 141–144
selecting, 144–146
setting expectations,
148–149
spam protections, 462–463
types of, 139–141
Internet Video Guy, 105, 132
interoperability, mobile
path, 750, 752
interstitial advertising,
802–803
interviews
as content, 527
professional SEO help, 259
inventory, mobile
advertising, 798, 799
involvement, membership
Web sites, 90
IP (Internet protocol)
address, 485
iPhone, 745, 749, 753
ipsh!, 744
ISP. *See* Internet service
provider (ISP)
iStockphoto (Web sites), 58
iTunes, 624, 629, 634
IVR (integrated voice
response), 745, 809

J

Jaguar XF, 802
JavaScript
AJAX, 188
funnel tracking for, 331
as reporting tool, 267, 268,
269
search engines, 188, 190,
196–197
setup for, 272
Jell-O, 50
Jingle Networks, 809, 810
JoeAnt, 240
johnarnold, 559

joint venture (JV) hosting,
14, 43–48
Joomla!, 91–93, 576
JPG images, 215, 499
jump-page advertising,
802–803
junk mail folders, 490–491
just-noticeable difference,
494

K

kapow, 827
Kelly, Lew (merchant
broker), 31–32
Kent, Peter (author)
Search Engine
Optimization for
Dummies, 2e, 153
key performance indicators
(KPIs), 264, 313–315,
317, 319
key phrases
title tags, 227–228
Web site relevance,
155–156
Keynote, 829
keyword density, 227
Keyword Discovery, 171
keyword diversity, 168,
252–253
keyword list
adjusting, 374–375
content networks, 435
destination URL, 393
editorial guidelines, 419
researching search
engines, 346
for sales, 379–390
search engine relevance
determination, 341
segmented keywords lists,
380–381, 383–385
tracking SEO results, 254
keyword match types, 365,
381–383
keyword meta tags, 156
keyword rankings, 168

keyword services, 171

keyword spreadsheet, 179–180

keyword stuffing, 228

keyword traffic, estimating, 428–431

keyword traffic tools, 428–431

keyword-rich URLs, 206

keywords
  bidding on, 409–415
  choosing from keywords lists, 379–380
  competition, 176–177, 180–181
  in conversion goal analysis, 324–325
  defined, 340
  deleting from keywords lists, 390
  image optimization, 215
  lists of, 379–390
  Microsoft adCenter, 370, 374
  PPC budgeting, 403–407
  quality links, 244
  referrals from, 296–297, 299–300
  as referrer data, 292
  report, for conversion analysis, 324–325
  reserved, 778
  search engine relevance determination, 340
  and SEO, 169–181

keyword-targeted campaign, 349–352, 355–357, 359–365

King, Julie Adair (author)
  Digital Photography For Dummies, 6e, 58

Kodak Gallery, 794

KPIs (key performance indicators), 264, 313–315, 317, 319

L

landing pages
  in conversion goal analysis, 326–327
  defined, 106–107, 326
  educational content pages, 107–109
  mobile Internet, 746, 826
  and PPC, 339
  referring data from, 297, 301
  sales pages, 111–113
  search engine relevance determination, 341
  site maps, 109
  squeeze pages, 110–111

large ISP, 139

layout, 59–69, 448, 495–498

lead-based worksheet, 723–724

leadershiparticles.net, 27

leads, 10, 318, 320, 330, 760

leasing, common short codes (CSC), 763, 766

LeClaire, Jennifer (author)
  Web Analytics For Dummies, 264, 301, 315

legacy tracking code, 273

legal and regulatory compliance
  Children's Online Privacy Protection Act (COPPA), 756–757
  click fraud, 422–423
  copyright, 58, 420–422
  editorial guidelines, 417–422
  e-mail marketing, 449, 451
  E-Mail Service Providers (ESPs), 451
  mobile channel, 753–757
  mobile content program certification, 755–756, 764, 776

mobile marketing, 753–757

National Do Not Call Registry, 756

personal information protections, 757

spam, 454–457

trademarks, 420–421

legitimacy of product/site, before checkout, 35

letters of recommendation, 104

Levi Strauss, 49

licensed mobile content, 837–838

lifetime value of conversion goal, 319–320

Lightpole, 794, 825, 827

Limelight Presentations, 100, 101, 125

link bait
  brainstorming, 347–348
  defined, 346
  images, 248–249
  in SEO, 246–250
  social media plan, 678, 679–680, 701
  video, 249–250

link exchange network, 257

link exchanges, 246

link text, Web site relevance, 157

link velocity, 236

link votes, 203, 235–237

LinkDiagnosis, 250

LinkedIn, 80, 643, 669–670, 677, 696–697

linking networks, 154, 246

links
  broken links, 195
  building, 235
  creating content clusters, 200–203
  deep linking, 199, 204
  in e-mail, 505–515

links *(continued)*
  e-mail text, 502
  to other blogs, 609–610
  and SEO, 235–250
    asking for links, 241–242
    buying and selling links, 245–246
    creating quality links, 244–245
    easy links, 238–241
    link bait, 246–250
    link exchanges, 246
    link networks, 246
    link votes, 203, 235–237
    researching competitor's links, 250
    tracking results, 254
    widget building, 242–244
    writing link-worthy content, 237–238
  Web site relevance, 157
list brokers, e-mail, 458–459, 480–482, 553
list members, protecting, mobile channel, 849
list rental, e-mail, 482
listening. *See* audio; podcasting
lists
  e-mail
    brokers, 458–459, 480–482, 553
    building quality, 469–482
    collecting addresses, and spam, 455
    contact information, collecting, 471–478
    database preparation, 469–471
    inherited lists, 460–462
    list brokers, 458–459, 480–482, 553
    permissions, 457–462, 480
    privacy, 480

    protecting, 462
    signup incentives, 473, 478–480
    Web site as, 10
  keyword
    adjusting, 374–375
    content networks, 435
    destination URL, 393
    editorial guidelines, 419
    researching search engines, 346
    for sales, 379–390
    search engine relevance determination, 341
    tracking SEO results, 254
  as social media bait, 679
  Web site relevance, 156
Live HTTP Headers, 159, 162
Live Local, 218
Live Search. *See* Microsoft Live Search
live testing of usability, 71–72
live-event voting, mobile, 788
LiveJournal, 576
local search optimization, 217–219, 257
location
  data regarding, 845
  e-mail From line, 486
  geographic targeting, 349, 359, 431–432
  horizontal navigation bar, 65
  mobile advertising, 806–807
  mobile information, 748–749
log files, 852
logic, social media site targeting, 677
logins
  control of, 11, 12
  forms as SEO roadblock, 186

logistics, E-Mail Service Providers (ESPs), 451
logos
  branding, 50, 51–53
  contest to design, 52–53
  developing branded, 50–52
  e-mail marketing, 491–492, 494
  and e-mail marketing, 448
  linking e-mail to Web site, 510
  and slogan, 50
logs (log files)
  referrer data from, 291
  as reporting tool, 267–268, 269
  server setup for, 272
long codes, 768
long-tail keyword, 380, 435
long-tail phrases, 170–171, 382
loyalty
  benchmarks, visit quality analysis, 305–306
  incentive rewards, 479
  loyalty point package promotions, 808
Lyris, 271

M

Ma.gnolia, 639, 698
making money. *See* monetization
managing
  content network campaign, 438–439
  membership Web sites, 86–91
  multiple PPC accounts, 347
  pay per click (PPC) drawbacks, 344
Manis, John (mobile industry player), 813

Mansfield, Richard (author)
*CSS Web Design For
Dummies*, 54, 190
manufacturers,
promotional content
from, 518
mapping, user flows,
777–778
market research, Web site
for, 10, 16
market share, calculating
potential, 16
market testing, Web site
for, 10
marketing
adding mobile to
marketing strategy,
736–741
defined, 734, 736
elements of, 734–735
experts, on marketing
team, 138
Web marketing process,
11–14
Marketing Makeover
Generator, 86, 111
marketing outlet, Web site
as, 10
marketing routine, social
media plan, 681–682
MarketingSherpa, 445
match types, keyword, 365,
381–383
maven social media style,
675
maximum CPC, 351, 410
MAXX Wireless, 747
McDonald's, 49
mCRM (mobile CRM), 743
media mailing list, 475
media-sharing sites
Flickr, 215, 639, 648,
702–703
friends, 714
social media, 639, 648,
701–704
TubeMogul, 704

YouTube
audio sharing, 639, 648
finding questions,
716–717
RSS feed, 216, 217
using, 703–704
video sharing, 132–133
viral marketing, 811
membership Web sites
anchoring, 88–89
calculating revenue
potential, 89–91
cost, 90–91
defined, 86–87
evaluating types of, 87–89
managing, 86–91
password-protected
directories, 87
third-party script on,
87–89
mentoring, marketing team,
138
menu trees, horizontal
navigation bar, 65
menus, building, 188–189
merchant brokers, 31–32
messages
color choices, 55–56
mobile, 804–806
paths, mobile content
delivery, 816–820
Premium Short Message
Service (PSMS), 805,
814, 834–838, 854
Short Message Service
(SMS)
for content delivery, 816
data collection through,
846–847
mobile content
certification, 755–756
mobile monetization,
805–806
for mobile monetization,
834–838
viral marketing,
742–744
social media plan,
674–675

meta description tags, 156,
230–231
meta robots tags, 184–185
meta tag optimization, SEO,
257
metadata, mobile channel,
773, 843
mFinity, 817
MGF (Mobile Giving
Foundation), 813
microblogs
building following,
708–709
defined, 707
friends, 714
for social media, 707–709
social media sites, 639,
646–648
as time waster, 709
microphones
for audio, 129, 132, 627
podcast, 624, 626–627
for video, 105
microsites, 745
micro-sites. *See* mini-sites
Microsoft Access, 842
Microsoft adCenter
A/B test, 399
account settings, 372–373
accounts, creating,
370–375
ad changing, determining
when, 402
ad groups, 377
adding tools, 378
advanced keyword
targeting, 386, 387
analytic package choices,
441
bidding, setting
incremental, 374–375
billing, 372
budgeting for keywords,
407
campaign, adding,
376–377
comparing search
engines, 346

Microsoft adCenter
    (continued)
  content network
    campaign, managing,
    438–439
  cost per click (CPC), 371,
    374–375
  demographic bidding,
    432–433
  expanding, 375–377
  keyword lists, adjusting,
    374–375
  keyword traffic tools,
    430–431
  scheduling, 414–415
  spending limits, PPC
    budget, 404
Microsoft adCenter
  Desktop, 370, 427
Microsoft adCenter Editor,
  427–428
Microsoft adCenter Labs,
  177, 667–672
Microsoft Excel, 19, 270, 842
Microsoft Live Cashback,
  370
Microsoft Live Search
  account settings, 372–373
  accounts, creating,
    370–375
  ad groups, 377
  adding tools, 378
  bidding, setting
    incremental, 374–375
  campaign, adding, 376–377
  comparing search
    engines, 346
  competitor links, 250
  expanding, 375–377
  image optimization,
    214–215
  keyword lists, adjusting,
    374–375
  local search optimization,
    218
  news optimization,
    213–214

  product optimization, 212
  tracking SEO results, 253
  Webmaster tools, 165,
    166–167
Microsoft MSN (search
  engine)
  advanced keyword
    targeting, 387
  cost per click (CPC),
    409–410
  expanding keywords lists,
    389
  multiple PPC accounts,
    347
  segmented keywords lists,
    385
Microsoft Office 2007, 449
Microsoft Outlook, 489, 583
Microsoft Sender ID, 559
mini-sites
  Ask sites, 82–84, 85–86
  auto-responder linking, 84
  connecting to main Web
    site, 82–84
  described, 82
  sales pages (one-page
    sales letters), 82
  squeeze pages, 82, 85
  text linking, 82
  thank you page linking,
    82–83
Mixx, 619
MMA Consumer Best
  Practices Guidelines,
  754, 756, 778, 800
M:Metrics, 829, 845
MMS (Multimedia Message
  Service), 744, 805, 806,
  816
MO (mobile originated)
  message, 772–773, 835
mobile ad players, 798–800
mobile advertising
  common short codes
    (CSC), 763, 766–767,
    837
  costs and budgeting,

    762–765
  coupons, 789, 790–793
  coverage, 760–761
  defined, 797
  elements and approaches,
    761–762
  giveaways, 789
  goal setting, 759–760
  incentives and giveaways,
    789–793
  integrated voice response
    (IVR), 745, 809
  location-based, 806–807
  mobile ad players,
    798–800
  mobile Internet, 746–747,
    800–804, 826–829
  mobile media property,
    797
  opt-ins, 769–773
  opt-outs, 774
  package-based, 807–809
  placing ads in mobile
    messages, 804–806
  planning for, 759–774
  point-of-sale (POS), 783,
    808–809
  polling, 786–788
  proximity advertising/
    marketing, 806–807
  social marketing, 812–813
  target-market focus, 753
  text promotions, 781–786
  tracking results, 841–855
  user (communication)
    flows, 775–781
  user-generated content
    (UGC), 793–796
  vanity marketing, 812
  viral marketing, 760,
    810–812
  voice-call ads, 809
Mobile Advertising
  Guidelines, 800
Mobile Advertising Network
  Aggregators, 799

mobile channel
  about, 5
  adding to marketing
    strategy, 736–741
  applications, 824–825
  audio, 829–830
  blogs and blogging,
    793–794
  branded utilities, 830
  complexities of, 736–737
  content certification,
    755–756, 764, 776
  content delivery, 815–830
  defined, 735
  elements of, 735–736
  e-mail, 745, 820, 852
  e-mail information, 820
  enablers, 748–750
  games, 824–825
  group text alerts, 816–819
  mesaging paths, 816–820
  mobile enhancements,
    820–824
  mobile Internet, 746–747,
    800–804, 826–829
  and mobile service
    providers, 738–741
  monetization, 831–840
  paths to, 741–748, 750–753
  personalization content,
    820–824
  personalized text alerts,
    819–820
  promotions, 781–786,
    831–832
  regulatory compliance,
    753–757
  ringtones, 823–824
  sales of, 838–840
  screen savers, 821–823
  social networking, 794
  sourcing, 815–816
  spam, 754–755
  subscriptions, 831–832
  video, 829–830
  wallpaper, 821–823
Mobile Complete
  DeviceAnywhere, 829

mobile content
  enhancements, 820–824
mobile CRM (mCRM), 743
Mobile Giving Foundation
  (MGF), 813
mobile Internet
  ads on network of sites,
    803
  bumper-screen
    advertising, 802–803
  creating, 827–828
  data collection, 848
  described, 746–747
  design issues, 828
  placing ads in your own
    site, 800–801
  placing ads on a branded
    site, 802
  placing outside ads on
    your site, 803
  testing, 829
  types of ads, 800
  using, 826–827
Mobile Marketing
  Association (MMA),
    754, 755, 756, 778, 800
mobile media property, 797
mobile operating systems,
  745, 825
mobile operators, 738
mobile originated (MO)
  message, 772–773, 835
mobile service providers,
  738–741
Mobile Streams, 834
mobile terminated (MT)
  call, 772–773
mobile Web. *See* mobile
  Internet
mobile-enhanced channel,
  735
mobileStorm, 745, 820
mobiThinking, 827
Moblog, 794
moderation of blog, 580

monetization. *See also*
  sales
  affiliates, 24–26, 40–42
  bidding on keywords,
    410–411
  customer revenue,
    increasing initial, 36–40
  defined, 27
  JV host, 43–48
  membership sites, 86–91
  mobile channel, 831–840
  online transactions, 30–36
  product and service sales,
    29–30
  selling products and
    services, 29–30
  of traffic, 27–28
  traffic monetization, 27–28
monitors, viewing colors
  on, 56–57
Monkeybizness, 52
monthly budget, 404
morale, and SEO tracking
  worksheet, 251
morewords, 50
Morris, Tee (author)
  Podcasting For Dummies,
    2e, 623
motivate by adding value
  and urgency
  C.O.N.V.E.R.T. M.E.
    formula, 114, 118–119
Movable Type, 78, 575–576,
  629, 634
Mozilla, 159
MP3 format, 130
MSN (search engine). *See
  also* under Microsoft
  advanced keyword
    targeting, 387
  cost per click (CPC),
    409–410
  expanding keywords lists,
    389
  multiple PPC accounts,
    347
  segmented keywords lists,
    385

MT (mobile terminated) call, 772–773
Multimedia Message Service (MMS), 744, 805, 806, 816
multimedia on MySpace, 694
multiple blogs, 574, 576
multiple e-mail addresses, 488
multiple Web sites, connecting
 Ask sites, 85–86
 blog sites, 77–81
 creating, 73–95
 membership sites, 87–88
 mini-sites, 82–84
 reasons for, 73–74
multi-step opt-in mobile call, 773
Music Mates, 84–85
MX Telecom, 839
My Yahoo!, 661–663
MyGoldSecurity, 56
MySpace, 639, 643, 692–696, 713
MySQL programming, 87, 93

N

name, e-mail From line, 485–486
naming the text link, 507–508
National Do Not Call Registry, 756
National Public Radio (NPR), 745
natural elements, video editing, 134
natural search, 154
natural search rankings, 341
navigation, e-mail, 497
navigation links, 510–511

negative keyword match types, 381–383
negative keywords, 364
Nellymoser, 825
Netbiscuits, 747
Netsuite, 34
Netvibes, 658–661
networking. *See also* content network
 events to find JV host, 44
 Facebook tools, 684–688
 linking, 154, 246
 Web sites, 77–88
new kid social media style, 676
New report, loyalty analysis, 306
New Tracking Code, 273
new-media channel, 735
new-media mobile service providers, 738
news
 optimization in blended search, 213–214
 social media site targeting, 677
news reference volume, 174
newsletter subscription forms, 124
Newsvine, 619
newswires, 250
NFC Nears Field Communication (NFC), 750
niche
 pay per click (PPC), 343, 415–416
 social media site targeting, 677–678, 712
Nielson Online, 674, 829, 845
99designs, 52–53
Noble, Jeff (author)
 HTML, XHTML & CSS For Dummies, 6e, 196
nofollow command, 236–237, 610

noise, unique visitors metric, 283
Nokia, 838
non-bounce response totals, e-mail, 533
non-click responses
 e-mail replies, 538–539
 event attendance, 538
 in-store purchases, 536–537
 phone calls, 538
 tracking, 536–539
Not Set item, non-referred source, 294, 295
now address your visitors, C.O.N.V.E.R.T. M.E., 113, 115
NPR (National Public Radio), 745
number of characters, subject line, 488
number of items on horizontal navigation bar, 65

O

Obama, Barack (U.S. President), 796
offerings, mobile marketing, 735, 760
offers
 coupons, 519–520
 creating valuable e-mail, 518–522
 defined, 518
 e-mail response tracking, 542–543
 facts, 529
 giveaways, 521, 522
 loss leaders, 521–522
 promotional content, 518–519
 testimonial in C.O.N.V.E.R.T. M.E., 113, 115
urgent offers, 522

offline editors, 425–428
offline efforts to generate
    traffic, 40
Ogilvy on Advertising
    (Ogilvy and Clark), 232
Omniture SiteCatalyst, 266,
    270, 331
1800MyLogo, 53
100 Clicks, 401
one-on-one assistance,
    training affiliates, 42
1ShoppingCart, 33–34, 88,
    124, 450
Online Commercial
    Intention, 668–669
online communities, 621,
    666–667, 721
online project tracker, 149
Open Directory Project, 80
open rate, e-mail, 533–535
open source software, 91
OpenCellID, 749
open-ended questions, 473,
    784–786
operating systems
    mobile, 745, 825
    Web design, 53–54
opinions, as content, 527,
    528
Optimize Ad Display,
    Yahoo! Search
    Marketing, 364
opt-ins
    call to action, mobile,
        770–773
    defined, 111, 849
    e-mail list with squeeze
        pages, 110–111
    forms, 123–125
    mobile channel campaign,
        769–773
    mobile channel tracking,
        849
    mobile messaging, 818
    signup links, e-mail, 476
    user-flow diagram, 777

opt-outs
    ad-group level, 438, 439
    campaign level, 437
    e-mail, 455
    mobile channel campaign,
        774
    mobile channel tracking,
        849
    user-flow diagram, 778
Oracle, 842
order of items on
    horizontal navigation
    bar, 65
organic search results, 154,
    168, 171, 252, 253
organize RSS feeds, 597,
    598–602, 604
outlined text boxes, 68
outsourcing ISPs, 148
ownership of Web site, by
    ISPs, 147

p

package-based advertising,
    743, 807–809
pages
    backup controls, 11–12
    homepages, 193–194, 311,
        393
    indexed, 168, 200, 253
    landing pages, 106–111
    loading speed, and PPC,
        343
    pasting code for mobile
        Internet, 801
    sales pages, 82, 111–113
    squeeze pages, 82, 85,
        110–111, 124
    thank you pages, 34, 38,
        82–83
Pages/Visit report, 304–305
pageviews
    AJAX reduces, 331
    as conversion goal, 318
    defined, 281

report options for, 285
time on site combined
    with, 286, 287
as traffic metric, 281
uses of tracking, 285–286
visit quality analysis from,
    304–305
pageviews per visit report,
    304–305
paid data services,
    audience research,
    673–674
paid search to generate
    traffic, 39–40
pairing mobile devices, 807
Pantone Matching System
    (PMS), 57
Papa John's International
    mobile service, 839
paragraph copy, 156,
    207–208, 232, 501
paralysis bounce rate
    study, 98
parentheticals, blog
    writing, 587
partner network, 364–365,
    434–439
partnering for sales growth,
    14
passion, of bloggers, 564
passive voice, 224–225
password-protected
    member directories, 87
pathfinder report, goal
    funnel tracking, 331
paths to mobile channel,
    741–748, 750–753
pay per call (PPC), 28
pay per click (PPC)
    about, 3–4
    benefits of using, 342–343
    bidding, 409–415
    budgeting, 342–343,
        403–416
    compared to CPC, 28.
        See also cost per
        click (CPC)

pay per click (PPC)
  (continued)
defined, 339
determining, 403–405
drawbacks, 343–344
expanding keywords lists,
  387–389
Google AdWords, 354–356,
  405–406
managing multiple
  accounts, 347
measurable results, 342
methods for, 339–344
Microsoft adCenter, 407
niche, finding, 343
selecting PPC search
  engine, 345–346
testing, 179
traffic report analyzes, 265
writing copy that earn
  clicks, 391–402
ad-serving percentages,
  401
benefits/features model,
  394
body, 392
call to action, 394–395
changing ad,
  determining when,
  400–402
click-through rate
  (CTR), 400
common mistakes, 396
conversion tracking,
  401–402
cost per click (CPC),
  400
destination URL,
  393–394
display URL, 393
frequency of checking,
  401
goal determined, 400
goals, 395
grammar and spelling,
  395

headlines, 391–392
100 Clicks, 401
PPC ads, 391–394
testing ads, 399–400
Yahoo! Search
  Marketing, 402
Yahoo! Search Marketing,
  406
pay per lead (PPL), 28
payment gateway, 32
payment options,
  1ShoppingCart, 33
payout, 855
PayPal, 31, 32, 362, 840
PDF converter, 29
pdfonline, 29
PDFs (Portable Document
  Format), 29, 515
Peacock Media, 168
Pearlman, Leah (author)
  Facebook For Dummies,
  692
permission
  to e-mail
    affirmative consent, 455
    confirmed, 458–459,
      481–482, 553
    e-mail lists, 457–460,
      480
    explicit, 458, 465
    implied, 457–458
    inherited lists, 460–462
    spam, 457–462
    trusted e-mail sender,
      457–462
  for testimonials use, 103,
    518
permission marketing, 766,
  816
persistent mobile Internet
  site, 826
personal e-mail filters,
  556–558
personal information,
  472, 757
personal ISP referrals, 141

personality in e-mail
  marketing, 493
personalization
  C.O.N.V.E.R.T. M.E.
    formula, 113, 115
  mobile content, 781,
    819–824
Pessemier, Marcia, 100, 101,
  125
phone communication, 34,
  102, 106, 538
photos. *See also* images
  buying, 58
  concept shots, 58
  creating your own, 58
  high-impact and Web site
    design, 57–59
  to introduce self, 100, 101
  JPG images, 215
  product shots, 57–58
  promotional content from,
    518
  selling the outcome with,
    59
  squeeze page, 110
PHP & MySQL For Dummies,
  3e (Valade), 79
PHP programming, 93
phrase keyword match
  types, 381–383
physical address, on e-mail,
  456
physical permission, to
  receive e-mail, 458
picture messaging, 744, 805
Picture2Screen, 743
ping, blogging, 580–582, 616
placement-targeted
  campaign, 355
plagiarism, 254–255,
  726–727
Plantronics, 627
platform approach, mobile
  marketing, 761
player health, mobile path,
  751, 752

Plime, 620

plug-ins, WordPress blogging tool, 80

Plurk, 639, 646, 647, 707

PMS (Pantone Matching System), 57

PNG images, 499

Podcast Maker, 62, 631, 632

PodcastAlley, 634

PodcastDirectory, 634

podcasting
  about, 4
  blog support, 629
  defined, 623
  encoding, 633–634
  listening to, 624
  promoting, 634
  recording first, 630–632
  script preparation, 630
  studio setup, 624–629
  testing studio setup, 628–629
  uploading, 633–634

Podcasting For Dummies, 2e (Morris, Tomasi, Terra, and Steppe), 623

PodProducer, 62, 626, 629

point-of-purchase, 808

point-of-sale (POS) mobile advertising, 783, 808–809

polling, 743, 786–788

popularity of product, 105

popularity sites, 639, 648–649

portable devices, text only, 509

Portable Document Format (PDF), 29, 515

Portent Interactive, 189–190

POS (point-of-sale) mobile advertising, 783, 808–809

post on blog. *See* blogs and blogging

post script reassurance statements, questions

before checkout, 36

post script statements, call to action, 120

postpay billing, 353

pound key, mobile call to action, 772

power-partnering, Internet marketing process, 14

PPC. *See* pay per click (PPC)

PPC (pay per call), 28

ppi, image resolution, 499

PPL (pay per lead), 28

preference data, 844

preferred cost bidding, 410

preferred CPC, 351

Premium Short Message Service (PSMS), 805, 814, 834–838, 854

prepay billing, 354

prepositions, simplicity in blog writing, 587

presence data, 844

press releases, 213–214

price
  for membership Web sites, 89–90
  price points, 36–37, 834
  questions to answer before checkout, 36

print media, 477–478, 492

prior consent, mobile, 816

privacy
  e-mail lists, 480
  mobile marketing to children, 756–757
  questions to answer before checkout, 35
  in referring data, 292
  by traffic report, 266

problem with product/ service, at checkout, 35

product feed, 212

product optimization, blended search, 212–213

products and services
  copy effectiveness, 104–105
  delivery, 10, 35
  establishing, Internet marketing process, 12
  high-impact photos, 57–58
  mobile marketing ecosystem, 740
  price points, 36–37
  types of, 29–30

professional appearance of ESPs, 450–451

professional help
  e-mail content, 529–530
  ISP, choosing, 139–150
  marketing team, 138
  SEO, 233, 257–260

professional standards, trusted e-mail sender, 453

profile
  mobile channel, 842–846
  social media, 676–677, 684–686, 694

profit per month, 17

profits. *See* monetization

program certification, mobile channel, 755–756, 764, 776

programming, as marketing task, 22

programming expert, marketing team, 138

project tracker, online, 149

proliferation of device, mobile path, 751, 752

promotion
  affiliates, 24–26, 42
  blogs, 615–621
  e-mail content, 518–519
  mobile channel, 781–786, 831–832
  podcasting, 634
  social media, 682, 717

proper credit on blogs, 610

Provide Support, 126

proximity advertising/ marketing, 748, 806–807

PSMS (Premium Short Message Service), 805, 814, 834–838, 854

psychographic data, 844

public timeline, microblogging, 646

publicity, as marketing task, 22

publicity expert, marketing team, 138

publish your blog post, 615–616

publishers, mobile, 798–799

Pudding Media, 809

punctuation, 100, 555, 587

purchasing. *See* buying

puzzling readers as link bait, 248

Q

QoolSqool, 677

QR Codes, 773, 792

qualifications, professional SEO help, 258–259

quality
  of images, 215
  link for SEO, 244–245
  LinkedIn, 697
  link-worthy content, 237–238

Quantcast, 16, 17, 672–673

questions and answers
  to answer before checkout, 35–36
  answering, as content, 528
  Ask Web site, 85–86
  audience research, and social media plan, 665–666
  friends, expanding network of, 715–716

LinkedIn, 697

for professional SEO help, 259

quizzes, mobile campaign, 782–784

as social media bait, 679

surveys, mobile, 743, 784–786

Quick Tip content, 526

quizzes, 743, 782–784

Qwikker, 748

R

Radio Frequency Identification (RFID), 750

random common short codes (CSC), 767

Rank Checker, 159

rankings, 255–257, 341

raw data dump, 853

reactivity, visitation and conversion rates, 20

readability of title tags, 229

recapture visitor attention, C.O.N.V.E.R.T. M.E., 113, 117

recordings, 42, 624–626, 630–632

red arrows, 67

red links, 68

Reddit, 619, 639, 649

redemption directions, coupons, 519–520

reducing blocked e-mail, 549–552

references, hiring professional SEO help, 258

referencing images in e-mails, 499–501

referrals, 40, 44, 141–144, 257

referrers
  advanced topics on, 301
  analyzing data from, 295–298
  defined, 281, 289
  importance of, 290, 291, 292
  keyword analysis of data from, 299–300
  privacy of data from, 292
  report from, for visit quality analysis, 308
  tracking, 289–290, 293–294
  understanding, 291–292
  visit quality analysis of, 308–309

referring keyword report, 299–300

Referring Sites report, 295–297

refresh and client-side redirect, 190

refunds, 35, 838

regex, 278

registration, 12, 79, 185–186

regulations. *See* legal and regulatory compliance

relevance
  of keywords, 176
  mobile content, 816
  product optimization, 212–213
  quality links, 244–245
  search engine determination of, 340–341
  SEO, 154, 155–157

RentACoder, 143, 144

renting, common short codes (CSC), 767

reporting. *See* specific topics

representative name, e-mail From line, 486

reputation. *See* trusted sender reputation

research
  audience and social media
    plan, 665–674
  competitor's links and
    SEO, 250
  as marketing task, 22
  as valuable e-mail
    content, 529
reserved keywords, 778
resolution of images, 499
return on investment (ROI),
  265, 271, 290, 536–539
returning report, loyalty
  analysis, 306
returning visitors report,
  306
ReturnPath, 533, 548, 552
returns, JV host, 46
revenue potential, 16, 89–91
revenue sharing, JV host,
  46
revenue-generating
  keywords, 392
review
  local search optimization,
    218
  RSS feeds with hot keys,
    602
  social media plan, 678–
    681
revised category-specific
  question, e-mail, 473
RFID (Radio Frequency
  Identification), 750
rhymezone, 50
right column showcase,
  layout, 68–69
ringtones, 823–824
robots (bots), 154
robots.txt file, 184
robotstxt.org, 184
rock star social media
  style, 676
ROI (return on investment),
  265, 271, 290, 536–539
Roland, 129
routine writing, setting,
  232–233

RSS feed readers, 583, 594,
  595–602, 680
RSS (really simple
  syndication) feeds
blog comments, 608
blogging, 571, 582–583
defined, 594
folders to organize feeds,
  597, 598–600
Google Reader, 583,
  595–602
organize feeds, 597,
  598–602, 604
podcasting, 629
review feeds with hot
  keys, 602
shared items page,
  603–604
social media, 651–663,
  678, 680
subscriptions, 678, 680
tags to organize feeds,
  597, 600–602
video, 216
Rumsey, Deborah (author)
  Statistics For Dummies,
    264
  *Statistics Workbook For
    Dummies*, 264

S

Sabah, Joe (radio guest), 40
sabahradioshows, 40
Sabin-Wilson, Lisa (author)
  WordPress For Dummies,
    2e, 575
Sahlin, Doug (author)
  *Building Web Sites All in
    One For Dummies*, 2e,
    30, 54
sales
  affiliates, 24–26, 40–42
  increasing initial, 36–40
  joint venturing (JV), 43–48
  as marketing task, 22
  mobile content, 837–840

online transactions, 30–36
selling products and
  services, 29–30
tracking SEO results, 251
traffic monetization, 27–28
Web site as tool, 10
writing copy for
  changing ad,
    determining when,
    400–402
  C.O.N.V.E.R.T. M.E.
    formula, 113–120
  elements of effective,
    97–106
  landing pages, 106–113
  as marketing task, 22
  pay-per-click (PPC),
    391–396
  testing ads, 396–400
sales expert, marketing
  team, 138
sales force, virtual, 14
sales pages, 82, 111–113
sales per year (SPY), 17
sales revenue goals
  formula, 19
samples, 744, 790
Sawmill, 271
ScanAlert, 209
scannability
  blogs, 586, 588–590
  e-mails, 496–497
scannable copy, 226
SEO, 238
social media bait, 679
scheduling, 404–405,
  411–415
Schell, Jim (author)
  *Small Business For
    Dummies*, 3e, 405
school drop-out mobile
  program, 812
screen savers, mobile,
  821–823
script preparation,
  podcasting, 630
scroll lines, 513

scrolling compared to
  clicking, 66–67
search engine(s)
  affiliate programs, finding,
    24, 25
  blog topic selection, 570
  blogs, 80
  comparing, 346
  ethics, 157–158
  generating traffic, 39–40
  Google
    Blogger, 571–574, 577
    for competition
      research, 16
    competitor links, 250
    cost per click (CPC),
      409–410
    duplicate content, 192
    FeedBurner RSS tool,
      583
    image optimization,
      214–215
    link buying/selling,
      245–246
    multiple PPC accounts,
      347
    news optimization,
      213–214
    product optimization,
      212
    as referrer, 295
    segmented keywords
      lists, 383–384
  MSN
    advanced keyword
      targeting, 387
    cost per click (CPC),
      409–410
    expanding keywords
      lists, 389
    multiple PPC accounts,
      347
    segmented keywords
      lists, 385
  PPC advertising, creating,
    339–340
  reasons for, 153–155
  referrals from, 292, 299

relevance of Web sites,
    155–158, 340–341
  researching, 345–346
  tracking SEO results,
    255–256
  Yahoo!
    advanced keyword
      targeting, 386
    competitor links, 250
    cost per click (CPC),
      409–410
    e-mail display header,
      484
    expanding keywords
      lists, 388–389
    image optimization,
      214–215
    local search
      optimization, 218
    multiple PPC accounts,
      347
    news optimization,
      213–214
    product optimization,
      212
    segmented keywords
      lists, 384–385
search engine optimization
    (SEO)
  about, 3
  black hat, 154, 157–158
  blended search (universal
    search), 211–219
  blogging platforms, 573,
    574, 575
  creating worksheet, 168
  ethics, 157–158
  hiring professional help,
    257–260
  keywords, selecting,
    169–181
  link building, 235–250
  preparing for, 153–168
  reasons for, 153–155
  relevance of Web sites,
    155–157
  roadblock removal,
    183–197

setting up toolbox,
    159–168
  structuring Web site,
    199–207
  toolbox
    Firefox browser,
      159–160
    Google Toolbar, 159,
      163
    Live HTTP Headers,
      159, 162
    SeoQuake, 159,
      160–162, 180–181
    Web Developer Toolbar,
      159, 163–164, 181,
      191
    Webmaster tools,
      165–167
    Xenu Link Sleuth,
      167–168, 195
    Yellowpipe Lynx Viewer
      Tool, 159, 164–165,
      180
  tracking results, 251–256
  white hat SEO, 154,
    157–158
  writing copy for, 221–233
*Search Engine Optimization
  For Dummies*, 2e (Kent),
  153
search engine ranking
  pages (SERPs), 153,
  154, 227
Search Marketing. *See*
  Yahoo! Search
  Marketing
search network, 364
search tracking, 276–277
search volume, 174,
  176–177
search-keywords report,
  265
second-chance offers, 542
security, 35, 209
segmented keywords lists,
  380–381, 383–385
selling. *See* sales
selling links, SEO, 245–246

semantic outline, traffic and SEO, 207–208

seminars, 37, 44

semi-pro ISP, 139

Sender ID, 559

Sender Policy Framework (SPF), 559

SenderScore, 553

SEO. *See* search engine optimization (SEO)

SEOmoz, 209

SeoQuake, 159, 160–162, 180–181

SERPs (search engine ranking pages), 153, 154, 227

server address, 485

server administration, as marketing task, 22

sessions
defined, 280
as general measure, 281
report for tracking, 281–282
reporting data affected by, 267
time on site combined with, 286, 287
as traffic metric, 280
unique visitors compared with, 284
uses of tracking, 282–283

Sessions Online by School of Design, 57

sexually-oriented e-mail, 456–457

shared items page, RSS feeds, 603–604

shared short code models, 768–769

sharing ease, social media plan, 678, 681

sharpness, writing blogs, 586, 590

shopping cart
abandonment point from, 333–334
configuration of, for goal tracking, 321

defined, 31
as funnel location, 329
in funnel-tracking setup example, 331
KPI mapping to, 319
membership Web sites, 88
traffic report capability for, 265

ShopText, 790, 839

short code. *See* common short codes (CSC)

Short Message Service (SMS)
for content delivery, 816
data collection through, 846–847
mobile content certification, 755–756
mobile monetization, 805–806
for mobile monetization, 834–838
mobile tracking, 852
viral marketing, 742–744

SHTML, SEO roadblock removal, 188–189

side loading, 747

signup links, e-mail, 475–477, 476

simplicity, writing blogs, 585, 586–587

single opt-in mobile call, 773

Singletouch, 772

site maps, 109, 207

size, font choice, 54

Skycore, 744

slogans, 50

Small Business For Dummies, 3e (Tyson and Shell), 405

small company team ISP, 139

SmartCast in FeedBurner, 624, 629

smartphones, 745, 749

SmartReply, 745

SMS. *See* Short Message Service (SMS)

Snafu, 167

SnapNow, 771

snapping/scanning, mobile call to action, 771

Snaptell, 771

sneeze principle
bookmark-driven, 698
described, 638
social media sites, 684, 691–692, 693, 695
social news, 701

Snell, Claudia (author)
Building Web Sites All in One For Dummies, 2e, 30, 54

snippet, 230

social marketing, mobile, 812–813

social media
aggregators, 639, 649–650
blogs, 639, 640–642
bookmarking sites, 639, 644–646
campaign creation, 721–729
categories of, 638–650
defined, 4–5, 637
desktop for, 651–663
friends, 713–719
media-sharing sites, 639, 648
microblogging sites, 639, 646–648
network building, 713–719
plan for, 665–682
popularity sites, 639, 648–649
power of, 639
profile, 676–677, 684–686, 694
sites for, 683–712
social networks, 80, 639, 642–644, 794
social news sites, 700–701, 714
social voting sites, blogs, 619–620
soft bounce e-mail, 548–549

solutions, communicating, 13
Sony fake PS3 blogs, 675
Sony Vegas Movie Studio 9, 105, 132
Sostre, Pedro (author)
  Web Analytics For Dummies, 264, 301, 315
sound card mixer, 129
sound files, e-mail links to, 514–515
Sound Forge Audio Studio, 129–130
Source Medical Equipment, 111, 112
sourcing content, 815–817
spam
  CAN-SPAM Act, 449, 454–457, 460, 463, 488, 491, 754
  collecting e-mail addresses legally, 455
  commercial e-mail, 454
  complaints, minimizing, 462–467, 553
  compliance with laws, 454–457
  defined, 754
  filtered e-mail, 552–558
  including required content, 455–457
  mobile marketing, 754–755
  origination of term, 464
  permission, asking for, 457–462
  social network, 645
  transactional/relationship e-mail, 454
SPAM lunch meat, 464
spam scores, 557
spam trap addresses, 550–551
spelling, writing PPC ad copy, 395–396
spending limits, PPC budget, 404
spending per visitor, 21
SPF (Sender Policy Framework), 559

Sphinn, 619
spiders, 154
splash advertising, 802–803
Sprint, 833
SPY (sales per year), 17
spying on competition, 10, 16
squeeze pages, 82, 85, 110–111, 124
Squidoo, 80
standards
  mobile path, 751, 752
  trusted e-mail sender, 453
  for usability, 71
star key, mobile call to action, 772
StarCut, 747
Start a Website Design Business, 124
stated feedback, e-mail, 446
Statistics For Dummies (Rumsey), 264
Statistics Workbook For Dummies (Rumsey), 264
status, Facebook, 685
Steppe, Kreg (author)
  Podcasting For Dummies, 2e, 623
steps in C.O.N.V.E.R.T. M.E. formula, 113–114
Stewart, Mike (video expert), 105, 132
stickiness, 138, 295
stock photos, buying, 58
stop characters, 224
stop words, 222–223
story telling, 229, 527, 529
strategic mobile marketing ecosystem, 740–741
strategy
  mobile marketing, 761, 762, 763
  Web sites, 15–22
streaming, mobile audio/video, 830
structuring Web site and SEO, 199–207

studio for podcasting, 624–629
StumbleUpon, 616–618, 639, 644–645, 698–699
style
  social media plan, 675–676
  Web site design, 54–55
  writing SEO copy, 224
sub-headlines, 115
Subject lines, e-mail
  creating effective, 483–485, 488–491
  filtered e-mail, 555
  misleading, 456
submission, Web site relevance, 157
submit button, forms, 122
submitting, mobile call to action, 772
subscription form on squeeze page, 111
subscriptions
  mobile, 247, 740, 831–832
  podcast, 624
  rewards for, 479
Superpages, 218
support, Web site for, 10
SurfKitchen, 825
surveys, 743, 784–786
Susan G. Komen for the Cure, 814
sweepstakes, 743
syllables, simplicity in blog writing, 586
Symbian, 745
syndicated data, 845
Syndicating Sites with RSS Feeds For Dummies (Finkelstein), 216

T

table of contents (TOC), e-mail links, 511–513
tactical planning, mobile marketing, 761, 764
tagging bookmarks, 699–700

tagging content,
    automated, 846
taglines, branding, 50, 51
tags to organize RSS feeds,
    597, 600–602
talking points, 630
targeting
  audience
    audience-driven terms,
      169–170
    e-mail information for,
      525–527
    horizontal navigation
      bar, 64
    mobile marketing, 760
    research, and social
      media plan, 665–674
    size analysis, 282, 283,
      568–570
  geotargeting, 349, 359,
    431–432
  placement-targeted
    campaign, 355
  sites and social media
    plan, 677–678
target-market focus, mobile
    channel, 753
technical support, as
    1ShoppingCart, 34
Technorati, 568, 616, 641
telephone communication,
    34, 102, 106, 538
television voting, mobile,
    788
tell your story, effective
    copy, 102
tell-a-friend marketing,
    125–126, 743, 760,
    795–796, 810–812
TemplateBox, 76
TemplateMonster, 59, 76
templates
  blogging platform,
    578–579
  defined, 75
  e-mail, 483
  layout, 59
  Web sites, 59, 75–76

TemplateTuning, 76
temporary blocked e-mail,
    547
Ten Foot Rule, to collect
    information, 477–478
terminal, mobile channel,
    735
Terra, Evo (author)
  Podcasting For Dummies,
    2e, 623
testimonials
  checklist for, 103
  C.O.N.V.E.R.T. M.E.
    formula, 113, 115
  in copy, 103
  creating valuable content,
    518
  permission to use, 103,
    518
  as sub-headline, 115
testing
  A/B tests, 396–399
  ads, writing copy that
    earn clicks, 396–400
  C.O.N.V.E.R.T. M.E.
    formula, 114, 117–118
  dynamic keyword
    insertion (DKI),
    399–400
  e-mail subject lines, 490
  pay per click (PPC), 179
  usability, 71–72
  visitation and conversion
    rates, 20
text, plain compared with
    HTML, 491, 501–505
text alerts, 743, 819–820
text banners, mobile ads,
    800, 802
text boxes, e-mail, 476
text links
  as call to action, 106
  defined, 505
  e-mail links, 505–509
  horizontal navigation bar,
    65
  inline text links, 68
  mini-sites, 82

naming, 507–508
signup links, e-mail, 476
text messaging. *See* Short
    Message Service (SMS)
text promotions, mobile
    campaign, 781–786
Text2Give, 743
Text2Screen, 743
texting, mobile call to
    action, 771
Textpattern, 576
text-to-screen mobile,
    794–795
textual components,
    layout, 62
thank you notes, 239
thank you pages, 34, 38,
    82–83
TheAccidentalLawyer, 52
thesaurus, simplicity in
    blog writing, 586
Think Like a Spy, 104
third-party forms
    processors, 123
3D codes, 792–793
301 redirect, 195, 209
throughput, mobile
    messaging, 818
Thumbplay, 834
Thunder Ridge ski resort,
    31, 32
Timacheff, Serge (author)
  *Digital Photography For
    Dummies*, 6e, 58
time
  ad changing, determining
    when to, 401–402
  bidding on keywords,
    411–415
  mobile marketing
    timelines, 762–763
  for SEO campaign, 252,
    259–260
  time on site, 281, 286–289,
    294, 305
  time until delivery,
    checkout, 35

timing of credit card
    charges, 36
tips as valuable e-mail
    content, 527–528
title tags
    brand placement, 227–228
    connecting headlines to
        copy, 231–232
    hiring professional SEO
        help, 258
    keyword stuffing, 228
    readability, 229
    semantic outline, 207–208
    telling story in, 229
    Web site relevance, 156
    writing SEO copy, 227–229
Tittel, Ed (author)
    *HTML, XHTML & CSS For
        Dummies*, 6e, 196
T-Mobile, 833
TOC (table of contents),
    e-mail links, 511–513
Tomasi, Chuck (author)
    Podcasting For Dummies,
        2e, 623
toolbar buttons,
    bookmarking sites, 699
tools
    adding, 369, 378
    -based social media
        campaign, 722–724
    keyword selection, SEO,
        171–175
    SEO set-up toolbox,
        159–168
Top 1000 Templates, 76
top content report, 285,
    307–308, 312, 324–326
top pages report, 285, 324
tracking
    blog comments, replies to,
        607–608
    conversion goals, 265, 272,
        321–324
    e-mail marketing, 531–543
    goal funnels, 331–333

keywords,
    underperforming,
        389–390
mobile campaign, 841–855
non-click responses,
    536–539
SEO, 251–256
social media desktop
    setup, 663–664
tracking code, 274–275, 420
trademarks, 420–421
traditional media, 740–741,
    764
traditional mobile service
    providers, 738, 739
traditional Web sites, 74–76
traffic analysis and
    reporting
    budgeting, 19–21, 407–408
    capabilities, 264–266
    content sites driving,
        84–85
    defined, 263
    educational content
        pages, 107–109
    estimating, 351–352,
        428–431
    generating, 39–40
    goal scenarios, 19–21
    hits on, 279–280
    monetization DP to
        monetization, 27–28
    privacy by, 266
    Quantcast, 16, 17, 672–673
    search engine
        optimization (SEO),
        199–209, 255–256
    setting up server for, 272
    site search tracking for,
        276–277
    tools for, 267–271
    tracking SEO results,
        255–256
    traffic monetization, 27
    traffic volume, 279–290
    visit quality analysis,
        303–312

    as Web analytic
        foundation, 263–264
traffic analysis and
    reporting, metrics
    described, 280–281
    pageviews
        AJAX reduces, 331
        as conversion goal, 318
        defined, 281
        report options for, 285
        time on site combined
            with, 286, 287
        as traffic metric, 281
        uses of tracking,
            285–286
        visit quality analysis
            from, 304–305
    referrers
        advanced topics on, 301
        analyzing data from,
            295–298
        defined, 281, 289
        importance of, 290, 291,
            292
        keyword analysis of data
            from, 299–300
        privacy of data from,
            292
        report from, for visit
            quality analysis, 308
        tracking, 289–290,
            293–294
        understanding, 291–292
        visit quality analysis of,
            308–309
    sessions
        defined, 280
        as general measure, 281
        report for tracking,
            281–282
        reporting data affected
            by, 267
        time on site combined
            with, 286, 287
        as traffic metric, 280
        unique visitors
            compared with, 284
        uses of tracking, 282–283

time on site
  combining other metrics
    with, 286–289
  as referring data, 294
  report, 305
  as traffic metric, 281
  visit quality analysis
    from, 305
  unique visitors
    defined, 280
    importance of tracking,
      284
    as referring data, 294
    in soft goal evaluation,
      320–321
    time on site combined
      with, 287
    tools for tracking, 284
    as traffic metric, 280
    uses of tracking, 282,
      283–284
trained content filters, 558
training, 37, 42, 44, 124
transaction page, 31
transactional/relationship
  e-mail, 454
transactions
  credit card
    Google AdWords,
      353–354
    merchant account,
      31–32
    mobile content, 839
    1ShoppingCart
      advantages, 33
    questions to answer
      before checkout,
      35–36
    Yahoo! Search
      Marketing, 362–364
  mobile marketing, 764
  shopping cart and
    checkout, 31–36
Trebuchet font, 54
troublemaker social media
  style, 675
trusted sender reputation.
  See also spam
  bookmarking, 698–699

CAN-SPAM Act, 449,
    454–457, 460, 463, 488,
    491, 754
  consumer standards, 453
  factors of, Web site
    relevance, 156
  and filtered e-mail,
    552–553
  list protection, 462
  optimization and SEO,
    208–209
  permission, asking for,
    457–462
  professional standards,
    453
  social media campaign
    creation, 728–729
  unsubscribe, 455, 458,
    463–467
TrustRank, 208–209
TubeMogul, 704
Twain, Mark (author), 586
TWCI (The Weather
    Channel Interactive),
    799, 804
Twitter, 80, 621, 639, 646,
    647, 649, 707, 716
2D codes, 792–793
TypePad, 78, 574
Tyson, Eric (author)
  *Small Business For
    Dummies*, 3e, 405

U

UGC (user-generated
    content), 554–556,
    793–796
UIEvolution, 825
U[insert umlat]bercaster,
    625
UK Mobile Network
    Operators, 766
Ultimate Dream Guide, 125
undeliverable e-mails,
    bounce rate, 532–533
unique affiliate link URL, 2
Unique Article Wizard, 85

unique visitors
  defined, 280
  importance of tracking,
    284
  as referring data, 294
  in soft goal evaluation,
    320–321
  time on site combined
    with, 287
  tools for tracking, 284
  as traffic metric, 280
  uses of tracking, 282,
    283–284
universal (blended) search,
    SEO, 211–219
Unlimited Mom, 114–115,
    116
unsolicited commercial
    e-mail, 462. *See also*
    spam
unsubscribe, e-mail, 455,
    458, 463–467
Unwired Nation, 809
up-front costs, mobile
    marketing, 762–763
uploading podcasts,
    633–634
upper-right quadrant
    (URQ), 62–64
upselling, 37
upside down blog writing
    style, 590
Urchin, 264, 267
urgent offers by e-mail, 522
URLs
  absolute, 239
  destination URLs
    A/B tests, 398
    editorial guidelines, 420
    PPC ad copy, 339,
      393–394
    segmented keywords
      lists, 383–385
  display URL
    A/B tests, 397–398
    editorial guidelines,
      419–420
    PPC ad copy, 393

URLs *(continued)*
  duplicate, 193–194
  ease of linking, 239
  image reference, 500–501
  keyword-rich URLs, 206
  Web site relevance, 157
URQ (upper-right
    quadrant), 62–64
usability, Web site design,
    70–72
USB headset, 627
USB mixing board, 627
user flows, mobile
    campaigns, 775–781
user-flow diagram, 776–779
user-generated content
    (UGC), 554–556,
    793–796

V

Vacancy (film), 745
Valade, Janet (author)
  *PHP & MySQL For
    Dummies*, 3e, 79
validation
  C.O.N.V.E.R.T. M.E., 113,
    115–117
  elements of effective
    solutions, 102–105
value. *See also* content
  of product/service, 36, 735
  of your company, and JV
    host, 47–48
vanity common short codes
    (CSC), 767–768
vanity mobile marketing,
    812
variables, A/B tests, 397
velocity, 216, 236
verbal meltdown, SEO copy,
    232
verbal permission, to
    receive e-mail, 458

Verdana font, 54
Verizon, 833
VerticalResponse, 450
Vibes Media, 744
Vice President Internet
    Marketing (VPIM), 138
video
  as content, 529
  as conversion goal, 318
  creating and adding,
    131–136
  delivering mobile, 829–830
  editing, 133–136
  equipment, 132
  file format, 134–135
  file formats, 215, 489–499,
    829
  getting started, 132–133
  to introduce self, 101–102
  link bait, 249–250
  linking to e-mail, 514
  media-sharing sites, 639,
    648
  mobile content delivery,
    829–830
  optimization, for blended
    search, 215–217
  podcasting, 624–634
    about, 4
    blog support, 629
    defined, 623
    encoding, 633–634
    listening to, 624
    promoting, 634
    recording first, 630–632
    script preparation, 630
    studio setup, 624–629
    testing studio setup,
      628–629
    uploading, 633–634
  producing your own, 105
  sales of, 29
video camera, 105, 132
viewable elements, video
    editing, 133
viral marketing, 125–126,
    743, 760, 795–796,
    810–812

virtual sales force,
    Internet, 14
visibility, SEO roadblock
    removal, 183–186
visibone, 57
visit quality analysis,
    303–312
visitation rates, 20, 43
Visitor Loyalty report, 306
visitors
  allowance per visitor, 21
  build traffic to Web site,
    13–14
  C.O.N.V.E.R.T. M.E.
    formula, 113–120
  layout evaluation, 62
  leaving Web sites, 62
  spending per visitor, 21
  visitors per month, 19–20
visits (sessions). *See also*
    traffic analysis and
    reporting
  defined, 280
  as general measure, 281
  report for tracking,
    281–282
  reporting data affected
    by, 267
  time on site combined
    with, 286, 287
  as traffic metric, 280
  unique visitors compared
    with, 284
  uses of tracking, 282–283
visual anchors, e-mail, 497
visual components, layout,
    62
visual editors for mobile
    Internet, 801
voice-call ads, mobile, 809
volume, pay per click (PPC)
    drawbacks, 343
voting
  link votes, 203, 235–237
  polling, 743, 786–788
  SMS application, 743

VPIM (Vice President
   Internet Marketing), 138

W

w3.org, 504
wallpaper, mobile, 821–823
walls, Facebook, 684
WAP (Wireless Application
   Protocol) billing, 839
Warner, Janine (author)
   *Web Sites Do-It-Yourself For
   Dummies*, 54
warning note, 264, 266
Watchee, 794
The Weather Channel, 799,
   804, 824
Web analytics. *See also*
   traffic analysis and
   reporting
   about, 3
   content report with dollar
      index, 325–326
   conversion goals, using,
      313–327
   e-commerce tracking, 272,
      322–323
   goal funnels, 329–335
   goal tracking, 272, 313,
      322–323, 324
   Google Analytics
   content report with
      dollar index in,
      325–326
   e-commerce tracking
      by, 272, 322–323
   goal funnel tracking,
      331–334
   goal tracking, 272, 313,
      322–324
   keywords report, 325
   landing page report,
      326–327
   loyalty benchmark,
      305–306

reputation of, 266
SEO results tracking,
   252–253
top content report,
   307–308
traffic analysis, 27, 267,
   270–289, 293–298
visit quality analysis,
   303–308, 310
Web site, 270, 272
key performance
   indicators (KPIs), 264,
   313–315, 317, 319
keywords report, 325
landing page report,
   326–327
loyalty benchmark,
   305–306
pay per click (PPC)
   drawbacks, 344
purpose of, 264
referrers, 291–301
reputation, 266
setting conversion goals,
   263–278
social media, 682
tools for, 267–271
tracking SEO results,
   252–253
visit quality, 303–312
Web Analytics For Dummies
   (Sostre/LeClaire), 264,
   301, 315
Web bugs, as traffic
   reporting tool, 267, 268,
   269
Web Developer Toolbar,
   159, 163–164, 181, 191
Web marketing process,
   11–14. *See also* specific
   topics
Web presence
   about, 2–3
   design for sales, 49–72

encouraging
   communication,
   121–136
hiring professional help,
   137–150
Internet business basics,
   9–22
making money online,
   23–48
multiple sites, creating/
   connecting, 73–95
writing copy for sales,
   97–120
Web sites. *See also* specific
   companies and
   products
   age of, Web site relevance,
      156
   building to degrade
      gracefully, 188–189
   business basics, 10–22
   connecting and
      networking, 77–88
   goal development, 17–22
   managing content, 91–95
   marketing process, 11–14,
      138
   SEO structuring, 199–207
   strategy, 15–22
   types of, 74–91
Web Template Biz, 76
Webalizer, 267, 271
Webalizer reporting tool,
   271
Webinars, 30, 37
Weblog. *See* blog
Webmaster tools, 165–167
Webmaster World, 644, 705
Web-safe colors, 56–57
Website Templates, 59, 76
Website Waves, 77–78, 79
WebTrends, 284
weekly conference call,
   affiliate training, 42
what-if scenarios Web sites,
   19–21

white hat SEO, 154, 157–158
white list e-mail, 552
whole product line, sales of, 30
widget, 835
Wi-Fi proximity marketing, 807
wiki, Facebook, 687
Windows Media Player, 624
Wireless Application Protocol (WAP) billing, 839
wireless mobile service providers, 738
wireless networks/ operators, 738
word-of-mouth marketing, 125–126, 743, 760, 795–796, 810–812
WordPress, 78–81, 571–574, 629, 639
WordPress For Dummies, 2e (Sabin-Wilson), 575
words on horizontal navigation bar, 65
Wordtracker, 171
Wordtracker (Web sites), 108
Wordze, 171, 172
worksheets
  creating SEO, 168
  lead-based, 723–724
  social media plan, 666, 676
  tracking SEO results, 251–254
writing content, 22, 237–238, 523–525
writing copy
  for advertising and sales
    changing ad, determining when, 400–402
    C.O.N.V.E.R.T. M.E. formula, 113–120
    elements of effective, 97–106

  landing pages, 106–113
  as marketing task, 22
  pay-per-click (PPC), 391–396
  testing ads, 396–400
  for search engine optimization (SEO), 221–233
writing link text, 205–206
written permission, to receive e-mail, 458

X

Xenu Link Sleuth, 167–168, 195
Xerox, 49
XHTML coding standards, 196
Xiosoft Audio, 130
XSitePro, 94, 95

Y

Yahoo! (search engine)
  advanced keyword targeting, 386
  competitor links, 250
  cost per click (CPC), 409–410
  e-mail display header, 484
  expanding keywords lists, 388–389
  image optimization, 214–215
  local search optimization, 218
  multiple PPC accounts, 347
  news optimization, 213–214
  product optimization, 212
  segmented keywords lists, 384–385
Yahoo! Answers, 643, 710–711

Yahoo! Buzz, 619
Yahoo! Directory (Web sites), 240
Yahoo! DomainKeys, 559
Yahoo! Groups, 87, 667, 706
Yahoo! Mail, 556
Yahoo! Search Marketing
  A/B test, 399
  account creating and configuring, 358–362, 364–365
  Account Tactic Settings, 364–365
  ad changing, determining when, 402
  ad groups, 362, 368–369
  adding campaign, 366–368
  adding tools, 369
  advanced keyword targeting, 386–387
  advertising, 358–369
  analytic package choices, 440–441
  billing, setting up, 362–364
  budgeting for keywords, 406
  comparing search engines, 346
  content network campaign, 437–438
  cost per click (CPC), 367
  expanding, 365–369
  first campaigns, 358–362
  keyword match types, 365
  keyword traffic tools, 429–430
  spending limits, PPC budget, 404
  writing copy that earn clicks, 402
Yahoo! Site Explorer, 165, 166, 180, 250, 253
Yahoo! Web Analytics, 266, 271, 313
Yellowpages, 218

Yellowpipe Lynx Viewer,
    159, 164–165, 180
Yelp!, 218
Your Website
    Domain/blog, 79
YouTube
  audio sharing, 639, 648
  finding questions, 716–717
  RSS feed, 216, 217
  using, 703–704
  video sharing, 132–133
  viral marketing, 811

Z

Zannel, 794
ZapFrog, 794
Zed, 834
ZIP code search, 319, 331
Zoom H2 microphone/
    audio recorder, 627
Zooomr, 702
Zoove, 772

Notes

Notes

Notes

Notes

BUSINESS, CAREERS & PERSONAL FINANCE

ounting For Dummies, 4th Edition*
-0-470-24600-9

okkeeping Workbook For Dummies†
-0-470-16983-4

mmodities For Dummies
-0-470-04928-0

ing Business in China For Dummies
-0-470-04929-7

E-Mail Marketing For Dummies
978-0-470-19087-6

Job Interviews For Dummies, 3rd Edition*†
978-0-470-17748-8

Personal Finance Workbook For Dummies*†
978-0-470-09933-9

Real Estate License Exams For Dummies
978-0-7645-7623-2

Six Sigma For Dummies
978-0-7645-6798-8

Small Business Kit For Dummies,
2nd Edition*†
978-0-7645-5984-6

Telephone Sales For Dummies
978-0-470-16836-3

BUSINESS PRODUCTIVITY & MICROSOFT OFFICE

ess 2007 For Dummies
-0-470-03649-5

el 2007 For Dummies
-0-470-03737-9

fice 2007 For Dummies
-0-470-00923-9

tlook 2007 For Dummies
-0-470-03830-7

PowerPoint 2007 For Dummies
978-0-470-04059-1

Project 2007 For Dummies
978-0-470-03651-8

QuickBooks 2008 For Dummies
978-0-470-18470-7

Quicken 2008 For Dummies
978-0-470-17473-9

Salesforce.com For Dummies,
2nd Edition
978-0-470-04893-1

Word 2007 For Dummies
978-0-470-03658-7

EDUCATION, HISTORY, REFERENCE & TEST PREPARATION

ican American History For Dummies
-0-7645-5469-8

ebra For Dummies
-0-7645-5325-7

ebra Workbook For Dummies
-0-7645-8467-1

t History For Dummies
-0-470-09910-0

ASVAB For Dummies, 2nd Edition
978-0-470-10671-6

British Military History For Dummies
978-0-470-03213-8

Calculus For Dummies
978-0-7645-2498-1

Canadian History For Dummies, 2nd Edition
978-0-470-83656-9

Geometry Workbook For Dummies
978-0-471-79940-5

The SAT I For Dummies, 6th Edition
978-0-7645-7193-0

Series 7 Exam For Dummies
978-0-470-09932-2

World History For Dummies
978-0-7645-5242-7

FOOD, HOME, GARDEN, HOBBIES & HOME

dge For Dummies, 2nd Edition
-0-471-92426-5

in Collecting For Dummies, 2nd Edition
-0-470-22275-1

oking Basics For Dummies, 3rd Edition
-0-7645-7206-7

Drawing For Dummies
978-0-7645-5476-6

Etiquette For Dummies, 2nd Edition
978-0-470-10672-3

Gardening Basics For Dummies*†
978-0-470-03749-2

Knitting Patterns For Dummies
978-0-470-04556-5

Living Gluten-Free For Dummies†
978-0-471-77383-2

Painting Do-It-Yourself For Dummies
978-0-470-17533-0

HEALTH, SELF HELP, PARENTING & PETS

ger Management For Dummies
-0-470-03715-7

xiety & Depression Workbook
r Dummies
-0-7645-9793-0

eting For Dummies, 2nd Edition
-0-7645-4149-0

g Training For Dummies, 2nd Edition
-0-7645-8418-3

Horseback Riding For Dummies
978-0-470-09719-9

Infertility For Dummies†
978-0-470-11518-3

Meditation For Dummies with CD-ROM,
2nd Edition
978-0-471-77774-8

Post-Traumatic Stress Disorder For Dummies
978-0-470-04922-8

Puppies For Dummies, 2nd Edition
978-0-470-03717-1

Thyroid For Dummies, 2nd Edition†
978-0-471-78755-6

Type 1 Diabetes For Dummies*†
978-0-470-17811-9

eparate Canadian edition also available
eparate U.K. edition also available

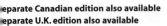
ailable wherever books are sold. For more information or to order direct: U.S. customers visit www.dummies.com or call 1-877-762-2974.
. customers visit www.wileyeurope.com or call (0)1243 843291. Canadian customers visit www.wiley.ca or call 1-800-567-4797.

INTERNET & DIGITAL MEDIA

AdWords For Dummies
978-0-470-15252-2

Blogging For Dummies, 2nd Edition
978-0-470-23017-6

Digital Photography All-in-One Desk Reference For Dummies, 3rd Edition
978-0-470-03743-0

Digital Photography For Dummies, 5th Edition
978-0-7645-9802-9

Digital SLR Cameras & Photography For Dummies, 2nd Edition
978-0-470-14927-0

eBay Business All-in-One Desk Reference For Dummies
978-0-7645-8438-1

eBay For Dummies, 5th Edition*
978-0-470-04529-9

eBay Listings That Sell For Dummies
978-0-471-78912-3

Facebook For Dummies
978-0-470-26273-3

The Internet For Dummies, 11th Edition
978-0-470-12174-0

Investing Online For Dummies, 5th Edition
978-0-7645-8456-5

iPod & iTunes For Dummies, 5th Editi◼
978-0-470-17474-6

MySpace For Dummies
978-0-470-09529-4

Podcasting For Dummies
978-0-471-74898-4

Search Engine Optimization For Dummies, 2nd Edition
978-0-471-97998-2

Second Life For Dummies
978-0-470-18025-9

Starting an eBay Business For Dumm◼ 3rd Edition†
978-0-470-14924-9

GRAPHICS, DESIGN & WEB DEVELOPMENT

Adobe Creative Suite 3 Design Premium All-in-One Desk Reference For Dummies
978-0-470-11724-8

Adobe Web Suite CS3 All-in-One Desk Reference For Dummies
978-0-470-12099-6

AutoCAD 2008 For Dummies
978-0-470-11650-0

Building a Web Site For Dummies, 3rd Edition
978-0-470-14928-7

Creating Web Pages All-in-One Desk Reference For Dummies, 3rd Edition
978-0-470-09629-1

Creating Web Pages For Dummies, 8th Edition
978-0-470-08030-6

Dreamweaver CS3 For Dummies
978-0-470-11490-2

Flash CS3 For Dummies
978-0-470-12100-9

Google SketchUp For Dummies
978-0-470-13744-4

InDesign CS3 For Dummies
978-0-470-11865-8

Photoshop CS3 All-in-One Desk Reference For Dummies
978-0-470-11195-6

Photoshop CS3 For Dummies
978-0-470-11193-2

Photoshop Elements 5 For Dummie◼
978-0-470-09810-3

SolidWorks For Dummies
978-0-7645-9555-4

Visio 2007 For Dummies
978-0-470-08983-5

Web Design For Dummies, 2nd Editi◼
978-0-471-78117-2

Web Sites Do-It-Yourself For Dummi◼
978-0-470-16903-2

Web Stores Do-It-Yourself For Dummi◼
978-0-470-17443-2

LANGUAGES, RELIGION & SPIRITUALITY

Arabic For Dummies
978-0-471-77270-5

Chinese For Dummies, Audio Set
978-0-470-12766-7

French For Dummies
978-0-7645-5193-2

German For Dummies
978-0-7645-5195-6

Hebrew For Dummies
978-0-7645-5489-6

Ingles Para Dummies
978-0-7645-5427-8

Italian For Dummies, Audio Set
978-0-470-09586-7

Italian Verbs For Dummies
978-0-471-77389-4

Japanese For Dummies
978-0-7645-5429-2

Latin For Dummies
978-0-7645-5431-5

Portuguese For Dummies
978-0-471-78738-9

Russian For Dummies
978-0-471-78001-4

Spanish Phrases For Dummies
978-0-7645-7204-3

Spanish For Dummies
978-0-7645-5194-9

Spanish For Dummies, Audio Set
978-0-470-09585-0

The Bible For Dummies
978-0-7645-5296-0

Catholicism For Dummies
978-0-7645-5391-2

The Historical Jesus For Dummies
978-0-470-16785-4

Islam For Dummies
978-0-7645-5503-9

Spirituality For Dummies, 2nd Edition
978-0-470-19142-2

NETWORKING AND PROGRAMMING

ASP.NET 3.5 For Dummies
978-0-470-19592-5

C# 2008 For Dummies
978-0-470-19109-5

Hacking For Dummies, 2nd Edition
978-0-470-05235-8

Home Networking For Dummies, 4th Edition
978-0-470-11806-1

Java For Dummies, 4th Edition
978-0-470-08716-9

Microsoft® SQL Server™ 2008 All-in-One Desk Reference For Dummies
978-0-470-17954-3

Networking All-in-One Desk Reference For Dummies, 2nd Edition
978-0-7645-9939-2

Networking For Dummies, 8th Edition
978-0-470-05620-2

SharePoint 2007 For Dummies
978-0-470-09941-4

Wireless Home Networking For Dummies, 2nd Edition
978-0-471-74940-0

ERATING SYSTEMS & COMPUTER BASICS

For Dummies, 5th Edition
0-7645-8458-9

tops For Dummies, 2nd Edition
0-470-05432-1

x For Dummies, 8th Edition
0-470-11649-4

Book For Dummies
0-470-04859-7

OS X Leopard All-in-One
k Reference For Dummies
0-470-05434-5

Mac OS X Leopard For Dummies
978-0-470-05433-8

Macs For Dummies, 9th Edition
978-0-470-04849-8

PCs For Dummies, 11th Edition
978-0-470-13728-4

Windows® Home Server For Dummies
978-0-470-18592-6

Windows Server 2008 For Dummies
978-0-470-18043-3

Windows Vista All-in-One
Desk Reference For Dummies
978-0-471-74941-7

Windows Vista For Dummies
978-0-471-75421-3

Windows Vista Security For Dummies
978-0-470-11805-4

ORTS, FITNESS & MUSIC

ching Hockey For Dummies
0-470-83685-9

ching Soccer For Dummies
0-471-77381-8

ess For Dummies, 3rd Edition
0-7645-7851-9

tball For Dummies, 3rd Edition
0-470-12536-6

GarageBand For Dummies
978-0-7645-7323-1

Golf For Dummies, 3rd Edition
978-0-471-76871-5

Guitar For Dummies, 2nd Edition
978-0-7645-9904-0

Home Recording For Musicians
For Dummies, 2nd Edition
978-0-7645-8884-6

iPod & iTunes For Dummies,
5th Edition
978-0-470-17474-6

Music Theory For Dummies
978-0-7645-7838-0

Stretching For Dummies
978-0-470-06741-3

Get smart @ dummies.com®

- **Find a full list of Dummies titles**
- **Look into loads of FREE on-site articles**
- **Sign up for FREE eTips e-mailed to you weekly**
- **See what other products carry the Dummies name**
- **Shop directly from the Dummies bookstore**
- **Enter to win new prizes every month!**

parate Canadian edition also available
parate U.K. edition also available

lable wherever books are sold. For more information or to order direct: U.S. customers visit www.dummies.com or call 1-877-762-2974.
customers visit www.wileyeurope.com or call (0) 1243 843291. Canadian customers visit www.wiley.ca or call 1-800-567-4797.

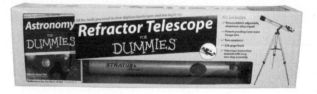